APTER, T.E.

VIRGINIA WOOLF, A STUDY
OF HER NOVELS

VIRGINIA WOOLF

THE GOTHAM LIBRARY
OF THE NEW YORK UNIVERSITY PRESS

The Gotham Library is a series of original works and critical studies published in paperback primarily for student use. The Gotham hardcover edition is primarily for use by libraries and the general reader. Devoted to significant works and major authors and to literary topics of enduring importance, Gotham Library texts offer the best in literature and criticism.

Comparative and Foreign Language Literature:
Robert J. Clements, Editor
Comparative and English Language Literature:
James W. Tuttleton, Editor

VIRGINIA WOOLF
A Study of her Novels

T. E. APTER

New York · New York University Press · 1979

Library of Congress Catalog Card Number: 78-78175
ISBN 0-8147-0568-5 (cloth)
ISBN 0-8147-0569-3 (paper)

Printed in Great Britain

To my Parents

Contents

Acknowledgements

The author and publisher wish to thank the following who have kindly given permission for the use of copyright material:

Jonathan Cape Ltd on behalf of the Executors of the James Joyce Estate and Viking Press Inc, for the extracts from *A Portrait of the Artist as a Young Man* by James Joyce;

Chatto and Windus Ltd and Random House Inc, for the extracts from *Swann's Way* by Marcel Proust, translated by C. K. Scott Moncrieff, © the Translator's Literary Estate, and *Time Regained* (U.S. title, *The Past Recaptured*) from *Remembrance of Things Past* by Marcel Proust, translated by Andreas Mayor, © the Translator's Literary Estate;

The Hogarth Press Ltd, the Literary Estate of Virginia Woolf and Harcourt Brace Jovanovich Inc, for the extracts from *The Voyage Out, Night and Day, Jacob's Room, Mrs Dalloway, Collected Essays Volume II, To the Lighthouse, Orlando, The Waves, The Years, Between the Acts, A Haunted House and Other Stories* and *Mrs Dalloway's Party* by Virginia Woolf, © 1920, by George H. Doran and Company; © 1922, 1925, 1927, 1931, 1937, 1941, 1944, 1972, by Harcourt Brace Jovanovich Inc; © 1928, by Virginia Woolf; © 1948, 1950, 1953, 1955, 1956, 1958, 1959, 1965, 1969, by Leonard Woolf; © 1973 by Quentin Bell and Angelica Garnett.

Laurence Pollinger Ltd on behalf of the Estate of the late Mrs Frieda Lawrence and Viking Press Inc, for an extract from *Sons and Lovers* by D. H. Lawrence.

Introduction

The recent abundance of material on Virginia Woolf as a literary personage certainly has its interest, but though it can be seen as relevant to her work, her fiction is far more rewarding when studied as art rather than as an emanation of the writer's personality. It is as art that this book approaches Virginia Woolf's fiction. More specifically, this book investigates the psychological and epistemological ideas which lie behind her characteristic use of symbols and which explain the sensibility that is so indubitably hers, and that arouses either sympathy or revulsion in her critics. For the strength of her writing, and the originality of her writing, reside in her presentation of a reality that is created and sustained by the perceiver; and this reality is far more substantial, coherent and complex than the novelist was able to explain in her critical essays, letters or diaries.

The centre of Virginia Woolf's artistic sensibility is the need of consciousness to establish its identity and integrity, and the vulnerability of consciousness to the constant barrage of impressions and feelings which can on the one hand vitalise, but, on the other, over-excite, destroy or deaden consciousness. The focus on consciousness is so great that it becomes the centre of the self: the self, primarily, is defined by the character of consciousness, by the manner in which the world is perceived, by the memories and moods which activate or inhibit the flow of consciousness. In her first two novels, *The Voyage Out* and *Night and Day*, Woolf's attention is on the need for isolation, which preserves the individual consciousness, in conflict with the need to extend consciousness beyond limits set by society—a need which can be fulfilled by love. Subsequently, the growth of consciousness is seen as a donnée of the creative perceiver, who is susceptible to the allusiveness of external objects, whose mind eagerly investigates those allusions and, in so doing, extends the 'objective' meaning of objects, lending his or her subjective discoveries to the external world. Thus Clarissa Dalloway suggests to Peter Walsh that she will live on in all those things she has looked upon lovingly, and thus Mrs Ramsay actually does haunt—or endow with her self—the house and its occupants at Skye.

The transition of focus from the need for isolation to the need for stimulus was made through her stories and sketches (now published in *A Haunted House*). In them she explores the various ways objects and situations can be viewed, or the various contexts objects or scenes suggest; and these exercises became investigations of the mind that was considering first this aspect and then that, or this possibility and then that. Frequently these stories end ('The Mark on the Wall', 'An Unwritten Novel') as reality eclipses the fantasy; the intricate musings of the narrator must submit to the commonplace reality. In other stories, however, in particular 'The Shooting Party', the imagined comic horror has a power that cannot be depleted by the narrator's discovery of the actual situation. Here Virginia Woolf launches into a new dimension of aspect-seeing and story-telling: once the aspect is revealed, once the story is told, the possibility revealed remains vivid and real. Moreover, in other stories she explores the problems which may arise when a character realises that he or she is an object whose various aspects are viewed by others, and that the reality of these aspects cannot be dismissed. 'The New Dress' presents a conflict of self-identity when Mabel Waring adores her dress in private and then, at Mrs Dalloway's party, sees it (through others' hypothetical visions) as ugly and absurd. The realisation that many possible views of her are both justifiable and unflattering, awakens in her a very narrow self: she must try, in self-defence, to deny the legitimacy of others' perceptions, and thus vanity limits and distorts her world.

For Virginia Woolf's emphasis on individual consciousness, and her attention to the world as something whose character is determined by individual perception, do not lead her to the conclusion that only one's own consciousness is real. If one character's world is created by his perception, if his responses to the world give that world a certain meaning, then the same type of power and reality must be granted to another's perceptions. Mabel Waring is disconcerted because she realises that others' views are as real as her own, and vanity, as frequently in Woolf's works, resists this realisation. Recognition of the reality of others' perceptions can threaten the certainty of one's own; and since one is so closely identified with one's perceptions, one can come, through others' views, to doubt the stability and reality of one's self. Yet to try to defend one's self against others' views, to construct a bulwark against others' reality is, generally, to create a falsely simple, mean consciousness.

However important one's individual vision, creative perception depends upon the capacity to share others' visions and to extend one's own through this participation. The light of one's own consciousness only falls here and there, and the recurring image of the searchlight or lighthouse (*Night and Day* [p. 418], 'The Searchlight' and, of course, *To the Lighthouse*) indicates perception in continuous motion. Yet the confidence and stateliness implicit in this image is something few of Woolf's characters actually attain—hence their attraction to the image. Usually the consciousness, influenced as it is by impressions received from the external world and by the fluctuation of one's own feelings, suffers a nearly paranoic uncertainty. Moments in which some coherence of past and present is attained, when the usual flux is at rest, when one has the opportunity to investigate and appreciate what one's consciousness has made of the world, are grasped with a peculiar joy.

To bring into one's own sphere of comprehension, into one's self, the enormous vision which the world and the process of life have to offer, to integrate the external, universal flux of life, death and time into the personal vision, is the challenge presented by the needs of Woolf's characters. In *The Waves*, with six characters sharing consciousness in a world that is described by the author in terms of the various stages of consciousness, this challenge is finally met. Death and time become part of consciousness, and the external world is reciprocally endowed with consciousness—yet there is not the stasis of a mystic consummation, nor does the individual self ever relinquish its identity.

Virginia Woolf's technique, language and psychology are based upon the importance and limitations of perception and awareness. The techniques employed in the novels from *Jacob's Room* to *The Waves* solve the problem of how to place various views of various characters (or, sometimes, of an unidentified narrator) alongside one another, so that they borrow from and clash with one another. Her extensive use of metaphor is a means of exploring the boundaries of moods and the allusiveness of the external world; it presents as fact the psychological and symbolic significance of received impressions. Virginia Woolf is not concerned with character primarily in terms of motive and action, but with character as perceiver. She is interested in the way the world takes on meaning, and in those attitudes which either impede or stimulate creative perception. A character's psychology is not revealed by the material or social conditions that would interest Bennett, Wells or Galsworthy; nor can a character's psychology be explained by general laws, such as Proust proposes. A character's psychology is best revealed by the images in which his or her perception is described.

Since the self's creation and exploration of its individual world is a fundamental need, Virginia Woolf's moral criticism focuses on that which thwarts individual perception and denies its reality. Even her feminist revolt against male domination is based in her fiction (though in *Three Guineas* she presents a far less subtle utilitarian argument) on the 'masculine' tendency to intrude upon consciousness, to limit its scope. She loathes the aridity of male reason which both scorns and feeds upon the sympathy and vision of 'female' consciousness. She loathes the childish dependence of the male, resulting from his failure to achieve his own vision, and she loathes his impulse to deprive others of their visions: this, in her works, is the meanest moral flaw.

Her social criticism, too, is based upon the way social responsibilities and modes of communication intrude upon thought and vision. Even in her early novels this is the point of her comedy of manners, and this emphasis marks her difference from Jane Austen's comedy of manners, with which many critics compare it. For in Jane Austen's novels, a character discovers that he or she actually adopts commonplace stupidities, which experience and intelligence can frequently correct; and corrected, one can then apply one's mind more fruitfully to one's society. In Virginia Woolf's novels, however, society itself limits one's thoughts: the fact of society, not this or that aspect of society, makes one lose one's grasp on one's own thoughts and impressions, and thus makes one lose one's grasp of one's self. The violence of society's attack, and the despair of the ensuing loss, is seen in Septimus Warren Smith's suicide, and in Mrs Dalloway's conviction that he was right to assert so aggressively his difference from the social norm.

The anger in Woolf's criticism, the paranoia in her criticism, brings her closer to D. H. Lawrence than to Jane Austen (she recognised that she shared with Lawrence 'the pressure to be ourselves'),[1] though Lawrence has a distinctive conviction in the potency of his anger, while Virginia Woolf (and this is partly, but only partly, due to her sense of suppression as a woman) speaks with a voice which knows it will not be heard. The purpose of that voice is to define and confirm the reality of the consciousness which will not be recognised by society; and the fear that personal vision will be thwarted—either because others will deny its validity when it is expressed or, more seriously, because the commonplace consciousness will infect one's own, or will deprive one of that privacy which is necessary to the development and flow of individual thought— creates a constant tension; and a vision of the frailty of consciousness haunts many of her characters. In her last novels this threat is realised. Imagination becomes badly constricted, and the struggle to preserve the self, especially in *The Years*, is primarily a negative struggle; it is no more than a struggle for momentary release from the disjointed and tawdry world. *Between the Acts*, her final novel, published posthumously and without the benefit of her customary revisions, presents a warmer world, but the warmth arises from the human comedy which is the comedy of building up, eternally, a vision that is the only source of happiness, but which is fundamentally ridiculous and which reveals the essentially changeless fragmentation of human life. In these last two novels the social and domestic settings dominate the imagination, stifle the imagination, and individual vision is mere fantasy, absurdly removed from reality, unable to transform and define reality. The mobile, joyful vision, with its other side of terror, has become enmeshed in a stagnant world.

I have chosen to discuss Virginia Woolf's fiction in chronological order as the best way of revealing the logic of her over-all vision. The novels from *Jacob's Room* to *The Waves* exhibit a progression of technique and theme, with two complementary culminations: *To the Lighthouse* and *The Waves*. In the former a single consciousness becomes effective in endowing a world with its own truth; in the latter, various consciousnesses contribute to wrest from the external world images which will help make sense of the characters' changing lives. Her style emerges from the concerns of her first two novels, *The Voyage Out* and *Night and Day*, in which the need for the development of individual sensibility is established, but for which an individual language is not yet found. The final two novels reveal a destruction of what has been so painstakingly established: the world is not transformed by vision; it shatters vision, and even the will to reconstruct is badly impaired. The drama of the sequence of her novels reveals a logic in the self as defined in any single one of her novels. The self as a perceiver of, rather than actor in, the world confronts the ultimate necessity of creating one's world, making one's position viable for one's self, through one's actions. And Virginia Woolf's characters cannot actively change the world, and thus the world eventually has its own way with their vision. Yet this ultimate defeat does not render her conception of the self invalid. For her novels have shown the truth of a certain type of need—the fact that 'normal' social conditions and 'normal' language cannot meet this need does not undermine its profundity.

1 The First Investigations: *The Voyage Out*

Though Virginia Woolf's first novel employs a romantic scheme within a Conradian setting, the traditional elements are used to explore her own interests and to establish her own reality. The association of love with death, the use of the sea as a symbol of mystery and release from conventional life, the journey into a wilderness as a means of psychic exploration, are here used by the author to investigate the needs of a self which seeks a definition of itself other than that offered by the social world. The first paragraphs of *The Voyage Out*, which depict the Ambroses' leave-taking of London, present the city as a narrowly conformist place. In its crowded streets beauty is disregarded, and eccentricity—which is defined as individual response and mood—is not tolerated. In contrast to the hectic practical world that dominates the city (the world Terence Hewet subsequently defines as constituted by judges, civil servants, navy, army, Houses of Parliament and lord mayors [p. 213] and which Woolf in *Mrs Dalloway* and *Three Guineas* associates with the masculine world, created and ruled by men), the flow of the River Thames invites the thoughtful eye and provides relief from the constricting atmosphere of the streets.

The image of a river is central to the novel, and confirms the identification of 'the voyage out' with Rachel's inward voyage. It is on a river journey that she realises her love for Hewet and contracts the disease that eventually kills her, thus completing her isolation. Moreover, as she discovers her more profound self, her simple perceptions have the distinctive combination of passivity and motion associated with a flowing river. Sitting among the guests of the Santa Marina hotel, she 'seemed to see and hear a little of everything, much as a river feels the twigs that fall into it and sees the sky above'. (p. 260) Her reception of external impressions is merely a passive reflection of objects; and throughout the novel there is a sense that something is

7

happening to the characters, that in embarking on their adventure they are relinquishing whatever power they might have to determine their behaviour.

Critics have complained that Virginia Woolf's emphasis on the passivity of perception[1] (specifically in her essay 'Modern Fiction', in which she suggests that the modern novelist tries to 'record the impressions as they fall') excludes the possibility that perceptions can form a pattern, or that perception, since passive, can reveal anything about the character. The passivity which interests Woolf, however, is actually the unconscious selection and interpretation of impressions: when the reception of impressions seems passive, because common-place association and logic are suppressed, then the course of perception is actually highly creative. It is the vagueness of passive perception, too, which makes it more profound than clear thought. Rachel's sense that she is like a fish at the bottom of the sea, that she can see nothing clearly, is opposed to St John Hirst's claim that everything is crystal clear to him; and her belief that she can see nothing clearly actually marks her keener, or more profound, awareness, which is at odds with quickness and assurance.

The course the mind takes in such a passive state, though aiding self-realisation, may be menacing and destructive, Helen Ambrose compares Rachel's mood, in the first stages of her love for Hewet, to the sliding of a river 'quicker, quicker still, as it races to a waterfall'. (p. 222) The excitement Rachel feels in face of that danger emerges clearly when she is engaged to Hewet. He tells her he enjoys being hostile to her, because she then looks at him as though she could throw him into the sea:

> To be flung into the sea, to be washed hither and thither, and driven about the roots of the world—the idea was incoherently delightful [. . .] He caught her in his arms as she passed him, and they fought for mastery, imagining a rock and the sea heaving beneath them [. . .] 'I'm a mermaid! I can swim,' she cried, 'so the game's up.' (p. 298)

The ability to swim, which will free Rachel from her lover's grip, will also free her from life. Her love itself presents her with this challenge: when she and Terence declare their love for one another, Rachel murmurs 'Terrible, terrible', thinking as much of the persistent churning of waters as of her own feelings. (pp. 271–2) There is no possible reconciliation between an awareness of a self and a reality extending conventional boundaries—which is what Rachel's love offers her—and the control necessary to living within society.

The society Rachel must reject is, first, the English spinsters' propriety of her childhood home, which seems to her totally hypocritical, totally false: 'It appeared that nobody ever said a thing they meant, or talked of a feeling they felt . . . ' (p. 37) Such a society denies the reality of individual responses and associations. Rachel is so bored by the volume of *Cowper's Letters* prescribed by her father that Cowper's praise of broom's scent sickens her, reminding her of the flowers that smelled so strong at her mother's funeral, that 'any flower-scent brought back the sickly horrible sensation'. But when she tries to express her impressions to her Aunt Lucy, she is told, 'Nonsense, Rachel [. . .] don't say such foolish things, dear. I always think [broom] a particularly cheerful plant.' (pp. 35–6)

In this society, then, it is nonsense to attend to one's own associations, or to endorse responses not in keeping with the bland cheerfulness of a tea-party atmosphere. When, after her aunts have had a disagreement, Rachel asks Aunt Lucy whether she is fond of Aunt Eleanor, the woman dismisses the query with, 'My dear child, what questions you ask!', and when Rachel asks whether her aunt is fond of her, the aunt kisses the girl 'and the argument was spilt irretrievably about the place like the proverbial bucket of milk'. (p. 36) The anger that emerges from this simile measures the cruelty behind the aunt's apparently innocuous behaviour. It is the cruelty of thwarting Rachel's critical responses, of alienating her because she is trying to understand other people's feelings and, through them, her own: 'To feel anything strongly was to create an abyss between oneself and others who feel strongly but perhaps differently. It was far better to play the piano and forget all the rest.' (p. 36)

The supposition that Rachel's dissatisfaction might be mere adolescence is cancelled by the repeated proofs that Rachel's ignorance is willed upon her by society, that people in general do not want her to discover through experience and experiment her individuality. Helen Ambrose's invitation to the girl to stay with her in Santa Marina and thus to improve her education is acceptable to Rachel's father only because he is thinking of standing for Parliament and might need a daughter with the skill and confidence of a hostess. Rachel has always been persuaded against effort or perseverence in her studies. Music is the only activity she pursues seriously and her dedication is permitted (though her aunts worry that her arm muscles will become over-developed as a result of her practising and that no one will then want to marry her) only as a suitably feminine activity. Her aunts do not realise that through music she develops that sensitivity and intelligence they would otherwise deny her.

The education society offers women is a training in submission to men and to masculine vanity. Helen and Rachel, 'after the fashion of their sex', promote men's conversation without actually listening to it; and when through boredom they leave Ridley and Mr Pepper, the gentlemen are surprised, for they 'had either thought them attentive or had forgotten their presence'. (p. 17) Such attitudes make it almost impossible for men and women to understand one another. Hirst blandly assumes that because he is able to intimidate Rachel she is in love with him; and even Hewet, who responds to Rachel's genuine desire to communicate, is at a loss to understand what Evelyn wants when she speaks to him as a friend—or tries to speak to him as a friend, for Evelyn herself suffers from the corruption of man/woman relations, and she cannot speak to a man without flirting with him. And just as man's self-interest encourages women's limitations, his selfishness makes it necessary: so this is why she has been crippled and suffocated, Rachel realises as Helen explains sex to her, because men are brutes. (p. 82) Neither Rachel nor Virginia Woolf carries the paradox further, and sees that the notion that men harm women by wanting to make love to them is itself frequently a case of masculine self-interest.

Repeatedly the author asserts, through her use of images, that the people on board the *Euphrosyne* are leaving behind the stagnant, restrictive social world. As the ship moves along the Thames it leaves London 'sitting on its mud', and the city shrinks to two lines of buildings on either side of them. London appears to the passengers as a place where swarms of people are imprisoned and, as the ship proceeds, all continents shrink into insignificance. Yet English social definitions are not forgotten. The Dalloways, who share part of the voyage, represent the totally committed social personality. There is little of the individuality and joy which characterises the Clarissa of *Mrs Dalloway*, for this version of a younger Clarissa never extends beyond her social self. Rooms are always in Virginia Woolf's novels an extention of a personality, and Mrs Dalloway's cabin on the ship immediately becomes the room of a lady of fashion. She both appears in the guise of a painting (she is like an eighteenth-century masterpiece) and sees things as paintings (she declares that the hills, from the ship, look just like Whistler). When she retires to her cabin she remains, except for a minor change of clothes, the same person she was at the formal dinner, and the letter she writes also expresses only that social self: her husband can read it without asking her permission, and the sentiments it contains are totally determined by and totally acceptable to her social *milieu*. Her pride in being English, her elation as she watches the Mediterranean fleet, are linked with her husband's belief that it would be disastrous if women had the vote: for Clarissa's love for England is constituted by a sense of honour, glory and propriety; her view is that which in *Three Guineas* is seen as responsible for the suppression of women and thus for war. In Clarissa's view the social reality is the most profound reality. Not surprisingly, therefore, her presence destroys Rachel's musical world: as the young woman plays a Bach fugue and feels the notes cohere and form a structure, Mrs Dalloway enters the room, and the fugue crashes to the ground. (p. 57)

Richard Dalloway, too, is constructed from his social self. Rachel's awareness of his presence is an awareness of his well-cut clothes, his crackling shirt-front, his very clean fingers. The storm which disturbs the order on the ship, and which so disturbs the passengers' minds that for a few days they are freed from their old emotions and their old selves, stirs in Richard Dalloway an impulse to be communicative, and an appreciation of the aesthetic personality which ordinarily he slights. But Richard Dalloway can understand this impulse only as a desire to make love to Rachel: it is almost as though he wants to condemn this impulse, so he expresses it crudely, knowing he will then condemn it. He values his work as a politician above everything else and declares that he is more proud of his contribution to the reduction of working hours for some women in his constituency than he would be to have written both Keats and Shelley. This problem of aesthetic versus utilitarian values, however, is unfortunately left merely as a presentation of dichotomous personalities. The value of the possible effectiveness of the politician is slighted because of the limitations of his personality, so that the value of his actual work is not considered. Furthermore, the value of the artist's work is too simply asserted by Hewet in his belief that the artist is the only person who genuinely wants to create something good and fine; and the artist's work is too simply set in opposition to society by Hewet's remark that society will be the first to discourage, mock and even condemn the artist.

Richard Dalloway's ideal of 'Unity', which impresses Rachel, is a desire to unify the masculine world—that is, the social and political world. His notion of Unity is the notion of the world as one huge machine, with everyone participating fully in the machine, so that it runs smoothly, without distraction or deviation. The effect of his utilitarian ideal (again, the effect of his belief, not of his political actions) is to present Rachel with a disturbing vision of alienation. Rachel's interest in unity is the unity between her inner reality and the social reality which she cannot herself bridge. When she considers Richard Dalloway's vision of the world as a machine, and sees herself as a part of that machine, she thinks about all the other human components, and in so doing she loses all sense of her self: she forgets not only to raise a finger to remind herself of her reality, but also forgets that she has a finger to raise. As a result of this self-annihilation, the world loses its wonder: 'The things that existed were so immense and so desolate.' (p. 125) When one's individual reality becomes submerged by others' reality and others' purposes, then one's own impressions cease to matter, and one's self ceases to exist. Repeatedly Rachel is threatened by this alienation. The social fact of her forthcoming marriage, as opposed to the personal reality of her feelings, is an important impediment to her ability to survive the marriage. As she finds her own replies to the letters of congratulation as platitudinous as the letters she received, she hears the clock ticking and feels the eerie distance that lies between her self and the sheet of paper on which she is writing. She wonders despairingly why it cannot be one indivisible world; she wonders why her inner self cannot be adequately expressed within her society.

This query, and the barrage of criticism against society, might make it seem that the personal world, the inner world, were not in itself problematic, as though the psyche could, freed from social constraint, be ultimately free. Virginia Woolf, however, makes it disturbingly clear that this is not the case. For in her presentation of Rachel's awakening consciousness Woolf shows grotesque and repelling aspects which cannot be resolved. Part of the difficulties within the psyche itself arise from the fact that in *The Voyage Out* the expansion of consciousness is linked to a sexual awakening. Though this theme is not worked out in detail (and, since Woolf never returned to it as a central theme, her subsequent works cannot throw light upon it), there is certainly a connection between Rachel's realisation of further possibilities of consciousness and feelings, and her response to Richard Dalloway's kiss, as there is a connection between her love for Hewet and her death. Despite Rachel's belief that something beautiful happened when Richard kissed her, she subsequently dreams that she is walking down a long tunnel which grows so narrow that she can touch the bricks on either side. The tunnel then becomes a vault, and she is trapped alone with 'a little deformed man who squatted on the floor gibbering, with long nails. His face was pitted and like the face of an animal. The wall behind him oozed with damp, which collected into drops and slid down. Still and cold as death she lay, not daring to move . . .' (p. 77) Richard Dalloway, with his well-kept nails, becomes this hideous figure, whose narrow views enclose her and freeze her; but this dream also registers the mind's terror of intruders, and thus the terror of mental expansion and change. This dream, somewhat transformed, recurs during the delirium preceding Rachel's death. Alone in her room, save for the pious hypocritical nurse whose shadows flick grotesquely on the wall, Rachel imagines herself in a cavern whose walls ooze with damp, and she believes she is alone save for an evil, sordid—this time, female—figure. Even the isolation illness offers Rachel cannot protect her from that tormentor and taunter.

Indeed, throughout the novel sex is presented as something which easily takes on a grotesque aspect, and therefore the liberating influence of sex is brought into question. As Helen explains to Rachel that men have a natural impulse to make love to women, she offers the young woman what she sees as a 'mature' escape from the revulsion Rachel expresses: she says, 'The pity is to get things out of proportion. It's like noticing the noises people make when they eat, or men spitting; or, in short, any small thing that gets on one's nerves.' (p. 81) The fastidiousness of Helen's response, however, is more repulsive than the facts she is trying to make palatable; and though this can be seen as part of the limitation of her personality (she is reluctant to join the expedition to the river because she is shy of the difficulties of bathing and undressing), her reaction is endorsed by the novel as a whole. When Rachel sees Susan and Arthur making love, she declares that she does not like what she sees. This could well be justified by her naïveté or by the unremarkable fact that love-making is very likely to appear peculiar when one's relation to it is that of a mere observer; but Terence confirms her response and admits that there is something horribly pathetic about two people being in love. The distaste St John Hirst feels for women's breasts and for their response to love-making, while clearly a comment on his own sexuality, also remains part of that reality which Rachel, in her death, rejects.

The grotesque face of sexuality, or of physical life in general, is aggravated in part by the use of animal imagery which here, as in *The Years*, reduces the dignity of human interest and impulse. For it is the appetitive aspect of animals and their indifference to beauty that emerge from the author's use of animal images. Mr Pepper, declaring lack of interest in the splendid view from the ship because it has no effect upon his uric acid, appears to Rachel like a fossilised fish. Arthur, making love to Susan, butts her as a lamb butts an ewe. The guests of the Santa Marina hotel are, when the mail arrives, like animals being fed. At the beginning of the hotel dance the dining room 'had a certain fantastic resemblance to a farmyard scattered with grain on which bright pigeons kept descending', (p. 151); and when the music begins the people are like rats following the piper, and a passing woman looks, as she dances, like a pig. Hewet reflects that he is unsure whether people are drawn together by love, or by the same instinct with which cows seek propinquity, and Hirst believes his intellect places him so far above ordinary people that they appear to him like rats squirming below him. Moreover, the animal appetites of the guests clearly set them at odds with the aspirations of the spirit, for the meals in the hotel 'served as an extinguisher upon any faint flame of human spirit that might survive the midday heat', and until the food is digested, the hotel is inhabited by bodies without souls. (p. 118) So there remains unresolved in the novel the theme of sex as a stimulus to consciousness, and the theme of physical aspects of human life as a negation of the spirit and a manifestation of society's limitations.

It is a disappointment that, after the imagery depicting the passengers' break with England and her society, after all continents have shrunk and disappeared from their world, after their emotions and thoughts have been disjointed by the storm at sea, that they should find themselves again in South America bound by a society from which they can only intermittently escape. The power of Conrad's *Heart of Darkness*, to which *The Voyage Out* is obviously related, resides to a large extent in the inescapability of the dark primitive world; the isolating force of the atmosphere creates its own logic, and the characters lose their grip on the meaning of that other, clearer, world. Yet the hotel in Santa Marina shows that the London the *Euphrosyne* had left 'sitting on its mud' is still with them, though the bustle of the city streets is replaced by society in repose, with all the ensuing pettiness and boredom. Little privacy is possible in the hotel with its many rooms and the thin partition walls. The clock, which reminds the guests when to eat, and the newspapers—both are symbols of public, impersonal reality—dominate the hotel sitting-room.

The contrasting primitiveness or savagery of the South American setting is, moreover, unwittingly conventional as a description of 'natives'. The physique of the 'majestic' South American makes the English Mr Flushing appear ugly and unnatural, and, according to Mrs Flushing, the peasants do not, like the English, seem small in contrast to nature. There is nothing here of the profound individuality of D. H. Lawrence's Mexican and South American natives, or of the vivid presence of Conrad's Africans. To some extent this is unimportant, for the voyage to Santa Marina and to the river are inward voyages: indeed, the success of the expedition to the river is seen by Rachel's increasing reluctance and inability to recognise external shapes and her irritation when people try to direct her vision to the external landscape. (p. 277)

This emphasis on the inner world, however, is unbalanced by the way in which the external world functions as a symbol for mental state and emotion. In her later work Virginia Woolf creates symbols from the external world by means of her characters' response to objects and situations in the world, yet in her first novel she uses the more conventional means of correlating an event with a psychological state or quality, and the correlation is the author's not the character's. Evelyn, who wants men to be interested in her but who refuses to commit herself to anyone, is firmly 'placed' in her self-induced loneliness by the author who, after describing her habitual behaviour with men, then adds: 'But her donkey stumbled to a jog-trot, and she had to ride in advance alone, for the path when it began to ascend one of the spines of the hill became narrow and scattered with stones.' (pp. 128–9) The crudeness of this image arises from the fact that in so ascending the hill, Evelyn is not herself expressing a state of mind. The description of her lonely ascent is the author's way of forcing a comment on the woman's self-defeating behaviour. Again, when Rachel flees the unsatisfactory company of the hotel guests, she sees a kitchen worker beheading a chicken 'with an expression of vindictive energy and triumph combined [. . .] The blood and ugly writhing fascinated Rachel . . . ' (p. 252) Here at least the character responds to that which is intended to express her mental state, but the external occurrence is already fully developed; Rachel's response adds nothing to it. Much of the description of the external world, then, suffers from the inadequacy of being little more than a 'literary' counterpart of a character's state and, at the same time, from being statically objective and separate from the character.

Despite the novel's flaws, the theme of Rachel's inward exploration has an undeniable power. The exploration is largely negative. It offers a statement of the difficulty of integrating the deepest needs of self-expression and self-realisation with the life one must lead as a social being. It offers a statement of the disturbing confusion of the self's own needs and impulses, of the horror contained in our own sexual feelings, in the fundamental inarticulacy of that part of the mind from which attraction and revulsion arise. The inadequacy of language, and the pressure of an inarticulate sensibility, are important themes. They are realised far more satisfactorily in Rachel's painful, vague gropings than in Hewet's often quoted and simplistic assertion that he wants to write a book about Silence. Rachel's appreciation of the power and necessity of silence—that is, of the omnipresence and enclosure of one's individual sensibility—is not an idea which appeals to her but a discovery forced upon her. She tries to explore the world; she is interested in discovering the world; but every response leads back to her private self, which is destructive in its privacy and vagueness.

Love acts as a catalyst for the inward voyage. This effect is the result not so much of love's capacity to extend consciousness as its tendency to cut one off from the social world. Rachel's and Terence's intimacy is described largely in terms of its isolating effect: the effect of their love is parallel to that of the isolating wilderness: 'The great darkness had the usual effect of taking away all desire for communication by making words sound thin and small' (p. 265); and when Terence and Rachel are alone, 'Silence seemed to have fallen upon the world.' (p. 271) When they again join the group the words of the others 'seemed to curl up and vanish as the ashes of burnt paper, and left them sitting perfectly silent at the bottom of the world'. (p. 276) When they first declare their love for one another they are sunk in deep waters, and the sounds of other people fail to reach them; when they do hear someone calling Hewet's name, the cry, dissevered into syllables, was 'to them like the crack of a dry branch or the laughter of a bird'. (p. 284) Words lack substance (p. 286) and their love leaves them only with a feeling of darkness (p. 289)—so not only are they left alone because others respect their desire to be alone, but because love itself leads them into a peculiar isolation from which even their mutual sympathy cannot protect them.

The death of Rachel is not a Romanticist's solution in which perfect love is realised in death. Rather, it is a denial of the possibility, even the desire, to join one's deepest self to another. In fact, the course which love has taken Rachel leads her to see love as an assault; her image of love becomes horrible and aggressive: during her illness Terence kisses her, and Rachel opens her eyes, 'but she saw only an old woman slicing a man's head off with a knife'. (p. 339) Terence's love has not brought Rachel into a larger world; it has confirmed the reality of her own sensibility, and confirmed her determination to cling to it. The people who try to speak to her during her illness are her 'tormentors' and their faces fade from her consciousness in her attempt to focus upon

> the hot, red, quick sights which passed incessantly before her eyes. She knew that it was óf enormous importance that she should attend to these sights and grasp their meaning [. . .] For this reason, the faces [. . .] which occasionally forced themselves very close to her, were worrying because they distracted her attention and she might miss some clue [. . .] The sights were all concerned in some plot, some adventure, some escape. (pp. 340– 1)

There is too much real horror in this submergence in her own mind, and in her release from external time (which means that the night hours can extend at their will to thirteen and fourteen and fifteen o'clock) to see her illness simply as the realisation of a death wish. Of course in death she can have that unity which, she realises as she sees her and Hewet's distinct reflections in the mirror, she cannot have in life. (p. 303) She also achieves some mystic union with nature, for during her illness Rachel's will is replaced by the movement of a wave, her body becomes a drift of melting snow above which her knees rise in huge peaked mountains of bare bone, and her voice becomes a bird which flies away from her. (p. 347) Nonetheless, her death is a defeat; she is locked away from life, and locked up with her own fragmenting thoughts. For Rachel, nothing is achieved by this terror and this loss.

There is both a disturbing sentimentality and a disturbing violence in the significance the author places upon Rachel's death. The sentimentality resides in the ease with which Rachel's vision is communicated after her death. Only while she is dying does Terence feel the same division between his emotions and the public world that Rachel always felt; only after her death does St John Hirst lose his shallow confidence and find himself content 'to sit silently watching the pattern build itself up, looking at what he hardly saw'. (p. 374)

And this sentimental ease of communication is linked to the disturbing violence; for, it seems, Rachel must die before her self and its confused pressure to understand can be made real to others; and, furthermore, the banal hypocrisy and ignorance of society must have this violent effect for its cruelty to be recognised.

This novel, with the exception of the simplistic communication through Rachel's death,—presents a study of the impotence of individual vision, and of the self-destruction that emerges from that frustration. Virginia Woolf was always to be interested in the clash between individual and public mentality, but she was to develop a vision of this clash as a creative challenge with the inevitable pitfalls as stimuli to self discovery.

2 An Uncertain Balance: *Night and Day*

Night and Day, despite the conventional form which disappointed Virginia Woolf's contemporary critics,[1] offers a more profound study than does her first novel of the clash between the person society expects and believes one to be, and the scope of that self one most values. The aspects of society which impede individual thought and feeling are frequently presented in a comedy of manners where the emphasis is on the way self-importance and emotional greed serve ignorance in the creation of moral principles. The shock Katherine's aunt, Mrs Milvain, suffers at the discovery of cousin Cyril's mistress and illegitimate children is a symptom of her desire to intrude upon others' lives and to deny others the emotional life she has been denied. Her moral fastidiousness is presented as a lack of vision; towards the end of the book she is about to lose the sight of one eye. (p. 517) Katherine's father shares this fastidiousness, but his limitation is the result of laziness. Refusing to consider as relevant Cyril's feelings, he concludes that the young man has behaved wrongly because he has not behaved acceptably: Mr Hilbery 'seemed to be looking through a telescope at little figures hundreds of miles in the distance'. (p. 111)

The actual effects of this narrow social vision on Katherine are rather slight. She has freedom both in decision and action, and there is never any danger that society will punish her transgressions with more than a paternal scolding. The author, then, gives her character trumped-up praise when she says that in deciding to encourage her fiancé's love for the more suitable Cassandra, Katherine 'let difficulties accumulate unresolved, situations widen their jaws unsatiated, while she maintained a position of absolute and fearless independence'. (p. 332) This monumental pose is far less subtle than her actual task, which is not that of staving off intruding gossips, but of defining that valuable self which has no simple, social means of expression, and of discovering a bridge between that self and one's daily life.

The division between self and society in Ralph Denham's life is in many respects more pronounced than in Katherine's. His work, his family responsibilities, his ambition and his conscientiousness lie beside, though with an unbridgeable gap between, his dreams. However much he values those dreams, however convinced he is that they point to a profound yet unrealised dimension of himself, they have the invalidity and escapism of daydreams. Indeed, much of his behaviour confirms the adolescent implications of his fantasies. He sulks because his family refuse him the privacy necessary for the development of his finer nature; he comforts himself with the reminder that he can at least keep his thoughts to himself—almost as though he were punishing his family by so doing; and he exhibits the adolescent vanity and ambivalence implicit in this supposition when, hearing his sister stand by his door and, frightened that she will pass by, he opens the door, feigning irritation at the intrusion. Even his love for Katherine, which he believes points to the realisation of his finer self, has a recalcitrant element of fantasy in that he is most confident of his love in her absence, and his dreams of her are constituted by egoism: he sees the woman descending from her perch to crown him with glory.

Ralph Denham bears some resemblance to the childish, vain men in Virginia Woolf's later fiction; but though he resents Katherine's self absorption—her 'lapses' as he calls them—his primary need is not for her sympathy and attention, but for his vision of her. The fact of her actual, physical humanity, separate from his dream, is only a distraction. When he stands by the Hilberýs' house and watches her through the window, he does not see a figure of flesh but of light. When he tells her of her love he explains that he *sees* her everywhere (p. 313), and when she does not respond to him he concludes there must be some 'blankness in the heart of his vision'. (p. 448) The fulfilment of love is marked by an ordering of vision. After seeing Katherine in the Strand, Ralph looks about, and the scene 'wore that curious look of order and purpose which is imparted to the most heterogeneous things when music sounds'. (p. 133) And as Katherine walks with Ralph 'it seemed to her the immense riddle was answered: the problem had been solved; she held in her hands for one brief moment the globe which we spend our lives in trying to shape, round, whole, and entire from the confusion of chaos'. (p. 533)

The emphasis is not on the need for love, but on the need for a coherent vision of life, a vision that is one's own and which is linked to that private sphere of sensibility which is generally ignored even by one's friends and family—partly because it is so difficult to find a language in which to express that sensibility. The first sentence of the novel introduces the type of problem involved. Katherine Hilbery is pouring out tea 'in common with many other young ladies of her class', (p. 1) but only one-fifth of her mind is occupied in this way. This partial involvement is alienation from her environment, and it is enforced by her belief that if someone were to open the door, he would suppose that she was a perfect participant of the tea-party. Anyone looking at her, that is, would identify her with the one-fifth of her mind. Though this aggravates her loneliness, she tries to take advantage of the fact that people see such a small part of her. Even among her family she must guard herself: 'Her mother always stirred her to feel and think quickly, and then she remembered that her father was there, listening with attention'. (p. 99) This frustrating contradiction of stimulus and suppression results not only in the belief that her real feelings are unacceptable, but also in a desire to protect herself from others' views of her, which are bound to be both incomplete and critical. As she looks out the window into the dark city—as she looks, that is, through her individual eye into the chaos and darkness in which she might begin to find her way within her self—she remembers that William Rodney is thinking of her and 'she wished that no one in the whole world would think of her'. (p. 107) Katherine's private view cannot be sustained in the cold ignorance of another's reality.

Inevitably the suppression of her self makes her angry, but Katherine is unable even to express anger. The only way she can show her annoyance at her aunt's behaviour (and Mrs Milvain's assessment of Cyril's predicament is a general denial of the right to individual emotion and behaviour) is to let the window shade up with a little snap. Her restricted means of expression are linked to her decision to marry William. By a vicious logic, it seems to her that she would have more freedom by conforming to society's expectations. To marry William would be to disguise further the broader scope of her self; then others would find her acceptable, and leave her alone. Yet her decision co-exists with a longing for an emotion which would sweep away the dominating falsehood of her daily life:

Splendid as the waters that drop with resounding thunder from high ledges of rock, and plunge downwards into the blue depths of night, was the presence of love she dreamt, drawing into it every drop of the force of life [. . .] in which everything was surrendered, and nothing might be reclaimed. (pp. 107–8)

As in *The Voyage Out*, the desire for release and dissolution is couched in the language of Romanticism, and the very excess of the language underlines Katherine's own sense that her desire is bound to be defeated. Her desires contain, moreover, a peculiar contradiction in that she both longs for perfect isolation and believes that this isolation can be achieved only with a heroic lover's aid. The acknowledgement of her desire's fantastical element and of the contradictions in her desires, does not lead her to integrate her self with reality but, rather, leads to an emotional paralysis. In Lincoln, when her disgust for her fiancé and her inability to break off the engagement act upon her with equal force, she rides in the carriage in a 'state of gloomy self-suppression which resulted in complete apathy'. (p. 228) (Mrs Hilbery, on the other hand, as she accompanies her daughter in the carriage, drops into a pleasant, inattentive state of mind in which she is conscious only of the passing countryside. She is a fore-runner of Mrs Dalloway in her ability to create a delightful world and to follow an individual flow of thought which at times makes her appear silly, but which gives her a respect for the individual differences of others.)

The need to discover and to confirm the reality of that four-fifths part of the mind not involved in the tea-party is in itself an acknowledge-ment of the reality of other people's responses; it is difficult to see things—even to see one's self—as different from others' views. When Mrs Milvain complains about Cassandra's and Rodney's behaviour Katherine suffers a loathing that makes her go rigid. It seems that however assured she is of her aunt's ignorance and shallowness, she must acknowledge it as a view with some kind of validity. For what she sees through her aunt's eyes is the indecent spectacle of 'her own action beheld for the first time from the outside; her aunt's words made her realise how infinitely repulsive the body of life is without its soul'. (p. 431) She must follow the wider implications of her aunt's view, and as she does so, it infects her own. After her conversation with her aunt everything seems poisoned: that is the effect of 'objectivity' or of a viewpoint determined by convention rather than empathy.

Katherine's conclusion that 'the only truth which she could discover was the truth of what she herself felt', clashes with the knowledge that her own view is 'a frail beam when compared with the broad illumination shed by the eyes of all the people who are in agreement to see together'. (p. 330) The dichotomy between the value of her individual view and its frailty frequently results in paranoia and snobbishness: the knowledge that people will not, in general, confirm her thoughts and attitudes leads her to make a crude assessment of the general view, and she assumes that because people will be different from her, they will therefore be in opposition to her. As Katherine walks, trying to focus her thoughts, the expression on her face 'would have made any passer-by think her reprehensibly and almost ridiculously detached from the surrounding scene', and only her beauty, the author explains, saves her from the worst fate that can befall a pedestrian: people looked at her, but did not laugh. (p. 330) This simplistic assumption, that all people one passes in the streets are cruel through limited imaginations, is enforced by Mrs Hilbery's pity for the workers, who cannot feel poetry as she and her daughter do.

This paranoic sensitivity to others' views becomes more discriminating with the development of Virginia Woolf's technique. As Katherine and Mary Datchet sit on the window ledge looking at the moon, someone in the crowded room makes a joke about star-gazing, thus destroying their privacy and their pleasure. (pp. 56–7) This is precisely what Peter Walsh does to Clarissa and Sally when he finds them together in the garden at Brouton, but in *Mrs Dalloway* the reductive remark is not a symptom of people's general insensitivity. In the later novel Virginia Woolf focuses on the specific context. Peter's jealousy at the communion of the two women, and his desire to bring them back to his plane, are expressed by the query, 'Star-gazing?', and it is Clarissa's particular vulnerability to Peter's opinion that makes his mockery so painful; so that we are given something more complex than a division between those characters who look out into the darkness of their minds and those who, representing the general mentality, demand that everyone participate in the shallow, lighted public gathering.

The limiting snobbishness of *Night and Day* is felt, too, in the attitude towards work which emerges in the novel. Though many critics have associated this flaw with all Virginia Woolf's fiction, it is in fact uncommon in her work (a few counter-examples to this charge would include Rezia's happiness as she sews the hat, Mrs Ramsay's concern for the welfare of her children and the running of the household, Mr Ramsay's need to have his work recognised, Lily Briscoe's need to get the painting right), and even in *Night and Day* it is partial and intermittent. Ralph Denham's view of his work as spiritual tedium might well be justified, but Katherine's depression upon visiting his home and realising that his family must work to earn their living, expresses a highly distasteful patronage. Certainly

Katherine's reaction measures her own state; the defensive conversation of Mrs Denham strikes 'upon a mind bereft of all defences, and, keenly conscious of the degradation which is the result of strife whether victorious or not, she thought gloomily of her loneliness, of life's futility, of the barren prose of reality, of William Rodney, of her mother, and the unfinished book'. (pp. 398—9) The focus is on the dreariness of Katherine's world, but the dreariness of the Denhams' domestic life and the fact that these people are not even in the running for dignity and happiness, are revealed as the author's view. The scenes in the Denham home imply that the need to work to get by in the world oppresses the spirit without qualification.

In Mary Datchet's case, too—though the dignity and force of this character more than balances any negative conclusions the author reaches—work acts towards the destruction of individuality. In her office she must think of only one thing (in this case her thought is: how to catch the eye of a Cabinet Minister and deliver the old arguments in favour of women's rights with unexampled originality [p. 77]), and as soon as her thoughts begin to follow their individual course, the office atmosphere stifles them and brings her back to the task at hand. Moreover, it seems that any concentration, any singleness of purpose, is a type of soul-murder. Mary herself is afraid, above all things, of never changing, of always holding the same thought in her head; and the aggressive quality of repetition can be felt in the way Rodney reads his lifeless drama: he delivers each line with the same lilt in the voice which seemed to nail each line firmly on to the same spot in the hearer's brain. (p. 143)

Mary's attitude towards her colleagues supports the implication that her dignity as a worker is exceptional. They appear to her with some substantial part of them cut off; they are not in the running for life. Though the author shares this attitude, the subsequent change in her depiction of such characters can measure the change in her sympathy. Mrs Seal, the passionate suffragette who nonetheless suffers without protest man's vanity and presumption (Mr Clacton teases her about her lunch habits much as he would a pet dog who had convenient tricks), looks out the window and wishes that she could draw all the people in Russell Square and Southampton Row together, if only for five minutes. Then, she is sure, she could make them understand: 'But they *must* see the truth some day . . . If only one could *make* them see it . . .' (p. 176) The woman's faith in her truth and her desire to share it as a vision, makes her a fore-runner of Miss La Trobe in *Between the Acts*. There is, in the later character's struggle to express her vision, something both pathetic and valuable. Such effort, in *Between the Acts*, becomes part of the mind's means of self-expression, not a negation of it.

What remains valid in the fastidiousness that sometimes emerges as snobbishness or paranoia is the sense of oppression from the commonplace needs of life. This oppression arises from the confusion not only of the life round one but of one's own feelings and responses. Katherine's interest in mathematics is an escape from the frustrations of a reserved nature and from the muddle of her own emotions; the longing for a precise, clear world is also expressed in her fascination with the stars, though even this desire is accompanied by a blatantly contradictory desire:

[. . .] after gazing for another second, the stars did their usual work upon the mind, froze to cinders the whole of our short human history, and reduced the human body to an ape-like, furry form, crouching amid the brushwood of a barbarous clod of mud. This stage was soon succeeded by another, in which there was nothing in the universe save stars and the light of stars; as she looked up the pupils of her eyes so dilated with starlight that the whole of her seemed dissolved in silver and spilt over the ledges of the stars for ever and ever indefinitely through space. Somehow simultaneously, though incongruously, she was riding with the magnanimous hero upon the shore or under forest trees . . .' (p. 205)

The squalid image of the human as ape-like and mud-inhabiting is less dominant here than in *The Years*, but it nonetheless functions as part of Katherine's reluctance to trust life and, also, it contributes to the author's presentation of vanity and self-importance (especially in William Rodney's case) as covering an ugly, pathetic nature. In face, then, of a fundamental human opposition to clarity and freedom, vision—the capacity, that is, to extend beyond our immediate reality and our immediate needs—offers a splendid release. Katherine is able to take into her self that which she sees ('the pupils of her eyes were so dilated with starlight that the whole of her seemed dissolved in silver and spilt over the ledges of the stars'); she becomes what she sees.

Mary Datchet, too, when—after losing Ralph—she becomes only a serviceable human being, when she decides that the world will not answer her more profound needs, can nonetheless discover the vitality and significance of personal vision:

In the eyes of every single person she detected a flame; as if a spark in the brain ignited spontaneously at contact with the things they met and drove them on. The young women looking into the milliners' windows had that look in their eyes; and elderly men turning over books in the second-hand bookshops, and eagerly waiting to hear what the price was [. . .] (p. 272)

It is clear, then, that individual vision is not individual feeling of the type D. H. Lawrence, for example, emphasises. For individual vision can release one even from one's own emotions by extending and vivifying the impersonal, visual world. On the other hand, mood and emotion can also determine vision, though in this novel the association of vision and feeling is clumsily portrayed. When Ralph discovers Katherine's engagement to Rodney he feels the chilly fog obscuring the further bank, and he sees the ugliness and depravity of the streets: here the character's vision underlines his emotion with a three-inch brush, but does not explore it or define its specific qualities. The use of nature as symbol, too, is over-obvious: 'the light of the late afternoon glowed green behind the straight trees, and became a symbol of her. The light seemed to expand his heart. She brooded over the grey fields, and was with him now in the railway carriage . . .' (p. 192) Compare this cumbersome assertion of a landscape endowed with one's own thoughts to the ease and simplicity of Clarissa's—in *Mrs Dalloway*—awareness of Peter's presence: 'some days, some sights bringing him back to her calmly, without the old bitterness: which was perhaps the reward of having cared for people; they came back in the middle of St James's Park on a fine morning—indeed they did'. (p. 9)

The heroic figure incongruously accompanying Katherine's celestial vision is not merely a comic reductive tag. It is necessary (as is the angelic figure of light in Ralph Denham's case) because the individual vision, and the individual self, are not assured. Nor are they stable, or even self-aware. Social and domestic demands do not entangle a self which would thrive without impediment. The larger part of the mind generally left out of account in 'normal' life must be created, and in *Night and Day* this part of the mind clearly seeks a response from another person who shares the pain of division between personal and public reality. Katherine's love of mathematics is a desire for mental certainty and a revulsion against her mother's inability to concentrate on one thing, or to think logically and sequentially; yet this desire is not satisfied by her own nature, either. Frequently her responses and emotions conflict, and cancel out one another. As she rides on the omnibus with Ralph she begins to believe that she can sympathise with him and his attitudes, yet her present responses confuse her, for she had already placed him among people she does not want to know well: she runs 'a bar through half her impressions, as one cancels a badly written sentence, having found the right one'. (p. 94) When she writes to him to try to tell him how she feels, all her thoughts seem to flow to the tip of her pencil and to stop there: the reserve which protects the greater part of her mind from society's ignorance and assaults also impedes the development of the thoughts and feelings which belong to that part of the mind. Her dislike of literature is a dislike for discussions about emotions which always seem to her inadequate and fictitious; she has no faith that any language—even that of art—could express her deepest thoughts and feelings. When her feelings are couched in ordinary language, in an ordinary social setting, she becomes alienated from them. She shares with Ralph and Mary the sense that, should she explain her self to another person, she would be robbed of that self.

People become different beings when they are with different people—not because they behave differently with different people, but because they are seen in different ways. Ralph knows there are certain things about himself he can tell Mary; he knows there are certain feelings she draws from him like a magnet which are truly his, yet he knows, too, that he cannot give expression to his deepest feelings. The knowledge that a good part of one's self cannot be expressed in given circumstances impinges very sorely upon one's vanity. Certainly Ralph Denham's discomfort at the opening tea-party stems from his awareness that his more profound qualities will not be recognised in that setting. At times vanity can lead to a vicious impulse to assert one's self, to assault people in order to gain recognition. Among the crowd gathered in Mary's rooms to hear William Rodney's paper, Katherine feels that she is nothing because she does not have a profession: the attitude, that is, which she attributes to others, becomes her own. As a result, she would like to trample on their bodies (p. 54), and this violent reaction is due to her sense of what they are doing to her; in thinking her unimportant, or in some way insufficient, they are slighting her in a way that seems to her paranoically sensitive self like a type of murder. This paranoia is not totally exaggerated, because society does at times kill the self she most values. Even the sensible Mary feels, when Katherine come to her office, that she represents another world, a world 'therefore sub-versive of her world'. (p. 83)

The alienation a character suffers from the knowledge that his most profound self has no recognition or expression in his social and inter-personal life, frequently makes it seem as though the character has no self. As Katherine is walking in Lincolnshire with Rodney, wishing she could tell him she does not want to marry him, she has the impression that all things round her are dimmed, and that she herself is incapable of passion: she feels herself to be insubstantial because she knows that she is not the person Rodney takes her to be, or the person he wants her to be. Since her real self is unknown, the people round her are strangers to her. She looks at William as though she were looking at someone on the opposite side of a window; she looks into the faces of passers-by and thinks only of their indifference to her, and of hers to them.

The vanity which makes one feel stifled at non-recognition can also, because it piques one's desire for self assertion, be a stimulus to communication. Mary, 'when she found herself in talk with Katherine [. . .] began to feel rapid alternations of opinion about her, arrows of sensation striking strangely through the envelope of personality, which shelters us so conveniently from our fellows'. (p. 285) The need of the women to justify themselves to one another becomes friendship. Moreover, Ralph's love for Katherine is a need for her to know him and to think well of him; and her desire for love is essentially a desire for 'an echo, a sound'—that is, for some response to that self which is normally incommunicable.

Love, in this novel, is seen to be important to self-realisation because a stable emotion stabilises the self: 'To seek a true feeling among the chaos of the unfeelings or half-feelings of life, to recognise it when found, and to accept the consequences of the discovery' quickens the light in the eyes, quickens one's vision. Love offers the only possibility of establishing the reality of the self while allowing one to function in society. Mary Datchet, who is unable to satisfy her love, suppresses her deeper self and directs her energy to a utilitarian goal: the public world eventually claims all of her. Ralph and Katherine, however, remain divided. Ralph feels that he has two bodies, one tied to the earth and one free. Initially, when at Kew Ralph offers friendship to Katherine, he proposed that friendship as a bridge between the private world, which is free, and the social world, which is constrained. Katherine, as she hears Ralph's idea, wonders why there should be this perpetual disparity between the thought and the action, between the life of solitude and the life of society, this astonishing precipice on one side of which the soul was active and in broad daylight, on the other side of which it was contemplative and dark as night? Was it not possible to step from one to the other, erect, and without essential change? Was this not the chance he offered her—the rare and wonderful chance of friendship? (pp. 358—9)

The balance, however, between the 'light' and 'dark' sides of the soul is bound to be unsatisfactory when they remain totally unintegrated, and connected only by a bridge. The solution in this novel is simply to make the opposition tolerable by having one's non-social self recognised by one person. This is the last novel in which Virginia Woolf proposes such a crudely schematic solution, nor does she subsequently see love as a solution to the self's need for realisation and expression and communication. Love can at times stimulate or at others suppress the self; but it never again forms the focus of the creative vision.

3 Image as Psychology: *Jacob's Room*

'So of course,' wrote Betty Flanders, pressing her heels rather deeper in the sand, 'there was nothing for it but to leave.'

Slowly welling from the point of her gold nib, pale blue ink dissolved the full stop; for there her pen stuck; her eyes fixed, and tears slowly filled them. The entire bay quivered; the lighthouse wobbled; and she had the illusion that the mast of Mr Connor's little yacht was bending like a wax candle in the sun. She winked quickly. Accidents were awful things. She winked again. The mast was straight; the waves were regular; the lighthouse was upright; but the blot had spread.

'. . . nothing for it but to leave,' she read.

'Well, if Jacob doesn't want to play' (the shadow of Archer, her eldest son, fell across the notepaper and looked blue on the sand, and she felt chilly—it was the third of September already), 'if Jacob doesn't want to play'—what a horrid blot! It must be getting late.

[. . .] Such were Betty Flanders's letters to Captain Barfoot—many-paged, tear-stained. Scarborough is seven hundred miles from Cornwall: Captain Barfoot is in Scarborough: Seabrook is dead. Tears made all the dahlias in her garden undulate in red waves and flashed the glass house in her eyes, and spangled the kitchen with bright knives, and made Mrs Jarvis, the rector's wife, think at church, while the hymn-tune played and Mrs Flanders bent low over her little boys' heads, that marriage is a fortress and widows stray solitary in the open fields, picking up stones, gleaning a few golden straws, lonely, unprotected, poor creatures. Mrs Flanders had been a widow for two years.

'Ja——cob! Ja——cob!' Archer shouted. (pp. 5–6)

These paragraphs, which open Virginia Woolf's third novel, *Jacob's Room*, the novel which clearly marks the realisation of her individual style and thought, present the themes and techniques which dominate the book. The novel is a series of sketches of Jacob's childhood and youth; it is a record of his own impressions, which are seen to form an isolated pattern amid others' impressions, and it is also a record of others' views of him. Virginia Woolf here depicts an individual personality while she underlines the difficulty of apprehending any person; and Jacob's early death in the First World War makes anything more than a fragmented picture impossible. The haunting question of what remains from a handful of incomplete impressions becomes central to the question of what a person is, for that, essentially, is all we have. The initial answer is offered through Betty Flanders's relation to her dead husband:

> Had he, then, been nothing? An unanswerable question, since even if it weren't the habit of the undertaker to close the eyes, the light so soon goes out of them. At first, part of herself; now one of a company, he had merged in the grass, the sloping hillside, the thousand white stones, some slanting, others upright, the decayed wreaths, the crosses of green tin, the narrow yellow paths, and the lilacs that drooped in April, with a scent like that of an invalid's bedroom, over the churchyard wall. Seabrook was now all that [. . .] (p. 13–14)

The supposition that the person has been nothing gains a foothold because the light of his eyes—his perceptions, his impressions—so quickly fade; yet the wife confirms his reality by drawing him into herself and therefore into her perceptions. The man's merging with the grass and sound of his voice in the church bell, is not symptomatic of a mystical union with nature and God; rather, it makes a statement about the relationship between consciousness and the person: the person extends beyond the living self, into the world everyone can see and hear, and one becomes aware of another person by seeing him within one's own world. It is only by relating a person to one's own interests and sensibility that one creates the other's qualities and, when he is himself no longer a perceiver, confirms his existence.

The opening paragraphs contain no specific statement about Mrs Flanders's feelings for her husband, yet they leave no doubt as to what her feelings are, and what his loss means to her. The effort of making a decision to leave Cornwall because some accident has occurred, the anxiety of a single parent's responsibility and her appeal to Captain Barfoot, who has become the focus of her romantic fantasies, to understand the logic of her decision, are connected by the image of something welling-up, which is of course the image of tears. First the pale blue ink wells up from the nib of Mrs Flanders's pen; then the tears well up in her eyes, and the blot caused by her distracted pressing of the nib on to the paper further disrupts her thoughts. The blue of the ink is transferred to her view of her son Archer, and the cold blue of his shadow makes her *feel* chilly. The day that quivers as she looks out towards the sea, the yacht that seems to bend like a wax candle, help define her vision of the world as a place subject to catastrophe. Her thought, 'Accidents were awful things', is also a thought about Seabrook's death, and thus tear images implicitly dominate the writing. It is not, however, the tears themselves as much as what she sees through the tears that precisely present her feelings. The undulation of the red dahlias, the flashing glass house, the scattering of knives in the kitchen (and since she is not now in the kitchen, this can be taken a statement of her general state) reveal her violent and threatening world. Even normal or apparently calm states of nature are violent: the moors 'shuddered and brightened as the clouds went over', and tulips 'burnt in the sun'. (p. 15)

The rector's wife sees Betty Flanders in her own melodramatic and Biblical terms (a widow straying solitary in the open fields, gleaning a few golden straws), but the image of her bending low over the boys' heads in church also offers a further picture of the widow's relation to her children: as a mother she is determined to deny the turbulence of the world and to protect her children from her own anxiety. A few pages later we are directly presented with this division between the vulnerable widow and the mother determined to show her strength:

'Don't lag, boys. You've got nothing to change into,' said Betty, pulling them along and looking with uneasy emotion at the earth displayed so luridly, with sudden sparks of light from the greenhouse in gardens, with a sort of yellow and black mutability, against this blazing sunset, this astonishing agitation and vitality of colour, which stirred Betty Flanders and made her think of responsibility and danger. She gripped Archer's hand. On she plodded up the hill. (p. 9)

Her grip on Archer's hand is undoubtedly firm and assured; her maternal power will try to defy nature's. But, inevitably, she is only partially successful, even at her strongest. At the close of one section a hurricane is described at sea (p. 10) and in the opening of the following section Mrs Flanders is trying to soothe her son. Despite the comfort she offers, the storm jerks the stars this way and that above the ships (the storm, then, causes the sky itself to move—that is the sense of its power), and the 'yellow-tinted and sulphrous' element in the darkness cannot—the images make it clear—be kept outside the boys' bedroom; for underneath their blankets they are not only warm but hot, 'sticky and steamy'. (p. 11) Moreover, Archer's frustrated cries as he searches the beach for his brother Jacob emphasise the boys' essential isolation and loneliness. The cry, as heard by Charles Steele, is one of extraordinary sadness: 'Pure from all body, pure from all passion, going out into the world, solitary, unanswered, breaking against rocks—so it sounded.' (pp. 6–7) Indeed, Mrs Flanders's frustration in not being able to control Jacob (he is the least obedient of her sons) is her frustration in not being able to protect him.

In *Mrs Dalloway* Virginia Woolf frequently passes from one character to another by means of a single object of focus; that is, the aeroplane or the car with the drawn blind will be the object of several people's attention, and the narration will pass from one person's thoughts to another's on the basis of each person's response to the object. In *Jacob's Room*, however, it is not a common object of perception, but a shared image, or an object as image, which provides a narrative bridge from one character to another. Archer's voice is heard by Charles Steele, and the author then introduces Charles Steele through his perception of the voice. He hears it as a disembodied thing breaking against rocks, and this image brings the author to Jacob, who is studying rocks along the coast. (pp. 6–7) Moreover, because Charles Steele's hearing of the voice makes the rocks appear hostile (they are the things against which the cry of 'Ja—cob!' breaks), they are ominous when Jacob views them even though he might not at that time be seeing them as ominous; and, when he runs to a rock, thinking it is his nanny, his disappointment is enforced by Charles Steele's previous juxtaposition of loneliness with the confrontation of rocks.

Sometimes this use of image as a bridge from one scene to another can be used with comic effect, especially when the image first presented as a metaphor is then used literally. Cambridge is said to be like a suburb where you go to see a view and eat special cakes (p. 37), where 'cake' refers to the luxuries and delicacies of Cambridge life, but the narrator uses it to jump into a room in Cambridge in which one of the students is cutting a cake.

An image can stand on its own—that is, it can be presented directly by the author and be independent of any character's consciousness

though, generally, in such cases the image represents the consciousness of a character. The crab in the half-filled child's bucket, circling
the bottom, trying again and again to climb the steep slippery side of
the bucket (p. 12) is described in language which mirrors the hypnotic
sound of the falling rain; and the image presents the continuous
mental effort of the sleeping boy. More commonly (and this is similar
to her technique in *To the Lighthouse* and *The Waves*) Virginia Woolf
shifts focus from one character to another as one character becomes
the object of another's thoughts. In *Jacob's Room* this technique
frequently has a comic effect, for it offers a means of juxtaposing one
character's consciousness with another's view of the character. Mrs
Flanders's naïve supposition that Scarborough is the hub of the
universe is teased by her inability to find a stamp for the letter she
wishes to post there. Her movements, as she searches her handbag, are
then seen through Charles Steele's eyes: she is an object to put in his
painting, and her movement annoys him. Charles Steele needs Mrs
Flanders as a violet-black dot on his canvas because, he reflects,
without it the critics would say the painting was too pale:

> for he was an unknown man exhibiting obscurely, a favourite with
> his landladies' children, wearing a cross on his watch and chain, and
> much gratified if his landladies liked his pictures—which they often
> did. (p. 6)

Here we have an introduction of the theme of people viewing others
according to their own limited needs and, also, a sardonic com-
mentary on the small things a person clings to in order to uphold his
self-image, and the way apparently disjointed things (Mr Steele's
critics and the cross on his watch and chain) can be signs of self-
esteem. The effect is absurd yet poignant, very much along the lines
of T. S. Eliot's 1920 poems.

The technique of placing quotidian limitations alongside spiritual
pretensions is also similar to T. S. Eliot's teasing presentation of a
person's haphazard and somewhat tawdry self-image. In *The Waste
Land* we are told that 'Mrs Sostris, famous clairvoyant/Had a bad
cold, nevertheless/Is known to be the wisest woman in Europe.'[1]
While in *Jacob's Room* Virginia Woolf remarks, 'As for Mrs Rossiter,
she had nursed cancer, and now painted water-colours', (p. 100) and
'Lady Rocksbier, whatever the deficiencies of her profile, had been a
great rider to hounds. She used her knife with authority, tore her
chicken bones, asking Jacob's pardon, with her own hands.' (p. 96)

The social comedy of emotional greed and ignorance and hypocrisy which characterised the comedy of her previous two novels is here replaced by an investigation of the way in which people manufacture self-importance. The gossips and the people with silly pretensions are no longer part of a world totally different from that of the 'serious' character, with his attempt to understood others and himself. The comedy forms one version of this attempt, though the qualities which the minor comic characters use to construct a self-image are, generally, qualities which their society would notice and which would be suitable subjects of gossip.

The romantic fantasies that in *Night and Day* stood on an uneasy border between the ridiculous and the serious now cross that border and stand firmly on comic ground. Dreams and fears and desires are presented in epigrammatic summaries. Mrs Jarvis, the rector's wife, shares with Prufrock an unenacted longing for mystery and love. The latter is succinctly expressed through a delicate balance between fear and hope ('Still, there is no need to say what risks a clergyman's wife runs when she walks on the moor.' [p. 25]) she tries to confront God with the universal, but, we are told, she never leaves her husband, never reads her poem through, and simply looks at the moon, watching the larks soar, thinking to herself, 'If only someone could give me . . . if I could give someone . . .' Unfortunately, the author becomes infected by the character's sentimentality and clumsily comments: 'But she does not know what she wants to give, nor who could give it her.' (p. 25)

There is in *Jacob's Room* a freshness and wit that is frequently lacking in her later novels, when the mind is oppressed by the need to discover its own logic and reality. Here she delights in the way the mind jumps from thought to thought, or from time to time, naïvely assured of its own laws. And, indeed, despite the disjointed movement and strange juxtaposition of thought, the author's presentations always have an unmistakable logic:

> 'Dear Mr Floyd,' [Betty Flanders] wrote. — 'Did I forget about the cheese?' she wondered, laying down her pen. No, she had told Rebecca that the cheese was in the hall. 'I am much surprised . . .' she wrote.
> But the letter Mr Floyd found on the table when he got up early the next morning did not begin 'I am much surprised,' and it was such a motherly, respectful, inconsequent, regretful letter that he kept it for many years; long after his marriage with Miss Wimbush,

of Andover; long after he had left the village. For he asked for a parish in Sheffield, which was given him; and, sending for Archer, Jacob, and John to say good-bye, he told them to choose whatever they liked in his study to remember him by. Archer chose a paper-knife, because he did not like to choose anything too good; Jacob chose the works of Byron in one volume; John, who was still too young to make a proper choice, chose Mr Floyd's kitten, which his brothers thought an absurd choice, but Mr Floyd upheld him when he said: 'It has fur like you.' Then Mr Floyd spoke about the King's Navy (to which Archer was going); and about Rugby (to which Jacob was going); and next day he received a silver salver and went—first to Sheffield, where he met Miss Wimbush, who was on a visit to her uncle, then to Hackney—then to Maresfield House, of which he became the principal, and finally, becoming an editor of a well-known series of Ecclesiastical Biographies, he retired to Hampstead with his wife and daughter, and is often to be seen feeding the ducks on Leg of Mutton Pond. As for Mrs Flanders's letter—when he looked for it the other day he could not find it, and did not like to ask his wife whether she had put it away. Meeting Jacob in Picadilly lately, he recognized him after three seconds. But Jacob had grown into such a fine young man that Mr Floyd did not like to stop him in the street. (pp. 19–20)

Virginia Woolf is here certainly not presenting a stream-of-consciousness narrative, even though the narrative does mark out various paths of thought. The author is virtually omniscient as she follows Mrs Flanders' distractions and Mr Floyd's assessment of the letter, and Archer's motive for choosing the paper-knife. She does not, however, describe the characters' emotions; rather, she presents them through the characters' thoughts and actions. This apparently casual, chequered story offers a condensed narrative of Mr Floyd's life, and the careful selection of actions and events reveals their meaning far more economically than a description of Mr Floyd's mental states. His anxiety over Mrs Flanders' reply is measured by the fact that he got up early, though, presumably, he did not have a sleepless night. He keeps the letter as a memento of past hope, but it is not so precious that he does not misplace it. More subtle, and revealing more of his deeper emotion, is his treatment of the Flanders children. Mr Floyd wants to be kind, but the boys are oppressed by his stilted regretful approach (thus Archer, knowing he cannot give Mr Floyd the emotion he wants, does not take anything 'too good'). His unfulfilled desire for sons is implicit partly in the mention of his one daughter; it is emphasised by his excessive admiration of Jacob and his own diffidence when he meets him in Picadilly. The silver salver is not presented as an object of Mr Floyd's thoughts, but the fact that it is mentioned makes it part of his life, part of his personality: he is the sort of man who receives such a public offering for his services, just as the fact that Miss Wimbush was on a visit to her uncle when Mr Floyd met her, paints her as a dutiful, somewhat subdued lady.

Despite her frequent use of images as independent of a character's consciousness, yet reflecting that consciousness, Virginia Woolf does show in this book the process by which images become psychological symbols, and she does this extremely well. As Mrs Flanders comes across the word 'love' in Mr Floyd's letter of proposal, she thinks of her dead husband and then, crumpling the letter in her hand, she shouts at her son John for chasing some geese with a stick. Later, when the boys are in bed, she re-reads the letter, and, thinking of John running after the geese with a stick, she realises she cannot marry Mr Floyd. Her initial anger at John, which occurred while she was reading the letter, can be understood as an expression of her anger at the presumption of the red-haired (sexually aggressive) suitor. Mr Floyd's proposal is to Betty Flanders a vulgar intrusion, an act of bullying, like that of chasing geese with a stick. The displaced anger makes the coincidental event a symbol for the real object of her anger. It becomes part of her mental logic; it explains, to her, her reason for refusing Mr Floyd; it justifies her refusal. This image is replaced, years later, by a related image. Mrs Flanders feels uncertain of the wisdom of her rejection after learning that Mr Floyd has been made principal of Maresfield House. Her anxiety is soothed by the memory of having gelded the cat Mr Floyd gave John, and of her dislike for men with red hair. Having escaped the man's attentions, she no longer identifies herself with the animals being chased with a stick; rather, she is complacent because she knows she has tamed the aggressor.

Here, as in all her other novels, images recur which mark two different aspects of consciousness: the eternal movement of life and death in waves crashing against the rocks 'with regular and appalling solemnity' (p. 50); and the marking of time by the sound of a bell which either startles one with the realisation of the impersonal passing of time (it scares 'sleepy wings into the air again' [p. 54]) or, as at Cambridge, gathers together the past and enriches the present moment. Because the mind is a creator of images, however, there are instances in which external objects form a focus for mood or emotion, but do not congeal into recurrent symbols: one moment the landscape appears to Jacob to constitute the substance of his gloom, and then, having shifted his focus, it becomes nothing more than a 'screen to hang straight behind as his mind marched up . . .' (p. 47) Without this capacity of objects to take on a mometary image, the symbols would become hardened and stylised. What in fact happens in the book is that the highly fanciful images, such as Jacob's shabby slippers, which are like 'boats burned to the water's rim' (p. 36), point to the mind's tendency to see one thing as another without insisting that the comparison made reveals a specific quality; their point is that the perceiver seeks symbolic meaning in even ordinary objects.

Jacob's Room investigates far more closely than her earlier books the unbounded nature of the personality. The indeterminate manner in which Mrs Flanders discovers the reality of her dead husband, the intricately personal patterns of thought, the various ways the external world can take on significance, indicate that there is, in consequence, a very high probability that one person will go wrong somewhere in his perception of another. Usually a person's needs and interests exacerbate the difficulty. Virginia Woolf presents cases in which perception can be so tied up with one's own thoughts and desires that the mistakes the character makes are not only mistakes about a person's characteristics but fundamental mistakes about what is seen. Jacob, having been frightened by the sight of two people making love on the beach, runs towards what he supposes to be his nanny, but what is in fact a rock. When Archer asks his mother, 'Who's that? That old man in the road?', Mrs Flanders, thinking the man is Captain Barfoot, denies that it is an old man; then, discovering it is Mr Floyd, she does not challenge Archer's description.

Our view of others depends upon what we are, and what we need; consequently, Virginia Woolf asserts, the independent reality of another person comes as a shock; the mind cannot sustain awareness of such reality; we are used to dealing with people as shadows:

> It seems then that men and women are equally at fault. It seems that a profound, impartial, and absolutely just opinion of our fellow-creatures is utterly unknown. Either we are men, or we are women. Either we are cold, or we are sentimental. Either we are young, or growing old. In any case life is but a procession of shadows, and God knows why it is that we embrace them so

eagerly, and see them depart with such anguish, being shadows. And why, if this and much more than this is true, why are we yet surprised in the window corner by a sudden vision that the young man in the chair is of all things in the world the most real, the most solid, the best known to us—why indeed? For the moment after we know nothing about him.

Such is the manner of our seeing. Such the conditions of our love. (p. 69)

This passage offers an interesting transformation of the close of 'Canto 21' of the *Purgatorio*:

Already he was bending to embrace my Teacher's feet; but he said to him: 'Brother do not do so, for thou art shade and a shade thou seest.'
And he, rising: 'Now thou canst understand the measure of the love that burns in me for thee, when I forget our emptiness and treat shades as solid things.'[2]

Dante's vision of the conditions of love in Purgatory becomes Woolf's vision of the conditions of love on earth: our customary supposition that the man in the chair is real and solid has no basis, for our knowledge of him is thoroughly inadequate.

Love, especially love between men and women, creates particular difficulties in knowledge of another. It does not occur to Jacob that Florinda has a mind; and, furthermore, even in this highly physical relationship, she appears to him as though she has no body, and her face is like a shell within its cap. At Cambridge Jacob does not see women as actual people; they are merely different coloured clothes, and it is his susceptibility to their charms, accompanied by this inability to accept their human reality, which makes them appear obscene to him and makes him see their presence in King's Chapel as tantamount to a dog peeing by a pillar. Woman's response to man complements his to her. Florinda sees Jacob as one of the statues in the British Museum. On Guy Fawkes' Night Jacob's female admirers wreath his head with paper flowers, thus making him into a figure-head. (p. 72) When Florinda tells Jacob that he is good, her apparent compliment is an attempt to define him to make him good, to protect herself from anything unkind in him. Similarly, Jacob's vision of Florinda as true and faithful and incapable of pretence in emotion is a protection against both jealousy and his own anxiety as to the true value of their relationship—just as Clara Durrant, wishing to preserve her sense of love's tenderness and purity, cannot know that at the moment she is thinking of Jacob, he is telling an 'indecent joke' to some friends.

The impediment to men's and women's knowledge of one another hinges, in this novel, largely upon the problematic aspects of sexuality. The most prominent symptoms of this problem are the ease with which sex turns into something bawdy, the difficulty of combining intellectual and sexual needs, and the failure of education to provide any help in this area: 'The problem is insoluble,' Jacob concludes. 'The body is harnessed to the brain. Beauty goes hand in hand with stupidity. There [Florinda] sat staring at the fire as she had stared at the broken mustard-pot. In spite of defending indecency, Jacob doubted whether he liked it in the raw.' (p. 79) This disgust and self-doubt impede his sympathy for the woman. Telling her he has a headache, he watches her half-understanding, half-apologetic face and concludes, again, that education is no help whatever, and that the problem is insoluble. (p. 79)

There is little in *Jacob's Room* to counter the identification of sexuality and indecency because the novel itself does not present any vigorous or tender sensuality. The grape and vine imagery in the scene in which Jacob discovers his attraction to Clara Durrant shows a would-be sensuality that remains essentially impotent. The white and purple bunches of grapes 'lay curled warm in the basket' (p. 60), and this cosiness is enforced by Clara's fear of anything different: she looks at the greenhouse door and thinks, ' "Don't break—don't spoil"— what? Something infinitely wonderful.' (p. 68) But this 'something wonderful' remains her fantasy; the novel offers it no support. For Jacob repeatedly sees the person he loves in a grotesque light. On Guy Fawkes' Night Florinda tells Jacob she is unhappy; thus she reaches out to him, makes an appeal to him, but he sees her not as a person with emotional needs; he sees only an eerie marionette or spectre:

> Of the faces which came out fresh and vivid as though painted in yellow and red, the most prominent was a girl's face. By a trick of the firelight she seemed to have no body. The oval of the face and hair hung beside the fire with a dark vacuum for background. As if dazed by the glare, her green-blue eyes stared at the flames. (p. 71)

The flames are then extinguished, and all the faces go out, so that the bodiless girl disappears altogether. Clara Durrant appears to Jacob in a more attractive light ('wonderfully beautiful, with lights swimming over her in coloured islands' [p. 60]), but she is 'semi-transparent' and thus this celestial vision, like the macabre one of Florinda, is another symptom of his inability to grasp the substance of the woman.

The converse to Jacob's viewing others in peculiar lights is that when he actually does grasp the other's reality, he himself becomes drenched in light, and this light destroys him; it makes him as unreal as those figures he sees. When he catches sight of Florinda turning up Greek Street on another man's arm, thus destroying his convenient assumption that she is incapable of deception:

> The light from the arc lamp drenched him from head to toe. He stood for a moment motionless beneath it. Shadows chequered the street. Other figures, single and together, poured out, wavered across, and obliterated Florinda and the man.
>
> The light drenched Jacob from head to toe. You could see the pattern on his trousers; the old thorns on his stick; his shoe-laces; bare hands; and face.
>
> It was as if a stone were ground to dust; as if white sparks flew from a livid whetstone, which was his spine; as if the switchback railway, having swooped to the depths, fell, fell, fell. This was in his face. (p. 91)

In being forced to realise the independent existence of another person Jacob himself becomes an object seen very clearly from the outside and inwardly annihilated. To be faced with another's independent reality is to be reminded of our essential ignorance of others and of the fantasies we construct when we think we know them.

Knowledge of another person is an alienating, not a unifying process. Always it is as a solitary figure watching another person (not sharing something with him or her) that Jacob realises some truth about another person. And always, when other people view him, he is trapped by the frozen quality of their perceptions: as the light at Mrs Durrant's party pours over Jacob, every cranny of his skin is illuminated, but not a muscle of his face moves. (p. 58) These static conditions make our perceptions both false and ugly. While trying to paint Fanny Elmer, Jacob's friend Nick Bramhan discovers that the fixed faces are the dull ones; beauty is motion, something that cannot be seized or possessed; it is the life in things that cannot be taken from them. (pp. 111–12)

Jacob cannot discover this living, moving reality of others, nor can they discover his. As a child everything he saw—the rocks, the sand, the jellyfish, the sheep's skull, the rain and the wind—had a life of its own; everything continually changed its aspect, was both intriguing and frightening, brought him knowledge of a world outside himself, but became part of—thus enlarging—himself. Yet his view of other people, and theirs of him, remain cramped and static.

Compare a passage in *Sons and Lovers* in which the love-object becomes illuminated and part of the landscape, as both Florinda and Clara do for Jacob:

> Then he left her again and joined the others. Soon they started home. Miriam loitered behind, alone. She did not fit in with the others; she could rarely get into human relations with anyone: so her friend, her companion, her lover, was Nature. She saw the sun declining wanly. In the dusky, cold hedgerows were some red leaves. She lingered to gather them, tenderly, passionately. The love in her finger-tips caressed the leaves; the passion in her heart came to glow upon the leaves.
>
> Suddenly she realised she was alone in a strange road, and she hurried forward. Turning a corner in the lane, she came upon Paul, who stood bent over something, his mind fixed upon it, working away steadily, patiently, a little hopelessly. She hesitated in her approach, to watch.
>
> He remained concentrated in the middle of the road. Beyond, one rift of rich gold in that colourless grey evening seemed to make him stand out in dark relief. She saw him, slender and firm, as if the setting sun had given him to her. A deep pain took hold of her, and she knew she must love him. And she discovered him, discovered in him a rare potentiality, discovered his loneliness. Quivering as at some 'annunciation', she went slowly forward.[3]

There is in this passage from D. H. Lawrence's novel the same mingling of emotion and perception ('the passion in her heart came to glow upon the leaves') and the same emphasis on atmosphere in the depiction of emotion that occur in Virginia Woolf's work; but here Miriam's perception reveals Paul's distinctive reality and also brings her closer to him. In her own subsequent writing Virginia Woolf was to show emotion-laden perception as a revelatory process, but in *Jacob's Room*, when such perception is of another person, emotion unbalances vision and creates a static, easily destroyed illusion.

The theme of Jacob's alienation through his sensitivity to others' unreal view of him and to his own inability to accept the substantial reality of others, is certainly powerfully realised. What is unsatisfactory, however, is Woolf's more general thesis that it is impossible, under any circumstances, to know another person and to appreciate that person's multiple reality. A modified thesis, nonetheless, is justified and explained by the novel. 'It is no use trying to sum people up,' the author declares. 'One must follow hints, not exactly what is said, nor yet entirely what is done.' (p. 150) Though if one does this—the novel shows, without the author actually admitting it—if one follows hints with a wide background knowledge of the person's responses and emotions, then something can be known about another person, something can be understood. Naturally one's knowledge of a person can never be complete, simply because of the sort of thing a person is: a person is always changing, each situation, each response and thought adds to the store of facts about him.

Yet the pessimistic tone of the novel rests to a great extent upon the poorly argued assumption that people are unknowable, and are therefore essentially and necessarily alone. Her argument is based upon situations which are either likely or bound to impede knowledge. Proust, for example, shows how love makes knowledge especially difficult, bound up as our perceptions are with desires and fears—and Virginia Woolf explores this, but not as a special case. Then, to support her assertion 'Nobody sees anyone as he really is [. . .] they see themselves . . .' (p. 28) she presents Mrs Norman staring at Jacob, with whom she happens to share a railway carriage, and constructing his personality through her fantasies of young men. Again, the author comments that people on an omnibus do not take the opportunity to look into one another's faces: 'Each had his past shut in him like the leaves of a book known to him by heart; and his friends could only read the title . . .' (p. 60) But these episodes are cases in which knowledge of other people is obviously impossible, and are not cases of interesting attempts to understand another. Moreover, in face of her insistence upon the opaque quality of a person, it is strange that she implies a person knows himself fully, or can know himself as he can read a book. Later, in particular in *The Waves*, she was to deny this simplistic assumption that one's own self is so easily open to one.

Our knowledge of others is fragmentary; our perception of others minimises their complexity; and, as a result, one carries the burden of one's multiplicity almost like guilt. These beliefs supply the brooding tone of the novel. Looking out upon the Greek landscape, Jacob watches the men in kilts: 'Their lack of concern for him was not the cause of his gloom; but some more profound conviction—it was not that he himself happened to be lonely, but that all people are.' (p. 136) Nonetheless it would seem that this loneliness is our only comfort, for it is the pleasures of solitude and the freedom of perception solitude engenders that carry the poetic force of the novel. As the omnibus moves forward each passenger feels relief at being a little closer to his destination: 'some cajoled themselves past the immediate engagement by promise of indulgence beyond—steak and kidney pudding, drink, or a game of dominoes in the smoky corner of a city restaurant.' (p. 60) The 'indulgences' imagined are either solitary or non-communicative. More significantly, solitude provides a rich opportunity for awareness. As Jacob leaves the omnibus he stands at the steps of St Paul's and watches the passers-by:

They have no houses. The streets belong to them; the shops; the churches; theirs the innumerable desks; the stretched office lights; the vans are theirs, and the railway slung high above the street. If you look closer you will see that three elderly men at a little distance from each other run spiders along the pavement as if the street were their parlour, and here, against the wall, a woman stares at nothing, boot-laces extended, which she does not ask you to buy. The posters are theirs, too; and the news on them. A town is destroyed; a race won. A homeless people, circling beneath the sky whose blue or white is held off by a ceiling cloth of steel filings and horse dung shredded to dust.

[. . .] Long past sunset an old blind woman sat on a camp-stool with her back to the stone wall of the Union of London and Smith's Bank, clasping a brown mongrel tight in her arms and singing aloud, not for coppers, no, from the depths of her gay wild heart—her sinful, tanned heart—for the child who fetches her is the fruit of sin, and should have been in bed, curtained, asleep, instead of hearing in the lamplight her mother's wild song, where she sits against the Bank, singing not for coppers, with her dog against her breast.

Home they went. The grey church spires received them; the hoary city, old, sinful, and majestic. One behind another, round or pointed, piercing the sky or massing themselves, like sailing ships, like granite cliffs; spires and offices, wharves and factories crowd the bank; eternally the pilgrims trudge; barges rest in mid stream heavy laden; as some believe, the city loves her prostitutes. (pp. 63—5)

Despite some uneven writing in this passage (for example, the forcing of sympathy in 'for the child that fetches her is the fruit of sin, and should have been in bed', and the sentimental *non sequitur*, 'as some believe, the city loves her prostitutes,') Virginia Woolf shows how Jacob's vision on the steps of St Paul's changes from a personal to a general one (forgetting her character the narrator points out what 'you can see' throughout the city) in which the eternity of joy and horror emerges from the quotidian setting. Only in undistracted solitude could Jacob achieve this breadth of vision.

The haunting eternity felt in this chant-like description of the London streets bears a strong resemblance to T. S. Eliot's London of *The Waste Land*:

> Unreal City,
> Under the brown fog of a winter dawn,
> A crowd flowed over London Bridge, so many,
> I had not thought death had undone so many.
> Sighs, short and infrequent were exhaled,
> And each many fixed his eyes before his feet.
> Flowed up the hill and down King William Street,
> To where Saint Mary Woolnoth kept the hours
> With a dead sound on the final stroke of nine.[4]

Yet Virginia Woolf relishes the squalor which Eliot sees as a type of death. However chained the people of London are to their street corners and poverty, the observer can seek out their individuality, can relish their existence as one form of vitality. The observer in *The Waste Land* is oppressed by his vision of the oppressed; in *Jacob's Room* the observer is free; he is not implicated in humdrum life; he is on an adventure, and the streets are uncharted; and through these uncharted streets he finds a response to those aspects of himself which are normally ignored: 'What are you going to meet when you turn this corner? [. . .] As frequent as street corners in Holborn are these chasms in the continuity of our ways. Yet we keep straight on.' (pp. 92—3) 'Street haunting', or the observation of a detached pedestrian, becomes a means of shedding one's limitations by shedding the limitations forced upon one in the social or personal world. The anonymity of the London crowds which horrifies T. S. Eliot provides Virginia Woolf with a vital stimulus:

The magnificent world—the live, sane, vigorous world. . . . These words refer to the stretch of wood pavement between Hammersmith and Holborn in January between two and three in the morning. [. . .] The street scavengers were the only people about at the moment. It is scarcely necessary to say how well-disposed Jacob felt towards them; how it pleased him to let himself in with his latch-key at his own door; how he seemed to bring back with him into the empty room ten or eleven people whom he had not known when he set out [. . .]

They cross the Bridge incessantly [. . .] Then the motor car in front jerks forward, and the tombstones pass too quickly for you to read more. All the time the stream of people never ceases passing from the Surrey side to the Strand; from the Strand to the Surrey side.

[. . .] That old man has been crossing the Bridge these six hundred years, with the rabble of little boys at his heels, for he is drunk, or blind with misery, and tied round with old clouts of clothing such as pilgrims might have worn. He shuffles on. No one stands still. It seems as if we marched to the sound of music; perhaps the wind and the river; perhaps these same drums and trumpets—the ecstasy and hubbub of the soul. (pp. 108–10)

This vision of changeless misery and static motion has more in common with the joy of Wordsworth's 'Woods decaying never to be decayed' than with the moral force of Eliot's spectral city. The emphasis is on the city as a natural phenomenon, and Jacob's observation of the city is very much like the impersonal participation one can enjoy with nature. Significantly, the ten or eleven people he brings back with him from these streets do not interrupt his solitude; in imagination he can enjoy people far more than in situations where demands are made upon his emotions and where his imagination is challenged by an independent reality. Even the author's praise of friendship reads as a eulogy of solitude: friendship is 'still, deep, like a pool. Without need of movement or speech it rose softly and washed over everything, mollifying, kindling, and coating the mind with the lustre of pearl . . .' (pp. 43–4) Friendship, then, at its best, does not extend the mind but, with a seductive coating, further encloses it.

At times Virginia Woolf speaks of reality as something the imagination discovers in the ordinary world, something external to one but created by one's vision and becoming part of one; at other times, she speaks of reality as the public world in opposition to individual vision, or as that view which defines the self in alienating terms—the Opera House the narrator-observer discovers at the end of the Strand represents the social, limiting view, for after the chaos and richness of the uncharted London streets, one runs up against the Opera House in which people are placed in compartments and are expected to conform: thus, 'Whenever I seat myself, I die in exile.' (p. 66) Luncheons and social engagements in general are part of the reality defined by 'Shaw and Wells and the sixpenny weeklies' (p. 33), and thus they deny Jacob's own identification of himself, of his reality, with the moors and Byron, the sea and the lighthouse, and the sheep's jaw he found on the beach as a child. Just as solitude stimulates the former type of reality, it protects one against the latter.

Jacob's determination—the determining force, in fact, of his thoughts—is to realise his individuality: 'I am what I am, and intend to be it,' he declares, and he understands that this self will have no form unless he creates it for himself. (p.33) Society will impede him, but opposition to society is seen as necessary to human survival. Indeed, social demands are suggested to be at the root of all personal distress and ignorance of the human heart:

> Indeed there has never been any explanation of the ebb and flow in our veins—of happiness and unhappiness. That respectability and evening parties where one has to dress, and wretched slums at the back of Gray's Inn—something solid, immovable, and grotesque—is at the back of it, Jacob thought probable. (pp. 134–5)

The connection, however, is not pursued. The destructiveness of society is felt most strongly on a personal, rather than an economic level; speeches in Parliament are useless (rather than harmful) as long as we have to give 'one inch to the dark waters' which drown our true self. Yet even at a modest University Professor's luncheon Jacob feels 'shock, horror and discomfort'. Fleeing from the party he finds immediate pleasure in his solitude:

> for he draws into him at every step as he walks by the river such steady certainty, such reassurance from all sides, the trees bowing, the grey spires soft in the blue, voices blowing and seeming suspended in the air, the springy air of May, the elastic air with its particles—chestnut bloom, pollen, whatever, it is that gives the

May air its potency, blurring the trees, gumming the buds, daubing the green. And the river too runs past, not at flood, nor swiftly, but cloying the oar that dips in it and drops white drops from the blade, swimming green and deep over the bowed rushes, as if lavishly caressing them. (p. 34)

This extended, wistful language, with its unoriginal imagery (one probable source is Matthew Arnold's *The Scholar-Gipsy*) is characteristic of much of her writing throughout her life; but her language is always careful, and the imagery, however indulgent or 'literary', offers a consideration of her themes. The air is elastic, thus giving the mind the opportunity to find its own form (and when Jacob rouses himself from this solitary musing, returning to a more public reality, he feels as though 'a piece of elastic had snapped in his face'); the 'blurring' and 'daubing' of colours, the 'gumming' of the buds, represent a softening of detail and focus; yet this softening is seen to be part of the air's 'potency' for the diminishing of ordinary boundaries and an increasing vagueness make the mind more potent. The movement of the river—'not at flood nor swiftly'—mirrors the semi-passive movement of the mind in its private and individual state; in such a state it seeks its own uninterrupted flow. As the mind receives impressions of the external world according to its own—not the public—law and logic, these impressions become part of the mind; they lead to further thoughts with the seductive ease of an oar dipping in gently flowing water, generating movement.

Society will not allow him any extension of this holiday. That which is absolute in us and despises qualification will be 'teased and twisted in society'. (p. 140) For lies are demanded as politeness, and gossips, who suppose they can define other people, 'stuff out their victims' characters till they are swollen and tender as the livers of geese exposed to a hot fire'. (p. 151) Through this angry metaphor Virginia Woolf again points to a causal analysis of political forces. Indeed, the sense of cruelty so violently exposed in this metaphor is felt to be as real as war. Juxtaposed to the gossips' torture of the true self and the ensuing destruction of human understanding (for in such an atmosphere, character-drawing becomes 'a matter of pins and needles, exquisite outlines enclosing vacancy, flourishes and mere scrawls' [p. 151]) is the image of young men descending into the depths of the sea to be blown up there. (p. 151) The death of the recognition of human complexity, the death of the recognition of its profundity, point towards the death of a satisfactory morality.

Society nonchalantly demands the death of these men because it is unable to appreciate their reality.

The freedom of self-realisation can be imagined only on the supposition that humanity is finished: 'To gallop intemperately; fall on the sand tired out; to feel the earth spin; to have—positively—a rush of friendship for stones and grasses, as if humanity were over, and as for men and women, let them go hang— . . .' (p. 137) Jacob can merely contemplate such release as he looks at a single wild red cyclamen which survives, somehow, amid the comedy of love and the tragedy of social restrictions that surround him. Jacob's strength lies in his assurance of this possibility of independence and release, and in his sensitivity to the cruelty that is usually imperceptibly inflicted upon its members. He has, however, no strength to resist that which he understands to be opposed to him, and when he dies, a victim of war and thus of society's ignorant cruelty, it seems that there is little left of him but—as his mother finds in the confusion of his room—a pair of old boots. *Jacob's Room* is a bitter novel, but that joy Jacob marks out as his own in solitary, vivid perception, is to be celebrated in Virginia Woolf's next novel.

4 Perception and Imagination: *Mrs Dalloway* and her Party

The eye is not a simple recording machine; the relation between eye and object is not like that of a seal upon wax. Karl Popper began a lecture with the following instructions: 'Take a pencil and paper; carefully observe, and write down what you have observed.' The students naturally asked what he wanted them to observe. Popper explained that this apparently straightforward instruction 'Observe!' is meaningless: 'Observation is always selective. It needs a chosen object, a definite task, an interest, a point of view, a problem. And its description presupposes a descriptive language, with property words; it presupposes similarity and classification, which in turn presupposes interests, points of views and problems.'[1] Virginia Woolf, throughout her mature fiction, is interested in exploring this selective aspect of observation. She is interested in the way one uses perception as a springboard for thoughts and memories, so that perception becomes laden with symbols. She is interested in the pace with which one passes from one point of focus to another, and in the way that pace measures individual, mental time outside the force of public time. She is interested in the different stories that can be told about what is seen, and she shows that these differences are not merely tales tagged on to the thing seen, but part and parcel of what a character observes.

In *Mrs Dalloway* everyone in the West End sees the same large car with the blind drawn, but each character makes a different inference about the person inside the car, according to his respective notion of greatness, just as each character offers a different reading of the aeroplane's sky-writing. There are cases in which it makes sense to say that the character's theory of what it is he perceives (behind the drawn blind, or in the sky) is either correct or mistaken. More commonly, however, individual interpretations cannot be either corrected or confirmed by further observation. Peter Walsh sees, in the woman singing outside the tube station in Regent's Park, the passing ages: he does not infer that she—or someone like her—has been standing there for centuries; he sees in her song something enduring and triumphant. The essential vitality of his vision of the woman is not denied by the essential pathos of Lucrezia's vision of her: Lucrezia hears the woman's song as an ancient song of love and, feeling the impotence of her own love for Septimus, she reveals her own state through her pity for that useless upsurge of love.

Just as the old woman and her song *are* these different things, the sounds of the bells, either to different people or to the same person at different times, reveal different aspects of the people who hear them. Outside the offices of Sir William Bradshaw the chimes of the clock shred and slice, divide and subdivide, nibble away at the June day to uphold authority and the advantages of a sense of proportion. As the young, shy Elizabeth Dalloway is presented to Peter, the chimes of Big Ben sound with extraordinary vigour, as if an inconsiderate young man were swinging dumb-bells: the image is shared by all of them, for to Clarissa and Peter, Elizabeth's youth represents the relentless vigour of time, while Elizabeth feels the chimes as a bullying force of the public, objective world. As Peter leaves Clarissa, he hears the chimes first, as he thinks about the woman's interminable parties, as leaden circles dissolving in the air; then, thinking of her as hostess, he hears church bells not as cold and dissolving, but as something which buries itself in the heart, 'something alive which wants to confide itself'. (p. 56) A moment later, through thoughts of Clarissa's illness and of the time that has passed since their youth and intimacy, the church bells become a tolling for death, so insistent that he has to protest that they are both still alive. The different things he hears cannot be accounted for by any difference of auditory sensation; yet he is not simply imagining what he hears. The sounds of the chimes and bells are open to many possible responses; these different responses are determined by the individual character's imagination, yet these different responses reveal not mere individual fantasies but different aspects of reality. Even Septimus Warren Smith's apparently mad visions have this kind of truth; the world makes sense that way, one can respond to it that way, one's response reveals new aspects of the world.

The perceiver who notes new possibilities, who vitalises new aspects of reality, is the creative perceiver, and this creativeness is Virginia Woolf's measure of truth. The perceiver who sees only what is publicly known and publicly accepted, kills the world as he observes it. Clarissa knows that through her observation of the world, she has given something of herself to the world, and that this extends beyond and will survive her individual life:

> [. . .] somehow in the streets of London, on the ebb and flow of things, here, there, she survived, Peter survived, lived in each other, she being part, she was positive, of the trees at home; of the house there, ugly, rambling all to bits and pieces as it was; part of people she had never met; being laid out like a mist between the people she knew best, who lifted her on their branches as she had seen the trees lift the mist, but it spread ever so far, her life, herself. (pp. 11–12)

Thus the idea that individual mood and thought-influenced perception highlights 'objective' or enduring truths about the world, functions as a literary device: personally developed symbols can be shared as easily and widely as qualities of an external object, and characters (such as Clarissa and Septimus) can be joined not through immediate contact but by various go-betweens—that is, by common objects of perception.

Virginia Woolf's investigations of imagination's role in perception began with stories and sketches originally published in *Kew Gardens* (1919), which now appear among the selections in *A Haunted House*. The story with that title is an experiment in passive reflection: a visitor becomes aware of the house as an object that has absorbed something of the lives of its previous inhabitants. The story makes use of the assumption that a person's impressions and responses are independent of the person, that an object takes on as its own qualities, perceivable by others, feelings and thoughts experienced in the presence of the object; but the crude version of this idea employed in the story renders it a failure. The point of interest—the process by which such an idea becomes plausible—is ignored, and nothing more is conveyed than a sensitive, eerie atmosphere.

In 'Monday or Tuesday' Woolf explores one of the more teasing philosophical problems of perception: we know objects only through our perception of them; how then can we be sure that we know the true character of an external object, or even that it exists at all? In this sketch the visual impressions, rather than the external object, are described. The flying heron is a dark mobile image that blocks out other images in the narrator's visual field. These images are continually changing; they are obliterated and then renewed. What kind of reality lies behind these images, the narrator wonders. After all, we suppose external objects to have spatial continuity and to change only according to various laws; but visual images, which we use to make suppositions about external objects, lack the solidity and continuity we attribute to objects. This puzzle is raised, but the author makes no attempt to answer it, and it is not a question which generally interests her. In 'An Unwritten Novel' the fragmentation of visual images leads the narrator to suppose that the story itself is fragmented ('She moved her knees—the map's in bits again.' [p. 21]); but here the simple behaviour of visual impressions reminds the narrator of the difficulty of establishing a satisfactory and stable view-point—it does not constitute the difficulty.

The narrator's delight in using one incident or impression as the starting point of a complex story, leads her to consider what impressions other people receive from the world and to confront the possibility of an observer who makes no use of imagination. The most frightening face, according to the narrator, is the face which coldly observes life, denying all hope and illusion. To escape this negative vision, she wants to hang still like a hawk, hovering above the ground: 'Alone, unseen; seeing all so still down there, all so lovely. None seeing, none caring. The eyes of others our prisons; their thoughts our cages . . .' (p. 20) The narrator is seeking some escape from others' vision, but the adequate point of view is crudely conceived as a spatial point: the problem becomes, in what place (literally) shall I stand to see the truth? This spurious posing of the problem is complemented by the notion that truth can be attacked head-on, as a physical fortress. The narrator determines; 'what I cannot thus eliminate, what I must, head down, eyes shut, with the courage of the battalion and the blindness of a bull, charge and disperse are, indubitably, the figures behind the ferns . . . ' (p. 21) The narrator does not escape the metaphor in which the challenge is conceived, and the attempts to come to grips with reality in terms of the metaphor make the attempt nothing more than a game with images.

'Kew Gardens' also opens with a description of the landscape primarily as a pattern of visual impressions: 'The petals were voluminous enough to be stirred by the summer breeze, and when they moved, the red, blue and yellow lights passed one over the other, staining an inch of the brown earth beneath with a spot of moist intricate colour.' (p. 32) The light that falls on the raindrops expands with such intensity that it seems the raindrops will burst: just as external objects are described as having the property of visual images, images are described as having the property of physical objects—the expanding light will burst the raindrop. Moreover, visual impressions are aggressive; as the breeze stirs colour is flashed into the eyes of the men and women who walk in the gardens. (p. 32) Somewhat clumsily, the anonymous observer becomes an individual reminiscing about a visit to Kew fifteen years before, when he had come with a woman he loved and when he had—so it seemed to him—seen his love settle upon the dragonfly he was watching. The story asserts that emotion can influence even the simplest perceptions, but it does not describe—as Woolf later does—precisely what happens in such cases.

In 'The Mark on the Wall' the question, 'What do I see?' is given several experimental answers. The simple definition of the mark as a thing seen is a 'small round mark, black upon the white wall, about six or seven inches above the mantel-piece'. (p. 40) The narrator guesses that it is a hook, and then uses this supposition as the basis for a sketch of the previous owners of the house, derived from the type of pictures the narrator imagines would have been hung on the hook. The black mark is a stimulus to the imagination, but it is a trivial stimulus and some of Woolf's critics have found it exasperating.[2] The arbitrary association of the mark with the story told is interesting, however, as sample of what was eventually to become a highly successful technique which reveals a great deal about the nature of perception. When William Empson complains that Virginia Woolf's method is impressionistic, that 'it tries to correlate sensations rather than the impulses that make the sensations interesting; even tries to define the impulse by an accumulation of the sensation it suggested to the author',[3] his criticism holds only for these experimental stories which merely indicate without developing Woolf's fascination with the way perception can be focused and coloured by feeling, and the way perception can open a door to memory or speculation.

In *A Haunted House* Virginia Woolf is generally interested in present observation as a stimulus to hypothesis; observation provides a starting point, and imagination fills in possible outlines, and muses upon something that is not observed. The most significant exercise of imagination, however, and that which the author developed in *Mrs Dalloway*, is not developing a fantasy but discovering a way of seeing the world that is both true and individual. The manner in which something is seen actually becomes part of what is seen. 'What a morning—fresh as if issued to children on a beach,' thinks Mrs Dalloway (p. 5), and the language in which her movements are described—she 'had burst open the French windows', and she had 'plunged at Bourton into the open air' (p. 5)—displays the eagerness of her vision. She recognises that part of her love for the world around her is the love for the creative act of perception itself:

> For Heaven only knows why one loves it so, how one sees it so, making it up, building it round one, tumbling it, creating it every moment afresh [. . .] In people's eyes, in the swing, tramp and trudge [. . .] in the triumph and the jingle and the strange high singing of some aeroplane overhead was what she loved; life; London; this moment of June. (p. 6)

The importance of imagination in this novel lies to a great extent in its capacity to make the present moment vivid, to endow the present with one's mood and memories, to draw the things one sees into one's own world and, at the same time, to discover the special vital qualities of the external objects. Repeatedly the characters focus on their immediate impressions: 'what she loved was this, here, now, in front of her.' (p. 11) The attributes upon which she focuses become substantives; in the florist's 'this beauty, this scent, this colour' appeal to her. (p. 16) Septimus, too, admires 'this exquisite beauty' (p. 25), but the vividness of objects also terrorises him: for, always in Virginia Woolf's writings, where there is the possibility of joy, there is the possibility of terror. The creativeness of perception can get out of hand; the vitality seen in the world can become aggressive; the part of one's self one gives to the world one sees can make one feel robbed of one's self.

Alongside their vivid immediacy, objects contain within them the sense of time. In her bedroom Mrs Dalloway sees 'the glass, the dressing-table, and all the bottles afresh' (p. 42) and the sight makes her feel the pressure of all other mornings. The capacity of the present to contain the past naturally makes the past appear as immediate. Memories become entangled in present thoughts and perceptions. There is a warmth, somewhat comical, in the way memories appear as present thoughts, and help one with one's present arguments; as a result, the mind, despite its sharp focus on the present, is seen as far-ranging and swift. Clarissa's meeting Hugh Whitbread in the West End leads her to reflect upon her reaction to him—and then to consider the reactions of people who matter to her. Clarissa's husband is driven mad by Hugh, and not only had Peter Walsh never a good word to say for Hugh, but he had never forgiven Clarissa for liking him. Thus Clarissa must defend her liking of Hugh; she begins to criticise Peter; she feels the tension of their past friendship and she tries to defend herself against his attack. Then she decides that this Peter who criticises her is Peter at his worst, and that, after all, he would be 'adorable to walk with on a morning like this'. (p. 9) She returns to her appreciation of the morning, and this appreciation makes the best in her past spring up before her: 'some days, some sights bringing him back to her calmly, without the old bitterness; which perhaps was the reward of having cared for people; they came back in the middle of St James's Park on a fine morning—indeed they did.' (p. 9) Peter's company—conjured through memory, sharing the vividness of the lovely day—is so real that the pleasant aspects of his company cannot remain—as they would in mere fantasy—unadulterated by the tension in their relationship, and by her own ambivalent feelings: 'So she would still find herself arguing in St James's Park, still making out that she had been right—and she had too—not to marry him.' (p. 10) However, if Peter were with her now, he would be looking at her, and she is afraid he would think her aged. In imagining Peter's company, she must imagine his independent vision. She tries to protect herself against it by clinging to this precious moment in June: to remind herself of her power to make the present real, and to make it hers, is to deny the reality of ordinary time.

Sensitivity to the present moment, to the vitality in the immediate surroundings, actually destroys the bounds of the present and the immediate. Following a description of Mrs Dalloway's delight and interest in Bond Street and the June morning is a paragraph describing all London—including what the King and Queen are doing and what people in shops are doing. Mrs Dalloway herself is not said to imagine these scenes, though this must be taken as an exaggerated statement of the way imagination can appear as actual vision. Her immediate, vivid perception opens the whole city to her; the imagination, stimulated by creative perception, becomes far-sighted, integrating perception.

This vision of London as a whole, with all its people connected, is linked to Clarissa's desire to give a party. The party is an expression of her vision; it is her means of realising and sharing it: 'she, too, was going that very night to kindle and illuminate; to give her party'. (p. 7) Her excitement is due to her sense that, in giving this party, 'she is part of it all'. (p. 7) Thus Lady Bruton's refusal to invite Clarissa to her luncheon not only inflicts the pain of a snub, but presents her with a vision of static deadliness: she sees Lady Bruton's face as a dial cut in impassive stone; she sees in it the dwindling of life, because it is excluding her from part of life.

The act of giving a party is not simply an offering of a completed, finished vision. Clarissa is so sensitive to Lady Bruton's exclusion of her because she must put forth a continuous effort to build up and integrate. When she looks in the glass, when she sees the reflection of 'the delicate pink face of the woman who was that night to give a party; of Clarissa Dalloway; of herself', (p. 42) the image she sees is not that of a single person. She tries to give her reflection a single point, but does not succeed. 'She alone knew how different the parts were' (p. 42) and this knowledge must be carefully protected. It is challenged by others because others tend to view her as a more simple, definite being. Her knowledge of her multiplicity thrives upon her sense of being 'invisible; unseen; unknown' (p. 13) and she refused Peter's proposal because he did not allow her this privacy, but wanted to go into every thought and feeling. Her fear of a profound exploration of her self, which is a fear of profound communication, makes the party suitable as a realisation of her sense of what it is to draw people together.

The images in *Mrs Dalloway* have neither the poetic independence (independence from any character's perception) nor the sardonic sharpness familiar in *Jacob's Room*. The responses of various characters are inter-linked; the response of one develops the response of another; the image used by one character is extended or modified by an image used by another character. The psychological truth underlying this technique is that however individual one's impressions, they are influenced—and in turn influence—the impressions of others. For, as Clarissa understands: 'she felt herself everywhere; not "here, here, here"; and she tapped on the back of the seat; but everywhere [. . .] so that to know her, or anyone, one must seek out the people who completed them . . .'. (pp. 168–169)

This novel is a brighter, more positive novel than *Jacob's Room*. Self-expression, self-realisation, emerge as real possibilities. Nonetheless, the deepest, the most real part of the self is hidden, and wants to keep itself hidden. Repeatedly the self is described as an underwater creature and, accordingly, it is seen to have a continuous motion, a peculiar freedom and isolation, a capacity to plunge deeper and deeper, a tendency to see objects as luminous and distorted. The mobility and freedom associated with an underwater creature are complemented by the similarity so many of the characters are said to have to birds: Scope Purvis, seeing Mrs Dalloway in the West End, thinks that she is perched on the curb like a bird, whereas she feels herself to be far out at sea (p. 10); Septimus Warren Smith is 'beak-nosed' and Lucrezia is like a bird in her vulnerability and timidity, surrounded by enormous trees (p. 73), and Sally Seton, with her brazen independence, reminds Clarissa of a cockatoo. The shared qualities of an underwater creature and a flying creature make these images virtually interchangeable. The birds indicate movement towards life, and the underwater creatures indicate movements towards death, but these two apparently opposing movements are closely related; they are different aspects of the same movement. The colours in the florist's shop flow over Mrs Dalloway like a wave (p. 16), and Septimus believes he might float away on the colours he sees. Clarissa's plunge into the morning-air as she bursts open the French windows, her participation in the rising and falling rooks, is the complement of Septimus's plunge to death from the high windows at the end of the book.

Since images of death are so similar to images of life, it is not surprising to discover that images of death are never merely deadly. The birds in Septimus's vision which sing to the dead in Greek proclaim there is no death. (p. 28) He has recurrent dreams of drowning, but these dreams or fantasies are always countered by a denial that to be drowned is to be dead. First he dreams that he has been drowned and has been dead, but that he is now alive, like a sleeper before waking, drawing towards the shore of life. Subsequently, Septimus's sense that he is drowned makes him feel separate from his body, so that only his body is drowned. This image is extended through Peter Walsh's ecstasy: 'It was as if he were sucked up to some very high roof by that rush of emotion, and the rest of him, like a white shell-sprinkled beach, left bare.' (p. 168) Clarissa, aware of the creeping approach of old age, of her diminishing sensibility and receptivity, finds excitement in the idea of death, and her feelings before entering her drawing room—before, that is, entering the room which is hers and in which she can, uninterrupted, follow her own thoughts—are anticipation and suspense 'such as might stay a diver before plunging while the sea darkens and brightens beneath him, and the waves threaten to break, but only gently split their surface, roll and conceal and encrust as they just turn over the weeds with pearl'. (pp. 34–5)

There is something here of a death wish as a desire for escape and relief, for freedom from the human world, freedom even from the physical world. This aspect is developed in Peter Walsh's desire

> for solace, for relief, for something outside these miserable pigmies,
> these feeble, these ugly, these craven men and women [. . .] So, he
> thinks, may I never go back to the lamplight; [. . .] rather let me
> walk straight on to this great figure, who will, with a toss of her
> head, mount me on her streamers and let me blow to nothingness
> with the rest. (pp. 64–5)

(Here again the image of flight and the image of descent are used to
the same effect.) Yet Clarissa's excitement at the prospect of solitude is
also excitement at the deepening of—not simple escape from—life.
This, too, is noted by Peter Walsh as he wonders whether to attend
the party:

> For this is the truth about our soul, he thought, our self, who fish-
> like inhabits deep seas and plies among obscurities threading her
> way between the boles of giant weeds, over sun-flickered spaces on
> and on into gloom, cold, deep, inscrutable: suddenly she shoots to
> the surface and sports on the wind-wrinkled waves; that is, has a
> positive need to brush, scrape, kindle herself, gossiping. (p. 178)

The need to sport on the surface is not the simple need for
relaxation. The images of 'brushing' and 'scraping' point to the
challenge the party presents to the self. The integration Clarissa hopes
to achieve can appear as a deluge amassing disparate people together.
As Peter Walsh approaches her house he sees the cabs rushing round
the corner 'like water round the piers of a bridge, drawn together, it
seemed to him, because they bore people going to her party' (p. 182)
and the image of the party as the deposit of flood victims is extended
by his image of the need to suppress his individual impressions:

> The cold stream of visual impressions failed him now as if the eye
> were a cup that overflowed and let the rest run down its china walls
> unrecorded. The brain must wake now. The body must contract
> now, entering the house, the lighted house, where the door stood
> open, where the motor cars were standing, and bright women
> descending: the soul must brave itself to endure. (p. 182)

The mind, then, is in some sense asleep when it is most individual and
active. To wake, to prepare itself for society, it must chill and drown

itself; the flame, which is the image of Peter's imaginaion as he walks round London, must now go out. The self must gather its defences and, before entering the house, Peter takes out his pocket knife; he must pare down his perceptions to fit them into a socially acceptable framework and to defend himself against others' views of him.

It is not in the novel itself, but in the collection of stories *Mrs Dalloway's Party*, that Virginia Woolf develops in detail the various challenges the self undergoes at a party. Under this pressure the self becomes an ego, trying to force others to accept a certain definition of it, trying to defy others' possible definitions. 'The Introduction' is the most touching portrayal of youthful sensibility—that is, of life-eagerness combined with a proud yet extremely fragile ego—in the midst of party conversation. Lily Evert both longs to accept the challenges presented and to flee from them; she feels 'the strangest mixture of excitement and fear, of desire to be left alone and of longing to be taken out and thrown into the boiling depths'. (p. 37) To maintain some stable self-identity she clings to a limited definition of her self, based on the praise she recently received for an essay on Swift. The stars marked on her essay become hard and fixed, like jewels inside her. She tries to associate reality with her essay, and to dismiss as fictions and froth the party activity. She tries to cling to the idea of her excellence 'as a drowning man might hug a spar in the sea', (p. 37) yet her anxiety reveals her inability to maintain this definition of reality versus fiction, and the diamond-like sharpness of her being turns into 'a mist of alarm, apprehension, and defence'. (p. 38) The sensibility of this young woman, who is like a 'butterfly with a thousand facets to its eyes', will be destroyed by the thrust and confidence and shallowness of that world consisting of 'telephone wires and Parliaments', the world that thrives upon easy com-munication, single-mindedness and general laws. Yet, in conclusion, the young woman sees that civilisation depends upon her—civilisation depends upon this many-faceted, fragile, individual vision.

Mrs Dalloway craves the challenge of a party because she has a distinctive power to integrate with her individual vision that which is normally opposed to such a vision. She is a perfect social being in that she can express and expand her self amid the anxiety and shallowness that are generally constricting. While Sally Seton must pretend she is satisfied with her life by bragging about her five sons, while Peter Walsh treats his failure to write as an amusement, while the middle-aged strut about with would-be self-importance, Clarissa constructs from all of it a glamour that transcends any individual failure; she constructs the glamour of a vivid, self-created vision.

Other people are able with more or less grace and agility to adapt or protect themselves from society's expectations and demands; but Septimus Warren Smith is unable to participate in any way in this society made up of 'telephone wires and Parliaments'. He cannot accept the viewpoint the world would have him accept, nor can he communicate his individual view in a way the world would accept. He cannot, for a few hours, pare down his perceptions to appear to be one of the crowd, nor can he find some comfortable perch (as Peter and Sally find self-irony) from which to defend himself from what he can guess to be others' view of him. Indeed, Septimus has no means of protecting himself. He knows this, and therefore his vulnerability becomes paranoia. Once you slip up, he thinks, you are in their power: once you show society you are not one of them, they are out to destroy you—and his thought is justified. He has said he wants to kill himself; he has shown himself to be opposed to 'normal' complacency and self-assertion. He is thus an example of the inefficacy of Dr Holmes's cures, which are derived from the assumption that pain and illness are unreal (Dr Holmes believes a little rest and a bromide will cure everything), and he thus becomes a pawn in the hands of Sir William Bradshaw, who uses weakness as an excuse to exercise his own power and as an opportunity to increase his fame. Septimus Smith is the perfect victim: his sensitivity to the pain in the world makes him intolerable to those who do not wish to see the pain; the individuality of his vision makes him unable to survive in a world that demands crafty self-defence and shallow self-assurance. At times even Lucrezia, who loves him, wishes him dead because his morbid vision affects her. A person lives with others' visions, and therefore a threatening, uncomfortable vision such as that of Septimus must be destroyed.

Mrs Dalloway, however well adapted she is to the social aspects of the public world, does not share the general denial of the reality of Septimus's vision. Her despairing thought, as she hears of the young man's act—'in the middle of my party, here's death' (p. 203)—is not the rejection of the idea of death that occurs in the social circles of Proust's novel, in which the assertion that someone has died or is going to die is said to be an 'exaggeration'. Clarissa's protest contains a sympathetic understanding of what it is that Septimus did; she understands what his action meant to him, and she rejects Sir

William's notion of the action, discovering, in her rejection, her hatred of the doctor. 'There he lay with a thud, thud, thud in his brain, and then a suffocation of blackness [. . .] And the Bradshaws talked of it at her party!' (p. 203) Her quick sense of the horror is a recognition of the reality of his death. Yet her party is her creative offering; it is a bringing together of various strands of life. Septimus's throwing away of life is therefore a denial of the value of her effort—his action presents a denial of the value of her party rather than a 'mad' action, because she understands the value of what he has done:

A thing there was that mattered; a thing, wreathed about with chatter, defaced, obscured in her own life, let drop every day in corruption, lies, chatter. This he had preserved. Death was defiance. Death was an attempt to communicate, people feeling the impossibility of reaching the centre which, mystically, evaded them; closeness drew apart; rapture faded; one was alone. There was embrace in death. (p. 204)

For Clarissa, despite her ability to thrive in society, shares with Septimus the need to preserve a private, unviolated self. And this need, necessarily, puts her at odds with 'normal' life.

Clarissa knows she lacks 'something central which permeated, something warm which broke up surfaces and rippled the cold contact of man and woman, or of women together'. (p. 36) Her solitary room with the narrow bed and tightly drawn sheet, her inability to respond to her husband's emotional appeals, are all part of her self-preservation, her attempt to protect the 'thing there was that mattered' that refuses to be shared and can rarely be communicated. (Mrs Ramsay is the exception.) She rejected Peter Walsh because he insisted upon going into everything, he wanted to share everything. The crude symbol of his all-too-present pocket knife is not a sign of sexual agression—at least there is nothing else in the novel other than the possible association of the knife with the phallus to support an erotic interpretation of Peter's pocket-knife; rather, it is a mark of his desire to intrude upon Clarissa's mental privacy, and to defend himself against others' scrutiny and criticism in a way which makes him insensitive to them. His teasing, cynical query, 'Star-gazing?', when he meets Sally and Clarissa in the garden at Bourton is, to Clarissa, like being smashed against granite. The focus of physical sensation is on the self's battle with other selves; the deepest physical feelings are a result of the mind's activity. Even Clarissa's memory of her ecstasy with Sally ('one yielded to its expansion, and rushed to the farthest verge and there quivered and felt the world come closer, swollen with some astonishing significance, some pressure of rapture, which split its thin skin and gushed and poured with an extraordinary alleviation over the cracks and sores', [p. 36]), though it follows a pattern similar to that of sexual intercourse, is certainly not about that, but about 'an inner meaning almost expressed'; the ecstasy is the expansion of one's mental world through this rare and momentary communication.

Clarissa may thrive upon the superficiality and frictions of society, but it is in solitude that she sinks into that state of consciousness which is the basis for the meaning she cannot discover in any other aspect of her life. Alone in the drawing room, without fear of interruption

> Quiet descends upon her calm, content, as her needle, drawing the silk smoothly to its gentle pause, collected the green folds together and attached them, very lightly, to the belt. So on a summer's day waves collect, overbalance, and fall; collect and fall; and the whole world seems to be saying 'that is all' more and more ponderously, until even the heart in the body which lies in the sun on the beach says too, that is all. Fear no more, says the heart. Fear no more says the heart, committing its burden to some sea, which sighs collectively for all sorrows, and renews, begins, collects, lets fall. And the body alone listens to the passing bee; the wave breaking; the dog barking, far away barking and barking. (pp. 44–5)

The seductive language of this passage reveals the peculiar passivity of creative consciousness. It is the passivity of being lulled by waves, of attending to the world partly as a sleeper in total acceptance; and such acceptance is possible because the self is safe in its hypnotic receptivity—'the body alone listens'—and is not actively engaged in the impressions it receives. Yet this passivity is, for Clarissa, the result of creative integration; it comes as she sews, and the drawing of folds together is the drawing of thoughts together, a healing of the disparate thoughts and responses that the morning has demanded of her. Septimus Smith's very similar vision of peace (he watches his hand which looks as it does when it floats in the bath, and he seems to be floating himself, while far away on the shore he hears the dogs barking and the heart in the body says, 'Fear no more') lacks this self-healing aspect. It is Lucrezia's sewing that lulls him, and he is at the mercy of others' will either to soothe or interrupt him.

Interruption, however—though it does not drive Clarissa, as it does Septimus, to suicide—is not easy to withstand. 'Who can—what can—' Mrs Dalloway demands at the announcement of a visitor, 'thinking it outrageous to be interrupted at eleven o'clock on the morning of the day she was giving a party'. (p. 45) Of course her outrage is comic, yet it immediately finds its justification in the sharpness and limitation of the visitor's—Peter Walsh's—view of her: 'here she's been sitting all the time I've been in India; mending her dress; playing about; going to parties . . .' (p. 46) Peter himself is humorously aware that his thoughts are an exaggeration; nonetheless they do express his attitude—critical and limited—and an attitude which shows ignorance of the self that dominated Clarissa before his entrance. Clarissa herself, aware of an undifferentiated consciousness at the core of the individual, would never say of anyone in the world 'that they were this or that', whereas Peter attacks her with fixed images, pinning them to her in a way that makes her feel pinned to one aspect of herself, robbed of the widening implications of that aspect. Peter told her, when she rejected him in favour of Richard Dalloway, that he could see her spending her life at the top of the stair case, forever presiding as hostess—and this image of a shallow, presumptuous character returns to haunt her. Contact with other people involves feeling the self chiselled into some unflattering image, as opposed to the fluidity and freedom of the self in solitude.

Yet Peter Walsh's view of others is not as unsatisfactory as his vanity at times makes it seem. Even his image of Clarissa as hostess contains a more profound understanding of what it is that she does as a hostess than his remark to her about spending her life at the top of the stair case would indicate. He hears the bells of St Margaret's trying to bury themselves in the heart, confiding like her a gentle hostess who seeks to communicate without changing either herself or her confidant; he feels Clarissa's presence in these sounds; he acknowledges the lack of presumption and warmth in Clarissa as hostess. He recognises, furthermore, that it is Clarissa who has given him the gift to see as much of life as he does see when he walks round London—though even here his limited sympathies are clear: he sees Septimus and Lucrezia as lovers engaged in a typical quarrel, and he sees the ambulance that carries away Septimus's dead body as a triumph of civilisation. Neither interpretation of what he sees is actually false, but its superficiality contains a cruel disregard for what the world is like for the people he sees. Yet his susceptibility to the breadth of Clarissa's vision does get the better of his reductive vanity: for just as he is trying, with Sally's help, to define Clarissa as a snob, as someone hard on other people, while he is playing with his knife, paring down his perceptions to suit his small-mindedness, he nonetheless is forced to see Clarissa's gift: 'to be; to exist; to sum it all up in the moment as she passed; turned, caught her scarf in some other woman's dress, unhitched it, laughed, all with the most perfect ease and air of a creature floating in its element'. (p. 192) The terror, ecstasy and extraordinary excitement she arouses in him are due to the immediate, vivid and unbounded vision of her—a vision, that is, that satisfies the requirements of truth.

Peter Walsh is a man with great imaginative capacity, though something has gone wrong with his vision. His responses to Clarissa are frustratingly ambivalent: he needs her, he feels inferior to Richard, he wants to impress her with a favourable image of himself—and these impulses make him suddenly burst into tears. While she is comforting him Clarissa feels a gaiety that, she supposes, would have been hers if she had married him. To her, Peter is 'blackberrying in the sun' while she is left alone in her chosen narrow tower. She envies his emotional capacity, and even as she mentally dismisses his claim that he has fallen in love with someone in India, she feels, all the same 'He has that [. . .] he is in love.' (p. 50) Yet her envy is misplaced. Peter is no better at joining his self to others than is Clarissa. In association with people his vision tends to malfunction badly, and he is left in a shambles. He needs help from others (he hopes that Richard will provide him with some career), he needs their love and admiration, yet his greatest need is to be left alone. The best, the most free and individual consciousness, emerges in solitude. Even thoughts of Clarissa—the person who has meant the most to him, the person who has been able to expand his vision—are frequently unwelcome; and it is obvious that he would have forced her to refuse him, if she had not chosen to do so. Walking alone, apart from anyone who knows him, who might try to define him, with no one other than Clarissa (who would not define him in any case) knowing that he is in England, he feels 'He had escaped! was utterly free—as happens in the downfall of habit when the mind, like an unguarded flame, bows and bends and seems about to blow from its holding.' (p. 59) He sees a passing woman whom he endows with all desirable qualities, he follows her, he feels himself to be in love with her. But it is clear that this fantasy is an end in itself; he does not desire the actual woman. His fantasy is part of his love for the city and the summer day; and this love, as it did for Clarissa, opens up to him the beauty and activity of all London. He sees 'young people slowly circling, conversations between men and women, maids idly looking out [. . .] stockings drying on top ledges, a parrot, a few plants. Absorbing, mysterious, of infinite richness, this life.' (pp. 180–1)

This is the finest achievement—to see and appreciate and discover the multiplicity and richness in life. To see clearly is to see without motive or presupposition or principle, and thus seeing clearly often involves a failure to see the point upon which other, less original people focus. In indicating the individuality of Clarissa's responses, however, the author makes her a little ridiculous, for Clarissa can never remember whether her husband is concerned with the plight of the Armenians or the Albanians. The point the author makes is nonetheless a valid one; Woolf is underlining the difficulty of bringing non-immediate causes to life. Clarissa's sympathies are easily aroused, but they are aroused by the people round her, not by causes or ideals. When causes and ideals rather than individual people and experiences become the object of passions, they can all too easily be used against people—they become a means of setting one's self apart from immediate contact and immediate experience and, as such, they become soul-destructive. For Lady Bruton, through whom Clarissa feels her fear of time and the dwindling of life, causes become the occasion for self-aggrandisement; they provide her with the reason to draw well-known people round her and to present her name to the public through letters to *The Times*. The unreality of her causes is emphasised by her inability to write the letters herself and her need to enlist the aid of Hugh Whitbread, the well-upholstered product of an English public school who is able to put worthy public issues in alphabetical order, but who is described at Clarissa's party as 'blind', looking as he does past everything except esteem and self comfort.

The most extreme case of principle combining with egoism to distort perception and sensibility is that of Miss Kilman, Elizabeth Dalloway's tutor and friend. To Clarissa the dog's mess is more palatable than the religious, self-righteous Doris Kilman, who 'starved herself for the Austrians, but in private inflicted positive torture'. (p. 14) The violence of Mrs Dalloway's response is endorsed by the author; and even although Clarissa understands that her real hatred is not for the woman herself but for what she represents (she is, to Clarissa, 'one of those spectres with which one battles in the night' [p. 15]) the presentation of Miss Kilman contains an anger which seems to enclose the character, so that one never gets beyond the spectre she represents. Compare, for example, the unqualified success of Sir

William Bradshaw, whose hatefulness emerges from the very blandness of his assumption that he is in the right, from the fact that his evil is oiled with sincerely felt concern; his cruelty is insidious—one can be caught off-guard by his apparent understanding. Miss Kilman, on the other hand, is so obviously hateful that she never has the chance to ingratiate herself; never could she obtain real power. She has the hatefulness of a 'loser', and this gives the author an unfair advantage in presenting her faults. For what emerges most strongly is Miss Kilman's defensiveness, and the way the world is awful for *her* because of what she is. We become, as Blake said, what we behold; and as Doris Kilman stands in the street, the scene is 'beaten up, broken up by the assault of carriages, the brutality of vans, the eager advance of myriads of angular men, of flaunting women . . .' (p. 142) If one compares the way the street appears to Mrs Dalloway ('to her it was absolutely absorbing; all this; the cabs passing, and she would not say of Peter, she would not say of herself, I am this, I am that.' [p. 11]), the difference between a hostile and appreciative approach to the world becomes clear. Miss Kilman would like to absorb the world as does Mrs Dalloway. Her voraciousness is a displaced desire to contain beauty within herself. Her love for Clarissa's daughter Elizabeth is felt as a desire to possess the girl and then to die. She cannot create in her vision her own beauty; she seeks possession of another's beauty and, in compensation for her failure, she gorges herself with food. What she cannot devour she despises. She sees the world as hostile, and she can imagine mitigating this hostility only by dominating it; she seeks vengeance upon the world whose awfulness she herself has created; she wants to bring the world to its knees crying, 'You are right!'

Virginia Woolf offers a finer, though not less grotesque, portrait of paranoia in 'The New Dress' which appears in the collection of stories, *Mrs Dalloway's Party*. Mabel Waring (her name alone places her in the same class as Doris Kilman) is similarly dominated by an awareness of her physical ugliness, but, defying this knowledge, she dresses herself in an orgy of self-love. Then, at the party, she feels she should be punished for her previous self-adoration. Her anger is now directed towards all the guests, whose admiration she had been hoping to win, who she now despises because her previous concern for their opinion has made her so foolish. She repeats to herself the phrase 'flies trying to crawl', which is both an expression of her detestation of everything round her and a means of numbing her contact with her immediate surroundings. This anger makes her create situations which are bound to aggravate it. She tells people she is certain she looks dowdy and, of course, they are forced to offer complimentary reassurances; as a result, she is convinced they are insincere. On the other hand, if someone does not mention her dress but makes commonplace conversation, she supposes that they are too ashamed of her dress to mention it; and when someone makes polite or conversational inquiries about an acquaintance, Mabel thinks she is being used merely as a source of information. She is a more successful character than Doris Kilman because her psychology is not a simple, fully established armour. Her defences are continually breaking down; she must search for some way to re-build them, whereas Miss Kilman's hatred is fully reinforced, and we barely see the pain behind it.

In contrast to these cases of egoistic distortion, Septimus Smith's paranoia is refreshingly sane—if 'sane' marks the ability to register reality. But reality is registered individually; its various aspects are revealed by individual responses which are then seen to have general meaning; and it is precisely Septimus's creative sensibilities which indicate to society 'insanity': the first symptoms of his madness are his symbolical interpretation of words. Yet his participation in the world he perceives is similar to that of Mrs Dalloway. Like Clarissa, who slices like a knife through everything and is at the same time outside looking on, who, while she is watching the passing scene feels herself far out to sea, alone (pp. 10–11), Septimus is part of his world, finds meaning in his world, and at the same time is isolated from the people round him, as someone out at sea.

For the vigorous, healthy world of Mrs Dalloway, because of its vigour and vitality, is not safe; 'it was very, very dangerous to live even one day' (p. 11), Clarissa feels. Nor is the danger simply that other people will mark one as insane. The danger is in the creative trend of vision; for, always, the joy one finds in life has another face of terror—participation in the world, in this active world, can reveal one aspect as easily as the other. And Septimus's vision is undoubtedly hellish. Even his vision of bliss with the birds singing in Greek, declaring death to be unreal, takes place in the land of the dead. His vision of universal love and the abolition of crime gives the trees round him a new life, but the vitality of the external world annihilates his own physical reality: 'His body was macerated until only the nerve fibres were left. It was spread like a veil upon a rock.' (p. 76) As the world comes alive to him its voices 'break inside his head'; he does not slice like a knife through things—they slice through him. He lacks that passive, integrating background of consciousness in which Clarissa rests as she sews her dress; his passivity contains no power to heal and soothe; rather, it increases his vulnerability. He receives impressions like a cushion receives pins, disjointed and penetrating; his impressions are created by him, but he can only suffer them, for this creativeness is not a healing, integrating process.

Septimus's capacity to see the universal and representative in the individual usually alienates him from the individual—even from himself. Lying on the grass in Regent's Park he is lying 'very high, on the back of the world. The earth thrilled beneath him. Red flowers grew through his flesh; their stiff leaves rustled by his head.' (p. 76) The flowers which are such a joy to Clarissa, which are a symbol of her husband's love, which communicate emotion, are for Septimus a symbol of something more powerful than himself. The red flowers which, for Peter Walsh, are associated with the fantasy lover he follows through London, which seems to burn his lips and which hang richly from her house, become for Septimus so powerful and so general a symbol that they attack him. The concentration of his symbols, the way he sees the entire world in his immediate setting, makes everything dangerously powerful and inescapable: 'The world has raised its whip', he thinks, 'where will it descend?' (p. 17)

Lucrezia directs Septimus's attention to the aeroplane because the doctors have said that he should take an interest in things outside himself. It is, however, impossible to emerge from the self by looking at something, because the way we see things is a symptom of what we are. Septimus does look at the aeroplane, just as everyone else in the Park looks at the aeroplane; but he does not thereby see what others see. Septimus sees someone trying to signal to him in a language he cannot understand. Indeed, the external world takes on his anguished projections with such bold outlines that Septimus has to close his eyes to preserve his sanity. (p. 26) He can see the world only as it has meaning for him.

Yet his insanity does reveal something real. Lucrezia protests that everyone has friends who were killed in the war; Septimus should therefore not be so upset by Evans's death. But there are grounds for saying that her implicit argument is more mad than Septimus's anguish: she assumes that it is 'normal' for men to die in wars, and 'normal' for their friends to accept this. The whimsical nature of this normal world is clear in the account of Septimus's reasons for joining the army. He was one of the first to volunteer. He 'went to France to save an England which consisted almost entirely of Shakespeare's plays and Miss Isabel Pole in a green dress walking in a square'. (p. 95) In so comically particularising his love for England the author indicates the emptiness in the bombastic notion of patriotism, or of patriotism as it motivated thousands of young soldiers. Septimus's decision to become a soldier was 'normal'; it sprang from a healthy, even admirable motive; but, at the same time, it was clearly mad.

Septimus's discovery that what the majority look upon with equanimity and approval can be actually barbaric, threatens the majority's complacency. Like Doris Kilman, the public want to bring dissenters to their knees crying, 'You are right!' For, as the author explains, the sister of Sir William Bradshaw's notion of proportion—the capacity, that is, to accept and perpetrate established opinion—is 'conversion', which feasts upon the human will: those who do not accept the public vision and who therefore have no friends, receive naked and defenceless the impress of Sir William's will. (p. 113) Even Lucrezia shares this impulse to destroy her husband, to convert his vision, though her aversion springs from terror rather than from a complacent adherence to the goodness of commonplace views. 'I am alone! I am alone!' she cries by the fountain in Regent's Park; but her desperate isolation is due to the fact that she is not alone, that she is intolerably close to her husband, sharing his awful vision, Septimus makes everything awful for her, even the trees and sky; she is so much a part of him that his nightmare becomes hers; she wishes him dead because his vision is infectious.

The deepest hell is discovered with the death of the soul, which is the death of feeling and imagination. This is the crux of Septimus's despair: he believes he felt nothing at the time of Evans's death; he believes he can see the world's beauty only as something behind a pane of glass. This alienation from one's own feelings is the same state Coleridge described in *Dejection: An Ode*. Looking at the stars and sky the speaker says, 'I see them all so excellently fair, /I see, not feel, how beautiful they are! In Proust's novel, Marcel's greatest anguish occurs when the train stops in the countryside outside Paris, and he notes the reddening light of sunset and the trees darkly marked against the sky, but he feels none of the longing and excitement, none of the creative quickening, that accompanies a vision deepened by imagination.

In all these cases, however, there is a paradox. There is, for example, an important difference between Septimus's sense of his own emptiness and the true imaginative poverty of Dr Holmes, Hugh Whitbread and Sir William Bradshaw. The latter accept as normal the absence of vitality and significance, whereas Septimus, the speaker in Coleridge's *Ode*, and Marcel find in such absence a definition of hell. But their very despair in their dissociation from beauty or feeling underlines their capacity for an imaginative vision which appreciates the special reality of the world around them. The paradox in the *Ode* is enforced by the fact that the poet's lament over the absence of imagination offers a finely imaginative picture of despair. In *Le Temps Retrouvé*, Marcel's apparently bland vision lays the groundwork for his realisation that what matters most is the condensed, profound vision achieved through the refining process of memory. Septimus's belief that he is without feeling and that beauty is beyond his reach is also one aspect of a highly developed imagination and sensibility. His sense of emotional poverty is actually a measure of the world's poverty; when Evans is killed Septimus is looking at his friend's death through the eyes of the public; his indifference, which is death, is 'normal'.

Septimus's belief in his inability to approach beauty, and the awful ease with which beauty is transformed into ugliness or with which ugliness eclipses beauty (in Shakespeare's language Septimus sees only hatred and disgust for mankind), links him to Miss Kilman, but there is an important difference in the fact that whereas Doris Kilman attacks the world with an unchanging vision, Septimus participates in it with a sympathetic and mobile vision. Indeed, it is his uncontrolled participation which robs him of his sanity, by robbing him of his self.

The participation of the self in perception indicates a continuing death: if what one perceives is part of the self, then changing, vanishing perceptions reveal a changing, vanishing self—yet only by so participating in perception does the world come alive. All the characters who are capable of bringing their world to life share an awareness of the passing of life; but each responds differently. Peter Walsh feels that his susceptibility to the moment when life and death come together has been his undoing; it has made it impossible for him to plan or to be practical. One impression after another falls upon him until it reaches the deep, dark cellar where he stands (p. 168); the deep, dark place of the self, the negative possessions of the self, are the result of the extent to which the self belongs to the external world. As Peter reflects, to know Clarissa is to know the things she loved, the things she observed and brought to life by her creative vision; and if, as Clarissa supposes, she will live on in those things after her death, she must also live on in them while she lives; it is not only in death that the world is haunted by fragmented, un-owned parts of the self.

Just as Clarissa believes, joyfully, that she will live on in the world she sees, that she gives her self to the world she sees, Septimus is robbed of his self by the external world. He endows objects with so much of himself that he has nothing left; he has nothing of the private, secluded self which both Peter and Clarissa relish. Septimus lacks the capacity to save anything of himself. Whereas Clarissa enjoys a sense of floating away on the colours in the florist's shop, Septimus will be carried irretrievably away by them. Whereas Clarissa feels the objects in the bedroom giving her back something of her past self, objects threaten Septimus either by penetrating him (as the flowers do when they grow through his hands) or by refusing to soften their distinction from him. Lucrezia leaves him to open the door to Dr Holmes, and Septimus is terrified of being alone forever among the sideboard and the bananas. The absurdity of his fear is eclipsed by the pathos of his terror. Alone, he can find no private flow of thought in which his perceptions become his own and which heals the fragmentation and alienation of interruption. A few minutes before, sitting with his wife, watching her sew and sharing her laughter, he had almost found it, but the entry of Dr Holmes is the entry of the complacent public who will rob him of this small chance of privacy and who will deny the reality of his own vision.

Even in his frantic throwing away of his own life, there is a sanity—that is, a legitimate response to reality—which Clarissa endorses as she retreats to the small room adjoining that in which her party is being held. She can understand why a young man would relinquish his own life to preserve that integrity which the party tends to destroy. The old woman Clarissa sees through the window, the complement of the old man Septimus sees across the street as he hurls himself from the window, represents the purely personal, private life which Clarissa has pilfered in her desire for social success, and she is ashamed to be forced to watch this woman—who is lost in the process of living—in her evening dress. (p. 205) Clarissa's gladness at the young man's suicide, while she and her friends go on living and throwing parties, is the relief of having part of her needs expressed by someone else. With this need fulfilled, she can 'assemble' and return to her task as hostess. In such a state she can deny the definitions her friends try to force upon her; she can communicate the individual and unbounded reality of her self.

5 Consciousness as Personality: *To the Lighthouse*

In the widely quoted essay 'Modern Fiction' (*Collected Essays, II*) Virginia Woolf develops a thesis about the nature of fiction which she had illustrated in 'Mr Bennett and Mrs Brown' (*Collected Essays, I*). In the earlier essay she supposes she is sitting opposite Mrs Brown in a railway carriage. The woman is engaged in a difficult and upsetting conversation with a gentleman. As such she offers the possibility of being a fictional character. If Wells or Galsworthy or Bennett were to use this woman as a character, then we would know the amount of rent she paid, we would know the material of her curtains and every other detail of her material conditions and social status; but the most important descriptions of her life would be ignored. The descriptions that Wells, Galsworthy and Bennett would offer would not, Virginia Woolf declares, reveal what these precisely defined material and social conditions meant to Mrs Brown.

In 'Modern Fiction' Woolf explains that these novelists fastened upon the trivial and tried to make it eternal and significant. She, in contrast, is interested in the inner reality of the character, in Mrs Brown's reactions and passions—but here Woolf can be understood merely as gesturing towards a dissatisfaction with conventional descriptions of 'inner reality', or the world as it appears to a character and the way in which a character responds to it, for these other novelists certainly do take responses and passions into account. Rather, it is the lack of emphasis and concentration and detail, the absence of a style that would place reactions and passions—especially their volatile and fragmentary character—under a very strong light. She explains:

> Life is not a series of gig-lamps symmetrically arranged; life is a luminous halo, a semi-transparent envelope surrounding us from

the beginning of consciousness to the end. Is not the task of the novelist to convey this varying, this unknown and uncircumscribed spirit, whatever aberration or complexity it may display, with as little mixure of the alien and external as possible? [. . .] Let us record the atoms as they fall upon the mind in the order in which they fall, let us trace the pattern, however disconnected and incoherent in appearance, which each sight or incident scores upon the consciousness. (pp. 106–7)

Woolf suggests that this is the aim of several modern writers, among whom James Joyce is the most notable, though this passage describes her own interests rather than Joyce's technique. (*Ulysses* presents a highly detailed picture of Dublin as an 'external' city, and the characters' impressions are selected according to the author's pattern, not vice versa.) Indeed, the assumption that haphazard impressions do form a pattern is an assumption about the way the mind works; the assumption is that impressions will be received according to some logic—in other words, that the mind, even while receiving impressions, is selective and therefore active. Turning from this somewhat poorly worded essay to her novels, it can be seen that the way impressions simply 'fall upon the mind' is through selection without reference to the will or to commonplace logic; the selection *reveals* a person's mind—it is not consciously determined by mind.

Furthermore, Joyce's method, and the method of Virginia Woolf herself, is misleadingly described as pointing to the 'messages received by the brain' without reference to 'external signposts'. (p. 107) For Woolf's interest in marking out 'the quick of the mind' (given the far wider implications of 'mind' as opposed to 'brain') makes external reference necessary. Emotions and thoughts can be identified only by reference to external objects, only through consideration of the situations in which they occur, the people towards whom they are directed, and the objects which awaken memories and responses.

It is generally recognised that Virginia Woolf cannot accurately be described as a stream-of-consciousness writer. She shifts from narrative of a character's feelings to a transcription of his thoughts, to a juxtaposition of thought and memory in ways that explain rather than simply present thoughts; and the narrative, moreover, is frequently taken up by an observer who, though not quite omniscient, is not to be identified with the character yet can describe the character's thoughts and also others' thoughts about the character. And though it is true that information about characters' material lives—that is, about their social situation, their past affairs, their external surroundings—is not presented by conventional description, it is neither ignored nor considered irrelevant. In *Mrs Dalloway*, for example, we are not told that Clarissa goes out of the house to buy flowers and that she walks along the street. Rather, her decision to buy flowers emerges—as does the fact that she is to give a party—from her thoughts about the work her maid has to do. That we are to assume she is walking along the street becomes very clear when the author writes, 'She stiffened a little on the kerb, waiting for Durtnall's van to pass. A charming woman, Scope Purvis thought her . . .' (p. 6) The author does give us, however sparsely, her physical movements; and here, the external signpost of her position—the kerb—is a pivot from Clarissa's consciousness to that of Scope Purvis.

If Virginia Woolf did, as she suggests the modern novelist tries to do, exclude external reality, there would be no fine June day for the various characters to enjoy, no real London streets where friends could be met and shops entered. Moreover, this 'external' or shared reality is not burdensome in its necessity; it is essential to her interests. For Woolf never tries to construct an Axel's Castle, where imagination rejects reality and chooses to dwell in fantasy; Woolf's account of imagination is bound up with an account of the way the world is discovered; imagination is a means not of constructing fantasy but of constructing truth. In *To the Lighthouse*, which is certainly one of her most successful novels, the consciousness, with its creative sensibility, not only discovers a true picture of the world but discovers a picture which can be shared. In *Jacob's Room* the depth of Jacob's consciousness and his discovery of the fragmentation of life alienated him from other people; in *Mrs Dalloway* the shallow people, to hold on to their own sense of truth, destroyed Septimus's more profound vision; but in *To the Lighthouse* the characters' personalities, or how he or she is known by others, are more closely linked to their respective consciousnesses, so that a personal vision can be communicated, and the reality discovered by one consciousness can be discovered by another.

External reality is something that is perceived by various people and known in various ways. One person, in trying to know another person, wants to understand how the world appears to the other person. In some cases, another's vision becomes part of one's own, part of the external reality one perceives. Andrew Ramsay tells Lily Briscoe that the problem his father works on—the subject and nature of reality—can be understood by thinking of a kitchen table when no one is perceiving it. Whenever Lily thinks about Mr Ramsay's work, she therefore thinks of a large, scrubbed kitchen table. The natural world round her disappears, and she sees only a solid, hard-wearing, scrubbed table, revealing grain after grain of many scrubbings. Indeed, Mr Ramsay's vision has influenced Lily's quite reasonably, despite her humorously literal interpretation of Andrew's example.

First, let us consider the problem with which Mr Ramsay as a philosopher would be actually concerned. The problem arises from the fact that people know about the existence of physical objects only through their perceptions of them, yet they assume these objects exist even when they are not being perceived. Thus Mr Ramsay's son instructs Lily to consider a kitchen table (he of course means 'any object') when it is not being perceived. The fact that this is, for Mr Ramsay, 'the subject and nature of reality', is not simply a fact about what a particular philosophical problem is generally called, but a fact about Mr Ramsay's personal vision. For Mr Ramsay, reality is simple objects and simple truths. He disregards a reality endowed with hope, beauty or sympathy. He is exultant when he can prove to others—as he does by insisting that the weather will not be fine in the morning, and that his young son James will not therefore be able to go to the Lighthouse—that a world other than his own is nonsense. The stark solid objects of his world—represented for Lily by the kitchen table— are repeatedly and scrupulously scrubbed; but all this scrubbing reveals is grain after grain. The repeated scrubbing in Lily's imagination is the futile effort of Mr Ramsay's mind, which sees truth as an alphabet. Mr Ramsay's life ambition is to get to R in the alphabet of knowledge; he is devoured by disappointment—a disappointment centred upon vanity rather than upon the value of a lost effort—that *he* will never reach Z.

Mr Ramsay denies the reality of a world permeated by sympathy, hope and beauty; and yet his own vision creates a world of impossible loneliness, so that he craves his wife's sympathy and the comfort of her beauty. His need for her becomes aggressive because it is a need which his own vision cannot fulfill. Mr Ramsay's fate is to stand on a cliff which is gradually being eaten away by the sea, to stare into the darkness of human ignorance, and to declare that we know nothing and that we never stand on firm ground. Mr Ramsay takes this position because his principles of knowledge prevent him from seeing anything in the darkness—in that same darkness which holds both terror and joy for his wife, which provides for his wife that inviolable inner space which is the source of her power and beauty. In looking into the darkness Mr Ramsay, like his wife, looks into himself; he finds within himself only ignorance and emptiness which continually eat away at him. The reality he creates is stark and immobile and deadly objective. He is unable to recognise his own individuality, to say 'this is what I like, this is what I am'. (p. 53) As a result, the world has no meaning for him; it is blankly opposed to him, and he can discover nothing in it.

The technique the author employs in *To the Lighthouse* continually enforces the theme of the interpenetration of consciousness and the external world. The following passage is a typical example. Every evening Lily and Mr Bankes walk to the break in the thick hedge where they can see the bay:

> They came regularly every evening drawn by some need. It was as if the water floated off and set sailing thoughts which had grown stagnant on dry land, and gave to their bodies even some sort of physical relief. First, the pulse of colour flooded the bay with blue, and the heart expanded with it and the body swam, only the next instant to be checked and chilled by the prickly blackness on the ruffled waves. Then, up behind the great black rock, almost every evening spurted irregularly, so that one had to watch for it and it was a delight when it came, a fountain of white water [. . .] (p. 24)

Perception involves participation, and just as the flood of colour and movement of the waves build up a sympathetic reaction in the observers' bodies, the observers must seek their own resolution of these feelings. Their gazes must complete the picture of the sea and its movement by turning to the distant sand dunes, which balance the merriment of the sailing boat with a melancholic peacefulness. The sadness the viewers find expressed by the dunes and sky is not nature's own sadness, nor even Lily's or Mr Bankes's sadness. The quiet, sloping dunes and evening sky present an image of eternity, of a world at rest; the viewers are not looking for projections of their own feelings, but for a stable point outside themselves. Strangely, they are comforted by this image of eternity which reminds them of their own mortality; they are drawn to the landscape by its ability to give them a vision which extends beyond their immediate concerns, beyond their personal lives; the participation in perception makes one's world much broader, and far more satisfying.

External objects, however, can become symbols for one's own feelings. As such they become a means of investigating one's feelings, or providing a focus for them. Reflecting upon his past association with Mr Ramsay, Mr Bankes remembers Ramsay remarking about the hen, 'Pretty, pretty', in a way that showed sympathy with humble things. This sympathy lead to Ramsay's marriage and, consequently, to the end of his close friendship with Mr Bankes. (Because it was Mr Ramsay's appreciation of a hen that warned Mr Bankes of his friend's susceptibility to the humble charms of marriage, Mr Bankes always associated the Ramsay family with 'fluttering wings and clucking domesticities'. [p. 27]) He sees how the 'pulp had gone out of their friendship',

> But in this dumb colloquy with the sand dunes he maintained that his affection for Ramsay had in no way diminished; but there, like the body of a young man laid up in peat for a century, with the red fresh on his lips, was his friendship, in its acuteness and reality laid up across the bay among the sandhills. (p. 25)

Mr Bankes finds—or creates—a confirmation of his attachment to Mr Ramsay as he looks at the landscape. His friendship is as safe and permanent as the scene; but now that this friendship is confirmed, it becomes part of Mr Bankes's personal world, something he must protect against conflicting views and something that can also threaten his own established views. He is anxious lest Lily disparage Mr Ramsay—yet he also needs Lily's sympathy, for this renewed sense of friendship has made him appreciate Mr Ramsay's assests; and among Mr Ramsay's many children, the widower feels shrunk and empty.

Mr Bankes's need to go over his past and get it straight, to lay it out before him, is similar to his and Lily's need to complete the view of the sea with the view of the sand dunes. There is in this novel no significant distinction between the need to clarify one's own thoughts and the course of one's life, and the need for aesthetic satisfaction. Certainly Lily's struggles with her painting are personal struggles. She feels she sees everything clearly, but as she applies her brush to the canvas a thousand forces wrest her vision from her, and this frustration is linked to the frustration of self-realisation; she thinks of her house-keeping for her father and of her inability to express her love for Mrs Ramsay. Mr Ramsay's need to confirm Scott's excellence is also a need for some personal confirmation. First, he reasons that if Tansley can say that Scott is no good, then the younger generation can say that his own work is no good. Secondly, the pleasure he has in reading Scott arises not only from the satisfaction of the vanity that led him to the book but, more importantly, from the growing irrelevance of his vanity: his involvement with the characters' joys and sorrows makes him forget the petty tensions of personal ambition. It is as though his real reason for reading Scott was not to confirm his own importance but to abolish his need for self-importance. Mr Bankes's aesthetic appreciation of the landscape also serves a double purpose. Not only does it provide a symbol for his friendship with Ramsay but also, as he turns away from the scene, the world becomes more vivid to him—he is 'alive to things which would not have struck him'. (p. 26) He sees Ramsay's daughter Cam picking Sweet Alice on the bank; he notes her words and gestures and the individual personality they express. He has not been given any new information as he watched the sandhills; he does not discover any new facts—yet a primarily aesthetic vision has affected all his perceptions.

Frequently an object takes on the quality of an eternal image, and a character uses it not exactly as a symbol, but as an external reference, and an external point of participation, for their own multiple and mobile thoughts. Lily, thinking about Mr Bankes, wondering whether she likes him, 'feels her thoughts flowing so quickly that she cannot note them'. Her intensity of perception is such that 'even the fissures and humps on the bark of the pear tree were irrevocably fixed there for eternity'. (p. 29) As Mrs Ramsay leaves the dining room to be alone, to reflect on the meaning and value of the tensions and emotions which emerged during the meal, she unconsciously uses the branches of the elm trees outside to help stabilise her position. (p. 130) As she admires the stillness of the branches and, subsequently, their fine upward, wave-like sweep in the wind, she feels that she will live on, this night will live on in the hearts of the newly engaged couple. She has achieved that

> community of feeling with other people which emotion gives as if the walls of partition had become so thin that practically (the feeling was one of relief and happiness) it was all one stream, and chairs, tables, maps, were hers, were theirs, it did not matter whose, and Paul and Minto would carry it on when she was dead. (p. 131)

Lily's sense of her own voice saying 'undeniable, everlasting, contradictory things' (p. 29) makes external objects irrevocably fixed, whereas Mrs Ramsay's vision is like flood which Lily, in the third section of the novel, tries to stabilise in her painting. The author emphasises in these cases the psychological fact of our use of external objects, of these objects' qualities, as a means of investigating or understanding our own thoughts. These cases further underline the futility of Mr Ramsay's scrubbed kitchen table from which one is expected to extract what perception has given to it, as though perception's offerings were opposed to the nature of reality.

In the above examples the perceiver either fixes the external object, or releases its potential mobility from the mass of impressions available to her; the character unconsciously, without any obvious directive, chooses the bark or the branches as a focus. Virginia Woolf has previously shown the importance of these perceptual choices, made without those interferences which challenge one's own mental logic and needs. However, in this novel in which there is frequently no distinction between investigating consciousness and observing the external world (thus Lily can dip into her consciousness to re-fashion her memory of Charles Tansley and keep it for herself almost like a work of art [pp. 182–3], and then she can turn from her canvas to the drawing-room steps to search 'the sky of the soul' for some revelation of the meaning of life, which will emerge as a re-fashioning of her memory of Mrs Ramsay [p. 183]), external events which demand attention can become easily and immediately a part of one's private train of thought. As Lily imagines eternal truth like a company of gnats, each separate but all 'marvellously controlled in an invisible elastic net', as her thoughts dance in the pear tree alongside the effigies of Mr Ramsay's scrubbed table, they become more intense until they finally explode. (p. 30) The explosion is the firing of Jasper's gun as he frightens the birds; but for Lily the explosion is simply the culmination of her own thoughts. As in a dream all sensations become part of the pattern or course already established in one's mind.

There is a *prima facie* case for Ramsay's dismissal of highly individual responses to the world, and the author herself admits some suspicion of them. Lily looks at the Ramsays and sees them as 'being in love'; they then become part of that 'unreal but penetrating and exciting universe which is the world seen through the eyes of love. The sky stuck to them; the birds sang through them.' (p. 55) From this 'unreal' point of view life becomes like a wave, bearing into one curved whole separate incidents; from this 'unreal' vision we receive the unity and integration that we always seek—just as Mrs Ramsay's vision of fluidity and eternity of objects arises from a mistaken supposition of

Paul and Minta's future hapiness. Lily wonders, 'Was it wisdom? Was it knowledge? Was it, once more, the deceptiveness of beauty, so that all one's perceptions, half-way to truth, were entangled in a golden mesh? or did she lock up within her some secret which certainly Lily Briscoe believed people must have for the world to go on at all?' (p. 59) The answer to this question inevitably hinges upon the truth and value and effectiveness of the short-sighted Mrs Ramsay's vision.

Despite Mrs Ramsay's disregard for facts, despite her outrage that her husband, when he declares that it will not be fine in the morning, should pursue truth with so little regard for people's feelings, she does not actually present people with falsehoods. She does not tell her son James that it will be fine in the morning; she tells him that it might be fine. She is showing him that hope makes sense. When James and Cam quarrel about the skull (Cam cannot sleep with it in the room and James screams when anyone tries to remove it), Mrs Ramsay covers the skull with her shawl and tells Cam that it is a bird's nest or a mountain with valleys and flowers and bells ringing, and she tells James that the skull is still in the room, just as he wanted. The fantasy she offers Cam is of course 'unreal' but what in all probability soothes both children is the love she offers them through her desire to comfort them.

It is impossible, in ordinary human intercourse, to separate a person's beliefs and remarks from their motives in stating them. Mr Ramsay's pursuit of truth is primarily egoistic. In particular, when he declares his belief about the morning's weather, he wants to destroy the communion between his son and his wife which rests upon an atmosphere penetrated by the mother's consciousness. Ramsay's attempt to play with the child by tickling his leg with a sprig is precisely the same type of aggression as his prediction of the morning's weather; in the one case he uses the guise of reason, in the other he uses a game to impress his will upon his son.

The truth of what people say is not a matter simply of the truth of the statements they make. People make statements in a given context, to bring others' attention to a certain point. In making a statement a person is not merely saying that something is—or is not—the case; he is implying that his statement is relevant, that it has some place among the set of beliefs and thoughts that are in that situation predominant. The manner in which something is said frequently indicates the position in the pattern the speaker believes his remark should take, and whether the statement lies beside other beliefs and thoughts, or whether it is meant to blot them out. All these things are seen in this novel as part of the truth of what a person says, and they all influence a character's response to statement.

The truth or falsity of Charles Tansley's repeated utterance, 'Women can't paint, can't write', is irrelevant, even to him. What matters is his reason for saying this (the remark seems to help him in some way) and the effect it has upon others. Tansley's remark constricts Lily's imagination, almost as though what he said were true—she cannot paint when he says such things, or even when she hears his words in her own mind. Moreover, she is compelled to participate in his cheap version of the man-versus-woman game. 'Oh, Mr Tansley, please take me to the Lighthouse with you', she says (p. 99); and though this is a request, not a statement, the author describes Lily as telling lies. For the lies she tells are not the lies of knowingly making untrue statements, but of false expression.

A true statement can be said to be false, or a false statement true, in regard to what the person making the statement is doing in making it. Mrs Ramsay gives her children hope and comfort in her remarks. Charles Tansley is always saying (whether he is denouncing Scott's novels, putting his colleagues in pecking order or reflecting upon women's limitations) 'I-I-I' and thinking about the impression he is making. At the dinner table the effect of his real assertion, underlying his discussion about other things, is to make everyone feel his or her own emptiness. Egoism, both in Tansley and Mr Ramsay, makes the individual null and void. For, paradoxically, egoism denies the validity of individual response and feeling. Egoism, and the need to assert one's own view upon others, stems from the poverty of one's own view; and no one, except Mrs Ramsay, finds a way out of this overpowering impression of inner emptiness. Mrs Ramsay, suffering with the others, reflects upon her husband's superiority to all this pettiness and, suddenly, she feels as though someone had praised their marriage. She glows all over and the egoist's spell is broken. (p. 110) Her husband, of course, is certainly not above such pettiness. A few hours before she had been outraged at his egoistic approach to James. What is true in her belief, however, is her love for him which can change (not disguise) the world round him, so that his consciousness does not have the same devastating effect Charles Tansley's has.

Mrs Ramsay's view of her husband can change him. Knowledge of another person, in the sense that matters here, is not knowledge merely of facts about a person, but a sympathy and understanding which may well find certain facts irrelevant or even intrusive, in the way that sympathy with the tensions and fluctuations of vanity might find the remark, 'He is a vain man', totally useless; though true, this fact, in certain cases, would indicate a more superficial knowledge of his vanity than the sympathy which knew the precise form the vanity took, and understood the difficulties that vanity caused to the person himself, and knew that at times the vanity ebbed, and that the ebbing brought relief. Therefore, one need not interpret Virginia Woolf's criticism of factual knowledge as a dismissal of the importance of factual truth; her point is that 'facts' about a person demand a complex balance.

Mrs Ramsay has this embracing, sympathetic knowledge. We are told that 'she knew without having learnt', (p. 34), that her knowledge follows from a kind of silence, that her mind falls like a plumb-line straight to the truth clever people falsify. The silence from which her knowledge springs is the area of privacy which has a depth and delicacy that is not amenable to the definitions commonly offered of other people. Mrs Ramsay's respect for her own private, submerged, only semi-articulate self, makes her recognise this privacy in other people. Her special knowledge of other people is therefore linked to her awareness that she does not know precisely what they are—not because, as in *Jacob's Room*, a person is purported to be unknowable, but because knowledge is difficult, and because there are limitless possibilities of thought and response. She is particularly sensitive to other people as perceivers; she knows their perceptions are bound up with their feelings and interests, that the 'public' world takes on a different form for each.

The author's assertion that Mrs Ramsay 'knew without having learnt' is not an assertion that she has some totally inexplicable knowledge, nor does the author attribute to Mrs Ramsay 'woman's intuition', which would simply be an admission that she could not account for Mrs Ramsay's knowledge. For Mrs Ramsay's knowledge is seen to be based upon a careful observation of people. Reading Grimm's tale about soldiers with kettle drums to James, she watches his eyes darken, and she thinks, 'Why should he grow up, and lose all that?' (p. 68) When she finishes the story, she sees another change in his eyes—'something wondering, pale, like the reflection of a light, which at once made him gaze and marvel'. (pp. 71–2) She sees that the Lighthouse has been lit, and she thinks, 'He will remember this disappointment all his life.' Her understanding, then, is based upon observation of James, on her knowledge of what has gone before (his father's declaration that he will not be able to go to the Lighthouse in the morning) and what is happening now (the light goes on in the Lighthouse). When, standing by the window, she knows without looking round that James is fidgeting and feeling himself to be out of things, her knowledge 'without looking round' emphasises rather than denies her careful observation. Presumably, she can hear him fidgeting, and she understands his mood from her knowledge of the situation, and she therefore understands what he is feeling at that moment.

Other, more general, developments in her children strike her as she observes them. At dinner, she guesses from the twitching of her children's lips that there is some joke going on among them. Her understanding is extended by her belief that their shared joke is important, by her belief that whatever they are thinking, whatever is happening to them, is important:

> What was it, she wondered, sadly rather, for it seemed to her that they would laugh when she was not there. There was all that hoarded behind those rather set, still, mask-like faces, for they did not join in easily; they were like watchers, surveyors, a little raised or set apart from the grown-up people. But when she looked at Prue tonight, she saw that this was not now quite true of her. She was just beginning, just moving, just descending. The faintest light was on her face, as of the glow of Minta opposite, some excitement, some anticipation of happiness was reflected in her [. . .] (pp. 125–6)

The subtlety of her observation, the patience she has in watching others, waiting for them to reveal themselves to her, is certainly at odds with her husband's decisiveness and quick assembling of facts. Since people tend to look at one another superficially, Virginia Woolf's characters cringe beneath another's scrutiny, and when a character is wooed into revealing something of his or her self, the character feels cruelly exposed and betrayed. As Mr Bankes looks at Lily's canvas—as he, that is, surveys her personal vision—she feels that 'the residue of her thirty-three years, the deposit of each day's living mixed with something more secret than she had ever spoken or shown in the course of all those days' (p. 61) is on view. To defend herself she tries to make him understand her vision; she explains why she needed Mrs Ramsay and her son in the picture, and why she represented Mrs Ramsay as a purple triangle. For a moment she is delighted at having shared her self with Mr Bankes, but, immediately, she nicks the catch of her paint-box firmly, suffering the humiliation that follows self-revelation, even as she appreciates the possibility of intimacy.

The special charm of intimacy with Mrs Ramsay is that it does not involve the type of self-revelation that seems to rob one of one's self—primarily because, as Lily realises, knowledge misfires at contact with another person; rather, what one seeks is union in which one realises that one does not know the other person yet in which one can share the world created by the other person. The notion, investigated in *Mrs Dalloway*, that people extend to the things they perceive, is developed more subtly here. In the earlier novel there was a clear separation between personality and objects surrounding the personality; even when objects absorbed a character's view, they were separate from the self, they could threaten or attack the self, and the ultimate emphasis in seeing Clarissa herself is the emphasis on an individual, if undefined, person. In *To the Lighthouse* the characters more convincingly permeate the world, and in seeking knowledge of them, one must not only, as in *Mrs Dalloway*, come to know the things the person loved, but the particular balance of responses and the position of the undisclosed self. Moreover, it is the character's vision and emotion which attract or repel one character to or from another; and it is understanding of that vision which brings one close to another. People are sealed, and in seeking knowledge of them one is like a bee 'drawn by some sweetness or sharpness in the air intangible to touch or taste, one haunted the dome-shaped hive, ranged the wastes of the air over the countries of the world alone, and then haunted the hives with their murmurs and stirrings; the hives which were people'. (p. 60)

The actual knowledge gleaned from intimacy is so evasive that Lily's initial reaction is, 'Nothing happened! Nothing! Nothing!' Yet the sound of the murmur in the hive grows louder, as though Mrs Ramsay herself had changed, as a person of whom we have dreamed seems changed. (p. 60) And, hypnotised by the new awareness, Lily is encouraged to engage in the exciting challenge of sharing her vision with Mr Bankes, and for one moment—only for a moment but a moment which is nonetheless permanently recorded—she feels what she had not hitherto suspected, 'that one could walk away down that long gallery not alone any more but arm-in-arm with somebody'. (p. 63)

Mrs Ramsay offers the possibility of sharing a vision. She seems, too, willing to give everything of her self to the people she loves, yet she has in her life 'something real, something private, which she had shared neither with her children or her husband'. (p. 69) (Somewhat too obviously the author repeats that Mrs Ramsay believes windows—that is, eyes—should be open, and doors—that is, the self—should be closed.) She does not protect this privacy cruelly, as does Mrs Dalloway, who, in protecting her privacy, denies her husband a full emotional response. Mrs Ramsay is relieved to be alone; she is pleased when the children are in bed and she can be herself, not to think as much as to be silent and solitary. This self, however, which emerges in total isolation, is not opposed to her responses to her family, but the basis of those responses; it is from this silence that her knowledge of others comes.

In her isolation she becomes, not—as Mrs Dalloway—a more highly individual, but a more universal perceiver; yet, like Mrs Dalloway, she loses that self which belongs to practical affairs. Her immediate frets and worries, her immediate surroundings, disappear, and she shrinks into a 'wedge-shaped core of darkness, something invisible to others'. (p. 72) Yet, in so shrinking, the range of experience becomes limitless. She 'meets the third stroke' of the Lighthouse, and the light searches as she alone can search her own mind and heart. But in this musing state, in which she is most intensely looking inside her self, she is no longer 'she' but 'one'. What is so profoundly one's own is not merely an individual possession. The trees and flowers now seem to express 'one' and she feels an irrational tenderness for that which is 'oneself' but which one discovers in the world round one. The identification of what one sees with what one is, is not an extension of the ego (as in *Mrs Dalloway*) but a dissolution of it. This dissolution offers a promise of union (there 'rose from the lake of one's being, a mist, a bride to meet her lover' [p. 74]) which is an ultimate fulfilment. The light strokes with 'its silver fingers some sealed vessel in her brain whose bursting would flood her with delight'. Waves of pure delight race over the 'floor of her mind' and she feels, 'It is enough! It is enough!' (pp. 75–6)

This complete identification of one's vision with the self, thus making one not a person with responsibilities, who lives in the world, but something like a disembodied perceiver, is of course interrupted by her husband (he believes, as he sees her through the window, that he wants to protect her, but he is actually frightened by the distance between them, and wants her attention) but the interruption is not a cruel one, nor is she outraged, as is Clarissa, by such an intrusion. She herself becomes aware of her husband's needs, and she goes to him; he does not have to force himself upon her.

As she gradually emerges from her solitude, which she does by fastening on to some sound or sight, her relations with the things round her change. Now the Lighthouse seems pitiless and remorseless; it still caresses her, but also has power over her; it is 'so much her, yet so little her'. (p. 75) She feels a strange division between the mind as investigator and the mind as the object of investigation, and she is aware how her previous perfect union with her surroundings has changed them; and, initially, the change is disturbing.

Since Mrs Ramsay so thoroughly penetrates her world, her death unbalances and distorts everything. The middle section of the novel, 'Times Passes', traces the effects of her illness and death from the point of view of a disembodied spectator in and around the house in Skye who reports fragments of the house's activities, thus giving each movement and each reported remark a symbolic point. An immense darkness falls upon the house which devours objects and obliterates identities; this darkness is not creative dissolution but annihilation. From the dominance of the house's atmosphere incidents of the character's lives are related in parentheses. We learn in this manner that Prue marries, and then dies from a disease related to childbirth. We learn that Andrew dies, too—a shell exploded in France killing, among others, Andrew Ramsay, 'whose death, mercifully, was instantaneous'; thus the author offers a sardonic comment on the casual disregard for young lives and on the letters officers wrote to inform relatives of their soldiers' deaths.

This world of battles now takes over. Even the landscape reflects the scars of war, though nature herself feels nothing and looks with equanimity upon man's meanness and misery:

> That dream, then, of sharing, completing, finding in solitude on the beach an answer, was but a reflection in a mirror, and the mirror itself was but the surface glassiness which forms in quiescence when the noble powers sleep beneath? Impatient, despairing, yet loth to go (for beauty offers her lures, has her consolations), to pace the beach was impossible; contemplation was unendurable; the mirror was broken. (p. 153)

The ability, shown in the first section, 'The Window', to use nature as a focusing symbol of the soul, revealing the creative harmony between what we see and what we seek to discover within ourselves, has been broken. The harmony was based upon a capacity for integration that has now been shattered; and, unsatisfactorily, the author purports two interchangeable causes for this destruction—Mrs Ramsay's death and the War. Alongside the exaggeration of the effect of the woman's death, mitigating the force of this section, is the self-consciously poetic or archaic language ('yet loth to go') and the sentimentality ('contemplation was unendurable; the mirror was broken').

In this middle section Mrs Ramsay's association with the house is portrayed in eerie effects, as though the narrator were both hyper-sensitive and partially blindfolded. (Doors open, admit nothing, and then slam shut.) This treatment of the house as an expression of her personality, or sorrow for the loss of her personality, is a disappointment after the careful writing in the first section, when the character of the house was clearly related to the woman. The clutter in the house, for example, was due to her refusal to prevent her children from pursuing their interests. If Andrew wants to dissect crabs, she decided, and if Jasper thinks you can make tea from seaweed, you have to let them try. So the resulting disarray is a symptom of the mother's special type of love, which regards her children's investigations as important. The variety of activity and emotion in the house, too—the Swiss girl's sobbing for her father and Mrs Ramsay's anger at being unable to help her, the freedom with which people seek their bedrooms after dinner to debate various matters—are part of Mrs Ramsay's sympathy joined with a respect for other's independent thoughts.

Nevertheless, the problem of how to salvage something of Mrs Ramsay's influence after her death is a real problem; and in the third section, 'The Lighthouse', it is investigated without the sentimental eerieness that burdens 'Time Passes'. The most prevalent symptom of Mrs Ramsay's absence and the intolerable difficulties it poses, is Lily's inability to see any meaning in the things or people or activities round her. She cannot understand why Mr Ramsay and the children want to go to the Lighthouse, nor can she understand why she herself returned to Skye, nor why she is sitting in the house. She feels no attachment to the place, nor any connection to the Ramsays. She feels, in general, that the link binding things together has suddenly been cut.

Lily's alienation is similar to that of Septimus Smith, and, as in Septimus's case, words and objects present themselves to her as nightmarishly disjointed symbols. Mr Ramsay's self-pitying, self-dramatised mutterings of 'Perished' and 'Alone' lodge as fragments in her mind; she is unable to construct a sentence, or any whole, from them. She escapes Septimus's impasse because in her case these incomplete responses form an incipient state of creative awareness. For though she is frightened by her own weird thoughts and by the unreality of her surroundings, she also is excited by this disorientation, demanding as it does the construction of new images.

As the others prepare their journey to the Lighthouse, she decides to finish the picture she had begun years ago, with Mrs Ramsay represented as a purple triangle. Lily's consideration of the proper relation among the masses on the canvas is interspersed with the tension between male and female. Because Mrs Ramsay is absent, Mr Ramsay appeals to Lily for sympathy and praise; but Lily's responses are clumsily aimed. After initial resistance, she grants him some meagre attention by praising his boots. His pleasure is so great that she finally feels real sympathy for him, because such a distinguished man can be so pathetic; but her sympathy comes when, satisfied by her admiration of his boots, he no longer needs it. Lily then recalls Tansley's (now disembodied) voice repeating, 'Can't write, can't paint', and thus she suffers the other side of man's attack upon women—not his devouring demands for their sympathy, but his need to think they are inferior.

Only when Lily is left alone, when she is able to forget the 'irrelevancies' that make her a specific person (as Mrs Ramsay became 'one' instead of 'she' during her musing), is integration and the healing investigation of the mind possible. Her mind throws up from its depths scenes, names, memories and voices, 'like a fountain spurting over that glaring, hideously difficult white space, while she modelled it in greens and blues'. (p. 181) The motion of her hand is described in terms of a water image (one line leads to another, as in the hollow of a wave one sees another wave rising) which, precisely, was the effect of Mrs Ramsay's presence: she made irrelevancies and irritations fall away like old rags, she brought fragments together and made everything curled and whole like a wave. Implicit in Lily's appropriation of this image is her need for the masculine element she has only resented and despised; for though Mrs Ramsay's affinity with waves was usually calm and soothing (they would be voices repeating, 'I am guarding you—I am your support'), they would at times become a drum remorselessly beating out the rhythm of life— and, in such a time, Mrs Ramsay was calmed by the sight of her husband walking up and down.

This unconscious borrowing of the woman's character is only the first step in the satisfaction of those needs created by Mrs Ramsay's absence. Even in memory her presence cannot be significantly realised. Though Mrs Ramsay has the power to reach out and wring one's heart, in Lily's memory she is nothing—only air and ghost. Memory only marks the woman's absence; and thus, in memory alone, Lily steps off her 'strip of board into the waters of annihilation'. (p. 205) Some further vision is necessary; memory must enlist imagination. The past must be re-fashioned and integrated with the present; the past must be re-created, and it must live within the present setting. Thus the boat, Mr Ramsay, and even Mr Carmichael—the totally negative personality, whose yellow cat's eyes merely reflect clouds and branches, and reveal no link with his inner being—contribute to Lily's reconstruction of Mrs Ramsay.

Lily's painting becomes an imaginative expression of Mrs Ramsay's personality. The painting is Lily's means of portraying what the woman meant to her, and will continue to mean to her, and the role of imagination is that of discoverer—not only of Lily's own feelings, but of Mrs Ramsay's own history. The woman's absence now acts as an impetus for discovery; Lily realises what she needs to know. One wanted fifty pairs of eyes to see with, she feels; fifty pairs of eyes would not be enough to see round that one woman. Thus Lily comes to understand what it is to know a person. She wants to know Mrs Ramsay's thoughts, musings, desires. She wants to know what the hedge and garden and breaking waves meant to her, and what stirred in her heart when she heard the children playing. And these finely focused questions themselves provide some answers. For in considering how the world appeared to Mrs Ramsay, and how she responded even to the smallest things, Lily can imagine how it was that Mrs Ramsay chose her husband. And, significantly, though Lily uses her imagination to understand the woman's choice, she is not inventing the story of the Ramsays' engagement: 'she was only trying to smooth out something she had been given years ago folded up; something she had seen'. (p. 226) The information necessary to the understanding of a person is not actually hidden in the sense of being behind or inside something; but the information must be noted carefully and then assembled with an intelligence that involves imagination. Once the process is begun, more and more information is brought to light and falls into place. Impressions follow one another, replace one another, and thereby set up an echo 'which chimed in the air and made it full of vibrations'. (p. 226)

Lily's completion of her painting, the completion of her vision, is linked with the Ramsays' journey to and arrival at the Lighthouse—as she paints, as she thinks about Mrs Ramsay, she is continually watching for the sail of the Ramsays' boat. During the journey the (now adolescent) children are in complete opposition to their father. Cam and James determine to form an alliance against him, lest he trick them into submission or sympathy. But as they approach the Lighthouse—as, that is, they realise the hope Mrs Ramsay offered James years ago when she said, 'Perhaps it will be fine'—the mother's sympathetic awareness penetrates their vision and, momentarily, they are all free from the resentment of one another's needs. Their father's faults cease to appear as attacks upon them, and they see his loneliness and the truth of his stark vision. The ability to accept this different view is based upon their new, different view of the Lighthouse. James had as a child seen it as a distant filmy thing; now, standing stark and straight, it confirms some obscure feeling about his own character. Thus his memory of being left impotent and ridiculous, clasping a pair of scissors, when his father stood strong and dominant before them (p. 212) is assuaged not only by his sympathy, but by this realisation of his own masculinity.

The Lighthouse is frequently identified as a male symbol complemented by the window which is seen as a female symbol; but such equations not only deny the flexibility of the symbols but also fail to make sense of them. 'Nothing was simply one thing,' James Ramsay reflects as he compares the immediate view of the Lighthouse tower with that he saw from the house. (p. 211) The tension and balance between man and woman, which is a tension and balance between male and female principle, is an important theme, but it is not actually worked out with reference to the Lighthouse. Obviously there are allusions to this theme in the third section, in the Ramsay children's reconciliation with their father, in Lily's sympathy for Mr Ramsay and her overcoming of Tansley's mocking voice; but the balance in the third section is schematic without having satisfactory substance. Moreover, the lack of conviction of the resolution in the third section of the novel is due in part to the excellent presentation of male and female principle in the first section of the novel, when the tensions are too profound to be, even momentarily, resolved. The tension itself is seen to be part of the male–female balance, and it is presented through a convincing involvement; whereas, in 'The Lighthouse' it is not clear that the characters have more at stake than a fluctuation of mood.

Initially it is through the child James's consciousness that the male and female are presented. He needs his mother for the world she creates. His own special child's world is vulnerable and unstable, though it has a potential richness. His feelings are not distinct; past and future influence the present, and 'any turn in the wheel of sensation has the power to crystallise and transfix the moment upon which its gloom or radiance rests'. (p. 5) His mother will crystallise the world with joy and hope, his father will make it dead and awful. (Mr Ramsay's references to his wife's 'pessimism' are attempts to deny as significant the darkness and terror which emerge in Virginia Woolf's novels as the other side of joy, and they are thus a denial of the sensibility that gives rise both to joy and terror—as such, his remedy for this 'pessimism' is far more pessimistic than the fears it dismisses.) The men pare down the richness of the world. The pocket knife with which Peter Walsh toyed in *Mrs Dalloway* here becomes a violent weapon. Mr Ramsay is 'lean as a knife' (p. 6) and he slices away everything but his meagre notion of truth. He sees this spareness of vision as a strength; he believes his attitude will provide people with courage and endurance. Indeed, his abilities are those that would be useful in extreme hardship; he would be a good leader of a polar expedition; he would fight on till the end. But these virtues are penetrated by egoism and self-dramatisation. Their effect, in normal circumstances, is to make life itself a polar expedition.

Mr Ramsay's colleague Charles Tansley joins him in this meagre world (Tansley is described as peeling the flesh and blood off everything), but he is totally dominated by egoism, and it is difficult to imagine any circumstances in which his characteristics would be virtues. All his conversation is aimed at proving his superiority. His consciousness is so different from Mrs Ramsay's that she cannot even understand the language he speaks or, rather, his 'ugly academic jargon'. As he talks she watches the distant, austere Lighthouse and the waving grasses on the dunes that seem to 'be running away into some moon country, uninhabited by men'. (p. 16) She must focus on some point outside this narrow egoism and the ugliness it creates.

Nevertheless, Mrs Ramsay is clearly bound to the male world. She feels protective towards it, the author says, for reasons Mrs Ramsay herself cannot understand—for its chivalry and valour, for its ruling of India and controlling of finance. (p. 8) She might seem to be undermining the male world by pitying it for those qualities which are commonly held to indicate strength; yet the comedy in her reasons for protectiveness are quite disingenuous, and she does revere the male world.

This reverence, moreover, defines her vis-à-vis man in an essentially subservient role. Mrs Ramsay feels that she is nothing more than a sponge to mop up other people's emotions, and her love finds expression in asking her husband whether there is anything she can do for him. She is governed by man's need for her, yet his needs for support, flattery and care are based upon pettiness, egoism and the domestic tyranny that would see the cost of mending the roof as the wife's fault. She needs him, too; but whereas man needs woman because he is mean-minded, she needs her husband's masculine vision to assuage the disturbing depth of her vision.

The negative aspect of man is continually stressed. He is seen as a symbol of sterility, craving the woman's fertility—and this bias indicates the bias of the novel as a whole. The success of Mrs Ramsay as a character, however, is such that this bias becomes part of the novel's tremendous strength, for her subservience to man becomes a service necessary to her own self-realisation, and we see, for the first time in Virginia Woolf's work, a consciousness that derives much of its strength through attachment to and active involvement with other people.

Though Mrs Ramsay feels taxed by man's need of her, she respects his need and therefore it is not through her, but through her son James, that we see the aggressive craving of the man and its effect upon her. With the special ambivalence, sensitivity and impotence a child feels in registering his parents' relations, James feels his father's 'beak of brass' and 'arid scimitar' swoop down upon his mother. (Later, in 'The Lighthouse', this hatred is directed not towards his father himself but some black-winged harpy with a cold hard beak that he sees in his father [p. 209], and his ability to separate his father's individual sufferings from his father as a representation of the male principle is the first step towards his ability to feel something like his mother's sympathy for the man.)

> But his son hated him. He hated him for coming up to them, for stopping and looking down on them; he hated him for interrupting them; he hated him for the exaltation and sublimity of his gestures; for the magnificence of his head; for his exactingness and egoism (for there he stood, commanding them to attend to him); but most of all he hated the twang and twitter of his father's emotion which, vibrating round them, disturbed the perfect

simplicity and good sense of his relations with his mother. By looking fixedly at the page, he hoped to make him move on; by pointing his finger at a word, he hoped to recall his mother's attention, which, he knew angrily, wavered instantly his father stopped. But no. Nothing would make Mr Ramsay move on. There he stood, demanding sympathy.

[. . .] Charles Tansley thought him the greatest metaphysician of the time, she said. But he must have more than that. He must have sympathy. He must be assured that he too lived in the heart of life; was needed; not here only, but all over the world. Flashing her needles, confident, upright, she created drawing-room and kit-chen, set them all aglow; bade him take his ease there, go in and out, enjoy himself. She laughed, she knitted. Standing between her knees, very stiff, James felt all her strength flaring up to be drunk and quenched by the beak of brass, the arid scimitar of the male, which smote mercilessly, again and again, demanding sympathy.

He was a failure, he repeated. Well, look then, feel then. Flashing her needles, glancing round about her, out of the window, into the room, at James himself, she assured him, beyond a shadow of a doubt, by her laugh, her poise, her competence (as a nurse carrying a light across a dark room assures a fractious child), that it was real; the house was full, the garden blowing. If he put implicit faith in her, nothing should hurt him; however deep he buried himself or climbed high, not for a second should he find himself without her. So boasting of her capacity to surround and protect, there was scarcely a shell of herself left for her to know herself by; all was so lavished and spent; and James, as he stood stiff between her knees, felt her rise in a rosy-flowered fruit tree with leaves and dancing boughs into which a beak of brass, the arid scimitar of his father, the egotistical man, plunged and smote, demanding sympathy. (pp. 43—5)

Mrs Ramsay's strength flares up, she rises, she flowers in these conditions of total demand. In her eyes the beating black wings of the rooks, which she watches as she dresses for dinner, are 'exquisite scimitar shapes'. The rooks are fighting desperately, absurdly, over nothing, yet they fascinate her. She can never describe the beating of their wings in a way that satisfies her, and she seeks help from her daughter: 'Look at that, she said to Rose, hoping that Rose would see it more clearly than she could. For one's own children so often gave one's own perceptions a little thrust forward.' (p. 93)

The extension of Mrs Ramsay's own consciousness rests upon her sympathy with the consciousnesses of others. She grants to others a reality which, usually in Virginia Woolf's works, is seen to be achieved only in isolation. What she gains from her sensitivity to her children's responses and thoughts, has an unquestionable value; yet the stimulus and taxation of her strength derived from her husband seems something like a cheat. 'For she had triumphed again', the author declares when, knowing that her husband is watching her and thinking her more beautiful than ever, Mrs Ramsay smiles and says, 'Yes, you were right. It's going to be too wet tomorrow.' (p. 142) She is triumphant because her protective consciousness is communicated through her beauty, or through her personality, which is her self as it appears to others. Her triumph, however, is disappointing. Though she is not actually denying her own view in giving way to him, and though, in this case, he is presumably right, the focus of her success is too narrowly on her ability to confirm and protect a far less profound consciousness, and her willingness to thus limit herself does not make her submission more acceptable.

One means of emphasising the diffusion of consciousness throughout the perceived world in *To the Lighthouse* is to contrast the passage quoted above, which fairly well represents James Ramsay's childhood awareness, with the awareness of the young Stephen Daedelus in Joyce's *A Portrait of the Artist as a Young Man*. Stephen's method of gathering information about the life round him is totally different from James's immediate, involuntary involvement. This is Stephen at Clongowes when he has been told by his mates to stay in bed because he is ill:

It was not Well's face, it was the prefect's. He was not foxing. No, no: he was sick, really. He was not foxing. And he felt the prefect's hand on his forehead; and he felt his forehead warm and damp against the prefect's cold damp hand. That was the way a rat felt, slimy and damp and cold. Every rat had two eyes to look out of. Sleek slimy coats, little feet tucked up to jump. But the minds of rats could not understand trigonometry. When they were dead they lay on their sides. Their coats dried then. They were only dead things.

The prefect was there again and it was his voice that was saying he was to get up, that Father Minister had said he was to get up and dress and go to the infirmary. And while he was dressing himself as quickly as he could the prefect said:

—We must pack off to Brother Michael because we have the collywobbles! Terrible thing to have the collywobbles! How we wobble when we have the collywobbles!

He was very decent to say that. That was all to make him laugh. But he could not laugh because his cheeks and lips were all shivery: and then the prefect had to laugh himself.

[. . .] He was sick then. Had they written home to tell his mother and father? But it would be quicker for one of the priests to go himself to tell them. Or he would write a letter for the priest to bring.

Dear Mother

I am sick, I want to go home. Please come and take me home. I am in the infirmary. [1]

Stephen's illness provides an isolation that encourages an intensified awareness of thoughts and sensations; and, as in Virginia Woolf's works, a fascination with an image and its associations directs the train of thought. In A Portrait, however, the image is independent of the circumstances in which it originally occurs and it therefore leads away from the immediate surroundings rather than to an investigation of one's total implication in those surroundings. As soon as the prefect leaves, Stephen no longer thinks of him, and the image which was brought to mind by the prefect's hand on his forehead becomes an independent train of thought. It leads to various similar sensations, and then to the association of rat, for these sensations apply, according to Stephen, to the sensations he would have in touching a rat. Then he continues to think about the rat—but all this has nothing to do with his response to the prefect himself. Compare, for example, James Ramsay's sensation when his father tickles his leg with a sprig, meaning to play with him. The boy associates this activity with what his father is doing at the time—or, rather, with the description of his father's activity that seems most important to James. His father is intruding upon the good and simple relations with his mother; he is demanding his mother's attention, his demand is an attack, and it devours all her energy. This image of something tickling his leg becomes associated with his father as an aggressor: later, as he and his father travel to the Lighthouse, he again sees everything his father does—even the turning of the pages of his book—as an aggressive act, and he feels himself to be a child again, with a cold hard beak tickling his leg. Never in Virginia Woolf's work could such an image be freed from the psychological situation in which it arose. Even when one image leads to another, the logic is not, as in Stephen Daedelus's case, a matter of associated sensations, but of emotionally associated thoughts; the thoughts direct one's attention to sensation and impression; psychology selects sensation and impression—whereas, for Stephen, sensation directs thought.

Both Stephen and James, with a child's powerlessness, hope that certain events will be seen by adults as reasons for fulfilling their respective wishes. James hopes that his pointing to a word on the page will recall his mother's attention to him and make his father move on. Stephen believes that his illness will be a reason for being sent home. But Stephen's world is far more his own than is James's, in the sense that Stephen is not participating in any adult drama through his child's hopefulness whereas James certainly is. Moreover, Stephen's understanding of the prefect's kindness in trying to make him laugh is understanding of the type necessary for commonplace politeness, such as smiling when one understands that someone is trying to make a joke rather than because one appreciates the joke; the prefect is not seen to be doing something else, something deeper, than playing with the boy, as characters in Woolf's works are always, even when involved in apparently innocuous behaviour, expressing themselves in a way that makes an intimately felt difference to the character towards whom their behaviour is directed. (This relentless intimacy, with all its tensions, resentments and uncertainties, is one reason solitude is so important to Woolf's characters.) Stephen's ability to be separate from that which he observes is maintained even among his family. He is not a participant, but an observer, trying to piece together the adult world:

It was not nice about the spit in the woman's eye. But what was the name the woman had called Kitty O'Shea that Mr Casey would not repeat? He thought of Mr Casey walking through the crowds of people and making speeches from a wagonette. That was what he had been in prison for and he remembered that one night Sergeant O'Neill had come to the house and stood in the hall, talking in a low voice and chewing nervously at the chinstrap of his cap. And that night Mr Casey had not gone to Dublin by train but a car had come to the door and he had heard his father say something about the Cabinteely road.

He was for Ireland and Parnell and so was his father: and so was

Dante too for one night at the band on the esplanade she had hit a
gentleman on the head with her umbrella because he had taken off
his hat when the band played 'God Save the Queen' at the end.

Mr Daedelus gave a snort of contempt.

—Ah, John, he said. It is true for them. We are an unfortunate
priest ridden race and always were and always will be till the end of
the chapter.

[. . . Mr Casey] stared before him out of his dark flaming eyes,
repeating:

—Away with God, I say!

Dante shoved her chair violently aside and left the table,
upsetting her napkinring which rolled slowly along the carpet and
came to rest against the foot of an easy chair. Mrs Daedelus rose
quickly and followed her towards the door. At the door Dante
turned round violently and shouted down the room, her cheeks
flushed and quivering with rage:

—Devil out of hell! We won! We crushed him to death! Fiend!

The door slammed behind her.

Mr Casey, freeing his arms from his holders, suddenly bowed his
head on his hands with a sob of pain.

—Poor Parnell! he cried loudly. My dead king!

He sobbed loudly and bitterly.

Stephen, raising his terrorstricken face, saw that his father's eyes
were full of tears.[2]

Stephen is certainly not a cold observer, but in observing he is
discovering something of the world round him; he is not, as James
Ramsay, standing stiff and straight between his mother's legs,
dramatically participating in the argument he observes. While James
sees his father as 'plunging' and 'smiting' Stephen notices the precise
gestures and words, and from these observations he comes to an
understanding of people's feelings, such as Sergeant O'Neill's
embarrassed self-importance as he takes a policeman's role among
acquaintances. He discovers the logic of events by reference to what
he has been told or remembers ('He was for Ireland and Parnell and so
was his father: and so was Dante . . .') and they involve him as
something which he learns is a part of him, but it is not immediately
felt to be a part of him. Stephen works hard to understand this world
of his, whereas James Ramsay has others' emotions—and their
significance—thrust upon him as inevitably as physical sensations.

Watching Rose choose the jewellery she will wear to dinner, Mrs

Ramsay reflects that the emotion she rouses in her children is so much larger than her self. However, in *To the Lighthouse* the emotion Mrs Ramsay rouses in others is identified with her self; the power and significance of her consciousness lies in the ease with which it is communicated, and it is communicated by being diffused through the world round her. People are not distinct beings; and however aggressive and disturbing this lack of separation may at times be, it also can provide the key to an extended awareness. The characters need to understand the minds of one another. The information they receive as immediately as they receive physical sensations is the starting point for the challenge to understand others' consciousness more fully. The need to achieve a satisfactory vision of others is, because no consciousness is separate and distinct, the same as the need to integrate one's own thoughts and visions.

6 *Orlando*, and the Problem of being a Woman

For it was this mixture in her of man and woman, one being uppermost and then the other, that often gave her conduct an unexpected turn. The curious of her sex would argue, for example, if Orlando was a woman, how did she never take more than ten minutes to dress? And were not her clothes chosen at random, and sometimes worn rather shabby? And then they would say, still, she has none of the formality of a man, or a man's love of power. She is excessively tenderhearted. She could not endure to see a donkey beaten or a kitten drowned. Yet again, they noted, she detested household matters, was up at dawn and out among the fields in summer before the sun had risen. No farmer knew more about crops than she did. She could drink with the best and liked games of hazard. She rode well and drove six horses at a gallop over London Bridge. Yet again, though bold and active as a man, it was remarked that the sight of another in danger brought on the most womanly palpitations. She would burst into tears on slight provocation. She was unversed in geography, found mathematics intolerable, and held some caprices which are more common among women than men, as for instance that to travel south is to travel downhill. Whether, then, Orlando was most man or woman, it is difficult to say [. . .] (p. 120)

This tongue-in-cheek account of Orlando's puzzling nature might be an attempt to do away with conventional notions of 'masculine' and 'feminine' and to show up the insignificance of acts such as galloping over London Bridge or the irrelevance of one's sex to one's knowledge of farming. In this fictional biography (based on the character of Virginia Woolf's friend Vita Sackville-West and on her family's history) the conventional 'male' and 'female' qualities are not themselves criticised here but only transferred from one sex to the other. Indeed, a certain amount of cliché and careless analysis characterises all Virginia Woolf's more direct and explicit treatment of the problem of being a woman. Both *A Room of One's Own* and *Three Guineas* share this shallow assessment of and random anger towards conventional distinctions.

In *A Room of One's Own* Woolf illustrates her argument that society thwarts female development with a tale based upon the supposition that Shakespeare had a sister with a genius equal to his and a similar love for the theatre. While William had the freedom and encouragement necessary to the development of his talent, the sister is scorned for her literary interests and scolded for her rejection of marriage. When she runs away from home to work in a London theatre she is first mocked and then seduced by the actor-manager. She becomes pregnant by him and takes her own life.

Virginia Woolf's bitterness towards the assumption that women are not entitled to the same education as men, and the assumption that they must engage in domestic drudgery for the sake of their brothers' education, is understandable; but an essayist's and novelist's attitudes must be soundly presented; it is not enough that they be understandable. Here the author's bitterness creates far too simple a story. We are told that Shakespeare's young sister was rendered susceptible to the actor-manager's seduction because he took pity on her. Yet we must also believe that, as William's counterpart, she has remarkable intellectual energy, and is eager for knowledge and experiment. Would pity seduce such a woman? She, presumably, has talent and a strong imagination: would not such qualities help her survive unwed motherhood, or worse? The cruelty she suffers at home is mockery and a father's wrath: but a lively imagination tends to see its own superiority, and it certainly survives petty-mindedness. Moreover, the mark of a literary genius is his or her ability to derive creative energy from hatred, pain and disgust, to discover in life's problems universal problems, to see stupidity and cruelty as a challenge to talent, to present all aspects, all levels of these limitations. The supposition that the girl, without further battle, takes her own life, marks her difference from Shakespeare, not society's different treatment of her. What the author does is to sketch an ordinary woman, and then to ask us to feel indignation as though a genius had been destroyed. Her legitimate point—that a woman should not have to be extraordinary to receive encouragement for her intellectual and creative inclinations—is lost in this careless overstatement.

In this same book Virginia Woolf argues that the lack of beautiful surroundings, and of good food and wine, inhibit both the intellect and the imagination. Yet in her novels she shows how imagination creates beauty, how beauty is not simply what Peter Walsh calls 'the crude beauty of the eye', but a vitality which is discovered. In her fiction Woolf reveals this truth, but as a woman's polemicist she forgets it. The narrator of *A Room of One's Own* despairs at the clear soup and homely pudding served at the women's college in contrast to the delicacies served at the men's college; but the comedy here is too ponderous to be effective. What is more disturbing is that the despair, despite its somewhat coy presentation, is seriously intended, and is therefore pathetic. The real point in this trivial instance is that women lack equal opportunities because their money is not theirs to use as they wish, nor is their leisure or energy.

Three Guineas, published ten years later in 1938, is a protest against the position of women, in particular against the position of the daughters of educated men, who are forced to work on behalf of their brothers' education, who are given virtually no paid education themselves, who have only very limited access to educational institutions and who are denied degrees and honours and posts from those institutions should they somehow have the opportunity to enter them, and who, if their fathers allow them to work, receive half a man's wages and have none of his chances of promotion. The five hundred pounds a year which gave the narrator of *A Room of One's Own* her special independence and equanimity have been taken away, and here the author's bitterness is forthright and persuasive; she fights as though she were demanding the right to breathe. Mrs Leavis's complaint in her *Scrutiny* review of *Three Guineas*[1] that there are as many if not more sons' lives ruined by possessive mothers as daughters' lives ruined by strict and demanding fathers, is hardly relevant. Virginia Woolf is saying, 'Look, these are instances of injustice.' It is not a contradiction to say, 'There are more instances here.'

In general, however, *Three Guineas* is too poorly argued to be of any value as a plea for women's rights. The main question posed is, 'How can we prevent war?' Almost blindly Woolf posits universal causes of war as those advantages men have over women. She sees the splendid robes, titles, degrees, honours available only to men as a means of labelling them brave and clever. Such labels, she continues, rouse the spirit of competition and jealousy, which encourage war. Women, who are denied these privileges and honours, have little call to love their country, nor have they access to those labels which rouse the fighting spirit, nor are they bound by loyalty to English institutions, such as school and college and club, which might inspire them to deeds of valour. Women's interest in the war effort is only an excuse to escape the tyranny of their domestic work.

For a better world, for a peaceful world, Virginia Woolf argues, women should not merely fight to be like men. They should cling to their old teachers: poverty, chastity, derision, and freedom from unreal loyalties—to country, school, club and college, institutions from which they are now excluded. Turning these conditions which have been forced upon them into wise precepts, women can abolish the inhumanity, beastliness, horror and folly of war. The narrator implies that if women are thus given power and made equal with men, the awfulness of men's work—the long hours, the inability to travel or to develop friendships or an interest in the arts—will disappear; for, through the training men have forced upon them, women will teach everyone the virtue of poverty, which is to earn enough, but no more than enough, to live independently of everyone else; of chastity, which is a refusal to sell your brain for advancement once your income is sufficient; of derision, which is to accept ridicule in preference to praise or fame; and of freedom from unreal loyalties. This simplistic cure is set beside a simplistic analysis of men's belief in the opposite of these virtues and thus in their penchant for war. Men suffer from an 'infantile fixation' which leads to obedience and respect for authority and the need to dominate others. This infantile fixation is the voice of the dictator and, it seems, disturbs all men. At this point the author's bitterness gives rise to random accusation rather than creative exploration, and the issues become hopelessly muddled.

Orlando was written in 1928, at about the same time as *A Room of One's Own.* (The companion novel to *Three Guineas* is *The Years,* in which women's freedom is denied by domestic tasks.) Virginia Woolf is here interested in the way conventions influence male and female characteristics, and she enjoys teasing established views by giving conventionally male characteristics to attractive women, and vice versa. The Muscovite Princess Sasha has the legs and movements of a boy, but the mouth and breasts of a woman. The Archduchess Harriet accosts Orlando (in his male phase) as a representative of the dreadful, lustful, decrepit side of romantic love; and, during Orlando's female phase, the (now) Archduke Harry exhibits the ridiculous aspect of romantic expectation. Sheldmarine, Orlando's husband, is so quick to understand his wife's feelings that she insists he must be a woman; and he, in turn, finds Orlando's virtues essentially manly.

Orlando undergoes one dramatic physical change from man to woman, and then undergoes more gradual psychological changes. First she discovers the pleasure of resisting, and then yielding to, men's advances. She becomes vain and timid and frightened of ghosts. She discovers the joy of having a protector, and this joy compensates her for the discomfort of her constricting skirts. Orlando realises that she must now suffer the culture her former male self endorsed: to be a woman means that she will never again be able to swear or to display violence or to sentence a man to death; nor will she be able to prance down Whitehall on a war-horse or lead an army or wear medals. Despite her regrets, she discovers that she is beginning to despise the sex to which she once belonged:

> 'To fall from a masthead,' she thought, 'because you see a woman's ankles; to dress up like a Guy Fawkes and parade the streets, so that women may praise you; to deny a woman teaching lest she may laugh at you; to be the slave of the frailest chit in petticoats, and yet to go about as if you were the Lords of creation. —Heavens!' she thought, 'what fools they make of us—what fools we are!' (p. 99)

What is worst in a man, then, is seen in his relation to woman. Clichés are self-propagating, and one sex frequently tries, for the sake of the other sex, to fulfil its stereotype. Thus the eighteenth-century prostitute abandons her frail, clinging manner when she discovers that Orlando is a woman; it is with relief she steps out of her ridiculous role and converses honestly with her companion, as she could not do with a man.

The difficulty is that in criticising stereotypes, Virginia Woolf does not escape them, but merely notes them with an expert eye. At their best the clichés are burlesqued, as when Orlando's conversation with Archduke Harry turns to love because they have exhausted the subject of the weather, and because men and women can converse only on these two subjects. In her anger the author sometimes twists clichés (as long as women are writing 'little notes' it is permissible for them to write; as long as they are thinking about men, it is permissible for them to think) but the result is neither startling nor remarkable. For the most part Woolf's criticism of society is a slip-shod mockery and analysis of customs. She makes much of the nineteenth-century crinoline which was an attempt to disguise woman's perpetual pregancy, and of the wedding ring which, the author claims, poisons the being. Her descriptions of the seventeeth-century coteries, however, read like a fine crib of Proust's account of various social circles: different hostesses create different illusions in their drawing-rooms—one creates an atmosphere of profundity, another of happiness, another of wit; but when Pope arrives and says three witty things all in the space of a few minutes, the atmosphere is destroyed. The poet is not a creator but a destroyer of illusions; that is his importance and power.

The novel itself tries to destroy the illusions that inhere in our notions of the different sexes, but the author gets lost in the fun of working within illusion. Yet the first part of the novel reveals a new dimension in Woolf's fine visual sensibility. The language has the preciousness common in her writing, but here it is a strength; it is the preciousness of whimsy and delight and fantasy:

> Birds froze in mid-air and fell like stones to the ground. At Norwich a young countrywoman started to cross the road in her usual robust health and was seen by the onlookers to turn visibly to powder and be blown in a puff of dust over the roofs as the icy blast struck her at the street corner. The mortality among sheep and cattle was enormous. Corpses froze and could not be drawn from the sheets. It was no uncommon sight to come upon a whole herd of swine frozen immovable upon the road. The fields were full of shepherds, ploughmen, teams of horses, and little bird-scaring boys all struck stark in the act of the moment [. . .] (pp. 14–5)

This naïvely exaggerated description of the Great Frost is composed of definite, succinct images which control the frequently distended quality of her metaphors. Compare the following passage from *Mrs Dalloway* in which the author seems to be roaming over wide ground to discover an appropriate image:

> There was nobody. Her words faded. So a rocket fades. Its sparks, having grazed their way into the night, surrender to it, dark descends, pours over the outlines of houses and towers; bleak hillsides soften and fall in. But though they are gone, the night is full of them; robbed of colour, blank of windows, they exist more ponderously, give out what the frank daylight fails to transmit— the trouble and suspense of things conglomerated there in the darkness; huddled together in the darkness; reft of the relief which

dawn brings when, washing the walls white and grey, spotting
each window-pane, lifting the mist from the fields, showing the
red-brown cows peacefully grazing, all is once more decked out to
the eye; exists again. I am alone; I am alone! she cried, by the
fountain in Regent's Park [. . .] (pp. 27–8)

with the following passage from *Orlando*:

All the colour, save the red of Orlando's cheeks, soon faded. Night
came on. [. . .] The Abbey appeared like the grey skeleton of a
leaf. Everything suffered emaciation and transformation. As they
approached the carnival they heard a deep note like that struck on a
tuning-fork which boomed louder and louder until it became an
uproar. [. . .] Above and around this brilliant circle like a bowl of
darkness pressed the deep black of a winter's night. And then into
the darkness there began to rise with pauses, which kept the
expectation alert and the mouth open, flowering rockets; crescents;
serpents; a crown. At one moment the woods and distant hills
showed green as on a summer's day; the next was all winter and
blackness again. (pp. 28–29)

In the passage from *Mrs Dalloway* an external image is used to
investigate Lucrezia's emotional and mental state, whereas in the
passage from *Orlando* the description of the external image is simply
the description of external events. In this respect the point and
purpose of the writing are quite different; but there is also a marked
difference in quality. In the former passage the writer elaborates her
image with fanciful detail, so fanciful that their presumed parallel to
Lucrezia's feelings makes them sentimental. The focus is on the
extension of the image, not on a probing of the psychological state;
the somewhat arbitrarily chosen image becomes a melancholic aside.
In *Orlando*, on the other hand, the image instills wonder, and sharpens
the impulse to investigate. The extension of the image is due to an
excited, probing observation.

Compare, again, the indulgent, lifeless language in which Peter's
and Clarissa's embrace is described: she 'actually had felt his face on
hers before she could down the brandishing of silver-flashing plumes
like pampas grass in a tropic gale in her breast, which, subsiding, left
her holding his hand', (p. 52) with Woolf's comment on Sasha's
and Orlando's love: 'And then they would marvel that the ice did not
melt with their heat, and pity the poor old woman who had no such
natural means of thawing it, but must hack at it with a chopper of

cold steel.' (p. 22) The latter pair of lovers marvel that their embraces, which are for them so powerful, do not affect physical reality, yet the second half of the sentence implies that their passion does actually thaw ice which ordinarily must be chopped. The lovers in *Orlando* find images for their emotions from their surroundings—they are, after all, making love in a winter landscape; whereas pampas grass in a tropical gale has a clichéd flamboyance due to its lack of connection with Clarissa's situation. The simple, naïve connection between feelings and surroundings in *Orlando* enables the author to be satisfyingly concise. When Sasha abandons Orlando the 'whole world seemed to ring with news of her deceit and derision', we are told (p. 33) and there is no need for over-insistence. We have already seen how the characters' conviction in their own emotions is linked to the world round them.

Also new, in the first part of *Orlando*, is an active, robust involvement in the world. In the opening paragraphs of *Mrs Dalloway* the initial thrust of the verbs ('she had burst open the French windows' and she had 'plunged at Bourton into the open air') is countered by the hypnotic swooping of the rooks, the wave imagery, and the rocking rhythm of the language. Activity in *Mrs Dalloway* is the peculiarly passive activity that comes from letting something outside the will guide one's thoughts and observations; it is the passivity of the unconscious in action. Orlando, however, directs his own investigations of the world; he is in motion, he loves motion, and his world mirrors this satisfying thrust forward in life: 'All the time they seemed to be skating on fathomless depths of air, so blue the ice had become; and so glassy smooth was it that they sped quicker and quicker to the city with the white gulls circling about them, and cutting in the air with their wings the very same sweeps that they cut on the ice with their skates.' (p. 28) In *Mrs Dalloway* the plunge into air is also a diver's plunge to that purely private area of mind in which the will is hypnotised, and to death. In *To the Lighthouse* the cutting of crescent shaped wings into the air was mean aggression. Only in *Orlando* is such movement vigorous and refreshing and freely chosen.

The concepts of knowledge, perception and the self deployed in this novel are not, however, fundamentally different from those in her other works. In fact, she offers here a more explicit (though not immaculately coherent) account of these concepts. More insistently than ever the author maintains that the person is a multitude of selves (thus she insists upon the legitimacy, as a biography, of Orlando's various histories, roles and sexes), though there is nonetheless a sense of a real self when the impulse to communicate something about one's true nature ends in failure, and one lights upon the truth in silence. Sometimes the conscious self, which is 'uppermost' and has 'the power to desire' longs to see the person as only one self, which is all the selves one might be, and which are guarded and unified by the Key self. This desire can be realised only in solitude and stillness:

> The whole of her darkened and settled, as when some foil whose addition makes the round and solidity of a surface is added to it, and the shallow becomes deep and the near distant; and all is contained as water is contained by the sides of a well. So she was now darkened, stilled, and become, with the addition of this Orlando, what is called, rightly or wrongly, a single self, a real self. And she fell silent. (p. 204)

All the discovery, then, made through Orlando's relations with people, through Orlando's observation of different societies, is, in the conclusion, seen to be less important than withdrawal into the private self. The purposiveness of Orlando's eager approach to life is also denied: the author declares that our lack of knowledge as to why we act as we do makes us like a ship passing along an unknown sea with no land in sight. (p. 44) After Orlando's careful observation of the world around him, the suggestion that all emotions and passions are not inspired by the outer world but are reflections from the depths and darkness of the mind is disappointing, as it is to be told that, in consequence, observation does not lead to understanding. Orlando muses:

> I am about to understand . . .
> Those were her words, spoken quite distinctly, but we cannot conceal the fact that she was now a very indifferent witness to the truth of what was before her and might easily have mistaken a sheep for a cow, or an old man called Smith for one who was called Jones and no relation of his whatever. For the shadow of faintness which the thumb without a nail had cast had deepened now, at the back of her brain (which is the part farthest from sight), into a pool where things dwell in darkness so deep that what they are we scarcely know. She now looked down into this pool or sea in which everything is reflected—and, indeed, some say that all our most

violent passions, and art and religion, are the reflections which we
see in the dark hollow at the back of the head when the visible
world is obscured for the time. She looked there now, long, deep,
profoundly, and immediately the ferny path up the hill along
which she was walking became not entirely a path, but partly the
Serpentine; the hawthorn bushes were partly ladies and gentlemen
sitting with card-cases and gold-mounted canes; the sheep were
partly tall Mayfair houses; everything was partly something else, as
if her mind had become a forest with glades branching here and
there; things came nearer; and farther, and mingled and separated
and made the strangest alliances and combinations in an incessant
chequer of light and shade. (p. 210)

To the theory (which is the reason for Mrs Ramsay's short-
sightedness and her inability to determine whether an object in the
water is a lobster-pot or an over-turned boat) that our deepest feelings
and most profound perceptions are focused inward and not outward,
is added another theory of what it is that we see, and the two are not
consistent. Her second theory is that a shadow comes from the eye to
transform the formless, immediate, terrifying impressions into
something recognisable and comprehensible. This transforming
shadow frees one from the terror and cruel beauty of the immediate
image and allows one the calm the self needs to maintain its sanity.
(p. 209) (Presumably Septimus Warren Smith lacked such a shadow,
and thus had to close his eyes to maintain his sanity. But such a fanciful
theory, with its spurious epistemology, cannot provide a satisfactory
psychological explanation for Septimus's madness.)
  On the one hand, therefore, it is only when we see into our own
minds, and construct the material world by our own thoughts, that
we come by the true perceptions; on the other hand, the true world is
the immediate, terrifying and beautiful external world which must be
moulded to accommodate our timid mental faculties. A similar
dilemma is felt by Orlando as he puzzles over the discrepancy
between plain facts and poetic language. The true colour of grass
seems to demand a more complex poetic statement than conventional
poetic diction will allow (this is in the seventeenth century) and
certainly a more complex statement than the simple ascription of
'green' to the grass. Yet, subsequently, he feels that factual and poetic
language are equally true; so there remains a discrepancy between the
assertion that factual language is true, and the assertion that to get at
the truth we need a new poetic language. Generally, there is no

disturbing inconsistency in Woolf's fiction, for she focuses at one time upon the way we transform the world according to our own thoughts, and at other times on the way the world is separate from us, and also vivid to us, so that we must assuage its immediacy by assuring ourselves that our minds are of paramount importance. Similarly, she sometimes sees truth as plain fact, and sometimes as imaginative perception, without inconsistency, with only a change of emphasis.

In any case, the novel concludes with an assertion of the need for silence and retreat as a healing and integrative process. This need was presented, for the first time in the novel, in Orlando's first long sleep, when life, apparently crippled forever, 'is brushed with a dark wing which rubs off the harshness of memories and gilds them'. (p. 37) The vigour which belonged to the first chapter is now denied, and after the second chapter Orlando undergoes no real growth. The now female character has many experiences; she romps gaily through the centuries and marries and has a child, but the originality of the opening is lost. This loss—or, rather, the first chapter's remarkable gain—is due in part to the special qualities of the seventeenth century when, according to the author, the sunsets were redder and everything was altogether more intense, when violence was law, and youth was brief, when it rained vigorously, or not at all. (p. 10) The appealing energy, too, may be a result of the fact that the active, spontaneous, free self could only be convincingly conceived in a masculine guise. Consequently, Virginia Woolf does not in *Orlando* solve the problem of the portrayal of a fully realised woman.

7 Metaphor and the Mind: *The Waves*

In 'Phases of Fiction' (*Collected Essays*, II) Virginia Woolf described, by means of her praise of Proust's novel *A la Recherche du Temps Perdu*, the type of mental investigation she herself embarked upon, and consummated, in *The Waves*. Woolf shared with Proust an interest in metaphor as an epistemological device; the process of forming and extending metaphors is an important vehicle for knowledge—and, in some cases, it is the only vehicle.

Virginia Woolf praised Proust's technique for its receptivity to all mental stimuli. His technique, she believed, provides a thin but elastic envelope that stretches wider and wider, and serves not to enforce a view, but to enclose a world. In other words, the view is not argued, but presented as part of a total consciousness, justified by cross-references (psychological and mnemonic) within that world. Anything at all can become an object of consciousness and, as such, can become part of the novel's world. The most common objects, Woolf noted, lose their simplicity and solidity, and become part of one's psychological history. The most common actions can bring a whole series of hitherto buried thoughts, sensations and memories to the surface. The characters themselves seem to be made of an immaterial substance:

> Thoughts, dreams, knowledge are part of them [. . .] As a consequence of the union of the thinker and poet, often, as on the heel of some fanatically precise observation, we come across a flight of imagery—beautiful, coloured, visual, as if the mind, having carried its powers as far as possible in analysis, suddenly rose in the air and from a station high up gave us a different view of the same object in terms of metaphor. (p. 89)

The assumption Woolf makes, then, is that precise observation and analysis can take us only so far, that to go further we need a different view altogether—and this is what metaphor can provide. In Proust's novel elaborate passages of metaphor 'spring out of the rock like a fountain of sweet water and serve as translation from one language into another. It is as though there were two faces to every situation. One turns towards the light to be analysed in detail; and the other, in shadow, can be described only in a moment of faith and vision by the use of metaphor.' (p. 97) The 'translation' which the metaphor offers is not a simple substitute for the first language; it is the only possible means of describing the other face of the situation.

Proust himself justifies his use of metaphor with a more developed epistemological theory. The theory is established through the narrator Marcel's relation to the external world. External objects may appear terrifying and strange through their independence from the viewer. Habit, however, makes one feel at home among certain objects and makes one forget that one is actually separate from these familiar objects. Any change in the familiar surroundings can destroy the habitual relation and remind one of one's alienation from the external world. Thus it is that the shadows cast by the moving lantern in Marcel's childhood bedroom introduce into the room which had previously been filled with Marcel's own personality, and which custom had made comfortable, a painful mystery and beauty. The figures in the lantern take possession of every object (the door knob is like a skeleton inside Golo's body[1]), thus terrifying the child with his own alienation and lack of control. Custom would eventually make the room his own again, but this custom would also dull his perceptions and deprive him of the beauty and glamour of the external world.

Some means other than habit must be discovered which allows the world its beauty and glamour but which, at the same time, protects one from the nightmare of looking upon that which is totally distinct from one's self. The beauty of external objects must be made part of one, not by mitigating the magic of the objects through habit, but by making that magic part of one's self. Marcel, struck by the beauty of the hawthorn's blossoming, wants 'to imitate, somewhere inside myself, the action of their blossoming'.[2] The process of internal imitation is achieved as he imagines the blossoming as 'a swift and thoughtless movement of the head with an enticing glance from her contracted pupils, by a young girl in white, careless and alive'.[3] With the help of a metaphor the life of the flowers becomes part of his own consciousness; the metaphor he constructs transforms that which is alien into something personally felt, personally imagined and therefore personally possessed.

The metaphor is not an arbitrarily chosen image. Nor does it register only individual response. Metaphor is an important means of discovering the world; it brings to light various aspects of the world. When the young Marcel is first introduced to Bergotte's novels he believes that the writer's images would make the beauty of a familiar object explode and drench one in its essence; Marcel longs to have some metaphor offered by Bergotte on everything in the world, especially on those objects with which he might one day become acquainted. The emphasis, then, is not on the capacity of metaphor to present to us that which we do not see, but on its capacity to reveal further aspects of that which we do see. In comparing the hawthorn's blossoming to the movement of a young girl's head Marcel is defining that aspect of the object he finds so exciting; he is intrigued by the *action* of their blossoming. He makes them part of himself through metaphor because metaphor isolates and defines special qualities; metaphor deepens his knowledge of the flowers.

Metaphor as a literary device is of secondary importance. What matters both to Proust and to Woolf is the mind's tendency to see one object or action in terms of another, for one object to reveal allusive potential which the mind seeks to complete, for one object to suggest another, perhaps, hidden, emotion or memory. Thus in *The Waves* the world becomes a psychological map; the external landscape is only that which the characters see and feel it to be. Though Proust's external world has more definite, objective outlines, the mind continuously seeks images to penetrate the psychological essence of the world. As Marcel sees the hedge of flowering hawthorn in Swan's Tansonville estate, the images of church and altar (for it was in the church at Combray that he was first so enchanted by the blossoms) are not sufficient to bring him into satisfactory contact with them:

> But it was in vain that I lingered before the hawthorns, to breathe in, to marshal before my mind (which knew not what to make of it), to lose in order to rediscover their invisible and unchanging odour, to absorb myself in the rhythm which disposed their flowers here and there with the light-heartedness of youth, and at intervals as unexpected as certain intervals of music; they offered me an indefinite continuation of the same charm, in an inexhaustible profusion, but without letting me delve into it any more deeply, like those melodies which one can play over a

hundred times in succession without coming any nearer to their secret. [4]

Marcel must seek further for an appropriate image. He tries looking away, and then looking again at the flowering hedge; he tries shaping his fingers into a frame to isolate the flowers; but the sentiment they arouse in him remains 'obscure and vague, struggling and failing to free itself, to float across and become one with the flowers'. [5] Only when his grandfather points out, hidden among the white bushes, a single pink hawthorn, is Marcel enlightened. It is like seeing a finished picture after struggling to understand the sketch alone, or like hearing a piece played by a full orchestra when before he knew only the piano transcription. It is not that he receives new information which might make a puzzle fall into place, but he sees something which enriches the picture.

At this point Marcel actually sees the young girl in white whose image had, in the Combray church, offered him an internal imitation of the flower's blossoming. At the appearance of Gilberte he stands still 'as happens when something appears that requires not only our eyes to take it in, but involves a deeper perception and takes possession of the whole of our being'. [6] Even when the image necessary to understanding is realised the mind cannot rest in satisfaction, but must assimilate the various stimuli aroused both by the object and the images it suggests. Even the most commonplace aspects of the external world demand a creative effort if they are to be appreciated. After having walked along the Guermantes' way, Marcel is ready to drop with sleep. He admits that at this time 'the balmy scent of the lime-trees seemed a consolation which I could obtain only at the price of great suffering and exhaustion, and not worthy of the effort'. [7]

Despite the importance of the perceiver's participation in perception, despite his emphasis on the necessity of creating images in order to come into contact with objects, Proust sees as problematic the fact that we know the world only through our perceptions of it. When Marcel looks at an object, he feels that his own vision lies like a barrier between him and the object, enclosing it in a 'slender, incorporeal outline' which prevents him from coming in direct contact with the object and from getting a true view of it—for, whenever he approaches the object, it in some way changes:

For even if we have the sensation of being always enveloped in, surrounded by our own soul, still it does not seem a fixed and immovable prison; rather do we seem to be borne away with it, and perpetually struggling to pass beyond it, to break out into the world, with a perpetual discouragement as we hear endlessly, all around us, that unvarying sound which is no echo from without, but the resonance of a vibration from within.[8]

Proust vacillates between using this fact as an explanation of the way mood, thought and desire influence our perceptions, and using it to insist that we neither see the material object as it really is, nor do we see it at all. He sometimes denies, then, what he elsewhere carefully shows: that our different ways of seeing the external world reveal various truths about the world which no single view could reveal.

In *The Waves* Virginia Woolf shows no such vacillation in her approach to truth. Always she focuses on that mobile shroud, and her aim in this novel is to create a language in which that shroud can be explored. Each stage in the characters' lives is prefaced by italicised lyric passages which present the whole world—the sun, sea and sky—in terms of various stages of perception and various stages of the ego which, as in her other novels, influence what one perceives and how one arranges one's perceptions. In the first lyric section the sea and sky are undifferentiated, for the characters are infants and cannot make a distinction; and the inside of the house, the inside of their minds, is 'dim and unsubstantial'. (p.6) Here the waves sigh like a sleeper who draws his breath unconsciously, but, subsequently, when the self becomes more aggressively aware of its individuality, they advance like turbaned warriors, or ripple proudly like a horse, or fall with the thud of a stamping beast. The waves are the undercurrent of life, the energy which defines one's relation to life, and which is linked to one's confidence in the continuation of one's own life. The birds, first singing their blank melody, then learning individual songs, able to be sung separately or together, are the selves which in adolescence and youth peck and peck at the snail which is the ego hardening round the self, and the self eventually becomes a worm retreating into its narrow hole. The rising sun marks the different relations to objects, the different stages of differentiation: gradually the sun reveals the opening of windows, gradually it shows objects to be distinct from one another until this distinctness becomes fanatical and aggressive (a knife is like a dagger of ice [p. 94]). Eventually a reddish light is poured over the entire landscape; the objects which had been so sharp and clear develop cracks and, as the sun sinks back into the horizon, objects vanish, sea and sky are again indistinguishable, and the unity of infancy is rediscovered in death.

These italicised passages are the least good in the novel. Their lyricism is forced, and the images are inadequate to the cosmic scope attempted: 'the dark bar on the horizon became clear as if the sediment in an old wine-bottle has sunk and left the glass green', and the bars of colour spread over the sky 'like the blades of a fan'. (p. 5) What these passages succeed in doing is marking stages of perception not as an individual psychological pattern but as a general fact of life, like the rising and setting sun. For the six characters' perceptions are not based upon an emotional-psychological setting in which, for example, James Ramsay sees his father's playful tickling of his leg as a beak pecking his soul and destroying his hope and dignity—an image based upon the son's relation to the father's personality, and the son's assessment of his father's relation with his mother. In *The Waves* there is little emphasis on interpersonal relations and psychological development through interpersonal situations. The children's parents (with the exception of Louis's, and then only in an extremely sketchy way) are not described, nor are Bernard's wife and family, nor are Susan's husband and children. The characters' psychology is an accumulation of images, of images determined by a private self, and of a private self given almost complete in infancy:

'I see a ring,' said Bernard, 'hanging above me. It quivers and hangs in a loop of light.'

'I see a slab of pale yellow,' said Susan, 'spreading away until it meets a purple stripe.'

'I hear a sound,' said Rhoda, 'cheep, chirp; cheep, chirp; going up and down.'

'I see a globe,' said Neville, 'hanging down in a drop against the enormous flanks of some hill.'

'I see a crimson tassel,' said Jinny, 'twisted with gold threads.'

'I hear something stamping,' said Louis. 'A great beast's foot is chained. It stamps, and stamps, and stamps.' (p. 6)

However one interprets *The Waves*—whether as a novel with various characters or as a prose poem representing various types of consciousness or different aspects of a single consciousness—this description of the infant's 'speech' describing visions which depend upon concepts they cannot possibly have, must be seen as unsatisfactory. What is legitimately implied in this highly stylised transcription of their impressions, is that from birth the characters' perception is selective and metaphorical, and that the manner of their selection and the metaphors chosen define the character. From the beginning each speaker has his or her own visionary, earthy, timid and repetitive, precise and abstract, sensual, or violent focus. From the beginning each character has his essential self which undergoes development and change more like the unfolding growth of a plant than the complex and haphazard changes which would be assumed by a less strictly determined development.

From the beginning the characters speak of what they perceive, yet the metaphorical quality of their perceptions indicates an interest not in the world around them, but in their particular relation to the world, their response to it, and their sense of the nature of their individual minds. Their entire consciousness is focused in their manner of seeing:

> 'I love,' said Susan, 'and I hate. I desire one thing only. My eyes are hard. Jinny's break into a thousand lights. Rhoda's are like those pale flowers to which moths come in the evening. [Bernard's] grow full and brim and never break.' (p. 12)

Susan's hard eyes follow from the singleness of her desire. In the meeting with Percival her eyes are lumps of crystal, and she sees all life as natural substance; even factories and battlements are huge, substantial blocks following an ancient pattern. Eyes can only be described in terms of what they see. Susan is not saying that Jinny's eyes sparkle, but that her vision is both exciting and dangerously fragmentary, that Rhoda's is nugatory and passive, that Bernard's easily won sympathy is partly controlled, partly distracted by his phrase-making and story-telling. Their manner of seeing is as definite a quality as would be green or sparkling eyes.

In *The Waves* Virginia Woolf believed she was eliminating the 'waste, deadness' that arises from the 'appalling narrative business of the realist',[9] for she presents as the only reality that which makes itself felt—and the manner in which it is felt—to the speakers. Again one can use Proust to argue her point:

> If reality were indeed a sort of waste product of experience, more or less identical for each one of us, [. . .] no doubt a sort of cinematographic film of these things would be sufficient and the 'style', the 'literature' that departed from the simple data that they

provide would be superfluous and artificial. But was it true that reality was no more than this? If I tried to understand what actually happens at the moment when a thing makes some particular impression on me [. . .] I realised that the words [I used at the time to express simply and easily my feelings] in each case were a long way removed from the impressions that I [. . .] had in fact received. So that the essential, the only true book, though in the ordinary sense of the word it does not have to be 'invented' by a great writer—for it exists already in each one of us—has to be translated by him. The function and task of a writer are those of a translator.[10]

Contrary to the assumptions of traditional rationalism and empiricism, the contents of the mind are not known simply and immediately. (Locke and Hume speak as though we can see the contents of our minds as we would see actors pass along a stage.) The process of mental investigation is such that categories of thought about thought must be created, and continuously re-created:

What an abyss of uncertainty whenever the mind feels that some part of it has strayed beyond its own borders; when it, the seeker, is at once the dark region through which it must go seeking, where all its equipment will avail it nothing. Seek? More than that: create. It is face to face with something which does not so far exist, to which it alone can give reality and substance, which it alone can bring into the light of day.[11]

This is each character's task in *The Waves*: to give reality and substance to that part of the mind which must be created, and which always threatens to be dissolved by coarse, commonplace categories or by one's own meagre abilities.

The creation of this language, the creation of the inner world itself, is seen both as the most significant activity of life and one that is separate from—even endangered by—one's relation with other people. Bernard cares nothing for his public, social self: they can murder this Bernard who is about to be married, he thinks, if only they leave untouched 'this margin of unknown territory' where he probes his mind, where he traces and constructs his stories in an attempt to put some order upon his thoughts. Though Louis values his public image, his businessman's personality, he values it not as a reality but as a protection against critical observation of his deeper self, or as a disguise for his real self which craves the sordidness and chaos his impeccable appearance denies. Rhoda, whose deepest self lacks protection to the extent that she sees herself as having no physical reality (she must press her toes against the bed rail to prevent herself from falling into space; she must hit her hand against something hard to be reassured of her solidity; always she feels she might be blown in the wind like a feather or mysteriously dissolved) angrily mocks the effectiveness of order, reducing it to an oblong placed upon a square. Because she has no protective covering, because she has no regard for simple, solid appearances, she gets lost in the regions of her mind and is destroyed by the terror she finds there.

The one character in *The Waves* who does not 'speak' is Percival. He does not need a voice because he lives in immediate, active involvement with the external world: there is not one piece of paper, Bernard reflects, between Percival and the sun. The other six characters value this friend, and his death intensifies their awareness of the fragility of their own respective consciousnesses. They must develop a voice because, unlike Percival, their position in the world is not that of actor but perceiver. They must develop a language which accounts for their position in the world because as perceivers they are nonetheless intricately involved in the world in a way no one else would appreciate. When others see him, Neville reflects, they see only Neville, but to himself he is immeasurable selves, 'a net whose fibres pass imperceptibly beneath the world. My net is almost indistinguishable from that which it surrounds. [. . .] I detect, I perceive.' (p. 183)

Throughout Virginia Woolf's novels mental states are described in terms of external landscapes. In *The Voyage Out* the entire journey can be seen as a metaphor of inward exploration. In *Mrs Dalloway* the drawing-room disappears as Peter kisses Clarissa, and she is among pampas grasses swayed by a tropical storm. In this case, one can see the swaying grasses as a means of saying, 'When Peter kissed her she felt like that.' Her emotion can be identified by her position in the drawing-room, by the fact that Peter is kissing her, by the fact we know she once loved him and is now married to Richard. In other words, her emotional state is partially described by the metaphor but it can be identified by other descriptions. In many cases, however, the emotional or psychological state cannot be identified by anything other than the metaphor. The wedge-shaped core of darkness into which Mrs Ramsay shrinks, for example, can be understood in part by her solitude and her musing, but a satisfactory description of her state can only be given by that metaphor; the metaphor could not be substituted by any descriptive terms, as could Mrs Dalloway's state when she feels herself to be among the pampas grasses (she could be said to feel exhilarated, strange, frightened). In *The Waves* it is impossible to give anything other than a metaphorical account of emotional and psychological states because the external context in which feelings occur, is virtually omitted. The metaphors ordinarily called in to extend a description of a psychological state already individuated by an external context, are the total constituents of any 'external' landscape the novel presents:

> 'I hear something stamping,' said Louis. 'A great beast's foot is chained. It stamps, and stamps, and stamps.'
> 'Look at the spider's web on the corner of the balcony,' said Bernard. 'It has beads of water on it, drops of white light.'
> 'The leaves are gathered round the window like pointed ears,' said Susan.
> 'A shadow falls on the path,' said Louis, 'like an elbow bent.'
> 'Islands of light are swimming on the grass,' said Rhoda.
> 'They have fallen through the trees.'
> 'The birds' eyes are bright in the tunnels between the leaves,' said Neville. (pp. 6–7)

The reader is directed towards what the characters see, but there is no distinction between the spider's web, which can be supposed to be an external object Bernard does see, and the stamping beast which is perhaps a dog but which appears to Louis as threatening, voracious and captive. One cannot here distinguish between a 'true' view of an external object and a character's view of it because there is no point to such a difference. It is not that the characters see the world as a symbol, but what they see is symptomatic of what they are. The light falling through the trees has for Rhoda, who always feels herself to be in danger of falling, the impression of falling as a physical object would fall through the trees. The characters' responses can be explained only by a description of how the world appears to them; their responses are defined not in terms of the emotional context but in terms of the metaphor that will reveal their manner of perception, and their psychological state. Reflecting upon his loneliness and his difference from others, Louis says:

'Up here Bernard, Jinny and Susan (but not Rhoda) skim the flower-beds with their nets. They skim the butterflies from the nodding tops of the flowers. They brush the surface of the world. Their nets are full of fluttering wings. "Louis! Louis! Louis!" they shout. But they cannot see me. I am on the other side of the hedge. [. . .] My hair is made of leaves. I am rooted to the middle of the earth [. . .] Now something pink passes the eyehole. Now an eye-beam is slid through the chink. Its beam strikes me. I am a boy in a grey flannel suit. She has found me. I am struck on the nape of the neck. She has kissed me. All is shattered.' (pp. 9–10)

The external event—the children skimming the flower beds with their nets—is for Louis an image of skimming the surface of the world. He feels not as though he were rooted to the earth—he feels himself to be rooted to the earth. Jinny, after kissing him, smells 'earth mould'. The reality of his metaphorical immersion in the earth is confirmed because another shares it. Yet Louis's fear that his own sense of what the world is, and what he is, will not be shared, makes the girl's glance and embrace appear destructive.

The characters' belief in a metaphorical description of their state as a literal description of their place in the world occurs repeatedly. Rhoda, while she is at school, looks forward to the time when she can turn out the light and lie suspended above the world, when the day drops below her and her tree grows 'quivering in green pavilions' above her head; whereas, when faced with the commonplace distractions of the day, her tree is attacked and cut down. There is a significant distinction made between her dreams in which she is an Empress commanding her people—a 'thin, papery' dream—and a dream which is not a fantasy but which is solid and satisfying, which creates images as an expression of one's true state. Abandoning her pretence of being an Empress Rhoda goes to the library:

'[. . .] Here is a poem about a hedge. I will wander down it and pick flowers, green cowbind and the moonlight-coloured May, wild roses and ivy serpentine. I will clasp them in my hands and lay them on the desk's shiny surface [. . .] I will bind flowers in one garland and clasp them and present them—Oh! to whom? There is some check in the flow of my being; a deep stream passes on some obstacle [. . .] Oh, this is pain, this is anguish! I faint, I fail. Now my body thaws; I am unsealed, I am incandescent. Now the stream pours on a deep tide fertilising, opening the shut, forcing the tight-folded, flooding tree. To whom shall I give all that now flows through me, from my warm, my porous body? I will gather my flowers and present them—Oh! to whom?' (p. 48)

In this passage we can see the way reality is supplanted by metaphor. The poem Rhoda is reading is about a hedge, and the hedge then becomes material—so truly material that there is no distinction between its reality and the reality of the desk at which she is sitting when she reads the poem: she picks flowers by the hedge and then lays them on the desk.

An important means by which metaphors and symbols are given the status of reality is the way in which they recur both in a single character's thoughts and among various characters as a shared object of thought. Rhoda's desire to offer flowers returns later, after Percival's death; she rips up 'flowers' from Oxford Street (that is, the colour and vitality of Oxford Street) and throws them on the waves in tribute to her dead friend. Waves, throughout the novel, are a symbol of continuing life, of the life outside that which is governed by the ego, yet in which each individual partakes, and which will, eventually, claim back the individual life. Rhoda, despising the 'antics of the individual', wanting to withdraw into darkness, has an affinity with death. Only in darkness will her tree grow; but this tree, which she feels to be her growing soul, is seen by Neville as a sign of death: as a child he overhears the cook speaking about a murder and he imagines an obstacle of an implacable tree with a greaved silver bark—an image of the fact that everyone is doomed to die—and he decides to call his vision 'death among the apple trees'. For Bernard, in his final soliloquy, both the tree and the waves become a positive force of life: the wave rises inside him and lifts him up; yet Rhoda, in maturity, sees the waves only as a force of dissolution:

'We launch out now over the precipice. Beneath us lie the lights of the herring fleet. The cliffs vanish. Rippling small, rippling grey, innumerable waves spread beneath us. I touch nothing. I see nothing. We may sink and settle on the waves. The sea will drum in my ears. The white petals will be darkened with sea water. They will float for a moment and then sink. Rolling over me the waves will shoulder me under. Everything falls in a tremendous shower, dissolving me.' (p. 177)

The metaphorical terms of the characters' visions do not merely offer an analogy of their state but become the focus of their actual sensations. Rhoda's vision of what will happen to her is the sensation of it happening to her. In middle age she looks forward to the time when she can be alone, when she will fall through this 'thin sheet into gulfs of fire'. She sees that her friends will not only let her fall, but will tear her to pieces when she has fallen. (p. 192) She does not believe that she is actually falling at the moment, in the way she did as a girl believe the stream to be flowing through her warm, porous body, yet she is no less involved in the vision she knows to be imagined. The metaphorical vision becomes a circumstance which must be endured as that circumstance would, if interpreted literally, have to be endured. For the metaphorical visions describe the characters' real stories. As Bernard reflects during his visit to Rome, the story-teller's art, the realist's design, is arbitrary and pointless; as he discovers in his final soliloquy, the important story is the history and integration of one's visions whose metaphorical nature present not simply an analogy of the characters' feelings, but the feelings themselves and the circumstances in which those feelings arise.

The six characters are brought together through association from infancy, but the significance of their bond is not primarily that of affection. The moments of communion, as they all feel at Hampton Court, are not in themselves enough to justify the presentation of characters as a body. Nor do the love affairs between Louis and Rhoda, and between Neville and Jinny, account for the coherence of the group. What binds them together is the fact that the vision of each character forms part of the bedrock of the others' visions, and that each discovers his or her self by reference to the others. Susan first feels the singleness of her desire, and the hardness of her eyes, by defining their difference from Rhoda's flower-like eyes and Jinny's glittering, fragmenting eyes. And alongside self-knowledge through comparison and contrast, is the need to defend one's self, and to criticise others, which inevitably creates friction among the characters.

This friction is as important as sympathy in binding the characters together. The alienation they suffer from failed attempts at communication is a stimulus to self-knowledge. When, at University, Neville shows Bernard one of his poems, the effect of this communication is to make Bernard feel alienated from himself. He feels that Neville has gone over him like a long wave, dragging him open, laying bare the pebbles on the shore of his soul. (p. 75) In intimacy all semblances are 'rolled up' and one suffers the humiliation of 'being contracted by another person into a single being'. (p. 76) In intimacy of this kind one person approaches the other as a single being, and the other then feels that the immeasurable selves he knows himself to be are denied. Moreover, intimacy makes the other's view infectious, and the friend's presence intervenes between one's consciousness and one's own self. Louis is turned into nothing but a boy in a grey flannel suit when Jinny looks at him, and the elderly Bernard cries out in protest that others see only an old man with a fixed body. Indeed, every meeting of the six characters arouses the need to defend one's self against the scrutiny of the others.

It is not active emotional attachment, then, that makes the characters important to one another. It is the simple fact of their shared visions—not because they all see the world in the same way but because one another's respective visions are among the possible views which each character feels he must balance, and because certain elements in the others' vision take part in his own. This participation in one another's thoughts does not involve actual communication. In solitude Bernard can reflect upon what the others would see, thus extending what he sees. As he looks out of the window and watches the merging crowds and an old, unsteady woman who pauses beneath a lighted window, he notes the contrast between her and the warmth inside the lighted room. He reflects that Neville would not appreciate this contrast, and that Neville will therefore succeed in realising his poetic vision—undeterred, like Bernard, by disjointed impressions. Thus, through his knowledge of Neville, Bernard analyses the reason for his own failure, and sees the possibility of a precise, productive but—for him—ultimately unsatisfactory vision. (It was as a child that he first realised he was himself and distinct from Neville when Susan's grief made him cry but left Neville unmoved.) Then Bernard thinks of Louis, and a different vision comes to life:

'[. . .] What malevolent yet searching lights would Louis throw upon this dwindling autumn evening, upon this china-smashing and trolling of hunting-songs, upon Neville, Byron and our life here? His thin lips are somewhat pursed; his cheeks are pale; he pores in an office over some obscure commercial document. "My father, a banker at Brisbane"—being ashamed of him he always talks of him—failed. So he sits in an office, Louis the best scholar in the school. But I, seeking contrasts, often feel his eye on us, his laughing eye, his wild eye, adding us up like insignifiant items in some grand total which he is forever pursuing in his office. And one day, taking a fine pen and dipping it in red ink, the addition will be complete; our total will be known; but it will not be enough [. . .] I feel Louis watching even my cigarette. And Louis says, "That means something. But what?"' (pp. 78–9)

Bernard, after noting what Neville would not see, considers what Louis would see. Bernard's own defensiveness as he recognises the probability of Neville realising his poetic vision, leads him to comment on Louis's defensiveness, and on the way that defensiveness prevents Louis from realising his intellectual potential. Bernard's thoughts of Louis lead directly to a presentation of Louis himself as he watches people from the window of an eating house. Continuity of time and space gives way to the continuity of thought and image.

Despite the author's emphasis on the reality of metaphor, the external world is seen to have a special, startling force. After all, there would be no point in showing the internal landscape to have the power of an external landscape, if an external landscape were not in itself powerful; and, of course, much of her metaphor is embedded in an external landscape which becomes personally significant. In Bernard's final soliloquy he reflects that external reality can sometimes strike one with the violence of a thunder clap, and that life frequently seems to concentrate itself in one vivid image. The shower of the willow's falling branches and its creased and crooked bark have 'the effect of what remains outside our illusions yet cannot stay them, is changed by them for the moment, yet shows through stable, still, and with a sternness that our lives lack. Hence the comment it makes, the standard it supplies, and the reason why, as we flow and change, it seems to measure.' (p. 216) But, immediately, Bernard then wonders: Can anything be as clear as Neville's gaze? He follows Neville's gaze through the branches of the willow tree to the punt on the river and to a young man eating bananas from a paper bag: 'The scene was cut out with such intensity and so permeated with the quality of his vision that for a moment I could see it too . . .' (p. 216)

The characters' respective consciousnesses form part of one another's reality. Even the apparently life-defeating visions cannot be dismissed. The willow tree, the symbol of external reality (just as the apple tree is the symbol of death and an obstacle no one can pass, and thus a symbol of external forces) which sometimes blocks windows— our perceptions—with its 'leaves of habit', is seen by Rhoda as growing on the verge of a grey desert where no bird sings: 'The leaves shrivelled as she looked at them, tossed in agony as she passed them.' (p. 216) To criticise the 'unhealthiness' of her vision is not sufficient to mitigate its hold upon the other characters. Bernard's fantasy about persuading her not to take her own life (after she has already done so) is an attempt to persuade himself to contain that vision she has given to him. For, as he reflects, this is not one life. His brow is the brow that was struck when Percival died. On his neck is the kiss Jinny gave Louis. His eyes fill with Susan's tears; and he sees the gold pillar Rhoda saw, and feels the rush of her flight when she leapt. (p. 249) The characters do not have the same consciousness ('the virginal wax that coats the spine melted in different patches for each of us' [p. 207]) yet the consciousness of each forms part of each character's reality and must, ultimately, be integrated with his own.

The friends' bonds send the individual back into himself, and then, as he emerges from the solitary journey, he joins his perceptions to those of the others. As they meet to bid farewell to Percival, Bernard wonders what it is that brings them all together. He rejects the explanation that it is love for Percival; 'love' is too small a word to mark the extent of their feelings: 'We have come together [. . .] to make one thing, not enduring—for, what endures?—but seen by many eyes simultaneously. There is a red carnation in that vase. A single flower as we sat here waiting, but now a seven-sided flower, many-petalled, red, puce, purple-shaded, stiff with silver-tinted leaves—a whole flower to which every eye brings its own contribution.' (p. 108) Even as the characters reflect upon their differences from one another, and their opposition to one another, their need for this balancing multiplicity is never diminished.

It is as a result of this need that Percival's death is felt so deeply by all of them. The carnation becomes a six, not a seven-sided flower, and each character's vision is thereby changed. Their grief is not depicted primarily in terms of what they feel, but in terms of what they see— or, more precisely, their emotions are explained by the way the world now appears to them. Neville believes that the lights of the world have gone out, and that his own past has been cut off from him: that past was shared by a consciousness that no longer exists, and thus his past itself no longer has confirmation. Bernard tries to conjure up the world Percival no longer sees—he tries to become the guardian of that lost vision upon which his own depends. Rhoda, however, suffers the greatest set-back from his death. She is halted by a puddle on the pavement: all palpable forms of life now fail her. She no longer focuses on her fear of external objects, but on her hatred of them. The faces that pass her are ugly and deformed. For one moment she tries to cling to the beauty that might be apprehended in the colour and bustle of the stocking shop, but as the shop assistant speaks, Oxford Street seems to disappear, and she plunges to the bottom of her inner world where, among the weeds, she sees 'envy, jealousy, hatred and spite scuttle like crabs over the sand'. (p. 137) Her world is now populated by images of life-inadequacy and torpidity. The violence of her imagination is such that all metaphorical investigation of the mind—which is the only method of investigating the mind—falls apart:

> '"Like" and "like" and "like"—but what is the thing that lies beneath the semblance of the thing? Now that lightning has gashed the tree and the flowering branch has fallen and Percival, by his death, has made me this gift, let me see this thing. There is a square; there is an oblong. The players take the square and place it upon the oblong. They place it very accurately; they make a perfect dwelling-place. Very little is left outside. The structure is now visible; what is inchoate is here stated; we are not so various or so mean; we have made oblongs and stood them on squares. This is our triumph; this is our consolation. (p. 139)

Her vision of humanity as grotesque and greedy is replaced by this vision of a sparse rigid world; it is the world of abstract figures which terrified her at school, which refused to provide her with an answer. With this metaphor depicting absence of all metaphors, she expresses her belief in an alien external world, a world which no longer has meaning. Her triumph, her consolation, is a terrible death of consciousness. She cannot withstand the destruction of the seventh side of the flower.

The characters need the balance of one another's vision, yet, when they meet, they feel that their respective selves are being threatened. They suffer what in Virginia Woolf's other works is frequently the result of a 'party consciousness', when characters search for a self-image that will protect them from others' scrutiny, from others' realisation of the passage of time, from others' criticism of the course their own lives have taken. In *The Waves*, even more clearly than in *Mrs Dalloway*, there is a balance between the pain of confrontation and reunion, and its necessity. Even Rhoda, who craves silence and darkness, who believes that the others will tear her to pieces as she falls into sheets of fire, who responds to commonplace greetings as to hooks sinking into her being, feels hopeful and excited by such meetings—at least until Percival dies. Louis reflects, 'We torture her. She dreads us, she despises us, yet comes cringing to our sides because for all our cruelty there is always some name, some face, which sheds a radiance which lights up her pavements and makes it possible for her to replenish her dreams.' (pp. 102—3) And as Neville notes the 'acid green' of Susan's eyes, he remembers that there is always someone who, when the friends meet, refuses to be submerged, who tries to enclose his or her self, to enclose individual consciousness and to resist a shared consciousness. This resistance is like an assertion of superiority. In trying to diminish the hostility in Susan's eyes, Neville tries to assure himself of his own merit and his own success. Susan understands this clash of egos and accepts it as a necessary prelude to communion, as the inevitable salute of old friends. For, gradually, the defensive reflection upon one's own status gives way to memories of past companionship and development. The egos formed by social contact are replaced by the sensibility of the private self.

When these characters merge into the social world, they identify themselves with their office work, their fame, their signatures, their toothbrushes, their clothes. They cling to such things as definitions of themselves, but what they are actually doing is making themselves anonymous; they see a self defined by others, and a self that merges easily with crowds in the streets and in railway carriages. This socially defined self protects one; it reduces one's susceptibility to criticism and disguises one's essential volatility. It is a convenience, and a sham. Meetings with old friends destroy the comfort of the social ego. Louis searches his pockets for papers to prove his importance; Neville wonders whether the waiter has heard of him; as long as they remain defined by their public image each is a statement contradicting the other, rather than a contributor to an expanding vision.

Food and wine make the world seem a safer place; the hazards of the crumbling public images are mitigated, and the friends are released from the dominion of the ego. Released from the ego, they are released from time and from the world: 'the earth is only a pebble flicked off accidentally from the face of the sun and [. . .] there is no life anywhere in the abysses of space'. (p. 193) Then they themselves become extinguished, and everything that is not part of them—the darkness, the rushing wind—becomes enlarged: Bernard reflects, 'To see things without attachment, from the outside, and to realise their beauty in itself—how strange!' (p. 226)

In his final soliloquy Bernard again finds the independence and detachment he had discovered with his friends and, in this soliloquy, his friends draw him towards a more concentrated and profound investigation than a single experience of joyful solitude would indicate. First, in his detachment, he feels the burden of pretence and unreality drop from him; he no longer sees himself as an object to be seen, and therefore as a self in need of protection, and this freedom from defensiveness leads to a penetrating vision: 'lightness has come with a kind of transparency, making onself invisible and things seen through as one walks . . .' (p.226) He ignores the newspapers and the placards—signs of the superficial public world—in his anticipation of new discoveries. Yet his elated independence is disturbed first by his memory of Percival, and then by his imaginary attempt to persuade Rhoda not to kill herself. His fulfilment must come in probing his self and, linked with this, his friends—not his wife and children, but the friends whose visions are felt to be part of his own.

When Bernard calls to his most familiar, his most private self, and it does not come, the doors of perception remain open, but the world appears barren and colourless: 'The heaviness of my despondency thrust open the gate I leant on and pushed me, an elderly man, a heavy man with grey hair, through the colourless field, the empty field.' (p. 246) Alienated from his familiar self, he is defined by his public appearance and, consequently, his own vision has no substance. But Bernard is now constantly changing—this vision constantly changes. The field gradually absorbs colour, like a sponge absorbs water. As the world around him becomes again full and substantial he emerges with something greater than his commonplace self—the heavy old man—and he discovers all his possible selves, and the selves of his friends. This extention of his self, and the abolition of personal desire and curiosity, makes him 'immeasurably receptive, holding everything, trembling with fullness, yet clear, contained'. (p. 250) He no longer attacks the problem of the mystery of life, yet it seems to lay itself out before him. He believes that pure contemplation has been achieved until he bangs into a pillar box, and is 'justly laughed at by any passer-by'. Having thought himself free forever of that self identified by others as 'Bernard', it returns to mock him: 'the wave has tumbled me over, head over heels, scattering my possessions, leaving me to collect, to assemble, to heap together, summon my forces, rise and confront the enemy'. (p. 252) He can never be merely possible selves; he can never be a purely contemplative being. Nor would such a state provide him with the balance and illumination he craves. Under the compulsion of another's gaze, under the blow dealt him by the pillar box, he is able to observe again details of his surroundings: 'Listen: a whistle sounds, wheels rush, and the door creaks on its hinges, I regain the sense of complexity and the reality and the struggle, for which I thank you.' (p.253) Moreover, the story of his life must include the hairy ape-like creature who belches and 'dabbles his fingers in ropes of entrails'. (p. 249) This ape-like aspect also contributes to the quality of perception; the ape has given a 'greener glow to green things, has held his torch with its red flames, its thick and smarting smoke, behind every leaf.' (pp. 249– 50)

Complete with all his selves, Bernard no longer fears the darkness that threatens the individual self. But this world without phantoms and without danger is again unsatisfactory; for it was danger and fear that stimulated Bernard to explore the world and self. Thus Rhoda's paranoid vision is vindicated: the self must be a fighter; it must acknowledge its own frailty; it must create its private space and its private time in opposition to outside forces.

In this soliloquy, which is an integration of all the novel's themes and all the characters' struggles, Bernard's impulses are to resolve, to balance, and then to withdraw. The eternal renewal, 'the incessant rise and fall and rise and fall again', comes upon him as an old man unable to believe in the relevance—for him—of a dawn. Yet the wave does rise in him, and he finds himself again fighting, again facing death and refusing to yield to the abolition of his life. For the forces of renewal are stronger than merely voluntary forces; they are contained in the simple fact of life, as is the creative impetus of perception and self-discovery. As Bernard sits at the restaurant table summing up his bill, which becomes one among many images of the summation of his life, he feels the effort of construction as relentless, facing obstacle after obstacle, coping with irreconcilable fragments. The intensity of the novel rests upon this unending effort of construction, which continues even after the will would let it cease.

The mind then acts as though its world could be ordered, even as experience repeatedly denies this supposition. Louis's anger and cynicism, which frequently make him sound like the speaker of T. S. Eliot's *The Hollow Men* while suffering at the same time the longings of J. Alfred Prufrock, are based upon his belief that there should be order and his opposing knowledge that the order he can achieve is false, and that an insidious chaos undermines all his actions:

'Supple-faced, with rippling skins, that are always twitching with the multiplicity of their sensations, prehensile like monkeys, greased to this particular moment, they are discussing with all the right gestures the sale of a piano [. . .] The streamers of my consciousness waver out and are perpetually torn and distressed by their disorder. I cannot therefore concentrate on my dinner.' (p. 79)

The sardonic conclusion does not mitigate the sincerity of his effort to understand multiplicity. To shut his eyes, to sleep and retreat to the past, to acquiesce (as he considers Bernard to do in his story-telling) is to defraud history of its rightful vision. (p. 56) Hating the disparate world, Louis nonetheless refuses to deny its disparateness. No ordered account of the world can be a true one; no definition of the self and its relation to the world can be complete, can be true. Therefore, in the end, not only does Bernard abandon his story-telling, but he feels that conventional language should itself be abandoned. He wants, in its place, a muffled language of the kind lovers use, or a howl, a cry, or the language children discover as, entering a room where their mother is sewing, they pick up a piece of bright wool or chintz or a feather. The metaphor, the means by which the mind is investigated, is abandoned: there is only this, and this.

The supposition that the only truth can be found in immediate emotions and immediate sights, isolated from any order, indicates that the truth about mental states cannot be communicated in anything other than an inarticulated 'language'; and the belief that the true states of mind cannot be communicated, leads to the pessimistic theme found previously in *Jacob's Room*. When Percival dies Bernard says that he will see through doors, that he will see memories which will make him weep, but which cannot be imparted. 'Hence,' he concludes, 'our loneliness; hence our desolation.' (p. 133)

The triteness of his conclusion can be seen when it is set against the positive side of the novel, which not only denies the assertion of incommunicability, but which also shows how mental states can be communicated: the form of the novel itself communicates these mental states. The suggestion that language be abandoned undermines the characters' efforts, as well as Bernard's ultimate triumph. For his triumph is the continuous effort of mind to understand itself and—what amounts to the same thing—to develop a language in which it can be described. Having paid his bill at the restaurant, having completed his (necessarily provisionary) summary, Bernard reflects:

'However beat and done with it all I am, I must haul myself up, and find the particular coat that belongs to me; must push my arms into the sleeves; must muffle myself up against the night air and be off. I, I, I, tired as I am, spent as I am, and almost worn out with all this rubbing of my nose against the surfaces of things, even I, an elderly man who is getting rather heavy and dislikes exertion, must take myself off and catch some last train.' (p. 255)

The triumph depends upon something outside the will, and it certainly is not a joyful or even an exuberant triumph. It depends, rather, upon the impulse, over-riding fatigue, laziness and a sense of failure, to create some definition—or, rather, a series of definitions—of one's self and the world one perceives. Thus it is that this depressed acknowledgement of a continued task and its meagre results leads to Bernard's vision of eternal renewal and to his resistance of annihilation. The creative, investigative vision is a fact about the mind. It is, moreover, the most important fact about the mind; and however clearly Virginia Woolf shows the creative effort to stumble and fail, she also presents it, in the conclusion of *The Waves*, as a complement of the proud action and life perfection the six characters saw in Percival. For it is Percival's horse Bernard rides, which is also the rising in him of the fundamental motion of life—the wave—as he confronts death, which is the enemy in virtue of its attempt to annihilate the individual vision, to make one again an undifferentiated and undifferentiating part of life.

8 The Narrowing Vision: *The Years*

The tragedy that besets the Pargiter family is unrelated to any specific set of events, nor is it a tragedy which besets them while leaving other characters in the novel untouched. Their tragedy is the imaginative stasis of their society and of the consequential poverty of life. The years which, in the opening paragraph, are said to pass one another across the sky 'like the rays of a searchlight' do not reveal anything profound, as did the rays of the Lighthouse of *To the Lighthouse*; instead, they reveal a vision of madness and despair, in contrast to which Septimus Smith's vision is a redeemed one. For though Septimus Smith saw hell in the world, his hell contained dynamic images, and his terror was the other face of a vital joy. In *The Years* there is no terror, only revulsion and banality and grotesqueness. The characters are defeated by their lack of imagination, by their acceptance of a dead world. To 'parget' is an English dialect word meaning 'to smooth over the cracks in a plastered surface', and a pargeter is a plasterer. The Pargiters are willing to maintain the fragmentary consciousness and shallow impressions conventional thought and conventional language allow them. Only momentarily are they relieved of the dominion of the commonplace, and never do their imaginations develop a resistance to the essential fissures of daily experience.

The conviction with which this failure of imagination is presented accounts for the inferior quality of *The Years*. In her diaries Virginia Woolf wrote that in this novel she was determined to stick to fact rather than to vision;[1] but she has shown throughout her fiction that there is no meaningful distinction between the two, that to see the world as constructed by fact alone is to employ a type of vision, and to present this limited, even distorted vision as a factual picture is to deny that these facts are interpreted and selected. To deny this is to deny there is any alternative to a treatment of the facts of the Pargiters' world; and thus the meagre vision becomes the restricted ambience of the book itself.

Many of the themes in this novel are familiar, but the problems which were previously seen as a whetstone for the imagination are here blank, confining walls. The difficulty of integrating various aspects of a person into the concept of a single person is one of the themes of *The Waves*, but there the difficulty is a challenge and stimulus to that eternal, instinctive probing and balancing; whereas in *The Years*, disparate images of a single person result in a mental numbness. After a period of separation only a gesture here and there makes one character recognisable to another; nor do these scattered gestures lead to anything more profound than a vague sense of familiarity. As Sara describes her guest to her telephone caller, North realises that his label is 'My cousin from Africa' and Sara, in turn, comes back to his consciousness 'in sections; first the voice; then the attitude; but something remained unknown.' (p. 239) That 'something' remains unknown is an understatement in virtue of the impoverished impressions one has of another person.

Even in *Jacob's Room*, when the assertion of an unknowable area was frequently the result of a confused resentment that others will not appreciate one's complexity, the theme was attacked with greater precision. As Eleanor reads Digby's obituaries she reflects that he was not at all as the newspapers describe him, and she concludes, 'It was odd how different the same person seemed to two different people,' (p. 119) Peggy, considering various facts about her Aunt Delia, realises that she is unable to describe people. Peggy is dissatisfied with her descriptions not because, as in *Jacob's Room*, people have a special self which cannot be expressed, but because other people are incapable of integrating their impressions of a person. In other words, the inability to know another person does not arise from the impossibility of receiving sufficient information about a person but from the inability to make use of information.

Indeed, the characters have the greatest difficulty making sense of anything, and the oppressive atmosphere of the novel arises from their knowledge of the futility of mental effort:

'Rose is coming?' [Sara] repeated.
'I told you,' said Maggie. 'I said to you, Rose is coming to luncheon on Friday [. . .]'
'It is Friday, and Rose is coming to luncheon,' Sara repeated.
'I told you,' said Maggie. 'I was in a shop. I was buying stuff.

And somebody'—she paused to make her fold more accurately—
'came out from behind a counter and said, "I'm your cousin. I'm
Rose," she said. "Can I come and see you? [. . .]" '

'Rose is coming,' [Sara] said, 'and this is where she'll sit . . . and
she'll take off her gloves; and she'll lay one on this side, one on that.
And she'll say, "I've never been in this part of London before."''

'And then?' said Maggie, looking at the table.

'You'll say "It's so convenient for the theatres."''

'And then?' said Maggie.

'And then she'll say rather wistfully, smiling, putting her head
on one side, "D'you often go to the theatre, Maggie?"''

'No,' said Maggie. 'Rose has red hair.'

'Red hair?' Sara exclaimed. 'I thought it was grey—a little wisp
straggling from under a black bonnet,' she added.

'No,' said Maggie. 'She has a great deal of hair; and it's red.'

[. . .] A door slammed below; they heard footsteps mounting
the stairs. 'There she is,' said Maggie.

[. . .] 'This is the worst torture . . .' Sara began, screwing her
hands together and clinging to her sister, 'that life . . .'

'Don't be such an ass,' said Maggie, pushing her away, as the
door opened. (pp. 126–7)

The familiar theme of the pain of confrontation here is a grotesque
comedy based upon the fear of being confronted with data one
cannot process. Sara tries to understand what led to the meeting and
she tries to prepare herself for it by enacting it. Her enactment
suggests a mockery of the assumption that anything new will happen
during such a meeting, yet her ignorance of the colour of Rose's hair
shows her inability to tame the confrontation by foresight. Her
anguish at Rose's approach is ridiculous, and Maggie's response is
justified; but the anguish itself is also justified by the mind's
helplessness in face of impressions which need to be processed. Sara is
an exception among the Pargiters in her sensitivity to this fragmentation; her madness, her inability to accept fragmentation placidly,
grants her a greater sanity than her 'no-nonsense' sister.

The triumph of *To the Lighthouse*, and the triumph of Mrs Ramsay, is
the ability to communicate effectively a personal vision and sensibility; but, in *The Years*, personal sensibility is so successfully
thwarted by quotidian concerns that communication is impossible,
not because sensibility itself cannot be communicated, but because it

contains nothing worth communicating. The failure of vision is a failure of thought, a failure for any pattern to congeal. Towards the close of the book Eleanor wonders, 'is there a pattern; a theme, recurring, like music; half remembered, half foreseen? . . . a gigantic pattern, momentarily perceptible? The thought gave her extreme pleasure: that there was a pattern. But who makes it? Who thinks it? Her mind slipped. She could not finish her thought.' (p. 282) The failure of imaginative construction is linked, furthermore, to a failure of language. Repeatedly words are dissociated from meaning, or wordless sounds take on strange, arbitrary meaning. The dance tune Sara hears as she tries to sleep on a hot summer's night with a party going on in the garden, takes on words from her musings, tosses the words about and, by repetition, cancels their meaning, so that the tune and its borrowed words are at first boring and subsequently intolerable. (p. 104) The cries of an old man selling iron in the noisy street have their meanings blotted out; only their rhythm remains. (p. 126) At Kitty's party Martin wonders what the stock vocabulary—'heavenly', 'amazing', 'marvellous'—mean. His lack of understanding is not actually ignorance but a symptom of his belief that the conversationalist's world has no substance. The conventional language used at the party marks no differentiation of response: Ann says that the tree is lovely in the same tone of voice she uses to proclaim that Martin is charming. (p. 196) Later, at Delia's party, North fastens his attention on the word 'adenoids' as it emerges from the hub of party conversation. The word takes on strange, repelling qualities; it becomes pinched in the middle, with a hard, shining, metallic abdomen; the word seems analogous to the appearance of an insect. (p. 285)

When words lose their proper meanings, their new associations are unstable; thus the mind is teased by its inability to focus and to make its thoughts cohere: later the word 'adenoids' recurs to North, but it suggests nothing; there is a gap in his memory because there is no coherent association among his memories. And the next generation passes further into the darkness of inarticulacy and its associated fragmentation of thought. When bribed by Delia with cake the caretaker's children begin to sing. Their's is the modern voice, the voice of the future; it is also incomprehensible and grotesque; the guests do not know whether to laugh or cry. Even the horrible manipulation of the song's words is abandoned in the middle of the third stanza; even the attempt to form words and music is broken off.

Characters' attempts to make sense of words frequently defeat their purpose. Words are repeated in order to force meaning from them, but such repetition only confounds their meaning. Concentration on words also distorts them. North listens to the strange, repetitive conversation: 'He felt that he had been in the middle of a jungle; in the heart of darkness; cutting his way towards the light; but provided only with broken sentences, single words, with which to break through the briar-bush of human bodies, human wills and voices, that bent over him, blinding him, blinding him . . . ' (p. 313) He continues to listen but words collide in his mind to form nonsense words.

All discussions about the characters' plight disintegrate as their language disintegrates. During the War (in 1917) Eleanor talks to Nicholas about the psychology of great men, and they also discuss the possibility of a new age and the conditions that must be made for improvement. She repeats Nicholas's phrases, and as she does so, she feels numb all over. As she repeats 'Napoleon' she knows she 'speaks without any meaning'. (p. 215) When Nicholas says that it is a great thing to be a son of a wine merchant, his sentence sounds like a quotation from the French grammar. Later, in the section 'Present Day', a similarly sententious and pointless conversation takes place about the necessity of knowing ourselves before we can know others and before we can make laws suitable to human needs. (p. 241) Everything that is said has been said over and over, to no effect. It seems that the characters do not know how to present an argument, and at a meeting Eleanor realises she does not even know what the discussion is about; the discussion is mere bickering in the form, 'I'm right—you're wrong.' Frequently the characters believe they are on the point of saying something significant, but always the significant point lies beyond their grasp.

Language is in so bad a state that even the simplest references are misunderstood. Sara overhears Rose's and Maggie's conversation as she prepares the lunch. She thinks they are talking about the Campagna in Italy, but subsequently discovers that they were talking about Waterloo Road—though they were not actually talking about Waterloo Road but about drunken men following women in the street. (p. 133) On another occasion Maggie is startled by a voice—presumably asking, 'Are you coming? for she replies, 'To Africa?' Yet the question was whether she was coming to Delia's party. (pp. 266–7).

Language fails not only because words behave strangely but also because the person speaking fails to make any sense to his interlocutor due to oddity of manner and tone of voice. As Sara describes to North how she presented a letter of introduction in an office, North tries to understand her: 'The actual words he supposed—the actual words floated together and formed a sentence in his mind—meant that she was poor; that she must earn her living, but the excitement with which she had spoken, due to wine perhaps, had created yet another person; another semblance, which one must solidify into one whole.' (p. 261) The difficulty in understanding conversation, then, arises in part from the inability to integrate various aspects of the speaker into a single person; if we do not understand what people are, we cannot understand what they say. And one's knowledge that others will see one as an oddity, that others will not understand one, inhibits one's attempts to make one's self understood. In 'Present Day' North and Eleanor encourage Edward to translate his Greek utterance. (They are speaking about *The Antigone* which previously, for Sara, was the focus of her image of her own dead state.) Edward refuses, and North realises that 'he can't say what he wants to say; he's afraid. They're all afraid; afraid of being laughed at; afraid of giving themselves away.' (p. 315) Paradoxically, this fear is greatest when there is the least possibility of communication, even when attempted.

Much of description of the dissociation of words from meaning reads as a description of incipient madness; but, in this novel, such madness is the norm. A sense of one's involvement in the world—which in Woolf's previous novels was seen to be creative—here results only in a sympathetic disintegration and sordid selectivity. As Sara Pargiter lies awake, listening to the party noises, she becomes (as did Louis in *The Waves*) a root lying sunken in the earth and her veins thread the cold mass. The tree she imagines as part of her self puts forth branches; but the tree that she sees as she opens her eyes is black and dead. (p. 103) Her imagined creative growth, however, only has a distorted and deadly flowering. Since she cannot sleep she reads the *Antigone*: 'At first she read a line or two at random; then, from the litter of broken words, scenes rose, quickly, inaccurately, as she skipped.' (p. 105) The distinction between her self and the characters she reads about is lost, as is the distinction between the object she reads about and the objects she sees: 'She glanced at the tree outside in the garden. The unburied body of the murdered man lay on the sand . . . ' (p. 105) The indistinct words of the people moving in and out of the garden become part of her nightmare:

'To the estimable court of the respected ruler?' she murmured, picking up a word or two at random, for she was still looking into the garden. The man's name was Creon. He buried her. It was a moonlight night. The blades of the cactuses were sharp silver. The man in the loincloth gave three sharp taps with his mallet on the brick. She was buried alive. The tomb was a brick mound. There was just enough room for her to lie straight out. Straight out in a brick tomb, she said. And that's the end, she yawned, shutting the book. (p. 105)

Her sympathy with her world, her acceptance of the cruel male phantom that dominates her world, leads to this dead end. Even more frightening is the fact that she does not protest against this deadliness. The narrow coffin is normal in this life; it is even comfortable:

She laid herself out, under the cold smooth sheets, and pulled the pillow over her ears. The one sheet and the one blanket fitted softly round her. At the bottom of the bed was a long stretch of cool fresh mattress. The sound of the dance music became dulled. Her body dropped suddenly; then reached ground. A dark wing brushed her mind, leaving a pause; a blank space. Everything—the music, the voices—became stretched and generalised. The book fell on the floor. She was asleep. (p. 106)

There is no vision beyond this darkness. Eleanor, as an old woman, falls asleep at a party and, as she dreams, she sees something beautiful which remains for a few moments after her sleep. Gradually, however, the world becomes more and more distinct; a pair of shoes is so clearly outlined that she can see the bunions of the feet. Distinctness is no longer vividness and vitality; now it destroys the beauty. She loses her dream vision and concludes, 'Directly something got together, it broke.' (p. 299) She knows she must try to make something new, but now there is really no energy for reconstruction. At the close of the novel she tries to hold her vision in cupped hands; again she sees the uselessness of trying to contain a vision. It must fall from her, and then she will have only endless night. Thinking of the darkness she is baffled by a sense of growing light; but the novel's emphasis is undoubtedly on restriction and darkness—so much so that nothing in the novel itself supports this assertion of hope, and it is difficult to see how light could survive in the world presented by the novel.

The loss of meaning through repetition of words is complemented by the constant mimickry of people and gestures confounding not only one's understanding of others but also of one's self. Milly, as a young girl, always imitates the manner of an older person, since her mother has been ill for some time and maternal duties fall upon her. The Colonel's cries, when he believes that his wife is dying, appear to his daughter Delia as a histrionic pretence, and she tells him that he performed very well. The Oxford streets appear to Kitty to be obsolete and inane; all the people in Oxford seem to be acting parts, and to her the butler does not even sound human as he utters his habitual remarks about the weather. Sara and Maggie and Rose talk about Abercorn Terrace, Rose's childhood home, as though it were a scene in a play. Sara, after her mother has come in from the party, imitates her manner perfectly and echoes her phrases, just as she repeats her father's words, giving them a comic effect. The sparse fantasies that comfort the characters—such as Rose's fantasy of being on a secret mission and Eleanor's fantasy (which the author later ascribes to Delia) of speaking about liberty and justice on a platform where she stands beside Parnell—are based upon acting parts. Even the twitter of sparrows in the London parks is a parody of street musicians' piping.

Mimickry destroys meaning, and pretence destroys any feeling language might convey. At her mother's funeral service Delia is initially attracted by the Church language, but is then disconcerted by the way the speaker—her cousin James—passes so easily into insincerity. The voice uttering sententious phrases about God's will and the deliverance from the sins and miseries of the world, spoils for Delia what she sees as her one true moment. On the other hand, an honest attempt to express feeling is seen as shameful or, at the very least, embarrassing. When Sara and Martin have lunch together after meeting outside St Paul's, Martin tries to draw Sara into conversation:

> 'And what, Sal,' he said, touching the little book, 'd'you make of it?'
> She opened the prayer-book at random and began to read:
> 'The father incomprehensible; the son incomprehensible—' She spoke in her ordinary voice.
> 'Hush!' he stopped her. 'Somebody's listening.' (p. 176)

The sense that things are spoiled is part of the general atmosphere of the novel. The world inhabited by the characters is repeatedly shown to be stained or dirty or deformed, despite the characters' almost obsessive efforts to keep things clean. In the first section, '1880', the large arm-chair upon which Abel rests his head has a dark stain. In Maggie's room the twisted cone of paper over the electric light is oddly stained. All ceilings suffer from damp, which makes a yellow stain, and Crosby, in knowing the house in Abercorn Terrace so well, is said to know every nook and stain. The caretaker of the house in Browne Street, who does not want the house sold, points out to prospective buyers the yellow stain on the ceiling. Even the buildings in Oxford are not red and yellow, but red-stained and yellow-stained. Mrs Pargiter's skin, as she lies in the sick room, is stained with brown patches and her hair has yellow patches as though it had been dipped in the yolk of an egg. Intermittently we see the stains and dirt as an expression of some mental horror the characters barely acknowledge: as Eleanor feels something awful, something hidden behind her eyes, she notices three drops of grease fall from the candle.

All the characters are concerned with cleanliness, but their concern seems to have little effect. The cleanliness of the linen in Mrs Pargiter's sick room makes everything seem unreal, with the unreality of things that are unused; the cleanliness itself seems unwholesome. Mrs Pargiter is annoyed to see that there is yet another clean cloth on the table, for she worries about the laundry bill—a legitimate enough worry, for when her husband Abel gives his mistress money for her favours, the woman pretends he is giving her money for the washing. Eleanor is described as a woman who would offer a dog a bone and wash her hands afterwards; and when her brother Morris enters the room, she jumps up and declares that she will have a bath. (Her reaction is not directed specifically towards Morris, any more than the author's comment about Eleanor's attitudes towards feeding a dog actually defines her special character; the nervousness about cleanliness reveals not individual psychologies, but a general trait.) When the retired Crosby meets Martin in Ebury Street he is taking his clothes to the laundry, and he complains that he needs a new laundress. When Eleanor returns from Spain she notices the number of different coloured soaps in the shop windows and reflects that people wash so throughly in England. When Rose comes home, she repeatedly tells Eleanor and Martin that she wants a bath, that she feels dirty. And at Maggie's and Renny's flat, just before the air raid, the bell sounds and Sara exclaims (incorrectly), 'That's the wash!'

The obsession with cleanliness and the images of stains are compounded by the number of scars and deformities that appear among the Pargiters and their acquaintances. Uncle Horace has one glass eye. Sara was dropped as an infant and her shoulders are permanently deformed. At one meeting with her brother and sister Rose is seen to have a scratch on her chin, and they all recall a former time when she had a gash on her wrist, and they recall that Eugenie had had a bad gash, too. They are blithely unaware of the suicidal tendency expressed by these wounds. They live in a world that is commiting suicide, and blandly they register this fact.

In the early part of the novel the sordid atmosphere seems to have a sexual basis. The eczema behind the dog's ear which distracts Abel from his fumbling caressing of his mistress (and he is stroking her with a deformed hand, for he lost two fingers in the Mutiny) offers itself as a comment on his activity. The child Rose's fantasy of being on a secret mission when she goes to the shop is destroyed by the white, peeled, pock-marked face of the exhibitionist who confronts her. After the encounter Rose feels that she herself is dirty, and she herself feels guilty. This sense of guilt, however illogical, is in Rose's case psychologically justified; but it prevails upon the entire household. Everyone shares the guilt of wanting the mother, finally, to die. Even the nurse shares this guilt, though, for her, guilt is occasioned by the fact that she has been gossiping rather than looking after Rose. The neurotic compulsion of guilt is perfectly portrayed in the scene between Martin and the waiter who tries to cheat him by hiding some change beneath the bill. In retaliation Martin refuses to leave him a tip. Ashamed of his meanness, Martin offers money to a violet seller. She looks up at him and he is appalled to see that she has no nose, only two hideous nostrils cut into her face. Any action taken to relieve oneself of guilt only pushes one deeper into the sordid atmosphere in which deformity and guilt are combined. It is impossible to reason freely in such a world, because one's involvement in the sordidness is too immediate to be allayed by reason.

The total world—not only the human world—participates in this squalor. Images borrowed from nature support the impression of decay and decrepitude. The spring light shows up the shabbiness of the chair-covers in Abercorn Terrace. The dying Mrs Levy whom Eleanor visits has an arm shrivelled and white like the roots of a tree. The rain falling on the pavements makes them greasy, and the bells in Oxford are heard like porpoises turning over slowly in a sea of oil. Rain also smears the air, and Mrs Porter's hands are 'knotted and grooved like the gnarled roots of a tree'. (p. 77) The March wind is cruel and unbecoming; it bleaches faces and raises red spots on noses, and reveals either stout legs or skeletal shins. (p. 113) There is no fullness, no fertility in this spring wind; it is like a scythe that cuts corn not usefully but destructively.

The natural world shares the ugliness of the human world; and, paradoxically, the natural world frequently provides images of deformity. Animal images repeatedly appear, and these mark not vitality or spontaneity, but grotesqueness and perversion. Abel Pargiter's deformed hand resembles the 'claw of some caged bird', (p. 12) and even the spring buds emerge from the branches like claws. Edward's college friend Gibbs has a hand like a great red paw, like a piece of raw meat (p. 42), and his homosexual friend Ashley moves like a cat. At the Law Courts the woman in furs who greets Eleanor has a face like a cat's, and the men in their wigs and gowns are like flocks of birds. (p. 84) Morris's mother-in-law has a hawk-like nose. Sara, when Martin catches sight of her outside St Paul's, is shuffling like some dishevelled fowl. Lady Warburton, at Kitty's party, descends the stairs like a crab; and the Italian gilt chair, which appears first in Browne Street and then in various other Pargiter apartments, has great paws for arms.

Both language and emotions are undermined by animal analogies. The conversation between the middle-aged Milly and her husband—representing, the author indicates, something common in long-term marriages—is like the half-articulate munching of animals in a stall. At the same party in which Milly and her husband appear in this light, Eleanor reflects that people cannot help one another because they are so interested in what belongs to them; when it comes to 'my children' it is always a question of animal protectiveness—of a rip down the belly or teeth in the soft throat. (p. 290) It is indeed symptomatic of the indiscriminate revulsion expressed in this novel that Eleanor cannot see that protecting one's children, even with an animal-like ferocity, is one means of helping other people. At this same party of Delia's, Peggy looks at the guests and sees them as cowards, drugged with cheap pleasures. It is impossible to be happy, she reflects, in a world that contains so much brutality and tyranny. Her irritable pessimism is shared by the author, and is heavily underlined by the imagery, but it is not otherwise developed or analysed; it is not brutality and tyranny the novel presents as much as drudgery and tedium.

The world of *Mrs Dalloway* was one of movement and change. In *To the Lighthouse*, too, much of the power arises from the varying impressions and emotions, and from the mind's volatility. The atmosphere of *The Years*, however, is remarkably static. Only a very narrow range of impressions and emotions is possible. Even the familiar street haunting which, in all her other works, vitalises the imagination, here provides only modest relief from daily constrictions. As Eleanor walks in the Strand she notes the violent and confused activity of the street, the splashing mud, the rushing traffic, and, in contrast, the free activity of the sky, sun, clouds and birds. Passively she accepts these disorganised impressions; the contrasts are not integrated, nor do they become a means of self-investigation. Only the absence of personal contact (when Morris passes her, he fails to recognise her) and freedom from domestic responsibility give her pleasure—there is no positive realisation of her relation to the world. As she reads of Parnell's death (the man who had at one time been the focus of an escapist fantasy) she sees a man chained to a pillar box, and a lion chained to the man. For her the scene is frozen, never to move again. This is not the stasis of eternal images formed by Mrs Dalloway's or Mrs Ramsay's imagination; this stasis is dead and cold and limiting.

The city that is presented in *The Years* is not Mrs Dalloway's London, which occasions so much joy. Here, as she walks the streets, Eleanor finds 'the vice, the obscenity, the reality of London'. (p. 88) The city appears both paltry and demonic. At Charing Cross men are sucked in at the gates of the station as through the gates of the underworld. There is some demon in them that would be enraged if they were kept waiting; they are hurrying to lose themselves in pointless, anonymous activity. The London of *The Years* is the sordid, conspiratorial and ignorant city of T. S. Eliot's *The Waste Land*. While Sara and North discuss the grease and hairs the Jewish lodger will leave in the bath, Sara describes her reaction when she had learned that she must share the Jew's bath. She had said:

> '"Polluted city, unbelieving city, city of dead fish and worn-out frying pans," [. . .] And there were people passing; the strutting; the tiptoeing; the pasty; the ferret-eyed; the bowler-hatted, servile innumerable army of workers. And I said, "Must I join your conspiracy? Stain the hand, the unstained hand,"'—he could see her hand gleam as she waved it in the half-light of the sitting-room, '"—and sign on, and serve a master; all because of a Jew in my bath, all because of a Jew?"' (p. 260)

So the ugliness of the city breeds ugliness of mind, and the imagination has no power to transform the city, and the anger one suffers in face of this ugliness only re-enforces one's participation in it.

Often the author records the details of street scenes which, in her previous novels, were recorded with delight, but here such details provide no magic; they reveal no vitality. As Delia rides in the carriage at her mother's funeral she looks out the window:

> Through the slit of the blind, Delia noticed dogs playing; a beggar singing; men raising their hats as the hearse passed them. But by the time their own carriage passed, the hats were on again. Men walked briskly and unconcernedly along the pavement. The shops were already gay with spring clothing; women paused and looked in at the windows. But they would have to wear nothing but black all summer, Delia thought, looking at Edward's coal-black trousers. (p. 66)

The tired rhythm of the writing, the blandness of Delia's vision, the limited response to the gay spring clothing, are not merely symptoms of a depression upon her mother's death, but are symptoms of characters' inability to transcend their immediate, practical concerns in an appreciation of the activity round them.

The stasis of the imagination is underlined by the characters' general inability to do anything. When Eleanor comes into the drawing-room she sees that the rest of her family are doing nothing. In the author's sketch of Peter Street, we are told that nothing is happening, and the eyes of the rapacious old woman who looks out the window have nothing upon which to feed their hunger. When North visits Sara, he waits for the servant girl, but again nothing happens. Characters wait for a kettle to boil or for a parent to die. Yet there is no true expectation in their waiting; they seek only relief from tedious tasks.

Indeed, the characters cannot even imagine a truly positive happiness. As Eleanor strolls about the law Courts her greatest pleasure—and the only pleasure she desires—is blankness of mind, and the knowledge that she need not be home for tea because her father is not coming home until dinner. In the omnibus ride, which for both Elizabeth Dalloway and Jacob Flanders led to an exciting release, Elizabeth Pargiter merely thinks about the leaking roof at Peter Street, wondering whether she has chosen the right man to mend it, of her Committee, of her sister's marriage. The rhythmical descriptions of the crowded streets and shops, which present the activity as rooks swooping in a field, are not a springboard for joy but merely an hypnotic escape. Even Regent's Park, visited by Sara and Martin on a beautiful spring day, provides only relief and temporary distraction, not a vital joy.

The most positive section in the novel is a description of Kitty's journey to her country home after she has given a party; though even her imagination is not active. As she is driven to the station her eyes alone register passing objects: 'After the talk, the effort and the hurry, she could add nothing to what she saw.' (p. 205) She has been busy throughout the day, but only in preparing for her solitary journey does she feel she is doing what she likes and that she is the person she likes. The private rail carriage, in which she will spend the night undisturbed, offers the best solace available in this world. In her isolated country house the world seems marvellous because it is indifferent to human life; she is happy, she is free from the irritations and criticisms of social life because she is among things that exist by themselves and for themselves. (p. 212) No such freedom, no such pleasure is possible amid the human arena. All people are the same, all lives are the same, she realises as she listens to the rhythm of the moving train. There is no life that can be seen to be more valuable or more significant than any other, nor can one successfully make anything of one's life.

Eleanor Pargiter, at seventy, reflects upon the value of her life, and on the definition of her life. She feels that even as an old woman she has only the present moment. She feels that she can make this sole possession meaningful only by connecting the present with the past and future. In such a process of integration will she find the key to life and happiness, and she will find happiness not only in dreams but in living people and ordinary rooms. Yet the novel cannot confirm this hope. Her vision of the young couple emerging from the carriage is far too bland to serve as a convincing image of future harmony. Even as she believes in this possibility of happiness and understanding, she knows that for her (as for her brother who still, as an old man, is repeating the same college stories) there will be endless dark. Life must fall, life must drop; but not as it did for Bernard in *The Waves*, when the image of dropping came from a congealing of life. There is no fullness in this falling of life, nor has it any consequence.

The characters in *The Years*, as are the characters in her other novels, are defined to a great extent in terms of how they see the world.

There is, however, nothing individual about the way the characters in *The Years* see the world; the poor quality of their society and their activities suppresses any development of response and imagination. As a result, the symbolism in this novel is different from that employed in her other works. Many of the images used in *The Waves* appear again. Kitty tears off Thursday from the calendar and screws it into a ball (pp. 49– 50) just as Susan, before she married and had her children, tore off each day, crumpled it in her fist and threw it away. Sara, trying to imagine herself as constituted by thought alone, becomes a root lying in the earth, just as Louis, alone, felt himself to be a root thrust into the earth. Martin, like Bernard, arranges pieces of bread by his plate and the bread pellets represent people and his playful control of their destinies. Yet the images in *The Waves* are formed and developed on a different basis.

Previously Virginia Woolf's symbols depended upon what her characters made of them. She saw symbolism as a psychological fact; that is, she believed external objects and events were perceived amid moods and feelings and thoughts that made the external object or event a participant in and focus for development of the perceiver's mental state: thus making it into a symbol. As such the external object or event could form not only part of the character's mental reference, but could stand in the novel as a mental or emotional reference independent of the character, and could be passed from one character to another. Yet even when a symbol became independent of a perceiver, it began with a perceiver, and its force was based upon the supposition that perceivers, not authors, create symbols; or, rather that authors use symbols because people in fact create them. In *The Years*, however, when the perceiver is no longer imaginatively susceptible to the world, when the perceiver no longer has the power to integrate his or her responses with the external world, it is the author who must create symbols which indicate general psychological states but which are not formed by them. Characters notice and fret about stains on ceilings and scars and deformities; they are frequently repelled by their world but they do not see their surroundings as symbols of themselves or of the the essential quality of their lives. Momentarily a character will understand the possibility of seeing in the landscape a sympathetic language: Kitty, alone in the country, hears the field and sky begin to sing; as Eleanor watches the searchlight during the air raid it seems 'to take what she was feeling and to express it broadly and simply, as if another voice were speaking in another language', (p. 229) but such connections are not sustained.

Typical of the way symbols work in this novel is the way various characters are fascinated by the rising flames of a fire, and are disturbed by the difficulty of keeping a fire in order, so that they are first cold and then over-heated. The characters themselves see the fire simply as a practical issue—whether it will get out of hand, whether it will make the room stuffy. It is the author who superimposes upon their merely practical concern a significance relating it to them. The stuffiness is readily seen to be part of the atmosphere, but the author must provide clues for a further interpretation. A poet at Delia's party, who shares Charles Tansley's habit of saying nothing but 'I, I, I', finds it intolerable whenever anyone else says 'I', for another's use of 'I' turns him into a 'you'. When Peggy says to him, 'I'm tired, I've been up all night', the fire goes out of the poet's face. (p. 276) So the author connects the fire image to the state of the ego and the difficulty of balancing the ego; though the characters themselves never feel their problems with fires as a problem with the ego. Again, the recurring image of the Italian chair with its paw-like arms is presented by the author in the absence of all perceivers. It is not one of those objects which takes on meaning because someone has perceived it (as the house in the section 'Time Passes' of To the Lighthouse or the objects on Mrs Dalloway's dressing-table); it is a symbol created by the author alone to portray emptiness and absence.

At the end of the novel Virginia Woolf offers her characters roses, and an open door, with a sky of 'extraordinary beauty, simplicity and peace', but she has shown previously that these characters will not be able to make use of such gifts. Beauty is useless if it cannot stimulate the imagination and be at least to some extent integrated with more than a momentary vision of the sky; and Virginia Woolf has shown that these characters cannot integrate one moment with another, nor can they extend the scope of their selves. Eleanor, hoping that she can confirm her desire for a pattern and develop her thoughts, longs for Nicholas's help; but she cannot even formulate the question she wants him to answer. Her frustration is taken up by North who concludes, after attempting to speak about a different and better life, that stillness and solitude are the only elements in which the mind is free. (p. 322) Communication is impossible, yet the solitary person does not have the equipment for his own rejuvenation.

The grotesque atmosphere of the novel, enforced by the fact that sexual desire is presented not as affection but as jealousy or lust, enforced too by others' will to spoil what is good for someone else (as Abel Pargiter reads of Parnell's death with pleasure, knowing it

defeats his daughter's fantasies), enforced too by the eternal bickering
of the characters (what they assume to be the sound of waves and thus
the sound of the eternal elements of life is only flak, for the eternal
elements of life are pettiness and strife), cannot be cancelled by the
faint promise offered in the conclusion. The novel's most striking
statement emerges in Sara Pargiter's belief that in time to come
people will look into their room, which she calls a little cave scooped
out of mud and dung, and hold their fingers to their noses as they
exclaim, 'Pah! They stink!' while Sara herself, in Maggie's eyes, looks
like a great ape crouching in a little cave of mud and dung. (p. 145)
The absence of vision itself becomes a viciously restricting vision; the
anger at a loss of vision creates this rigid distortion.

9 Approaching a Breakthrough: *Between the Acts*

The characters in *Between the Acts* are not happier than those in *The Years*. They are not more fulfilled; they have no greater sense of purpose; nor have they more satisfactory relations with one another. They, also, are ensnared in a petty, limiting domesticity. Isa, as she chats to her father-in-law about the fish they will have for lunch, about the price of veal, and about her son, is 'pegged down on a chair arm, like a captive balloon, by a myriad of hair-thin ties into domesticity.' (p. 17) Her fondness for the word 'abortive' further marks her attitude towards her life and her society.

In this last novel, which was finished but never revised, Virginia Woolf carries the oppression of *The Years* to its conclusion and shows how, nonetheless, imagination develops—somewhat like a healthy midget—within the restrictions of life. Imagination reappears not as vital, transforming perception, not as a powerful creator, but as an activity which seems valuable, seems profound, seems to realise our deepest needs, yet which always remains somewhat ridiculous and incomplete. For however strongly the author sympathises with the effort of imagination, with its intensity and purpose, she also reduces its claims by means of a comedy new to her style, something warm and earthy and pathetic—apparent, for example, when the cows' bellows take up the emotion left suspended by an awkward pause in the pageant.

To a great extent, Isa's imagination remains mere day-dream, and registers her inability either to accept or to change her life. The need for fantasy guides her reading and her interest in books in general; but fantasy is not a modest diversion; it is a powerful need. She runs her eye over the books in the library as a person with a raging tooth runs his eye over bottles in a chemist's to see if one provides a cure. (p. 18) For her generation, the author explains, a newspaper is as good as a book; and Isa choses elements from various news items to construct a fantasy about a guard who drags her to the barrack room and removes a piece of her clothing, whereupon she screams and slaps him. The fantasy takes over the narrative, so that the author, somewhat gauchly, interposes real events in parenthesis:

> That was real; so real that on the mahogany door panels she saw the Arch in Whitehall; through the Arch the barrack room; in the barrack room the bed, and on the bed the girl was screaming and hitting him about the face, when the door (for in fact it was a door) opened and in came Mrs Swithin carrying a hammer. (p. 19)

When Lucy Swithin enters Isa can predict the conversation that will take place between the woman and her father-in-law; it is the same as last year's discussion about the pageant and the prospect of the weather. The only difference is that this year Isa hears in addition, 'The girl screamed and hit him about the face with a hammer.' Only the hammer, which fits into her fantasy, marks a change. The external world is viciously repetitive; day-dream alone gives the impression of variety. This is the modern age which, like the gramophone (referred to as a machine and thus as a symbol of the modern age) is always breaking down; the world around the village is being devastated (the novel is set in June, 1939), yet two thoughts dominate the pageant: that the Victorians would never have changed if they had not been forced to change, and, secondly, that nothing has in fact changed, only the clothes styles are different.

When imagination is day-dream rather than the vital perception of Mrs Dalloway or the perceptive sympathy of Mrs Ramsay, there will naturally be a gap between imagination and reality. Isa's bitterness is frequently caused by this discrepancy. Her longings are projected on to a gentleman farmer Rupert Haines (the connection between her fantasies and her sympathy for her husband's desires is marked by the fact that her husband Giles believes he would have become a farmer rather than a stockbroker if he had had the choice). Rupert Haines's face is beautifully mysterious to Isa, and when he quotes Byron it seems that the two of them float like swans downstream—but his snow-white breast is encircled with a tangle of dirty duck-weed, and her webbed feet are entangled by her husband. This squalor in her fantasy, this frustration, arises from her recognition of the ultimate impossibility of the realisation of her day-dream, not only because of the actual circumstances of her life, but also because of the conditions of life itself. The conversation which opens the novel concerns the. village cesspool, and Isa wonders what Rupert Haines would have to say about that; she cannot reconcile the subject of cesspools with the mystery he represents to her. Isa's weakening faith in her imagination when it is placed alongside general facts makes her cynical. She is suspicious of the viability of others' fantasies because she must suspect her own. In the sky which has a 'pure blue, black blue that never filtered down, that had escaped registration' she supposes that Lucy Swithin, her father-in-law's sister, sees God, and she wonders—thus reducing the power she herself has felt in the sky—whether the woman has invested this Godhead with toe-nails. (p. 20)

This tendency to destroy the beauty in fantasy is complemented by the common impulse to destroy in others those emotions which lie outside convention, which help to define the private self. Mrs Haines, the gentleman farmer's wife, senses Isa's emotion and waits for it to die, knowing she will be able to destroy it as 'a thrush pecks wings off a butterfly'. Bartholomew Oliver, who has some of the masculine egoism and accompanying mental precision of Mr Ramsay (he pretends to know exactly how far they are from the sea, as though he had just whipped out a tape measure, and he aggrandises his control over the dog by calling it a wild beast), tries to frustrate the flights of his sister Lucy's religious fantasy which is, despite some ridiculous aspects, a true religious sensibility. Lucy Swithin, who is the least restricted of all the characters, who is able to increase the bounds of the present by adventures into the past and future, who walks as if the floor were fluid, wears a crucifix—which William Dodge sees as a stamp upon her volatile nature. Yet this apparent limitation is a protection against her brother's mockery; she must cling to a conventional symbol to disguise the reality of her non-conventional thoughts. As in *To the Lighthouse*, mockery—that is, the refusal to grant sympathy to individual responses—stems from a belief in the reality of reason, but reason is shown to permit all sorts of stupidities. Old Mr Oliver applauds Reason as she steps on to the pageant stage; but this Reason is a complacent and mute observer of greed, lust and farcical connivance.

The tensions among the characters, the meagre sympathy they have for one another's imaginations, lead to immense difficulties in communication. Yet in this novel words promise some richness; their potential is acknowledged, and this provides a refreshing contrast to the hopelessly grotesque presentation of language in *The Years*. The nurses, as they trundle perambulators, roll out words, like sweets on their tongues, and their words, 'as they thinned to transparency, gave off pink, green and sweetness'. (p. 11) Bartholomew Oliver believes that treasures are released when great names are mentioned; and, to Miss La Trobe, at the end of the pageant, it seems that from the fertile mud round, her words rise above the dumb oxen. Yet the potential of language cannot be realised. The nurses, as they so lovingly roll out their words, do not exchange information. The words that arise for Miss La Trobe from the mud are, though wonderful, 'words without meaning'. Lucy Swithin repeats to herself that we 'haven't the words', and concludes that it is not on the lips but behind the eyes that true emotion is communicated. Unlike *The Years*, this novel insists that there is something real to be communicated, but language is always insufficient. The language used by the characters is, generally, that of conventional phrases and greetings and sentiment; their language cannot express—nor can they develop—their individuality.

Because imagination is separate from the shared language, the references a person makes to his or her own thoughts are frequently misunderstood. Mrs Sands tells Mrs Swithin that her nephew, who is apprenticed to a butcher, has been cheeking the master, and Mrs Swithin says, 'That'll be all right', half referring to the boy, and half referring to the neat, trimmed triangular sandwich she has been making. (pp. 29–8) When Isa sees her husband flirting with Mrs Manressa, she exclaims, 'Oh, that idiot!', and her companions believe she is referring to the idiot in the play, which every traditional play must have. The widow Etty Springett says it is cheap and nasty, referring to the play, but she shoots a vicious glance at Dodge's green trousers, yellow spotted tie and unbuttoned waistcoat. (p. 121)

The vagueness, or open-endedness, of reference is essential to the meaning of the pageant. The actors sometimes bawl so loudly that their words are unintelligible, and Isa can make nothing of the plot; but this allows the audience more easily to project itself on to the stage. Mrs Manressa, who imagines herself to be a 'wild child of nature', though who is actually more like a spoiled lady of society, believes that she is the Queen of the event; and Lucy Swithin declares that she might have been Cleopatra. The people who hear Mrs Swithin's declaration, naturally enough, laugh, but her identification is based upon her sense of an unacted part—and that is the point of the pageant, which depicts the audience's possibilities as well as their reality.

Alongside the tension between the actual world and fantasy—a tension which results in the fragmentation of both—is the difficult balance between the need for solitude and silence (in which fantasy develops) and the need for society, the fear of loneliness. The characters need others' approval; they need others to help them enact their fantasies; they wish to communicate these fantasies, to have their underlying reality (which is the reality of their personal needs) realised. As a result, the conventions that the characters themselves perpetrate are highly unsatisfactory. The audience cannot indulge their personal desires to sleep and to dream in one another's company; for company impedes such self-involvement. Miss La Trobe actually wishes she could be free of her audience, for then she would not have to suffer distorted interpretations of a poorly realised vision. But at the same time, the characters are afraid to be alone; their fantasies are frequently symptoms of their loneliness and the pageant is an attempt to mend the fragmentation which each in isolation suffers. They resist being drawn together, yet only as a group—because what they are depends so much on what their society is—can they achieve any vision of themselves.

The images of loneliness are in this novel devoid of the individual personalities that distinguished Woolf's presentation of mood and atmosphere in her earlier works. The characters see their loneliness in opposition to a crowded world, while the author presents the world itself as lonely: 'Empty, empty, empty: silent, silent, silent. The room was a shell, singing of what was before time was; a vase stood in the heart of the house, alabaster, smooth, cold, holding the still, distilled essence of emptiness, silence.' (p. 30) Though the writing here is, to say the least, unremarkable (none of the lyric passages in this book are very good, but this is an unrevised novel), the image of loneliness as a cold, smooth alabaster centre offers a fine expression of the static, haunted loneliness the characters only half-consciously endure. Nor can society in any simple way assuage their loneliness, for they want to be alone; some part of them.needs solitude. As Bartholomew, Isa and Lucy meet Mrs Manressa and Dodge, the confrontation is like running into a rock; their initial response is outrage: 'Utterly impossible, was it, even in the heart of the country, to be alone?' (p. 30) Gradually, however, they see the encounter as a pleasant diversion; for people are drawn together by the same instinct that makes cows and sheep seek physical propinquity. The characters illustrate Schopenhauer's fable of the porcupine who seeks company for warmth and then, driven mad by the discomfort of other porcupines' spikes, flees into isolation, until, driven mad by loneliness and cold, he forgets his past experience of companionship and again eagerly seeks it. For as the characters wait for the pageant to begin, the inactivity which is pleasant in solitude becomes a burden, and they look for ways to camouflage their desires to slip back into their private sleepy thoughts. This unhappy balance between the need for solitude and the need for company, the desire for company and the discomfort suffered in company, stems from the characters' inability to communicate: 'Their minds and bodies were too close, yet not close enough. We aren't free, each one of them felt separately to feel or think separately, nor yet to fall asleep. We're too close; but not close enough. So they fidgeted.' (p. 50)

The society these people share is one that thwarts vision. Isabella, as she sits among the audience—which is the village population—feels imprisoned, with the bars deflected by a haze of sleep. Her vision of a world governed by love and hate grows dim because, among these people, she can feel neither love nor hate distinctly. Her strongest conscious desire is, because she had a glass of sweet wine with lunch, for a glass of cold water. This desire dominates her imagination; she sees 'water surrounded by walls of shining glass'. (p. 50) The vividness and glamour of her vision, alongside the pettiness of the desire, is certainly comic; and the pathos of that comedy arises from her inability to imagine in broader or more profound terms what it is to be free. Water is Isa's image of release. Her belief that they are a hundred miles from the sea is one aspect of her oppression, as is her continuous worry that the fish they eat will not be fresh. She fell in love with her husband Giles when she saw the water rushing between his legs and saw the salmon leap in front of him; her image of love, too, was one of freedom and excitement. But her married life has only imposed restrictions upon her. She must disguise her poetry writing in the covers of an accounts book; she finds that her love has become absorbed by convention while real love, which lies 'in the eyes', is ignored. Her imagination becomes more and more constricted as convention seems more and more real. Even her meagre imagination, expressed in the vision of the shining glass, is suppressed by 'the leaden duty she owed to others'. Indeed, imagination itself is lazy. The excitement and creativeness of visual stimuli portrayed in Woolf's other books cannot develop among these people. Visual beauty only leads to sleep: 'How tempting, how very tempting, to let the view triumph; to reflect its ripple; to let their own minds ripple; to let outlines elongate and pitch over—so—with a sudden jerk.' (p. 50)

The release of imaginative perception topples into a surreptitious dozing.

Yet the absence of vision, or the inadequacy of vision, is as terrifying here as in any of Virginia Woolf's previous books. During the pageant, when the stage is empty and the breeze blows away the last words of the singers, Miss La Trobe thinks, 'This is death.' (p. 99) For all the goodness and effectiveness of imagination seems to be gone. Communication is at a standstill; the wind rises and the villagers, who still open and shut their mouths, utter inaudible words. Miss La Trobe's creative power leaves her; she leans against a tree, paralysed. Illusion has failed, and this is death.

The general paralysis of vision can be linked to the stagnant, dying community. The old families of the village intermarried, 'and lay in their deaths intertwisted, like ivy roots beneath the churchyard wall'. (p. 9) The surprising juxtaposition of intermarriage and graveyards places that which might be expected to renew life alongside death. Similarly, images of death permeate both the actual and the dream world. Old Mr Oliver's dog is like a stone figure guarding, even in the realms of death, the sleep of his dreaming master. (p. 16) The master, however, is not dead: he is dreaming of his youth in India—but the landscape of which he dreams is filled with images of death (in the sand there is a hoop of ribs, and a maggot-eaten bullock lies in the sun); yet it is only his dream hand that clenches in protest and determination; his real hand lies still on the chair with veins swollen with a brownish fluid. (p. 17) The image of death (the stone dog guarding the dead) is really alive, and sits beside a living but decaying master, dreaming of a youth that itself was steeped in death.

Pointz Hall is said to be out of harmony with nature; for though nature had provided a perfect site for a house, raised up and in the light, the Hall was built in a hollow, facing north, and in winter the damp sweeps upon the panes and chokes the gutter with dead leaves. The characters' alienation from natural life and their bondage to convention enrages them. Giles feels himself to be 'manacled to a rock' and 'forced passively to behold indescribable horror' as he observes the commonplace quality of their lives. (p. 46) His wife, understanding his state, can only express her response by turning over a coffee cup—only that slight breach of etiquette seems possible to her. Giles, trying to integrate his thoughts, repeats 'I . . . I' and then he glares at his Aunt Lucy: the conventional education she has thrust upon him has deprived him of his self. Miss La Trobe who, unlike

Giles, has the courage to dress unconventionally, reflects that people who are blinded by convention do not see that a dish cloth wound round the head appears, in the open air, to represent a silk turban better than real silk; convention, then, prevents others from knowing what looks real.

The characters who try to break free of convention generally do so in a highly conventional way. Mrs Manressa, who supposes herself to be free of convention and at one with nature, breaks convention simply to break it. Yet the author's hatred of convention is here so uncontrolled that she seems to think Mrs Manressa is doing something fine in defying it. When Mrs Manressa does anything or says anything, the author declares that one feels 'she's said it, she's done it'. Her breach of decorum is a breath of fresh air which restores to Bartholomew his spice islands, (p. 33) and when Isa hears that the first thing the woman does when she arrives in the country is take off her stays and roll in the grass, Isa thinks, 'That's genuine.' (p. 34)

Far more convincing a rejection of convention is the presentation of savagery as a fundamental element of life, and one which is not in the least modified by convention. As Giles plays the child's game of kicking a stone to a goal, he attacks it first as Mrs Manressa (lust), then as William Dodge (perversion), then as himself (coward), and thereafter all the kicks are the same. The description of the landscape then becomes part of Septimus Smith's violent world:

> He reached [his goal] in ten. There, crouched in the grass, curled in an olive ring, was a snake. Dead? No, choked with a toad in its mouth. The snake was unable to swallow; the toad was unable to die. A spasm made the ribs contract; blood oozed. It was birth the wrong way round—a monstrous inversion. So, raising his foot, he stamped on them. The mass crushed and slithered. The white canvas on his tennis shoes was bloodstained and sticky. But it was action. Action relieved him. He strode to the Barn, with blood on his shoes. (pp. 72−73)

Giles, like Septimus, is angry at society for failing to recognise the violence it has inflicted upon its people. His anger, however, is itself a wish to inflict that same violence upon society—whereas Septimus's wish was to preserve himself from violence, and the violence of his visions registered not his wish to be violent but the fact that society was violent. While the villagers are thinking about the loveliness of the view, Giles is thinking about the sixteen men who have just been blown up across the gulf, and he believes he would like to see these people and their pretty views blasted to bits. His disgusting cruelty towards the snake actually relieves him. He even expects to be admired for his deed—and, after all, society does admire its soldier-murderers. Society wishes to destroy the 'monstrous inversion' of its own creation.

It is this see-saw between convention and savagery that makes what is essentially a comic novel so disturbing. Lucy Swithin, reminded by her brother that her visions of England as a primeval and savage place are unreal, sits down to tea like any other old woman. (p.11) Convention denies the reality of primitive reality; yet the novel itself is immersed in it. At both the opening and close of the book Lucy Swithin is reading Wells' *Outline of History*, which describes the world—even Piccadilly Circus—as populated by elephant-bodied, seal-necked, heavy, surging, slowly writhing and, Lucy Swithin supposes, barking monsters 'from whom we presumably descend'. (p. 10) This musing vision of the old woman is the actual vision of young George Oliver:

The flower blazed between the angles of the roots. Membrane after membrane was torn. It blazed a soft yellow, a lambent light under a film of velvet; it filled the caverns behind the eyes with light. All that inner darkness became a hall, leaf smelling, earth smelling of yellow light. And the tree was beyond the flower; the grass, the flower and the tree were entire. Down on his knees grubbing he held the flower complete. Then there was a roar and a hot breath and a stream of coarse grey hair rushed between him and the flower. Up he leapt, toppling in his fright, and saw coming towards him a terrible peaked eyeless monster moving on legs, brandishing arms. (pp. 12–13)

Young George's vision of the flower is a return to the active vital world created by an imaginative perceiver. The flower he holds is not a simple and safe flower. His awareness of it the violates him, invades him, destroys the boundaries of his self; yet the monster that so terrifies him and alienates him from his self-created joy is his grandfather, Bartholomew Oliver. The man who prides himself upon being a man of reason and convention is seen to be some primeval creature without eyes. Unable to see himself, he must destroy others' vision. The moment of true imagination gives way to the savagely destructive conventional adult world.

The extensive animal imagery, which is as prevalent as in *The Years*, enforces the fact of the characters' prehistoric natures, despite their rejection of nature. Mrs Swithin has knobbed shoes, as if she had claws like a canary's. Hens stare into the Barn where the pageant is being held; cows stray past and participate in the emotion of the play. The Barn is built high to protect it from rats and damp, though it is nonetheless populated by mice and swallows and a stray bitch. The Barn reminds some people of a Greek temple: animals are the gods who dwell in the temple. The animals' eyes are as keen as the human; they can easily replace human observers as they pass the Barn and supply a continuation of the narrative.

Animals can give the lie to the respectability and dignity of convention, as when pigeons are described as ladies in ornate ball dresses, mincing tiny steps on their little pink feet. (p. 53) More commonly, however, they actually participate as equals in the human world. The swallows, retreating and advancing, are the melodic movements of the pageant's music, while the trees prevent what is fluid in the pageant's atmosphere from over-flowing. (p. 127) When jazz is played—representing the young who, the author declares, cannot construct but only destroy—the music is like a woodpecker flitting from tree to tree, and the cows and dogs and Afghan hound join the music. Yet the animal imagery does not have the same reductive effect it had in *The Years*. Even the blue vein on Mrs Swithin's forehead that wriggles like a worm is pathetic rather than grotesque. Animals, who do not have a changing society or conventions, show that this *entr'acte* presentation of characters' lives is also part of a changeless recurrent, involuntary drama.

It is very clearly a community of people being described in the novel, a community bound by their relation to one another in a way characters were not bound together in *The Years*. In *Between the Acts* solid human connection, both for good and evil, is always felt. Flesh and blood are not barriers to Bartholomew and Lucy, but a mist covering their criticisms of one another; nothing changes their affection—no argument, no fact, no truth. (p. 22) When Bartholomew muses over the harvests his mind has reaped, he feels that, next to his son's unhappiness, nothing matters. (p. 84) Isa and Giles, too, are bound by emotions far more vivid than any emotion presented in *The Years*—and this, despite the confusion and squalor of their feelings, is refreshing. These bonds, however, also have a totally negative and limiting aspect; nor is any possible escape imagined. At the end of the book Isa and Giles are outlined against the window; the window is all sky, and the sky is without colour. Their situation, which is not individual but universal, is this:

> Alone enmity was bared; also love. Before they slept, they must fight; after they fought, they would embrace. From that embrace another life might be born. But first they must fight, as the dog fights with the vixen, in the heart of darkness, in the fields of night. [. . .] The house had lost its shelter. It was a night before roads were made, or houses. It was the night that dwellers in caves had watched from some high place among the rocks.
> Then the curtain rose. They spoke. (p. 152)

The tension and dissatisfaction they suffer is part of the human play that has been enacted from the beginning of human time, and they cannot change their condition.

But this assertion of the stasis of human connection does not completely override Virginia Woolf's belief that creative, integrating perception, is a key to a better life, that all hope is hope for a better vision. The special cruelty of the modern age is seen in its fragmentation, presented in the pageant by jazz and a revolving cheval glass scattering its piecemeal images:

> Out they leapt, jerked, skipped. Flashing, dazzling, dancing, jumping. Now old Bart . . . he was caught. Now Manressa. Here a nose . . . There a skirt . . . Then trousers only . . . Now perhaps a face . . . Ourselves? But that's cruel. To snap us as we are, before we've had a chance to assume . . . And only, too, in parts. . . . That's what's so distorting and upsetting and utterly unfair. (p. 128)

The glass's revolutions stop when the young man carrying it runs out of muscle, and the audience is shown a reflection of their present selves—'not whole by any means, but at any rate standing still'. (p. 29) Subsequently, however, a familiar contrapuntal work is played; one note points to another, one note reveals another; the base line opens up a force of opposition, and then the two disparate lines are united; on different levels they diverge and move forward, all wrestling with meaning and finally comprehended. Thus the author insists that even such apparently hopeless fragmentation can be integrated, and that the ridiculous, greedy, licentious people—the people of England throughout her history—who have been displayed in the pageant, have something in them that refuses to be sold. (pp. 130–1) This, too, is Lucy Swithin's vision when she looks into the lily pond and sees 'ourselves' in the fish (and Giles has seen himself as a fish caught in water); there she retrieves 'some glint of faith from the grey waters, hopefully, without much help from reason, she followed the fish; the speckled, streaked, and blotched; seeing in that vision beauty, power, and glory in ourselves'. (p. 142)

Between the Acts attempts to divulge the most pessimistic and ridiculous aspects of human life; it portrays in the pageant the continuing history of tension, frustration and comedy—and then it attempts to reconcile all this with the insistence that there is something noble and steadfast in human nature. One's conclusion must be that if the positive assertion is justified, then it is justified by something other than that world presented in the novel. And the pessimism is further aggravated by the loss of the belief in the truth or profundity of vision. This loss is disguised by comedy; but it is nonetheless present. The comic reduction of vision's purpose is seen in the Reverend Streatfield's speech, which boasts of the thirty-six pounds, ten shillings and eight pence that have been raised by the pageant for the illumination of the church. The purpose of the pageant was to increase illumination, certainly, but this kind of illumination serves no real purpose.

The creative effort behind the pageant is presented seriously. The description of Miss La Trobe's feelings reveals the earnest and unconditional commitment of the artist, as well as the way creative effort supplies its own impetus for further work and investigation. Miss La Trobe feels that there is always another play behind the play she has just written. The thing completed, the thing expressed, is inadequate to her creative needs; the thing that needs expression has changed, or seeks a new, broader expression. What turns this theme back into comedy, however, is the fact that the artistic value of the play, so lovingly and painstakingly achieved, is nil. The author makes no attempt to present the play as anything other than a typical village pageant, with fluffed lines, mechanical mishaps and bored audiences. But at the same time the author describes the effects of this pageant as the effects of great art; it has the revitalising force of great art. Even as Miss La Trobe recognises the failure of her play the flowers appear to be incandescent, and from the earth green waters seem to rise over her, and as she drinks her whisky the mud becomes fertile and words rise above the laden, dumb oxen. (p. 147) Even poor art provides a language and releases one from that irritable wordless state in which Isa crushed the leaves of Old Man's Beard in her fingers and sought the faces of the crowd for the face of her fantasy lover.

Not only the author of the play, but the audience, too, are affected as though by great art. During the interval they feel they are neither here nor there; they are released from specific time and place: the play had jerked the ball out of the cup, 'and what I call myself was still floating unattached'. (p. 105) The confused execution of the play acts as an artistic asset, for the characters see themselves in the pageant as they might see themselves in a Rorschach test; the allusiveness of the characters and situations in the pageant play is not that of powerful artistic images. The pessimism lying behind this comic replacement of symbolic allusiveness with vagueness and incomprehensibility is the assumption that any focus of fantasy leads to the impression of integration, and that even the most serious artistic effort will give rise only to ridiculous fragments.

After the total disintegration of The Years, the charm and poignancy of Between the Acts does point to the possibility of a new type of integration among a decaying society. The eternal recurrences of the characters' sufferings are not, in Virginia Woolf's final novel, as oppressive as the series of banalities that confronted the Pargiters; the fact that Isa and Giles enact ancient quarrels and reconciliations provides some explanation for their confusion and dissatisfaction. The criticism of her society is more pointed and forceful than in any other of her works (with the exception of Mrs Dalloway) and, what is so striking and significant, is the insistence that vision depends upon a shared vision, that vision depends upon communication, that one's possible visions depend upon one's society. Here, if an integrated vision is possible, then it must have wide implications; it must affect not only individual consciousness but also communal life and language; it must affect what can be said and what can be generally understood and what one will assume other people to be. Between the Acts points to a Mrs Dalloway of a different order, in which language as a society-dependent tool and a person as a being bound to a community would be integrated with the private vision and would be shown to be linked to the question of what private visions were possible—but this promise was not fulfilled.

References

Page references to Virginia Woolf's texts are from the following editions:

The Voyage Out (New York: Harcourt Brace and World, 1975)
Night and Day (London: Duckworth, 1920)
Jacob's Room (St Albans: Triad/Panther, 1976)
Mrs Dalloway (Harmondsworth: Penguin, 1967)
To the Lighthouse (Harmondsworth: Penguin, 1969)
Orlando (New York: Penguin, 1946)
The Waves (Harmondsworth: Penguin, 1968)
The Years (St Albans: Triad/Panther, 1977)
Between the Acts (Harmondsworth: Penguin, 1976)
A Haunted House and Other Stories (London: Hogarth Press, 1973)
Mrs Dalloway's Party, Stella McNichol (ed.), (London: Hogarth Press, 1973)
A Room of One's Own (Harmondsworth: Penguin, 1970)
Collected Essays, L. Woolf (ed.), 4 vols. (London: Chatto and Windus, 1966, 1967)
A Writer's Diary, L. Woolf (ed.), (London: Hogarth Press, 1959)

Notes

INTRODUCTION
  1. Virginia Woolf, *A Writer's Diary*, p. 177.

CHAPTER 1: *The Voyage Out*
  1. J. W. Beach, 'Virgina Woolf', The English Journal, vol. 26 (1937), pp. 603–12, and F. R. Leavis, 'After *To the Lighthouse: Between the Acts* by Virginia Woolf', *Scrutiny*, vol. X (1938)

CHAPTER 2: *Night and Day*
  1. R. M. Underhill, review in *Bookman* (New York; August 1920), pp. 685–6

CHAPTER 3: *Jacob's Room*
  1. T. S. Eliot, 'The Waste Land', *Collected Poems* (London: Faber, 1963), p. 64.
  2. Dante Alighieri, *Purgatorio*, J. D. Sinclair (ed.) (Oxford University Press, 1971).
  3. D. H. Lawrence, *Sons and Lovers* (New York: Random House, 1922), p. 196.
  4. T. S. Eliot, op. cit., p. 65.

CHAPTER 4: *Mrs Dalloway*
  1. Karl Popper, *Conjectures and Refutations* (London: Routledge and Kegan Paul, 1972), p. 46.
  2. M. C. Bradbrook, 'Notes on the Style of Mrs Woolf', *Scrutiny* (May 1932), pp. 33–8).
  3. W. Empson, 'Virginia Woolf', in E. Rickworth (ed.), *Scrutinies by various Writers*, vol. 2 (1931), pp. 204–16.

CHAPTER 5: *To the Lighthouse*
  1. James Joyce, *A Portrait of the Artist as a Young Man* (London: Jonathan Cape, 1975), p. 22.
  2. *Ibid.*, pp. 38–41.

CHAPTER 6: *Orlando*
  1. Q. D. Leavis, review in *Scrutiny* (September 1938), pp. 203–14.

CHAPTER 7: *The Waves*
  1. Marcel Proust, *Swann's Way*, vol. 1, C. K. Scott Moncrieff (trans.) (London: Chatto and Windus, 1966), p. 10.
  2. *Ibid.*, p. 151.
  3. *Ibid.*, p. 151.
  4. *Ibid.*, pp. 188–189.
  5. *Ibid.*, p. 190.

6. *Ibid.*, p. 192.

7. *Ibid.*, p. 155.

8. *Ibid.*, p. 115.

9. Virginia Woolf, *A Writer's Diary*, L. Woolf (ed.) (London: Hogarth Press, 1953), p. 134.

10. Marcel Proust, *Time Regained*, A. Mayor (trans.) (London: Chatto and Windus, 1970), p. 255.

11. Marcel Proust, *Swann's Way*, vol. 1, p. 59.

CHAPTER 8: *The Years*

1. Virginia Woolf, *A Writer's Diary*, L. Woolf (ed.) (London: Hogarth Press, 1953), p. 189.

Virginia Woolf Bibliography

The Voyage Out (London: Duckworth, 1915)

Night and Day (London: Duckworth, 1919)

Jacob's Room (London: Hogarth Press, 1922)

Mrs Dalloway (London: Hogarth Press, 1925)

To the Lighthouse (London: Hogarth Press, 1927)

Orlando (London: Hogarth Press, 1928)

A Room of One's Own (London: Hogarth Press, 1929)

The Waves (London: Hogarth Press, 1931)

Flush: A Biography (London: Hogarth Press, 1933)

The Years (London: Hogarth Press, 1937)

Three Guineas (London: Hogarth Press, 1938)

Roger Fry: A Biography (London: Hogarth Press, 1940)

Between the Acts (London: Hogarth Press, 1941)

A Haunted House and Other Short Stories (London: Hogarth Press, 1944)

A Writer's Diary: Being Extracts from the Diary of Virginia Woolf, L. Woolf (ed.), (London: Hogarth Press, 1953)

Virginia Woolf and Lytton Strachey: Letters, L. Woolf and James Strachey (ed.), (London: Hogarth Press, 1956)

Contemporary Writers, (London: Hogarth Press, 1965)

Collected Essays, 4 vols., L. Woolf (ed.), (London: Chatto and Windus, 1966, 1967)

Mrs Dalloway's Party, Stella McNichol (ed.), (London: Hogarth Press, 1973)

Letters, 2 vols, Nigel Nicholson (ed.), (London: Hogarth Press, 1975, 1976)

Freshwater, Lucio P. Ruotolo (ed.), (London: Hogarth Press, 1976)

Diaries 1915–1919, Anne Oliver Bell (ed.), (London: Hogarth Press, 1977)

Moments of Being (London: Hogarth Press, 1978)

The Pargiters, Mitchell Leaska (ed.), (London: Hogarth Press, 1978)

Index

There is no entry for Virginia Woolf in the index. Reference to Woolf's works are entered by their titles.

LOGIC-BASED
0-1 CONSTRAINT
PROGRAMMING

OPERATIONS RESEARCH / COMPUTER SCIENCE
INTERFACES
SERIES

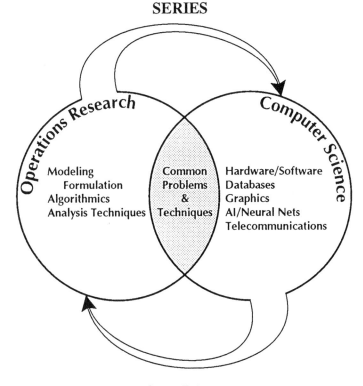

Series Editor

Ramesh Sharda
Conoco/Dupont Chair of Management of Technology
Oklahoma State University
Stillwater, Oklahoma U.S.A.

Other published titles in the series:

Brown, Donald/Scherer, William T.
University of Virginia
   Intelligent Scheduling Systems

Nash, Stephen G./Sofer, Ariela
George Mason University
   *The Impact of Emerging Technologies on Computer Science
   and Operations Research*

LOGIC-BASED
0-1 CONSTRAINT
PROGRAMMING

Peter Barth
Max Planck Institute
Saarbrücken, Germany

KLUWER ACADEMIC PUBLISHERS
Boston/London/Dordrecht

Distributors for North America:
Kluwer Academic Publishers
101 Philip Drive
Assinippi Park
Norwell, Massachusetts 02061 USA

Distributors for all other countries:
Kluwer Academic Publishers Group
Distribution Centre
Post Office Box 322
3300 AH Dordrecht, THE NETHERLANDS

Library of Congress Cataloging-in-Publication Data

A C.I.P. Catalogue record for this book is available from the Library of Congress.

Printed on acid-free paper.

Printed in the United States of America

CONTENTS

FOREWORD

Constraint programming has become a major area of interaction between operations research and computer science over the last few years. It combines new programming language paradigms from computer science, like *constraint logic programming* and *concurrent constraint programming*, with efficient constraint solving techniques from mathematics, artificial intelligence, and operations research. Constraint programming allows the user both to build and to solve a model in the same framework:

- Expressive programming language constructs make it possible to formulate the problem in a natural and declarative way.

- Powerful constraint handling techniques supporting these language constructs provide for efficiency in problem solving.

Compared to other approaches, constraint programming offers incremental development, flexibility for modifications and extensions, and interactivity, without sacrificing efficiency. Constraint technology has been applied successfully to a large variety of practical problems arising in industry, for example in production planning, scheduling, and resource allocation.

0-1 constraint programming, where constraints are defined over 0-1 variables, corresponds to 0-1 integer programming in operations research. 0-1 constraints are a special form of finite domain constraints, which are used in most existing constraint programming systems and which are usually solved by local consistency techniques from artificial intelligence. In his book, Peter Barth develops a new *logic-based* approach for 0-1 constraint solving in constraint programming, which combines methods from 0-1 integer programming with techniques from automated deduction in computational logic. The basic formulas of his constraint solver are extended clauses saying that at least m out of n literals have to be true, where a literal is either a 0-1 variable or its negation. He has developed a comprehensive collection of new techniques for transforming general, possibly non-linear, 0-1 constraints into extended clauses, for simplifying sets of extended clauses by the generation of *logic cutting planes*, and

for computing solved forms in the context of constraint programming. For the first time, a complete account of the techniques needed for a logic-based 0-1 constraint solver, or a logic-based 0-1 optimizer, is given.

This logic-based approach is complementary to the more classical polyhedral approach in combinatorial optimization, which is based on linear programming relaxations. Practical experience shows that logic-based methods can be very effective where polyhedral methods fail and vice versa. There are many interesting parallels between the two approaches, but the relationship between them is still not fully understood. This book makes a significant contribution to the area. It lays the foundation for future research, which has to show how logic-based and polyhedral methods can be combined in the most fruitful way.

Alexander Bockmayr

PREFACE

Logic-based methods for modelling and solving combinatorial problems have recently started to play a significant role in both theory and practice. The application of logic to combinatorial problems is twofold. On one hand, *constraint logic programming* allows one to declaratively model combinatorial problems over an appropriate constraint domain, which are then solved by a corresponding constraint solver. Besides being a high-level declarative interface to the constraint solver, the logic programming language allows one to implement also those subproblems that cannot be naturally expressed with constraints. On the other hand, logic-based methods can be used as a *constraint solving* technique inside a constraint solver for combinatorial problems modelled as 0-1 integer programs. A logic view of 0-1 integer programming problems provides new insights into the problem structure and may lead to more effective solving techniques depending on the problem class. The combination of operations research techniques and deductive methods provides effective constraint solving techniques from operations research integrated in a logic programming environment.

Pseudo-Boolean or 0-1 constraints are expressive enough to formulate a wide range of practical problems. We develop a set of techniques needed for building a logic-based constraint solver for 0-1 integer programming problems and demonstrate their integration into classical operations research methods. Logic-based methods are neither a priori superior to classical polyhedral techniques nor do they entail a completely different constraint solving methodology. Instead, there are many parallels to the polyhedral approach and achievements in one area carry over to the other. In polyhedral theory we can find the notion of a solved form, i.e., an inequality description of the convex hull of the 0-1 solution points of a pseudo-Boolean problem. We introduce an analogous logic-based solved form consisting of extended clauses. Extended clauses state that at least k out of n facts need to hold and hence are suitable for combinatorial problems. Lying halfway between expressive linear pseudo-Boolean constraints and manageable classical clauses (where $k = 1$), extended clauses are a good compromise w.r.t. expressibility and manageability. Since the possibly exponential size of the ideal solved form forbids its generation in general, the logic-based

constraint solver works on a mixture of linear pseudo-Boolean inequalities and extended clauses. The techniques for extended clauses are expanded to cope with linear pseudo-Boolean inequalities and simplification methods for linear pseudo-Boolean inequalities are included. The logic-based methods can also co-operate with polyhedral methods. For instance, extended clauses generated by our transformation technique correspond to extended cover inequalities, which have been successfully used as cutting planes in linear programming based systems. Logic based simplification methods can yield even stronger polyhedral cuts. Ultimately, an integration of both approaches will yield more stable and efficient optimization tools.

Overview

We introduce constraint logic programming in Chapter 2. After a motivating example and a presentation of semantic issues and problems, we illustrate modelling techniques in CLP($\mathcal{PB}$), a constraint logic programming language over pseudo-Boolean constraints. We also discuss other constraint logic programming systems and constraint domains that are suitable for handling combinatorial problems. After reviewing previous work on pseudo-Boolean problems, we focus on a logic-based constraint solving approach in Chapter 3. An ideal logic-based solved form consisting of extended clauses in defined in Section 3.3. We present a complete logic-based pseudo-Boolean constraint solver in Chapter 4 and motivate each of the techniques developed in the following chapters. We start with a generalization of the unit resolution procedure for classical clauses to the pseudo-Boolean case in Chapter 5, which serves as a discrete relaxation replacing the classical linear programming relaxation. An implicit enumeration procedure based on this discrete relaxation is presented, which compares well with traditional linear programming based branch-and-bound. Next, we show in Chapter 6 how to use this enumerative method in order to generate valid constraints, i.e., logic cuts, replacing classical polyhedral cuts in a logic view of pseudo-Boolean constraints. Since extended clauses constitute the ideal solved form, we present techniques transforming linear pseudo-Boolean constraints into extended clauses in Chapter 7. Specialized simplification techniques for extended clauses are developed in Chapter 8, which are the logical counterparts of strong cutting planes in polyhedral theory. In order to handle non-linear pseudo-Boolean constraints we develop a linearization technique in Chapter 9. Finally, we present in Chapter 10 a projection technique in order to eliminate auxiliary variables, which is needed in the context of constraint logic programming.

Audience

The intended audience of this book can be divided into two groups. First, developers and users of constraint logic programming systems will be interested in using operations research techniques for combinatorial optimization problems. We discuss the requirements of an integration of such techniques in constraint logic programming, state upcoming problems, and present solutions for our logic-based approach. Since our constraint solver is able to decide entailment problems, the techniques are also relevant for designers of concurrent constraint languages. From a user's perspective, a complete constraint solver for 0-1 problems allows for a more declarative programming style and hence eases implementation.

Second, people interested in operations research will find new logic-based techniques for solving 0-1 problems. In some applications, exploiting the logical structure turns out to be superior to the classical polyhedral view underlying linear programming based systems. Software engineers faced to practical problems will be interested in applicable solving techniques. A prototype implementation of some of the presented techniques has been released as the system OPBDP [Bar95] and about hundred users successfully have applied the system to 0-1 problems coming from such diverse areas as statistics, VLSI-CAD, scheduling, and others. Researchers interested in the logic view of 0-1 constraints will find a well developed set of logic-based techniques, which can be used, refined, and may stimulate the development of new logic-based methods.

Acknowledgements

This book is a revised version of my PhD thesis, submitted at the University of Saarbrücken in February 1995. I am indebted to many people who made this work possible. First, I would like to thank my supervisors Prof. Dr. Harald Ganzinger and Dr. Alexander Bockmayr. Many thanks to Prof. Dr. Harald Ganzinger for his interest in my research and his support during my studies. He gave me the opportunity to work in an excellent research group at the Max Planck Institute in Saarbrücken. I am indebted to Dr. Alexander Bockmayr for his strong encouragement and constant support for this work. I took advantage of his valuable comments and many fruitful discussions. I thank him for his patience in reading and correcting numerous draft versions, which substantially improves this work. He introduced me to the problem area and kindly supported and advised me through my PhD studies. Special thanks to Prof. Dr. John N. Hooker for his instant commitment to become one of the referees, for his careful reading of the entire text, and for his helpful comments.

Finally, I am very grateful to my room-mates Manfred Jaeger and Peter Graf for the nice atmosphere and for spending time for discussions and reading draft versions.

1

INTRODUCTION

We present two orthogonal ways of using logic for modelling and solving combinatorial optimization problems. First, we demonstrate the use of *Constraint Logic Programming* (CLP) in order to model combinatorial problems and handle non-constraint aspects of real-life problems. Second, we propose and evaluate a *logic-based constraint solving* approach for pseudo-Boolean constraints, exemplify the potential of combining logic-based and polyhedral methods, and develop all the essential elements of a logic-based constraint solver for pseudo-Boolean constraints that can be used in the context of constraint logic programming.

1.1 CLP AND COMBINATORIAL OPTIMIZATION

Constraint logic programming combines the declarative nature of logic programming with the computational power of constraint solvers over specific domains. The logic programming language PROLOG, emerging from the work of Colmerauer [CKPR73] and Kowalski [Kow74], has introduced a subset of first-order logic, namely Horn clause logic, as a programming language. Programming in logic supports the writing of clear, readable, and concise programs. Although common constraint systems, like arithmetic, can be defined from scratch in logic, efficiency considerations forbid that. The CLP($\mathcal{X}$)-scheme of Jaffar and Lassez [JL87] merges logic programming and constraint solving, and thus provides a framework for both declarative and efficient programming. Given a constraint solver over a computational domain $\mathcal{X}$ that is able to decide the consistency of a set of constraints over $\mathcal{X}$, the CLP($\mathcal{X}$)-scheme provides a semantic

basis for the corresponding constraint logic programming language $\text{CLP}(\mathcal{X})$. Instantiating $\mathcal{X}$ by a domain of computation, such as linear arithmetic, Boolean algebra, finite domains, or lists, has been an active research area in recent years. Several constraint logic programming systems have been developed. Among the pioneering systems are $\text{CLP}(\mathcal{R})$ [JL87], PROLOG III [Col87], CAL [ASS⁺88], and CHIP [DvHS⁺88a, vH89a].

Handling combinatorial optimization problems within a logic programming language is one of the aims of CHIP. With its finite domain constraint solver, based on local consistency techniques [Mac77, vH89a], the system has been successfully applied to a large variety of combinatorial optimization problems coming from operations research; e.g., graph coloring, disjunctive scheduling, car-sequencing, warehouse location, and cutting-stock problems [DvHS⁺88b, DSvH88b, DSvH88c, DSvH88a, DSvH90]. In a CLP-language over finite domain constraints with a constraint solver based on local consistency techniques, a combinatorial problem is viewed as a constraint satisfaction problem. The main task of such a language is the implementation of specific *constraint solvers* [vH89a]. Local consistency based solvers are also called incomplete constraint solvers, since they do not solve a combinatorial problem but a relaxation of the problem. For deciding global consistency of a set of constraints, the programmer has to rely on enumeration. Handling combinatorial problems with local consistency techniques inside a CLP-language has the following features:

Modelling: Inherited from the logic-programming paradigm the use of CLP allows for a declarative modelling of combinatorial optimization problems. Aspects of a real-life problem that are not (or not naturally) expressible as constraints, i.e., interactivity, incrementality, rule-based conditions, dynamic modifications, etc., can be handled by exploiting the programming language aspect of CLP. This tight coupling of constraint solving and programming offers a flexibility that favors CLP w.r.t. pure 'modelling languages' like GAMS [MB93] and AMPL [FGK90].

Constraint Solving: Embedding local consistency techniques, coming from AI, into logic programming offers a convenient environment for handling constraints (CHIP = Constraint Handling In Prolog) arising in combinatorial optimization problems. Search and backtracking, the main paradigms for solving constraint satisfaction problems with local consistency techniques, are naturally available in PROLOG. This yields a clean and straightforward integration. Constraint solvers based on the constraint satisfaction approach can be implemented in a logic programming language with integrated local consistency based finite domain constraint solving featuring a short development time and great flexibility.

A different approach for handling combinatorial problems inside logic programming is to embed a complete constraint solver for combinatorial problems ensuring global consistency. This enables us to model and program with combinatorial problems without caring about constraint solving and hence emphasizes the declarative modelling aspect. Non-constraint aspects of the problem then can be freely mixed with constraints without worrying about semantic problems arising in the obligatory enumeration phase of a local consistency based solver. Furthermore, in such a language the constraint solver can exploit any constraint solving technique available, and thus use achievements from the operations research community, and need not rely on local consistency techniques combined with enumeration. Disadvantages of the local consistency approach are discussed in Section 2.4. The features of a CLP-system offering constraint solving for combinatorial problems are presented in Section 2.5.2.

Pseudo-Boolean constraints have long been used for modelling combinatorial problems in the operations research community. They can be viewed as a restriction of finite domain constraints where each variable has the special domain $\{0, 1\}$. Modelling with pseudo-Boolean constraints covers a large fraction of typical operations research problems like scheduling and sequencing [For59, For60, HR68, PWW69, Tah71], time-table scheduling, coding theory [HR68], plant location [Ham68], inter-city traffic [Rhy70], kinetic energy in spin glass models [KGV83], fault diagnosis [WYO81], cutting problems [CW77, Bea85], or supply support of space stations [FGGB66]. In mathematics and operations research solving optimization problems over pseudo-Boolean constraints ($\mathcal{PB}$) is also known as *constrained non-linear 0-1 programming* [HJM93]. We obtain the constraint logic programming language CLP($\mathcal{PB}$), introduced by Bockmayr [Boc91, Boc93b], when instantiating the computational domain $\mathcal{X}$ of the CLP($\mathcal{X}$)-scheme to pseudo-Boolean constraints.

Our aim is to design a complete constraint solver for pseudo-Boolean constraints that can be embedded in a logic programming language, i.e., in CLP($\mathcal{PB}$). The main differences w.r.t. a finite domain constraint solver based on local consistency techniques and our complete solver for pseudo-Boolean constraints are:

- *We always ensure global consistency.* Unlike local consistency based systems, we ensure at each point of the computation that the set of collected constraints is consistent. Hence, the CLP($\mathcal{X}$)-scheme gives us a clean semantics of our logic programming language.

- *We provide a solved form of the collected constraints.* A solved form of the collected constraints constitutes the output of a CLP-system. It should nicely describe the solution set of the modelled problem.

- *We support deciding entailment of constraints.* The solved form eases deciding entailment problems. The design of concurrent constraint logic programming (CCLP)languages necessitates a new functionality, namely deciding whether a constraint is entailed by a set of constraints, which we want to support. Additionally, entailment questions can be used for investigating a modelled problem.

In the context of constraint logic programming an appropriate solved form for finite domain constraints is not yet known. The restriction to the special domain $\{0, 1\}$ allows us to provide a constraint solver that fits the requirements of a constraint logic programming language, while a large fraction of combinatorial problems remains in the scope of the language. A CLP-language with a complete constraint solver encourages declarative programming and allows the use of constraints in order to guide the computation. A solved form that supports entailment allows a declarative reading of the solution set of the specified problem.

1.2 LOGIC-BASED PSEUDO-BOOLEAN CONSTRAINT SOLVING

Solving pseudo-Boolean constraints has a long tradition in the operations research community. In the last twenty years, most of the research in this field concentrated on linear programming based methods combined with branch-and-bound and polyhedral cutting plane techniques [NW88]. These methods have been very successful in solving some large instances of notoriously hard combinatorial problems, the most prominent example being the traveling salesman problem [PR91], by the development of polyhedral cutting plane techniques [Gom58, Chv73, CJP83, BCC94] yielding so-called branch-and-cut systems, e.g., MINTO [NSS94]. They have also been successfully applied to pure logical problems [Hoo88a]. On the other hand, logic-based methods for solving pseudo-Boolean problems have also been developed [HR68]. Interesting connections between cutting plane theory and logical inference have been established [Hoo88b, HF90, Hoo92b, Hoo94b, Hoo94a]. In this book we exploit a logic-based approach for solving pseudo-Boolean constraints in the context of constraint logic programming. We design an incremental logic-based constraint

solver that is able to ensure global consistency and provides a solved form that eases deciding entailment, which meets the requirements of constraint logic programming.

In the late sixties, Hammer and Rudeanu [HR68] wrote a classical book on Boolean methods in operations research. Recently, there has been renewed interest in logic-based methods for combinatorial optimization. Hooker [Hoo94b] states that "Logic-based methods provide not only another point of view but an entire body of theory and algorithms that parallels the classical material. Linear relaxations, cutting planes, facet-defining cuts, convex hulls, etc. all have logical parallels". We elaborate on this connection and propose a logical view of pseudo-Boolean constraints that is based on the deductive system *Generalized Resolution* [Hoo92a] and fits into the framework of constraint logic programming.

Granot and Hammer [GH71] showed how to express pseudo-Boolean constraints by an equivalent set of classical clauses. Pseudo-Boolean constraints could then be solved with resolution-based methods [Rob65] in an incremental way [Jac92]. The solved form would then be a set of prime implicates[1], which fits exactly the requirements imposed by constraint solving in the context of constraint logic programming. Since a clause is entailed by a complete set of prime implicates if and only if it is implied by a single clause in that set, one of the main requirements is satisfied. The solved form makes deciding entailment trivial. Since a set of clauses is inconsistent if and only if the empty clause is a prime implicate, the solved form provides an easy check of consistency. So why are we not satisfied with that solution? The problem is that transforming arbitrary pseudo-Boolean constraints into an equivalent set of clauses typically generates an exponential number of clauses [GG80], which caused the failure of early attempts of solving pseudo-Boolean problems with clausal-based methods.

Recently, Hooker [Hoo92a] has presented a deductive system *Generalized Resolution* working with linear pseudo-Boolean inequalities and *extended clauses*, an extension of classical clauses. Semantically, a classical Boolean clause states that at least one of its literals has to be true. So a classical Boolean clause

$$L_1 \vee \ldots \vee L_n$$

can be expressed as linear pseudo-Boolean inequality

$$L_1 + \cdots + L_n \geq 1 \; ,$$

---

[1]The word "prime implicant" is used when we work with disjunctive normal form, opposed to "prime implicate" with conjunctive normal form.

where a negated literal $\overline{X_i}$ corresponds to $(1-X_i)$ and the truth values *false* and *true* correspond to 0 and 1 respectively. Extended clauses generalize classical clauses by allowing values other than 1 on the right-hand side. An extended clause is of the form

$$L_1 + \cdots + L_n \geq d \ ,$$

expressing that at least d of the n literals in the extended clause have to be 1. Hooker [Hoo92a] shows that there exists an equivalent notion of prime implicates for a set of extended clauses, and the deductive system *Generalized Resolution* generates such a set of *prime extended clauses*. Prime implicates and prime extended clauses are the logical counterparts to facet-defining cuts [NW88], the strongest polyhedral cuts.

We propose the use of extended clauses as basic constraints in our complete constraint solver for pseudo-Boolean constraints [Bar93a, Bar92b], because

- there is a method for computing a solved form and, given the solved form, deciding satisfiability and logical entailment is easy,

- the solved form describes all possible solutions and is explanatory, because of the natural d out of n interpretation,

- extended clauses are more expressive than classical clauses and provide a much more compact representation of information while preserving computational manageability.

For the latter point, note that the equivalent representation of the extended clause $L_1 + \cdots + L_n \geq d$ using classical clauses without introducing new variables is

$$\bigwedge_{I \subseteq \{1,\ldots,n\}:|I|=n-d+1} \left(\vee_{i \in I} L_i \right) \ ,$$

a conjunction of $\binom{n}{n-d+1}$ classical clauses. The more compact representation often enables us to represent pseudo-Boolean constraints as an equivalent set of extended clauses, since the number of extended clauses needed is typically much smaller than the number of equivalent classical clauses.

When designing a pseudo-Boolean constraint solver based on extended clauses we are faced with two problems:

- Representing an arbitrary set of pseudo-Boolean constraints as an equivalent set of extended clauses.

- Computing the set of prime extended clauses equivalent to a set of extended clauses.

Both problems can be viewed as a reformulation of a set of constraints into an equivalent, but somehow simpler, set of constraints.

We break down the reformulation of pseudo-Boolean constraints into two parts. Given an arbitrary pseudo-Boolean constraint, we present reformulation techniques that allow us to

- linearize non-linear pseudo-Boolean constraints, i.e., reformulate an arbitrary pseudo-Boolean constraint as a set of linear pseudo-Boolean inequalities.

- transform a linear pseudo-Boolean inequality to an equivalent set of extended clauses.

Since there may be an exponential blow up in the size of the formulas when transforming them down to extended clauses, we present techniques that are sensitive to that blow up and only partially transform these formulas so that subsequent simplifications will make a full transformation easier. We also present a compact representation of pseudo-Boolean constraints that speed up the transformation process. In the context of constraint logic programming it is helpful to consider the set of already collected constraints while the transformation takes place. Thus, we can reduce the number of generated constraints and may generate immediately stronger constraints.

Powerful simplification of pseudo-Boolean constraints w.r.t. a set of pseudo-Boolean constraints is the key feature in order to process large pseudo-Boolean constraint sets. We present methods that strengthen linear pseudo-Boolean inequalities and extended clauses. We adapt the rules of the deductive system *Generalized Resolution* in order to generate *simplifying extended clauses*. The intention is that these extended clauses better approximate the set of prime extended clauses and thus approach the solved form. The simplification phase is the logical counterpart to the cut-generation phase in 0-1 integer programming. The simplifying extended clauses correspond to strong valid inequalities in polyhedral theory.

Pseudo-Boolean unit relaxation, a generalization of classical unit relaxation for linear pseudo-Boolean inequalities, is the logical counterpart to the linear

programming relaxation in polyhedral theory. We present a logical branch-and-bound method for solving 0-1 integer programming methods based on a generalization of the well-known Davis-Putnam [DP60] enumeration algorithm for solving clausal satisfiability problems and show that this method is comparably efficient to state-of-the-art branch-and-bound systems based on linear programming.

In the context of constraint logic programming we favor a pure logic cut system, since there should be no branching inside the constraint solver. We show how to generate logic cuts by considering the pseudo-Boolean unit relaxation of the problem. In combination with simplification methods, this pure cut generation system will generate a complete set of prime extended clauses equivalent to an arbitrary set of pseudo-Boolean constraints.

The logic cut generation techniques and reformulation methods can also be applied inside linear programming based methods. We demonstrate this with several examples, i.e., preprocessing, coefficient reduction, extended cover generation, and simplification techniques are evaluated in the context of polyhedral methods. Moreover, these techniques can also be made available within a logic programming language suitable for implementing constraint solvers, like local consistency based systems whose solving approach can also be viewed as a logic-based branch-and-bound system. Then the generation of problem-specific cuts can be implemented and the development of logic-based branch-and-cut systems is supported on the language level.

Using logic-based techniques for solving pseudo-Boolean problems does not entail a radically different solution strategy; mainly important polyhedral concepts are replaced by their logical counterparts. Instead of the linear programming relaxation, a discrete relaxation is solved. Cutting plane generation techniques are replaced by the generation of logical implications. Modelling and solving experience collected by the operations research community can hence carry over to the logic-based approach. Furthermore, the logic view of pseudo-Boolean problems can be more natural than the polyhedral view. It turns out that exploiting the logic structure of a pseudo-Boolean problem is advantageous if the exploitation of the polyhedral structure seems to be inefficient or is just too complex. Logic-based methods already have found their way into polyhedral approaches. For example, the generation of cover inequalities, which are in fact logical implications of pseudo-Boolean constraints, has been widely recognized as an effective method in practice. Further exploration of logic-based methods and their combination with polyhedral approaches can yield a large contribution to the solution of pseudo-Boolean problems.

2

CONSTRAINT LOGIC
PROGRAMMING

The declarative paradigms *constraint solving* and *logic programming* are successfully merged in constraint logic programming. Integrating constraint solving techniques into logic programming increases expressibility, efficiency, and flexibility and therefore encourages declarative programming. Efficient special purpose algorithms, coming from mathematics, operations research, or artificial intelligence, can be embedded into the logic programming language. The logic programming language allows one to declaratively state the problem, which is solved by the underlying constraint solver. Besides being a high-level declarative interface to the constraint solver, the logic programming language allows the implementation of subproblems that do not fit into the constraint domain.

First, we introduce the basic concepts of constraint logic programming by an example in Section 2.1. A more formal definition, which can be skipped on a first reading, is given in Section 2.2. We extract the special functionality of a constraint solver in the context of constraint logic programming in Section 2.3. The local consistency approach for solving combinatorial problems embedded in logic programming is compared with complete constraint solving inside CLP in Section 2.4. We introduce the constraint logic programming language CLP($\mathcal{PB}$), which handles combinatorial problems using pseudo-Boolean constraints in Section 2.5, and discuss programming examples for modelling typical practical problems. Finally, we review and compare existing logic programming systems for handling combinatorial problems in Section 2.6.

2.1 CLP BY EXAMPLE

We illustrate some crucial CLP-concepts by an example. For a detailed introduction in PROLOG we refer to [CM87]. In the program-fragments we use an *italic* font for constraints over $\mathcal{X}$. Here, $\mathcal{X} = \mathcal{PB}$, i.e., finite domain variables restricted to the domain $\{0,1\}$ and constraints stated over these variables. For the rest of the code we use a `typewriter` font. Variables begin with an uppercase character.

Programming in a CLP($\mathcal{X}$)-language means declaring *facts* and *rules* about objects and their relationship, including constraints over $\mathcal{X}$. Facts and rules are also called *predicates*. Suppose we want to declare a relation `sequence` that holds for all lists of Boolean values where no consecutive chain of 3 zeros is allowed. A list containing the elements $X_1, X_2, \ldots, X_n$ is denoted by $[X_1, X_2, \ldots, X_n]$. Hence, the relation `sequence` consists of all lists

$$\{[X_1, X_2, \ldots, X_n] \mid X_i + X_{i+1} + X_{i+2} \geq 1 \text{ for all } 1 \leq i \leq n - 2\} \ ,$$

where the X_i are Boolean variables and $X_i + X_{i+1} + X_{i+2} \geq 1$ is a pseudo-Boolean constraint.

A CLP-program that defines the relation `sequence` consists of 3 facts and one rule. First, we state the facts that the empty list and the one- and two-element-lists are `sequences`.

```
sequence([]).
sequence([X]).
sequence([X,Y]).
```

For lists that have more than two elements we define a recursive rule modelling the `sequence` property[1].

```
sequence([X,Y,Z|L]) :-
        X + Y + Z ≥ 1,
        sequence([Y,Z|L]).
```

The rule can be read as "A list containing at least three elements, where X, Y, Z are the first, second, and third elements respectively and L is the remaining list,

---

[1]The term $[X_1, X_2, \ldots, X_k | L]$ denotes the first k elements of a list by $X_1, X_2, \ldots, X_k$ and the remaining list by L.

is a sequence if $X + Y + Z \geq 1$ holds and the list without the first element, i.e., $[Y, Z | L]$, is a sequence".

Once we have a CLP-program consisting of facts and rules we can ask *queries* w.r.t. this program. For example, we might be interested in knowing whether the list $[A, A, B, B, C, C]$ is a sequence. The query

$$?\text{-}sequence([A, A, B, B, C, C]).$$

gives rise to the answer

$$A + B \geq 1,$$
$$B + C \geq 1$$
yes.

This can be read as "The list $[A, A, B, B, C, C]$ is a sequence if $A + B \geq 1$ and $B + C \geq 1$ holds". Hence, in CLP, constraints constitute the output of a program. Operationally, this query is processed as follows. We search for a fact or a rule applicable to the query $sequence([A, A, B, B, C, C])$. If there are several applicable rules or facts these possibilities are tried on backtracking. Since the list $[A, A, B, B, C, C]$ contains more than two elements none of the facts apply, but the rule does. If $X = A, Y = A, Z = B$, and $L = [B, C, C]$, then the rule says that $[A, A, B, B, C, C]$ is a sequence if $A + A + B \geq 1$ and $[A, B, B, C, C]$ is a sequence. In other words, we replace the initial query by

$$A + A + B \geq 1, sequence([A, B, B, C, C]) \ .$$

Computation now continues until only constraints remain or no rule or fact is applicable in which case *backtracking* takes place. Note that in order to apply the rule we have generated some equality constraints, which equalize the query and the left-hand side of the rule. The equality constraints together with the pseudo-Boolean constraints of the rule are added to the so-called *constraint store*. A rule or fact is only applicable if the constraint store remains consistent after adding the generated constraints, that is, the constraint store must admit a least one solution. Since rules and facts can be applied several times, all variables in a rule or fact are replaced by fresh ones at each invocation. We model this by subscripting the variables in the rules and facts by new indices whenever they are applied. For illustrative purposes we give the complete computation sequence of the previous query, i.e., the state of the constraint store and the remaining queries after a rule or fact has been applied.

`sequence([A, A, B, B, C, C]).`

$A = X_1, A = Y_1, B = Z_1, X_1 + Y_1 + Z_1 \geq 1,$
   `sequence([A, B, B, C, C]).`

$A = X_2, B = Y_2, B = Z_2, X_2 + Y_2 + Z_2 \geq 1, A = X_1, A = Y_1, B = Z_1, X_1 + Y_1 + Z_1 \geq 1,$
   `sequence([B, B, C, C]).`

$B = X_3, B = Y_3, C = Z_3, X_3 + Y_3 + Z_3 \geq 1, A = X_2, B = Y_2, B = Z_2, X_2 + Y_2 + Z_2 \geq 1, A = X_1, A = Y_1, B = Z_1, X_1 + Y_1 + Z_1 \geq 1,$
   `sequence([B, C, C]).`

$B = X_4, C = Y_4, C = Z_4, X_4 + Y_4 + Z_4 \geq 1, B = X_3, B = Y_3, C = Z_3, X_3 + Y_3 + Z_3 \geq 1, A = X_2, B = Y_2, B = Z_2, X_2 + Y_2 + Z_2 \geq 1, A = X_1, A = Y_1, B = Z_1, X_1 + Y_1 + Z_1 \geq 1,$
   `sequence([C, C]).`

$B = X_4, C = Y_4, C = Z_4, X_4 + Y_4 + Z_4 \geq 1, B = X_3, B = Y_3, C = Z_3, X_3 + Y_3 + Z_3 \geq 1, A = X_2, B = Y_2, B = Z_2, X_2 + Y_2 + Z_2 \geq 1, A = X_1, A = Y_1, B = Z_1, X_1 + Y_1 + Z_1 \geq 1.$

For all but the last step the rule has been applied. By replacing the X_i, Y_i and Z_i with their defining equalities, we see that the last state is equivalent to

$$B + C + C \geq 1, B + B + C \geq 1, A + B + B \geq 1, A + A + B \geq 1, B = X_4, C = Y_4, C = Z_4,$$
$$B = X_3, B = Y_3, C = Z_3, A = X_2, B = Y_2, B = Z_2, A = X_1, A = Y_1, B = Z_1.$$

Note that both $B + C + C \geq 1$ and $B + B + C \geq 1$ are equivalent to $B + C \geq 1$ and both $A + B + B \geq 1$ and $A + A + B \geq 1$ are equivalent to $A + B \geq 1$. Boolean variables that do not occur in the query should not occur in the answer. The auxiliary Boolean variables introduced by the execution of the CLP-program are projected away and the answer constraint $A + B \geq 1, B + C \geq 1$ is hence implied (and not necessarily equivalent) to the constraints in the final state.

Next, we trace the execution of a query that has no solution.

$?- A + C \leq 1,$ `sequence([A, A, 0, 0, C, C]).`

The computed answer is **no**. We start with a similar sequence of states, but the fourth computation state is then

$$0 = X_3, 0 = Y_3, C = Z_3, X_3 + Y_3 + Z_3 \geq 1, A = X_2, 0 = Y_2, 0 = Z_2, X_2 + Y_2 + Z_2 \geq 1, A = X_1, A = Y_1, 0 = Z_1, X_1 + Y_1 + Z_1 \geq 1, A + C \leq 1,$$
$$\texttt{sequence([0, C, C])} \;.$$

which is equivalent to

$$0 + 0 + C \geq 1, A + 0 + 0 \geq 1, A + A + 0 \geq 1, 0 = X_3, 0 = Y_3, C = Z_3, A = X_2, 0 = Y_2, 0 = Z_2, A = X_1, A = Y_1, 0 = Z_1, A + C \leq 1,$$
$$\texttt{sequence([0, C, C])} \;.$$

Since $0+0+C \geq 1$ implies $C = 1$ and $A+A+0 \geq 1$ implies $A = 1$, we know that $A+C \leq 1$ is violated. Therefore, the constraint set is unsatisfiable, and in CLP no further computation is allowed. Since no other rule or fact is applicable on backtracking, the query fails and yields the answer **no**. This means that whatever the Boolean values of A and C are, the list $[A, A, 0, 0, C, C]$ is not a sequence if $A + C \leq 1$.

Finally, we show queries with their answers that nicely exemplify the descriptive power of constraints constituting the answer. The query

$$?-\texttt{sequence}([A, B, \overline{A}, \overline{B}, A]).$$

where $\overline{X}$, the negation of a Boolean value, is an abbreviation for $1 - X$, yields the answer **yes** with no constraints imposed. From this we can conclude that *every* five element list of Boolean values where the successor of the successor is the negation of itself is a **sequence** regardless of the actual Boolean values. As we have seen not only simple Boolean variables can be used in a query but also more complicated pseudo-Boolean expressions. Consider for example the query

$$?-\texttt{sequence}([A \cdot B, \overline{A} \cdot B, C \cdot A, A + B, D + \overline{A}]).$$

Note that also non-linear expressions are used. By applying the rule of our CLP-program the first time, we dynamically create and add the Boolean equations

$$
\begin{aligned}
A \cdot B &= X_1 \\
\overline{A} \cdot B &= Y_1 \\
C \cdot A &= Z_1
\end{aligned}
$$

together with the constraint $X_1 + Y_1 + Z_1 \geq 1$. These constraints are checked for satisfiability and computation then continues. At the end of computation and after projecting away auxiliary Boolean variables we obtain the answer

$A + B \geq 1$,
$B + C \geq 1$
yes.

as for the query ?-sequence($[A, A, B, B, C, C]$). This answer gives a nice and concise description of a complicated dynamically created pseudo-Boolean problem. Furthermore, since the Boolean variable D does not occur in the answer constraint, we know that the property of being a sequence does not depend on the value of D. Hence, constraint logic programming allows one to model, solve and investigate pseudo-Boolean problems. We have the following key features of constraint logic programming [JM94]:

- Constraints are used to specify the query as well as the answers.

- During execution, new variables and constraints are created.

- The collection of constraints in every state is tested as a whole for satisfiability before execution proceeds further and thus allows for control of execution.

2.2   SEMANTICS

The declarative and operational semantics of a $\text{CLP}(\mathcal{X})$-language is based on the semantics of pure logic programs, but parameterized by a choice of $\mathcal{X}$, the domain of computation and constraints. Let $\mathcal{X}$ be a 4-tuple $(\Sigma, \mathfrak{D}, \mathfrak{L}, \mathfrak{T})$, where Σ is a signature, $\mathfrak{D}$ is a Σ-structure, and $\mathfrak{T}$ is a first order Σ-theory [JM94]. The domain of computation is $\mathfrak{D}$, over which constraints of a class $\mathfrak{L}$ of Σ-formulas can be expressed, and $\mathfrak{T}$ axiomatizes properties of $\mathfrak{D}$. We assume that Σ contains the binary predicate $=$, which is interpreted as identity in $\mathfrak{D}$.

A *constraint domain* $(\mathfrak{D}, \mathfrak{L})$ is *solution compact* [JM94] if every element in $\mathfrak{D}$ can be defined by a conjunction of constraints of $\mathfrak{L}$ and if the negation of each constraint of $\mathfrak{L}$ can be defined by a disjunction of constraints of $\mathfrak{L}$. The corresponding theory $\mathfrak{T}$ is *satisfaction complete* [JM94] w.r.t. $\mathfrak{L}$ if either $\mathfrak{T} \models \exists C$ or

$\mathfrak{T} \models \not\exists C$ for all $C \in \mathfrak{L}$. A solution compact constraint domain with a satisfaction complete theory constitutes an appropriate framework for a $\text{CLP}(\mathcal{X})$-language.

A $\text{CLP}(\mathcal{X})$-program consists of a finite set of constraint rules of the form

$$h :\text{-} b_1, \ldots, b_n \quad ,$$

where h is an atom and the b_i are either atoms over a signature Σ', not sharing any function or predicate symbols with Σ, or a constraint of $\mathfrak{L}$. A $\text{CLP}(\mathcal{X})$-goal is of the form

$$?\text{-}b_1, \ldots, b_n \quad .$$

By the results of Jaffar and Lassez [JL87, JM94], we have the existence of a canonical domain of computation, the existence of a least and greatest model semantics, the existence of a least and greatest fixed point semantics, soundness and completeness results for successful derivation of the underlying implementation model, soundness and completeness results for finitely failed derivations of the underlying implementation model, and soundness and completeness results for negation-as-failure.

An operational model [JM94] that describes the operational semantics of many CLP-systems is given by a transition system on *states*, i.e., tuples $\langle A, C \rangle$, where A is a multiset of atoms and C is a multiset of constraints[2], also called *constraint store*. The special state $\bot$ denotes failure. Intuitively, A is the set of not yet considered goals and C is the set of constraints collected so far. We assume to have a *computation rule* that selects an element of A and an appropriate transition rule for each state. The transition system is parameterized by a predicate consistent and a function infer corresponding to the specific constraint solver. An initial CLP-goal ?-$b_1, \ldots, b_n$ is represented by the state $\langle \{b_1, \ldots, b_n\}, \emptyset \rangle$. Suppose that the computation rule selects a constraint c in A, then rewriting the state $\langle A, C \rangle$ is defined by

$$\langle A, C \rangle \rightarrow \begin{cases} \langle A \setminus \{c\}, C' \rangle & \text{if} \quad \begin{array}{c} \text{consistent}(C \cup \{c\}) \\ C' = \text{infer}(C \cup \{c\}) \end{array} \\ \bot & \text{if} \quad \neg\text{consistent}(C \cup \{c\}) \; . \end{cases}$$

Suppose that the computation rule selects an atom a in A and a constraint rule h :- $b_1, \ldots, b_n$ of the constraint logic program such that a and h have the

---

[2]Note that C also contains equality constraints over finite trees over the signature Σ', introduced by unification when constraint rules are applied.

same predicate symbol, then

$$\langle A, C \rangle \rightarrow \begin{cases} \langle (A \setminus \{a\}) \cup \{b_1, \ldots, b_n\}, C' \rangle & \text{if} & \begin{aligned} & \text{consistent}(C \cup \{h = a\}) \\ & C' = \text{infer}(C \cup \{h = a\}) \end{aligned} \\ \perp & \text{if} & \neg\text{consistent}(C \cup \{h = a\}) \ , \end{cases}$$

where $h = a$ is an abbreviation for the conjunction of equations between corresponding arguments of a and h, extends the transition system $\rightarrow$. If there is an atom a in A, but no constraint rule in the CLP-program having the same predicate symbol, we have a failure.

$$\langle A, C \rangle \rightarrow \perp$$

The predicate consistent checks for consistency of a set of constraints C and is defined by

$$\text{consistent}(C) \quad \text{if and only if} \quad \mathfrak{D} \models \exists \vec{x} \colon C$$

where $\vec{x}$ is the set of free variables in C. The function infer is responsible for simplifying a set of constraints C. We require that

$$\mathfrak{D} \models \text{infer}(C) \Leftrightarrow C$$

and so preserve equivalence of the simplified constrained set. Jaffar and Maher [JM94] present a more sophisticated transition system that allows the distinction between active and passive constraints and the use of an incomplete consistency check. Furthermore, the infer function is split and a separate simplification transition rule is introduced. The presented operational semantics of a CLP-system described by $\rightarrow$ is called "ideal" in [JM94].

A *derivation* is a finite or infinite sequence of transition states

$$\langle A_0, C_0 \rangle \rightarrow \cdots \rightarrow \langle A_i, C_i \rangle \rightarrow \cdots \ .$$

A *final state* is a state that cannot be rewritten by $\rightarrow$. A derivation is *successful* if its final state is of the form $\langle \emptyset, C \rangle$. Let G be a goal with free variables $\vec{x}$ that gives rise to a successful derivation with final state $\langle \emptyset, C \rangle$. Then $\exists \vec{x} : C$ is the *answer constraint* of this derivation. A derivation is *failed* if the final state is $\perp$. A derivation is *fair* if it is failed or if for all i each $a \in A_i$ is rewritten in a later transition. A computation rule is fair if it generates only fair derivations. A CLP-goal is finitely failed if all derivations from the state representing the goal are failed.

The *computation tree* of a goal for a CLP-program in a CLP-system is a tree with nodes labeled by states, where the state of a direct subnode of a node is the state

of the node rewritten once by →. The root node of the tree has as label the state of the initial CLP-goal. In the computation tree each possible derivation for each possible computation rule is a branch of the computation tree. Executing a CLP-program, i.e., finding the answers of a CLP-goal w.r.t. a CLP-program, means searching all non-failed finite derivations in the computation tree and returning their answer constraint.

Most CLP-systems employ a standard depth-first search, which is not fair. The soundness and completeness results for an "ideal" CLP-system can be found in [JM94].

2.3 CONSTRAINT SOLVING

Let us investigate the domain specific predicate consistent and the function infer. We neglect the equality constraints over finite trees[3]. Along a derivation we have to perform a sequence of consistency checks, where at each step a new set of constraints is incrementally added to the previously consistent constraint set. For reasons of efficiency, it is advantageous to use information from the previous consistency checks in the sequence of current consistency checks. Simplification of the current constraint set by the function infer is one of the possible ways to achieve incrementality.

We again consider finite domain constraints over the domain $\{0, 1\}$ and follow a derivation of the goal

$$?\text{-}b_1(A, B, C), b_2(A, B, C), b_3(A, B, C)$$

w.r.t. the CLP-program consisting of the three constraint rules

$$b_1(A, B, C) \; :\text{-} \; A + B \geq 1$$
$$b_2(A, B, C) \; :\text{-} \; A + (1 - B) \geq 1$$
$$b_3(A, B, C) \; :\text{-} \; A + C \geq 1 \; .$$

---

[3]Strictly speaking, a CLP($\mathcal{X}$)-language is a statically typed language, i.e., each argument in an atom and each variable must be used in a consistent way. Here, we also neglect the type problems and assume the presence of only well typed CLP($\mathcal{X}$)-programs [HJM+92].

First, assume that $\mathsf{infer}(C) = C$ for all constraints C. Then a possible finite derivation sequence[4] is

$$\langle \{A + B \geq 1, A + (1 - B) \geq 1, A + C \geq 1\}, \emptyset \rangle \rightarrow$$
$$\langle \{A + (1 - B) \geq 1, A + C \geq 1\}, \{A + B \geq 1\} \rangle \rightarrow$$
$$\langle \{A + C \geq 1\}, \{A + B \geq 1, A + (1 - B) \geq 1\} \rangle \rightarrow$$
$$\langle \emptyset, \{A + B \geq 1, A + (1 - B) \geq 1, A + C \geq 1\} \rangle$$

since the constraint sets of all states are consistent. The satisfiability check performed by consistent has to recheck satisfiability from scratch 4 times. Next, suppose that we have an infer that is more clever, i.e., infer is able to detect that $\{A + B \geq 1, A + (1 - B) \geq 1\}$ is equivalent to $\{A = 1\}$. Then the derivation sequence is

$$\langle \{A + B \geq 1, A + (1 - B) \geq 1, A + C \geq 1\}, \emptyset \rangle \rightarrow$$
$$\langle \{A + (1 - B) \geq 1, A + C \geq 1\}, \{A + B \geq 1\} \rangle \rightarrow$$
$$\langle \{A + C \geq 1\}, \{A = 1\} \rangle \rightarrow$$
$$\langle \emptyset, \{A = 1, A + C \geq 1\} \rangle \ .$$

and checking consistency of the fourth state is much simpler. Note that the constraint set of the third state entails the newly added constraint of the constraint set of the fourth state. Therefore, consistency is trivially ensured and the new constraint is not needed. Given an infer[5] that eliminates entailed constraints, we obtain the derivation sequence

$$\langle \{A + B \geq 1, A + (1 - B) \geq 1, A + C \geq 1\}, \emptyset \rangle \rightarrow$$
$$\langle \{A + (1 - B) \geq 1, A + C \geq 1\}, \{A + B \geq 1\} \rangle \rightarrow$$
$$\langle \{A + C \geq 1\}, \{A = 1\} \rangle \rightarrow$$
$$\langle \emptyset, \{A = 1\} \rangle \ .$$

Therefore, an *incremental check of consistency* for a set of constraints and *deciding entailment* of a constraint w.r.t. a set constraints are the basic operations to be provided in an implementation of consistent and infer.

Deciding entailment of a set of constraints is a basic functionality of a constraint solver in CCLP-systems [Sar89, HJ90, AK93, SHW93a]. This functionality is used for the synchronization of concurrent processes. We refer to [JM94, PS95] for an overview of CCLP-languages and the requirements on a constraint solver for CCLP-systems.

---

[4]For the sake of simplicity, we neglect the introduction of new variables like $A_i = A$.

[5]In an implementation infer and consistent are not strictly separated, but work hand in hand, e.g., it may be useful to eliminate entailed constraints before checking satisfiability.

Projecting a set of constraints onto a set of variables in order to eliminate extra variables not occurring in the initial CLP-goal has to be done at the end of computation in order to present a user-friendly answer constraint. Additionally, it may be useful to immediately project away variables that do not occur in the initial CLP-goal and that are no longer visible in the computation of the following states, i.e., no new constraints can be added involving these variables.

When we abstract away the inference machine from the operational semantics, we see that the following operations provide the basis for an implementation for a constraint solver over a specific domain [JM94].

consistency: Given a set of constraints $C \in \mathfrak{L}$, decide whether the set is consistent, i.e., whether $\mathfrak{D} \models \exists \vec{x} : C$, where $\vec{x}$ is the set of free variables in C.

entailment: Given a set of constraints $C \in \mathfrak{L}$, decide whether a constraint $C' \in \mathfrak{L}$ is entailed by C, i.e., whether $\mathfrak{D} \models \forall \vec{x} : C \Rightarrow C'$, where $\vec{x}$ is the set of free variables in C and C'.

projection: Let C be a set of constraints in $\mathfrak{L}$ and $\vec{x}$ be the set of free variables in C. Let $\vec{y} \subseteq \vec{x}$ be a set of variables that we want to project away. The problem is to calculate a simplified form C' of the constraint $\exists \vec{y} : C$. We require that $\mathfrak{D} \models C \Rightarrow C'$.

Instantiating the computational domain $\mathcal{X}$ of the CLP($\mathcal{X}$)-scheme and providing a constraint solver for the specific selected constraint domain has been an active research area in recent years. Before we formally instantiate the computational domain $\mathcal{X}$ of the CLP($\mathcal{X}$)-scheme to pseudo-Boolean constraints in Section 2.5, we will first point out some conceptual differences and semantic as well as practical problems that arise when viewing a logic-programming language with a local consistency based solver as a CLP-*language* over finite domain constraints.

2.4 LOCAL CONSISTENCY AND CLP

Logic programming languages with a local consistency based solver for finite domain constraints, like CHIP, is commonly viewed as a constraint logic programming language over finite domain constraints. However, contrary to common belief, this is not the case. As already mentioned, such a language is

intended to ease the *implementation of user-defined constraint solvers using constraint satisfaction techniques* [vH89a] and therefore has a different intention than a CLP-language offering complete constraint solving of combinatorial problems. In the following we will demonstrate with examples what happens if one views a logic programming language with local consistency methods as CLP-language over finite domain constraints. We point out the pitfalls and problems and also motivate the need for a real CLP-language for modelling and solving combinatorial problems.

2.4.1   Local Consistency

Since combinatorial problems fall into the class of NP-complete problems, van Hentenryck [vH89a] concludes that "backtracking is an important technique for solving these problems". Since backtracking is naturally available in PROLOG, in CHIP the "most important operation on constraints ...a test for consistency" [JM94] of the current set of finite domain constraints is relaxed to local consistency and global consistency is no longer ensured. Instead, the programmer has to ensure global consistency by an extra enumeration predicate. A typical CLP-program for a system based on local consistency techniques therefore has the form

```
problem(<Variables>) :-
        <state constraints over Variables>,
        <enumerate domain of Variables>.
```

The search for a solution of the collected constraints is carried out by the PROLOG backtracking mechanism and the finite domain constraint solver is responsible for pruning the search tree. Logically, there is no need for an extra enumeration predicate. Given an "ideal" [JM94] constraint solver for finite domain constraints, a sufficient formulation of a CLP-program over finite domain constraints is

```
problem(<Variables>) :-
        <state constraints over Variables>.
```

For this kind of CLP-programs, a finite domain solver based on local consistency techniques will not generate a concise and simplified solved form. Consider the following query and assume that all variables are restricted to the domain $\{0, 1\}$.

?-$A + B \geq 1, A + (1 - B) \geq 1.$

The answer of a constraint logic programming language based on local consistency techniques (here we use ECLIPSE [MAC+89], which has a similar finite domain constraint solver as CHIP) is

Delayed goals: $A + B \geq 1, A - B \geq 0$ yes.

which is correct, since the constraint set is satisfiable, but not what we expect from a CLP-system. By adding an extra enumeration predicate to the previous query

?-$A + B \geq 1, A + (1 - B) \geq 1, \texttt{enum}([A, B]).$

we obtain the following solutions from ECLIPSE.

$A = 1, B = 0$ More?   (;) ;
$A = 1, B = 1$ yes.

By investigating the two solutions, we see immediately that the variable A has to be 1 for all possible solutions and that the variable B is arbitrary. Thus, a *good* answer of a CLP-system to the query

?-$A + B \geq 1, A + (1 - B) \geq 1.$

is

$A = 1$ yes.

The behavior is worse if the set of collected constraints is unsatisfiable. Assume again that all variables are restricted to the domain $\{0, 1\}$ and consider the following query.

?-$A + B \geq 1, A + 1 - B \geq 1, 1 - A + B \geq 1, 1 - A + 1 - B \geq 1.$

The answer of ECLIPSE,

Delayed goals: $A + B \geq 1, A - B \geq 0, B - A \geq 0, 1 - A - B \geq 0$ yes.

in particular, the yes is wrong, which can be verified by adding an extra enumeration predicate.

?- $A + B \geq 1, A + 1 - B \geq 1, 1 - A + B \geq 1, 1 - A + 1 - B \geq 1$,
   enum($[A, B]$).
no.

Unfortunately, adding an extra enumeration predicate does not ensure detection of failure in practice. Consider the following CLP-program over finite domain constraints, where the domain of the variables is restricted to $\{0, 1\}$.

f($[A, B]$) :-
       $A + B \geq 1, A + 1 - B \geq 1, 1 - A + B \geq 1, 1 - A + 1 - B \geq 1$,
       f($[A, B]$).

In ECLIPSE the query

?-f($[A, B]$), enum($[A, B]$).

goes into an infinite loop.   If the underlying constraint solver ensures global consistency of the collected constraints, then the computed correct answer is no.

2.4.2   Global Consistency

Since the problems we consider are NP-complete, in the worst case assuring global consistency may require an exponential computation time in problem size (unless P = NP). Therefore, it has been argued that ensuring global consistency in the context of constraint logic programming is not efficiently achievable.

It is obvious that a CLP-program over finite domain constraints with a constraint solver based on local consistency techniques has to have an extra enu-

meration predicate in order to produce correct results. The advantage of delaying constraint solving until all constraints are known is that all constraints can be used for pruning the search space. So it might be the case that assuring global consistency at each step of the computation requires exponential computation time w.r.t. the problem size, whereas deciding consistency of the complete constraint set at the end is trivial. However, we feel that for a large fraction of practical problems this is not the case. In particular, this is true for optimization problems, which are formulated as

```
problem(<Variables>) :-
        <state constraints over Variables>,
        <maximize objective function over Variables>.
```

Typically, the constraint set that is generated by `<state constraints over Variables>` is easily shown to be consistent. Only optimizing the objective function is problematic. For these kind of problems, assuring global consistency is no problem.

Furthermore, we feel that if executing a CLP-program generates an unsatisfiable set of constraints, one should be immediately informed. This enables one to react at the precise point of failure. For example, consider the following fragment of a CLP-program.

```
problem(<Variables>) :-
        constraintA(<Variables>),
        constraintB(<Variables>),
        constraintC(<Variables>).
constraintB(<Variables>) :-
        <state constraints over Variables>.
constraintB(<Variables>) :-
        <react to failure>.
```

Given the common execution mechanism of logic programs, the programmer intends to react immediately in `<react to failure>` to an inconsistency encountered when adding the constraints of the first rule of `constraintB` to the current constraint set. Suppose that adding the constraint of the first rule of `constraintB` generates an unsatisfiable set of constraints, which is of course detected by a constraint solver assuring global consistency. As intended by the programmer, `<react to failure>` is invoked. Assume that a constraint solver

based on local consistency techniques does not detect inconsistency, then computation goes on and the constraints of constraintC are added. Inconsistency is then detected by the extra enumeration predicate, but the precise point of failure is not known. Suppose that constraintC invoked heavy computation; it was useless, since it must be undone by backtracking in order to execute <react to failure>. In this case, providing a complete solver increases efficiency. Suppose that constraintC is implemented in the same way as constraintB, i.e., the programmer intends to react to failure caused by adding the constraints of constraintC. In case of inconsistency caused by constraintB, backtracking, caused by the failure of the extra enumeration predicate, will nevertheless first try to fix the problem by <react to failure> of constraintC, which is not what the programmer intended.

2.4.3   Solved Form and Entailment

For a CLP-program the simplified set of constraints collected at the end of execution is called the *answer constraint* and constitutes the solved form. It should provide a *good* and *explanative* description of all solutions of the current constraint set. An example is the answer constraint $A = 1$ to the previous query

$$?\text{-}A + B \geq 1, A + (1 - B) \geq 1.$$

In our opinion a good and explanative solved form should also allow entailment of constraints to be easily tested. Deciding entailment of constraints allows the interpretation of the presented results and enables the programmer to better understand the dependencies of the specified constraint problem. Furthermore, deciding entailment of constraints is essential for a new class of declarative programming languages; Concurrent Constraint Logic Programming (CCLP) languages [SHW93a, FHJ91], based on the ask and tell framework defined by Saraswat [Sar88, Sar89]. In CCLP-languages, deciding entailment and disentailment of constraints is needed for identifying determinate computation paths. Moreover, program execution can be guided not only by detecting inconsistency of a constraint set, but also by detecting entailment of constraints w.r.t. the current constraint set.

In CLP-languages based on local consistency techniques, like CHIP, there is no solved form for finite domain constraints and thus there is no obvious way to decide entailment of constraints, besides assuming the converse and trying to show unsatisfiability by enumeration. Providing a solved form is nevertheless

necessary if we want to avoid an extra enumeration predicate. Furthermore, a solved form is typically more compact than an explicit enumeration of all possible solutions. For example, the query

$$?\text{-} \ A + B + C + D + E + F + G + H + I + J + K + L + M +$$
$$N + O + P + Q + R + S + T + U + V + W + X + Y + Z \geq 13 \ .$$

has $\sum_{i=13}^{26} \binom{26}{i} = 38,754,732$ different solutions, whereas the solved form is simply the constraint itself, naturally stating that at least 13 out of the 26 variables have to be 1. Constraints stating that at least n out of m variables have to be 1, appropriate for combinatorial problems, are the kind of constraints that are allowed in our solved form.

2.4.4 Conclusion

Constraint logic programming is intended to provide a declarative programming environment where subproblems over a specific domain are handled by a domain specific constraint solver. The semantic problems of current PROLOG implementations, caused by the standard PROLOG execution of logic programs, should, whenever possible, not be additionally merged with semantic problems caused by incomplete constraint solvers. Providing a complete constraint solver surely enhances the declarative reading of CLP-programs and encourages writing of declarative programs. Furthermore, the underlying constraint solving techniques can be enhanced without changing the program behavior. Hence, there is a need for a CLP-language solving combinatorial problems. Despite the fact that a complete constraint solver necessarily has to solve an NP-complete problem at each step, computation time need not always be exponential. Local consistency based methods also solve NP-complete problems, although the possible exponential blow up is bound to happen in the enumeration phase. Although both approaches essentially attack the same kind of problems, their application areas differ. On one hand, if the specified problem can be attacked by the underlying complete solver, there is no need to use local consistency based techniques and write a specific solver. If global consistency is needed because there are problem aspects that call for the control of execution by deciding NP-complete problems or if a description of the complete solution set is required, a CLP-system including a complete solver is the only possible choice. On the other hand, if local consistency based techniques have proven to be applicable to a class of constraint satisfaction problems and special heuristics, enumeration orderings and other tricks must be included, then writing

a constraint solver in a logic programming system including local consistency techniques is the right choice. Hence, there is no a priori better approach.

2.5   LOGIC PROGRAMMING WITH PSEUDO-BOOLEAN CONSTRAINTS

The constraint logic programming language $\text{CLP}(\mathcal{PB})$, introduced by Bockmayr [Boc91, Boc92b], aims to be a logic programming environment suitable for various applications where 0-1 or pseudo-Boolean problems naturally arise, which is the case for many AI-applications and operations research [BB93]. In this section we formally define the constraint domain $\mathcal{PB}$ of pseudo-Boolean constraints and instantiate the $\mathcal{X}$ in the $\text{CLP}(\mathcal{X})$-scheme to $\mathcal{PB}$. We then illustrate modelling combinatorial problems and programming techniques in $\text{CLP}(\mathcal{PB})$ by some typical examples.

2.5.1 $\text{CLP}(\mathcal{PB})$

A pseudo-Boolean function is a mapping $f : \{0,1\}^n \to \mathbb{Z}$, where $\mathbb{Z}$ denotes the ring of integer numbers. Pseudo-Boolean functions are a generalization of Boolean functions, since the codomain of Boolean functions, $\{0,1\}$, is enlarged to $\mathbb{Z}$. First, we define a signature that allows the representation of pseudo-Boolean functions as pseudo-Boolean terms.

Definition 2.5.1 [Boc91] Let Σ_{psbool} be a signature with the sort symbol integer and the set of function symbols

$$
F_{\text{psbool}} := \begin{array}{lll}
\{ & 0,1 & : & \to \text{integer}, \\
& +,-,\cdot & : & \text{integer} \times \text{integer} \to \text{integer}, \\
& - & : & \text{integer} \to \text{integer}\}
\end{array}
$$

and let

$$\text{Var}_{\text{bool}} := \{X, Y, Z, X_1, X_2, \ldots\}$$

denote a countable infinite set of Boolean variables, i.e., the domain of the variables is $\{0,1\}$. The terms in the term algebra $\mathcal{T}(F_{\text{psbool}}, \text{Var}_{\text{bool}})$ are called *pseudo-Boolean terms*. By interpreting the function symbols $+, \cdot, -$ as the usual arithmetic operations on integer numbers any pseudo-Boolean term $t \in \mathcal{T}(F_{\text{psbool}}, \text{Var}_{\text{bool}})$ containing n Boolean variables *generates* an n-ary pseudo-Boolean function $f : \{0,1\}^n \to \mathbb{Z}$.

We allow the abbreviation $n \cdot t$ for $\overbrace{t + \cdots + t}^{n \times}$, where n is a positive integer and t is a pseudo-Boolean term. Next, we define constraint relations between pseudo-Boolean terms that are allowed in our constraint logic programming language.

Definition 2.5.2 We extend the signature Σ_{psbool} to Σ by adding the binary predicate symbols

$$P_{\mathsf{psbool}} := \{=, <, >, \leq, \geq : \mathsf{integer} \times \mathsf{integer}\} \ .$$

Predicates of the form $t_1 \bowtie t_2$, where t_1 and t_2 are pseudo-Boolean terms and $\bowtie \in P_{\mathsf{psbool}}$ are called *primitive constraints*. Let $\mathfrak{L}$ be the constraints generated by the primitive constraints and let $\mathfrak{D}$ interpret the symbols of Σ as usual in arithmetics. Then $\mathcal{PB} = (\mathfrak{D}, \mathfrak{L})$ is the pseudo-Boolean constraint domain.

The structure $\mathcal{PB}$ is solution compact, since it has no limit elements (limit elements are those that can be defined only by an infinite number of constraints [JL87]). From the general results of Jaffar and Lassez [JL87, JM94] for $\text{CLP}(\mathcal{X})$ we obtain a semantic basis (see page 15) for the constraint logic programming language $\text{CLP}(\mathcal{PB})$.

2.5.2 Programming in $\text{CLP}(\mathcal{PB})$

A typical $\text{CLP}(\mathcal{PB})$-program, namely **sequence**, has already been presented in Section 2.1. Another example, coming from operations research, is the following knapsack problem [Boc91]. Suppose there is a vessel with capacity w and goods g_i with weight w_i and value v_i for $i = 1, \ldots, n$. Let us introduce a Boolean variable X_i for all $1 \leq i \leq n$ that indicates whether the goods g_i are loaded on the vessel. The possible cargos not exceeding the capacity of the vessel can be determined by the following constraint rule.

```
cargo(X₁,...,Xₙ) :-
        w₁ · X₁ + ··· + wₙ · Xₙ ≤ w.
```

The goal $\mathtt{cargo}(X_1, \ldots, X_n)$ adds the constraint over the variables $X_1, \ldots, X_n$ that only admissible cargos are consistent. If we want to find the most valuable cargo, this can be done using a meta-predicate max $/2$ that maximizes a pseudo-Boolean function subject to some goal.

```
most_valuable_cargo(X_1, ..., X_n) :-
    max(v_1 · X_1 + ··· + v_n · X_n, cargo(X_1, ..., X_n)).
```

The semantic problems introduced by the meta-predicate max are discussed in [Fag93, MS94].

Next, we present a typical problem where a pseudo-Boolean formulation is suitable and show how to solve the problem with a corresponding $\text{CLP}(\mathcal{PB})$-program. The problem is to assemble a radio set under the following conditions [Boc91, HR68].

- Any one of the three types T_1, T_2, T_3 of tubes may be utilized, but only one.
  $\rightsquigarrow T_1 + T_2 + T_3 = 1$

- The box may be either of wood W, or of plastic material P.
  $\rightsquigarrow W + P = 1$

- When using P, dimensionality requirements impose the choice of T_2, and as there is no place for a transformer F, a special power supply S is needed.
  $\rightsquigarrow P \leq T_2 \cdot S$

- T_1 needs F.
  $\rightsquigarrow T_1 \leq F$

- when choosing T_2 or T_3 we need S
  $\rightsquigarrow T_1 + T_2 \leq S$
  (and not F).
  $\rightsquigarrow F + S = 1$

The prices of the above components are:

one series of tubes T_1	28 units
one series of tubes T_2	30 units
one series of tubes T_3	31 units
one transformer F	25 units
one special power supply S	23 units
one wooden box W	9 units
one plastic material box P	6 units

The other necessary components of the radio set cost

27 units,   if the tubes T_1 are utilized,
28 units,   if the tubes T_2 are utilized,
25 units,   if the tubes T_3 are utilized.

The price of production is 10 units for each set in all the cases and a set is sold at 110 units when it is enclosed in a wooden box, and at 105 units in the other case. Which model is to be constructed in order to maximize the profit? The following CLP-program implements the specification.

```
assemble(T₁, T₂, T₃, F, S, W, P) :-
        T₁ + T₂ + T₃ = 1,
        W + P = 1,
        P ≤ T₂ · S,
        T₁ ≤ F,
        T₁ + T₂ ≥ S,
        F + S = 1.

maximal_profit(T₁, T₂, T₃, F, S, W, P) :-
        max(110 · W + 105 · P−
                (28 · T₁ + 30 · T₂ + 31 · T₃ + 25 · F + 23 · S + 9 · W+
                6 · P + 27 · T₁ + 28 · T₂ + 25 · T₃ + 10),
                        assemble(T₁, T₂, T₃, F, S, W, P).
```

The query

```
?-maximal_profit(T₁, T₂, T₃, F, S, W, P).
```

yields the unique answer

$$T_1 = 0, T_2 = 0, T_3 = 1, F = 0, S = 1, W = 1, P = 0.$$

Interesting perspectives of the specified problem can be obtained by fixing some components of the problem and investigating the generated solved form. For example, the query

```
?-assemble(T₁, 1, T₃, F, S, W, P).
```

gives rise to the answer

$$T_1 = 0, T_3 = 0, F = 0, S = 1, W + P = 1.$$

from which we conclude that using tubes T_2 left no choices, except that of the material of the box.

Insight about a specified problem can be obtained by interpreting the declarative answer constraint returned by the CLP-system. For example, suppose that we want to install an alarm system containing 10 equivalent detectors [BB93]. Each of them has two possible states OK or ALERT. The problem is to deduce a warning level that can be either green, orange or red. The specification defines the warning level red if the state of 5 or more detectors is ALERT, orange if the number of detectors that are in the state ALERT lies between 1 and 4 and green if no detector is in the state ALERT. With each of the detectors we associate a Boolean variable D_i, which has the value 0 if the detector is in the state OK and the value 1 if the detector is in the state ALERT. This specification can be implemented in CLP($\mathcal{PB}$) by the following rules

$$\text{warning\_level}(D_1, D_2, \ldots, D_9, D_{10}, \text{red}) : -$$
$$D_1 + D_2 + \cdots + D_9 + D_{10} \geq 5.$$
$$\text{warning\_level}(D_1, D_2, \ldots, D_9, D_{10}, \text{orange}) : -$$
$$D_1 + D_2 + \cdots + D_9 + D_{10} \leq 4,$$
$$D_1 + D_2 + \cdots + D_9 + D_{10} \geq 1.$$
$$\text{warning\_level}(D_1, D_2, \ldots, D_9, D_{10}, \text{green}) : -$$
$$D_1 + D_2 + \cdots + D_9 + D_{10} = 0.$$

To compute the warning level we use a logical variable Warninglevel, which is instantiated by the query

$$?\text{-warning\_level}(D_1, \ldots, D_{10}, \text{Warninglevel}).$$

where $D_i \in \{0, 1\}$ for all $1 \leq i \leq 10$. Suppose now that the detectors associated with D_2, D_5, and D_9 are broken and hence no value is assigned. Furthermore, suppose that D_1, D_6, and D_7 are in the state ALERT and the remaining ones are in the state OK. Then the query

$$?\text{-warning\_level}(1, D_2, 0, 0, D_5, 1, 1, 0, D_9, 0, \text{Warninglevel}).$$

can succeed with the following two answer constraints

$$D_2 + D_5 + D_9 \geq 2, \texttt{Warninglevel} = \texttt{red}$$
$$\overline{D_2} + \overline{D_5} + \overline{D_9} \geq 2, \texttt{Warninglevel} = \texttt{orange}$$

So unifying `Warninglevel` with warning level `red` succeeds, which is important for safety-critical applications, where detectors may indeed fail. Furthermore, we derive from the answer constraints that if at least two of the three failed detectors are in the state `ALERT`, we have warning level `red` and on the other hand, that if at least two of the three failed detectors are in the state `OK`, we ensure warning level `orange`.

Suppose that D_2, D_5, and D_9 are repaired and that all are in the state `OK`. This can be modelled by adding the constraints $D_2 = 0, D_5 = 0$, and $D_9 = 0$. Since then the constraint $D_2 + D_5 + D_9 \geq 2$ is violated, the system correctly deduces the only possible answer constraint `Warninglevel = orange`.

As demonstrated in this `warning_level`-example, using classical Boolean constraints does not always yield the most adequate problem description. For example, constraints like "at least or at most d out of n facts need to hold" cannot be expressed directly as Boolean constraints. On the other hand, representing classical Boolean constraints as pseudo-Boolean constraints is straightforward. Thus, pseudo-Boolean constraints often allow a given problem to be more naturally expressed.

For example, suppose that D_1, D_2, D_3, D_4, and D_5 represent detectors as in the `warning_level`-example and that the following Boolean specification defines the warning level `red`.

$$(D_1 \vee (D_2 \wedge (D_3 \vee D_4)) \vee (D_3 \wedge D_4 \wedge d_5)) \quad \Longrightarrow \quad \texttt{red} \qquad (2.1)$$

We can immediately translate this specification into an equivalent pseudo-Boolean specification, namely

$$D_1 + D_2 \cdot (D_3 + D_4) + D_3 \cdot D_4 \cdot D_5 \geq 1.$$

If the number of detectors and the number of conditions increase, then Boolean specifications become more and more complicated and difficult, or even impossible, to understand due to their size. In that case a more compact and understandable specification may become necessary. For example, we can introduce weights for each detector expressing its importance. Deciding the warning level is then done by giving lower bounds for some combinations of detectors. In the example above, the pseudo-Boolean constraint

$$5 \cdot D_1 + 3 \cdot D_2 + 2 \cdot D_3 + 2 \cdot D_4 + D_5 \geq 5$$

is again equivalent to the Boolean specification (2.1). A complete specification can be investigated by studying the solved form, i.e., checking the entailed constraints.

Finally, we present some generic examples that can be used in several applications, which show how to implement in $\text{CLP}(\mathcal{PB})$ some typical problems arising in the modelling phase of a combinatorial problem [Wil90]. In many applications one wants to express a logical relationship between Boolean variables like conjunction, disjunction, etc.. In the standard reference on modelling [Wil90], we can find how to express these logical conditions using linear pseudo-Boolean constraints.

```
or(X_1, X_2) :-      X_1 + X_2 ≥ 1.
and(X_1, X_2) :-     X_1 + X_2 = 2.
implies(X_1, X_2) :- X_1 - X_2 ≤ 1.
equiv(X_1, X_2) :-   X_1 - X_2 = 1.
```

With these declarations we can now use an appropriate name whenever we intend to use a logical connective and we are not forced to translate it directly to a linear pseudo-Boolean constraint. This increases readability. Note that since $\text{CLP}(\mathcal{PB})$ also accepts non-linear pseudo-Boolean constraints, a thorough treatment of the conversion of complex logic relations into linear pseudo-Boolean constraints [MW89] is not necessary, although possible.

Another common modelling problem is that we want to decide with the help of a Boolean variable, whether a linear pseudo-Boolean inequality should hold or whether it may be violated. Again in [Wil90], we find that for a linear pseudo-Boolean inequality

$$L \geq R \qquad\qquad (2.2)$$

the linear pseudo-Boolean inequality

$$-M \cdot \overline{B} + L \geq R\ , \qquad\qquad (2.3)$$

where M is a lower bound of $L - R$ and B is a new Boolean variable, is the desired formulation. If B is 1 then (2.3) is equivalent to (2.2). If B is 0 then (2.3) is equivalent to

$$L - R \geq M,$$

which always holds, since M is a lower bound of $L - R$. Hence, setting B to 1 activates the constraint and setting B to 0 deactivates it. We give a $\text{CLP}(\mathcal{PB})$-program that attaches a Boolean variable B to a linear pseudo-Boolean inequality with the above described behavior.

$$\texttt{switchconstraint}(L \geq R, B) \text{ :-}$$
$$\texttt{lowerbound}(L - R, M),$$
$$-M \cdot \overline{B} + L \geq R.$$

A simple implementation of `lowerbound` computes the sum of all negative coefficients of the linear pseudo-Boolean term. Having `switchconstraint` available we can express a disjunction between two constraints C_1 and C_2. We model this by introducing two switching variables B_1 and B_2 for C_1 and C_2 respectively. Between these switching variables, the logical or relation is established.

$$\texttt{orcs}(C_1, C_2) \text{ :-}$$
$$\texttt{switchconstraint}(C_1, B_1),$$
$$\texttt{switchconstraint}(C_2, B_2),$$
$$\texttt{or}(B_1, B_2).$$

Since we have a complete constraint solver providing a nice solved form, we can also find out to what the disjunction of two constraints is equivalent. For example, the query

$$\texttt{orcs}(4 \cdot A + 3 \cdot B + 2 \cdot C \geq 3, 4 \cdot A + 2 \cdot B + 3 \cdot C \geq 3).$$

yields the answer

$$A + B + C \geq 1 \text{ yes.}$$

Hence, a possible use of $\text{CLP}(\mathcal{PB})$ is the preprocessing of disjunctive constraints in order to avoid the introduction of additional Boolean variables. A more general tool in modelling are cardinality constraints, which state that from a list of constraints at least L constraints and at most U constraints must hold. Using `switchconstraint`, implementing a generic cardinality constraint is straightforward.

$$\texttt{card}(L, \text{Cs}, U) \text{ :-}$$
$$\texttt{switchsum}(\text{Cs}, S), L \leq S, S \leq U.$$

$$\texttt{switchsum}([], 0).$$
$$\texttt{switchsum}([C \mid \text{Cs}], S + B) \text{ :-}$$
$$\texttt{switchconstraint}(C, B), \texttt{switchsum}(\text{Cs}, S).$$

Let Cs be a list $[C_1, \ldots, C_n]$ of pseudo-Boolean constraints. The predicate switchsum associates a Boolean variable B_i to each constraint, with help of switchconstraint. In the second argument S of switchsum the pseudo-Boolean term $\sum_{i=1}^{n} B_i$ is constructed. In order to ensure that at least L and at most U constraints must hold we add the constraints $L \leq S$ and $S \leq U$ respectively. We can now model a disjunction of two constraints by

```
orcs(C₁, C₂) :-
        card(1,[C₁,C₂],2).
```

Of course a solved form can be inspected, which may help to understand and improve the model. For example, we obtain for the disjunction

?- card(1,[$4 \cdot A + 3 \cdot B + 2 \cdot C \geq 3, 4 \cdot A + 2 \cdot B + 3 \cdot C \geq 3$],2).
$A + B + C \geq 1$ yes.

and for the conjunction

?- card(2,[$4 \cdot A + 3 \cdot B + 2 \cdot C \geq 3, 4 \cdot A + 2 \cdot B + 3 \cdot C \geq 3$],2).
$A + B \geq 1, B + C \geq 1$ yes.

The flexible and powerful modelling technique using cardinality is made generically available with just a few lines of code, which shows the merits of the combination of constraint solving and logic programming.

2.6   EXISTING CLP-SYSTEMS FOR COMBINATORIAL OPTIMIZATION

Combinatorial problems arise in a large number of applications. They appear in such diverse areas as in operations research (scheduling and assignment), hardware design (circuit verification and layout), decision making (portfolio management and option trading), or even biology (DNA-sequencing). Consequently, there is not a single general method for solving all kinds of combinatorial problems, but a wide range of specific problem classes together with dedicated constraint solving techniques. This diversity is also reflected in the different instances of the CLP-scheme, where each instance has its advantages

and disadvantages w.r.t. the problem to be solved. We organize this overview of CLP-systems by constraint domain. For each constraint domain typical application areas and CLP-systems that support this constraint domain are mentioned.

First, we introduce finite domain constraint solving in logic programming based on local consistency techniques. Most of the successful, and in the meantime also commercial, applications have been developed with such systems. For Boolean problems typically a complete constraint solver is used, which has its main application in hardware verification. Although the whole book is about pseudo-Boolean constraints, we also list pseudo-Boolean constraints in this summary but with other constraint solving techniques proposed. Linear arithmetic constraints are typically completely solved inside CLP, but can also be used for combinatorial problems by viewing the global consistency w.r.t. the linear arithmetic constraint domain as relaxation w.r.t. the integer constraint domain and relying on enumeration. Finally, we briefly mention some other constraint domains.

2.6.1   Finite Domain Constraints

We illustrate solving finite domain problems with help of local consistency in a logic programming language on a well-known crypto-arithmetic problem; the "SEND+MORE=MONEY" example [Col86, vH89b]. The problem is to assign to each digit in the set {S,E,N,D,M,O,R,Y} a different digit from {0,...,9} such that the equation

$$
\begin{array}{cccccc}
 & & S & E & N & D \\
+ & & M & O & R & E \\
= & M & O & N & E & Y \\
\end{array}
$$

is satisfied. A logic program for solving this crypto-arithmetic problem consists of the two parts constraint generation and enumeration.

```
sendmory([S,E,N,D,M,O,R,Y]) :-
        generate_constraints([S,E,N,D,M,O,R,Y],[C1,C2,C3,C4]),
        enumerate([C1,C2,C3,C4,S,E,N,D,M,O,R,Y]).
```

First, we restrict the domain of the variables in the set {S,E,N,D,M,O,R,Y} to {0,...,9}. We also need carries in order to add two digits. The carries {C1,C2,C3,C4} are hence restricted to the domain {0,1}. Next, we state that all

digits must be pairwise different and finally the arithmetic conditions between
the digits and the carries are written down.

```
generate_constraints([S,E,N,D,M,O,R,Y],[C1,C2,C3,C4]) :-
        [S,E,N,D,M,O,R,Y] :: [0 .. 9],
        [C1,C2,C3,C4] :: [0 .. 1],
        alldiff([S,E,N,D,M,O,R,Y],
        S ≠ 0,
        M ≠ 0,
                     C1 = M ,
        C2 + S + M  = O + 10·C1,
        C3 + E + O  = N + 10·C2,
        C4 + N + R  = E + 10·C3,
             D + E  = Y + 10·C4.
```

Enumeration is implemented by

```
enumerate([V|Vs]) :-
        indomain(V),
        enumerate(Vs).
```

where `indomain` is typically a built-in predicate that assigns a value from the
current domain of V to V. Via backtracking all possible values in the current
domain are tried. The query

```
?- sendmory([S,E,N,D,M,O,R,Y]).
```

then yields the, in this case unique, answer

$$S = 9, E = 5, N = 6, D = 7, M = 1, O = 0, R = 8, Y = 2 \ \ .$$

Given a complete constraint solver for finite domain constraints the enumeration part could have been skipped. The local consistency solver only eliminates
impossible values from the domain of the variables which are detected by some
consistency procedure. For a detailed introduction into consistency techniques
we refer to [vH89a, Kum92, Tsa93]. We follow the first steps of a typical propagation mechanism. Since $M \neq 0$, $C1 = M$, and C1 is either 0 or 1, we derive that

M = C1 = 1. The value 1 is removed from all the variables in {S,E,N,D,O,R,Y} due to the `alldiff` constraint. Since M = C1 = 1, the constraint

$$C2 + S + M = O + 10 \cdot C1$$

reduces to

$$C2 + S = O + 9 \quad .$$

Since O + 9 is greater than or equal to 9 in all possible assignments, we conclude that S must be greater than or equal to 8, because C2 is at most 1. Hence, the domain of S is reduced to {8,9}. Furthermore, the domain of O is reduced to {0}, since C2 + S is at most 10. Hence, O must be smaller than 2, but 1 is already eliminated from the domain. Proceeding further we obtain the following state before starting the enumeration.

$$S=9, M=1, O=0, C1=1, C2=0, \text{ and } E,N,D,R,Y \in \{2,\ldots,8\}$$

While enumerating we choose a value from a not yet fully determined finite domain variable and fix this variable. With this information the domains of the other variables are further reduced until either a solution is found or inconsistency is detected in which case backtracking takes place. What is still missing is an implementation of `alldiff`.

```
alldiff([]).
alldiff([X|Y]) :-
        outof(X,Y),
        alldiff(Y).

outof(X,[]).
outof(X,[F|T]) :-
        X ≠ F,
        outof(X,T).
```

The predicate `alldiff` imposes the constraint X ≠ Y for all pairs of elements in the list in its argument. Note that we are creating a quadratic number of constraints w.r.t. the number of variables. But, the `alldiff` constraint could also be handled algorithmically. Whenever a value is assigned to a variable in an

alldiff relation, then for all remaining variables this value is removed. Such an algorithmic treatment avoids the creation of a quadratic number of constraints while the same pruning effect is achieved. Furthermore, even better pruning can be obtained by using information about the alldiff relation. The property that for every subset of k variables the cardinality of the union of the associated domains must be greater than or equal to k [Hal35] can be exploited, which is done in commercial systems like CHIP [DvHS+88a] and ILOG-Solver [Pug94].

There are other common complex constraints, so-called *global constraints*[6], which occur very often in practical applications. For these constraints often an effective algorithmic treatment is possible [BC94, AB93, BLPN95]. Among them are the cumulative constraint, which handles typical resource constraints occurring in scheduling problems, the among constraint, which is a generalization of the atleast and atmost constraints stating that from a list of constraints at least or at most n constraints must hold, the diffn constraint, a generalization of the alldiff constraint, and the cycle constraint, which is designed for solving complex vehicle routing problems. There are several advantages of introducing these special purpose constraints into a logic programming language:

- Special purpose algorithms for specific problem types coming from operations research are made available. Hence, efficiency is greatly enhanced while declarativity is still preserved.

- Due to their integration in the propagation paradigm these special purpose algorithms can be combined. Hence, complex problems where several special constraint types occur can be handled.

The propagation-based approach for solving combinatorial problems requires a good knowledge of the problem to be solved and of the techniques used inside the constraint solver in order to attack the problem with the right propagators.

Application areas of finite domain constraint solving with local consistency techniques inside a logic programming language include car sequencing [vH89a, DSvH88c], scheduling [DSvH88b, vH92, Wal94, LP94, BC94, BL95, BLPN95], cutting stock problems [DSvH88a, vH89a], test pattern generation [vHSD92], graph coloring [vH89a], microcode label assignment [vH89a], financial decision

---

[6]Although such a special treatment of constraints typically results in a better pruning and hence reduces the search space, the word *global* has nothing to do with ensuring global consistency.

making [Ber90], planning [Ber88, BDP93], frequency assignment for cellular telephones [CG93], and many others.

Finite domain constraint handling techniques are integrated in many CLP-systems including CHIP [DvHS$^+$88a], ECLIPSE [MAC$^+$89], ECHIDNA [HJO$^+$92], CLP($\mathcal{FD}$) [DC93], IFPROLOG [IFP95], and Oz [SSW94]. SICStus [CW90] should also have finite domain constraints included at the time you hold this book in your hands. There are also systems that emphasize on the constraint programming aspect and no longer include a logic programming language like ILOG [Pug94] and CHARME [OMT89].

2.6.2 Boolean Constraints

Büttner and Simonis [BS87] embedded Boolean constraints into logic programming. Many constraint solvers for Boolean problems are based on Boolean unification [BS87, MN88, MN89] (cf. Section 3.2.2) and are implemented with help of binary decision diagrams [Bry86, Bry92]. They provide complete constraint solving and a solved form. The constraint solver handles equations between Boolean terms over Boolean variables and the connectives $\vee, \wedge$, and $\oplus$ as in Definition 3.1.5 For example, we show how to model a digital circuit, here, a full adder, in a constraint logic programming language over Boolean constraints [BS87].

We describe Boolean circuits by predicates whose arguments represent the Boolean signals. The logic programming language then allows one to build complex Boolean circuits by using simpler ones. As primitive circuits we have the built-in Boolean connectives. First, we implement a half adder.

```
half_adder(X,Y,X ⊕ Y,X ∧ Y).
```

where X and Y represent the inputs. The third argument represents the sum, whose value is the **exor** of the input arguments. The fourth argument represents the carry, whose value is the **and** of the input arguments. A full adder can be built from two half adders where the connections of the input and output arguments are as follows.

```
full_adder(X,Y,Cin,S,C1 ∨ C2) :-
        half_adder(X,Y,S1,C1),
        half_adder(S1,Cin,S,C2).
```

The query

>   ?-full_adder(X,Y,Cin,S,Cout).

yields a symbolic solution, i.e., a most general Boolean unifier, of the generated
Boolean equations.

$$S = X \oplus Y \oplus Cin,$$
$$Cout = X \wedge Y \oplus X \wedge Cin \oplus Y \wedge Cin \text{ yes}.$$

We see that full_adder has the expected functionality. Queries like

>   ?-full_adder(X,Y,Cin,1,0).
> $X = A$
> $Y = A \wedge B \oplus B$
> $C = A \wedge B \oplus A \oplus B \oplus 1$ yes.

show the potential of using Boolean unification embedded in logic programming
for testing and analyzing digital circuits [SND88].

Boolean constraint solving based on Boolean unification is available in the
logic programming systems CHIP [DvHS+88a] and SICStus [CW90]. The main
application area is hardware verification, but whenever a complete symbolic
description of all solutions of a Boolean problem is needed it might be applicable. Other methods for solving Boolean constraints are integrated in
PROLOG III [Col90, Ben93] based on resolution and in CAL [ASS+88] based
on Buchberger's algorithm for Gröbner bases. Boolean problems can also be
handled by finite domain techniques if just one solution is needed and the
problem class is sensible to finite domain techniques [SD90, CD93, CD94].

2.6.3   Pseudo-Boolean Constraints

Beside the logic-based approach for handling pseudo-Boolean constraints we
can also exploit a polyhedral approach for pseudo-Boolean constraint solving
inside CLP, as proposed by Bockmayr [Boc93c, Boc94] (see also Section 3.2.4).
Furthermore, a generalization of Boolean unification to the pseudo-Boolean
case [Boc93b] can be used (see also Section 3.2.2). Another possibility is to

convert pseudo-Boolean constraints into Boolean constraints, which seems to be impractical because of the size of the generated constraints. Moreover, finite domain techniques based on local consistency techniques can also handle pseudo-Boolean constraints, which is discussed in Section 2.4 and Section 3.2.3.

2.6.4 Linear arithmetic

CLP($\mathcal{R}$) was one of the first instances of a CLP-system. Jaffar and Lassez [JL87] illustrated the CLP($\mathcal{X}$)-scheme by instantiating the computational domain $\mathcal{X}$ to linear arithmetic constraints. First, a CLP($\mathcal{R}$)-interpreter has been made available and later a compiler was developed [JMSY90, HJM+92], which also allowed meta-programming with linear arithmetic constraints [HMSY89]. The CLP($\mathcal{R}$)-system has been used for many problems, including electrical engineering problems [HMS87], options trading [LMY87, HL88], and temporal reasoning [Brz91].

Currently, many logic programming environments provide linear arithmetic constraint solving, among them CHIP [DvHS+88a], ECLIPSE [MAC+89], and SICStus [CW90, Hol95]. Many use rational constraints with infinite precision arithmetic in order to avoid numerical problems. All systems can also handle non-linear constraints by delaying them and reactivate them in case they become linear.

The underlying constraint solvers are specialized simplex algorithms combined with Gaussian elimination and Fourier-Motzkin elimination [JMSY90]. They provide complete constraint solving for linear arithmetic inequalities, equations, and disequations. We show the features of constraint logic programming with linear arithmetic constraints on the standard mortgage-example [HJM+92].

```
mortgage(P, Time, IntRate, Bal, MP) :-
      Time = 1,
```
$$\text{Bal} = P \cdot (1 + \text{Time} \cdot \frac{\text{IntRate}}{1200}) - \text{Time} \cdot \text{MP}.$$
```
mortgage(P, Time, IntRate, Bal, MP) :-
      Time > 1,
```
$$\text{mortgage}(P \cdot (1 + \frac{\text{IntRate}}{1200}) - \text{MP}, \text{Time-1}, \text{IntRate}, \text{Bal}, \text{MP}).$$

The parameters of a mortgage, i.e., the principal P, the duration of the mortgage in months Time, the annual interest rate in % IntRate, which is compounded monthly, the monthly payment MP, and the outstanding balance Bal, is related

naturally by these two rules. In order to find out how much it would cost to finance a mortgage with a principal of 100000 at 12 percent for 15 years we ask the query

?-mortgage(100000, 180, 12, 0, MP).

which yields the answer

MP = 1200.17 yes.

The advantages of using CLP are again the bidirectionality and the output of constraints as answers. For example, the query

?-mortgage(P, 180, 12, Bal, MP).

yields the answer

P = 0.166783 * Bal + 83.3217 * MP yes.

naturally relating the principal to the balance and the monthly payment if the duration is 180 months and the interest rate is 12 %.

Combinatorial problems can be handled within CLP($\mathcal{R}$) by viewing the complete solver over linear arithmetic constraints as an approximative solver for integer domain constraints. Just ensuring local consistency is replaced by solving the linear programming relaxation of the integer programming problem. For example, the crypto-arithmetic problem in Section 2.6.1 runs with almost no changes[7]. CLP($\mathcal{R}$) should be preferred if solving the linear programming relaxation of a combinatorial problem turns out to achieve a better pruning than using local consistency techniques. The advantage of CLP($\mathcal{R}$) is that also mixed-integer programming problems can be handled. But, like in local consistency based systems, constraint solving relies on enumeration. Unfortunately, commercial linear programming systems are typically much faster than the constraint solvers inside a CLP-system for linear arithmetic [Cra93, CFGG95]. Hence, main application areas of CLP($\mathcal{R}$) are problems that either rely on the

---

[7]Just the domain constraints X :: [L .. U] have to be replaced by X $\geq$ L and X $\leq$ U, and the indomain predicate has to be implemented.

declarative and simplified answer constraint or problems where exploiting the programming language aspect is necessary.

2.6.5 Other constraint domains

Several other constraint domains have been proposed that are more or less well suited for handling combinatorial problems.

Interval Constraints

Older [OV90] has introduced interval constraints into logic programming. Handling arithmetic constraints with interval techniques is based on the same idea as handling finite domain constraints with local consistency techniques, i.e., bound propagation combined with enumeration. The advantage of using interval constraints is that also non-linear arithmetic can be handled. Furthermore, interval arithmetic can also be used to solve discrete problems [BO93]. Interval constraints are available in CLP(BNR) [OB93], NEWTON [BMvH94], CIAL [CL94], and PROLOG-IV.

Set Constraints

Constraints over finite sets are available as an extension of ECLIPSE [MAC+89, Ger94]. Their application areas are combinatorial problems based on sets, relations, or graphs like warehouse location, resource allocation, bin packing and others [Ger94]. They may provide a more natural formulation of a problem than a finite domain or (0-1) integer programming formulation.

Non-linear Arithmetic Constraints

As already mentioned interval methods can also handle non-linear constraints. CLP-systems that support linear arithmetic constraints accept also non-linear constraints, but these are typically completely delayed and not solved. However, there is one CLP-system, RISC-CLP($\mathcal{R}$) [Hon92], that is able to handle non-linear constraints over the real numbers with computer algebra techniques based on quantifier elimination (Partial Cylindrical Algebraic Decom-

position) [Tar51, Col75, Hon90]. The applicability of these constraint solving techniques to *just* NP-hard problems seems limited[8].

---

[8]Hoon Hong once said: "Other people build black-box solvers, we build black-hole solvers. Once called they never return."

3

PSEUDO-BOOLEAN
CONSTRAINTS

After a formal presentation of the constraint domain $\mathcal{PB}$ we investigate several methods for solving pseudo-Boolean constraints and examine their applicability in the context of constraint logic programming. We adopt a logical view of pseudo-Boolean constraints and propose a solved form suitable for the constraint logic programming language $\text{CLP}(\mathcal{PB})$.

3.1 PRELIMINARIES

3.1.1 Basic Definitions

Pseudo-Boolean Terms

With the signature Σ_{psbool} of Definition 2.5.1 we can represent pseudo-Boolean functions as pseudo-Boolean terms. A unique representation of a pseudo-Boolean term is the *polynomial normal form* of pseudo-Boolean functions.

Proposition 3.1.1 *[HR68] For any pseudo-Boolean function $f : \{0,1\}^n \to \mathbb{Z}$ there is a unique, up to associativity and commutativity of $+$ and $\cdot$, pseudo-Boolean term of the form*

$$\sum_{I \in \Omega} c_I \prod_{i \in I} X_i \,, \tag{3.1}$$

where Ω is a collection of subsets of $\{1, \ldots, n\}$ and the c_I are coefficients in $\mathbb{Z} \setminus \{0\}$, that generates f.

We shall adopt the usual convention of identifying a pseudo-Boolean term and the pseudo-Boolean function it generates.

Example 3.1.2 Let the function $f : \{0,1\}^3 \to \mathbb{Z}$ be defined by the following table.

X	0	0	0	0	1	1	1	1
Y	0	0	1	1	0	0	1	1
Z	0	1	0	1	0	1	0	1
f(X,Y,Z)	-5	0	0	0	-3	8	0	6

The polynomial normal form of $f(X,Y,Z)$ is

$$-5 + 2 \cdot X + 5 \cdot Y + 5 \cdot Z - 2 \cdot X \cdot Y + 6 \cdot X \cdot Z - 5 \cdot Y \cdot Z \ .$$

An important class of pseudo-Boolean terms are linear pseudo-Boolean terms.

Definition 3.1.3 Let $\sum_{I \in \Omega} c_I \prod_{i \in I} X_i$ be the polynomial normal form of a pseudo-Boolean term t. The pseudo-Boolean term t is *linear* if $|I| \leq 1$ for all $I \in \Omega$.

We introduce the abbreviation $\overline{X_i}$ for the pseudo-Boolean term $(1 - X_i)$, where X_i is a Boolean variable. We say $\overline{X_i}$ is the *negation* of the Boolean variable X_i. A *literal* L_j is either a Boolean variable X_i or the negation of a Boolean variable $\overline{X_i}$. Let $\mathcal{L}$ be the set of all literals. The negation of a negative literal $\overline{\overline{X_i}}$ is always simplified to X_i. We denote by $\mathsf{Var}(X_i) = \mathsf{Var}(\overline{X_i}) = X_i$ the variable of a literal.

Definition 3.1.4 An *assignment* is a mapping $\alpha : \mathsf{Var}_{\mathsf{bool}} \to \{0,1\}$. We extend an assignment to a mapping $\alpha : \mathcal{T}(F_{\mathsf{psbool}}, \mathsf{Var}_{\mathsf{bool}}) \to \mathbb{Z}$ by defining

$$
\begin{aligned}
\alpha(0) &:= 0 \\
\alpha(1) &:= 1 \\
\alpha(t_1 + t_2) &:= \alpha(t_1) + \alpha(t_2) \\
\alpha(t_1 \cdot t_2) &:= \alpha(t_1) \cdot \alpha(t_2) \\
\alpha(t_1 - t_2) &:= \alpha(t_1) - \alpha(t_2) \\
\alpha(-t_1) &:= -\alpha(t_1) \ ,
\end{aligned}
\tag{3.2}
$$

where $t_1, t_2 \in \mathcal{T}(F_{\mathsf{psbool}}, \mathsf{Var}_{\mathsf{bool}})$ and $+, -$, and $\cdot$ have the usual meaning of addition, subtraction, and multiplication respectively in $\mathbb{Z}$.

Boolean functions, i.e., mappings $g : \{0,1\}^n \to \{0,1\}$, are a restriction of pseudo-Boolean functions. We introduce a signature with the usual Boolean operators that allows the representation of Boolean functions as Boolean terms.

Definition 3.1.5 [Boc91] Let Σ_{bool} be a signature with the sort symbol bool $\subseteq$ integer and the set of function symbols

$$F_{bool} := \left\{ \begin{array}{rcl} 0,1 & : & \to \text{bool}, \\ \overline{} & : & \text{bool} \to \text{bool}, \\ \wedge, \vee, \oplus & : & \text{bool} \times \text{bool} \to \text{bool} \end{array} \right\} .$$

The terms in the term algebra $\mathcal{T}(F_{bool}, \text{Var}_{bool})$ are called *Boolean terms*. By interpreting $\overline{}$ as negation, $\oplus$ as sum modulo 2, $\wedge$ as conjunction, and $\vee$ as disjunction, any pseudo-Boolean term $t \in \mathcal{T}(F_{bool}, \text{Var}_{bool})$ containing n Boolean variables *generates* an n-ary Boolean function $f : \{0,1\}^n \to \{0,1\}$. Again, we adopt the convention to identify a Boolean term and the Boolean function it generates.

We can represent every Boolean term t as an equivalent pseudo-Boolean term by normalizing t with the following canonical term rewrite system.

$$\begin{array}{rcl} X \oplus Y & \to & X + Y - (X \cdot Y + X \cdot Y) \\ X \wedge Y & \to & X \cdot Y \\ \overline{X} & \to & 1 - X \\ X \vee Y & \to & X + Y - X \cdot Y \end{array}$$

We denote by $PB(t)$ the pseudo-Boolean term obtained by applying the above given rewrite system on a Boolean term t.

Pseudo-Boolean constraints

Pseudo-Boolean constraints are equations or inequalities between two pseudo-Boolean functions. They are represented as pseudo-Boolean constraints between two pseudo-Boolean terms according to Definition 2.5.2.

Definition 3.1.6 A pseudo-Boolean constraint $t_1 \bowtie t_2$ with $\bowtie \in P_{psbool}$ and $t_1, t_2 \in \mathcal{T}(F_{psbool}, \text{Var}_{bool})$ is *satisfied* by an assignment α if

$$\alpha(t_1) \bowtie \alpha(t_2)$$

holds, where $\bowtie \in P_{psbool} = \{=, <, >, \leq, \geq : \text{integer} \times \text{integer}\}$ has its usual meaning in $\mathbb{Z}$. An assignment satisfying a pseudo-Boolean constraint is also

called a *solution* of the pseudo-Boolean constraint. A pseudo-Boolean constraint $t_1 \bowtie t_2$ is *satisfiable* if there exists a solution α of $t_1 \bowtie t_2$.

A pseudo-Boolean constraint that is satisfied by any assignment is called *tautology* and simplified to $\top$. A pseudo-Boolean constraint that is not satisfiable is called *contradiction* and simplified to $\bot$.

The *extension* $\mathsf{Ext}(C)$ of a pseudo-Boolean constraint C is the set of assignments satisfying C. The extension of a set of pseudo-Boolean constraints S is the intersection of the extensions of the pseudo-Boolean constraints in S. A set of pseudo-Boolean constraints is satisfiable if $\mathsf{Ext}(S)$ is non-empty. A set of pseudo-Boolean constraints S *(strictly) dominates* a set of pseudo-Boolean constraints S' if $\mathsf{Ext}(S)$ is a (proper) subset of $\mathsf{Ext}(S')$. We also write $S \models S'$ if S dominates S'. We abbreviate $\{C\} \models S'$ by $C \models S'$ and $S \models \{C\}$ by $S \models C$. Two sets of pseudo-Boolean constraints S, S' are *equivalent* if $\mathsf{Ext}(S) = \mathsf{Ext}(S')$. If a set of pseudo-Boolean constraints S dominates a pseudo-Boolean constraint C, we say C is *valid* w.r.t. S.

Solving a set of pseudo-Boolean constraints means to check it for satisfiability and, optionally, to represent the set of all its solutions, i.e., its extension.

Optimization

In practical applications an important problem is to solve a *pseudo-Boolean program*, which means minimizing or maximizing a pseudo-Boolean function, possibly subject to a set of pseudo-Boolean constraints.

Definition 3.1.7 Let C be a set of pseudo-Boolean constraints and let t be a pseudo-Boolean term. An assignment $\alpha \in \mathsf{Ext}(C)$ is *globally maximizing* for C if

$$\alpha(t) \geq \alpha'(t) \quad \text{for all } \alpha' \in \mathsf{Ext}(C) \ .$$

The value $\alpha(t)$ for a globally maximizing α is called the *maximum* of t subject to C.

Minimization is defined in a similar way. Given the optimal value z of a pseudo-Boolean program max t subject to C, we can represent the solution set of the optimization problem by solving $C \cup \{t = z\}$ [Boc91].

3.1.2 Normal Forms

We classify pseudo-Boolean constraints and present for each kind of pseudo-Boolean constraints an appropriate normal form.

Non-linear Pseudo-Boolean Constraints

The most general class of pseudo-Boolean constraints are non-linear pseudo-Boolean constraints. In Section 3.1.1 we already have seen a normal form for pseudo-Boolean terms. We adopt this normal form to represent arbitrary non-linear pseudo-Boolean constraints. We distinguish between non-linear pseudo-Boolean equations and non-linear pseudo-Boolean inequalities.

It is sufficient to consider only non-linear pseudo-Boolean inequalities of the form $t_1 \geq t_2$, since the following equations obviously hold.

$$
\begin{aligned}
\mathrm{Ext}(t_1 > t_2) &= \mathrm{Ext}(t_1 \geq t_2 + 1) \\
\mathrm{Ext}(t_1 \leq t_2) &= \mathrm{Ext}(t_2 \geq t_1) \\
\mathrm{Ext}(t_1 < t_2) &= \mathrm{Ext}(t_2 \geq t_1 + 1)
\end{aligned}
\tag{3.3}
$$

Next, we define a unique normal form for non-linear pseudo-Boolean inequalities.

Definition 3.1.8 A non-linear pseudo-Boolean inequality

$$
\sum_{I \in \Omega} c_I \prod_{i \in I} X_i \geq d \; ,
\tag{3.4}
$$

where Ω is a collection of subsets of $\{1, \ldots, n\} \neq \emptyset$ and coefficients $c_I \in \mathbb{Z} \setminus \{0\}$ is in *(non-linear pseudo-Boolean) normal form*.

Proposition 3.1.9 *For each non-linear pseudo-Boolean inequality there exists an equivalent non-linear pseudo-Boolean inequality in normal form.*

Proof. Let $t_1 \geq t_2$ be an arbitrary non-linear pseudo-Boolean inequality. Obviously, $t_1 \geq t_2$ is equivalent to $t_1 - t_2 \geq 0$. By Proposition 3.1.1 there is a unique normal form for the pseudo-Boolean term $t_1 - t_2$. For the left-hand side of the pseudo-Boolean inequality the only additional restriction is that we require the index sets $I \in \Omega$ to be non-empty. For an empty index set the pseudo-Boolean term $c_\emptyset \prod_{i \in \emptyset} X_i$ is simply $c_\emptyset$. By adding $-c_\emptyset$ on both sides of the non-linear pseudo-Boolean inequality we obtain the desired normal form. $\qquad \square$

The non-linear pseudo-Boolean normal form of a pseudo-Boolean equation is defined in a similar way. Note that

$$\mathsf{Ext}(t_1 = t_2) = \mathsf{Ext}(\{t_1 \geq t_2, t_2 \geq t_1\})$$

and therefore non-linear pseudo-Boolean inequalities are sufficient to describe arbitrary non-linear constraints.

Linear Pseudo-Boolean Constraints

Linear pseudo-Boolean constraints are an important subclass of general pseudo-Boolean constraints. In most applications linear pseudo-Boolean constraints are sufficiently expressive to naturally formulate the problem. Linear 0-1 integer programming [NW88], a discipline of mathematics and operations research, deals with the problem of solving linear pseudo-Boolean programs. Furthermore, each non-linear pseudo-Boolean constraint is equivalent to a set of linear pseudo-Boolean constraints. We will present in Chapter 9 methods that transform a non-linear pseudo-Boolean constraint into an equivalent set of linear pseudo-Boolean constraints.

A linear pseudo-Boolean constraint is a pseudo-Boolean constraint between linear pseudo-Boolean terms. As for non-linear pseudo-Boolean constraints it is sufficient to consider only linear pseudo-Boolean inequalities of the form $t \geq d$, where t is a linear pseudo-Boolean term and d is an integer. We assume that all linear pseudo-Boolean terms are of the form

$$c + \sum_{i \in I} c_i \cdot L_i \ ,$$

where $c, c_i \in \mathbb{Z}$ and the L_i are literals for all $i \in I$. A product $c_i \cdot L_i$ is abbreviated by $c_i L_i$. Next, we define a normal form for linear pseudo-Boolean inequalities that allows us to detect immediately whether the pseudo-Boolean inequality is a tautology or a contradiction.

Definition 3.1.10 A linear pseudo-Boolean inequality $c_1 L_1 + \cdots + c_n L_n \geq d$ is in *(pseudo-Boolean) normal form* if

$$d \geq c_1 \geq \cdots \geq c_n \geq 1 \text{ and } \mathsf{Var}(L_i) \neq \mathsf{Var}(L_j) \text{ for all } 1 \leq i < j \leq n \ .$$

We assume that $d \geq 1$, since otherwise the linear pseudo-Boolean inequality in normal form is a tautology and therefore need not be considered.

Proposition 3.1.11 *[HR68] For each linear pseudo-Boolean inequality, which is not a tautology, there exists an equivalent linear pseudo-Boolean inequality in normal form.*

Proof. We constructively describe how to obtain the pseudo-Boolean normal form of a linear pseudo-Boolean inequality. We begin with an arbitrary linear pseudo-Boolean inequality

$$e_1 L'_1 + \cdots + e_m L'_m \geq d' \; . \tag{3.5}$$

First, we apply several arithmetic equivalence transformations. We rewrite (3.5) such that literals containing the same variable are grouped together and obtain

$$a_1 X_1 + b_1 \overline{X_1} + \cdots + a_n X_n + b_n \overline{X_n} \geq d' \; ,$$

where the X_i are pairwise different. For each i such that $a_i = b_i$ we can simplify $a_i X_i + b_i \overline{X_i}$ to the constant a_i and move the constant a_i to the right-hand side. So let us assume that $a_i \neq b_i$ for all $1 \leq i \leq n$. Next, we replace $a_i X_i + b_i \overline{X_i}$ by $c'_i L_i + c''_i$ for all $1 \leq i \leq n$ according to

$$c'_i L_i + c''_i := \begin{cases} (a_i - b_i) X_i + b_i & \text{if} \quad a_i > b_i \\ (b_i - a_i) \overline{X_i} + a_i & \text{if} \quad b_i > a_i \; . \end{cases}$$

Note that the c'_i are all positive. Bringing the constants c''_i to the right-hand side gives us the new right-hand side $d = d' - \sum_{i=1}^{n} c''_i$. After re-indexing according to the ordering restriction we have brought the linear 0-1 inequality into the form

$$c'_1 L_1 + \cdots + c'_n L_n \geq d \; , \tag{3.6}$$

where $c'_1 \geq \cdots \geq c'_n \geq 1$ and $\mathsf{Var}(L_i) \neq \mathsf{Var}(L_j)$ for all $1 \leq i < j \leq n$. Note that $d \geq 1$, since otherwise (3.5) is a tautology. So far we have only applied arithmetic equivalence transformations, hence an assignment α satisfies (3.5) if and only if α satisfies (3.6). When constructing the pseudo-Boolean normal form of a linear pseudo-Boolean inequality we can detect at this point whether we have a tautology or not.

Suppose that $c'_i > d$ for some i, then every assignment α with $\alpha(L_i) = 1$, maps the left-hand side of (3.6) to an integer greater than d and satisfies (3.6). For all assignments α with $\alpha(L_i) = 0$, the value of the left-hand side is independent of c'_i. Hence, we can safely replace each c'_i by d if $c'_i > d$. Formally, we define

$$c_i := \begin{cases} c'_i & \text{if} \quad c'_i \leq d \\ d & \text{if} \quad c'_i > d \end{cases} \tag{3.7}$$

for all $1 \leq i \leq n$, and thereby obtain the pseudo-Boolean normal form

$$c_1 L_1 + \cdots + c_n L_n \geq d \qquad (3.8)$$

of (3.5) with $d \geq c_1 \geq \cdots \geq c_n \geq 1$. Obviously, an assignment α satisfies (3.5) if and only if α satisfies (3.6) if and only if α satisfies (3.8).   □

The last step of the normalization process as described by (3.7) is also called *coefficient reduction* [CJP83].

We abbreviate a linear pseudo-Boolean inequality in normal form $c_1 L_1 + \cdots + c_n L_n \geq d$ by $cL \geq d$ and view cL as a set of products $\{c_i L_i \mid 1 \leq i \leq n\}$. For a set of products cL we denote by $\sum c := \sum_{i=1}^{n} c_i$ the sum over the coefficients of cL. Note that a linear pseudo-Boolean inequality in normal form $cL \geq d$ is satisfiable if and only if $\sum c \geq d$, because $c_i > 0$ for all $1 \leq i \leq n$. Hence, $cL \geq d$ is unsatisfiable if and only if $\sum c < d$, and we can easily decide whether $cL \geq d$ is $\perp$.

Example 3.1.12 Let us transform the linear pseudo-Boolean inequality

$$\begin{aligned} -6 \cdot X_1 + -5 \cdot X_6 + 4 \cdot X_3 + 3 \cdot X_6 + 3 \cdot X_4 + \\ 3 \cdot X_3 + 2 \cdot X_1 + 2 \cdot \overline{X_3} + 2 \cdot X_5 + -2 \cdot \overline{X_6} + 1 \cdot X_2 \geq 7 \end{aligned} \qquad (3.9)$$

into pseudo-Boolean normal form using Proposition 3.1.11. First, we regroup the products and obtain

$$\begin{aligned} 4 \cdot X_3 + 3 \cdot X_3 + 2 \cdot \overline{X_3} + -6 \cdot X_1 + 2 \cdot X_1 + \\ 3 \cdot X_4 + 2 \cdot X_5 + 1 \cdot X_2 + -5 \cdot X_6 + 3 \cdot X_6 + -2 \cdot \overline{X_6} \geq 7 \ , \end{aligned}$$

which simplifies to

$$\begin{aligned} 7 \cdot X_3 + 2 \cdot \overline{X_3} + -4 \cdot X_1 + 0 \cdot \overline{X_1} + 3 \cdot X_4 + 0 \cdot \overline{X_4} + \\ 2 \cdot X_5 + 0 \cdot \overline{X_5} + 1 \cdot X_2 + 0 \cdot \overline{X_2} + -2 \cdot X_6 + -2 \cdot \overline{X_6} \geq 7 \ . \end{aligned}$$

Because $a_6 = -b_6 = -2$, we simplify $-2 \cdot X_6 + -2 \cdot \overline{X_6}$ to -2, and derive

$$\begin{aligned} 7 \cdot X_3 + 2 \cdot \overline{X_3} + -4 \cdot X_1 + 0 \cdot \overline{X_1} + 3 \cdot X_4 + 0 \cdot \overline{X_4} + \\ 2 \cdot X_5 + 0 \cdot \overline{X_5} + 1 \cdot X_2 + 0 \cdot \overline{X_2} \geq 7 + 2 = 9 \ . \end{aligned}$$

Next, we replace the $a_i X_i + b_i \overline{X_i}$ by $c'_i L_i + c''_i$ according to Proposition 3.1.11 and obtain

$$5 \cdot X_3 + 2 + 4 \cdot \overline{X_1} + -4 + 3 \cdot X_4 + 0 + 2 \cdot X_5 + 0 + 1 \cdot X_2 + 0 \geq 9 \ .$$

By bringing the constants to the right-hand side we have

$$5 \cdot X_3 + 4 \cdot \overline{X_1} + 3 \cdot X_4 + 2 \cdot X_5 + 1 \cdot X_2 \geq 9 - 2 + 4 = 11 \ .$$

Since all coefficients are less than or equal to the right-hand side, coefficient reduction does not apply. After re-indexing we obtain the pseudo-Boolean normal form

$$5 \cdot L_1 + 4 \cdot L_2 + 3 \cdot L_3 + 2 \cdot L_4 + 1 \cdot L_5 \geq 11 \qquad (3.10)$$

of (3.9) with $L_1 = X_3$, $L_2 = \overline{X_1}$, $L_3 = X_4$, $L_4 = X_5$, and $L_5 = X_2$.

Assumption 3.1.13 From now on we assume that all linear pseudo-Boolean inequalities are in pseudo-Boolean normal form. Furthermore, we assume that in all sets of linear pseudo-Boolean inequalities each of the linear pseudo-Boolean inequalities in the set is in pseudo-Boolean normal form.

Next, we show how to derive valid linear pseudo-Boolean inequalities from a given one. A linear pseudo-Boolean inequality $cL \geq d$ *reduces* to $c'L \geq d'$ (the *reduction*) if $0 \leq c'_i \leq c_i$ for all $1 \leq i \leq n$ and $d' = d - (\sum c - \sum c')$. We require that $d' \geq 1$ and hence forbid reduction to tautologies. Because $0 \leq \alpha(cL) - d \leq \alpha(c'L) - d'$ for all solutions α, a linear pseudo-Boolean inequality dominates all its reductions. We denote by $\mathsf{Red}(cL \geq d)$ the set of all reductions of a linear pseudo-Boolean inequality $cL \geq d$. We say a linear pseudo-Boolean inequality $cL \geq d$ *strictly reduces* to $c'L' \geq d'$ if $c'L' \geq d'$ is a reduction and either $c'_i = c_i$ or $c'_i = 0$ for all $1 \leq i \leq n$. We say we have *eliminated* the literal L_i if $c'_i = 0$. We denote by $\mathsf{SRed}(cL \geq d)$ the set of all strict reductions of a linear pseudo-Boolean inequality $cL \geq d$. Note that $cL \geq d \in \mathsf{SRed}(cL \geq d)$.

Extended Clauses and Classical Clauses

A linear pseudo-Boolean inequality $cL \geq d$ whose coefficients are all 1 is called an *extended clause* and abbreviated by $L \geq d$. A *classical clause* is an extended clause with right-hand side $d = 1$.

The problem of whether a set of classical clauses is satisfiable (SAT) has been extensively studied in the past [DP60, vG84, MS85, GU89, JW90, HHT94]. It was the first problem proven to be NP-complete [Coo71, Kar72, GJ79]. Extended clauses are a generalization of classical clauses, where one of the main properties, namely domination, remains easily decidable. Note that a reduction of an extended clause $L \geq d$ is $L \setminus L' \geq d - |L'|$ with $L' \subseteq L$.

Lemma 3.1.14 $L \geq d$ *dominates* $L' \geq d'$ *if and only if*

$$|L \setminus L'| \leq d - d' \ . \tag{3.11}$$

Proof.

"$\Leftarrow$": First, we compute a reduction of $L \geq d$ by eliminating all literals that
are not in L', i.e., $L \setminus L'$. The reduction is $L \setminus (L \setminus L') \geq d - |L \setminus L'|$,
which is equivalent to $L \cap L' \geq d - |L \setminus L'|$. Thus, $L \geq d$ dominates
$L \cap L' \geq d - |L \setminus L'|$. Since $|L \setminus L'| \leq d - d'$, we have $0 \leq d' \leq d - |L \setminus L'| \leq d$
and therefore $L \geq d$ also dominates $L \cap L' \geq d'$. Since $L \cap L' \subseteq L'$, we
know that $L \cap L' \geq d'$ dominates $L' \geq d'$. Hence, $L \geq d$ dominates $L' \geq d'$.

"$\Rightarrow$": We assume that $|L \setminus L'| > d - d'$ and show that in that case $L \geq d$ does
not dominate $L' \geq d'$ by constructing an assignment α satisfying $L \geq d$,
but not $L' \geq d'$. We choose $\alpha \in \text{Ext}(L \geq d)$ such that $\alpha(L) = d$ and
$\alpha(L_i) = 0$ for all $L_i \in L' \setminus L$. Then we know that $\alpha(L') = d - |L \setminus L'|$.
Since $|L \setminus L'| > d - d'$, we have $d - |L \setminus L'| < d'$ and therefore $\alpha(L') < d'$.
But then α is not in the extension of $L' \geq d'$. Thus, $L \geq d$ does not
dominate $L' \geq d'$. $\square$

When deciding domination between two classical clauses $L \geq 1$ and $L' \geq 1$,
condition (3.11) reduces to $|L \setminus L'| \leq 0$, which is equivalent to $L \subseteq L'$; the usual
condition for deciding domination (or implication) between classical clauses.

Note that deciding domination between two arbitrary linear pseudo-Boolean
inequalities is an NP-complete problem[1]. So extended clauses are a restriction
of linear pseudo-Boolean inequalities that make an important problem easily
decidable. On the other hand, we can view extended clauses as a generalization of classical clauses, where we retain computational manageability while
increasing expressiveness.

We say a set of extended clauses S is in *normal form* if no extended clause in
S dominates another extended clause in S. Obviously, every set of extended
clauses S can be easily brought into normal form by deleting all extended
clauses that are dominated by other extended clauses in S.

---

[1] A linear pseudo-Boolean inequality $cL \geq d$ dominates another linear pseudo-Boolean
inequality $c'L' \geq d'$ if and only if the minimum of $c'L'$ subject to $cL \geq d$ is greater than
d'. So deciding domination between two linear pseudo-Boolean inequalities involves solving
a knapsack problem [NW88].

No.	X_1	X_2	X_3	X_4	X_5	X_6	X_7
1	1	-	-	-	-	-	-
2	0	1	1	-	-	-	-
3	0	1	0	1	-	-	-
4	0	1	0	0	1	-	-
5	0	1	0	0	0	1	-
6	0	0	1	1	-	-	-
7	0	0	1	0	1	1	-
8	0	0	1	0	1	0	1
9	0	0	0	1	1	1	-

Table 3.1   Families of Solutions

3.2   PREVIOUS WORK

Solving pseudo-Boolean programs has been an active research area since the early works from Dantzig [Dan57], Fortet [For59, For60], and Hammer [HRR63, HR68]. We present in this section an overview of the work on solving pseudo-Boolean constraints having in mind their applicability in the context of constraint logic programming.

3.2.1   Boolean Methods

One of the early attempts to solve pseudo-Boolean problems was to explicitly construct the set of solutions and represent them in a table of *families of solutions* [Ham64, HR68]. For example, consider the linear pseudo-Boolean inequality in normal form [HR68]

$$9 \cdot X_1 + 7 \cdot X_2 + 5 \cdot X_3 + 4 \cdot X_4 + 3 \cdot X_5 + 2 \cdot X_6 + X_7 \geq 9 \ . \qquad (3.12)$$

The solutions of (3.12) can be represented as in Table 3.1. Each solution is implicitly given by taking one line of Table 3.1 and assigning each variable the value indicated in the table if it is 0 or 1 and arbitrary otherwise. For example, line 4 represents one family of solutions, i.e., the set of all assignments α such that $\alpha(X_1) = \alpha(X_3) = \alpha(X_4) = 0$, $\alpha(X_2) = \alpha(X_5) = 1$, and $\alpha(X_i)$ arbitrary for all $i \geq 6$.

For a linear pseudo-Boolean inequality in normal form constructing a table representing families of solutions is straightforward. We define a procedure

`families` that constructs the families of solutions of a linear pseudo-Boolean inequality. We use the following non-standard conventions. By $cL = c_1 L_1 + c'L'$ we express splitting the non-empty set of products cL such that $c_1 L_1$ is a product with the largest coefficient in cL and $c'L'$ is $cL \setminus \{c_1 L_1\}$. The first argument of `families` is a list, the empty list is denoted by $[\,]$. We denote by $A@B$ the list, where B is appended to A. We define

$$
\texttt{families}(A, cL, d) := \begin{cases} [\texttt{fill}(A)] & \text{if} \quad d \le 0 \\ [\,] & \text{if} \quad d > 0 \text{ and } cL = \emptyset \\ L_1 @ L_2 & \text{if} \quad d > 0, cL = c_1 L_1 + c'L' \\ & \qquad L_1 := \texttt{families}(A@[1], c'L', d - c_i) \\ & \qquad L_2 := \texttt{families}(A@[0], c'L', d) \ , \end{cases}
$$

where `fill` is a function that fills a list with "-"-signs. Then $\texttt{families}([\,], cL, d)$ computes the table of families of solutions of the linear pseudo-Boolean inequality $cL \ge d$.

The main problem with representing the solutions of a linear pseudo-Boolean inequality as a table of families of solutions is that the table tends to blow up exponentially even on simple linear pseudo-Boolean inequalifies, like extended clauses of the form

$$
L_1 + \cdots + L_{2n} \ge n \ .
$$

Constructing a table of families of solutions for a set of linear pseudo-Boolean inequalities is described in [HR68]. Maintaining a table of families of solutions for a set of pseudo-Boolean constraints is not advantageous in the context of constraint logic programming, since incrementality is hard to achieve and typically the size of the table forbids its use.

Hammer et al. [HR68, GH71] already proposed another way to represent the families of solutions. The key idea is to construct a Boolean formula that has the same set of satisfying solutions than the pseudo-Boolean constraint. Given the table of families of solutions, it is straightforward to give an equivalent Boolean formula. Since each family of solutions is characterized by one line where some variables are fixed, we immediately have a Boolean formula that has the same set of solutions as represented by that line. We take the conjunction of the variables that are fixed to 1 and their negation if they are fixed to 0. For the

pseudo-Boolean inequality (3.12) we obtain

$$
\begin{aligned}
&X_1 \vee \\
&(\overline{X_1} \wedge X_2 \wedge X_3) \vee \\
&(\overline{X_1} \wedge X_2 \wedge \overline{X_3} \wedge X_4) \vee \\
&(\overline{X_1} \wedge X_2 \wedge \overline{X_3} \wedge \overline{X_4} \wedge X_5) \vee \\
&(\overline{X_1} \wedge X_2 \wedge \overline{X_3} \wedge \overline{X_4} \wedge \overline{X_5} \wedge X_6) \vee \\
&(\overline{X_1} \wedge \overline{X_2} \wedge X_3 \wedge X_4) \vee \\
&(\overline{X_1} \wedge \overline{X_2} \wedge X_3 \wedge \overline{X_4} \wedge X_5 \wedge X_6) \vee \\
&(\overline{X_1} \wedge \overline{X_2} \wedge X_3 \wedge \overline{X_4} \wedge X_5 \wedge \overline{X_6} \wedge X_7) \vee \\
&(\overline{X_1} \wedge \overline{X_2} \wedge \overline{X_3} \wedge X_4 \wedge X_5 \wedge X_6) \ .
\end{aligned}
\tag{3.13}
$$

It was realized in [GH71] that the negated variables are not needed in order to preserve equivalence. A simplified equivalent formula to (3.13) is therefore

$$
\begin{aligned}
&X_1 \vee \\
&(X_2 \wedge X_3) \vee \\
&(X_2 \wedge X_4) \vee \\
&(X_2 \wedge X_5) \vee \\
&(X_2 \wedge X_6) \vee \\
&(X_3 \wedge X_4) \vee \\
&(X_3 \wedge X_5 \wedge X_6) \vee \\
&(X_3 \wedge X_5 \wedge X_7) \vee \\
&(X_4 \wedge X_5 \wedge X_6) \ .
\end{aligned}
\tag{3.14}
$$

The Boolean formula 3.14 is called *resolvent* [GH71]. Similarly, we can compute a set of classical clauses that is equivalent to a linear pseudo-Boolean inequality $cL \geq d$. For this purpose we consider the negation of $cL \geq d$, namely $cL < d$, and bring it in pseudo-Boolean normal form. From the family of the solutions we construct again the resolvent. Since this resolvent is true if and only if the linear pseudo-Boolean inequality $cL \geq d$ is not satisfied, we obtain a Boolean formula that is equivalent to $cL \geq d$ by negating the obtained resolvent. With De Morgan's Law we obtain a conjunction of classical clauses. For the pseudo-Boolean inequality (3.12) we construct the following set of classical clauses.

$$
\begin{aligned}
\{ \ &X_1 + X_2 + X_3 + X_4 \geq 1, X_1 + X_2 + X_3 + X_5 \geq 1, \\
&X_1 + X_2 + X_3 + X_6 \geq 1, X_1 + X_2 + X_4 + X_5 \geq 1, \\
&X_1 + X_2 + X_4 + X_6 + X_7 \geq 1, X_1 + X_3 + X_4 + X_5 + X_6 \geq 1 \ \}
\end{aligned}
\tag{3.15}
$$

So apparently in [GH71] an algorithm was constructed generating a set of classical clauses[2] equivalent to a linear pseudo-Boolean inequality. The basic idea of *simplifying* the resulting set of clauses was also present in [GH71],

---

[2]The classical clauses generated by the resolvent method are so called *cover inequalities* and play today an important role in 0-1 integer programming [NW88].

although restricted to obvious simplifications like fixing variables and deleting
dominated classical clauses. As a "promising idea" in the appendix of [GH71]
"a B-B-B (Boolean branch-and-bound) type approach" is suggested for solving pseudo-Boolean optimization problems. Unfortunately, the method failed,
mainly because of the large number of constraints in the equivalent set of classical clauses [GG80]. As already mentioned, reducing constraint solving of
pseudo-Boolean constraints to constraint solving of classical clauses is interesting in the context of constraint logic programming, since

- SAT-procedures, deciding whether a set of clauses admits a satisfying assignment, have evolved recently [JW90, Zha93, HV94] and even efficient
  incremental SAT-procedures are available [Hoo93].

- there is an appropriate solved form, i.e., the set of prime implicates [JP90],
  and incremental algorithms for maintaining the solved form are available [KT90, Jac92].

We show that *extended clauses* provide the same good properties in the context of constraint logic programming as classical clauses. We develop methods
transforming pseudo-Boolean constraints into an equivalent set of extended
clauses and managing the solved form. The main advantage w.r.t. classical
clauses is that typically a set of extended clauses is much more compact than
an equivalent set of classical clauses.

3.2.2   Pseudo-Boolean Unification

The first constraint solver that embeds Boolean constraint-solving in a constraint logic programming language was based on *Boolean unification* [MN86,
BS87, MN88, BR89, MN89]. Efficient implementations were possible using
specialized data structures [Bry86, Kar88, Bry92].

Bockmayr [Boc91, Boc93b] generalizes Boolean unification to pseudo-Boolean
unification. Since arbitrary pseudo-Boolean constraints can be formulated as a
pseudo-Boolean unification problem, although more of theoretical interest, we
consider as pseudo-Boolean constraints only pseudo-Boolean equations.

A *pseudo-Boolean unification problem* is a set of pseudo-Boolean equations

$$\{s_1 = t_1, \ldots, s_n = t_n\}$$

with $s_i, t_i \in \mathcal{T}(F_{\mathsf{psbool}}, \mathsf{Var}_{\mathsf{bool}})$ for all $1 \leq i \leq n$. A *pseudo-Boolean uni-fier* of a pseudo-Boolean unification problem is a substitution $\tau : \mathsf{Var}_{\mathsf{bool}} \rightarrow \mathcal{T}(F_{\mathsf{bool}}, \mathsf{Var}_{\mathsf{bool}})$ such that $\mathsf{Ext}(\tau(s_i)) = \mathsf{Ext}(\tau(t_i))$ for all $1 \leq i \leq n$. A *most general pseudo-Boolean unifier (mgu)* of a pseudo-Boolean unification problem is a substitution $\sigma : \mathsf{Var}_{\mathsf{bool}} \rightarrow \mathcal{T}(F_{\mathsf{bool}}, \mathsf{Var}_{\mathsf{bool}})$ such that for all pseudo-Boolean unifiers τ of the pseudo-Boolean unification problem there is a sub-stitution $\lambda : \mathsf{Var}_{\mathsf{bool}} \rightarrow \mathcal{T}(F_{\mathsf{bool}}, \mathsf{Var}_{\mathsf{bool}})$ such that for all Boolean variables $X \in \mathsf{Var}_{\mathsf{bool}}$ the normal forms of the pseudo-Boolean terms $PB(\lambda(\sigma(X)))$ and $PB(\tau(X))$ are identical. Bockmayr [Boc93b] shows that pseudo-Boolean unifi-cation is unitary, which means that for any two unifiable pseudo-Boolean terms there is a most general pseudo-Boolean unifier, and gives a variable elimination procedure, which is a generalization of the Boolean unification algorithm of Büttner and Simonis [BS87] to the pseudo-Boolean case. We present another variable elimination procedure that needs not convert a pseudo-Boolean term into its Boolean equivalent.

It is sufficient to consider the pseudo-Boolean unification problem $t = 0$. First, suppose that t does not contain any Boolean variable, then the empty substi-tution is a mgu of t and 0 if the normal form t is identical to 0, otherwise t and 0 are not unifiable. Let t be a pseudo-Boolean term containing the Boolean variables $\{X_1, \ldots, X_{n+1}\}$. We can rewrite t into the form

$$t_1 \cdot X_{n+1} + t_2 \cdot \overline{X_{n+1}} \tag{3.16}$$

equivalent to t, where $t_1, t_2 \in \mathcal{T}(F_{\mathsf{psbool}}, \mathsf{Var}_{\mathsf{bool}})$ do not contain X_{n+1}. Con-structing a mgu of t and 0 is possible, given a mgu of $t_1 = 0$ and $t_2 = 0$. First, we state an easy lemma.

Lemma 3.2.1 *[Boc91] Let t_1 and t_2 be pseudo-Boolean functions and s be a Boolean function. If $t_1 \cdot s + t_2 \cdot \overline{s} = 0$, then $t_1 = t_2 = 0$.*

Proof. Suppose that $t_1 \cdot s + t_2 \cdot \overline{s} = 0$. Multiplying this equation by s yields $t_1 \cdot s \cdot s + t_2 \cdot s \cdot \overline{s} = t_1 \cdot s = 0$. Similarly, multiplying with $\overline{s}$ yields $t_2 \cdot \overline{s} = 0$. Hence, $t_1 \cdot t_2 = t_1 \cdot t_2 \cdot (s + \overline{s}) = t_1 \cdot t_2 \cdot s + t_1 \cdot t_2 \cdot \overline{s} = 0 + 0 = 0$. Therefore, both $t_1 = 0$ and $t_2 = 0$. $\qquad\square$

Next, we show how to a construct a mgu of (3.16) and 0, given a mgu of $t_1 = 0$ and $t_2 = 0$.

Proposition 3.2.2 *Let the pseudo-Boolean term t over the Boolean variables $\{X_1, \ldots, X_{n+1}\}$ be equivalent to $t_1 \cdot X_{n+1} + t_2 \cdot \overline{X_{n+1}}$ such that the Boolean*

variable X_{n+1} occurs in t but neither in t_1 nor in t_2. Let σ_1 be a mgu of $t_1 = 0$ and σ_2 be a mgu of $t_2 = 0$. Then the substitution σ defined by

$$\begin{aligned} \sigma(X_{n+1}) &:= Y & \text{where } Y \text{ is a new Boolean variable} \\ \sigma(X_i) &:= \sigma_1(X_i) \wedge Y \oplus \sigma_2(X_i) \wedge \overline{Y} & \text{for all } 1 \leq i \leq n \end{aligned}$$

(3.17)

is a most general pseudo-Boolean unifier of $t = 0$. If either t_1 or t_2 is not unifiable with 0, then the substitution σ defined by

$$\sigma(X_{n+1}) := \begin{cases} 1 & \text{if } t_1 \text{ is unifiable with 0} \\ 0 & \text{if } t_2 \text{ is unifiable with 0} \end{cases}$$

$$\sigma(X_i) := \begin{cases} \sigma_1(X_i) & \text{if } \sigma_1 \text{ is the mgu of } t_1 \text{ and 0} \\ \sigma_2(X_i) & \text{if } \sigma_2 \text{ is the mgu of } t_2 \text{ and 0} \end{cases} \quad \text{for all } 1 \leq i \leq n$$

(3.18)

is a most general pseudo-Boolean unifier of $t = 0$. If neither t_1 nor t_2 is unifiable with 0, then t is not unifiable with 0.

Proof. Because of Lemma 3.2.1, we know that a mgu σ' of $t = 0$ has to satisfy $\sigma'(t_1 \cdot X_{n+1}) = \sigma'(t_2 \cdot \overline{X_{n+1}}) = 0$. If neither t_1 nor t_2 is unifiable with 0, then t is obviously not unifiable with 0. Let t_1, but not t_2, be unifiable with 0. Since t_2 is not unifiable with 0, we have $\sigma'(\overline{X_{n+1}}) = 0$. Therefore, $\sigma'(X_{n+1}) = 1$ and $\sigma'(t_1) = 0$. Hence, a mgu σ' of $t = 0$ must be a mgu of $t_1 = 0$, except that $\sigma'(X_{n+1}) = 1$. Thus, σ is a mgu of $t = 0$ by construction. Similarly, if t_2, but not t_1, is unifiable with 0.

In the remaining case t_1 and t_2 are unifiable with 0. First, we show that σ is a pseudo-Boolean unifier of $t = 0$. Since $\sigma(t) = \sigma(t_1) \cdot Y + \sigma(t_2) \cdot \overline{Y}$, we know by Lemma 3.2.1 that σ is pseudo-Boolean unifier of $t = 0$ if it is a pseudo-Boolean unifier of $t_1 \cdot Y = 0$ and $t_2 \cdot \overline{Y} = 0$. We show that σ is a pseudo-Boolean unifier of $t_1 \cdot Y = 0$. The proof that σ is a unifier of $t_2 \cdot \overline{Y} = 0$ is similar.

Let $\sum_{I \in \Omega} c_I \prod_{i \in I} X_i$ be the pseudo-Boolean normal form of t_1, then $t_1 \cdot Y$ is equivalent to

$$\sum_{I \in \Omega} c_I \prod_{i \in I} (X_i \cdot Y) \ .$$

Hence, $\sigma(t_1 \cdot Y)$ is equivalent to

$$\sum_{I \in \Omega} c_I \prod_{i \in I} ((\sigma_1(X_i) \wedge Y \oplus \sigma_2(X_i) \wedge \overline{Y}) \cdot Y)$$

by definition of σ. The inner term $(\sigma_1(X_i) \wedge Y \oplus \sigma_2(X_i) \wedge \overline{Y}) \cdot Y$ is equivalent to $\sigma_1(X_i) \cdot Y$. Thus, $\sigma(t_1 \cdot Y)$ is equivalent to

$$\sum_{I \in \Omega} c_I \prod_{i \in I} (\sigma_1(X_i) \cdot Y)$$

and therefore to $\sigma_1(t_1) \cdot Y$. But σ_1 is a pseudo-Boolean unifier of $t_1 = 0$ and thus of $t_1 \cdot Y = 0$.

It remains to show that σ is a mgu of $t = 0$. Let τ be an arbitrary pseudo-Boolean unifier of $t = 0$, then τ is a pseudo-Boolean unifier of $t_1 = 0$ and $t_2 = 0$. Since σ_1 is a mgu of $t_1 = 0$, we know that there is a substitution λ_1 such that $\lambda_1(\sigma_1(X_i)) = \tau(X_i)$ for all $1 \leq i \leq n$. Likewise, there is a substitution λ_2 such that $\lambda_2(\sigma_2(X_i)) = \tau(X_i)$ for all $1 \leq i \leq n$. We define the substitution λ by

$$\lambda(Y') := \lambda_1(Y') \wedge \tau(X_{n+1}) \oplus \lambda_2(Y') \wedge \overline{\tau(X_{n+1})} \qquad \text{for all } Y' \in V$$
$$\lambda(Y) := \tau(X_{n+1})$$

where V is the set of all Boolean variables occurring in $\sigma_1(X_i)$ or $\sigma_2(X_i)$ for all $1 \leq i \leq n$. Similar to the proof of $\sigma(t_1) \cdot Y = \sigma_1(t_1) \cdot Y$, we can show that $\lambda(\sigma_1(X_i)) \wedge \lambda(Y) = \lambda_1(\sigma_1(X_i)) \wedge \lambda(Y)$ for all $1 \leq i \leq n$ and therefore $\lambda(\sigma_1(X_i)) \wedge \lambda(Y) = \tau(X_i) \wedge \lambda(Y)$ for all $1 \leq i \leq n$. Similarly, we have
• $\lambda(\sigma_2(X_i)) \wedge \lambda(\overline{Y}) = \tau(X_i) \wedge \lambda(\overline{Y})$ for all $1 \leq i \leq n$. In summary, we have for all $1 \leq i \leq n$

$$\begin{aligned} \lambda(\sigma(X_i)) &= \lambda(\sigma_1(X_i)) \wedge \lambda(Y) \oplus \lambda(\sigma_2(X_i)) \wedge \lambda(\overline{Y}) \\ &= \tau(X_i) \wedge \lambda(Y) \oplus \tau(X_i) \wedge \lambda(\overline{Y}) \\ &= \tau(X_i) \end{aligned}$$

and $\lambda(\sigma(X_{n+1})) = \tau(X_{n+1})$ by definition. $\qquad\square$

A variable elimination algorithm constructing a mgu of a pseudo-Boolean term t and 0 based on Proposition 3.2.2 is straightforward. We define

$$\begin{aligned} \texttt{vemgu}(0) &:= id \\ \texttt{vemgu}(1) &:= \bot \\ \texttt{vemgu}(t_1 \cdot X + t_2 \cdot \overline{X}) &:= \texttt{combine}(\texttt{vemgu}(t_1), \texttt{vemgu}(t_2), X) \end{aligned}$$

$$\begin{aligned} \texttt{combine}(\bot, \bot, X) &:= \bot \\ \texttt{combine}(\sigma, \bot, X) &:= \{X \mapsto 1, Z \mapsto \sigma(Z) \mid Z \neq X\} \\ \texttt{combine}(\bot, \sigma, X) &:= \{X \mapsto 0, Z \mapsto \sigma(Z) \mid Z \neq X\} \\ \texttt{combine}(\sigma_1, \sigma_2, X) &:= \{X \mapsto Y, Z \mapsto \sigma_1(Z) \cdot Y \oplus \sigma_2(Z) \cdot \overline{Y} \mid \\ &\qquad Z \neq X, Y \text{ and } Y \text{ is a new Boolean variable}\} , \end{aligned}$$

where id denotes the identity substitution. We assume that the argument term of $\texttt{vemgu}$ is brought to the form $t_1 \cdot X \oplus t_2 \cdot \overline{X}$ if it contains a variable and to either 0 or 1 otherwise. Since the number of Boolean variables in the recursion of $\texttt{vemgu}$ is strictly decreasing, $\texttt{vemgu}$ is well defined. If t is unifiable with 0, then $\texttt{vemgu}(t)$ is a mgu of $t = 0$, otherwise $\texttt{vemgu}(t)$ is $\bot$. Correctness follows from Proposition 3.2.2.

In the context of constraint logic programming a mgu is an appropriate solved form. Global consistency is ensured and all possible solutions can be obtained by instantiating the new variables in the mgu. The algorithm can be made incremental as done for Boolean unification [BS87]. Problematic is the size of the mgu. Practical experience shows that even a small pseudo-Boolean unification problem can generate a very complex mgu. Another drawback is that deciding entailment of pseudo-Boolean constraints is not obvious, given a mgu.

3.2.3   Finite Domain Techniques

Local propagation methods for solving finite domain constraints [Mac77], introduced by van Hentenryck [vH89a] in the context of constraint logic programming and incorporated in the CHIP-system [DvHS+88a], have been successfully applied to many problems from operations research and artificial intelligence. Pseudo-Boolean constraints can be seen as finite domain constraints over the integers, where all constraint variables are restricted to the special domain $\{0, 1\}$.

Solving Boolean constraints with finite domain techniques in CLP-systems is evaluated in [SD90, CD93]. The efficiency of the finite domain constraint solver on some typical Boolean benchmark problems is comparable to special purpose Boolean constraint solvers [CD93, CD94].

The idea of finite domain constraint solving is to reduce the domain of the variables whenever possible by the inference rules *forward checking* and *(partial) lookahead* [vH89a]. The only restriction possible when working with the restricted domain $\{0, 1\}$ is to fix a Boolean variable either to 0 or to 1. Thus, domain reduction methods developed for arbitrary finite domains are too general for the domain $\{0, 1\}$. The inference rules reduce to a consistency check described by the procedure `fixing` presented in Section 7.5 in the case of linear pseudo-Boolean inequalities. But, general finite domain techniques do not exploit the special structure of pseudo-Boolean constraints. In particular, non-linear finite domain constraints are typically suspended until they become linear and therefore are not actively used to prune the search space, whereas non-linear pseudo-Boolean constraints can be reformulated as an equivalent set of linear pseudo-Boolean inequalities with the method presented in Chapter 9. Moreover, powerful reformulation techniques, which are available for pseudo-Boolean constraints, are not yet fully investigated for finite domain constraint

solvers based on local consistency techniques but can be used in order to enhance constraint solving [BB95].

The semantic problems of local consistency techniques in the context of constraint logic programming is discussed in Section 2.4 and we do not elaborate further on finite domain techniques for solving pseudo-Boolean constraints.

3.2.4 0-1 Integer Programming

Linear programming based methods are currently the most evolved tools for solving linear pseudo-Boolean optimization problems [NW88]. In particular, polyhedral cutting plane techniques have been successfully applied to a large variety of hard combinatorial problems [Gom58, Chv73, CJP83, BCC94]. The basic idea of solving pseudo-Boolean constraints with 0-1 integer programming methods is to solve first a *relaxation* of the original problem. Assuring local consistency in a finite domain solver can also be seen as solving a relaxation of the original problem. Unlike the obligatory enumeration in finite domain constraint solving, polyhedral cutting plane techniques can be used to generate valid inequalities that yield a stronger relaxation of the problem. A pure cutting plane algorithm reformulates the problem until the relaxation of the reformulated problem is sufficiently strong, i.e., until solving the relaxation solves the initial problem. In the context of constraint logic programming this means reformulating a set of constraints until satisfiability (and entailment) becomes easily decidable. Moreover, the reformulated problem serves as solved form. The use of cutting plane techniques in the context of constraint logic programming was first proposed by Bockmayr [Boc92a, Boc93a, Boc93c] and is currently an active research area [Boc94, Boc95]. After introducing the polyhedral view of a set of linear pseudo-Boolean inequalities and the relaxation of the problem, we review some basic results from polyhedral theory [NW88] and investigate the approach in the context of constraint logic programming [Boc94, Boc95].

In 0-1 integer programming a set of linear pseudo-Boolean inequalities is formulated as matrix

$$
\begin{array}{ccccc}
a_{11}X_1 & + \cdots + & a_{1n}X_n & \leq & b_1 \\
\vdots & & \vdots & & \vdots \\
a_{m1}X_1 & + \cdots + & a_{mn}X_n & \leq & b_m
\end{array}
\qquad (3.19)
$$

or shortly as $aX \leq b$ with $a \in \mathbb{Z}^{m \times n}$, $X \in \{0,1\}^n$ and $b \in \mathbb{Z}^m$. From a mathematical point of view $aX \leq b$ describes a possibly empty set of 0-1 points in $\mathbb{R}^n$. By replacing the condition $X \in \{0,1\}^n$ by $X \in [0,1]^n$, i.e.,

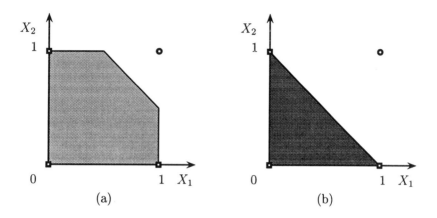

Figure 3.1 (a) Polyhedron of $2 \cdot X_1 + 2 \cdot X_2 \leq 3$ and $X_1, X_2 \in [0,1]$. (b) The convex hull of its 0-1 solutions.

$0 \leq X_i \leq 1$ for all $1 \leq i \leq n$, we obtain the *linear programming relaxation* of $aX \leq b$. Thus, system (3.19) becomes a system of linear arithmetic constraints over the real numbers. The set of points $X \in [0,1]^n$ satisfying (3.19) defines a *polytope P* in $\mathbb{R}^n$. The set of 0-1 points in the polytope is the extension of the original problem, i.e., $\mathsf{Ext}(aX \leq b) = P \cap \{0,1\}^n$.

Example 3.2.3 Let $aX \leq b$ be

$$2 \cdot X_1 + 2 \cdot X_2 \leq 3 \ .$$

The corresponding polytope P is given in Figure 3.1(a) as gray region. The 0-1 solutions points $(0,0), (0,1), (1,0)$ lying in P are marked by ▪ .

For a full-dimensional polytope $P \subseteq [0,1]^n$ there is up to multiplication of inequalities by positive real numbers a unique representation consisting of the set of all *facet defining inequalities* of P. A facet defining inequality of a polytope P is an inequality for which n affinely independent points in P are satisfied at equality. Note that there are several different polyhedra containing the same set of 0-1-solution points. A particularly strong polytope is the convex hull $conv(P \cap \{0,1\})$.

Example 3.2.4 Let $aX \leq b$ be $2 \cdot X_1 + 2 \cdot X_2 \leq 3$, as in Example 3.2.3, and P be the corresponding polytope. The convex hull of $P \cap \{0,1\}^n$ is the gray region in Figure 3.1(b). For example, an inequality description of this convex

hull is $X_1 + X_2 \leq 1$ plus the trivial inequalities $0 \leq X_1, X_2 \leq 1$. Note that $conv(P \cap \{0,1\}^n) \subset P$.

Bockmayr [Boc94, Boc95] compares several kinds of solved forms for pseudo-Boolean constraints and shows that an inequality description of the convex hull of the 0-1 solutions points can be seen as (ideal) solved form in the context of constraint logic programming. The convex hull is empty if and only if the set of pseudo-Boolean inequalities is unsatisfiable and thus has a trivial inequality description. Furthermore, deciding entailment, given an inequality description of the convex hull, reduces to solving a linear program. Note that a linear pseudo-Boolean inequality $cX \leq d$ is entailed by a set of linear pseudo-Boolean inequalities $aX \leq b$ if and only if the maximum of cX subject to $aX \leq b$ is smaller than or equal to d. When solving the linear program $\max\{aX \mid a'X \leq b'\}$, where $a'X \leq b'$ is the inequality description of the non-empty convex hull of $aX \leq b, X \in \{0,1\}^n$, the optimal solution is ensured to be a 0-1 solution.

Enumeration and cutting plane generation are the standard techniques of linear programming based 0-1 integer programming for solving linear pseudo-Boolean optimization problems. A pure enumeration algorithm, *branch-and-bound*, solves first the linear programming relaxation of the problem. If the solution happens to be 0-1, then the problem is solved. Otherwise, a branching variable having a fractional value in solution of the linear programming relaxation, is selected and the two subproblems, where the branching variable is set to 0 and 1 respectively, are solved. The optimal solution is the better of the optimal solutions of the two subproblems. When a subproblem is solved, then all other subproblems whose solution of the linear programming relaxation is not as good as the current integer solution can be deleted, since they cannot contain the optimum. This step is also called bounding.

Instead of branching whenever a fractional solution of the current problem shows up, we can also generate a valid pseudo-Boolean inequality w.r.t. the 0-1 solutions that invalidates the current fractional solution. These valid inequalities are called *cutting planes*, or *cuts*. We say that an inequality $cX \leq d$ is *stronger* than $c'X \leq d'$ w.r.t. a set of points M, if each $X \in M$ satisfying $cX \leq d$ satisfies $c'X \leq d'$ [Boc94]. Generating strong cuts, ideally facet defining inequalities of the convex hull of the 0-1 solution points, may reduce the number of enumeration steps by an order of magnitude [PR91, CCT87]. Whether a cut is generated or branching takes place is typically decided by heuristics. Algorithms that combine cutting plane generation and enumeration are called *branch-and-cut*.

A pure cutting plane algorithm allows the generation of a cutting plane only if a fractional solution occurs. This process is repeated[3] until a 0-1 solution is reached or the problem is found to be infeasible. In other words, the original inequality description is reformulated and getting closer and closer to an inequality description of the convex hull of the 0-1 solutions of the problem. A cutting plane algorithm fits well the requirements imposed by constraint logic programming [Boc94].

- The algorithm is incremental in nature. Incremental algorithms for maintaining a set of linear inequalities in the context of constraint logic programming are available [JMSY90].

- The solved form provides an easy check of satisfiability and entailment.

The ideal solved form, i.e., the inequality description of the convex hull of the 0-1 solution points, may require an exponential number of inequalities. However, we can stop the algorithm if the problems imposed by the current state of the CLP-program are solved. The idea is to compute an approximation of the convex hull that allows one to decide satisfiability of the current set of constraints and answer the current queries about entailment. The approximation is computed by adding cutting planes and simplifying the inequality description. The advantage of this approach is that cutting planes are added only when needed and there is a constant progress towards the solved form. Bockmayr [Boc94] presents such a constraint solver for $CLP(\mathcal{PB})$ based on the new and powerful cutting plane method *lift and project* [BCC93b, BCC93a].

In the next section we investigate a logical view of linear pseudo-Boolean inequalities and adopt the idea of generating valid inequalities in order to approximate a solved form.

3.3   GENERALIZED RESOLUTION

Generating strong valid inequalities w.r.t. $\mathbb{R}^n$ is the aim of the cutting plane methods presented in Section 3.2.4. The inequalities representing the facets of the convex hull of the 0-1 solutions points are strongest valid inequalities w.r.t. $\mathbb{R}^n$. Hooker [Hoo92a] investigates strong valid inequalities w.r.t. $\{0,1\}^n$ and presents a deductive system to generate them.

---

[3]Termination of this process can be enforced by several restrictions depending on the kind of cutting planes that are added. We refer to [NW88] for further explanation.

Definition 3.3.1 A linear pseudo-Boolean inequality $cL \geq d$ is *stronger* than $c'L' \geq d'$ w.r.t. a set of 0-1 points *Sol*, if

$$Sol \subseteq \text{Ext}(cL \geq d) \subseteq \text{Ext}(c'L' \geq d') \; .$$

A *logic cut* w.r.t. a set of linear pseudo-Boolean inequalities is a linear pseudo-Boolean inequality dominated by S, but not dominated by any linear pseudo-Boolean inequality in S.

Basic principles of linear programming based methods for 0-1 integer programming carry over to the "logical view" [Hoo94b] of linear pseudo-Boolean optimization problems. The linear programming relaxation is replaced by a discrete relaxation and cutting planes are replaced by logical implications. The nice properties of cutting plane algorithms still hold for logic cut algorithms. The two views of pseudo-Boolean problems do not exclude each other. Exploiting the structure of particular problems by generating cuts, either logic or polyhedral ones, is possible. Moreover, the logical view often provides a better intuitive way of finding strong logic cuts when the analysis of the polyhedron is far too complex [Hoo94b, Hoo94a]. Although strong cuts w.r.t. $[0.1]^n$ and $\{0,1\}^n$ are quite different concepts, there are parallels (see for example Section 8.2).

3.3.1 Prime Inequalities

We investigate strong inequalities w.r.t. $\{0,1\}^n$. The strongest inequalities w.r.t. $\{0,1\}^n$ are so-called *prime inequalities* [Hoo92a].

Definition 3.3.2 A linear pseudo-Boolean inequality $cL \geq d$ is *prime* w.r.t. a set of linear pseudo-Boolean inequalities S if S dominates $cL \geq d$, but S dominates no other linear pseudo-Boolean inequality that strictly dominates $cL \geq d$.

A prime inequality is a strongest possible linear pseudo-Boolean inequality in the sense that its extension properly contains that of no other valid linear pseudo-Boolean inequality. Unfortunately, a prime inequality is not necessarily unique, i.e., a prime inequality may be equivalent to a number of other prime inequalities. The notion of prime inequality can also be defined w.r.t. a class T of linear pseudo-Boolean inequalities. Extended clauses are a class of linear pseudo-Boolean inequalities for which a unique set of prime inequalities exists.

Definition 3.3.3 An extended clause $L \geq d$ is *prime* w.r.t. a set of linear pseudo-Boolean inequalities S if S dominates $L \geq d$, but S dominates no other extended clause strictly dominating $L \geq d$.

A prime extended clause is necessarily unique, since different extended clauses necessarily have different extensions. We propose to regard *the equivalent set of all prime extended clauses as solved form of a set of pseudo-Boolean constraints.* This solved form satisfies the requirements imposed by constraint solving in the context of constraint logic programming.

Proposition 3.3.4 *Let S be a set of linear pseudo-Boolean inequalities. An extended clause $L \geq d$ is dominated by S if and only if $L \geq d$ is dominated by a prime extended clause w.r.t. S.*

Proof.

$\Leftarrow$: If $L \geq d$ is dominated by a prime extended clause w.r.t. S, then obviously $L \geq d$ is dominated by S.

$\Rightarrow$: Let S dominate $L \geq d$. It remains to show that there is a prime extended clause w.r.t. S that dominates $L \geq d$. If $L \geq d$ is prime w.r.t. S, then the proposition holds, since each extended clause dominates itself. Let $L \geq d$ be not prime w.r.t. S. Then, by Definition 3.3.3, there exists an extended clause $L' \geq d'$ dominated by S that strictly dominates $L \geq d$. Suppose that there is no prime extended clause w.r.t. S dominating $L \geq d$. Then there is no prime extended clause w.r.t. S dominating $L' \geq d'$, since it would also dominate $L \geq d$. Therefore, we have an extended clause strictly dominating $L \geq d$ for which there is no prime extended clause w.r.t. S strictly dominating it. We conclude that there must be an infinite chain of different extended clauses, each of them strictly dominating its predecessor. Therefore, there is an infinite chain of extensions such that each extension is a proper subset of its predecessor. Since any extension is finite, there cannot be such a chain. Hence, $L \geq d$ is dominated by a prime extended clause w.r.t. S.   □

By Proposition 3.3.4 the basic functionalities of a pseudo-Boolean constraint solver, i.e., entailment and consistency check, are supported, when choosing the set of all prime extended clauses as solved form.

■ An extended clause is dominated by a set of pseudo-Boolean constraints if and only if it is dominated by one prime extended clause of the set of pseudo-Boolean constraints.

■ A set of pseudo-Boolean constraints is unsatisfiable if and only if its solved form is $\{\perp\}$. Note that $\perp$ dominates all extended clauses and that $\perp$ is dominated if and only if the set of pseudo-Boolean constraints is unsatisfiable.

Since deciding domination between extended clauses is easy (see Lemma 3.1.14), we have an easy check of entailment. In order to decide whether an arbitrary pseudo-Boolean constraint is dominated by a set of pseudo-Boolean constraints, we have to reformulate these constraints into an equivalent set of extended clauses. Techniques for such a reformulation are presented in Chapter 7 and Chapter 9.

The notion of prime inequalities and facet defining inequalities of the convex hull of a 0-1 solution set are not equivalent. A prime inequality need not be facet defining and a facet defining inequality may fail to be prime.

Example 3.3.5 [Hoo92a] Let S be the set of linear pseudo-Boolean inequalities

$$\{X_1 + X_2 \geq 1, X_1 + X_3 \geq 1\} \ .$$

The extension of S is given in the following table.

	α_1	α_2	α_3	α_4	α_5
X_1	1	1	0	1	1
X_2	0	0	1	1	1
X_3	0	1	1	0	1

The linear pseudo-Boolean inequality $X_1 + X_2 \geq 1$ is facet defining but not prime, since it is strictly dominated by the valid linear pseudo-Boolean inequality $2 \cdot X_1 + X_2 + X_3 \geq 2$. Note that the point $(0,1,0)$ satisfies the former inequality but not the latter. On the other hand, the latter inequality is not facet defining although it is prime.

3.3.2 The Deductive System

Having defined the solved form, we are now interested in how to obtain it. Hooker [Hoo92a] presents the deductive system *Generalized Resolution* that

generates a set of prime inequalities given a set of linear pseudo-Boolean inequalities, including a specialized version working on sets of extended clauses.

Definition 3.3.6 The deductive system *Generalized Resolution* consists of the transition rules, *resolution*, *diagonal sum*, and *simplify*. We denote by $\overline{L} := \{\overline{L_i} \mid L_i \in L\}$ the set of all negated literals of a set of literals L. Let S be a set of linear pseudo-Boolean inequalities.

Resolution : Add an extended clause $L \geq 1$, a *resolvent* of S, to S if

[a] Each of the classical clauses $L' \geq 1$ and $L'' \geq 1$ is dominated by a linear pseudo-Boolean inequality in S,

[b] $L' \cap \overline{L''} = \{L_i\}$, and

[c] $L = (L' \cup L'') \setminus \{L_i, \overline{L_i}\}$.

Diagonal Sum Rule : Add a linear pseudo-Boolean inequality of the form $\sum_{1 \leq i \leq n} c_i L_i \geq d+1$, a *diagonal sum* of S, to S if

[a] for all $1 \leq j \leq n$ the linear pseudo-Boolean inequality $(c_j - 1)L_j + \sum_{1 \leq i \neq j \leq n} c_i L_i \geq d$, which is a reduction of $\sum_{1 \leq i \leq n} c_i L_i \geq d+1$, is dominated by a linear pseudo-Boolean inequality in S,

[b] there is no linear pseudo-Boolean inequality in S that dominates $\sum_{1 \leq i \leq n} c_i L_i \geq d+1$, and

[c] $\mathsf{Var}(L_i) \neq \mathsf{Var}(L_j)$ for all $i \neq j$.

Simplify : Delete a linear pseudo-Boolean inequality in S if it is dominated by another linear pseudo-Boolean inequality in S.

A resolvent is a resolvent in the classical sense (see Section 7.8 and 8.3 for a more general notion of resolvents), but we forbid construction of tautologies. The diagonal sum rule has no obvious relation to classical resolution. Intuitively, its role is to increase the coefficients and the right-hand side. We illustrate the diagonal sum rule by an example.

Example 3.3.7 [Hoo92a] Let S contain the following 4 linear pseudo-Boolean inequalities.

$$
\begin{aligned}
L_1 &+ 5 \cdot L_2 + 3 \cdot L_3 + L_4 \geq 4 \\
2 \cdot L_1 &+ 4 \cdot L_2 + 3 \cdot L_3 + L_4 \geq 4 \\
2 \cdot L_1 &+ 5 \cdot L_2 + 2 \cdot L_3 + L_4 \geq 4 \\
2 \cdot L_1 &+ 5 \cdot L_2 + 3 \cdot L_3 \geq 4
\end{aligned}
$$

Note that all linear pseudo-Boolean inequalities are identical, except that the coefficients of the diagonal term, highlighted by the box, are reduced by one. The diagonal sum rule states that the linear pseudo-Boolean inequality obtained by taking a coefficient/literal pair with the maximal coefficient of each column for the left-hand side and taking the right-hand side plus one, is a valid linear pseudo-Boolean inequality. In our example we derive that

$$2 \cdot L_1 + 5 \cdot L_2 + 3 \cdot L_3 + L_4 \geq 5$$

is dominated by S.

Hooker [Hoo92a] shows that the transition rules of *Generalized Resolution* generate a complete set of prime inequalities.

Theorem 3.3.8 *[Hoo92a] The repeated application of the transition rules* **Resolution, Diagonal Sum,** *and* **Simplify** *on a set of linear pseudo-Boolean inequalities S until none of the rules is applicable yields a complete set of prime inequalities of S.*

Proof. Can be found in [Hoo92a](pp. 277–278). □

It is interesting to note that the two transition rules resolution and diagonal sum generate a subclass of so-called *Chvátal-Gomory cutting planes* [Gom58], which are used in linear programming based 0-1 integer programming. A Chvátal-Gomory cutting plane is obtained from a non-negative linear combination of a set of linear pseudo-Boolean inequalities followed by integer rounding [NW88]. Let

$$r_1 L_1 + \cdots + r_n L_n \geq s \qquad (3.20)$$

be a linear pseudo-Boolean inequality obtained by a non-negative linear combination of a set S of linear pseudo-Boolean inequalities, where the r_i and s may be fractional but greater zero. The linear pseudo-Boolean inequality (3.20) is obviously valid. We round up the fractional coefficients of the left-hand side yielding

$$\lceil r_1 \rceil L_1 + \cdots + \lceil r_n \rceil L_n \geq s$$

with $\lceil a \rceil = \min(\{b \in \mathbb{N} \mid b \geq a\})$. Because rounding only increases the left-hand side, we have generated a valid inequality w.r.t. S. Since the coefficients $\lceil r_i \rceil$ are integer and $L_i \in \{0,1\}$ for all $1 \leq i \leq n$, the left-hand side is integer for all assignments. Therefore, the right-hand side s can be round up to the next integer, i.e to $\lceil s \rceil$. We obtain the valid linear pseudo-Boolean inequality

$$\lceil r_1 \rceil L_1 + \cdots + \lceil r_n \rceil L_n \geq \lceil s \rceil \ ,$$

dominated by S. Next, we show that the resolution and diagonal sum rule generate Chvátal-Gomory cutting planes.

Let $(L \cup L') \setminus \{L_i, \overline{L_i}\} \geq 1$ be the resolvent of the two classical clauses $L \geq 1$ and $L' \geq 1$. The sum, a linear combination, of the classical clauses is $L + L' \geq 2$. The subterm $L_i + \overline{L_i}$ can be simplified to 1, which is brought to the right-hand side. Because only one literal occurs positively in one and negatively in the other classical clause, we know that $L + L' \geq 2$ is equivalent to

$$2(L \cap L') + 1((L \cup L') \setminus ((L \cap L') \cup \{L_i, \overline{L_i}\})) \geq 1 \ .$$

We divide this inequality[4] by 2 and after integer rounding we obtain

$$1(L \cap L') + 1((L \cup L') \setminus ((L \cap L') \cup \{L_i, \overline{L_i}\})) \geq 1 \ ,$$

which simplifies to the resolvent $(L \cup L') \setminus \{L_i, \overline{L_i}\} \geq 1$.

For the diagonal sum rule we consider the weighted reductions

$$(c_j - 1)L_j + \sum_{1 \leq i \neq j \leq n} c_i L_i \geq d - 1 \qquad | \cdot c_j/(W-1) \qquad \text{for all } 1 \leq j \leq n \quad (3.21)$$

of the diagonal sum $\sum_{1 \leq i \leq n} c_i L_i \geq d + 1$ with $W := \sum_{i=1}^{n} c_i$. The sum over all the weighted reductions (3.21) is then

$$\sum_{i=1}^{n} c_i L_i \geq (d-1)W/(W-1) \ . \tag{3.22}$$

Since $W \geq d$, otherwise the linear pseudo-Boolean inequality is unsatisfiable, we have

$$d - 1 < (d-1)W/(W-1) \leq d \ .$$

Thus, $\lceil (d-1)W/(W-1) \rceil = d$ and integer rounding of (3.22) yields the desired diagonal sum.

As for polyhedral cutting planes it is not necessary that the logic cuts are generated by a specific method. Any method generating valid linear pseudo-Boolean inequalities can be used, if we assure that all possible resolvents and diagonal sums, or linear pseudo-Boolean inequalities dominating them, are generated. For extended clauses we discuss in detail how to generate "good logic cuts" in Chapter 6 and Chapter 8. The performance of our constraint solver depends heavily on the logic cut generation process. Studying the generation of logic cuts is a new promising field that combines operations research and theorem proving.

---

[4]Since the right-hand side is 1, coefficient reduction can be applied. Thus, bringing the sum into normal form also yields the resolvent.

3.3.3 Logic Cuts in Constraint Logic Programming

In the context of constraint logic programming a pure logic cut algorithm has the same advantages as a pure polyhedral cutting plane algorithm. By choosing extended clauses as a class of linear pseudo-Boolean inequalities for the solved form, we have a user-friendly and natural description of the 0-1 solutions. In order to cope with the exponential blow up in the number of extended clauses that are needed to represent the 0-1 solutions, we show how to relax our solved form such that just satisfiability and entailment can be decided easily. A pure logic cut algorithm is suitable in the context of constraint logic programming, since:

- The algorithm is incremental in its nature. Adding more information and asking more questions about entailment gives a constant progress versus the solved form, the set of prime inequalities.

- When choosing extended clauses as basic constraints, there is a unique normal form that allows for an easy test of satisfiability and entailment.

We believe that logic cut algorithms can be as efficient as polyhedral cutting plane methods and that many constraint sets that arise while executing constraint logic programs are better thought of logically.

Logic-based methods for solving pseudo-Boolean constraints in the context of constraint logic programming constitute a constraint solver for $\mathrm{CLP}(\mathcal{PB})$ providing global consistency and a user-friendly solved form. With the logic view of pseudo-Boolean constraints, we merge polyhedral techniques with automated theorem proving. Global consistency and support for entailment make 'real' CLP-programs handling combinatorial problems possible. To this end we present in the following chapters a collection of methods, including a pure logic cut algorithm and several reformulation and simplification techniques, whose combination result in a constraint solver for pseudo-Boolean constraints suitable in the context of constraint logic programming. We contribute to the study of logic cuts and present several logic cut generation and reformulation techniques with an emphasis on their applicability in the context of constraint logic programming.

4

A LOGIC CUT BASED CONSTRAINT SOLVER

We outline a constraint solver for pseudo-Boolean constraints based on the generation of logic cuts. The principle idea is to *add logic cuts to the current set of constraints as long as an appropriate relaxation of the problem is not able to answer the questions imposed by the current state of the* CLP-*program.*

4.1 THE SOLVED FORM

Constraint solving in the context of constraint logic programming means reformulating a set of pseudo-Boolean constraints into a solved form such that the solution space remains invariant. Unsatisfiability of a set of pseudo-Boolean constraints must be detected and the solved form should ease deciding entailment. For a set of pseudo-Boolean constraints we propose to regard its set of all prime extended clauses, as in Definition 3.3.3, as a solved form [Bar93b]. Providing the fully solved form at each step of computation is useless, since it may change completely while the constraint logic program proceeds. It is sufficient if the constraint solver is able to answer the satisfiability and entailment questions imposed by the current state of the CLP-program.

Since we assume that non-linear pseudo-Boolean constraints have been linearized in advance, using the techniques given in Chapter 9, we consider only linear pseudo-Boolean inequalities as pseudo-Boolean constraints. The current set of constraints, the *constraint store* [Sar93], then consists of a set of linear pseudo-Boolean inequalities. Because our ideal solved form consists of a set of extended clauses, it is convenient to separate the extended clauses from the set of linear pseudo-Boolean inequalities. Hence, the constraint store consists of

a set of extended clauses E and a set of linear pseudo-Boolean inequalities I, written (I, E), and is equivalent to $I \cup E$.

Ideally, the set of linear pseudo-Boolean inequalities is empty and the set of extended clauses is the set of all prime extended clauses of the current constraint set. Since the number of all prime extended clauses of a set of pseudo-Boolean constraints may be exponentially large, we relax the solved form, at least while the computation continues. We do **not** relax the satisfiability test, and require that if the current set of pseudo-Boolean constraints is unsatisfiable, then the constraint store is $(\emptyset, \{\bot\})$.

If the current satisfiable constraint store is (I, E), we allow in principle any (I', E') such that $\mathsf{Ext}(I \cup E) = \mathsf{Ext}(I' \cup E')$. We only require that progress is made versus the solved form.

4.2   REACHING THE SOLVED FORM

Adding a new constraint to the constraint store gives rise to further reformulation of the constraint store. Satisfiability of the enlarged constraint set needs to be ensured and the entailment questions have to be answered[1].

First, we reformulate each pseudo-Boolean constraint that is added to the constraint store into an equivalent set of linear pseudo-Boolean inequalities and then add this set of linear pseudo-Boolean inequalities to the constraint store. Then we have to decide satisfiability of the current constraint store. A variant of the Davis-Putnam implicit enumeration method generalized for handling linear pseudo-Boolean inequalities, which is explained in detail in Chapter 5, serves for this purpose. The Davis-Putnam method for linear pseudo-Boolean inequalities is tailored to generate strong logic cuts in Chapter 6 as long as satisfiability is not ensured. For reasons of efficiency, we develop sophisticated simplification techniques that reformulate a current constraint store (I, E) into (I', E') such that $\mathsf{Ext}(I \cup E) = \mathsf{Ext}(I' \cup E')$, but (I', E') is in some sense *simpler* or *closer to the solved form*. Among these techniques we mainly distinguish between techniques working on linear pseudo-Boolean inequalities and techniques working only on extended clauses. The principle idea is to generate strong logic cuts that are not yet dominated by any single pseudo-Boolean constraint in the constraint store.

---

[1]In a traditional CLP-system, employing a standard depth-first search, entailment questions do not arise.

Since our ultimate goal is a solved form consisting only of extended clauses, we need to transform a linear pseudo-Boolean inequality into an equivalent set of extended clauses. We develop an efficient transformation method in Chapter 7. Although an exponential number of extended clauses may be generated, typically fewer extended clauses than classical clauses are needed to represent a linear pseudo-Boolean inequality. Moreover, we investigate the concept of symmetries in linear pseudo-Boolean inequalities that speeds up the transformation method and suggests a more compact representation of a set of linear pseudo-Boolean inequalities. Additionally, the method is refined in order to suit the needs of constraint logic programming and to avoid the exponential blow up in the number of extended clauses that may be necessary for representing a linear pseudo-Boolean inequality. We present techniques, like coefficient reduction and the generalization of the transformation method to constrained transformation, that *strengthen* linear pseudo-Boolean inequalities w.r.t. the current constraint store. Such a strengthened linear pseudo-Boolean inequality can also be seen as a logic cut, since the strengthened linear pseudo-Boolean inequality typically has fewer 0-1 solutions than the original one. We also show how to split linear pseudo-Boolean inequalities into several smaller ones when a complete transformation is unsuitable because of excessive storage requirements. The smaller linear pseudo-Boolean inequalities are more easily reformulated and strengthened. Furthermore, partially transforming a linear pseudo-Boolean inequality into an equivalent set of extended clauses is needed when deciding entailment of a linear pseudo-Boolean inequality.

The transformation techniques of Chapter 7 push information into the set of extended clauses. The efficiency of the constraint solver depends highly on a powerful simplification of the set of extended clauses. We present efficient simplification methods for extended clauses in Chapter 8. We restrict the application of the inference rules of *Generalized Resolution* [Hoo92a] to the production of stronger extended clauses, i.e., strong logic cuts, and show in detail how to obtain them efficiently.

Whenever a Boolean variable does not appear in the top level goal and is not visible in subsequent goals, we can project it away by the techniques presented in Chapter 10. At the latest, when the computation ends and the answer constraint has to be prepared, projecting away Boolean variables that do not occur in the top level goal is required.

In practice it is useful to maintain the fixed literals separately and ensure that none of the fixed literals occur in the remaining parts of the constraint store. Furthermore, equations between Boolean variables have no good representation as extended clauses. Thus, we present methods that detect equations between

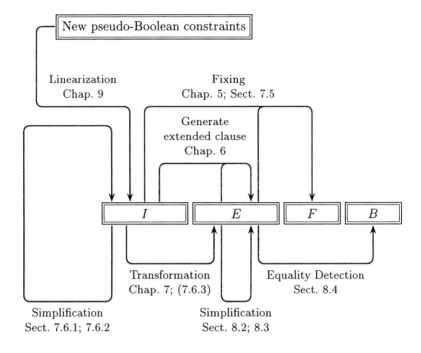

Figure 4.1 Overview of our pseudo-Boolean constraint solver

Boolean variables in Section 8.4 and also keep these equations separately. The constraint store is then of the form (I, E, F, B), where I is a set of linear pseudo-Boolean inequalities, E is a set of extended clauses, F is a set of fixed literals, and B is a set of equations between Boolean variables.

In Figure 4.1 we give an overview of the basic parts of this logic-based pseudo-Boolean constraint solver. In summary, the main goals are

- to push all information from I to E and convert E into a set of prime extended clauses.

- to detect all fixed literals, moving them to F and updating the constraint store.

- to detect all equations between Boolean variables, moving them to B and updating the constraint store.

While computation continues, we relax our requirements and just *do what can easily be done* by the following simplification techniques:

- coefficient reduction, constrained simplification and constrained transformation for linear pseudo-Boolean inequalities.

- simplifying diagonal sums, simplifying resolvents, equality detection and fixing literals for extended clauses.

- logic cut generation w.r.t. the whole constraint store by enumeration techniques, if satisfiability is not yet ensured.

The different parts of the constraint solver and the parts of the constraint store on which they depend are represented graphically in Figure 4.1. Using specific parts of the constraint store (I, E, F, B) the different techniques either reformulate constraints or derive new constraints for some other parts of the constraint store. In Figure 4.1 the techniques are listed together with the number of the section or chapter where they are presented. Each technique generates information for the part of the constraint store where it is connected with an arrow and uses information from the other connected parts.

Operationally, this logic-based constraint solver is best viewed as a collection of independently working agents that try to apply the presented techniques whenever possible. Simplification techniques are preferred and always applied in advance. If satisfiability or entailment questions cannot be answered, the logic cut generation technique of Chapter 6 is invoked and gives rise to further simplifications. This is continued as long as there are open questions. When implementing this logic-based constraint solver, the main difficulties are an efficient representation of the constraint store and a triggering of the simplification techniques such that simplification is only attempted when it seems promising. Many of the logic-based constraint processing techniques presented in this book are available in the 0-1 integer optimization package OPBDP[2].

---

[2] FTP: ftp.mpi-sb.mpg.de:pub/guide/staff/barth/opbdp/opbdp.tar.Z
    WWW: http://www.mpi-sb.mpg.de/~barth/opbdp/opbdp.html

PSEUDO-BOOLEAN UNIT RESOLUTION

The traditional approach of solving a linear pseudo-Boolean optimization problem (maximize a linear pseudo-Boolean term cL subject to a set of linear pseudo-Boolean inequalities S) is to solve the linear programming relaxation of the problem and then to branch on a variable X_i having a fractional value in the current LP-solution. If there is no such variable, then the LP-optimum is the integer optimum. Branching on X_i yields the two subproblems maximize cL subject to $S, X_i = 1$ and maximize cL subject to $S, X_i = 0$, which are solved recursively by the same approach. The desired optimum is the maximum of the optima of the two subproblems. Subproblems need not be split further if either all variables are integral or if there is another subproblem having an integral solution with a greater value of the objective function.

We present an optimization method that follows a similar enumeration scheme. The main difference is that we do not consider the linear programming relaxation of the problem, but a relaxation of the problem more suitable to the logic view of a set of linear pseudo-Boolean inequalities, namely *pseudo-Boolean unit relaxation*, a generalization of the *unit relaxation* of a set of classical clauses [Hoo88a, Hoo89] to the pseudo-Boolean case. The implicit enumeration procedure can be seen as a generalization of the well-known Davis-Putnam enumeration method [DP60, Lov78] (DP) for solving the propositional satisfiability problem of a set of classical clauses (SAT).

DP-based algorithms have evolved recently into the fastest known methods for solving SAT [JW90, HHT94, Hoo93, Zha93]. This is due to proper implementation techniques and the development of good variable selection heuristics [JW90, HV94]. We present a generalization of the DP-procedure for linear pseudo-Boolean inequalities and make use of the achievements for DP. The

algorithm compares well with traditional linear programming based methods on a variety of standard 0-1 integer programming benchmarks.

Pseudo-Boolean unit relaxation is the logical counterpart to the linear programming relaxation. Solving the pseudo-Boolean unit relaxation is the heart of our pseudo-Boolean constraint solver based on the logic view of pseudo-Boolean constraints. In this chapter we focus on a pure enumerative approach for solving linear pseudo-Boolean optimization problems, which corresponds to branch-and-bound in linear programming based 0-1 integer programming.

5.1 THE CLASSICAL DAVIS-PUTNAM PROCEDURE

First, we recall the classical Davis-Putnam enumeration method (DP) for solving SAT.

A classical clause $L \geq 1$ with $|L| = 1$, i.e., there is only one literal, is called a *unit clause*. The literal L_i of a unit clause is called a *unit literal*. We know that in all satisfying assignments α of a SAT-problem containing a unit clause $\{L_i\} \geq 1$, abbreviated by $L_i \geq 1$, we have $\alpha(L_i) = 1$. Given a unit literal L_i, the basic step of the DP-procedure is to replace L_i by 1 and $\overline{L_i}$ by 0 in all classical clauses followed by a simplification step. Such a step is called a *unit resolution step*. Formally, we define

$$\text{ures}(L_i \geq 1, L \geq 1) := \begin{cases} L \setminus \{\overline{L_i}\} \geq 1 & \text{if } \overline{L_i} \in L, \\ \top & \text{if } L_i \in L, \\ L \geq 1 & \text{otherwise .} \end{cases} \qquad (5.1)$$

Then $\text{ures}(L_i \geq 1, L \geq 1)$ is the classical clause obtained from $L \geq 1$ after replacing L_i by 1 and $\overline{L_i}$ by 0 followed by the simplification step. Since we have $\alpha(L_i) = 1$ for all solutions α of a SAT-problem containing $L_i \geq 1$, we know that each solution of $\{\text{ures}(L_i \geq 1, L \geq 1), L_i \geq 1\}$ is a solution of $L \geq 1$. Therefore, $L \geq 1$ is dominated by $\{\text{ures}(L_i \geq 1, L \geq 1), L_i \geq 1\}$ and can be replaced by $\text{ures}(L_i \geq 1, L \geq 1)$ in a SAT-problem containing $L_i \geq 1$. For a set of classical clauses S we define

$$\text{ures}(L_i \geq 1, S) := \{\text{ures}(L_i \geq 1, L \geq 1) \mid \begin{array}{l} L \geq 1 \in S \text{ and} \\ \text{ures}(L_i \geq 1, L \geq 1) \neq \top \end{array} \}. \qquad (5.2)$$

Note that there are no tautologies $\top$ in $\text{ures}(L_i \geq 1, S)$. When applying ures to a set of classical clauses, we may generate further unit clauses and ures may

be applicable again. *Unit resolution*, or *clausal chaining*, for a set of classical clauses S means to apply **ures** as long as there is a unit clause in S.

In the following we describe algorithms as a *transition system*, i.e., a set of *transition rules* of the form

$$\frac{\mathsf{State}_i}{\mathsf{State}_{i+1}} \text{ if } C \; , \tag{5.3}$$

which say that we replace a state State_i by a state State_{i+1} if the condition C holds. States State_i are typically tuples of the form $\langle X, Y \rangle$. A state State_n is a *normal form* of State_1 if State_n can be obtained by applying a set of transition rules to State_1 and for State_n no rule is applicable i.e., for each transition rule its condition C does not hold. In our algorithms we take care that at most one transition rule may apply to a state. Hence, if there exists a normal form, i.e., the algorithm is terminating, the normal form is unique.

Unit resolution for a set of classical clauses S is described by the following transition rule, where S is a set of classical clauses and U is a set of literals.

$$\frac{\langle S, U \rangle}{\langle \mathsf{ures}(L_i \geq 1, S), U \cup \{L_i\} \rangle} \text{ if } L_i \geq 1 \in S \tag{5.4}$$

We denote by $\langle \mathsf{ur}(S), \mathsf{ul}(S) \rangle$ the normal form obtained by applying the transition rule (5.4) as long as possible starting with $\langle S, \emptyset \rangle$. The set $\mathsf{ul}(S)$ then contains the set of all literals that occurred in a unit clause during the application of unit resolution. Moreover, $\mathsf{ur}(S)$ does not contain a unit clause and we have

$$\mathsf{Ext}(\mathsf{ur}(S) \cup \{\mathsf{ul}(S) \geq |\mathsf{ul}(S)|\}) = \mathsf{Ext}(S) \; . \tag{5.5}$$

If $\mathsf{ur}(S)$ contains the empty clause $\bot$, then S is unsatisfiable and we say that the *unit relaxation* of S is unsatisfiable. On the other hand, we know that S is satisfiable if and only if $\mathsf{ur}(S)$ is satisfiable, since each solution α of S is a solution of $\mathsf{ur}(S)$ and $\alpha(L_i) = 1$ for all $L_i \in \mathsf{ul}(S)$. Note that $\mathsf{Var}(L_i) \neq \mathsf{Var}(L_j)$ for all different L_i and L_j in $\mathsf{ul}(S)$. It is well known that the unit relaxation of S is unsatisfiable if and only if the linear programming relaxation of S is unsatisfiable [BJL86].

Given a set S of classical clauses, the DP-procedure searches a solution α of S by exploring a search tree, where each node of the tree represents a SAT-problem. Next, we define a transition system that operates on states $\langle P, Sol \rangle$. Here, P is a set of tuples $\langle S, U \rangle$, where S is a SAT-problem and U is a set of literals that have been fixed so far, representing the nodes that still need

to be explored. We collect the sets of fixed literals that generate an empty SAT-problem as a set of sets of literals Sol.

$$\texttt{dp\_clash:} \quad \frac{\langle\{\langle S,U\rangle\}\uplus P, Sol\rangle}{\langle P, Sol\rangle} \quad \text{if } \perp\, \in S$$

$$\texttt{dp\_sol:} \quad \frac{\langle\{\langle S,U\rangle\}\uplus P, Sol\rangle}{\langle P, Sol \cup \{U\}\rangle} \quad \text{if } S = \emptyset$$

$$\texttt{dp\_split:} \quad \frac{\langle\{\langle S,U\rangle\}\uplus P, Sol\rangle}{\langle\{P_1, P_2\}\cup P, Sol\rangle} \quad \text{if } \begin{array}{l} \perp\, \notin S, S \neq \emptyset, \\ L_i = \texttt{select\_literal(S)}, \\ S' = S \cup \{L_i \geq 1\}, \\ P_1 = \langle\texttt{ur}(S'), \texttt{ul}(S')\cup U\rangle, \\ S'' = S \cup \{\{\overline{L_i}\} \geq 1\} \text{ and} \\ P_2 = \langle\texttt{ur}(S''), \texttt{ul}(S'')\cup U\rangle \end{array}$$

In $\texttt{dp\_split}$ we select a so-called *branching literal* L_i occurring in some classical clause of the current SAT-problem by a procedure $\texttt{select\_literal}$. Applying the transition system defined by the three rules $\texttt{dp\_clash}$, $\texttt{dp\_sol}$, and $\texttt{dp\_split}$ as long as possible on $\langle\{\langle\texttt{ur}(S), \texttt{ul}(S)\rangle\}, \emptyset\rangle$, where S is a set of classical clauses, yields the normal form $\langle\emptyset, Sol\rangle$. Note that unit resolution applies at least once for each of the two subproblems introduced by $\texttt{dp\_split}$, since we add a unit clause. Therefore, the number of literals in each of the two subproblems is smaller than the number of literals in the selected problem. Hence, the above defined transition system always terminates. We know that S is satisfiable if and only if $Sol \neq \emptyset$. From each element $U \in Sol$ we can construct a solution $\alpha \in \texttt{Ext}(S)$ by defining $\alpha(L_i) := 1$ for all $L_i \in U$ and arbitrary otherwise. The set of all solutions of S is obtained by building all solutions α for each $U \in Sol$.

For reasons of efficiency, the search tree is typically explored depth first, i.e., the set of subproblems is implemented as a "Last In, First Out"(LIFO) data structure. Since we are only interested in whether the SAT-problem is satisfiable or not, we stop as soon as the first solution is found. We define

$$\texttt{dp}(S) := \begin{cases} (\top, U) & \text{if} \qquad\quad S \text{ is satisfiable and } U \in Sol \\ (\perp, \emptyset) & \text{otherwise ,} \end{cases} \tag{5.6}$$

which yields $(\top, U)$ if and only if S is satisfiable and U is the first set of literals that is added to Sol.

5.2 DAVIS-PUTNAM FOR LINEAR PSEUDO-BOOLEAN INEQUALITIES

We obtain a DP like procedure for solving the satisfiability problem of a set of linear pseudo-Boolean inequalities by generalizing unit resolution to *pseudo-Boolean unit resolution*. The key idea of the unit resolution procedure is to fix unit literals to their only possible value and then to make obvious inferences, i.e., fixing literals and detection of (un)satisfiability. Therefore, we first need to determine whether a linear pseudo-Boolean inequality implies the fixing of a literal.

Lemma 5.2.1 *A linear pseudo-Boolean inequality* $cL \geq d$ *dominates* $L_i \geq 1$ *if and only if* $c_i L_i \in cL$ *and* $\sum c - c_i < d$, *where* $\sum c$ *denotes the sum over all coefficients of* c.

Proof. Let $c'L'$ be $cL \setminus \{c_i L_i\}$ and α be a solution of $cL \geq d$. Then $\alpha(c_i L_i) + \alpha(c'L') \geq d$ and $\sum c' = \sum c - c_i$.

$\Leftarrow$: Suppose that $\sum c' < d$. Because $\alpha(c'L') \leq \sum c' < d$, we must have $\alpha(c_i L_i) > 0$ and thus $\alpha(L_i) = 1$. Hence, $L_i \geq 1$ is dominated by $cL \geq d$.

$\Rightarrow$: We assume that $\sum c' \geq d$ and show that then $L_i \geq 1$ is not dominated by $cL \geq d$. Let $\alpha(L_i) = 0$ and $\alpha(L_j) = 1$ for all $L_j \in L'$, then $\alpha(cL) = \alpha(c_i L_i) + \alpha(c'L') = \sum c' \geq d$. Hence, α is a solution of $cL \geq d$, but not of $L_i \geq 1$. □

If a linear pseudo-Boolean inequality $cL \geq d$ dominates $L_i \geq 1$, we call L_i *unit literal* of $cL \geq d$.

Lemma 5.2.2 *If a linear pseudo-Boolean inequality* $cL \geq d$ *dominates* $L_i \geq 1$ *with* $c_i L_i \in cL$, *then* $cL \geq d$ *dominates* $L_j \geq 1$ *for all* $c_j L_j \in cL$ *with* $c_j \geq c_i$.

Proof. If $\sum c - c_i < d$ then $\sum c - c_j < d$, because $c_j \geq c_i$ and therefore Lemma 5.2.1 applies. But then we know that $cL \geq d$ dominates $L_j \geq 1$. □

Using Lemma 5.2.2, we see that a linear pseudo-Boolean inequality $cL \geq d$ dominates $L_i \geq 1$ for some L_i if and only if $cL \geq d$ dominates $L_1 \geq 1$, since L_1 is a literal with the largest coefficient in a linear pseudo-Boolean inequality

$cL \geq d$ in normal form. We define

$$\texttt{fixed}(cL \geq d) := \begin{cases} L_1 & \text{if } \sum c - c_1 < d \\ \bot & \text{otherwise .} \end{cases} \tag{5.7}$$

Then $\texttt{fixed}(cL \geq d) = L_1$ if and only if $cL \geq d$ dominates $L_1 \geq 1$. Moreover, if $\texttt{fixed}(cL \geq d) = \bot$, then $cL \geq d$ does not dominate any unit clause. Given a unit clause $L_i \geq 1$, we can simplify a linear pseudo-Boolean inequality $cL \geq d$ by replacing L_i by 1 and $\overline{L_i}$ by 0. Resulting constants on the left-hand side are brought to the right-hand side. Special cases arise when the linear pseudo-Boolean inequality becomes tautologous after fixing ($\top$) or unsatisfiable ($\bot$). We define

$$\texttt{fix}(L_i, cL \geq d) := \begin{cases} \top & \text{if } d - c_i \leq 0 \text{ and } c_i L_i \in cL, \\ cL \setminus \{c_i L_i\} \geq d - c_i & \text{if } d - c_i > 0 \text{ and } c_i L_i \in cL, \\ \bot & \text{if } \sum c - c_i < d \text{ and } c_i \overline{L_i} \in cL, \\ cL \setminus \{c_i \overline{L_i}\} \geq d & \text{if } \sum c - c_i \geq d \text{ and } c_i \overline{L_i} \in cL, \\ cL \geq d & \text{if } \text{neither } L_i \text{ nor } \overline{L_i} \text{ in } L \text{ .} \end{cases} \tag{5.8}$$

Then $\texttt{fix}(L_i, cL \geq d)$ denotes the linear pseudo-Boolean inequality obtained by fixing a unit literal L_i in $cL \geq d$ followed by the simplification step. We have

$$\text{Ext}(\{cL \geq d, L_i \geq 1\}) = \{\texttt{fix}(L_i, cL \geq d), L_i \geq 1\} \ .$$

Note that fixing a literal L_i in a linear pseudo-Boolean inequality $cL \geq d$ may produce a tautology only if $L_i \in L$ and may produce a contradiction only if $\overline{L_i} \in L$. Given a set of linear pseudo-Boolean inequalities S, we denote by $\texttt{fix}(L_i, S)$ the set of all linear pseudo-Boolean inequalities $\texttt{fix}(L_i, cL \geq d) \neq \top$ with $cL \geq d \in S$. Note that no tautologies are in $\texttt{fix}(L_i, S)$. Next, we define *pseudo-Boolean unit resolution* for a set of linear pseudo-Boolean inequalities S, the generalization of the unit resolution procedure for classical clauses to the pseudo-Boolean case.

$$\frac{\langle S, U \rangle}{\langle \texttt{fix}(L_i, S), U \cup \{L_i\} \rangle} \quad \text{if } cL \geq d \in S \text{ and } L_i = \texttt{fixed}(cL \geq d) \neq \bot \tag{5.9}$$

We denote by $\langle \texttt{pbur}(S), \texttt{pbul}(S) \rangle$ the normal form obtained by applying the transition rule (5.9) as long as possible starting with $\langle S, \emptyset \rangle$. The set $\texttt{pbul}(S)$ then contains the set of all unit literals detected by $\texttt{fixed}$ during the application of pseudo-Boolean unit resolution. Moreover, $\texttt{pbur}(S)$ does not contain a linear

pseudo-Boolean inequality $cL \geq d$ with $\texttt{fixed}(cL \geq d) \neq \perp$ and we have

$$\text{Ext}(\text{pbur}(S) \cup \{\text{pbul}(S) \geq |\text{pbul}(S)|\}) = \text{Ext}(S) . \qquad (5.10)$$

The *pseudo-Boolean unit relaxation* of S is the set of all assignments α such that $\alpha(L_i) = 1$ for all $L_i \in \text{pbul}(U)$ if $\perp \notin \text{pbur}(S)$ and $\emptyset$ otherwise. If $\perp \in \text{pbur}(S)$, we say that the pseudo-Boolean unit relaxation of S is unsatisfiable. On the other hand, S is satisfiable if and only if $\text{pbur}(S)$ is satisfiable, since each solution α of S is a solution of $\text{pbur}(S)$ and $\alpha(L_i) = 1$ for all $L_i \in \text{pbul}(S)$. If S contains only classical clauses, then $\text{ur}(S) = \text{pbur}(S)$ and therefore $\perp \in \text{pbur}(S)$ if and only if $\perp \in \text{ur}(S)$. If the pseudo-Boolean unit relaxation of S is unsatisfiable, then the linear programming relaxation of S is unsatisfiable. The converse no longer holds. For example, consider

$$S = \{1 \cdot A + 1 \cdot B + 1 \cdot C \geq 2, 1 \cdot \overline{A} + 1 \cdot \overline{B} + 1 \cdot \overline{C} \geq 2\} . \qquad (5.11)$$

Since $\texttt{fixed}(1 \cdot A + 1 \cdot B + 1 \cdot C \geq 2) = \texttt{fixed}(1 \cdot \overline{A} + 1 \cdot \overline{B} + 1 \cdot \overline{C} \geq 2) = \perp$, we have $\text{pbur}(S) = S$ and $\text{pbul}(S) = \emptyset$, thus $\perp \notin \text{pbur}(S)$. On the other hand, the sum of both linear pseudo-Boolean inequalities simplifies to $3 \geq 4$ and therefore the linear programming relaxation is unsatisfiable.

Next, we generalize DP to the pseudo-Boolean case. Again, we define a transition system that operates on states $\langle P, Sol \rangle$, but here P is a set of tuples $\langle S, U \rangle$, where S is a set of linear pseudo-Boolean inequalities. For the sake of completeness we include the transition system, which is almost identical to the one for classical clauses.

$$\texttt{pbdp\_clash:} \quad \frac{\langle \{\langle S, U \rangle\} \uplus P, Sol \rangle}{\langle P, Sol \rangle} \quad \text{if } \perp \in S$$

$$\texttt{pbdp\_sol:} \quad \frac{\langle \{\langle S, U \rangle\} \uplus P, Sol \rangle}{\langle P, Sol \cup \{U\} \rangle} \quad \text{if } S = \emptyset$$

$$\texttt{pbdp\_split:} \quad \frac{\langle \{\langle S, U \rangle\} \uplus P, Sol \rangle}{\langle \{P_1, P_2\} \cup P, Sol \rangle} \quad \text{if } \begin{array}{l} \perp \notin S, S \neq \emptyset, \\ L_i = \texttt{select\_literal}(S), \\ S' = S \cup \{L_i \geq 1\}, \\ P_1 = \langle \text{pbur}(S'), \text{pbul}(S') \cup U \rangle, \\ S'' = S \cup \{\{\overline{L_i}\} \geq 1\} \text{ and} \\ P_2 = \langle \text{pbur}(S''), \text{pbul}(S'') \cup U \rangle \end{array}$$

Only the unit resolution procedure is replaced by its generalization to the pseudo-Boolean case. Applying the transition system defined by the three rules pbdp_clash, pbdp_sol, and pbdp_split as long as possible starting with $\langle\{\langle\text{pbur}(S),\text{pbul}(S)\rangle\},\emptyset\rangle$, where S is a set of linear pseudo-Boolean inequalities, yields the normal form $\langle\emptyset, Sol\rangle$ and Sol represents the set of all solutions of S. We define

$$\text{pbdp}(S) := \left\{ \begin{array}{ll} (\top, U) & \text{if} \qquad\qquad S \text{ is satisfiable and } U \in Sol \\ (\bot, \emptyset) & \text{otherwise ,} \end{array} \right. \tag{5.12}$$

which yields $(\top, U)$ if and only if S is satisfiable and U is the first set of literals that is added to Sol when exploring the search tree depth first and stopping after the first solution has been found.

5.3   OPTIMIZING WITH PSEUDO-BOOLEAN DAVIS-PUTNAM

Optimizing a linear pseudo-Boolean term cL subject to a set of linear pseudo-Boolean inequalities S can be done by solving a sequence of pseudo-Boolean satisfiability problems. We consider the problem of maximizing cL subject to S. Minimization works in a similar way.

The goal is to find a solution α of S such that $\alpha(cL) \geq \alpha'(cL)$ for all solutions α' of S. We will find such an assignment by solving a sequence of pseudo-Boolean satisfiability problems of the form $S_i := S \cup \{cL \geq \max_i\}$, where only $\max_i$ differs from problem to problem. We call $cL \geq \max_i$ *objective function inequality*. Suppose that $\max_0$ is such that $cL \geq \max_0$ is a tautology. Solving S_0 yields a solution α_0 of S_0 and therefore of S. A lower bound of the optimum is then $\alpha_0(cL)$. We define $\max_{i+1} := \max_i + 1$ and so exclude assignments yielding no better lower bounds than the current one. Obviously, we have $\alpha_{i+1}(cL) > \alpha_i(cL)$ for all satisfying assignments α_i of S_i and α_{i+1} of S_{i+1}. If S_i is satisfiable and S_{i+1} is unsatisfiable, then $\alpha_i(cL)$ is the desired maximum.

We can incorporate this idea into pbdp by replacing just the rule pbdp_sol. Instead of adding a computed solution that fixes the literals U, we construct a solution α such that $\alpha(L_i) = 1$ for all $L_i \in U \cup (L \backslash \overline{U})$, where $\overline{U} := \{\overline{L_i} \mid L_i \in U\}$ is the set of all negated literals in U. Then $\alpha(cL)$ is the maximal value of $\max cL$ subject to $\{U \geq |U|\}$. We add to the remaining satisfiability problems the linear pseudo-Boolean inequality $cL \geq \alpha(cL) + 1$. Thus, we ensure that for

each further solution the value of the objective function is larger. If there are no remaining nodes, then the last computed $\alpha(cL)$ was optimal.

Suppose that cL is a linear pseudo-Boolean term with $c_i > 0$ for all $c_i \in c$. We define a transition system that operates on states $\langle P, \max \rangle$, where P is a set of tuples $\langle S, U \rangle$, S is a set of linear pseudo-Boolean inequalities, and U is a set of literals that are fixed so far. The current lower bound of the maximization problem is max.

$$\text{opbdp\_clash:} \quad \frac{\langle \{\langle S, U \rangle\} \uplus P, \max \rangle}{\langle P, \max \rangle} \quad \text{if } \bot \in S$$

$$\text{opbdp\_climb:} \quad \frac{\langle \{\langle S, U \rangle\} \uplus P, \max \rangle}{\langle \text{prop}(P, \max' + 1), \max' \rangle} \quad \text{if } \begin{array}{l} S = \emptyset, \\ \forall L_i \in L' \setminus \overline{U} : \alpha'(L_i) = 1 \\ \text{and } \max' = \alpha'(cL) \end{array}$$

$$\text{opbdp\_split:} \quad \frac{\langle \{\langle S, U \rangle\} \uplus P, \max \rangle}{\langle \{P_1, P_2\} \cup P, \max \rangle} \quad \text{if } \begin{array}{l} \bot \notin S, S \neq \emptyset, \\ L_i = \text{select\_literal}(S), \\ S' = S \cup \{L_i \geq 1\} \text{ and} \\ P_1 = \langle \text{pbur}(S'), \text{pbul}(S') \cup U \rangle, \\ S'' = S \cup \{\{\overline{L_i}\} \geq 1\} \text{ and} \\ P_2 = \langle \text{pbur}(S''), \text{pbul}(S'') \cup U \rangle \end{array}$$

It remains to define **prop**, which updates the remaining satisfiability problems such that only better lower bounds are generated.

$$\text{prop}(\langle S, U \rangle \uplus P, \max) := \{ \begin{array}{l} \langle \text{pbur}(S \cup \{cL \geq \max\}), \\ \text{pbul}(S \cup \{cL \geq \max\}) \cup U \rangle \end{array} \} \cup \text{prop}(P, \max)$$

$$\text{prop}(\emptyset, \max) \qquad := \emptyset$$

Applying the transition system defined by the rules opbdp_clash, opbdp_climb, and opbdp_split as long as possible starting with $\langle \{\langle \text{pbur}(S), \text{pbul}(S) \rangle\}, -1 \rangle$ yields the normal form $\langle \emptyset, \max \rangle$, where $\max \geq \alpha(cL)$ for all $\alpha \in \text{Ext}(S)$ and $\max = -1$ if and only if S is unsatisfiable. We define the optimization procedure $\text{opbdp}(S, cL) := \max$, where max is the value computed by the above given transition system.

It is no restriction to require that cL contains only positive coefficients. Each term $c_i L_i$ with $c_i < 0$ is equivalent to $c_i + |c_i| \overline{L_i}$, since

$$c_i L_i \quad = \quad c_i - c_i + c_i L_i$$

$$= c_i - c_i \cdot (1 - L_i)$$
$$= c_i - c_i \overline{L_i} \ .$$

Optimizing a linear pseudo-Boolean term $\sum_{i=1}^{n} c_i L_i$ containing also negative coefficients is done by optimizing $\sum_{i=1}^{n} |c_i| L_i'$, where L_i' is L_i if $c_i > 0$ and $\overline{L_i}$ otherwise, and adding the sum over the negative coefficients c_i to the positive result of opbdp.

5.4 IMPLEMENTATION

Proper implementation and the use of appropriate data structures are important factors for the efficiency of the DP-procedure [Hoo93, HHT94, Zha93]. In a naive implementation of dp a satisfiability problem has to be copied at each node which may require excessive storage. We use the following data structure for implementing dp. Given a set of classical clauses S and the set of variables V occurring in S, we compute in advance the following index data structures. Each classical clause can be referenced by a unique identifier cid. The set of literals in a classical clause with identifier cid can be referenced by lids(cid). We can obtain a list of clause identifiers where a literal L_i occurs by cids(L_i). We represent a sub-problem of S by a list of *active variables* av, i.e., variables that are not yet fixed, and a list of *clause states*, where a clause state is a clause identifier and the number of literals nl currently active in that classical clause. Applying unit resolution for the literal L_i is done by

- deleting each element in the clause state list, where the identifier in the clause state is in cids(L_i)

- and decreasing nl by one if the identifier in the clause state is in cids($\overline{L_i}$).

We obtain a unit clause if nl is set to 1. The new unit literal is then determined by lids(cid) $\cap$ (av $\cup$ $\overline{\text{av}}$) and its variable is deleted from av. The empty clause is derived if nl is set to 0. Copying a sub-problem is now done by just copying the active clause list and the clause state list. The advantage of this data structure is that the index data structure does not change while exploring the search tree. The representation of the sub-problem in a node is very compact and detection of unit literals is straightforward.

For pbdp each linear pseudo-Boolean inequality can be referenced by a unique inequality identifier iid. Given a literal L_i, we can obtain a list of inequality

identifiers where L_i occurs by $\mathsf{iids}(L_i)$. We need an additional index data structure in order to access the coefficient $c_i = \mathsf{coeff}(L_i, \mathsf{iid})$ of a given literal L_i and an inequality identifier iid. A sub-problem is represented by a list of active variables av and a list of inequality states. An inequality state consists of an inequality identifier iid, a current right-hand side d of the linear pseudo-Boolean inequality, and a current sum $\sum c$ over all coefficients of the active literals of the linear pseudo-Boolean inequality. For applying pseudo-Boolean unit resolution for the literal L_i we do the following for all inequality states, where the inequality identifier iid is in $\mathsf{iids}(L_i)$:

- Delete the inequality state if $\mathsf{coeff}(L_i, \mathsf{iid}) \geq d$ (eliminate tautologies).

- Otherwise decrease the current right-hand side d and the current sum over all coefficients $\sum c$ by $\mathsf{coeff}(L_i, \mathsf{iid})$.

For all inequality states, where the inequality identifier iid is in $\mathsf{iids}(\overline{L_i})$ we do the following:

- Decrease the sum over all coefficients $\sum c$ by $\mathsf{coeff}(\overline{L_i}, \mathsf{iid})$. If $\sum c$ is smaller than the current right-hand side, then the sub-problem is unsatisfiable.

- Compute the active literal $L_j \in$ av for which $\mathsf{coeff}(L_j, \mathsf{iid})$ is maximal. L_j is a new unit literal, i.e., it can be fixed, if $\sum c - \mathsf{coeff}(L_j, \mathsf{iid}) < d$.

For large linear pseudo-Boolean inequalities, computing the active literal $L_j \in$ av $\cup \overline{\mathsf{av}}$ for which $\mathsf{coeff}(L_j, \mathsf{iid})$ is maximal will often yield the same literal. One improvement is to store the maximal coefficient with its literal in the inequality state and to update it only if this literal is fixed.

We implement opbdp as a slight variation of pbdp. When a satisfiable solution is found (i.e an empty inequality state list) we do not return $\top$, but calculate the maximal value max of the objective function under the current assignment. We then change destructively all copied right-hand sides d of the objective function inequality states to the new value $d - (\mathsf{max} + 1 - \mathsf{max}')$, where max' is the previous calculated maximal value. Hence, the current node becomes unsatisfiable and we backtrack until the objective function constraint is no longer violated. Then standard pbdp depth first search is continued. We follow roughly the ideas presented by Hooker [Hoo93] for incrementally solving SAT.

5.5   HEURISTICS

The selection of the branching literal [JW90, HHT94, HV94] is another important factor for the efficiency of the DP-procedure. Good literal selection heuristics can reduce the number of explored nodes by an order of magnitude. Hooker
et al. [HV94] investigate several branching heuristics for the clausal case. The
"Two-Sided Jeroslow-Wang" rule has been justified by a Markov chain analysis
of a simplification model that selects the literal L_i when $\text{pbur}(S \cup \{L_i \geq 1\})$ is
the *mostly simplified* problem [HV94]. The rule says that we should branch on
a variable X_i which maximizes $J(X_i) + J(\overline{X_i})$, with

$$J(L_i) := \sum_{L \geq 1 \in S : L_i \in L} 2^{-|L|} . \tag{5.13}$$

If $J(X_i) \geq J(\overline{X_i})$, then X_i should be selected, otherwise $\overline{X_i}$. The intention
of the rule is that we branch on a variable that occurs often in short clauses
and so get a small sub-problem with an increasing probability that unit literals
occur.

For linear pseudo-Boolean inequalities we adapt the two-sided Jeroslow-Wang
rule and branch on a variable X_i that maximizes $PBJ(X_i) + PBJ(\overline{X_i})$, with

$$PBJ(L_i) := \sum_{cL \geq d \in S : c_i L_i \in cL} \frac{c_i}{\sum c - d} \cdot 2^{-|\sum c/d|} . \tag{5.14}$$

If $PBJ(X_i) \geq PBJ(\overline{X_i})$, then X_i is selected, otherwise $\overline{X_i}$. We replace $|L|$,
which is a measure of the length of a clause, by $|\sum c/d|$, which reduces to the
length if we have classical clauses and so is a straightforward generalization.
The idea is that we prefer linear pseudo-Boolean inequalities, where many of the
coefficients are needed in order to satisfy the linear pseudo-Boolean inequality.
We weight this preference by multiplying $2^{-|\sum c/d|}$ by $c_i/(\sum c - d)$ and so take
into account the relative improvement of reaching the right-hand side when
fixing the literal to 1. Alternatively, we use

$$PBJ(L_i) := \sum_{cL \geq d \in S : c_i L_i \in cL} \frac{c_i \cdot d}{(\sum c)^2} ,$$

which has a similar intention than (5.14) but is easier to compute and takes
also very weak inequalities, i.e., where $|\sum c/d|$ is much larger than 1, into ac-
count. Further analysis is required in order to obtain a more efficient branching
heuristics. For opbdp we use as alternative a greedy-like heuristics depending
only on the objective function. We simply select a literal L_i with the maximal

coefficient in the objective function. The idea is that a better approximation of the optimal value is obtained earlier. A better literal selection heuristics that takes into account the goal of maximizing an objective function *and* reducing the search space needs to be found.

5.6   COMPUTATIONAL RESULTS

We have implemented the procedure opbdp in C++ and made it available in the 0-1-optimization package OPBDP [Bar95]. First, we compare OPBDP and SATO 2.0 [Zha93], a state-of-the-art implementation of the DP-procedure, on propositional satisfiability problems in classical clausal form. We use OPBDP for solving the satisfiability problem of a set of classical clauses S by maximizing a new single variable w.r.t. S. The set of classical clauses S is satisfiable if and only if OPBDP computes the optimum 1. SATO [Zha93] uses the heuristics to branch on a literal of a shortest positive clause. We use the variant of the two-sided Jeroslow Wang heuristics, presented in Section 5.5, for OPBDP.

In Figure 5.1 we present the results running SATO and OPBDP on a variety of propositional satisfiability problems from the DIMACS test set [Tri93]. In the column "Name" we give the name of the problem. In "# V" we mention the number of variables and in "# C" the number of clauses of the problem. In "SAT" we indicate whether the problem is satisfiable or not. "Nodes" is the number of nodes explored while solving the problem and "Time" is the user cpu time used for solving the problem by OPBDP resp. SATO on a SPARC-10/31. In the average case OPBDP is about 6 times slower than SATO w.r.t. the number of nodes explored per second. Considering only hard problems, where both algorithms explore more than a million nodes, OPBDP is about 2 times slower than SATO. Taking into account that OPBDP is able to solve linear pseudo-Boolean optimizations problems, whereas SATO can just check the satisfiability of a set of classical clauses, and the use of a computationally more difficult variable selection heuristics, the implementation is reasonably efficient w.r.t. SATO.

In Figure 5.2 we present computational results obtained by solving a variety of pure 0-1 integer programming problems found in MIPLIB [BBI92] with OPBDP. In the column "Name" we give the name of the problem. In "# V" we mention the number of variables and in "# I" the number of inequalities of the problem. "Nodes" is the number of nodes explored for solving the problem and "Time" is the user cpu time used for solving the problem with OPBDP on a SPARC-10/31.

Name	# V	# C	SAT	SATO Nodes	SATO Time	OPBDP Nodes	OPBDP Time
aim-100-20-n-1	100	200	N	92442475	12368.59	32	0.05
aim-100-20-n-2	100	200	N	53797042	6196.75	1642700	363.18
aim-100-20-y1-1	100	200	Y	271346	24.75	68181	19.11
aim-100-20-y1-2	100	200	Y	32300	3.90	14723	4.69
hole6	42	133	N	770	0.05	1438	0.28
hole9	90	415	N	362880	50.15	725758	312.25
dubois20	60	160	N	2097152	155.34	4194302	546.98
dubois21	63	168	N	4194304	350.31	8388606	1011.75
ssa0432-003	435	1027	N	268848	109.09	12366	16.93
ii32b3	348	5734	Y	55	0.19	274	14.35
ii32c3	279	3272	Y	20	0.09	70	3.55
ii32e3	330	5020	Y	65	0.23	322	12.46
par-8-2-c	68	270	Y	41	0.03	20	0.06
par-8-4-c	67	266	Y	15	0.01	17	0.06
par-16-2-c	324	1292	Y	?	&	66596	185.26
par-16-4-c	349	1392	Y	2886	2.72	34495	110.43
pret60_25	60	160	N	2236416	243.67	4194302	578.00
pret60_75	60	160	N	1589784	129.20	4194302	578.76

& : aborted after 30000 seconds

Figure 5.1   Clausal Boolean Satisfiability Problems

In the "DS-JW" columns we use OPBDP with the adapted two sided Jeroslow Wang heuristics. The columns "...(opt)" describe when the optimal value is found and the columns "...(V)" describe when the optimal result is verified and OPBDP terminates. In the column "OF" we first select the literal with the largest coefficient in the objective function. Typically, this heuristics finds good or even optimal solutions quickly, whereas the verification of optimality takes too long. Hence, we only measure the time to find the optimal solution "...(opt)".

In Figure 5.3 we report the results for solving the same 0-1 integer optimization problems with CPLEX 3.0 and MINTO 1.5 [NSS94]. CPLEX is a commercial mixed integer solver based on the simplex algorithm. Integer problems are solved by a standard branch-and-bound method. In CPLEX 3.0 also cutting plane techniques are incorporated. MINTO is based on CPLEX, but additionally generates strong cuts, e.g., clique inequalities and lifted knapsack covers, at each node if possible. For CPLEX and MINTO the time when the optimal solution was found is not given. MINTO does not mention the node where the optimal solution was found. The other columns in Figure 5.3 are similar to those in Figure 5.2.

Name	#I	#V	DS-JW (opt)		DS-JW (V)		OF (opt)	
			Nodes	Time	Nodes	Time	Nodes	Time
air01	46	771	2094	6.33	6302	17.68	1549	10.11
p0033	15	33	126	0.00	1083	0.05	890	0.05
p0040	23	40	215263	8.42	277520	10.81	61	0.01
p0201	133	201	51489055	18023.29	190836287	69130.40	493	0.30
bm23	20	27	6203	0.68	7165	0.79	4510	0.34
enigma	42	100	2534	0.33	2534	0.34	681	0.18
lseu	28	89	1415427	130.30	2967299	279.28	650191	59.88
misc01	70	82	214	0.06	1566	0.29	19740	2.15
misc02	52	58	114	0.01	293	0.04	141	0.06
misc03	122	159	54046	13.86	72065	20.21	425	0.13
misc07	246	259	9782421	6056.60	12037880	7552.70	164544	83.53
sentoy	30	60	312155	91.09	446968	147.09	778	0.14
stein15	36	15	9	0.00	436	0.02	6	0.01
stein27	118	27	2451	0.12	29138	1.60	17	0.01
stein45	331	45	159133	18.89	1535290	198.00	9170	1.83

& : aborted after 30000 seconds

Figure 5.2 0-1 Integer Optimization Problems from MIPLIB

Name	# I	# V	CPLEX (opt)	CPLEX (V)		MINTO(V)	
			Nodes	Nodes	Time	Nodes	Time
air01	23	771	3	3	0.35	2	955.00
p0033	16	33	662	694	2.23	31	1.00
p0040	23	40	51	54	0.17	1	0.00
p0201	133	201	760	1023	25.83	841	129.00
bm23	20	27	452	452	1.88	201	27.00
enigma	21	100	22086	22086	214.68	2466	786.00
lseu	28	89	10811	15889	82.05	187	15.00
misc01	54	82	76	721	6.97	283	18.00
misc02	39	58	29	60	0.60	46	2.00
misc03	96	159	24	527	16.77	2569	378.00
misc07	212	259	2601	22832	1450.48	?	&
sentoy	30	60	595	723	4.92	162	80.00
stein15	36	15	7	85	0.38	91	1.00
stein27	118	27	8	4061	32.87	4861	125.00
stein45	331	45	29373	71595	2910.18	103207	20904.00

& : aborted after 30000 seconds

Figure 5.3 0-1 Integer Optimization Problems from MIPLIB

The presented system OPBDP compares well w.r.t. the two linear programming based systems. For the problems enigma and steinxxx we gain a least an order of magnitude. Other problems, e.g., air01 and p0201, where the optimal value of the linear programming relaxation is already near the integer optimal value, but the number of variables is high, appear to be more difficult for OPBDP. It is interesting to note that in most of the problems the optimal solution was found early when using the greedy like heuristics "OF". This indicates that better variable selections heuristics that take into account both the objective function and the reduction of the search tree need to be found. Better implementation techniques (like the one from SATO) and special handling of equality constraints are further possible ways to improve the algorithm. Note that all occurring equalities $cL = d$ have been replaced by the two inequalities $cL \leq d$ and $cL \geq d$. Therefore, the row "# I" differ from the "ROWS" column found in MIPLIB. Direct use of the equality constraints would reduce the problem size and might help to decrease the number of explored nodes.

Currently, we require that all the coefficients are integer. The results still hold when rational coefficients are allowed in the constraint inequalities and adapting the presented method is easy. This has not yet been done and therefore some problems ("p0281", "mod008", "mod010", and "pipex") have not been considered. Furthermore, we have not tried some problems with a very large number of variables. We believe that a version of OPBDP using a full repertory of logic-based constraint processing techniques could also be applied on larger problems.

5.7   PSEUDO-BOOLEAN DAVIS-PUTNAM FOR CLP

An incremental version of the pseudo-Boolean Davis-Putnam algorithm pbdp is suitable in the context of constraint logic programming, if we do not require a solved form, but global consistency. The advantage is that satisfiability is ensured at each step of computation and, as computational experience indicates, the performance is acceptable even compared to specialized 0-1 integer programming tools. Thus, a first step to a more sophisticated and efficient constraint solver for constraint logic programs over pseudo-Boolean constraints is to use incremental pbdp as constraint solver. We then satisfy at least the most important requirement imposed by constraint logic programming; global consistency. Thus, we are sure that each CLP($\mathcal{PB}$) program is executed in the

same way, regardless to other improvements that may or may not speed up constraint solving.

Instead of a logic branch-and-bound algorithm, we can also use a logic branch-and-cut algorithm, which not only yields a solved form but, just as polyhedral cuts in 0-1 integer programming, may significantly reduce the number of nodes necessary to exhibit (un)satisfiability of a set of pseudo-Boolean constraints. Instead of exploring a search tree, we reformulate the current constraint store by adding valid constraints and strengthening existing constraints. The key to an efficient and powerful constraint solver is thus the development of methods for generating strong logic cuts. In the next chapter we show how to generate strong logic cuts that better approximate the set of prime extended clauses of the current constraint store by using **pbdp**.

6

LOGIC CUTS AND ENUMERATION

An unsatisfiable branch of the pseudo-Boolean Davis-Putnam enumeration algorithm pbdp of Chapter 5 provides information that allows us to generate a new valid extended clause that is not yet dominated by any single linear pseudo-Boolean inequality in the set of linear pseudo-Boolean inequalities to which pbdp is applied. Thus, we have a method for generating a logic cut for a set of linear pseudo-Boolean inequalities. This cut generation is complete, i.e., if the set of linear pseudo-Boolean inequalities is unsatisfiable, then the repeated generation of these logic cuts will detect unsatisfiability, otherwise a satisfiable branch will be hit. Thus, we have a complete pure logic cut algorithm for solving linear pseudo-Boolean constraints. Moreover, we show how to tailor the logic cut algorithm to generate logic cuts that help to decide entailment of extended clauses.

6.1 VALID EXTENDED CLAUSES BY ENUMERATION

Let us recall pbdp and apply it to a set of linear pseudo-Boolean inequalities S. Suppose that pbdp_clash applies, because we have $\perp \in S'$ in a state $\langle S', U \rangle$. For pbdp we delete that state, which contains useful information. Since $\perp \in S'$, we know that the set of linear pseudo-Boolean inequalities $S \cup \{U \geq |U|\}$ is unsatisfiable and that unsatisfiability is detected by pseudo-Boolean unit resolution, i.e., we have $\perp \in \text{pbur}(S \cup \{U \geq |U|\})$.

From the unsatisfiability of $S \cup \{L \geq |L|\}$ we know that S dominates the negation of $L \geq |L|$. The negation of $L \geq |L|$ is $L < |L|$ and after bringing

$L < |L|$ into pseudo-Boolean normal form we obtain

$$\overline{L} \geq 1 \ , \tag{6.1}$$

where $\overline{L}$ is $\{\overline{L_i} \mid L_i \in L\}$. In summary, S dominates $\overline{L} \geq 1$, since $S \cup \{L \geq |L|\}$ is unsatisfiable. Hence, we can generate a valid extended clause w.r.t. S, whenever fixing of literals yields $\bot$. We define

$$\text{gvec}(S, U) := \begin{cases} \overline{U} \geq 1 & \text{if} \quad \bot \in S \\ \top & \text{if} \quad S = \emptyset \\ \text{gvec}(S', U') & \text{if} \quad \bot \notin S, S \neq \emptyset, \\ & \quad L_i = \text{select\_literal}(S), \\ & \quad S' = \text{pbur}(S \cup \{L_i \geq 1\}) \text{ and} \\ & \quad U' = \text{pbul}(S \cup \{L_i \geq 1\}) \cup U \ . \end{cases} \tag{6.2}$$

Operationally, we explore the search tree of pbdp depth first without backtracking. If a solution is found, we return $\top$, otherwise we construct a valid extended clause w.r.t. S. Hence, S dominates $\text{gvec}(S, \emptyset)$. Furthermore, if $\text{gvec}(S, \emptyset) = \top$, then S is satisfiable.

Let us investigate the extended clause $\overline{U} \geq 1$ returned by pbdp_gvec(S) in the case that $\text{pbul}(S) = \emptyset$ and $\bot \notin S$, i.e., the pseudo-Boolean unit relaxation of S is satisfiable. Its most interesting property is that it is not yet dominated by any single linear pseudo-Boolean inequality in S.

Proposition 6.1.1 *Let S be a set of linear pseudo-Boolean inequalities, where* $\text{pbul}(S) = \emptyset$ *and* $\bot \notin S$*. Let* $\overline{U} \geq 1 \neq \top$ *be the result of* gvec(S)*. Then there is no linear pseudo-Boolean inequality* $cL \geq d$ *in S such that* $cL \geq d$ *dominates* $\overline{U} \geq 1$*.*

Proof. Suppose that there is a linear pseudo-Boolean inequality $cL \geq d$ in S such that $cL \geq d$ dominates $\overline{U} \geq 1$. Because $\bot \notin S$ we know that $U \neq \emptyset$. Let $L_i \in U$ be the last literal that is selected by select_literal. We then know that $\bot \in \text{pbur}(S \cup \{U \geq |U|\})$ and that $\bot \notin \text{pbur}(S \cup \{U \setminus \{L_i\} \geq |U|-1\})$, since otherwise $\text{gvec}(S, \emptyset) = \overline{U \setminus \{L_i\}} \geq 1$. Furthermore, we have $\overline{L_i} \notin \text{pbul}(S \cup \{U \setminus \{L_i\} \geq |U| - 1\})$, since otherwise L_i cannot be selected. Let $c'L' \geq d'$ be the linear pseudo-Boolean inequality obtained from $cL \geq d$ by fixing all the literals in $\text{pbul}(S \cup \{U \setminus \{L_i\} \geq |U|-1\})$ with the procedure fix defined by (5.8). Then $c'L' \geq d'$ is not $\bot$, since otherwise unsatisfiability would have been detected. If $c'L' \geq d'$ dominates $\overline{L_i} \geq 1$, then it is detected by pseudo-Boolean unit resolution because of Lemma 5.2.1 and thus $\overline{L_i} \in \text{pbul}(S \cup \{U \setminus \{L_i\} \geq |U|-1\})$, which is a contradiction. Therefore, $c'L' \geq d'$ does not dominate $\overline{L_i} \geq 1$.

But then there is an assignment α in $\mathsf{Ext}(c'L' \geq d')$ such that $\alpha(L_i) = 1$. Since no variable occurring in $\mathsf{pbul}(S \cup \{U \setminus \{L_i\} \geq |U| - 1\})$ occurs in $c'L' \geq d'$, let $\alpha(L_j) = 1$ for all $L_j \in \mathsf{pbul}(S \cup \{U \setminus \{L_i\} \geq |U| - 1\})$. Note that then $\alpha \in \mathsf{Ext}(cL \geq d)$. Since $cL \geq d$ dominates $\overline{U} \geq 1$, we know that $\alpha \in \mathsf{Ext}(\overline{U} \geq 1)$. But $\alpha(L_j) = 1$ for all $L_j \in U$ and thus $\alpha(\overline{U}) = 0$, which is a contradiction. Therefore, $cL \geq d$ does not dominate $\overline{U} \geq 1$. □

A straightforward way of checking whether we can derive a stronger extended clause than $\overline{U} \geq 1$ is to check whether $S \cup \{(U \setminus \{L_j\}) \cup \overline{L_j} \geq |U|\}$ is unsatisfiable for some $L_j \in U$, since then S dominates the stronger extended clause $\overline{U \setminus \{L_j\}} \geq 1$. Note that $S \cup \{U \setminus \{L_j\} \geq |L| - 1\}$ dominates $\overline{L_j} \geq 1$, since we already have derived that S dominates $\overline{U} \geq 1$. The simplest way to check unsatisfiability is to test whether $\bot \in \mathsf{pbur}(S \cup \{(U \setminus \{L_j\}) \cup \overline{L_j} \geq |U|\})$. Such a test requires at most $|U|$ times the application of pbur. Since pbur can be efficiently implemented, as shown in Section 5.4, such a test is suitable. Whenever we have eliminated a literal L_j, we can still try to eliminate not yet tried literals by the same method. If the generated extended clause is still too weak, we can also apply a restricted version of pbdp for the unsatisfiability test. For example, we can limit the depth of the search tree to a fixed bound. Note that if exploring this search tree yields a solution, we have also shown satisfiability of the current constraint store.

6.2 A PURE LOGIC CUT ALGORITHM

By Proposition 6.1.1 the procedure $\mathsf{pbdp\_gvec}$ generates a logic cut not yet dominated by any single linear pseudo-Boolean inequality in S or detects satisfiability of a set of pseudo-Boolean inequalities S. Since only variables from S occur in the logic cut, there is a finite number of not yet dominated logic cuts. Thus, repeatedly adding the result of gvec to S and applying gvec again will finally either generate $\top$, indicating that S is satisfiable, or the pseudo-Boolean unit relaxation will become unsatisfiable. We define

$$\mathsf{plc}(S, F) := \begin{cases} \{\bot\} & \text{if} \quad \bot \in S \\ S \cup \{F \geq |F|\} & \text{if} \quad \bot \notin S \text{ and } \mathsf{gvec}(S) = \top \\ \mathsf{plc}(S', F') & \text{if} \quad \bot \notin S, \\ & \qquad \mathsf{gvec}(S, \emptyset) = \overline{U} \geq 1 \neq \top, \\ & \qquad S' = \mathsf{pbur}(S \cup \{\overline{U} \geq 1\}) \text{ and} \\ & \qquad F' = \mathsf{pbul}(S \cup \{\overline{U} \geq 1\}) \cup F \ ; \end{cases}$$

$$(6.3)$$

a pure logic cut algorithm for solving linear pseudo-Boolean inequalities.

Theorem 6.2.1 *Let $S' = \text{plc}(\text{pbur}(S), \text{pbul}(S))$, where S is a set of linear pseudo-Boolean inequalities. Then $\text{Ext}(S) = \text{Ext}(S')$ and $S' = \{\bot\}$ if S is unsatisfiable.*

Proof. By definition (6.3) of `plc`, we know that `gvec` is only applied on a set of linear pseudo-Boolean inequalities S'' with $\text{pbul}(S'') = \emptyset$. By Proposition 6.1.1 we know that each clause generated by `gvec` is valid w.r.t. S. Since `plc` repeatedly adds valid extended clauses, we have $\text{Ext}(S) = \text{Ext}(S')$. Furthermore, we know that `gvec` always generates $\top$, or a clause consisting of variables from S that is not yet dominated by the current set of linear pseudo-Boolean inequalities. Since there is only a finite number of these clauses, either $\top$ is generated, or the pseudo-Boolean unit relaxation of the current problem is unsatisfiable. If $\top$ is generated, then the current equivalent problem is returned and the problem is known to be satisfiable. If the pseudo-Boolean unit relaxation of the current problem is unsatisfiable, then $\bot$ is in the current problem and $\{\bot\}$ is returned. $\square$

We say that $S' = \text{plc}(\text{pbur}(S), \text{pbul}(S))$ is closer to the solved form than S. Note that if S dominates an extended clause $L \geq d$, then there is a single extended clause in the solved form of S, the set of all prime extended clauses of S, dominating $L \geq d$. Obviously, there are more extended clauses that are dominated by an extended clause in S' than in S, if at least one clause generated by `gvec` is added.

The pure logic cut algorithm `plc` always adds a new extended clause. Despite the advantage that `plc` produces a stronger reformulation of the current problem, and therefore is suitable in the context of constraint logic programming, one may argue that `pbdp` would always be faster in deciding satisfiability than `plc`. We think that `plc` has two properties that allow for a more efficient handling of the pseudo-Boolean satisfiability problem than `pbdp`.

- Adding strong logic cuts changes the problem and so the variable selection heuristics may decide to try other branches. In other words, we do not completely explore a subtree if we choose the wrong literal early.

- We can simplify the current problem after the generation of a strong logic cut, which may change the problem completely. In particular, if the problem is unsatisfiable it is likely that simplification techniques apply and the

problem is solved much faster. Since the reformulation of the problem is closer to the set of its prime extended clauses, again the variable selection heuristics may try out completely different branches that are more promising.

In Chapter 8 we discuss several simplification techniques working on extended clauses and in Section 7.6 simplification techniques for linear pseudo-Boolean inequalities. Suppose that these simplification techniques are realized by a procedure `simplify`, then we obtain an enhanced pure logic cut algorithm by redefining

$$S' = \text{simplify}(S \cup \{\overline{U} \geq 1\})$$

in (6.3). The efficiency of a pure logic cut constraint solver depends heavily on the simplification techniques and the logic cuts that these simplification techniques generate. In an implementation we have to provide an incremental version of the simplification methods that are triggered by the newly added logic cut generated by `gvec`, where we assume that the set of linear pseudo-Boolean inequalities is initially in fully simplified form.

Example 6.2.2 We apply `plc` on $S :=$

$$\{A+F \geq 1, \overline{A}+B+\overline{C} \geq 1, \overline{A}+\overline{B}+D+E \geq 1, \overline{A}+\overline{C}+\overline{D} \geq 1, \overline{A}+\overline{B}+D+\overline{E} \geq 1\} \ .$$

We start fixing $A = 1$ and obtain $\text{pbur}(S') := \text{pbur}(S \cup \{A \geq 1\}) =$

$$\{B + \overline{C} \geq 1, \overline{B} + D + E \geq 1, \overline{C} + \overline{D} \geq 1, \overline{B} + D + \overline{E} \geq 1\} \ .$$

Next, we select $B = 1$ and get $\text{pbur}(S'') := \text{pbur}(\text{pbur}(S') \cup \{B \geq 1\}) =$

$$\{D + E \geq 1, \overline{C} + \overline{D} \geq 1, D + \overline{E} \geq 1\} \ .$$

By selecting $C = 1$ we get a contradiction, since we derive as fixed literals first $\overline{D} = 1$ from the second clause in $\text{pbur}(S'')$ and then the first clause implies $E = 1$, whereas the third implies $\overline{E} = 1$. Thus, we know that

$$\overline{A} + \overline{B} + \overline{C} \geq 1$$

is dominated by S. Let us check whether all selections are necessary for deriving the contradiction. Indeed, we see that already $\perp \in \text{pbur}(S \cup \{A+C \geq 2\})$, since the second extended clause of S forces $B = 1$. Thus, we derive the stronger extended clause

$$\overline{A} + \overline{C} \geq 1 \ .$$

Next, we add $\overline{A} + \overline{C} \geq 1$ to S and delete dominated extended clauses. We obtain $\hat{S} :=$

$$\{A + F \geq 1, \overline{A} + \overline{C} \geq 1, \overline{A} + \overline{B} + D + E \geq 1, \overline{A} + \overline{B} + D + \overline{E} \geq 1\} .$$

We restart solving $\hat{S}$ by again selecting first $A = 1$ and obtain $\text{pbur}(\hat{S}') :=$

$$\{\overline{B} + D + E \geq 1, \overline{B} + D + \overline{E} \geq 1\} .$$

Note that $\overline{C} = 1$ is now already detected. We have a stronger formulation and pseudo-Boolean unit resolution can detect more fixed literals. We again may select B, but after selecting D we obtain $\emptyset$ and thus S is satisfiable. Hence, we replace S by $\hat{S}$ in the current constraint store.

Suppose that our variable selection heuristics selects $A = B = \overline{D} = 1$ for $\hat{S}$ and thus again derives $\bot$. Then we obtain the valid extended clause

$$\overline{A} + \overline{B} + D \geq 1$$

and adding $\overline{A} + \overline{B} + D \geq 1$ to $\hat{S}$ yields, after deleting dominated extended clauses, $\widetilde{S} :=$

$$\{A + F \geq 1, \overline{A} + \overline{C} \geq 1, \overline{A} + \overline{B} + D \geq 1\} .$$

Now for $\widetilde{S}$ any variable selection heuristics in gvec derives satisfiability. We again have a stronger formulation of S and replace $\hat{S}$ by $\widetilde{S}$ in the current constraint store.

6.3   ENTAILMENT AND LOGIC CUTS

Deciding entailment of pseudo-Boolean constraints is a basic functionality in the context of concurrent constraint logic programming [JM94]. It is sufficient to decide entailment of extended clauses, since arbitrary entailment questions can be reformulated by the linearization technique of Chapter 9 and transformation technique of Chapter 7 to a set of entailment questions on extended clauses. Let S be the set of linear pseudo-Boolean inequalities representing the current constraint store. The problem is to check whether an extended clause $L \geq d$ is dominated by S.

We know that S dominates $L \geq d$ if and only if S together with the negation of $L \geq d$, i.e., $\overline{L} \geq |L| + 1 - d$, is unsatisfiable. A straightforward way for checking entailment of $L \geq d$ is therefore pbdp. We know that S dominates $L \geq d$ if and only if

$$\text{pbdp}(S \cup \{\overline{L} \geq |L| + 1 - d\}) = (\bot, \emptyset) .$$

Checking entailment by that method has the disadvantage that we have to explore a search tree for each entailment question and that after having decided domination, we have not gained any new information and the constraint store is unchanged. Therefore, we introduce a logic cut generation method that successively generates new logic cuts until entailment becomes easily decidable.

First, we restrict ourselves to the case $d = 1$, i.e., deciding whether or not a classical clause $L \geq 1$ is dominated by S. We know immediately that $L \geq 1$ is dominated by S if there is an extended clause in S dominating $L \geq 1$. If there is no such extended clause we try to generate it with our logic cut generation method based on the enumeration technique of Chapter 5. Again, the basic idea is to check unsatisfiability of the negation of $L \geq 1$ and S. The negation of $L \geq 1$ is $\overline{L} \geq |L|$, i.e., all literals in L are fixed to 0. Thus, we first apply pseudo-Boolean unit resolution and calculate

$$S' = \text{pbur}(S \cup \{\overline{L} \geq |L|\}) \ .$$

If $\bot \in S'$, we know that $L \geq 1$ is dominated. If S' is empty, we know that $S \cup \{\overline{L} \geq |L|\}$ is satisfiable and thus S does not dominate $L \geq 1$. The remaining case is that S' still contains linear pseudo-Boolean inequalities. We then apply gvec on S'. If $\text{gvec}(\text{pbur}(S'), \text{pbul}(S'))$ is $\top$, then $L \geq 1$ is not dominated, since S', and thus $S \cup \{\overline{L} \geq |L|\}$, is satisfiable. The other possibility is that gvec generates a clause $L' \geq 1$ dominated by S'. But our goal is to generate a valid extended clause dominated by S. Since we know that $S \cup \{\overline{L} \geq |L|, \overline{L'} \geq |L'|\}$ is unsatisfiable, we know that $S \cup \{\overline{L \cup L'} \geq |L| + |L'|\}$ is unsatisfiable. Thus, we obtain a valid extended clause dominated by S, namely $L \cup L' \geq 1$, which is a logic cut of S. By a repeated application of that procedure, we add not yet dominated logic cuts of the form $L \cup L' \geq 1$, where L' varies and L is fixed. Since there is only a finite number of these logic cuts, again, we are sure that either satisfiability of $S \cup \{\overline{L} \geq |L|\}$ is detected, and thus $L \geq 1$ is not dominated, or unsatisfiability of $S \cup \{\overline{L} \geq |L|\}$ is detected, and thus $L \geq 1$ is dominated. We restart the enumeration each time after adding a generated clause, since simplification may lead to a stronger formulation of the current constraint store and thus deciding entailment becomes more efficient. We get the following algorithm deciding entailment of a classical clause $L \geq 1$ w.r.t. S.

Algorithm 6.3.1 *Entailment of a classical clause*

> $\text{entail\_classclause}(S, L \geq 1)$
> > **if** $\exists L' \geq d' \in S : L' \geq d' \models L \geq 1$ **then return** $(S, \top)$ **endif**
> > $S' := \text{pbur}(S, \overline{L} \geq |L|)$

if $\bot \in S'$ **then return** $(\mathtt{simplify}(S \cup \{L \geq 1\}), \top)$
elseif $S' = \emptyset$ **then return** $(S, \bot)$
endif
$R := \mathtt{gvec}(\mathtt{pbur}(S'), \mathtt{pbul}(S'))$
if $R = \top$ **then return** $(S, \bot)$
elseif $R = L' \geq 1$ **then**
        $S'' := \mathtt{simplify}(S \cup \{L \cup L' \geq 1\})$
        return $\mathtt{entail\_classclause}(S'', L \geq 1)$
endif
end $\mathtt{entail\_classclause}$

We know that $\mathtt{entail\_classclause}(S, L \geq 1)$ returns $(S', \top)$ if and only if S dominates $L \geq 1$ and it returns $(S', \bot)$ if and only if S does not dominate $L \geq 1$. In both cases we have $\mathsf{Ext}(S') = \mathsf{Ext}(S)$ and S' is stronger than S. We replace the current constraint store S by S'. Thus, Algorithm 6.3.1 decides entailment of a classical clause and strengthens the current constraint store.

When deciding entailment of an extended clause $L \geq d$ with $d > 1$, we apply in principle the same algorithm. First, we check whether $L \geq d$ is dominated by an extended clause in S. If yes, it is entailed. Otherwise we choose a strict reduction $L' \geq 1$ of $L \geq d$ with $L' \subseteq L$ and $|L \setminus L'| = d - 1$. Additionally, we require that $L' \geq 1$ is not yet dominated by an extended clause in S. If all reductions $L' \geq 1$ of $L \geq d$ are dominated by an extended clause in S, then $L \geq d$ is dominated by S, since the set of all reductions $L' \geq 1$ is equivalent to $L \geq d$, see Theorem 7.1.5, and we have decided entailment. Next, we check whether $L' \geq 1$ is dominated by S with $\mathtt{entail\_classclause}$. If this is not the case, we know that $L \geq d$ is not dominated by S. If $L' \geq 1$ is dominated, then the constraint store is modified and there exists an extend clause in the current constraint store dominating $L' \geq 1$. Next, we again select a strict reduction of $L \geq d$, which cannot be $L' \geq 1$, and iterate the whole process. Since there are only finitely many reductions of $L \geq d$, the iteration must terminate. Hence, we have a decision procedure for deciding entailment of an extended clause $L \geq d$.

Algorithm 6.3.2 *Entailment of an extended clause*

$\mathtt{entail\_extendedclause}(S, L \geq d)$
    if $\exists \hat{L} \geq \hat{d} \in S : \hat{L} \geq \hat{d} \models L \geq d$ **then return** $(S, \top)$ **endif**
    if $\exists L' \geq 1 \in \mathsf{SRed}(L \geq d) \land \forall \hat{L} \geq \hat{d} \in S : \hat{L} \geq \hat{d} \not\models L' \geq 1$ **then**
        if $\mathtt{entail\_classclause}(S, L' \geq 1) = (S', \bot)$ **then**
            return $(S', \bot)$

        elseif entail_classclause$(S, L' \geq 1) = (S', \top)$ **then**

            return entail_extendedclause$(S', L \geq d)$

      endif

    else

        return $(\texttt{simplify}(S \cup \{L \geq d\}), \top)$

    endif

end entail_extendedclause

At a first sight it seems that Algorithm 6.3.2 would not be very efficient, since in the extreme case all strict reductions have to be checked for entailment. Again, the key point is that simplification takes place. In Section 8.2 we present an efficient method that generates extended clauses with right-hand side greater than 1. So, for example, when adding a classical clause $L' \geq 1$ it is likely that an extended clause $L' \cup \{L_j\} \geq 2$ is generated, which dominates $L' \geq 1$. Or even $L' \cup \{L_j, L_k\} \geq 3$ and so on. Thus, we hope that the simplification techniques of Section 8.2 will generate an extended clause dominating $L \geq d$ after only a few classical clauses have been generated.

The most important advantage of the presented entailment procedure is that not only entailment is decided, but the current constraint store is reformulated and gets closer to the solved form, the set of all prime extended clauses. Hence, the constraint solver is in a state where current questions about entailment can be answered, but the set of all prime extended clauses is not necessarily generated. Therefore, we spend computation time to answer questions and not to provide a solved form when unnecessary.

7

LINEAR PSEUDO-BOOLEAN
INEQUALITIES AND EXTENDED
CLAUSES

Transforming linear pseudo-Boolean inequalities into an equivalent set of extended clauses allows us to handle linear pseudo-Boolean constraints with specialized methods for extended clauses [Bar93c, Bar94]. Furthermore, deciding whether a linear pseudo-Boolean inequality is dominated by a set of pseudo-Boolean constraints reduces to the simpler problem of deciding whether extended clauses are dominated; an issue for which our solved form of pseudo-Boolean constraints is well-suited.

The idea of reformulating linear pseudo-Boolean inequalities in a simpler class of formulas without changing the solution space goes back to Hammer and Granot [HR68, GH71]. They showed how to express linear pseudo-Boolean inequalities as an equivalent set of classical clauses. Their attempt failed mainly because of the large number of generated classical clauses [GG80]. We express a linear pseudo-Boolean inequality as an equivalent set of extended clauses. Typically, substantially fewer extended clauses than classical clauses are needed to represent a linear pseudo-Boolean inequality.

In this chapter we present a transformation method efficiently producing prime extended clauses of a linear pseudo-Boolean inequality. We adapt cutting plane techniques, known from 0-1 integer programming, for generating valid extended clauses w.r.t. a linear pseudo-Boolean inequality in Section 7.1 and prove the equivalence of the set of generated extended clauses and the linear pseudo-Boolean inequality. Specialized strong redundancy criteria, that ensure that the minimal number of needed extended clauses is generated and that allow for an efficient redundancy test, are presented in Section 7.2. We sketch an implementation of the transformation method in Section 7.3. An important improvement is the use of symmetries along with a compact representation

of linear pseudo-Boolean inequalities and extended clauses, introduced in Section 7.4. We use pseudo-Boolean unit resolution, introduced in Chapter 5, in order to detect some of the fixed literals of a set of linear pseudo-Boolean inequalities. In the context of constraint logic programming, we typically already have a set of pseudo-Boolean constraints in the constraint store. Hence, we need not generate extended clauses that are already dominated by the constraint store. *Constrained transformation*, presented in Section 7.6, takes the information of the constraint store into account and thus we may reduce the number of generated extended clauses. In this context we also present simplification methods that strengthen a linear pseudo-Boolean inequality w.r.t. the constraint store and introduce methods that only partially transform a linear pseudo-Boolean inequality.

Besides the use inside our constraint solver for CLP($\mathcal{PB}$), we also relate the produced set of extended clauses to extended cover inequalities [NW88]. We show in Section 7.7 that the method generates the set of all *strongest, non-redundant* extended cover inequalities w.r.t. a linear pseudo-Boolean inequality, which are used as cutting planes in traditional 0-1 integer programming [NW88]. We apply the presented technique in a preprocessing phase for 0-1 integer programming problems and give some encouraging computational results. Another application is the implementation of one of the basic deduction rules of *Generalized Resolution* [Hoo92a], introduced in Section 7.8, that allows us to apply several resolution steps at once.

7.1 GENERATING VALID EXTENDED CLAUSES

We show how to generate a set of extended clauses equivalent to a linear pseudo-Boolean inequality. We define the *strongest extended clause* of a linear pseudo-Boolean inequality, and relate it to *cutting plane* inequalities known from 0-1 integer programming [NW88]. The equivalence of the set of all strongest extended clauses of all strict reductions of a linear pseudo-Boolean inequality and the linear pseudo-Boolean inequality itself is the main theorem of this section.

7.1.1 The Strongest Extended Clause

We already have seen in Section 3.3.2 that linear combination and integer rounding are well-known techniques of 0-1 integer programming for deriving

valid inequalities [NW88]. We adopt these techniques in order to generate valid extended clauses.

Let us divide a linear pseudo-Boolean inequality in normal form

$$c_1 L_1 + \cdots + c_n L_n \geq d \tag{7.1}$$

by a positive integer k and round the fractional coefficients of the left-hand side yielding

$$\lceil c_1/k \rceil L_1 + \cdots + \lceil c_n/k \rceil L_n \geq d/k$$

with $\lceil a \rceil := \min(\{b \in \mathbb{N} \mid b \geq a\})$. Because rounding only increases the left-hand side, we have generated a valid inequality w.r.t. (7.1). Since the coefficients $\lceil c_i/k \rceil$ are integer, the left-hand side is integer for all assignments. Therefore, the right-hand side d/k can be replaced by the largest integer less than or equal to d/k, which is $\lceil d/k \rceil$. We obtain the valid linear pseudo-Boolean inequalities

$$\lceil c_1/k \rceil L_1 + \cdots + \lceil c_n/k \rceil L_n \geq \lceil d/k \rceil \ ,$$

dominated by (7.1), for all positive integers k. These linear pseudo-Boolean are a subclass of the so-called *Chvátal-Gomory cutting plane* inequalities [Gom58, NW88], obtained from a linear combination of the linear pseudo-Boolean inequality and the valid bounds $L_i \geq 0$ and $-L_i \geq -1$ for the literals L_i followed by integer rounding of the coefficients and the right-hand side. We obtain the valid extended clause

$$L_1 + \cdots + L_n \geq \lceil d/c_1 \rceil \ , \tag{7.2}$$

dominated by (7.1), if we set $k = c_1$, since then the $\lceil c_i/k \rceil$ are all 1. The extended clause (7.2) derived from a linear pseudo-Boolean inequality $cL \geq d$ is denoted by $\mathsf{CP}(cL \geq d)$ and is dominated by $cL \geq d$.

Example 7.1.1 Let $cL \geq d$ be

$$5 \cdot L_1 + 4 \cdot L_2 + 3 \cdot L_3 + 2 \cdot L_4 + 1 \cdot L_5 \geq 11$$

then $\mathsf{CP}(cL \geq d)$ is

$$L_1 + L_2 + L_3 + L_4 + L_5 \geq 3 \ .$$

For a set of linear pseudo-Boolean inequalities S we denote by $\mathsf{CP}(S)$ the set of extended clauses $\mathsf{CP}(cL \geq d)$ for all $cL \geq d$ in S. The cutting plane operation CP generates a valid extended clause $L \geq d'$ dominated by the linear pseudo-Boolean inequality $cL \geq d$. We are now interested in the greatest integer β such that $L \geq \beta$ is dominated by $cL \geq d$. We call $L \geq \beta$ *strongest extended clause* of $cL \geq d$.

Proposition 7.1.2 *The strongest extended clause of a linear pseudo-Boolean inequality $cL \geq d$ is*

$$L \geq \beta \, , \tag{7.3}$$

where β is the smallest β such that $\sum_{i=1}^{\beta} c_i \geq d$, determined by the condition

$$\sum_{i=1}^{\beta-1} c_i < d \leq \sum_{i=1}^{\beta} c_i \, . \tag{7.4}$$

The extended clauses $L \geq \beta + l$ are not dominated by $cL \geq d$ for all $l \geq 1$.

Proof.

[a] First, we show that $cL \geq d$ dominates $L \geq \beta$. Because $cL \geq d$ is in pseudo-Boolean normal form, we know that $c_1 \geq \cdots \geq c_n$. Thus, for all $1 \leq k \leq n$ we have $\sum_{i=1}^{k} c_i \geq \sum_{i \in K} c_i$ for all $K \subseteq \{1, \ldots, n\}$ with $|K| = k$. Let k be $\beta - 1$. Since $\sum_{i=1}^{\beta-1} c_i < d$, we know that $\sum_{i \in K} c_i < d$ for all $K \subseteq \{1, \ldots, n\}$ with $|K| = \beta - 1$. Consequently, for all solutions $\alpha \in \text{Ext}(cL \geq d)$ we have $\alpha(L) > \beta - 1$ and therefore $\alpha(L) \geq \beta$.

[b] Next, we show that $cL \geq d$ does not dominate $L \geq \beta + l$ for all $l \geq 1$. Let α be an assignment such that $\alpha(L_1) = \ldots = \alpha(L_\beta) = 1$ and $\alpha(L_{\beta+1}) = \ldots = \alpha(L_n) = 0$. Then $\alpha \in \text{Ext}(cL \geq d)$ because $\sum_{i=1}^{\beta} c_i \geq d$, but $\alpha \notin \text{Ext}(L \geq \beta + l)$ for all $l \geq 1$ because $\alpha(L) = \beta$. $\square$

For a linear pseudo-Boolean inequality $cL \geq d$ we denote by $\text{SCP}(cL \geq d)$ the strongest extended clause $L \geq \beta$ of Proposition 7.1.2. For a set of linear pseudo-Boolean inequalities S we denote by $\text{SCP}(S)$ the set of all extended clauses $\text{SCP}(cL \geq d)$ with $cL \geq d$ in S. From Proposition 7.1.2 we know that the degree of $\text{SCP}(cL \geq d)$ is greater than or equal to the degree of $\text{CP}(cL \geq d)$; therefore $\text{SCP}(cL \geq d)$ dominates $\text{CP}(cL \geq d)$.

Example 7.1.3 Let $cL \geq d$ again be

$$5 \cdot L_1 + 4 \cdot L_2 + 3 \cdot L_3 + 2 \cdot L_4 + 1 \cdot L_5 \geq 11$$

as in Example 7.1.1, then

$$\text{CP}(cL \geq d) = \text{SCP}(cL \geq d) = L_1 + L_2 + L_3 + L_4 + L_5 \geq 3 \, .$$

If $cL \geq d$ is

$$5 \cdot L_1 + 4 \cdot L_2 + 3 \cdot L_3 + 2 \cdot L_4 + 1 \cdot L_5 \geq 10 \, ,$$

then

$$\mathsf{CP}(cL \geq d) \quad = \quad L_1 + L_2 + L_3 + L_4 + L_5 \geq 2$$

and

$$\mathsf{SCP}(cL \geq d) \quad = \quad L_1 + L_2 + L_3 + L_4 + L_5 \geq 3 \ .$$

Note that $\mathsf{SCP}(cL \geq d)$ strictly dominates $\mathsf{CP}(cL \geq d)$.

7.1.2   Strict Reductions

We know that all reductions of a linear pseudo-Boolean inequality $cL \geq d$ are valid w.r.t. $cL \geq d$. Hence, for all strict reductions $c'L' \geq d'$ of $cL \geq d$ we know that $\mathsf{SCP}(c'L' \geq d')$ is a valid extended clause w.r.t. $cL \geq d$.

Example 7.1.4 A strict reduction of

$$5 \cdot L_1 + 4 \cdot L_2 + 3 \cdot L_3 + 2 \cdot L_4 + 1 \cdot L_5 \geq 11$$

is

$$5 \cdot L_1 + 4 \cdot L_2 + 3 \cdot L_3 + 2 \cdot L_4 \geq 10$$

obtained by eliminating L_5. Its strongest extended clause is

$$L_1 + L_2 + L_3 + L_4 \geq 3 \ .$$

We now show that $\mathsf{SCP}(\mathsf{SRed}(cL \geq d))$, the set of strongest extended clauses derived from all strict reductions of a linear pseudo-Boolean inequality $cL \geq d$, is equivalent to $cL \geq d$.

Theorem 7.1.5 *Let $cL \geq d$ be an arbitrary linear pseudo-Boolean inequality, then*

$$\mathsf{Ext}(cL \geq d) = \mathsf{Ext}(\mathsf{SCP}(\mathsf{SRed}(cL \geq d))) \ . \tag{7.5}$$

Proof.

[a] $\mathsf{Ext}(cL \geq d) \subseteq \mathsf{Ext}(\mathsf{SCP}(\mathsf{SRed}(cL \geq d)))$:
   For all strict reductions $c'L' \geq d'$ of $cL \geq d$ we know that $\mathsf{Ext}(cL \geq d) \subseteq \mathsf{Ext}(c'L' \geq d')$ because $cL \geq d$ dominates $c'L' \geq d'$. Hence,

$$\mathsf{Ext}(cL \geq d) \subseteq \bigcap_{c'L' \geq d' \in \mathsf{SRed}(cL \geq d)} \mathsf{Ext}(c'L' \geq d') = \mathsf{Ext}(\mathsf{SRed}(cL \geq d)) \ .$$

It remains to show $\mathsf{Ext}(\mathsf{SRed}(cL \geq d)) \subseteq \mathsf{Ext}(\mathsf{SCP}(\mathsf{SRed}(cL \geq d)))$. Since a strongest extended clause of a linear pseudo-Boolean inequality is valid w.r.t. this inequality, we have $\mathsf{Ext}(c'L' \geq d') \subseteq \mathsf{Ext}(\mathsf{SCP}(c'L' \geq d'))$ for all $c'L' \geq d'$ of $cL \geq d$. Because the intersection of sets T_i is a subset of the intersection of sets T_i' if $T_i \subseteq T_i'$, we have $\mathsf{Ext}(\mathsf{SRed}(cL \geq d)) \subseteq \mathsf{Ext}(\mathsf{SCP}(\mathsf{SRed}(cL \geq d)))$.

[b] $\mathsf{Ext}(\mathsf{SCP}(\mathsf{SRed}(cL \geq d))) \subseteq \mathsf{Ext}(cL \geq d)$:

We show that $\alpha \notin \mathsf{Ext}(\mathsf{SCP}(\mathsf{SRed}(cL \geq d)))$ if $\alpha \notin \mathsf{Ext}(cL \geq d)$ from which the theorem follows. Suppose that $\alpha \notin \mathsf{Ext}(cL \geq d)$. We show that in this case there is a strict reduction of $cL \geq d$ such that α is not a solution of the strongest extended clause of this reduction, and therefore $\alpha \notin \mathsf{Ext}(\mathsf{SCP}(\mathsf{SRed}(cL \geq d)))$. Since $\alpha \notin \mathsf{Ext}(cL \geq d)$, we know that $\alpha(cL) = d' < d$. Let Y be the set of literals $\{L_i \mid \alpha(L_i) = 1\}$ and $Z = L \backslash Y$, then $\sum_{i:L_i \in Y} c_i = d' < d$. Let $c'L' \geq d'$ be $\sum_{i:L_i \in Z} c_i L_i \geq d - d'$. Because $d' < d$, we know that $d - d' \geq 1$, and therefore $c'L' \geq d'$ is a strict reduction of $cL \geq d$, obtained by eliminating the literals that are mapped to zero by α. Let $\mathsf{SCP}(c'L' \geq d')$ be $L' \geq \beta$. We know that $\beta \geq 1$ because $d - d' \geq 1$. Because $\alpha(L') = 0$, we derive that $\alpha \notin \mathsf{Ext}(\mathsf{SCP}(c'L' \geq d'))$, and therefore $\alpha \notin \mathsf{Ext}(\mathsf{SCP}(\mathsf{SRed}(cL \geq d)))$, which proves the theorem. $\qquad\square$

Theorem 7.1.5 suggests a simple procedure for transforming a linear pseudo-Boolean inequality into an equivalent set of extended clauses. Unfortunately, a large number of extended clauses may be produced. Obviously, we preserve equivalence if we consider only extended clauses that are not dominated by others.

Example 7.1.6 The set of all strongest extended clauses of all strict reductions of

$$5 \cdot L_1 + 4 \cdot L_2 + 3 \cdot L_3 + 2 \cdot L_4 + 1 \cdot L_5 \geq 11 \tag{7.6}$$

is

$L_1 + L_2 + L_3 + L_4 + L_5 \geq 3$	$L_1 + L_2 + L_3 \geq 2$	$L_1 + L_2 + L_3 + L_5 \geq 2$	
$L_1 + L_2 + L_4 + L_5 \geq 2$	$L_1 + L_3 + L_4 \geq 2$	$L_2 + L_3 + L_4 + L_5 \geq 2$	
$L_1 + L_2 + L_3 + L_4 \geq 3$	$L_1 + L_2 + L_4 \geq 2$	$L_1 + L_2 + L_5 \geq 2$	
$L_1 + L_3 + L_4 + L_5 \geq 2$	$L_1 + L_3 + L_5 \geq 1$	$L_1 + L_4 + L_5 \geq 1$	
$L_2 + L_3 + L_4 \geq 2$	$L_2 + L_3 + L_5 \geq 1$	$L_2 + L_4 + L_5 \geq 1$	
$L_3 + L_4 + L_5 \geq 1$	$L_1 + L_2 \geq 1$	$L_1 + L_3 \geq 1$	
$L_1 + L_4 \geq 1$	$L_1 + L_5 \geq 1$	$L_2 + L_3 \geq 1$	
$L_2 + L_4 \geq 1$	$L_2 + L_5 \geq 1$	$L_3 + L_4 \geq 1$	$L_1 \geq 1$.

Note that there are 25 strict reductions and therefore 25 extended clauses. If we delete all extended clauses that are dominated by others, we obtain

$$L_1 + L_2 + L_3 + L_4 \geq 3 \qquad L_1 + L_2 + L_5 \geq 2 \qquad L_1 \geq 1 \ .$$

The set of these 3 extended clauses is equivalent to (7.6).

An interesting property is that the normal form of $\mathsf{SCP}(\mathsf{SRed}(cL \geq d))$ consists of the set of all prime extended clauses of $cL \geq d$.

Proposition 7.1.7 *For all extended clauses $L' \geq d'$ dominated by $cL \geq d$ there exists an extended clause in $\mathsf{SCP}(\mathsf{SRed}(cL \geq d))$ dominating $L' \geq d'$.*

Proof. Suppose that $L' \geq d'$ is dominated by $\mathsf{SCP}(\mathsf{SRed}(cL \geq d))$. Because $\mathsf{Ext}(cL \geq d) = \mathsf{Ext}(\mathsf{SCP}(\mathsf{SRed}(cL \geq d)))$, we know that $cL \geq d$ dominates $L' \geq d'$. Obviously, $cL \geq d$ dominates $L' \geq d'$ only if it dominates $L'' \geq d'$ with $L'' = L' \cap L$. We consider the strict reduction $c''L'' \geq d''$ of $cL \geq d$ and its corresponding strongest extended clause $L'' \geq \beta$. From Proposition 7.1.2 we know that $\beta \geq d'$, and therefore $L'' \geq \beta$ in $\mathsf{SCP}(SRed(cL \geq d))$ dominates $L' \geq d'$. □

For a single linear pseudo-Boolean inequality $cL \geq d$ the normal form of $\mathsf{SCP}(\mathsf{SRed}(cL \geq d))$ is already the *ideal solved form* that should be extracted by our constraint solver. Note that if there are two or more linear pseudo-Boolean inequalities, then the union of the sets of generated extended clause does not contain all prime extended clauses of the set of these linear pseudo-Boolean inequalities. We then have to apply *Generalized Resolution* in order to obtain the ideal solved form.

The challenge is to find the normal form of $\mathsf{SCP}(\mathsf{SRed}(cL \geq d))$ without completely constructing the dominated and therefore *redundant* extended clauses, and to minimize the number of domination checks. In the following we describe strong redundancy criteria identifying extended clauses that are dominated by other extended clauses.

7.2 IDENTIFYING REDUNDANT EXTENDED CLAUSES

The normal form of $\mathsf{SCP}(\mathsf{SRed}(cL \geq d))$, i.e., the set of all non-redundant extended clauses in $\mathsf{SCP}(\mathsf{SRed}(cL \geq d))$, is the set of extended clauses, equivalent to $cL \geq d$, that we want to build. A naive way is to completely generate $\mathsf{SCP}(\mathsf{SRed}(cL \geq d))$, and then delete the redundant extended clauses. Typically, many of the generated extended clauses are redundant. We develop strong redundancy criteria that minimize the number of domination checks needed for deciding whether an extended clause is redundant, i.e., is dominated by another extended clause. We show how to decide redundancy of an extended clause in $\mathsf{SCP}(\mathsf{SRed}(cL \geq d))$ by checking domination against *two* other extended clauses. For this purpose we first arrange the elements of $\mathsf{SCP}(\mathsf{SRed}(cL \geq d))$ as a directed acyclic graph.

Let $T = T(cL \geq d)$ be a finite acyclic graph with root node, where the nodes are labeled with the strict reductions of $cL \geq d$. The root of T is labeled by $cL \geq d$. The direct subgraphs of T are the graphs $T(c'L' \geq d')$ for all strict reductions $c'L' \geq d'$ of $cL \geq d$, where exactly one literal has been eliminated. We denote by $\mathcal{T}(T, j)$ the direct subgraph of T with the label $\sum_{1 \leq i \neq j \leq n} c_i L_i \geq d - c_j$, provided that $d - c_j \geq 1$. We abbreviate $\mathcal{T}(\mathcal{T}(\ldots(\mathcal{T}(T, j_1), j_2), \ldots), j_k)$ by $T(\{j_1, \ldots, j_k\})$. We say $j_1 \ldots j_k$ is a *path* to the graph $T(\{j_1, \ldots, j_k\})$. Note that every permutation of $j_1 \ldots j_k$ is a path to $T(\{j_1, \ldots, j_k\})$, and that every element of $\mathsf{SRed}(cL \geq d)$ is the label of exactly one node in $T(cL \geq d)$. We denote by T_j the strongest extended clause of the root label of $\mathcal{T}(T, j)$. The strongest extended clause of the root label of $T(\{j_1, \ldots, j_k\})$ is referenced by $T_{\{j_1, \ldots, j_k\}}$. Note that the extended clause $T_{\{j_1, \ldots, j_k\}}$ has $n - k$ literals, therefore the length of the path determines the number of literals of the label. A part of the graph view of $\mathsf{SCP}(\mathsf{SRed}(cL \geq d))$ is shown in Figure 7.1. For each node we show the strict reduction and its corresponding strongest extended clause. Additionally, the arcs are labeled by the literal L_i that we eliminated from the father node to the son node.

In the following we denote by $J_k := \{j_1, \ldots, j_k\} \subset \{1, \ldots, n\}$ a set of indices such that $T(J_k)$ is a valid strict reduction of $cL \geq d$. Furthermore, we denote by $\overline{J_k} := \{j'_1, \ldots, j'_{n-k}\}$ the set of indices of the remaining literals in $T(J_k)$. Thus, $\overline{J_k} \cup J_k = \{1, \ldots, n\}$ and $\overline{J_k} \cap J_k = \emptyset$. We then have

$$T(J_k) = \sum_{i=1}^{n-k} c_{j'_i} L_{j'_i} \geq d - \sum_{i=1}^{k} c_{j_i} .$$

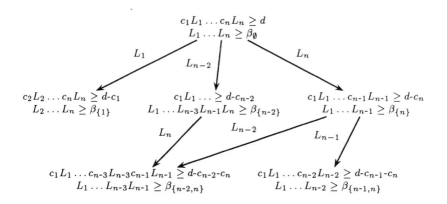

Figure 7.1   Part of a graph view of $\mathsf{SCP}(\mathsf{SRed}(cL \geq d))$

We abbreviate $\sum_{i=1}^{n-k} c_{j'_i} L_{j'_i}$ by $c(J_k)L(J_k)$ and $\sum_{i=1}^{n-k} L_{j'_i}$ by $L(J_k)$. First, we investigate the degrees of the strongest extended clauses along a path.

Lemma 7.2.1 *For all J_k and $J_{k+1} = J_k \cup \{j_{k+1}\}$ we have*

$$\deg(T_{J_k}) \geq \deg(T_{J_{k+1}}) \geq \deg(T_{J_k}) - 1 \ . \tag{7.7}$$

Furthermore, for all $J_k \subset J_l$ we have

$$|J_l| - |J_k| \geq \deg(T_{J_k}) - \deg(T_{J_l}) \ . \tag{7.8}$$

Proof. First, we show (7.7). Let T_{J_k} be $L_{j_{k+1}} + L(J_{k+1}) \geq \beta$ and let $T_{J_{k+1}}$ be $L(J_{k+1}) \geq \beta'$. We need to show that $\beta \geq \beta' \geq \beta - 1$.

$\beta \geq \beta'$: We know that $L(J_{k+1}) \geq \beta'$ dominates $L_{j_{k+1}} + L(J_{k+1}) \geq \beta'$. Since $L_{j_{k+1}} + L(J_{k+1}) \geq \beta$ is the strongest extended clause, we have $\beta \geq \beta'$.

$\beta' \geq \beta - 1$: We know that $L_{j_{k+1}} + L(J_{k+1}) \geq \beta$ dominates its own reduction $L(J_{k+1}) \geq \beta - 1$. Because $L(J_{k+1}) \geq \beta'$ is a strongest extended clause, we have $\beta' \geq \beta - 1$.

Therefore, the degree of the strongest extended clauses along a path from the root at each step either decreases by 1 or stays equal. By induction, we conclude that (7.8) holds for all $J_k \subset J_l$.   □

Lemma 7.2.2 Let $T(J_k)$ be $c_{j_{k+1}}L_{j_{k+1}} + \sum_{i=1}^{n-(k+1)} c_{j'_i} L_{j'_i} \geq d' + c_{j_{k+1}}$. W.l.o.g. we assume that $c_{j'_p} \geq c_{j'_q}$ for all $1 \leq p < q \leq n - (k+1)$. Let $\deg(T_{J_k}) = \beta$ and $\deg(T_{J_{k+1}}) = \beta'$. If $c_{j_{k+1}} \geq c_{j'_{\beta'}}$, then $\beta' + 1 = \beta$.

Proof. The strict reduction $T(J_{k+1})$ of $T(J_k)$ is $\sum_{i=1}^{n-(k+1)} c_{j'_i} L_{j'_i} \geq d'$. From equation (7.4) in Proposition 7.1.2 we know that

$$\sum_{i=1}^{\beta'-1} c_{j'_i} < d' \leq \sum_{i=1}^{\beta'} c_{j'_i} .$$

By adding $c_{j_{k+1}}$ to the left inequality, we derive

$$c_{j_{k+1}} + \sum_{i=1}^{\beta'-1} c_{j'_i} < d' + c_{j_{k+1}} . \tag{7.9}$$

According to Proposition 7.1.2, β is the smallest number of the largest coefficients such that the sum of the largest coefficients is greater than the right-hand side $d' + c_{j_{k+1}}$. From $c_{j_{k+1}} \geq c_{j'_{\beta'}}$ and (7.9) we know that $c_{j_{k+1}}$ is one of the coefficients of this sum, and therefore $\beta > \beta'$. By Lemma 7.2.1 we have $\beta \leq \beta' + 1$, and therefore $\beta' + 1 = \beta$. $\qquad\square$

The converse does not necessarily hold.

Example 7.2.3 Let the strict reduction $T(J_{k+1})$ be

$$6 \cdot L_1 + 5 \cdot L_2 + 4 \cdot L_3 + 3 \cdot L_4 \geq 12 .$$

Its strongest extended clause is

$$L_1 + L_2 + L_3 + L_4 \geq 3$$

with degree 3, because $6 + 5 < 12 \leq 6 + 5 + 4$. Let $c_i L_i$ be the product that has been eliminated, thus the inequality at the father node is

$$c_i \cdot L_i + 6 \cdot L_1 + 5 \cdot L_2 + 4 \cdot L_3 + 3 \cdot L_4 \geq 12 + c_i ,$$

and its strongest extended clause is

$$L_i + L_1 + L_2 + L_3 + L_4 \geq \beta .$$

By Lemma 7.2.2 we know that if $c_i \geq 4$ then $\beta = 4$. Suppose that $c_i = 4$, then condition (7.4) becomes $6 + 5 + 4 < 16 \leq 6 + 5 + 4 + 4$ and, as expected, the degree β is 4. Note that if $c_i = 3$, then β is still 4.

We now give a complete redundancy criterion for $\text{SCP}(cL \geq d) = T_\emptyset$.

Lemma 7.2.4 $T_\emptyset$ *is redundant if and only if* $\deg(T_\emptyset) = \deg(T_{\{n\}})$.

Proof. We show that $T_\emptyset$ is dominated by a strongest extended clause if and only if it is dominated by $T_{\{n\}}$. Let $T_\emptyset$ be $L \geq \beta$, let L' be $L \setminus \{L_n\}$ and let $T_{\{n\}}$ be $L' \geq \beta'$. Note that $c_n \leq c_i$ for all $1 \leq i \leq n$.

$\Leftarrow$: Since $\beta = \beta'$, we know that $L' \geq \beta$ dominates $L \geq \beta$ because $L' \subset L$. Hence, $L \geq \beta$ is redundant.

$\Rightarrow$: Let us assume that $L \geq \beta$ is redundant. Then there exists $L'' \geq \beta''$ in $\text{SCP}(\text{SRed}(cL \geq d))$ that dominates $L \geq \beta$, and thus $\beta'' \geq \beta$. Since $L'' \geq \beta''$ is the strongest extended clause of a strict reduction of $cL \geq d$, we have by Lemma 7.2.1 that $\beta \geq \beta''$ and therefore $\beta = \beta''$. Because the degree of the strongest extended clauses along a path always decreases by 1 or stays equal, see (7.8), and since $L'' \subset L$, we know that all strongest extended clauses along the path from the root to the node with strongest extended clause $L'' \geq \beta$ have the degree β. Thus, for some direct son of the root we have a strongest extended clause $L \setminus \{L_j\} \geq \beta$ dominating $L \geq \beta$. From Lemma 7.2.2 we know that the coefficient c_j of the eliminated literal L_j is smaller than $c_{\beta-1}$, because otherwise $\beta'' + 1 = \beta + 1 = \beta$. From $c_j < c_{\beta-1}$ we derive $j \geq \beta - 1$, since $cL \geq d$ is in pseudo-Boolean normal form and therefore $\sum_{i=1}^{\beta-1} c_i < d - c_j$. Because $c_j \geq c_n$, we have $d - c_j \leq d - c_n$, and therefore $\sum_{i=1}^{\beta-1} c_i < d - c_n$. But then $\beta' \geq \beta$, and because β' is the degree of a strongest extended clause on a path from the root, we have $\beta' \leq \beta$ and therefore $\beta' = \beta$. $\qquad\square$

Proposition 7.2.5 *If* T_{J_k} *is dominated by* T_{J_l} *and* $J_l \supset J_k$*, then* $T_{J_{k+1}} := T_{J_k \cup \{j_{k+1}\}}$ *dominates* T_{J_k} *with* $c_{j_{k+1}} \leq c_i$ *for all* $i \in \overline{J_k}$.

Proof. The proposition follows immediately from Lemma 7.2.4 if we view $T(J_k)$ as an independent graph. The specific son is then the one, where the literal with the smallest coefficient has been eliminated. $\qquad\square$

With Proposition 7.2.5 we can decide whether T_{J_k} is dominated by an extended clause in a subgraph of the graph with root label $T(J_k)$ by checking domination against one specific extended clause, i.e., the strongest extended clause from the strict reduction of $T(J_k)$, where we have eliminated the literal with the smallest coefficient. In Figure 7.2 the basic idea of Lemma 7.2.4 is illustrated.

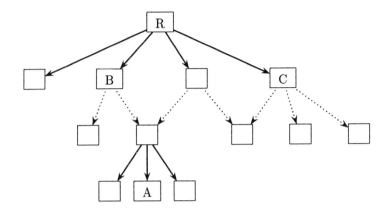

Figure 7.2 Redundancy caused by an extended clause in the subgraph

The graph corresponds to a part of the graph view of $\mathsf{SCP}(\mathsf{SRed}(cL \geq d))$. Assume that the sons of each node are ordered such that the coefficient of the eliminated literal of a son node is greater than or equal to all the coefficients of the eliminated literals of its right brothers. Now Lemma 7.2.4 says that there is an extended clause A under the extended clause R dominating R if and only if C dominates R. In the proof of Lemma 7.2.4 we show that if there is an A dominating R, then B is dominating R, from which we show that C is dominating R. The key idea is to show that the strongest extended clauses A,B, and C all have the same degree.

We now give a similar criterion for extended clauses lying on a path to $T(J_k)$, and, as in Proposition 7.2.5, identify a single specific extended clause that needs to be considered.

Lemma 7.2.6 For $J_p \subset J_k$ the extended clause T_{J_k} is dominated by T_{J_p} if and only if

$$|J_k| - |J_p| \leq \deg(T_{J_p}) - \deg(T_{J_k}) \ .$$

Proof. Because $|\{1, \ldots, n\} \setminus J_p| - |\{1, \ldots, n\} \setminus J_k| = |J_k| - |J_p|$, the lemma follows immediately from Lemma 3.1.14.   □

Lemma 7.2.7 If $T_{J_{k+1}}$ is dominated by T_{J_p} with $J_p \subset J_{k+1}$, then $T_{J_{k+1} \setminus \{j_i\}}$ dominates $T_{J_{k+1}}$ for all $j_i \in J_{k+1} \setminus J_p$.

Proof. From (7.8) we know that $|J_{k+1}| - |J_p| \geq \deg(T_{J_p}) - \deg(T_{J_{k+1}})$ and from Lemma 7.2.6 we know that $|J_{k+1}| - |J_p| \leq \deg(T_{J_p}) - \deg(T_{J_{k+1}})$, therefore we have $|J_{k+1}| - |J_p| = \deg(T_{J_p}) - \deg(T_{J_{k+1}})$. Since in this case the degree of all extended clauses on a path from T_{J_p} to $T_{J_{k+1}}$ decreases always by one, we know that the degree of all direct fathers, $T_{J_{k+1}\backslash\{j_i\}}$ for all $j_i \in J_{k+1} \backslash J_p$, is the degree of $T_{J_{k+1}}$ plus one. Thus, for all $j_i \in J_{k+1} \backslash J_p$ we have $\deg(T_{J_{k+1}\backslash\{j_i\}}) - \deg(T_{J_{k+1}}) = 1$ and since $|J_{k+1}| - |J_{k+1} \backslash \{j_i\}| = 1$, we have domination by Lemma 7.2.6.   □

We identify similar to Proposition 7.2.5 a single specific extended clause that needs to be tested for application of Lemma 7.2.6.

Proposition 7.2.8 *If $T_{J_{k+1}}$ is dominated by T_{J_p} with $J_p \subset J_{k+1}$, then there exists $T_{J_{k+1}\backslash\{j_{max}\}}$ that dominates $T_{J_{k+1}}$, where $c_{j_{max}} \geq c_{j_i}$ for all $1 \leq i \leq k+1$.*

Proof. Let us consider a specific path $H_{k+1} := h_1 \ldots h_{k+1}$ from the root to $T(J_{k+1})$, where $c_{h_1} \leq \cdots \leq c_{h_{k+1}} = c_{j_{max}}$ and $h_{k+1} = j_{max}$, i.e., we always eliminate the literal with the smallest coefficient first. For all direct fathers of $T(J_{k+1})$ the coefficient of the literal that is eliminated is therefore less than or equal to $c_{h_{k+1}}$. Let $\beta = \deg(T_{J_{k+1}})$. Because of Lemma 7.2.7, we have a strict reduction

$$R := \sum_{i \in J_{k+1}} c_i L_i + c_x L_x \geq d + c_x - \sum_{i \in J_{k+1}} c_i$$

with $x \in J_p$ and $\deg(\mathsf{SCP}(R)) = \beta + 1$. Using our fixed path H_{k+1}, we know that there is another strict reduction

$$H := \sum_{i \in J_{k+1}} c_i L_i + c_{j_{max}} L_{j_{max}} \geq d + c_{j_{max}} - \sum_{i \in J_{k+1}} c_i \ .$$

We now show that $\deg(\mathsf{SCP}(R)) = \deg(\mathsf{SCP}(H)) = \beta + 1$.

Suppose that $c_{j_{max}} \geq c_{j'_\beta}$. As in Lemma 7.2.2 we derive that $\deg(\mathsf{SCP}(H)) > \beta$, hence $\deg(\mathsf{SCP}(H)) = \beta + 1$.

Now suppose that $c_{j_{max}} < c_{j'_\beta}$. Since we have $c_{j_{max}} \geq c_x$, we also have $c_x < c_{j'_\beta}$. Because $\deg(\mathsf{SCP}(R)) = \beta + 1$, we have

$$\sum_{1 \leq i \leq \beta} c_{j'_i} < d + c_x - \sum_{i \in J_{k+1}} c_i \ .$$

With $c_{j_{max}} \geq c_x$ we get

$$\sum_{1 \leq i \leq \beta} c_{j'_i} < d + c_{j_{max}} - \sum_{i \in J_{k+1}} c_i \ ,$$

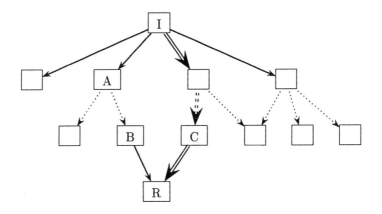

Figure 7.3   Redundancy caused by an extended clause above in the graph

which also implies $\deg(\mathsf{SCP}(H)) > \beta$ and therefore $\deg(\mathsf{SCP}(H)) = \beta + 1$. Let $J_{k+1} \setminus \{j_{\max}\}$ be $\{h_1, \ldots, h_k\}$, then the proposition follows. $\qquad\qquad\square$

We illustrate the basic idea of Proposition 7.2.8 in Figure 7.3. Proposition 7.2.8 says that there is an A dominating R if and only if C dominates R. In the graph we assume that the fathers of each node are ordered such that the coefficient of the eliminated literal to come from a father node to a son node is greater than or equal to all the coefficients of the eliminated literals of its *left* neighbors. In the proof of Proposition 7.2.8 we show that if A dominates R, then there is a B dominating R, and that all degrees along a path from R to A decrease by one. The double line corresponds to the specific path H_{k+1}, and we show that C, lying on this path, has the same degree as B and therefore dominates R.

We combine now Proposition 7.2.5 and Proposition 7.2.8 to a complete redundancy criterion.

Theorem 7.2.9 *The strongest extended clause $T_{J_{k+1}}$ is redundant if and only if*

[a] $T_{J_{k+1} \cup \{j_{k+2}\}}$ *dominates* $T_{J_{k+1}}$ *with* $c_{j_{k+2}} \leq c_i$ *for all* $i \in \overline{J_{k+1}}$,   *or*

[b] $T_{J_{k+1} \setminus \{j_{\max}\}}$ *dominates* $T_{J_{k+1}}$ *with* $c_{j_{\max}} \geq c_i$ *for all* $i \in J_{k+1}$.

Proof.

$\Leftarrow$: [a] from Proposition 7.2.5 and [b] from Proposition 7.2.8.

$\Rightarrow$: Suppose that neither [a] nor [b] is satisfied for $T_{J_{k+1}}$, but $T_{J_{k+1}}$ is redundant. Then there is a strongest extended clause $L'' \geq \beta$ that dominates $T_{J_{k+1}} := L' \geq \beta'$ and $L'' \neq L'$. From Proposition 7.2.8 we have $L'' \not\supseteq L'$ and from Proposition 7.2.5 we have $L'' \not\subseteq L'$. Therefore, there is at least one literal in L'' that is not in L'. Following the proof of Lemma 3.1.14 a valid reduction of $L'' \geq \beta$ is $L'' \cap L' \geq \beta - |L'' \setminus L'|$, which also dominates $L' \geq \beta'$. The strongest extended clause containing exactly the literals in $L'' \cap L'$ therefore dominates $L \geq \beta'$ and hence $T_{J_{k+1}}$. Since $L'' \cap L' \subset L''$, because $L'' \setminus L' \neq \emptyset$, Proposition 7.2.5 applies, and therefore condition [a].

$\square$

For illustrating statement [b] of Theorem 7.2.9 we look again at Figure 7.2. We have shown that if there is an X dominating R and X is not on a path also including R, then we will find an A in the subgraph under X such that Proposition 7.2.5 applies.

By Theorem 7.2.9 we can decide redundancy of a strongest extended clause by investigating exactly 2 other strongest extended clauses. We end this section with an example.

Example 7.2.10 Let us transform the linear pseudo-Boolean inequality

$$5 \cdot L_1 + 4 \cdot L_2 + 3 \cdot L_3 + 2 \cdot L_4 + 1 \cdot L_5 \geq 11 .$$

Its strongest extended clause is

$$L_1 + L_2 + L_3 + L_4 + L_5 \geq 3 .$$

Let us compute the strict reductions $T(\{i\})$ and their corresponding strongest extended clauses $T_{\{i\}}$.

i	$T(\{i\})$	$T_{\{i\}}$
1	$4 \cdot L_2 + 3 \cdot L_3 + 2 \cdot L_4 + 1 \cdot L_5 \geq 6$	$L_2 + L_3 + L_4 + L_5 \geq 2$
2	$5 \cdot L_1 + 3 \cdot L_3 + 2 \cdot L_4 + 1 \cdot L_5 \geq 7$	$L_1 + L_3 + L_4 + L_5 \geq 2$
3	$5 \cdot L_1 + 4 \cdot L_2 + 2 \cdot L_4 + 1 \cdot L_5 \geq 8$	$L_1 + L_2 + L_4 + L_5 \geq 2$
4	$5 \cdot L_1 + 4 \cdot L_2 + 3 \cdot L_3 + 1 \cdot L_5 \geq 9$	$L_1 + L_2 + L_3 + L_5 \geq 2$
5	$5 \cdot L_1 + 4 \cdot L_2 + 3 \cdot L_3 + 2 \cdot L_4 \geq 10$	$L_1 + L_2 + L_3 + L_4 \geq 3$

We see that $T_{\{5\}}$ dominates $T_\emptyset$ (Theorem 7.2.9[a] $\Leftarrow$) and that $T_{\{1\}}, T_{\{2\}}, T_{\{3\}}$, and $T_{\{4\}}$ are dominated by $T_\emptyset$ (Theorem 7.2.9[b] $\Leftarrow$). We calculate $T_{\{4,5\}} =$

$L_1 + L_2 + L_3 \geq 2$ and conclude that $T_{\{5\}}$ is not redundant(Theorem 7.2.9; completeness). Proceeding further, we arrive at the set of non-redundant extended clauses given in Example 7.1.6.

7.3   IMPLEMENTATION

We sketch an implementation of the transformation algorithm using the strong redundancy criteria presented in Section 7.2.

Theorem 7.2.9 is a complete redundancy criterion for a strongest extended clause that reduces the number of needed domination checks to 2. We denote by $\beta' = \deg(T_{J_k \setminus \{j_{\max}\}})$ the degree of the strongest extended clause of the specific father of $T(J_{k+1})$ and by $\beta'' = \deg(T_{J_{k+1} \cup \{j_{k+2}\}})$ the degree of the strongest extended clause of the specific son of $T(J_{k+1})$. The degree of the extended clause for which we want to check redundancy is denoted by $\beta = \deg(T_{J_{k+1}})$. From Theorem 7.2.9 we see immediately that $T_{J_{k+1}}$ is redundant if and only if

$$\beta' - 1 = \beta \qquad \text{or} \qquad \beta = \beta'' .$$

Hence, for deciding redundancy of a strongest extended clause only the degrees of two strongest extended clauses (the specific father and the specific son) are needed. We describe an algorithm that computes from a linear pseudo-Boolean inequality $cL \geq d$ in normal form a set of equivalent non-redundant extended clauses. We assume that $\sum_{i=1}^{n} c_i \geq d$, since otherwise $cL \geq d$ is unsatisfiable. We also assume that $\sum_{i=2}^{n} c_i \geq d$, since otherwise $\alpha(L_1) = 1$ for all $\alpha \in \text{Ext}(cL \geq d)$, and we can consider the simpler problem of transforming

$$\sum_{i=2}^{n} c_i L_i \geq d - c_1 .$$

In the following we assume that the linear pseudo-Boolean inequality $cL \geq d$ is satisfiable, in pseudo-Boolean normal form and that for every literal $L_i \in L$ there are assignments $\alpha_1, \alpha_2 \in \text{Ext}(cL \geq d)$ such that $\alpha_1(L_i) = 1 - \alpha_2(L_i)$. Note that for all generated strongest extended clauses $L' \geq \beta$, we have $|L'| > \beta$, since otherwise $\alpha(L_i) = 1$ for all $L_i \in L'$, which we have excluded. We can always ensure this condition by applying pseudo-Boolean unit resolution in advance.

In the program fragments we use the following non-standard notation. Given a linear pseudo-Boolean term cL, we select the last (resp. first) coefficient/literal pair $c_l L_l$ and the remaining term $c'L'$ by $cL = c'L' + c_l L_l$ (resp. $cL = c_l L_l + c'L'$).

First, we give the procedure **get_beta** calculating the degree β of the strongest extended clause of its argument, a strict reduction, and β'', the degree of the strongest extended clause of the strict reduction, where we have eliminated the literal with the smallest coefficient. The right-hand side β'' is then the degree of the strongest extended clause of the specific son node as in Proposition 7.2.8.

Algorithm 7.3.1 *Get greatest possible right-hand side*

```
get_beta(cL ≥ d)
        (i, β, sum, prevsum) := (1, 0, 0, 0)
        while sum < d
              cL = c_l L_l + c' L'
              prevsum := sum
              (sum, β, cL) := (sum + c_l, β + 1, c' L')
        endwhile
        while cL = c_l L_l + c' L'
              cL := c' L'
        endwhile
        (* c_l is the smallest coefficient *)
        β'' := if prevsum ≥ d - c_l then β - 1 else β endif
        return (β, β'')
end get_beta
```

We obtain β by summing up the coefficients according to (7.3), and count the number of added coefficients until we reach the right-hand side. Since the specific son is the one where the literal with the smallest coefficient has been eliminated, this coefficient cannot be part of the sum. Note that $\sum_{i=2}^{n} c_i \geq d$. Therefore, the degree of the specific son is one smaller if and only if the current sum minus the last added coefficient, i.e., the previous sum, is greater than or equal to the right-hand side $d - c_l$ of the specific son. Hence, the overhead for calculating β'' is not high. In the actual implementation we store the value of the smallest coefficient for each strict reduction and so avoid searching for it.

In an efficient implementation we do not generate the whole graph. Instead, we implicitly visit the nodes, i.e., the strict reductions, in a specific order such that for each strict reduction the redundancy test becomes trivial. We ensure that each strict reduction $T(J_{k+1})$ is visited only once through the path H_{k+1} (see Proof of Proposition 7.2.8). This is achieved by splitting the linear pseudo-Boolean term (the left-hand side of the linear pseudo-Boolean inequality) into two parts, one containing the literals that must be eliminated and the other one containing the literals that need not be eliminated. We eliminate literals having a smaller coefficient first and then forbid further reduction on these literals by moving them from the first part to the second part. Thus, we make sure that the strict reductions are visited only through the specific path. We give a recursive procedure transform generating each possible strict reduction only once and adding its strongest extended clause to the output set if and only if it is not redundant. As parameters we have a linear pseudo-Boolean inequality, which is split into two parts and the right-hand side, and the right-hand side β' of the strongest extended clause of the father in the path H_{k+1}.

Algorithm 7.3.2 *Transform a linear pseudo-Boolean inequality*

```
transform(cL, ĉL̂, d, β')
    S := ∅
    (β, β'') = get_beta(cL + ĉL̂ ≥ d)
    if β' − 1 ≠ β ∧ β'' ≠ β then (* not redundant *)
        S := S ∪ {L + L̂ ≥ β} (* add it *)
    endif
    (* cL is non-empty and there are valid strict reductions *)
    while c'L' + c_l L_l = cL ∧ d − c_l ≥ 1 (* eliminate c_l L_l *)
        S := S ∪ transform(c'L', ĉL̂, d − c_l, β)
        ĉL̂ := ĉL̂ + c_l L_l (* forbid further reduction on L_l *)
        cL := c'L'
    endwhile
    return S
end transform
```

Note that in the **while**-loop we select first the product with the smallest coefficient and then forbid further reduction on it by moving the product to the second part. The set of all non-redundant strongest extended clauses equivalent to the linear pseudo-Boolean inequality $cL \geq d$ is transform($cL, \emptyset, d, 0$). We finish this section with some examples.

Example 7.3.3 The examples are taken from [NW88].

[a] [NW88, page 266] Let $cL \geq d$ be

$$79 \cdot X_1 + 53 \cdot X_2 + 53 \cdot X_3 + 45 \cdot X_4 + 45 \cdot X_5 \leq 178 \ .$$

The pseudo-Boolean normal form of $cL \geq d$ is

$$79 \cdot \overline{X_1} + 53 \cdot \overline{X_2} + 53 \cdot \overline{X_3} + 45 \cdot \overline{X_4} + 45 \cdot \overline{X_5} \geq 97 \ .$$

The equivalent set of extended clauses is

$$\begin{aligned} \{\overline{X_1} + \overline{X_2} + \overline{X_3} + \overline{X_4} + \overline{X_5} &\geq 2, \\ \overline{X_1} + \overline{X_2} + \overline{X_3} &\geq 1\} \ . \end{aligned}$$

[b] [NW88, page 460] Let $cL \geq d$ be

$$\begin{aligned} 774 \cdot X_1 + 76 \cdot X_2 + 22 \cdot X_3 + 42 \cdot X_4 + 21 \cdot X_5 + \\ 760 \cdot X_6 + 818 \cdot X_7 + 62 \cdot X_8 + 785 \cdot X_9 \leq 1500 \ . \end{aligned}$$

The transformation procedure generates the single extended clause

$$\overline{X_1} + \overline{X_6} + \overline{X_7} + \overline{X_9} \geq 3 \ ,$$

which is equivalent to $cL \geq d$.

[c] [NW88, page465] Let $cL \geq d$ be

$$\begin{aligned} 300 \cdot X_3 + 300 \cdot X_4 + 285 \cdot X_5 + 285 \cdot X_6 + 265 \cdot X_8 + 265 \cdot X_9 + \\ 230 \cdot X_{12} + 230 \cdot X_{13} + 190 \cdot X_{14} + 200 \cdot X_{22} + 400 \cdot X_{23} + \\ 200 \cdot X_{24} + 400 \cdot X_{25} + 200 \cdot X_{26} + 400 \cdot X_{27} + 200 \cdot X_{28} + \\ 400 \cdot X_{29} + 200 \cdot X_{30} + 400 \cdot X_{31} \leq 2700, \end{aligned}$$

which is a linear 0-1 inequality from the constraint set of the 0-1 integer programming problem p0033 [CJP83, BBI92]. Transforming $cL \geq d$ generates 4282 non-redundant strongest extended clauses. They have been calculated with a PROLOG-implementation of the algorithm in 4.8 seconds cpu-time on a SPARC-10/31. All 15 inequalities of the problem produce together 8710 extended clauses, where 749 extended clauses are dominated by extended clauses generated from another inequality such that 7961 extended clauses remain. Note that the number of non-redundant classical clauses that are equivalent to $cL \geq d$ is 117520.

Example 7.3.3[c] demonstrates the advantage of using extended clauses instead of classical clauses. Because of the large number of classical clauses needed to represent a linear pseudo-Boolean inequality, clausal satisfiability methods cannot be applied to typical 0-1 integer programming problems [GG80]. The reformulation of a linear pseudo-Boolean inequality as a set of extended clauses is more likely to be applicable to general 0-1 problems because of its more compact representation.

In the next section we give an even more compact representation of linear pseudo-Boolean inequalities and extended clauses, which allows us to speed up the computation and brings even larger problems into the scope of this symbolic method.

7.4 SYMMETRIES

We introduce the concept of symmetries for a set of literals w.r.t. a linear pseudo-Boolean inequality and then define the *compact set* representation of linear pseudo-Boolean inequalities and extended clauses. This more compact formulation helps to avoid *redundant computations* in the transformation method.

Let us transform the linear pseudo-Boolean inequality

$$5 \cdot A + 5 \cdot B + 4 \cdot C + 3 \cdot D + 3 \cdot E + 3 \cdot F \geq 12 \ . \tag{7.10}$$

For example, three strict reductions of (7.10) are

$$5 \cdot A + 5 \cdot B + 4 \cdot C + 3 \cdot E + 3 \cdot F \geq 9 \tag{7.11}$$

$$5 \cdot A + 5 \cdot B + 4 \cdot C + 3 \cdot D + 3 \cdot F \geq 9 \tag{7.12}$$

$$5 \cdot A + 5 \cdot B + 4 \cdot C + 3 \cdot D + 3 \cdot E \geq 9 \tag{7.13}$$

obtained by eliminating D for (7.11), E for (7.12) and F for (7.13). Note that these three strict reductions are identical, except for the names of the last two literals. Therefore, these three extended clauses yield exactly the same set of non-redundant extended clauses except for the names of the literals. We say that D, E and F are *symmetric* in (7.10). The study of symmetries for propositional calculus problems [BS92] is not directly related to the presented approach. Although the main idea, i.e., avoiding redundant computation by exploiting symmetry properties, is similar. In the following we describe how to avoid redundant computations occurring while eliminating symmetric literals. For this purpose we first define a compact representation of a set of linear pseudo-Boolean inequalities.

Definition 7.4.1 For all $1 \le i < j \le m$ let S_i and S_j be sets of literals such that $\mathsf{Var}(L_l) \ne \mathsf{Var}(L_k)$ for all $L_l \in S_i$ and $L_k \in S_j$. We say that

$$\sum_{i=1}^{m} c_i S_i^{k_i} \ge d \; , \tag{7.14}$$

where $d \ge c_1 > \cdots > c_m \ge 1$ and $1 \le k_i \le |S_i|$ for all $1 \le i \le m$, is a *compact pseudo-Boolean inequality set* of a set of linear pseudo-Boolean inequalities. The compact pseudo-Boolean inequality set (7.14) represents the set of all linear pseudo-Boolean inequalities

$$\mathsf{expand}\left(\sum_{i=1}^{m} c_i S_i^{k_i} \ge d\right) := \left\{ cL \ge d \; \middle| \; \begin{array}{l} |L| = \sum_{i=1}^{m} k_i, \\ \forall c_l L_l \in cL : \exists S_i : L_l \in S_i \wedge c_l = c_i, \\ |S_i \cap L| = k_i \text{ for all } 1 \le i \le m \end{array} \right\} . \tag{7.15}$$

In other words, all linear pseudo-Boolean inequalities, where from each set of literals S_i exactly k_i occur in the linear pseudo-Boolean inequality with coefficient c_i. We say we *expand* a compact pseudo-Boolean inequality set if we replace $\sum_{i=1}^{m} c_i S_i^{k_i} \ge d$ by $\mathsf{expand}(\sum_{i=1}^{m} c_i S_i^{k_i} \ge d)$. For a set S of compact pseudo-Boolean inequality sets we define $\mathsf{expand}(S) := \bigcup_{I \in S} \mathsf{expand}(I)$.

Example 7.4.2 We can represent the single linear pseudo-Boolean inequality (7.10) by the compact pseudo-Boolean inequality set

$$5 \cdot \{A, B\}^2 + 4 \cdot \{C\}^1 + 3 \cdot \{D, E, F\}^3 \ge 12 \; .$$

The three strict reductions (7.11), (7.12) and (7.13) can be represented by

$$5 \cdot \{A, B\}^2 + 4 \cdot \{C\}^1 + 3 \cdot \{D, E, F\}^2 \ge 9 \; .$$

Note that every single linear pseudo-Boolean inequality can be represented as compact pseudo-Boolean inequality set. Then for all sets of literals S_i in its compact representation, we have $k_i = |S_i|$.

The compact pseudo-Boolean inequality set representation is the key to exploit the symmetry property of literals in a linear pseudo-Boolean inequality. The possible strict reductions that lead to an identical search can now be represented by a single compact pseudo-Boolean inequality set. We define similar to Definition 7.4.1 a compact set representation for extended clauses.

Definition 7.4.3 For all $1 \le i < j \le m$ let S_i and S_j be sets of literals such that $\mathsf{Var}(L_l) \ne \mathsf{Var}(L_k)$ for all $L_l \in S_i$ and $L_k \in S_j$. We say that

$$\sum_{i=1}^{m} S_i^{k_i} \ge \beta \tag{7.16}$$

with $1 \leq k_i \leq |S_i|$ for all $1 \leq i \leq m$, is a *compact extended clause set* of a set of extended clauses. The compact extended clause set (7.16) represents the set of all extended clauses

$$\text{expand}(\sum_{i=1}^{m} S_i^{k_i} \geq \beta) := \left\{ L \geq \beta \;\middle|\; \begin{array}{l} |L| = \sum_{i=1}^{m} k_i \text{ and} \\ |S_i \cap L| = k_i \text{ for all } 1 \leq i \leq m \end{array} \right\} . \quad (7.17)$$

We say we *expand* a compact extended clause set $\sum_{i=1}^{m} S_i^{k_i} \geq \beta$, if we replace it by $\text{expand}(\sum_{i=1}^{m} S_i^{k_i} \geq \beta)$. For a set S of compact extended clause sets we define $\text{expand}(S) := \bigcup_{I \in S} \text{expand}(I)$.

We generalize now the generation of strongest extended clauses of Proposition 7.1.2. For a compact pseudo-Boolean inequality set $\sum_{i=1}^{m} c_i S_i^{k_i} \geq d$ the corresponding strongest compact extended clause set is

$$\sum_{i=1}^{m} S_i^{k_i} \geq \beta \quad (7.18)$$

with

$$\sum_{i=1}^{\beta-1} c_i \cdot k_i < d \leq \sum_{i=1}^{\beta} c_i \cdot k_i . \quad (7.19)$$

Note that (7.19) corresponds to (7.3), but takes into account the compact set representation. We denote by $\text{SCP}'(\sum_{i=1}^{m} c_i S_i^{k_i} \geq d) := (\sum_{i=1}^{m} S_i^{k_i} \geq \beta)$ the strongest compact extended clause set of a compact pseudo-Boolean inequality set. Obviously, for each linear pseudo-Boolean pseudo-Boolean inequality in $\text{expand}(\sum_{i=1}^{m} c_i S_i^{k_i} \geq d)$ there is a corresponding strongest extended clause in $\text{expand}(\sum_{i=1}^{m} S_i^{k_i} \geq \beta)$ and we have

$$\text{expand}(\text{SCP}'(\sum_{i=1}^{m} c_i S_i^{k_i} \geq d)) = \text{SCP}(\text{expand}(\sum_{i=1}^{m} c_i S_i^{k_i} \geq d)) .$$

A compact strict reduction of a compact pseudo-Boolean inequality set of the form $\sum_{i=1}^{m} c_i S_i^{k_i} \geq d$ is

$$\sum_{i=1}^{m} c_i S_i^{k_i'} \geq d - \sum_{i=1}^{m} c_i \cdot (k_i - k_i')$$

with either $k_i' = k_i$ or $k_i' = k_i - 1$ for all $1 \leq i \leq m$. Note that $c_i S_i^{k_i'}$ disappears if $k_i' = 0$. We denote by $\text{SRed}'(\sum_{i=1}^{m} c_i S_i^{k_i} \geq d)$ the set of all compact strict

reductions of a compact pseudo-Boolean inequality set. Obviously, we have

$$\mathsf{expand}(\mathsf{SRed}'(\sum_{i=1}^{m} c_i S_i^{k_i} \geq d)) = \mathsf{SRed}(\mathsf{expand}(\sum_{i=1}^{m} c_i S_i^{k_i} \geq d)) \ .$$

The transformation method using compact sets is now straightforward. For a compact pseudo-Boolean inequality set $\sum_{i=1}^{m} c_i S_i^{k_i} \geq d$ we have

$$\mathsf{expand}(\mathsf{SCP}'(\mathsf{SRed}'(\sum_{i=1}^{m} c_i S_i^{k_i} \geq d))) = \mathsf{SCP}(\mathsf{SRed}(\mathsf{expand}(\sum_{i=1}^{m} c_i S_i^{k_i} \geq d))) \ .$$

The practical advantage is that we avoid redundant computation of identical strict reductions modulo literal renaming because they are grouped together in a single compact pseudo-Boolean inequality set. Generalizing Theorem 7.2.9 for compact sets is immediate and an implementation of the transformation method using compact sets is similar to the implementation sketched in Section 5.4.

Example 7.4.4

[a] When transforming the linear pseudo-Boolean inequality

$$5 \cdot A + 5 \cdot B + 4 \cdot C + 3 \cdot D + 3 \cdot E + 3 \cdot F \geq 12 \ ,$$

we have to consider 32 strict reductions. If we transform the equivalent compact pseudo-Boolean inequality set

$$5 \cdot \{A, B\}^2 + 4 \cdot \{C\}^1 + 3 \cdot \{D, E, F\}^3 \geq 12 \ ,$$

then only 11 compact strict reductions are possible and the following set of compact extended clause sets is generated.

$$\begin{aligned} \{\{A\}^1 + \{B\}^1 + \{C\}^1 + \{D\}^1 + \{E\}^1 + \{F\}^1 &\geq 3, \\ \{A\}^1 + \{B\}^1 + \{C\}^1 + \{D, E, F\}^1 &\geq 2\} \ . \end{aligned}$$

The set of equivalent strongest extended clauses is

$$\begin{aligned} \{A + B + C + D + E + F &\geq 3, \\ A + B + C + D &\geq 2, \\ A + B + C + E &\geq 2, \\ A + B + C + F &\geq 2\} \ . \end{aligned}$$

So by exploiting the symmetry property of literals we avoid redundant computation and obtain a more compact result.

[b] The linear pseudo-Boolean inequality of Example 7.3.3[c] generates 4282 extended clauses in 4.8 seconds cpu time on a SPARC-10/31. The implementation using symmetries takes 0.77 seconds cpu time for generating the 4282 extended clauses, where 0.49 seconds are used to expand the 253 compact non-redundant extended clause sets. The transformation itself takes only 0.18 seconds.

The very compact representation of Example 7.4.4[b] suggests to further investigate the compact extended clause set representation of extended clauses. Generalizing symbolic methods for solving linear pseudo-Boolean problems, e.g., pseudo-Boolean unit resolution and *Generalized Resolution*, to work directly on the compact representation, brings even larger 0-1 problems in the scope of these methods. This issue will be investigated in the future.

7.5   DETECTION OF FIXED LITERALS

We present a method detecting some of the literals L_i for which the extended clause $L_i \geq 1$ is dominated by a set of linear pseudo-Boolean inequalities S. Given such an L_i, we have $\alpha(L_i) = 1$ for all assignments $\alpha \in \text{Ext}(S)$. Hence, the literal L_i is fixed, and S can be simplified to a set of linear pseudo-Boolean inequalities S' not containing L_i or $\overline{L_i}$ such that

$$\text{Ext}(S) = \text{Ext}(S' \cup \{L_i \geq 1\}) \ .$$

A similar simplification is possible if several literals can be fixed. Let L be a set of literals such that S dominates $L_i \geq 1$ for all $L_i \in L$. We then can simplify S to a set of linear pseudo-Boolean inequalities S' not containing L_i or $\overline{L_i}$ for all $L_i \in L$ such that

$$\text{Ext}(S) = \text{Ext}(S' \cup \{L \geq |L|\}) \ .$$

Note that $L \geq |L|$ dominates $L_i \geq 1$ for all $L_i \in L$. We show how to find some of the fixed literals in L with help of pseudo-Boolean unit resolution of Chapter 5.

A subset of these literals that can be fixed is the set of unit literals $\text{pbul}(S)$, defined on page 86. Pseudo-Boolean unit resolution is a procedure detecting this set of literals.

Example 7.5.1 Let S be

$$\{5 \cdot A + 4 \cdot B + 3 \cdot C + 2 \cdot D \geq 10,$$
$$8 \cdot \overline{A} + 6 \cdot D + 4 \cdot E + 3 \cdot F \geq 8\}$$

and let us follow a computation of $\text{pbur}(S)$, defined on page 86. First, we obtain $\text{fixed}(5 \cdot A + 4 \cdot B + 3 \cdot C + 2 \cdot D \geq 10) = A$ and simplify S to $\text{fix}(A, S)$.

$$\{4 \cdot B + 3 \cdot C + 2 \cdot D \geq 5,$$
$$6 \cdot D + 4 \cdot E + 3 \cdot F \geq 8\}$$

Next, we have $\text{fixed}(6 \cdot D + 4 \cdot E + 3 \cdot F \geq 8) = D$ and obtain $\text{fix}(D, \text{fix}(A, S))$.

$$\{3 \cdot B + 3 \cdot C \geq 3,$$
$$2 \cdot E + 2 \cdot F \geq 2\}$$

Since now for all linear pseudo-Boolean inequalities fixed returns $\perp$, we have

$$\text{Ext}(S) = \text{Ext}(\{3 \cdot B + 3 \cdot C \geq 3, 2 \cdot E + 2 \cdot F \geq 2, A + D \geq 2\}) \ .$$

Transforming the remaining linear pseudo-Boolean inequalities is trivial and we obtain

$$\text{Ext}(S) = \text{Ext}(\{B + C \geq 1, E + F \geq 1, A + D \geq 2\}) \ .$$

When a linear pseudo-Boolean inequality has been simplified by fixing literals, then transforming it is simpler and typically fewer strongest extended clauses are generated.

We know that a set of linear pseudo-Boolean inequalities S dominates $L_i \geq 1$ for some literal L_i if and only if $(S \cup \{\overline{L_i} \geq 1\})$ is unsatisfiable. We approximate the unsatisfiability test by checking whether the pseudo-Boolean unit relaxation of $S \cup \{\overline{L_i} \geq 1\}$ is unsatisfiable, i.e., whether $\perp \in \text{pbur}(S \cup \{\overline{L_i} \geq 1\})$. We get the procedure fixing that detects some of the literals L_i for which $\alpha(L_i) = 1$ for all solutions α of a set of linear pseudo-Boolean inequalities S.

Algorithm 7.5.2 *Detect Fixed Literals*

```
fixing(S)
      K := ∅
      while ∃Lᵢ : ⊥ ∈ pbur(S ∪ {L̄ᵢ ≥ 1})
            K := K ∪ pbul(S ∪ {Lᵢ ≥ 1})
            S := pbur(S ∪ {Lᵢ ≥ 1})
      endwhile
      return K
end fixing
```

Note that S dominates $\texttt{fixing}(S) \geq |\texttt{fixing}(S)|$. Let K be $\texttt{fixing}(S)$, then

$$\text{Ext}(S) = \text{Ext}(\texttt{pbur}(S \cup \{K \geq |K|\}) \cup \{K \geq |K|\}) \ .$$

Note that $\texttt{fixing}$ is a stronger procedure for detecting fixed literals of a set of linear pseudo-Boolean inequalities than pseudo-Boolean unit resolution and we have

$$\texttt{fixing}(S) \supseteq \texttt{pbul}(S) \ .$$

Example 7.5.3 Let S be

$$\begin{aligned}\{5 \cdot A + 4 \cdot B + 3 \cdot C + 2 \cdot D &\geq 7, \\ 3 \cdot \overline{B} + 3 \cdot D + 2 \cdot \overline{C} &\geq 4\} \ ,\end{aligned}$$

then none of the two linear pseudo-Boolean inequalities dominates $L_i \geq 1$ for some literal L_i. Let us apply $\texttt{fixing}$ to S and start with calculating $\texttt{pbur}(S \cup \{\overline{A} \geq 1\})$. First, we obtain $\texttt{fix}(\overline{A}, S)$.

$$\begin{aligned}\{4 \cdot B + 3 \cdot C + 2 \cdot D &\geq 7, \\ 3 \cdot \overline{B} + 3 \cdot D + 2 \cdot \overline{C} &\geq 4\}\end{aligned}$$

Now $\texttt{fixed}(4 \cdot B + 3 \cdot C + 2 \cdot D \geq 7) = B$ and we calculate $\texttt{fix}(B, \texttt{fix}(\overline{A}, S))$.

$$\begin{aligned}\{3 \cdot C + 2 \cdot D &\geq 3, \\ 3 \cdot D + 2 \cdot \overline{C} &\geq 4\}\end{aligned}$$

Next, we derive $\texttt{fixed}(3 \cdot C + 2 \cdot D \geq 3) = C$ and $\texttt{fix}(C, \texttt{fix}(B, \texttt{fix}(\overline{A}, S)))$ gives

$$\begin{aligned}\{ \quad &\top, \\ 3 \cdot D &\geq 4\} \ ,\end{aligned}$$

where $3 \cdot D \geq 4$ is $\bot$. We conclude that $S \cup \{\overline{A} \geq 1\}$ is unsatisfiable. Thus, S dominates $A \geq 1$ and we can replace S by $\texttt{fix}(A, S) \cup \{A \geq 1\}$.

$$\begin{aligned}\{2 \cdot B + 2 \cdot C + 2 \cdot D &\geq 2, \\ 3 \cdot \overline{B} + 3 \cdot D + 2 \cdot \overline{C} &\geq 4, \\ A &\geq 1\} \ .\end{aligned}$$

Note that $2 \cdot B + 2 \cdot C + 2 \cdot D \geq 2$ is already normalized. There is no further literal L_i such that $\bot \in \texttt{pbur}(\texttt{fix}(A, S) \cup \{A \geq 1\} \cup \{\overline{L_i} \geq 1\})$ and so $\texttt{fixing}$ ends.

For example, on the constraint set of a 0-1 integer optimization problem "air01" found on MIPLIB [BBI92] $\texttt{fixing}$ detects that 130 out of the 771 Boolean

variables have to be fixed. But, `fixing` is a rather costly process. Suppose that n variables occur in S, then for a complete application of `fixing` we have to compute $2n$ pseudo-Boolean unit resolutions if `fixing` detects no fixed literals.

7.6 CONSTRAINED SIMPLIFICATION

In the context of constraint logic programming a linear pseudo-Boolean inequality $cL \geq d$ is typically part of a set of linear pseudo-Boolean inequalities S which are already in the constraint store. We now present reformulation techniques for a linear pseudo-Boolean inequality that *constrain* the reformulation of $cL \geq d$ w.r.t. S. In the previous sections we presented a method that reformulated a linear pseudo-Boolean inequality $cL \geq d$ as a set of extended clauses S' such that

$$\mathsf{Ext}(cL \geq d) = \mathsf{Ext}(S') \ .$$

Since $cL \geq d$ is part of a set of linear pseudo-Boolean inequalities S, it is sufficient if $cL \geq d$ is equivalent to S' w.r.t. the context S, i.e., only

$$\mathsf{Ext}(S \cup \{cL \geq d\}) = \mathsf{Ext}(S \cup S')$$

needs to hold. Assume that S' consists not only of extended clauses, i.e., arbitrary linear pseudo-Boolean inequalities are allowed. Then replacing $cL \geq d$ by S' is useful only if S' is in some sense *simpler* than $cL \geq d$.

We will present in Section 7.6.1 a method that generates a *stronger* linear pseudo-Boolean inequality $c'L' \geq d'$ from $cL \geq d$ with $\mathsf{Ext}(c'L' \geq d') \subseteq \mathsf{Ext}(cL \geq d)$ and

$$\mathsf{Ext}(S \cup \{cL \geq d\}) = \mathsf{Ext}(S \cup \{c'L' \geq d'\}) \ .$$

Thus, if $cL \geq d$ is part of the set of linear pseudo-Boolean inequalities S, we can replace $cL \geq d$ by the stronger linear pseudo-Boolean inequality $c'L' \geq d'$. It is often possible to transform some simple linear pseudo-Boolean inequalities in S into a small equivalent set of extended clauses, which then can be used to strengthen $cL \geq d$. Since extended clauses are computationally easier to handle, and nevertheless are the ultimate goal in our solved form, we restrict ourselves mainly to the case that the context S is a set of extended clauses. Hence, the goal is to generate a linear pseudo-Boolean inequality $c'L' \geq d'$ that dominates $cL \geq d$ with equivalence w.r.t. S being preserved, which means that $\mathsf{Ext}(S \cup \{cL \geq d\}) = \mathsf{Ext}(S \cup \{c'L' \geq d'\})$ still holds. Transforming such

a strengthened linear pseudo-Boolean inequality $c'L' \geq d'$ instead of $cL \geq d$ generates stronger extended clauses.

In Section 7.6.2 we show how to replace $cL \geq d$ by a set of linear pseudo-Boolean inequalities S' in the context S such that $\mathsf{Ext}(S \cup \{cL \geq d\}) = \mathsf{Ext}(S \cup S')$. The linear pseudo-Boolean inequalities in S' are simpler in the sense that each of them contains fewer literals than $cL \geq d$. The method can be applied when the original linear pseudo-Boolean inequality $cL \geq d$ is too large to be transformed completely. We then hope to transform more easily some of the linear pseudo-Boolean inequalities in S' and afterwards strengthen the set of extended clauses, which again may lead to a strengthening of the remaining linear pseudo-Boolean inequalities in S'.

We will present a variant of the transformation method in Section 7.6.3. We again assume that the context of the linear pseudo-Boolean inequality $cL \geq d$ is a set of extended clauses S. We transform $cL \geq d$ into an equivalent set of extended clauses S' such that $\mathsf{Ext}(S \cup \{cL \geq d\}) = \mathsf{Ext}(S \cup S')$, but the number of extended clauses in S' is reduced or, optionally, the generated extended clauses are stronger than the one of the unconstrained transformation.

The *simplification* of a linear pseudo-Boolean inequality *constrained* by a context S is common to the methods presented in this section. In the context of constraint logic programming equivalence preserving reformulation of constraints into simpler ones in a context is called *relative simplification* [Smo94]; an essential functionality of constraint solvers for concurrent constraint languages.

7.6.1   Coefficient Reduction

Let S be a set of linear pseudo-Boolean inequalities, the context, and $cL \geq d$ be the linear pseudo-Boolean inequality that we want to replace. We will present a method that reduces a coefficient of $cL \geq d$ such that the modified linear pseudo-Boolean inequality dominates $cL \geq d$, but is still equivalent to $cL \geq d$ in the context S.

Let $c_i L_i$ be a product of $cL \geq d$ and let $c'L'$ be $cL \setminus \{c_i L_i\}$. We search for a linear pseudo-Boolean inequality $c'_i L_i + c'L' \geq d$ with $c'_i < c_i$, which implies that $c'_i L_i + c'L' \geq d$ dominates $cL \geq d$, and

$$\mathsf{Ext}(S \cup \{c'_i L_i + c'L' \geq d\}) = \mathsf{Ext}(S \cup \{cL \geq d\}) \ . \tag{7.20}$$

Since $c'_i L_i + c' L' \geq d$ dominates $cL \geq d$, we know that $\mathsf{SCP}(\mathsf{SRed}(c'_i L_i + c' L' \geq d))$ dominates $\mathsf{SCP}(\mathsf{SRed}(cL \geq d))$. Because our transformation method generates a set of prime extended clauses, we further know that each extended clause in $\mathsf{SCP}(\mathsf{SRed}(cL \geq d))$ is dominated by an extended clause in $\mathsf{SCP}(\mathsf{SRed}(c'_i L_i + c' L' \geq d))$. Transforming $c'_i L_i + c' L' \geq d$ instead of $cL \geq d$ generates therefore only stronger extended clauses, since every extended clause we obtain by transforming $cL \geq d$ is dominated by an extended clause obtained by transforming $c'_i L_i + c' L' \geq d$.

Next, we describe how to derive a coefficient c'_i such that (7.20) holds. The key idea is to deduce a lower bound b for the linear pseudo-Boolean term $c' L'$ w.r.t. $S \cup \{L_i \geq 1\}$.

Proposition 7.6.1 *If $S \cup \{L_i \geq 1\}$ dominates $c' L' \geq b$ and $c_i > d - b$ then*

$$\mathsf{Ext}(S \cup \{c_i L_i + c' L' \geq d\}) = \mathsf{Ext}(S \cup \{(d - b)L_i + c' L' \geq d\}) \ .$$

We then have reduced the coefficient c_i to $c'_i = d - b < c_i$.

Proof. The direction $\supseteq$ is obvious, since $c_i > d - b$ and thus $(d - b)L_i + c' L' \geq d$ dominates $c_i L_i + c' L' \geq d$. It remains to show $\subseteq$. Let α be in $\mathsf{Ext}(S \cup \{c_i L_i + c' L' \geq d\})$. We show that then α is in $\mathsf{Ext}(S \cup \{(d - b)L_i + c' L' \geq d\})$ by case analysis on $\alpha(L_i)$.

$\alpha(L_i) = 0$: Then $\alpha(c_i L_i + c' L') = \alpha((d - b)L_i + c' L') = \alpha(c' L')$, and thus we know that $\alpha(c_i L_i + c' L') \geq d$ if and only if $\alpha((d - b)L_i + c' L') \geq d$.

$\alpha(L_i) = 1$: Then $\alpha((d - b)L_i + c' L') = (d - b) + \alpha(c' L')$. It remains to show that $(d-b)+\alpha(c' L') \geq d$, or $\alpha(c' L') \geq b$, which follows from the hypothesis that $S \cup \{L_i \geq 1\}$ dominates $c' L' \geq b$. $\square$

Dietrich et al. [DEC93] present a similar coefficient reduction technique, where essentially the bounds are obtained in a different way. A necessary condition for the application of coefficient reduction is that $S \cup \{L_i \geq 1\}$ dominates $cL \geq d$. Otherwise S does not dominate $c' L' \geq d - c_i$ and therefore for each lower bound b for $c' L'$ w.r.t. $S \cup \{L_i \geq 1\}$ we have $b \leq d - c_i$, which contradicts $c_i > d - b$.

Example 7.6.2 Let $cL \geq d$ be

$$10 \cdot A + 5 \cdot B + 4 \cdot C + 3 \cdot D + 3 \cdot E \geq 10 \ . \tag{7.21}$$

Good candidates for coefficient reductions are obviously coefficient/literal pairs $c_i L_i$, where the coefficient c_i is relatively large w.r.t. the right-hand side, because then the necessary condition, $S \cup \{L_i \geq 1\}$ dominates $cL \geq d$, is more

likely to hold. Let us choose $10 \cdot A$ and, since the coefficient 10 equals the right-hand side, we know that $S \cup \{A \geq 1\}$ dominates (7.21) for all sets of extended clauses S. We can reduce the coefficient 10 if we find some lower bound $b > 0$ for the linear pseudo-Boolean term $5 \cdot B + 4 \cdot C + 3 \cdot D + 3 \cdot E$. Suppose that S contains the extended clause $\overline{A} + B + C + F \geq 2$. Since $\{\overline{A} + B + C + F \geq 2, A \geq 1\}$ dominates $B + C \geq 1$, we know that either B or C has to be 1. Therefore, we can derive the lower bound $b = 4$.

$$\{\overline{A} + B + C + F \geq 2, A \geq 1\} \text{ dominates } 5 \cdot B + 4 \cdot C + 3 \cdot D + 3 \cdot E \geq 4$$

Following Proposition 7.6.1 we obtain $c_i' = 6$ and $c_i' L_i + cL \geq d$ is

$$6 \cdot A + 5 \cdot B + 4 \cdot C + 3 \cdot D + 3 \cdot E \geq 10 \ .$$

When transforming both linear pseudo-Boolean inequalities $c_i L_i + c' L' \geq d$ and $c_i' L_i + c' L' \geq d$ into an equivalent set of extended clauses, we see that the former generates only extended clauses with right-hand side 1, whereas the latter generates for example the strongest extended clause $A + B + C + D \geq 2$.

In order to obtain an ideal coefficient reduction we need to derive the maximal lower bound $b_{\min}$ for $c' L'$ w.r.t. $S \cup \{L_i \geq 1\}$. Because this involves solving the NP-complete problem

$$\min : c' L' \qquad \text{w.r.t.} \quad S \cup \{L_i \geq 1\} \ ,$$

we only approximate the best lower bound $b_{\min}$.

We propose the following procedure to obtain a valid lower bound b. Since the constraint set contains the unit literal L_i, we first simplify the set of extended clauses by replacing $S \cup \{L_i \geq 1\}$ by $\mathtt{pbur}(S \cup \{L_i \geq 1\})$. Note that $S \cup \{L_i \geq 1\}$ dominates $\mathtt{pbur}(S \cup \{L_i \geq 1\})$. We then fix the literals of $\mathtt{pbul}(S \cup \{L_i \geq 1\})$ in the objective function. For a set of literals K we define

$$\mathtt{o\_reduce}(c' L', K) := \{c_j L_j \mid c_j L_j \in c' L', L_j \notin K \text{ and } \overline{L_j} \notin K\}$$

and the new objective function is $\hat{c}\hat{L} := \mathtt{o\_reduce}(c' L', \mathtt{pbul}(S \cup \{L_i \geq 1\}))$. Summing up the coefficients of the literals that are fixed to 1 yields the constant $\hat{b}$, which can be added to the lower bound that we obtain from the approximation of the minimum for $\hat{c}\hat{L}$. For a set of literals K we define

$$\mathtt{sum\_fixed}(c' L', K) := \sum_{c_j L_j \in c' L' : L_j \in K} c_j$$

and the desired constant is then

$$\hat{b} := \texttt{sum\_fixed}(c'L', \texttt{pbul}(S \cup \{L_i \geq 1\})) \ .$$

The minimum of $c'L'$ w.r.t. $S \cup \{L_i \geq 1\}$ is then the same as the minimum of $\hat{c}\hat{L} + \hat{b}$ w.r.t. $\texttt{pbur}(S \cup \{L_i \geq 1\})$.

We restrict ourselves to a context S consisting of extended clauses and consider the problem of approximating the minimum of $\hat{c}\hat{L}$ w.r.t. the set of extended clauses $\texttt{pbur}(S \cup \{L_i \geq 1\})$, where no extended clause in $\texttt{pbur}(S \cup \{L_i \geq 1\})$ dominates an extended clause of the form $L_i \geq 1$. In other words, no more obvious fixings apply. Next, we will derive a set of extended clauses S' from the set $\texttt{pbur}(S \cup \{L_i \geq 1\})$ such that S' is dominated by $\texttt{pbur}(S \cup \{L_i \geq 1\})$ and S' contains only literals also occurring in $\hat{L}$. For a set of literals K and a set of extended clauses T we define

$$\texttt{c\_reduce}(T, K) := \left\{ K' \geq \beta' \; \middle| \; \begin{array}{l} K' \uplus K'' \geq \beta \in T, \\ \beta' = \beta - |K''| \geq 1, \\ K'' \subseteq K \text{ and } K \cap K' = \emptyset \end{array} \right\} \ ,$$

which is the set of all strict reductions of the extended clauses in T, where all literals in K have been eliminated. The set of extended clauses is then

$$S' = \texttt{c\_reduce}(\texttt{pbur}(S \cup \{L_i \geq 1\}), \mathcal{L} \setminus (\hat{L} \cup \overline{\hat{L}})) \ ,$$

where $\mathcal{L}$ is the set of all literals. We now give a greedy like approach to obtain a valid lower bound b for $\hat{c}\hat{L}$ w.r.t. the set of extended clauses S'. For each extended clause $K' \geq \beta'$ in S' we define

$$b_{K' \geq \beta'} := s(\hat{c}') \qquad \text{where} \qquad \left\{ \begin{array}{l} \hat{c}'\hat{L}' \subseteq \hat{c}\hat{L}, \\ \hat{L}' \subseteq K', \\ |\hat{L}'| = \beta' \text{ and} \\ \max(\hat{c}') \leq \min(\hat{c} \setminus \hat{c}') \ . \end{array} \right.$$

That is, $b_{K' \geq \beta'}$ is the sum of the smallest β' coefficients of $\hat{c}\hat{L}$ whose literals are in K'. So for each $\alpha \in \text{Ext}(K' \geq \beta')$ we have $\alpha(\hat{c}\hat{L}) \geq b_{K' \geq \beta'}$ and so a first valid lower bound for $\hat{c}\hat{L}$ is $b_{K' \geq \beta'}$. Let us select some bound $b_{K' \geq \beta'}$. For deriving the bound $b_{K' \geq \beta'}$ we considered all literals occurring in K'. Note that the bound is also valid for the subterm of the objective function containing only the literals of K'. We can therefore safely replace this subterm in the objective function by the bound $b_{K' \geq \beta'}$ and minimize the simpler objective function. Hence, a valid lower bound for $\hat{c}\hat{L}$ can be obtained by solving a simpler minimization problem

$$\min : \texttt{o\_reduce}(\hat{c}\hat{L}, K') + b_{K' \geq \beta'} \qquad \text{subject to} \quad S' \ ,$$

where $K' \geq \beta' \in S'$, which can again be solved by the same approach. We obtain the following algorithm computing a valid lower bound b for $\hat{c}\hat{L}$ w.r.t. S'.

Algorithm 7.6.3 *Lower bound for a linear pseudo-Boolean term*

```
lower_bound(ĉL̂, S')
      b := 0
      while ĉL̂ ≠ ∅ ∧ S' ≠ ∅
            K' ≥ β' := select_clause(ĉL̂, S')
            b := b + b_{K'≥β'}
            S' := c_reduce(S', K')
            ĉL̂ := o_reduce(ĉL̂, K')
      endwhile
      return b
end lower_bound
```

The procedure select_clause selects an extended clause that is used for deriving the current bound. We use the following heuristics. We choose the extended clause $K' \geq \beta'$ that maximizes

$$\frac{b_{K'\geq\beta'}}{\sum_{c_i L_i \in \hat{c}\hat{L}: L_i \in K'} c_i} \ .$$

The heuristics reflects that the bound is the largest or best w.r.t. the sum of the coefficients it has consumed. The computed lower bound b for $c'L'$ w.r.t. $S \cup \{L_i \geq 1\}$ is then

sum_fixed($c'L', K$)+
lower_bound(o_reduce($c'L', K$), c_reduce(pbur($S \cup \{L_i \geq 1\}$), $L' \setminus K$))

with $K = \text{pbul}(S \cup \{L_i \geq 1\})$.

Example 7.6.4 Let $cL \geq d$ be

$$5 \cdot A + 4 \cdot B + 4 \cdot C + 4 \cdot D + 3 \cdot E + 2 \cdot F \geq 11 \tag{7.22}$$

and let the set of extended clauses S be

$$\{\overline{A} + B \geq 1, C + D + G \geq 2, D + E + F \geq 1\} \ .$$

Let us reduce the coefficient 5 of the literal A. We apply pseudo-Boolean unit resolution to $S \cup \{A \geq 1\}$ and obtain

$$\text{pbur}(S \cup \{A \geq 1\}) \; = \; \{C + D + G \geq 2, D + E + F \geq 1\} \text{ and}$$
$$\text{pbul}(S \cup \{A \geq 1\}) \; = \; \{A, B\} \; .$$

Next, we reduce $\text{pbur}(S \cup \{A \geq 1\})$ such that only the literals of the objective function remain, i.e., we eliminate all literals in $\mathcal{L} \setminus \{C, D, E, F, \overline{C}, \overline{D}, \overline{E}, \overline{F}\}$. and obtain

$$S' = \{C + D \geq 1, D + E + F \geq 1\} \; .$$

We update the objective function $c'L'$ by calculating

$$\text{sum\_fixed}(4 \cdot B + 4 \cdot C + 4 \cdot D + 3 \cdot E + 2 \cdot F, \{A, B\}) = 4$$
$$\text{o\_reduce}(cL, \{A, B\}) = 4 \cdot C + 4 \cdot D + 3 \cdot E + 2 \cdot F = \hat{c}\hat{L}$$

and then call lower_bound. Calculating the $b_{K' \geq \beta'}$ yields

$$b_{C+D \geq 1} = 4 \qquad b_{D+E+F \geq 1} = 2$$

and since $4/8 > 2/9$, we select $C + D \geq 1$. Updating the objective function and the extended clause set gives

$$\text{o\_reduce}(4 \cdot C + 4 \cdot D + 3 \cdot E + 2 \cdot F, \{C, D\}) \; = \; 3 \cdot E + 2 \cdot F$$
$$\text{c\_reduce}(\{C + D \geq 1, D + E + F \geq 1\}, \{C, D\}) \; = \; \emptyset$$

and hence lower_bound stops and returns 4. The overall bound b is then $4 + 4 = 8$ and therefore $S \cup \{A \geq 1\}$ dominates

$$4 \cdot B + 4 \cdot C + 4 \cdot D + 3 \cdot E + 2 \cdot F \geq 8 \; .$$

By Proposition 7.6.1 we have $5 = c_i > d - b = 11 - 8 = 3$ and can so reduce the coefficient 5 of A to 3. Finally, we obtain the stronger linear pseudo-Boolean inequality

$$4 \cdot B + 4 \cdot C + 4 \cdot D + 3 \cdot A + 3 \cdot E + 2 \cdot F \geq 11 \; ,$$

which is equivalent to (7.22) in the context S.

The presented method for deriving a lower bound for $c'L'$ w.r.t. $S \cup \{L_i \geq 1\}$ yields good bounds when the set of extended clauses S is sparse or if the set of extended clauses S is nearly prime. Note that any method can be used to obtain a valid lower bound and the better the approximation of $b_{\min}$ the more likely it is that coefficient reduction applies.

The coefficient reduction method is useful for strengthening 0-1 problems that contain so-called *big-M-constraints* of the form

$$M \cdot X_i + cL \geq d$$

with $M = d$. We call X_i a *decision variable*, since setting it to 0 activates the constraint $cL \geq d$, whereas setting it to 1 makes $M \cdot X_i + cL \geq d$ a tautology [Wil90]. For these linear pseudo-Boolean inequalities all generated extended clauses obtained by the transformation process have the right-hand side 1. But, it is likely that coefficient reduction applies, since even a lower bound 1 for cL reduces M by 1. Note that then the transformation also generates stronger extended clauses with a right-hand side greater than 1.

7.6.2 Constrained Strict Reductions

Next, we introduce a method that replaces a linear pseudo-Boolean inequality $cL \geq d$ by a set of linear pseudo-Boolean inequalities S' such that $cL \geq d$ is equivalent to S' w.r.t. a set of extended clauses S.

$$\mathsf{Ext}(S \cup \{cL \geq d\}) = \mathsf{Ext}(S \cup S')$$

In the previous section we focused on deriving a lower bound for a linear pseudo-Boolean subterm of the original linear pseudo-Boolean inequality. With help of this lower bound we strengthened the linear pseudo-Boolean inequality and therefore the extended clauses generated by the transformation method. Application of coefficient reduction is always an improvement. In contrast to the method of Section 7.6.1 we allow here that S' is weaker than $cL \geq d$, which means $\mathsf{Ext}(S') \supseteq \mathsf{Ext}(cL \geq d)$. The set S' is simpler because the linear pseudo-Boolean inequalities in S' contain fewer literals than $cL \geq d$. Unfortunately, we may lose strong extended clauses when transforming the linear pseudo-Boolean inequalities in S' instead of $cL \geq d$. On the other hand, we possibly reduce the number of generated extended clauses. The idea is that some of the linear pseudo-Boolean inequalities in S' are easier to transform than $cL \geq d$. Combining the obtained strongest extended clauses with S may strengthen S, which again may lead to further simplifications.

When transforming a linear pseudo-Boolean inequality $cL \geq d$ we need to calculate all strict reductions $\mathsf{SRed}(cL \geq d)$. We show how to *constrain* the generation of strict reductions, and thus reduce their number with equivalence still being preserved.

Proposition 7.6.5 *Let $cL \geq d$ be a linear pseudo-Boolean inequality and let $L' \geq \beta$ be an extended clause with $L' \subseteq L$. Let S' be the set of linear pseudo-Boolean inequalities*

$$\left\{ \hat{c}\hat{L} \geq \hat{d} \,\middle|\, \begin{array}{l} \hat{c}\hat{L} = cL \setminus c''L'', \hat{d} = d - \sum c'', \\ c''L'' \subseteq cL, L'' \subseteq L' \text{ and } |L''| = \beta \end{array} \right\},$$

then $\mathsf{Ext}(\{L' \geq \beta, cL \geq d\}) = \mathsf{Ext}(\{L' \geq \beta\} \cup S')$. *Note that S' is the set of all strict reductions of $cL \geq d$, where the set of literals L'' for all $L'' \subseteq L'$ with $|L''| = \beta$ has been eliminated.*

Proof. Since $S' \subseteq \mathsf{SRed}(cL \geq d)$, we know that $cL \geq d$ dominates S'. It remains to show that every solution α of $\{L' \geq \beta\} \cup S'$ is a solution of $cL \geq d$. Let α be in $\mathsf{Ext}(\{L' \geq \beta\} \cup S')$. Let $L''' \subseteq L'$ be the set of all literals $L_i \in L'$ with $\alpha(L_i) = 1$. Because $L' \geq \beta$, we know that $|L'''| \geq \beta$. Let L'' be a subset of L''' such that $|L''| = \beta$. We select the strict reduction $\hat{c}\hat{L} \geq d - \sum c''$ from S', where L'' has been eliminated. Because α is a solution of S', we know that $\alpha(\hat{c}\hat{L}) \geq d - \sum c''$ and therefore $\alpha(\hat{c}\hat{L}) + \sum c'' \geq d$. Because $\alpha(\hat{c}\hat{L}) + \sum c'' = \alpha(cL)$, we have $\alpha(cL) \geq d$. □

Example 7.6.6 Let $cL \geq d$ be a linear pseudo-Boolean inequality and let $\{c_i \cdot A, c_j \cdot B, c_k \cdot C\} \subseteq cL$. We suppose that the extended clause $A + B + C \geq 2$ is dominated by an extended clause in the context S. Note that c_i, c_j, c_k can be any coefficients of $cL \geq d$, not necessarily the largest ones. Let $\hat{c}\hat{L} = cL \setminus \{c_i \cdot A, c_j \cdot B, c_k \cdot C\}$. We then can replace $cL \geq d$ by

$$\begin{aligned} S' = \{ c_i \cdot A + \hat{c}\hat{L} &\geq d - (c_j + c_k), \\ c_j \cdot B + \hat{c}\hat{L} &\geq d - (c_i + c_k), \\ c_k \cdot C + \hat{c}\hat{L} &\geq d - (c_i + c_j) \} \end{aligned}$$

according to Proposition 7.6.5, where $L' \geq \beta$ is $A + B + C \geq 2$, and have $\mathsf{Ext}(S \cup \{cL \geq d\}) = \mathsf{Ext}(S \cup S')$.

The use of Proposition 7.6.5 is only practicable if the number of linear pseudo-Boolean inequalities it generates is not too high. Note that Proposition 7.6.5 generates $\binom{|L'|}{\beta}$ extended clauses. The most interesting cases are if β is close to $|L'|$, since then the number of linear pseudo-Boolean inequalities is small and the number of deleted literals is high. In Example 7.6.6 we used an extended clause with $|L'| - \beta = 1$ and so $\binom{|L'|}{\beta} = |L'|$. Extended clauses of the form $L' \geq |L'| - 1$ are also called *clique inequalities* or *special ordered set*

constraints [NW88] and frequently occur in practical linear pseudo-Boolean constraint sets.

One problem of the application of Proposition 7.6.5 is that we may lose strong extended clauses.

Example 7.6.7   [a] Let $cL \geq d$ be

$$5 \cdot A + 4 \cdot B + 3 \cdot C \geq 6$$

then $cL \geq d$ is equivalent to $A + B + C \geq 2$. Applying Proposition 7.6.5 on $cL \geq d$ with the extended clause $A + B \geq 1$ gives the set of linear pseudo-Boolean inequalities

$$\{5 \cdot A + 3 \cdot C \geq 2, 4 \cdot B + 3 \cdot C \geq 1\} \tag{7.23}$$

equivalent to $cL \geq d$ w.r.t. $\{A + B \geq 1\}$. Transforming the linear pseudo-Boolean inequalities in (7.23) yields

$$\{A + C \geq 1, B + C \geq 1\} \ .$$

Now Proposition 7.6.5 assures that

$$\mathsf{Ext}(\{A + C \geq 1, B + C \geq 1, A + B \geq 1\}) = \mathsf{Ext}(\{A + B + C \geq 2\}) \ ,$$

but the *better* formulation of $cL \geq d$ is obviously $\{A + B + C \geq 2\}$. Indeed, in Section 8.2 we describe how to obtain this better formulation if only $\{A + C \geq 1, B + C \geq 1\}$ and $A + B \geq 1$ are given.

[b] Let $cL \geq d$ be

$$d \cdot A + c_i \cdot B + \hat{c}\hat{L} \geq d \ ,$$

where $c_i \cdot B$ can be any coefficient literal pair in $cL \setminus \{d \cdot A\}$. Then we know that all generated extended clauses have degree 1, since there is a coefficient in $cL \geq d$ that equals the right-hand side. Note that there is no strict reduction on A, because eliminating A would give a tautology. Suppose that there is a clique inequality in S dominating $A + B \geq 1$. Because of Proposition 7.6.5, we know that $cL \geq d$ is equivalent to

$$(d - c_i) \cdot A + \hat{c}\hat{L} \geq d - c_i$$

and we are sure that we do not miss any strongest extended clause. So applications of Proposition 7.6.5, where all but one[1] of the generated strict reductions are dominated by the context are safe.

---

[1] Of course, if all generated strict reductions are dominated by the context, then the whole linear pseudo-Boolean inequality is dominated by the context and can be ignored.

Another problem is that transforming the linear pseudo-Boolean inequalities in the set S' of Proposition 7.6.5 may invoke redundant computation. While transforming the linear pseudo-Boolean inequalities of S' in Example 7.6.6 we fully transform 3 times the strict reduction $cL \geq d - (c_i + c_j + c_k)$. We avoid the redundant computation by using Proposition 7.6.5 directly in the transformation routine.

Example 7.6.8 Let $cL \geq d$ be a linear pseudo-Boolean inequality and let $\{c_i \cdot A, c_j \cdot B, c_k \cdot C\} \subseteq cL$ as in Example 7.6.6. Let $\hat{c}\hat{L} = cL \backslash \{c_i \cdot A, c_j \cdot B, c_k \cdot C\}$ and $c_i \geq c_j \geq c_k$. We assume that the extended clause $A + B + C \geq 2$ is dominated by an extended clause in the context. Because of Proposition 7.6.5, we know that $cL \geq d$ is equivalent to the set of linear pseudo-Boolean inequalities

$$
\begin{aligned}
S' = \{ c_i \cdot A + \hat{c}\hat{L} &\geq d - (c_j + c_k), \\
c_j \cdot B + \hat{c}\hat{L} &\geq d - (c_i + c_k), \\
c_k \cdot C + \hat{c}\hat{L} &\geq d - (c_i + c_j) \} \ .
\end{aligned}
$$

We transform $c_i \cdot A + \hat{c}\hat{L} \geq d - (c_j + c_k)$ completely by the standard transformation method, but we start the transformation of $c_j \cdot B + \hat{c}\hat{L} \geq d - (c_i + c_k)$ with the forbidden elimination on B, since all extended clauses generated when B is eliminated are already obtained by the full transformation of $c_i \cdot A + \hat{c}\hat{L} \geq d - (c_j + c_k)$. Likewise, we forbid elimination of C when transforming $c_k \cdot C + \hat{c}\hat{L} \geq d - (c_i + c_j)$ and so avoid the redundant transformation of $\hat{c}\hat{L} \geq d - (c_i + c_j + c_k)$.

7.6.3 Constrained Transformation

Finally, we present a variant of the transformation method that restricts the number of generated extended clauses while transforming a linear pseudo-Boolean inequality $cL \geq d$ w.r.t. a set of extended clauses S. Let E be the set of non-redundant extended clauses generated by the transformation of $cL \geq d$, then *constrained transformation* generates a smaller set $E' \subseteq E$ such that

$$
\mathsf{Ext}(S \cup \{cL \geq d\}) = \mathsf{Ext}(S \cup E') \ .
$$

While transforming a linear pseudo-Boolean inequality $cL \geq d$ we need to compute all strict reductions $\mathsf{SRed}(cL \geq d)$. When proving the equivalence of $\mathsf{SCP}(\mathsf{SRed}(cL \geq d))$ and $cL \geq d$ in Theorem 7.1.5 we showed that for each non-satisfying assignment α of $cL \geq d$, we find an extended clause $L' \geq \beta$ in $\mathsf{SCP}(\mathsf{SRed}(I))$ such that α is not a solution of $L' \geq \beta$. If α is not a solution of the

context S, then we need not find an extended clause in $\mathsf{SCP}(\mathsf{SRed}(cL \geq d))$ for which α is not a solution. Hence, the corresponding generated extended clause need not be added for preserving equivalence. We can so restrict the number of needed strict reductions and therefore the number of generated extended clauses. First, we define a set of strict reductions of $cL \geq d$ taking into account the context S.

Definition 7.6.9 Let $cL \geq d$ be a linear pseudo-Boolean inequality, let S be a set of extended clauses and let $c'L' \geq d'$ be a strict reduction of $cL \geq d$. The set of literals $L \setminus L'$ is the set of literals that have been eliminated from $cL \geq d$ in order to obtain $c'L' \geq d'$. We denote by $\mathsf{SRed}(cL \geq d, S) \subseteq \mathsf{SRed}(cL \geq d)$ the set of strict reductions of $cL \geq d$ such that

$$c'L' \geq d' \in \mathsf{SRed}(cL \geq d, S)$$
$$\text{if and only if} \quad S \cup \{L \setminus L' \geq |L \setminus L'|\} \text{ is satisfiable.}$$

We now show that the set $\mathsf{SCP}(\mathsf{SRed}(cL \geq d, S))$ of strongest extended clauses obtained from the smaller set of strict reductions $\mathsf{SRed}(cL \geq d, S)$ is sufficient for the equivalence with $cL \geq d$ w.r.t. a set S of linear pseudo-Boolean inequalities.

Theorem 7.6.10 *Let $cL \geq d$ be a linear pseudo-Boolean inequality and let S be a set of extended clauses, then*

$$\mathsf{Ext}(S \cup \{cL \geq d\}) = \mathsf{Ext}(S \cup \mathsf{SCP}(\mathsf{SRed}(cL \geq d, S)s)) \ .$$

Proof.

- $\mathsf{Ext}(S \cup \{cL \geq d\}) \subseteq \mathsf{Ext}(S \cup \mathsf{SCP}(\mathsf{SRed}(cL \geq d, S)))$: as in Theorem 7.1.5.
- $\mathsf{Ext}(S \cup \{cL \geq d\}) \supseteq \mathsf{Ext}(S \cup \mathsf{SCP}(\mathsf{SRed}(cL \geq d, S)))$:
  We show that $\alpha \notin \mathsf{Ext}(S \cup \mathsf{SCP}(\mathsf{SRed}(cL \geq d, S)))$ if $\alpha \notin \mathsf{Ext}(S \cup \{cL \geq d\})$ from which the theorem follows.
  Suppose that $\alpha \notin \mathsf{Ext}(S \cup \{cL \geq d\})$. If $\alpha \notin \mathsf{Ext}(S)$ then obviously $\alpha \notin \mathsf{Ext}(S \cup \mathsf{SCP}(\mathsf{SRed}(cL \geq d, S)))$.
  Suppose that $\alpha \in \mathsf{Ext}(S)$, but $\alpha \notin \mathsf{Ext}(cL \geq d)$. We show that in this case there is a strict reduction in $\mathsf{SRed}(cL \geq d, S)$ such that α is not a solution of this reduction, hence $\alpha \notin \mathsf{Ext}(\mathsf{SCP}(\mathsf{SRed}(cL \geq d, S)))$ and thus $\alpha \notin \mathsf{Ext}(S \cup \mathsf{SCP}(\mathsf{SRed}(cL \geq d, S)))$. Since $\alpha \notin \mathsf{Ext}(cL \geq d)$, we know that $\alpha(cL) = d' < d$. Let Y be the set of literals L_i such that $\alpha(L_i) = 1$ and $L' = L \setminus Y$, then $\sum_{i|L_i \in Y} c_i = d' < d$ and $c'L' \geq d'$ is

$\sum_{i|L_i \in L'} c_i L_i \geq d - d'$. Because $d' < d$, we know that $d - d' \geq 1$, and therefore $c'L' \geq d'$ is a strict reduction of $cL \geq d$, obtained by eliminating the literals that are mapped to zero by α. Furthermore, we know that $Y = L \setminus L'$, hence $\alpha(L \setminus L') = |L \setminus L'|$. Because $\alpha \in \mathsf{Ext}(S)$, we know that $\alpha \in \mathsf{Ext}(S \cup \{L \setminus L' \geq |L \setminus L'|\})$ and therefore $c'L' \geq d'$ in $\mathsf{SRed}(cL \geq d, S)$. Let $\mathsf{SCP}(c'L' \geq d')$ be $L' \geq \beta$. We know that $\beta \geq 1$ because $d - d' \geq 1$. Because $\alpha(L') = 0$, we derive that $\alpha \notin \mathsf{Ext}(\mathsf{SCP}(c'L' \geq d'))$, and therefore $\alpha \notin \mathsf{Ext}(\mathsf{SCP}(\mathsf{SRed}(cL \geq d)))$, which establishes the theorem. □

The proof of Theorem 7.6.10 is similar to the proof of Theorem 7.1.5. The main difference is that we additionally show that each strict reduction we need is in the restricted set of strict reductions. Theorem 7.1.5 can be seen as an instance of Theorem 7.6.10, where the set of extended clauses S is the empty set.

An implementation of the constrained transformation algorithm is now straightforward. For each strict reduction $c'L' \geq d'$ of $cL \geq d$ we maintain a set of extended clauses $S_{c'L' \geq d'} := S \cup \{L \setminus L' \geq |L \setminus L'|\}$. By Theorem 7.6.10 we can eliminate the strict reduction $c'L' \geq d'$ from the transformation process if $S_{c'L' \geq d'}$ is unsatisfiable. Note that if $S_{c'L' \geq d'}$ is unsatisfiable, then for each strict reduction $c''L'' \geq d''$ of $c'L' \geq d'$ the corresponding set of extended clauses $\{S \cup \{L \setminus L'' \geq |L \setminus L''|\}$ is unsatisfiable. Care must be taken when applying the strong redundancy criteria presented in Section 7.2. Suppose that a strict reduction $c'L' \geq d'$ is eliminated because $S_{c'L' \geq d'}$ is unsatisfiable. Furthermore, suppose that $\mathsf{SCP}(c'L' \geq d')$ dominates an extended clause $\mathsf{SCP}(c''L'' \geq d'')$, where $c''L'' \geq d''$ is a strict reduction of $c'L' \geq d'$ and there is no other non-redundant extended clause dominating $\mathsf{SCP}(c'L' \geq d')$. In that case we have to add $\mathsf{SCP}(c''L'' \geq d'')$ or $\mathsf{SCP}(c'L' \geq d')$ for preserving equivalence. The simplest way is to add $\mathsf{SCP}(c'L' \geq d')$ always, if $S_{c'L' \geq d'}$ is unsatisfiable, and then forbid further strict reductions of $c'L' \geq d'$, i.e., not to transform recursively $c'L' \geq d'$. When later inserting the transformed set of extended clauses into a larger set, redundant extended clauses can be deleted.

In the constrained transformation algorithm we need to solve again a satisfiability problem for the set of extended clauses $S \cup \{L \setminus L' \geq |L \setminus L'|\}$. Because this is an NP-complete problem, we relax the problem again and check only whether the pseudo-Boolean unit relaxation of $S \cup \{L \setminus L' \geq |L \setminus L'|\}$ is unsatisfiable. That is, at each node we check whether $\bot \in \mathsf{pbur}(S \cup \{L \setminus L' \geq |L \setminus L'|\})$. Note that all literals in $L \setminus L'$ are unit literals and therefore unsatisfiability of $S \cup \{L \setminus L' \geq |L \setminus L'|\}$ is likely to be detected by pseudo-Boolean unit resolution.

Example 7.6.11 Let $cL \geq d$ be

$$6 \cdot A + 5 \cdot B + 4 \cdot C + 3 \cdot D + 2 \cdot E + F \geq 13$$

and suppose that the extended clause $\overline{B} + \overline{C} \geq 1$ is dominated by an extended clause in the context S. Hence, $S \cup \{B + C \geq 2\}$ is unsatisfiable which is detected by pseudo-Boolean unit resolution. The full transformation of $cL \geq d$ generates the five extended clauses

$$\{ \quad A + B + C + D + E \geq 3, A + B + C \geq 2, A + D \geq 1,$$
$$A + B + D + F \geq 2, A + E + F \geq 1\} \ .$$

One strict reduction of $cL \geq d$ is

$$6 \cdot A + 3 \cdot D + 2 \cdot E + F \geq 4 \tag{7.24}$$

from which the two non-redundant extended clauses

$$A + E + F \geq 1 \qquad A + D \geq 1$$

are derived. Since the set of extended clauses $S_{6 \cdot A + 3 \cdot D + 2 \cdot E + F \geq 4}$ is unsatisfiable, and therefore $\mathsf{SRed}(6 \cdot A + 3 \cdot D + 2 \cdot E + F \geq 4, S) = \emptyset$, we need not consider $6 \cdot A + 3 \cdot D + 2 \cdot E + F \geq 4$ and constrained transformation generates only three extended clauses. Note that $\mathsf{SCP}(6 \cdot A + 3 \cdot D + 2 \cdot E + F \geq 4)$ is redundant and dominated by another extended clause from the remaining three. Hence, we need not include $\mathsf{SCP}(6 \cdot A + 3 \cdot D + 2 \cdot E + F \geq 4)$.

Instead of deleting the strict reduction $c'L' \geq d'$ if $S_{c'L' \geq d'}$ is unsatisfiable, we can also use this fact for strengthening the generated extended clause. We explain the idea first by an example. Let $cL \geq d$ be

$$c_1 \cdot A + c_2 \cdot B + cL \geq d$$

and suppose that $S \cup \{A + B \geq 2\}$ is unsatisfiable. Hence, the strict reduction

$$cL \geq d - (c_1 + c_2) \ . \tag{7.25}$$

need not be considered. However, because $S \cup \{A + B \geq 2\}$ is unsatisfiable we know that $\overline{A} + \overline{B} \geq 1$ is a valid extended clause w.r.t. S. So we can derive an upper bound for the linear pseudo-Boolean term $c_1 \cdot A + c_2 \cdot B$, namely $\{\overline{A} + \overline{B} \geq 1\}$ dominates $c_1 \cdot A + c_2 \cdot B \leq \max(c_1, c_2)$. Therefore, we derive the stronger linear pseudo-Boolean inequality

$$cL \geq d - \max(c_1, c_2) \ . \tag{7.26}$$

We miss no extended clause if we replace the strict reduction (7.25) by (7.26), but may only generate stronger extended clauses. Note that we derive here an *upper bound* for a linear pseudo-Boolean term and use the bound in order to strengthen the generated extended clauses.

Lemma 7.6.12 *Let* $cL \geq d$ *be a linear pseudo-Boolean inequality and let* $c'L' \geq d'$ *be a strict reduction of* $cL \geq d$. *Let* S *be a set of extended clauses such that* $S_{c'L' \geq d'}$ *is unsatisfiable. Let* $c''L''$ *be* $cL \setminus c'L'$, *then*

$$\mathsf{Ext}(S \cup \{cL \geq d\}) = \mathsf{Ext}(S \cup \mathsf{SCP}(\mathsf{SRed}(cL \geq d, S)) \cup \{c'L' \geq d' + \min(c'')\}) \ .$$

Proof. The direction $\supseteq$ is immediate by Theorem 7.6.10. It remains to show $\subseteq$, which means $S \cup \{cL \geq d\}$ dominates $c'L' \geq d' + \min(c'')$. Let α be in $\mathsf{Ext}(S \cup \{cL \geq d\})$, then we have $\alpha(cL) \geq d$ and therefore $\alpha(c'L') + \alpha(c''L'') \geq d$. Since $S_{c'L' \geq d'} = S \cup \{L'' \geq |L''|\}$ is unsatisfiable, we know furthermore that S dominates $\overline{L''} \geq 1$, i.e., at least one literal of L'' is mapped to 0 by α. We conclude that $\alpha(c''L'') \leq \sum c'' - \min(c'')$ and, since $\alpha(c'L') + \alpha(c''L'') \geq d$, we have $\alpha(c'L') + \sum c'' - \min(c'') \geq d$. Because $d' = d - \sum c''$, we derive $\alpha(c'L') + \sum c'' - \min(c'') \geq d' + \sum c''$ which simplifies to $\alpha(c'L') \geq d' + \min(c'')$.
□

With Lemma 7.6.12 we can replace the strict reduction $c'L' \geq d'$ by the stronger linear pseudo-Boolean inequality $c'L' \geq d' + \min(c'')$ while preserving equivalence w.r.t. the context S.

Example 7.6.13 Let $cL \geq d$ again be

$$6 \cdot A + 5 \cdot B + 4 \cdot C + 3 \cdot D + 2 \cdot E + F \geq 13$$

and suppose that $S \cup \{B + C \geq 2\}$ is unsatisfiable. A non-redundant extended clause dominated by $cL \geq d$ is $A + E + F \geq 1$. While eliminating B and C we detect unsatisfiability of $S \cup \{B + C \geq 2\}$ and can replace the reduction

$$6 \cdot A + 3 \cdot D + 2 \cdot E + F \geq 4$$

by

$$6 \cdot A + 3 \cdot D + 2 \cdot E + F \geq 8$$

from which we derive the non-redundant extended clause $A + E \geq 1$ dominating $A + E + F \geq 1$. Note that $6 \cdot A + 3 \cdot D + 2 \cdot E + F \geq 8$ dominates $A \geq 1$, which is obtained from the strongest extended clause of the strict reduction obtained when further eliminating $\{D, E, F\}$. So in this case we replace a non-redundant extended clause by a stronger one, but we may also derive new extended clauses that do not dominate other generated extended clauses.

We propose the use of Lemma 7.6.12 in the constrained transformation algorithm and to consider no further strict reductions of the stronger strict reduction $c'L' \geq d' + \min(c'')$, but only add $\mathsf{SCP}(c'L' \geq d' + \min(c''))^2$ to the set of extended clauses. Note that we get the stronger extended clause $\mathsf{SCP}(c'L' \geq d' + \min(c''))$ with minimal computational effort and we have to add $\mathsf{SCP}(c'L' \geq d')$ in any case in order to apply the redundancy criteria presented in Section 7.2.

7.7   CUT GENERATION FOR 0-1 INTEGER PROGRAMMING

Extended cover inequalities of a linear 0-1 inequality, well known in 0-1 integer programming, can be related to the extended clauses generated by our transformation method. In linear programming based 0-1 optimization algorithms (branch-and-bound), valid extended cover inequalities can be added to the current constraint set in order to strengthen the linear programming relaxation of the problem [NW88, NSS94].

We show how to use our transformation method for generating these extended cover inequalities and how to restrict the transformation method in order to produce *strong* extended cover inequalities or extended cover inequalities over a special subset of variables. We test the method on a subset of 0-1 integer programming problems and report computational results.

7.7.1   Extended Clauses and Extended Cover Inequalities

Reformulating 0-1 integer programming problems and applying constraint generation techniques make large scale 0-1 optimization problems solvable in reasonable time [CJP83, JKS85]. The widely used branch-and-bound method for 0-1 integer optimization problems solves the linear programming (LP) relaxation of the problem and then branches on variables with fractional values in the current LP-solution. At each node valid 0-1 inequalities may be generated, so-called strong cuts, that better approximate the integral solutions of

---

[2]Or better the non-redundant extended clause dominating $\mathsf{SCP}(c'L' \geq d' + \min(c''))$ on the path H_{k+1} of Proposition 7.2.8.

the problem. Therefore, solving the reformulated problems typically requires fewer branch and bound cycles.

The constraint set of a linear 0-1 integer programming problem consists of a set of linear 0-1 inequalities of the form

$$c_1 \cdot X_1 + \cdots + c_n \cdot X_n \leq d \qquad (7.27)$$

which is equivalent to

$$-c_1 \cdot X_1 - \cdots - c_n \cdot X_n \geq -d$$

and then can be brought into pseudo-Boolean normal form.

An important constraint generation technique is presented in [NW88]. It is based mainly on the notion of *minimal covers* or *minimal dependent sets*.

Definition 7.7.1 [NW88] A set $C \subseteq \{1, \ldots, n\}$ is a minimal dependent set of a linear 0-1 inequality (7.27) if

$$\sum_{i \in C \setminus \{j\}} c_i \leq d < \sum_{i \in C} c_i$$

for all $j \in C$.

Proposition 7.7.2 [NW88] If C is a minimal dependent set for a linear 0-1 inequality $\sum_{i=1}^{n} c_i X_i \leq d$, then

$$\sum_{i \in E(C)} X_i \leq |C| - 1 , \qquad (7.28)$$

where

$$E(C) = C \cup \{k \mid 1 \leq k \leq n \text{ and } c_k \geq c_j \text{ for all } j \in C\}$$

is a valid inequality w.r.t. $\sum_{i=1}^{n} c_i X_i \leq d$. The set of indices $E(C)$ is called the extension of C and we call (7.28) an extended cover inequality.

Proof. We show that if α is not in $\text{Ext}(\sum_{i \in E(C)} X_i \leq |C| - 1)$ then α is not in $\text{Ext}(\sum_{i=1}^{n} c_i X_i \leq d)$.

Let α be an assignment that is not in $\text{Ext}(\sum_{i \in E(C)} X_i \leq |C| - 1)$. Then $\alpha(\sum_{i \in E(C)} X_i) \geq |C|$. Therefore, $\alpha(\sum_{i=1}^{n} c_i X_i)$ is a sum of at least $|C|$ coefficients c_i with $i \in E(C)$. The sum of $|C|$ coefficients c_i with $i \in E(C)$ is greater than d by construction. Hence, $\alpha(\sum_{i=1}^{n} c_i X_i) > d$, which means $\alpha \notin \text{Ext}(\sum_{i=1}^{n} c_i X_i \leq d)$. $\qquad \square$

Note that

$$\sum_{i \in E(C)} X_i \leq |C| - 2$$

is not valid w.r.t. $\sum_{i=1}^n c_i X_i) > d$. Let $\alpha(X_i) = 1$ for all $i \in C \setminus \{j\}$ for some $j \in C$ and $\alpha(X_i) = 0$ otherwise. Then $\alpha \notin \mathsf{Ext}(\sum_{i \in E(C)} X_i \leq |C| - 2)$, but $\alpha \in \mathsf{Ext}(\sum_{i=1}^n c_i X_i \leq d)$.

Let us write (7.28) in pseudo-Boolean normal form.

$$\sum_{i \in E(C)} \overline{X_i} \geq |E(C) \setminus C| + 1 \qquad (7.29)$$

We know that

$$\sum_{i \in E(C)} \overline{X_i} \geq |E(C) \setminus C| + 2$$

is not a valid inequality, because otherwise

$$\sum_{i \in E(C)} X_i \leq |C| - 2$$

would be valid, which is not the case. Hence, (7.29) is the strongest extended clause containing exactly the literals X_i for all $i \in E(C)$. Because each extended cover inequality of $cL \geq d$ corresponds to a strongest extended clause in $\mathsf{SCP}(\mathsf{SRed}(cL \geq d))$, we can use our transformation procedure to systematically construct the set of all strongest *non-redundant* extended cover inequalities.

In a preprocessing phase of linear programming based 0-1 integer programming systems, extended cover inequalities are generated and *added* to the original constraint set. Because of our equivalence result, we can replace the original inequality by its set of equivalent extended clauses. For a branch-and-cut system, where valid constraints may be added at each node, we can generate all extended cover inequalities, but store them separately. At each node we can then select just one, if it violates the current LP-solution.

Example 7.7.3 Let us look again at Example 7.3.3 on page 127.

[a] By writing the extended clauses as "$\leq$-inequalities" we see that the two extended cover inequalities

$$\begin{aligned} X_1 + X_2 + X_3 + X_4 + X_5 &\leq 3 \\ X_1 + X_2 + X_3 &\leq 2 \end{aligned}$$

p0033	# I	# EC	# Nodes	PrePro	Solve	LP-Sol.	Optimum
Original	11	4	9685	0.00	59.89	2520.57	3089
Normal	11	4	1289	0.00	6.47	2819.36	3089
Simple	2	80	124	0.04	1.42	2846.00	3089
Full	0	8710	118	0.90	237.30	2846.00	3089

Figure 7.4   Computational Results for "p0033"

are equivalent to the linear 0-1 inequality

$$79 \cdot X_1 + 53 \cdot X_2 + 53 \cdot X_3 + 45 \cdot X_4 + 45 \cdot X_5 \leq 178 \ .$$

[b] The single extended cover inequality

$$X_1 + X_6 + X_7 + X_9 \leq 1$$

is equivalent to the linear 0-1 inequality

$$774 \cdot X_1 + 76 \cdot X_2 + 22 \cdot X_3 + 42 \cdot X_4 + 21 \cdot X_5 + \\ 760 \cdot X_6 + 818 \cdot X_7 + 62 \cdot X_8 + 785 \cdot X_9 \leq 1500 \ .$$

So for Example 7.7.3[a] and [b] a full transformation is suitable. For Example 7.3.3[c] the number of extended clauses is too large and we need to restrict the number of extended clauses we generate. A trivial, but powerful, approach is to transform only *simple* linear pseudo-Boolean inequalities. The transformation algorithm can easily be changed to just count the number of extended clauses that will be generated, which will be much faster than generating the extended clauses. We can then only transform linear pseudo-Boolean inequalities that generate fewer extended clauses than a given upper bound.

For example, the constraint set of the 0-1 optimization problem p0033 [NW88, page 465] (also available in MIPLIB [BBI92]) consists of 15 inequalities, where 4 of them are already extended clauses. From the remaining 11 inequalities 9 are *simple*, since they are equivalent to only a few extended clauses, and just 2 inequalities produce more than 4000 extended clauses. Thus, a naive approach is to transform the 13 simple inequalities completely in advance and leave the 2 *hard* inequalities unchanged. We ran the commercial mixed integer solver CPLEX 2.1 on the original and the preprocessed problem. The results are reported in Figure 7.4. We denote by "# I" the number of linear pseudo-Boolean inequalities where some coefficients on the left-hand side are greater than 1, and

by "# EC" the number of extended clauses. "# Nodes" denotes the number of nodes explored by CPLEX in order to find the optimal solution and to prove optimality. "PrePro" is the time in user cpu seconds on a SPARC-10 used by a PROLOG-implementation of the transformation method in order to preprocess the problem. "Solve" is the time in user cpu seconds CPLEX needed to solve the preprocessed problem. By "LP-Sol." we denote the optimal solution of the linear programming relaxation of the problem and by "Optimum" the integer optimal solution. The rows describe 4 different formulations of "p0033". In "Original" we solve the original problem as found in MIPLIB. In "Normal" we solve the problem after bringing each inequality into pseudo-Boolean normal form.

Bringing an inequality into pseudo-Boolean normal form includes coefficient reduction as presented in [CJP83] and for "p0033" we obtain a speedup of factor 9. This is reflected by the better optimal solution of the linear programming relaxation of the problem and the fewer number of linear programs solved ("Nodes"). Transforming the *simple* inequalities completely generates a larger problem (82 versus 15 constraints), but we obtain an additional speedup of factor 4, which is again due to a better linear programming relaxation. Note that the time consumed by the preprocessing phase is very small w.r.t. the "Solve"-time. A complete transformation of all inequalities shows to be too clumsy. The size of the problem (8710 versus 15 inequalities) slows down the linear programming solver, although even fewer nodes are needed. Using constrained transformation as presented in Section 7.6.3, which means transforming each inequality completely in the context of all remaining inequalities, generates only 4484 extended clauses. So when a complete transformation is required, constrained transformation is advantageous. Complete transformation of a constraint set of a 0-1 integer optimization problem is not always well-suited. Therefore, we need to make our transformation method more flexible.

7.7.2   Restrictions

By restricting the number of generated extended clauses, we can use the transformation method as generator of extended cover inequalities, i.e., strongest extended clauses, in a branch-and-cut system for solving 0-1 integer optimization problems. We show how to focus on extended clauses that are sufficiently strong and restrict the number of extended clauses by focusing on some set of variables.

First, we give a measure of extended clauses describing their *quality* and show how to adopt the transformation method in order to obtain only extended clauses better than or equal to a given quality border. The *weakness* of an extended clause $L \geq d$ is defined by $w(L \geq d) := |L| - d$ (see Definition 8.1.1). Note that $w(L \geq d) \leq w(L' \geq d')$ is a necessary condition for $L \geq d$ dominates $L' \geq d'$, which is obvious from Lemma 3.1.14. We say that $L \geq d$ is *stronger* than $L' \geq d'$ if $w(L \geq d) \leq w(L' \geq d')$.

Given a linear pseudo-Boolean inequality, we can easily determine the minimal weakness of all extended clauses the transformation method generates.

Lemma 7.7.4 *Let $cL \geq d$ be a linear pseudo-Boolean inequality in normal form and let β be such that*

$$\sum_{i=1}^{\beta} c_{n-i+1} < d \leq \sum_{i=1}^{\beta+1} c_{n-i+1} \ , \tag{7.30}$$

then $\beta' = |L| - \beta - 1$ is the smallest weakness of all extended clauses generated by the transformation method.

Proof. We know that

$$\sum_{i=1}^{n-\beta} c_i L_i \geq d - \sum_{i=1}^{\beta} c_{n-i+1}$$

is a valid strict reduction of $cL \geq d$. The right-hand side of its corresponding strongest extended clause is 1 because of (7.30) and therefore its weakness is $n - \beta - 1 = \beta'$. Next, we show that there is no stronger extended clause, i.e., no extended clause with a smaller weakness. Let us recall (7.8), which states that the degrees of the extended clauses along a path are either equal or decrease by one from father node to son node. On the other hand, the number of literals in the extended clauses along a path decrease always by one from father node to son node. So, we conclude that the weakness of the extended clauses along a path are either equal or decrease by one from father node to son node. In order to determine the minimal weakness, it is therefore sufficient to consider only the leaves of the graph, i.e., all extended clauses, where the right-hand side is 1. Hence, we only need to investigate all strict reductions

$$\sum_{i \in M} c_i L_i \geq d - \sum_{i \in N \setminus M} c_i \tag{7.31}$$

with $M \subseteq N$ such that $\sum_{i \in M} c_i < d$ and $c_{\max(N \setminus M)} + \sum_{i \in M} c_i \geq d$. The weakness of these extended clauses is $|M| - 1$ and we search for an M with a

minimal cardinality. Obviously, $M' = \{1, \ldots, \beta\}$ has minimal cardinality, since $\sum_{i=1}^{\beta} c_i \geq \sum_{i \in M} c_i$ for all M satisfying (7.31).   □

We can easily adapt our transformation method to generate only extended clauses having a weakness less than or equal to a given bound by applying Lemma 7.7.4 to every strict reduction we construct and abandon further strict reductions, if the minimal weakness is greater than the bound. So, by Lemma 7.7.4 we can filter out the generation of extended clauses that do not have a weakness less than or equal to the bound. Note that we avoid unnecessary computation of branches that do not lead to extended clauses that are strong enough.

A very popular and strong class of extended clauses that can be generated this way are extended clauses with weakness 1.

Definition 7.7.5 An extended clause of the form $L \geq |L| - 1$, i.e., an extended clause with weakness 1, is called *clique inequality* or *special ordered set constraint* [NW88].

Clique inequalities have proven to be useful in 0-1 integer programming. With the method presented here in combination with Lemma 7.7.4 we can generate extended clauses having an arbitrary weakness limit and generalize so existing methods that generate only cliques.

Another possibility is to generate only extended clauses from a linear pseudo-Boolean inequality containing a special subset of variables. Suppose that we have a clique inequality for some variables and have no extended clauses containing the remaining variables. So we are interested in generating extended clauses, where this set of remaining variables V occurs. Another interesting set of variables is the one with large coefficients in the objective function, since they are mainly responsible for the resulting objective function value.

We obtain valid extended clauses containing a special set V of variables, if we transform a strict reduction of the linear pseudo-Boolean inequality, where we have eliminated in advance all literals containing the variables that are not in V. Another reason to transform a strict reduction and not the whole linear pseudo-Boolean inequality is given, if the linear pseudo-Boolean inequality contains some relatively large and some relatively small coefficients. The generated strongest extended clauses typically contain the literals with the largest coefficients and eliminating literals with small coefficients in advance focuses on

Name	# I	# EC	# Nodes	PrePro	Solve	LP-Sol.	Opt.
p0033-Original	11	4	9685	0.00	59.89	2520.57	3089
p0033-Normal	11	4	1289	0.00	6.47	2819.36	3089
p0033-Simple	2	80	124	0.04	1.42	2846.00	3089
p0040-Original	23	20	96	0.00	0.55	61796.54	62027
p0040-Normal	23	20	59	0.00	0.32	61829.08	62027
p0040-Simple	0	24	0	0.03	0.05	62027.00	62027
p0201-Original	33	100	5238	0.00	167.95	6875.00	7615
p0201-Normal	33	100	2775	0.00	90.42	7125.00	7615
p0201-Simple f	30	106	2273	0.33	84.83	7125.00	7615
p0201-wl(9) f	30	112	1258	0.43	47.47	7125.00	7615
p0548-Original	89[1]	63	&	0.00	&	315.25	8691
p0548-Normal	89	63	&	0.02	&	4568.75	8691
p0548-Simple f	52	508	&	0.54	&	6617.47	8691
p0548-wl(1) cr f	52	672	&	8.10	&	7306.68	8691
p2756-Original	378[2]	352	&	0.00	&	2688.75	3124
p2756-Normal	378	352	&	2.35	&	2701.14	3124
p2756-wl(1) cr f	343	2096	&	256.50	&	2701.75	3124
lseu-Original	11	17	55526	0.00	791.60	834.68	1120
lseu-Normal	11	17	28551	0.00	465.65	944.75	1120
lseu-Simple	7	22	18032	0.00	275.02	985.54	1120

[1] From 176 inequalities are 10 tautologies and 14 become tautologous after fixing
[2] From 755 inequalities are 6 tautologies and 19 become tautologous after fixing
& out of memory

Figure 7.5   Some Computational Results

these strong extended clauses. Note that we can obtain strong extended clauses also by restricting the weakness as showed at the beginning of this section. By eliminating literals in advance, we reduce the size of the search tree of the transformation method, but in exchange only approximate the strongest extended clauses. The approach can be used if the linear pseudo-Boolean inequalities are too large to be transformed completely.

7.7.3   Computational Results

We have tested the preprocessing approach on some pure 0-1 integer programming problems found in MIPLIB [BBI92]. For the format of the figures see Section 7.7.1, page 153. Additionally, we denote by "f" whether variables have been fixed using the fixing procedure presented in Section 7.5, and with "wl(w)"

that for the non-simple inequalities the generation of extended clauses has been limited to the maximal weakness w.

We obtain encouraging results on the "pxxxx" problem set [CJP83], since these are sparse problems and considering each inequality on its own is promising under this premise. On dense problems we cannot expect similar improvements. We denote by "cr" whether coefficient reduction, as presented in Section 7.6.1, has been successfully applied to problem. Coefficient reduction is tried on the literal with the largest coefficient in each linear pseudo-Boolean inequality that cannot be simply transformed. The set of extended clauses that is used for the coefficient reduction is the set of extended clauses generated by the transformation of all simple linear pseudo-Boolean inequalities. Coefficient reduction was not very successful in the preprocessing phase. Coefficient reduction would be more successful when applied on the linear pseudo-Boolean inequalities constructed while exploring the branch-and-bound tree, since then some literals are fixed and so better bounds may be obtained for the simpler linear pseudo-Boolean inequalities.

The presented techniques can be used in a branch-and-bound method when solving 0-1 integer programming problems. On spare problems the techniques are useful even in a preprocessing phase. Significant speedups can be obtained when the optimal solution of the linear programming relaxation of the partially transformed problem is better than in the original problem. In the context of 0-1 integer optimization we generalize the generation of clique inequalities (extended clauses with weakness 1) to the generation of extended clauses with an arbitrary weakness limit. The transformation method can be used as a cut generator in a branch-and-bound algorithm. When searching an extended clause violating the fractional solution of the current linear programming relaxation, we can extract just the needed extended clause. With the given redundancy criteria we assure that we select the best possible extended clause. For example, assume that the variables A, B have the fractional value 0.5 in the current LP-solution, and that a linear pseudo-Boolean inequality $cL \geq d$ of the constraint set dominates the non-redundant extended clause $A + B + C \geq 2$, i.e., $A + B + C \geq 2$ is in $\mathsf{SCP}(\mathsf{SRed}(cL \geq d))$. When searching some polyhedral cut that violates the current fractional solution, we may just compute the extended clause $A + B \geq 1$, which is also in $\mathsf{SCP}(\mathsf{SRed}(cL \geq d))$, and add it to the problem. Because of the redundancy criteria, we choose with our approach $A + B + C \geq 2$ and so forbid further fractional solutions, among them, for example, $B = C = 0.5$.

Note that the main feature of the transformation method is that on the obtained set of extended clauses the deductive system *Generalized Resolution* [Hoo92a]

can be applied. Thus, information coming from several linear pseudo-Boolean inequalities are used and may lead to stronger extended clauses. In Chapter 8 we investigate how to strengthen extended clauses by using a restricted version of *Generalized Resolution*. The output of the transformed and strengthened constraint set can be stored separately and extended clauses serving as cuts then can be selected when needed by the branch-and-cut algorithm.

7.8   IMPLEMENTING RESOLUTION

Hooker [Hoo92a] defines a *resolvent* of two extended clauses as the classical resolvent of two classical clauses, each of them dominated by one of the extended clauses. We enhance the notion of resolvents between extended clauses and show how to efficiently implement the inference rule with the help of our transformation method.

Example 7.8.1 Let

$$A + B + \overline{D} + E + \overline{F} + \overline{G} \geq 4 \tag{7.32}$$

$$\overline{A} + \overline{C} + \overline{D} + \overline{E} + F + G \geq 3 \tag{7.33}$$

be two extended clauses. The classical clause $A + B + \overline{D} \geq 1$ is dominated by (7.32) and $\overline{A} + \overline{C} + \overline{D} + \overline{E} \geq 1$ is dominated by (7.33). From these two classical clauses we obtain the classical resolvent $B + \overline{C} + \overline{D} + \overline{E} \geq 1$ by resolving on A.

As shown in Section 3.3, the resolvent of two classical clauses can be obtained by linear combination of the two classical clauses and the valid bounds $L_i \geq 0$ and $-L_i \geq -1$ for all literals L_i, and integer rounding. Thus, resolvents are also cutting plane inequalities. It is easy to see that resolvents of extended clauses can also be obtained by linear combination and rounding, since classical clauses dominated by extended clauses are strict reductions that are obtained by adding the valid bound $-L_i \geq -1$ for all literals L_i that are eliminated. In the following we show that each resolvent of two extended clauses is dominated by an extended clause obtained by transforming the sum of these two extended clauses. The *sum* of two linear pseudo-Boolean inequalities $cL \geq d$ and $c'L' \geq d'$ is the linear pseudo-Boolean inequality $cL + c'L' \geq d + d'$. As usual, we assume that the sum of two linear pseudo-Boolean inequalities is brought into pseudo-Boolean normal form.

Proposition 7.8.2 *Each resolvent of two extended clauses $L \geq d$ and $L' \geq d'$ is dominated by an extended clause in* $\mathsf{SCP}(\mathsf{SRed}(cL + c'L' \geq d + d'))$.

Proof. We construct two classical clauses that are dominated by $L \geq d$ resp. $L' \geq d'$ and have a resolvent. We then show that this resolvent is dominated by an extended clause in $\mathsf{SCP}(\mathsf{SRed}(cL + c'L' \geq d + d'))$.

First, we extract the literals that occur positively in one extended clause and negatively in the other. Let $L_R + K = L$ and $L'_R + \overline{K} = L'$ with $K = \{L_i \mid L_i \in L$ and $\overline{L_i} \in L'\}$ and $\overline{K} = \{\overline{L_i} \mid L_i \in K\}$. Next, we construct two classical clauses that are dominated by $L \geq d$ resp. $L' \geq d'$ and have a resolvent. The general representation[3] of such a classical clause that is dominated by $L \geq d$ is $L_C + K_C \geq 1$ with $|K_C| = 1$ and $|L_R \setminus L_C| + |K \setminus K_C| \leq d - 1$, where $L_C \subseteq L_R$ and $K_C \subseteq K$. Similarly, the general representation of such a classical clause that is dominated by $L' \geq d'$ is $L'_C + K'_C \geq 1$ with $|K'_C| = 1$ and $|L'_R \setminus L'_C| + |\overline{K} \setminus K'_C| \leq d' - 1$, where $L'_C \subseteq L'_R$ and $K'_C \subseteq \overline{K}$. Furthermore, $K_C = \overline{K'_C}$ must hold. Now, we extract the literals that occur in both L_C and L'_C. Let $P \cup Q = L_C$ and $P \cup Q' = L'_C$ with $L_C \cap L'_C = P$ and $Q \cap Q' = \emptyset$. So, the general representation of a classical resolvent of $L \geq d$ and $L' \geq d'$ is

$$P \cup Q \cup Q' \geq 1 \ .$$

Since $|L_R \setminus L_C| + |K \setminus K_C| \leq d - 1$ and $|L'_R \setminus L'_C| + |\overline{K} \setminus K'_C| \leq d' - 1$ we have

$$d + d' \geq |L_R \setminus L_C| + |L'_R \setminus L'_C| + 2 + 2 \cdot (|K| - 1) \ ,$$

which simplifies to

$$d + d' \geq |L_R \setminus L_C| + |L'_R \setminus L'_C| + 2 \cdot |K| \ . \tag{7.34}$$

Let us investigate the sum of $L \geq d$ and $L' \geq d'$. We know that $L + L' \geq d + d'$ is equivalent to

$$L_R + L'_R + |K| \geq d + d' \ .$$

A strict reduction of $L + L' \geq d + d'$ is

$$L_C + L'_C \geq d + d' - |K| - |L_R \setminus L_C| - |L'_R \setminus L'_C| \ ,$$

obtained by eliminating the literals in $(L_R \setminus L_C) \cup (L'_R \setminus L'_C)$, which dominates

$$L_C + L'_C \geq |K| \ ,$$

---

[3]Note that we consider only classical clauses that contain only literals occurring in the extended clause dominating it, because otherwise their resolvent is dominated by either one of the fathers, or by the resolvent of the valid classical clauses that contain only literals occurring in the extended clause dominating it.

because of (7.34). Note that $|K| \geq 1$. We rewrite L_C and L'_C and obtain

$$2 \cdot P + Q + Q' \geq |K| \ .$$

We apply the cutting plane operation of Section 7.1 and obtain

$$P + Q + Q' \geq \left\lceil \frac{|K|}{2} \right\rceil \geq \left\lceil \frac{1}{2} \right\rceil = 1 \ .$$

Hence, $P+Q+Q' \geq 1$ is dominated by the extended clause $P+Q+Q' \geq \lceil |K|/2 \rceil$. Because each extended clause obtained by linear combination and rounding is dominated by a strongest extended clause, the proposition is established. □

By Proposition 7.8.2 we can replace the original resolution rule of *Generalized Resolution* by a rule generating the equivalent set of extended clauses of the linear pseudo-Boolean inequality $L + L' \geq d + d'$ while preserving completeness.

Example 7.8.3 [Hoo92a] We again consider Example 7.8.1. Let

$$A + B + \overline{D} + E + \overline{F} + \overline{G} \geq 4$$
$$\overline{A} + \overline{C} + D + \overline{E} + F + G \geq 3$$

be two extended clauses. With the enhanced resolution rule of Hooker [Hoo92a] we may generate 12 different resolvents, where

$$B + \overline{C} + \overline{D} + \overline{E} + F + \overline{G} \geq 2$$

is one of them. The sum of the two extended clauses brought in normal form is $2 \cdot \overline{D} + B + \overline{C} \geq 3$. After the transformation we obtain the two extended clauses

$$\overline{D} + \overline{C} + B \geq 2 \qquad \overline{D} \geq 1 \ ,$$

where each of the 12 resolvents is dominated by one of them.

Using the presented transformation method we generate fewer and stronger extended clauses than with the original resolution method. Note that there are no further non-redundant resolution steps, since resolution between the extended clauses in $\mathsf{SCP}(\mathsf{SRed}(L + L' \geq d + d'))$ is not possible, because no literal occurs negatively in one and positively in another of them. Additionally, there is no literal occurring positively in $L \geq d$ or $L' \geq d'$ and negatively in an extended clause in $\mathsf{SCP}(\mathsf{SRed}(L + L' \geq d + d'))$. Thus, the only possible resolution steps are the ones between $L \geq d$ and $L' \geq d'$. But these are all

dominated by an extended clause in $\mathsf{SCP}(\mathsf{SRed}(L + L' \geq d + d'))$, because of Proposition 7.8.2. Note that we generate not only resolvents but also *diagonal sums* [Hoo92a], generated by the other rule of *Generalized Resolution*. The sum of $A + B \geq 1$ and $C + D \geq 1$ is $A + B + C + D \geq 2$, which is already an extended clause. Since there is no other extended clause dominating $A + B + C + D \geq 2$ that is derivable from $A + B \geq 1$ and $C + D \geq 1$, the strongest extended clause $A + B + C + D \geq 2$ is non-redundant.

8

SIMPLIFICATION

Simplifying a constraint w.r.t. a set of given constraints is a powerful constraint solving technique, particularly in the context of constraint logic programming. In this chapter we consider only simplification techniques for a set of extended clauses. Simplification techniques for linear pseudo-Boolean inequalities were introduced in Section 7.6 (as they fit better into a chapter dealing mainly with linear pseudo-Boolean inequalities).

The basic idea of the simplification rules in this chapter is that we take an inference rule generating a valid extended clause $L \geq d$ from a set of extended clauses S and then restrict its application to the case that $L \geq d$ strictly dominates at least one other extended clause in S. Thus, an inference rule $S \to L \geq d$ is restricted to the case where

$$\exists L' \geq d' \in S : L \geq d \text{ strictly dominates } L' \geq d'$$

holds. We say that $L \geq d$ is a *simplifying* extended clause. Given a simplifying extended clause $L \geq d$, we replace the dominated extended clause $L' \geq d'$ by $L \geq d$ without changing the set of solutions. The idea is that we explicitly generate an extended clause such that an existing extended clause in S becomes *redundant* and thus we *simplify* the set of constraints.

Assumption 8.0.1 Throughout this chapter we assume that all sets of extended clauses are in *normal form*, i.e., in a set of extended clauses there is no extended clause dominating another extended clause in that set.

We define a complete order for extended clauses in Section 8.1 and show that the simplification rules generate smaller extended clauses w.r.t. that order. In Section 8.2 we restrict the diagonal sum rule to be simplifying and show in

detail how to efficiently obtain a simplifying extended clause. Furthermore, we apply the simplification to combinatorial clausal satisfiability problems, which are solved with traditional 0-1 integer programming techniques, since diagonal sums are typically also strong cuts w.r.t. $[0,1]^n$. The simplification idea is applied to the resolution rule in Section 8.3.

We show how to detect equations between two Boolean variables in Section 8.4. Since an equation between two Boolean variables is not obviously representable given only extended clauses as basic formulas, equality detection by a special treatment helps to simplify the constraint store.

8.1 AN ORDER FOR EXTENDED CLAUSES

We define a complete ordering for extended clauses that is an approximation of the domination relation.

Definition 8.1.1 We denote by $\mathrm{w}(L \geq d) := |L| - d$ the *weakness* of an extended clause $L \geq d$.

By rewriting an extended clause $L \geq d$ as a $\leq$-inequality we get $\overline{L} \leq \mathrm{w}(L \geq d)$ with $\overline{L} = \{\overline{L_i} \mid L_i \in L\}$. Note that $\mathrm{w}(L \geq d) + 1$ is the number of literals of all shortest classical clauses dominated by C.

Lemma 8.1.2 If an extended clause $L \geq d$ dominates an extended clause $L' \geq d'$, then $\mathrm{w}(L \geq d) \leq \mathrm{w}(L' \geq d')$.

Proof. If $L \geq d$ dominates $L' \geq d'$, then we have $|L \setminus L'| \leq d - d'$ by Lemma 3.1.14. Since $|L| - |L'| \leq |L \setminus L'|$, we know that $|L| - |L'| \leq d - d'$, which is equivalent to $|L| - d \leq |L'| - d'$ and therefore $\mathrm{w}(L \geq d) \leq \mathrm{w}(L' \geq d')$.   □

We define the following irreflexive and transitive ordering over $\mathcal{L}$. Let ϕ be the function from $\mathcal{L}$ to $\mathbb{N}$ with $\phi(X_j) = 2j$ and $\phi(\overline{X_j}) = 2j + 1$. Then ϕ maps each literal to a unique natural number. We say a literal L_i is smaller than a literal L'_i (written $L_i \lhd L'_i$) if and only if $\phi(L_i) < \phi(L'_i)$. Let us view a set of literals L as an ordered n-tuple $(L_1, \ldots, L_n)$ with $L_i \lhd L_j$ if $i < j$. We then have the total ordering $\ll$ for sets of literals, where $\ll$ is the lexicographic ordering over $\lhd$. We define the following total ordering for extended clauses.

Definition 8.1.3 We say that an extended clause $L \geq d$ is *smaller* than an extended clause $L' \geq d'$ (written $L \geq d \prec L' \geq d'$) if

- $\mathrm{w}(L \geq d) < \mathrm{w}(L' \geq d')$ or

- $\mathrm{w}(L \geq d) = \mathrm{w}(L' \geq d')$ and $d > d'$ or

- $\mathrm{w}(L \geq d) = \mathrm{w}(L' \geq d')$ and $d = d'$ and $L \ll L'$.

We use $\preceq, \succ$ and $\succeq$ with their obvious meaning. For classical clauses the ordering reduces to the weakness, the length of a classical clause, i.e., the number of its literals, and the lexicographic ordering $\ll$. This is the usual ordering for classical clauses.

Proposition 8.1.4 *If $L \geq d$ dominates $L' \geq d'$, then $L \geq d \preceq L' \geq d'$.*

Proof. Suppose that $L \geq d$ dominates $L' \geq d'$, then from Lemma 8.1.2 we know that $\mathrm{w}(L \geq d) \leq \mathrm{w}(L' \geq d')$ and from Lemma 3.1.14 we have $d \geq d'$. Suppose that $L' \geq d' \prec L \geq d$, then $\mathrm{w}(L \geq d) = \mathrm{w}(L' \geq d')$, $d = d'$ and therefore $|L| = |L'|$. Because of Lemma 3.1.14, we have $|L \setminus L'| = d - d' = 0$, and thus $L = L'$. But then $L' \geq d'$ equals $L \geq d$, which contradicts $L' \geq d' \prec L \geq d$. Therefore, $L \geq d \preceq L' \geq d'$. $\qquad\square$

Note that the ordering is not well founded given an infinite number of Boolean variables. For example,

$$\sum_{1 \leq i \leq n} X_i \geq n \quad \text{is dominated by} \quad \sum_{1 \leq i \leq n+1} X_i \geq n + 1$$

for all $n > 0$, but the latter extended clause is smaller than the former. We assume that the number of variables, and thus the number of literals, is finite, which is reasonable for all practical applications, and then the ordering $\prec$ is well founded.

8.2 SIMPLIFYING DIAGONAL SUMS

First, we restate the diagonal sum rule of *Generalized Resolution* [Hoo92a] for extended clauses and then restrict its application to generate only simplifying diagonal sums.

Definition 8.2.1 [Hoo92a] An extended clause $DS := \sum_{1 \le i \le n} L_i \ge d+1$ is a *diagonal sum* of a set S of extended clauses if

[a] for all $1 \le j \le n$ the extended clause $DS_j := \sum_{1 \le i \neq j \le n} L_i \ge d$ is dominated by an extended clause in S,

[b] there is no extended clause in S that dominates DS, and

[c] $\mathsf{Var}(L_i) \neq \mathsf{Var}(L_j)$ for all $i \neq j$.

We say S *supports* DS. A set $S' \subseteq S$ supporting DS is called *minimal support* of DS if S' supports DS but no proper subset of S'. We denote by $DSF := \{DS_j \mid 1 \le j \le n\}$ the set of *fathers* of DS.

If a set of extended clauses S supports a diagonal sum DS, then there exists a minimal supporting set $S' \subseteq S$.

Proposition 8.2.2 *A diagonal sum DS of a set of extended clauses S is a valid extended clause with respect to S.*

Proof. Summing up all the DS_j yields the linear pseudo-Boolean inequality $(n-1) \cdot L \ge n \cdot d$. Dividing this inequality by $n-1$ yields $L \ge n \cdot d/(n-1)$. Because each L_i is either 0 or 1, the sum of the L_i is integral. Therefore, it is valid to round up the right side to the next integral value. Since $n/(n-1) > 1$, we have $\lceil n \cdot d/(n-1) \rceil \ge d+1$. $\square$

Note that a diagonal sum is a *rank 1 Chvátal-Gomory cutting plane* [Gom58, NW88], obtained from a positive linear combination of valid inequalities and integer rounding.

Definition 8.2.3 Let S be a set of extended clauses supporting a diagonal sum DS. If there is an extended clause $C \in S$ that is dominated by DS, then we call DS a *simplifying diagonal sum* with respect to S.

Given a simplifying diagonal sum DS of S, we can add DS to S and delete dominated extended clauses in S yielding a *simpler* set S'. Note that $\mathsf{Ext}(S') = \mathsf{Ext}(S)$ and $|S'| \le |S|$, since at least one extended clause $C \in S$ is dominated by DS. Since DS is smaller than C w.r.t. the ordering $\prec$ of Definition 8.1.3, and

thus we replace a larger element by a smaller one, we have another justification of the simplification argument. Because $\prec$ is well founded, we know that the simplification algorithm terminates, and that there is a fully simplified form.

The simplification argument is also valid w.r.t. $[0,1]^n$. If we compare the polytope of the linear programming relaxation of the set of fathers of the simplifying diagonal sum and the linear programming relaxation of the simplifying diagonal sum, then we see that the latter is included in the former, i.e., the latter better approximates the convex hull of the 0-1 solutions points. To see this assign to each $L_i \in DS$ the value $d/(n-1)$, then each DS_j is satisfied but not DS. We say we have simplified the problem w.r.t. $[0,1]^n$. In many cases we even cut off solutions of the linear programming relaxation of S and then S' is a better approximation[1] of $\text{Ext}(S)$ (cf. [HF90]).

Example 8.2.4 Let S be $\{X_1+X_2 \geq 1, X_1+X_3+X_4 \geq 1, X_2+X_3+X_4 \geq 1\}$. By adding the diagonal sum $X_1+X_2+X_3+X_4 \geq 2$ and deleting the dominated extended clauses we obtain a simplified set $S' = \{X_1 + X_2 + X_3 + X_4 \geq 2, X_1 + X_2 \geq 1\}$. Then $X_1 = X_2 = 0.5$ and $X_3 = X_4 = 0.3$ is a solution of the linear programming relaxation of S but not of the linear programming relaxation of S'.

Instead of first generating diagonal sums and afterwards checking whether there is one dominating an extended clause, which is rather inefficient, we show how to search for a simplifying diagonal sum dominating a specific extended clause of the current set of extended clauses. In other words, we pick an extended clause of the set of extended clauses and try to construct a valid diagonal sum dominating it.

8.2.1 Properties of Simplifying Diagonal Sums

We show some useful properties of simplifying diagonal sums. First, we want to restrict the search for fathers of a simplifying diagonal sum.

Proposition 8.2.5 *Let S be a set of extended clauses supporting the diagonal sum $L \geq d+1$ and let $S' \subseteq S$ be a minimal support of $L \geq d+1$. Then for all $L' \geq d' \in S'$ we have $w(L' \geq d') \leq w(L \geq d+1)$ and $d' \geq d$.*

---

[1] Note that in general we do not cut off solutions of the linear programming relaxation. For example, suppose that the linear programming relaxation is infeasible (let S contain $A + B + C \geq 2$ and $\overline{A} + \overline{B} + \overline{C} \geq 2$), then we cannot cut off anything.

Proof. If S' is a minimal support, then each $L' \geq d' \in S'$ dominates at least one $DS_i := L \setminus \{L_i\} \geq d$. Because of Proposition 8.1.4, we know that $L' \geq d' \preceq DS_i$, and therefore $w(L' \geq d') \leq w(DS_i) = w(DS)$ and $d' \geq d$. □

Given an extended clause $L' \geq d' \in S$, we are searching for a simplifying diagonal sum $L \geq d+1$ supported by S that dominates $L' \geq d'$. We restrict ourselves to simplifying diagonal sums $L \geq d+1$ with $d+1 > d'$, i.e., we want to replace $L' \geq d'$ by an extended clause with a greater right-hand side.

Next, we show that if there is a diagonal sum $L \geq d+1$ supported by a set of extended clauses S such that $L \geq d+1$ dominates the extended clause $L' \geq d' \in S$ with $d+1 > d'$, then it is sufficient to search for a specific simplifying diagonal sum dominating $L' \geq d'$.

Proposition 8.2.6 *Let S be a set of extended clauses supporting a diagonal sum $L \geq d+1$ that dominates an extended clause $L' \geq d' \in S$ with $d+1 > d'$. Then S supports a diagonal sum of the form $\{L_?\} \cup L' \geq d'+1$, where $L_? \in L \setminus L'$.*

Proof. Since $L \geq d+1$ dominates $L' \geq d'$, we have $|L \setminus L'| \leq d+1-d'$ by Lemma 3.1.14. We split L into two disjoint sets M and N, such that $M \subseteq L'$, $N \cap L' = \emptyset$ and $M \cup N = L$. Note that $M = L \setminus L'$. Since

$$|L \setminus L'| = |(M \cup N) \setminus L'| = |M \setminus L'| + |N \setminus L'| = |N| \leq d+1-d' ,$$

we have

$$|M \setminus L'| = 0 \leq d+1-|N|-d' \tag{8.1}$$

and thus $L \geq d+1$ dominates its reduction $M \geq d+1-|N|$, which dominates $L' \geq d'$, because $M \subseteq L'$ and $d+1-|N| \geq d'$.

Next, we show that $N \neq \emptyset$. Suppose the converse, then $M = L \subseteq L'$. Since

$$|(L \setminus \{L_j\}) \setminus L'| = 0 \leq d-d'$$

because $d \geq d'$, we know that $L' \geq d'$ is dominated by a father $L \setminus \{L_j\} \geq d$ of $L \geq d+1$ for any $L_j \in L$. Hence, $L' \geq d'$ is dominated by an extended clause in S, which contradicts the normal form condition and therefore $N \neq \emptyset$.

Let $L_?$ be an arbitrary literal in N. It remains to show that each extended clause

$$\{L_?\} \cup (L' \setminus \{L_i\}) \geq d' \tag{8.2}$$

for all $L_i \in L'$ is dominated by an extended clause in S, since then the diagonal sum rule generates $\{L_?\} \cup L' \geq d'+1$. Because $L \geq d+1$ is supported by S,

we know that each extended clause $L \setminus \{L_j\} \geq d$ for all $L_j \in L$ is dominated by an extended clause in S. We show that the extended clauses (8.2) for all $L_i \in L'$ are dominated by a father $L \setminus \{L_j\} \geq d$ of $L \geq d + 1$ for some $L_j \in L$. Thus, we have to show for each $L_i \in L'$ that there exists an $L_j \in L$ such that

$$|(L \setminus \{L_j\}) \setminus (L_? \cup (L' \setminus \{L_i\}))| \leq d - d' \ ,$$

which is equivalent to

$$|((M \cup N) \setminus \{L_j\}) \setminus (L_? \cup (L' \setminus \{L_i\}))| \leq d - d' \ .$$

We choose L_j such that $L_? \neq L_j$. Hence, we have to show

$$|N| - 1 + |(M \setminus \{L_j\}) \setminus (L' \setminus \{L_i\})| \leq d - d'$$

We choose $L_j = L_i$ and since $M \subseteq L'$, we obtain

$$|N| - 1 + 0 \leq d - d' \ ,$$

which is equivalent to

$$0 \leq d + 1 - |N| - d' \ .$$

But $0 \leq d + 1 - |N| - d'$ is (8.1). □

8.2.2 Finding Simplifying Diagonal Sums

We discuss now how to construct a simplifying diagonal sum DS of S dominating a given extended clause $L \geq d \in S$. Because of Proposition 8.2.6, we know that it is sufficient to search for simplifying diagonal sums of the form $\{L_?\} \cup L \geq d + 1$ for some literal $L_?$. In the following we abbreviate $\{L_?\} \cup L$ by $L_? + L$ and thus

$$DS \equiv L_? + L \geq d + 1 \ . \tag{8.3}$$

The goal is to find a literal $L_?$ such that each extended clause in

$$DSG := \{L_? + \sum_{1 \leq i \neq j \leq n} L_i \geq d \mid \text{ for all } 1 \leq j \leq n\} \tag{8.4}$$

is dominated by an extended clause in S, i.e., we search for a supporting set $S' \subseteq S$ of DS for some $L_?$. Note that we can identify each extended clause in DSG by the missing literal L_j. We show that each extended clause in S that dominates an extended clause in DSG has a special form. Hence, we can restrict the number of extended clauses that need to be investigated.

Proposition 8.2.7 If $L' \geq d' \in S$ dominates an extended clause in DSG, then $L' \geq d'$ is of the form

$$(L \setminus M) \cup N \geq d + |N| - 1 \tag{8.5}$$

with $M \subset L$, $|M| \geq 1$, $N \cap L = \emptyset$, and $L_? \in N$.

Proof. We know that $L' \geq d'$ must dominate an extended clause in DSG of the form $L_? + (L \setminus \{L_j\}) \geq d$ with $L_j \in L$. Note that $L_? \in L'$ because otherwise $L' \geq d'$ dominates $L \setminus \{L_j\} \geq d$ and therefore the given extended clause $L \geq d$, which contradicts the normal form condition. We split L' into $(L \setminus M) \cup N$ such that N contains the literals in L' that are not in L and M contains the literals of L that are missing in L'. Note that then $M \subseteq L$, and $L \cap N = \emptyset$ and $L_? \in N$.

First, suppose that $M = \emptyset$. Therefore, we have $L' = L \cup N$. Since $L' \geq d'$ dominates $L_? + (L \setminus \{L_j\}) \geq d$ for some $L_j \in L$, we have

$$|(L \cup N) \setminus (L_? + (L \setminus \{L_j\}))| \leq d' - d .$$

Because

$$|(L \cup N) \setminus (L_? + (L \setminus \{L_j\}))| = |N| = |(L \cup N) \setminus L| ,$$

we have $|(L \cup N) \setminus L| \leq d' - d$. Therefore, $L \cup N \geq d'$ dominates $L \geq d$, which contradicts the normal form condition. Hence, we know that $|M| \geq 1$.

Since $L' \geq d'$ dominates $L_? + (L \setminus \{L_j\}) \geq d$ for some $L_j \in L$, we have

$$|((L \setminus M) \cup N) \setminus (L_? + (L \setminus \{L_j\}))| \leq d' - d .$$

Because $L_? \in N$ and N is disjoint with L, we have $|\{L_j\} \setminus M| \leq d' - d - (|N| - 1)$ and therefore

$$d' \geq d + |N| - 1 + |\{L_j\} \setminus M| . \tag{8.6}$$

Suppose that $d' > d + |N| - 1$, then $L' \geq d'$ dominates $L_? + (L \setminus M) \geq d + 1$, since

$$
\begin{aligned}
|((L \setminus M) \cup N) \setminus (L_? + (L \setminus M))| &= |N \setminus \{L_?\}| \\
&= |N| - 1 \\
&= d + |N| - (d + 1) \leq d' - (d + 1) .
\end{aligned}
$$

Therefore, $L' \geq d'$ dominates DS and $L \geq d$, which contradicts the normal form condition. We conclude that $L_j \in M$, because of (8.6), and $d' = d + |N| - 1$. □

Note that while searching for extended clauses $L' \geq d'$ dominating an element of DSG, it is sufficient to consider only extended clauses in S, for which condition (8.5) holds. If we have found such an extended clause of the form $(L \setminus M) \cup N \geq d + |N| - 1$, then it dominates all extended clauses $\{L_? + L \setminus \{L_j\} \geq d \mid L_? \in N \text{ and } L_j \in M\}$. We define now the set of possible literals (candidates) for $L_?$ provided by the investigation of each father DS_j.

$$\text{Cand}_{L_j} := \{L_? \mid (L \setminus M) \cup N \geq d + |N| - 1 \in S, L_? \in N \text{ and } L_j \in M\} \quad (8.7)$$

The set of literals Cand_{L_j} is the complete set of literals that can be substituted for $L_?$ such that the father clause DS_j is dominated by an extended clause in S. We see immediately that DS is valid for a specific $L_?$, if substituting it yields a dominated father for all DS_j, i.e., if

$$L_? \in \bigcap_{j=1}^{n} \text{Cand}_{L_j} . \quad (8.8)$$

Example 8.2.8 From the set of extended clauses

$$S := \{X_1 + X_2 \geq 1, X_2 + X_3 \geq 1, X_2 + X_4 \geq 1, X_1 + X_3 + X_5 \geq 2\}$$

we select $X_1 + X_2 \geq 1$ and show how to derive a simplifying diagonal sum for it. We start calculating Cand_{X_1}, i.e., we search for literals $L_?$ such that $L_? + X_2 \geq 1$ is dominated by an extended clause in S. From $X_2 + X_3 \geq 1$ we see that X_3 is a valid choice for $L_?$. Similarly, we see that X_4 is a valid choice for $L_?$ from the extended clause $X_2 + X_4 \geq 1$. The other extended clauses do not satisfy (8.5) and thus we know that $\text{Cand}_{X_1} = \{X_3, X_4\}$. When calculating Cand_{X_2} we see that condition (8.5) only applies for $X_1 + X_3 + X_5 \geq 2$ and we know that X_3 and X_5 are valid choices for the literals $L_?$ such that $L_? + X_1 \geq 1$ is dominated by an extended clause in S. Therefore, $\text{Cand}_{X_2} = \{X_3, X_5\}$ and with (8.8) we have $L_? = X_3$. We then know that $X_1 + X_2 \geq 1, X_1 + X_3 \geq 1$, and $X_2 + X_3 \geq 1$ are all dominated by extended clauses in S. Hence, we derive with the diagonal sum rule the extended clause $X_1 + X_2 + X_3 \geq 2$. We add the diagonal sum $X_1 + X_2 + X_3 \geq 2$ of these 3 extended clauses to S and by construction we know that $X_1 + X_2 \geq 1$ is dominated by it. Furthermore, $X_2 + X_3 \geq 1$ is also dominated and both are eliminated. We obtain the simpler set of extended clauses

$$\{X_1 + X_2 + X_3 \geq 2, X_2 + X_4 \geq 1, X_1 + X_3 + X_5 \geq 2\} .$$

8.2.3   Improved Diagonal Sum Rule

In Definition 8.2.1 we require that all DS_j are dominated by an extended clause in S. We show that only a subset of these extended clauses is needed.

Proposition 8.2.9 *An extended clause $DS := L \geq d+1$ is valid with respect to a set of extended clauses S if $n-d+1$ extended clauses of DSF are dominated by extended clauses in S.*

Proof. Suppose that $n - d + 1$ extended clauses of DSF are dominated by extended clauses in S. W.l.o.g. suppose that the set of these dominated extended clauses is $DSF' = \{DS_j \mid 1 \leq j \leq n - d + 1\} \subseteq DSF$. Summing up the extended clauses in DSF' yields

$$(n - d + 1) \cdot \sum_{1 \leq i \leq d-1} L_i + (n - d) \cdot \sum_{d \leq i \leq n} L_i \geq (n - d + 1) \cdot d \ .$$

We add the valid bounds $-L_i \geq -1$ for all $1 \leq i \leq d - 1$ and obtain

$$(n - d) \cdot \sum_{1 \leq i \leq n} L_i \geq (n - d + 1) \cdot d - (d - 1) = (n - d) \cdot d + 1 \ .$$

Dividing this inequality by $(n - d)$ yields $L \geq d + 1/(n - d)$. We reason as in Proposition 8.2.2 and, since $1/(n - d) > 0$, we round up the right-hand side to $d + 1$ and obtain DS.   □

Note that the computed diagonal sum is still a Chvátal-Gomory rank 1 cut. Using Proposition 8.2.9, we can relax condition (8.8). We know that DS is valid if $L_?$ is in the intersection of at least $n - d + 1$ of the Cand_{L_i}, i.e., if

$$\exists I \subseteq \{1, \ldots, n\} : |I| \geq n - d + 1 \qquad \text{and} \qquad L_? \in \cap_{i \in I} \mathsf{Cand}_{L_i} \ . \qquad (8.9)$$

Example 8.2.10 From the set of extended clauses

$$\{X_1 + X_2 + X_3 \geq 2, X_1 + X_2 + X_4 \geq 2, X_1 + X_2 + X_5 \geq 2, X_1 + X_3 + X_4 \geq 2\} \qquad (8.10)$$

we can derive the simplifying extended clause $X_1 + X_2 + X_3 + X_4 \geq 3$. While trying to eliminate $X_1 + X_2 + X_3 \geq 2$, we obtain the following Cand_{L_i}.

$$\mathsf{Cand}_{X_1} = \emptyset \qquad \mathsf{Cand}_{X_2} = \{X_4\} \qquad \mathsf{Cand}_{X_3} = \{X_4, X_5\} \qquad (8.11)$$

Condition (8.8) does not apply but (8.9) does, because $n - d + 1 = 2$ and X_4 is in the intersection of two of the Cand_{L_i}.

8.2.4 Temporary Diagonal Sums

We again consider Example 8.2.10, but we replace $X_1 + X_2 + X_4 \geq 2$ by $X_2 + X_4 \geq 1$. Therefore, Cand_{X_3} becomes $\{X_5\}$, and we can no longer derive the extended clause $X_1 + X_2 + X_3 + X_4 \geq 3$. Obviously, it would be possible if S contains $C := X_1 + X_2 + X_4 \geq 2$ or if $S \models C$. One approach to approximate $\models$ is to check whether C is a diagonal sum. By applying Definition 8.2.1 we see that C is a diagonal sum (and therefore valid) if $X_1 + X_2 \geq 1$, $X_1 + X_4 \geq 1$ and $X_2 + X_4 \geq 1$ are dominated by extended clauses in S. Since this is the case, we derive C and therefore $X_1 + X_2 + X_3 + X_4 \geq 3$. In other words, we enlarge the set Cand_{X_3} with the literal X_4 by recursively searching for a diagonal sum $L_? + X_2 + X_4 \geq 2$. In some sense we *temporarily* add the father $X_2 + X_4 \geq 1$ to the set of extended clauses, eliminate it with a simplifying diagonal sum, and use the computed candidates to construct the originally sought simplifying diagonal sum. In the following we generalize the idea of recursively searching for simplifying diagonal sums for the fathers of a simplifying diagonal sum.

Throughout this section let S be a set of extended clauses and $L \geq d \in S$ an extended clause for which we search a simplifying diagonal sum $L_? + L \geq d+1$. Let M always denote a subset of L. We call an extended clause of the form $L_? + L \setminus M \geq d + 1 - |M|$ also a *goal*. We denote by $\theta(M) := \{M \cup \{L_i\} \mid L_i \in L \setminus M\}$ the set of all sets of literals containing M and one more literal of L. We denote by

$$\mathsf{Cand}_M := \{L_? \mid C \models L_? + L \setminus M \geq d + 1 - |M| \text{ for a } C \in S\} \qquad (8.12)$$

the set of literals $L_?$ for which $L_? + L \setminus M \geq d + 1 - |M|$ is dominated by an extended clause in S. We reformulate Proposition 8.2.9 to be suitable for arbitrary goals.

Lemma 8.2.11 *The extended clause $L_? + L \setminus M \geq d + 1 - |M|$ is valid if*

$$\exists \Theta \subseteq \theta(M) : |\Theta| \geq n - d + 1 \qquad \text{and} \qquad L_? \in \bigcap_{M' \in \Theta} \mathsf{Cand}_{M'} \, . \qquad (8.13)$$

Proof. Note that $|L \setminus M| - (d - |M|) + 1 = |L| - d + 1 = n - d + 1$, because $M \subset L$. But then Proposition 8.2.9 applies, since we have (8.13). □

We say that we *expand* a goal $L_? + L \setminus M \geq d + 1 - |M|$ if we calculate all $L_?$ satisfying (8.13) and add them to Cand_M. In the example we obtained the new

candidate X_4 for $L_?$ in $\mathsf{Cand}_{\{X_3\}}$ by expanding $L_? + X_1 + X_2 \geq 2$. Next, we define the set Cand_M^k of literals $L_?$ obtained by expanding k times $L_? + L \setminus M \geq d + 1 - |M|$. Cand_M^k is the set of literals such that $L_? + L \setminus M \geq d + 1 - |M|$ is valid w.r.t. S in the kth expansion. For $k = 0$ we define $\mathsf{Cand}_M^0 := \mathsf{Cand}_M$. For $k \geq 1$ we recursively define

$$\mathsf{Cand}_M^k := \{L_? \mid \exists \Theta \subseteq \theta(M) : |\Theta| \geq n - d + 1 \text{ and } L_? \in \cap_{M' \in \Theta} \mathsf{Cand}_{M'}^{k-1}\} . \tag{8.14}$$

By construction we see that $L_? + L \geq d + 1$ is valid if there exists a k such that $L_? \in \mathsf{Cand}_\emptyset^k$. Note that (8.9) is equivalent to $L_? \in \mathsf{Cand}_\emptyset^1$. Obviously, $k \leq d$ because the degree must be greater than 1.

Lemma 8.2.12 *The number of goals in the k-th expansion of $L_? + L \geq d + 1$ is $\sum_{i=0}^{k} \binom{n}{i}$.*

Proof. While expanding a goal $L_? + L \geq d + 1$ we create all new goals where exactly 1 literal is missing, which are $\binom{n}{1} = n$ goals. Recursively expanding each of the new goals gives all goals, where exactly 2 literals are missing, which are $\binom{n}{2}$ goals. At level k we have $\binom{n}{k}$ new goals. The number of all goals is therefore $\sum_{i=0}^{k} \binom{n}{i}$. $\square$

Next, we show that if we recursively search for candidates of $L_?$, then we only enlarge the set of candidates. For this purpose we first relate the expansion level and the number of literals that are missing in a goal.

Lemma 8.2.13 *If $M \subseteq M'$, then $\mathsf{Cand}_M^k \subseteq \mathsf{Cand}_{M'}^k$.*

Proof. Let $M \subseteq M'$ and suppose that $M' \in \theta(M)$. Let L_j be in Cand_M^k. We show that $L_j \in \mathsf{Cand}_{M'}^k$ by induction over k.

$k = 0$: $\quad L_j + L \setminus M \geq d + 1 - |M|$ dominates $L_j + L \setminus M' \geq d + 1 - |M'|$.

$k - 1 \to k$: $\quad$ Because $L_j \in \mathsf{Cand}_M^k$, we have $\exists \Theta' \subseteq \theta(M) : |\Theta'| \geq n - d + 1$ and $L_? \in \cap_{N \in \Theta'} \mathsf{Cand}_N^{k-1}$. By induction hypothesis, we know that $\exists \Theta' \subseteq \theta(M') : |\Theta'| \geq n - d + 1$ and $L_? \in \cap_{N \in \Theta'} \mathsf{Cand}_N^{k-1}$ Therefore, $L_j \in \mathsf{Cand}_{M'}^k$. $\square$

By induction $\mathsf{Cand}_M^k \subseteq \mathsf{Cand}_{M'}^k$ follows for any $M \subseteq M'$.

Lemma 8.2.14 *For all $l \geq k$, $\mathsf{Cand}_M^k \subseteq \mathsf{Cand}_M^l$ holds.*

Proof. It is sufficient to proof the lemma for $l = k + 1$. Let $L_j \in \mathsf{Cand}_M^k$, then we know by Lemma 8.2.13 that for all M' in $\theta(M)$ we have $L_j \in \mathsf{Cand}_{M'}^k$. By definition (8.14) we have $L_j \in \mathsf{Cand}_M^{k+1}$. $\qquad\square$

We show now that the candidates obtained in all goals of a level are necessarily candidates of the original goal.

Lemma 8.2.15 $\bigcap_{M:|M|=l} \mathsf{Cand}_M \subseteq \mathsf{Cand}_\emptyset^l$.

Proof. We know that if $L_j \in \mathsf{Cand}_M^k$ for all M with $|M| = l$, then $L_j \in \mathsf{Cand}_M^{k+1}$ for all M with $|M| = l - 1$ by repeated application of definition (8.14). So if $L_j \in \bigcap_{M:|M|=l} \mathsf{Cand}_M^0$, then we have $L_j \in \bigcap_{M:|M|=l-1} \mathsf{Cand}_M^1$ and by induction $L_j \in \bigcap_{M:|M|=0} \mathsf{Cand}_M^l = \mathsf{Cand}_\emptyset^l$. $\qquad\square$

Note that the converse does not necessarily hold. It is only true if we consider the case $|M| = d$. The idea is to restrict the number of levels that need to be expanded. For this purpose we need a technical lemma.

Lemma 8.2.16 *Let N be $\{1, \ldots, n\}$, $n \geq 2$ and let M be a subset of N. Let P be a property of subsets of N such that if $P(M)$ holds, then $P(M')$ holds for at least $t + 1$ subsets M' of M with $|M'| = |M| - 1$ and $1 \leq t \leq n - 1$. Now if $P(N)$ holds, then $P(M)$ holds for all subsets M of N with $|M| = t$.*

Proof. We show the lemma by induction on n.

$n = 2$: obvious.

$n - 1 \rightarrow n$: If $t = n - 1$ the lemma trivially holds, so assume $t < n - 1$. Suppose that $P(N)$ holds. Then by definition we have $t + 1$ different subsets N' of N such that $|N'| = n - 1$ and $P(N')$ holds. Let N_i be $N \setminus \{i\}$ and w.l.o.g. suppose that $P(N_i)$ for all $1 \leq i \leq t + 1$. By induction hypothesis we have for all $1 \leq i \leq t + 1$ that $P(M_i)$ holds for all subsets M_i of N_i with $|M_i| = t$. It remains to show that every subset M of N such that $|M| = t$ is a subset of one of the N_i. Suppose otherwise, then there is $M \subset N$ that is not a subset of any of the N_i. But then for all N_i we derive that M must contain i and therefore $\{1, \ldots, t + 1\} \subseteq M$, which contradicts $|M| = t$. $\qquad\square$

We use Lemma 8.2.16 for showing that there is a literal for which we have a simplifying diagonal sum, obtained from any expansion level, if and only if this literal is in all the goals of the maximal expansion level.

Proposition 8.2.17 *There exists an expansion level k such that $\mathsf{Cand}_\emptyset^k$ is not empty if and only if $\bigcap_{M:|M|=d} \mathsf{Cand}_M$ is not empty.*

Proof. If $\bigcap_{M:|M|=d} \mathsf{Cand}_M$ is not empty, then by Lemma 8.2.15 we know that $\mathsf{Cand}_\emptyset^d$ is not empty. If $\mathsf{Cand}_\emptyset^k$ is not empty, then by Lemma 8.2.14 we know that $\mathsf{Cand}_\emptyset^d$ is not empty, since $k \leq d$. Let L_j be in $\mathsf{Cand}_\emptyset^d$. It remains to show that L_j in Cand_M for all M with $|M| = d$. For this we use Lemma 8.2.16. We know by Definition (8.14) that if $L_j \in \mathsf{Cand}_M$, then $L_j \in Cand_{M'}$ for $n - d + 1$ sets $M' \in \Theta(M)$. We associate with Cand_M^k the set of indices of the literals in the corresponding goal. We associate with $Cand_\emptyset^d$ the set $\{1, \ldots, n\}$ and with the Cand_M the subsets of $\{1, \ldots, n\}$ with cardinality $n - d$. We associate with $n - d$ the value t and with the property $P(M)$ the property $L_i \in \mathsf{Cand}_M^{d-|M|}$, then the proposition follows.   □

With Proposition 8.2.17 we can restrict the number of possible goals to be at most

$$\sum_{i=0}^{\min(n-d,d)} \binom{n}{i} \ .$$

Note that $\binom{n}{d} = \binom{n}{n-d}$ and each level k of a valid k-expansion for $k \geq n-d$ has more goals than the level d of the d-expansion. Because of Proposition 8.2.17, we can replace each k-expansion by level d of the d-expansion and lose no possible candidates. In particular, this is useful for extended clauses with weakness 1, so-called *cliques*[2] (Definition 7.7.5).

Corollary 8.2.18 *Let $L_1 + \cdots + L_n \geq n - 1$ be a clique. Then there exists a simplifying diagonal sum $L_? + L_1 + \cdots + L_n \geq n$ if and only if one of the following equivalent conditions holds.*

■ *For each $M \subset \{1, \ldots, n\}$ and $|M| = n - 1$ we have $L_? \in \mathsf{Cand}_M$.*

■ *For all $1 \leq i \leq n$ there is a $L_?$ such that the extended clause $L_? + L_i \geq 1$ is dominated by an extended clause in S.*

---

[2]In 0-1 integer programming *cliques* are usually written as $\leq$-inequalities and, then, are of the form $L_1 + \cdots + L_n \leq 1$.

Note that a simplifying diagonal sum obtained by a k-expansion is not necessarily a rank 1 cut, but may be a rank k cut.

8.2.5 Simplifying Clausal Satisfiability Problems

We apply the presented simplification algorithm on some combinatorial satisfiability problems and solve the 0-1 integer formulation of the simplified and the original problem with a linear programming based branch-and-bound algorithm. We use the commercial, state-of-the-art, mixed integer solver CPLEX.

We present some details of the implemented prototype. Given a set of extended clauses S, we try to find a simplifying diagonal sum and then simplify the problem. This is continued until no simplifying diagonal sum can be found. Searching for a simplifying diagonal sum is done incrementally, that is computed values for the different $Cand_M$ in the different goals of the different extended clauses in S are not recomputed, but stored and reused after a successful search. As strategy, extended clauses having smaller weakness are preferred, because

- their simplifying diagonal sums are likely to dominate more other extended clauses.

- their maximal number of goals is smaller in the average case.

- the set of extended clauses that can contribute to the diagonal sum is smaller.

Note that the weakness of an extended clause is related to the length of classical clauses. If there are several extended clauses with the same weakness, then extended clauses with greater degree are preferred. We try to find a diagonal sum by $(k + 1)$-expansion only if no diagonal sum is found for all extended clauses by k-expansion. We use Proposition 8.2.17 to restrict the maximal number of goals. If no further diagonal sum is found the simplified problem is given to CPLEX.

The examples, taken from [MR91], are combinatorial problems formulated as satisfiability problems. The "ulm..."-problems include n-queens problems, the "hole..."-problems are pigeon hole problems and the "nod..."-problems are

Table 8.1 FAWULM (combinatorial problems (dataset 2/7))

Name	Vars	Clauses	SDS	SClauses	Cplex	Simp	SCplex
ulmbc024	24	164	60	38	0.15	0.52	0.02
ulmbc040	40	340	126	69	0.32	1.98	0.03
ulmbc060	60	610	218	108	3.22	5.40	0.35
ulmbc084	84	994	340	158	1.62	12.90	0.40
ulmbp048*	48	99	20	29	6.87	0.28	0.02
ulmbp070*	70	161	30	41	49.15	0.54	0.03
ulmbp096*	96	244	42	55	364.23	1.28	0.05
ulmbp126*	126	351	56	71	>1000	2.30	0.07
ulmbp160*	160	485	72	89	>1000	4.18	0.10
ulmbp198*	198	649	90	109	>1000	7.21	0.12
ulmbs040	40	70	15	25	0.07	0.14	0.02
ulmbs060	60	120	24	36	0.95	0.36	0.03
ulmbs084	84	189	35	49	6.70	0.78	0.03
ulmbs112	112	280	48	64	89.70	1.50	0.07
ulmbs144	144	396	63	81	0.45	2.94	0.08
ulmbs180	180	540	80	100	0.65	6.30	0.10
hole6*	42	133	30	13	25.02	0.38	0.02
hole7*	56	204	42	15	306.90	0.87	0.03
hole8*	72	297	56	17	>1000	1.71	0.02
hole9*	90	415	72	19	>1000	3.44	0.07
hole10*	110	561	90	21	>1000	5.86	0.08
hole20*	420	4221	380	41	>1000	291.30	0.10
nod5col4*	40	130	55	45	2.20	0.70	0.22
nod6col4*	60	255	97	64	12.68	2.21	0.05
nod6col5	75	315	130	87	0.27	3.40	0.03
nod7col4*	84	441	154	91	86.98	6.25	0.12
nod7col6*	126	651	225	120	>1000	11.91	797.42

graph-coloring problems. Table 8.1 is read as follows. In the first column the name of the problem is given, followed by * if the problem is unsatisfiable. The second column is the number of boolean variables in the original problem followed by the number of classical clauses. In column "SDS" we count the number of simplification steps and in column "SClauses" we count the number of extended clauses in the simplified problem. In column "Simp" we find the time needed by the simplification algorithm prototyped in Prolog. In column "Cplex" we find the time Cplex needs to solve the original problem. In the last column "SCplex" we find the time Cplex needs to solve the simplified problem. All examples are run on a SPARC-10/31, all times are user-CPU-

seconds. The presented preprocessing method behaves well on combinatorial satisfiability problems.

Example 8.2.19 The presented algorithm solves hard instances of the pigeon hole problems [Hak85] in sub-exponential time, see Table 8.1 (hole...). The problem is to fit m pigeons into n pigeonholes. Each pigeonhole may hold at most one pigeon, each pigeon must be placed into some hole. Let P_{ij} denote whether to place pigeon i in hole j. The problem is described by the following extended clauses. Each pigeon must be placed in one hole:

$$\sum_{j=1}^{n} P_{ij} \geq 1 \qquad \text{for all } 1 \leq i \leq m \qquad (8.15)$$

Each hole can hold at most one pigeon:

$$\sum_{i=1}^{m} P_{ij} \leq 1 \quad (\equiv \sum_{i=1}^{m} \overline{P_{ij}} \geq m - 1) \qquad \text{for all } 1 \leq j \leq n \qquad (8.16)$$

Hard instances are obtained for $m = n + 1$. Using classical clauses the latter constraints are

$$\overline{P_{i_1 j}} + \overline{P_{i_2 j}} \geq 1 \qquad \text{for all } 1 \leq j \leq n, 1 \leq i_1 < i_2 \leq m \ . \qquad (8.17)$$

Our simplification method deletes all classical clauses of (8.17) and replaces them with (8.16) by just generating simplifying clique inequalities. No more simplifications apply. For $m = n + 1$ the sum of all extended clauses in (8.15) and (8.16) is $0 \geq 1$. Therefore, the linear programming relaxation is unsatisfiable. The number of simplification steps is bounded by $O(n^3)$ like in [CCT87]. For each clique simplification we have at most n goals. Therefore, our simplification algorithm in combination with a linear programming solver solves the pigeon hole problems in polynomial time.

The main point here is that we have found a short proof of the pigeon hole formulae *automatically* with our simplification algorithm. So we exploit the theoretical power of cutting planes [CCT87] in a practical framework.

8.3 SIMPLIFYING RESOLVENTS

The resolution rule of *Generalized Resolution* [Hoo92a] is just classical resolution. We have presented in Section 7.8 a stronger inference rule that replaces

resolution and allows us to generate immediately the strongest extended clauses derivable from two given extended clauses.

Restricting resolution to be simplifying turns out to be easy for classical resolution, as presented in Section 8.3.1. Since classical resolution only generates extended clauses with right-hand side 1, no extended clauses with right-hand side greater than 1 can be eliminated. In Section 8.3.2 we restrict the enhanced resolution rule of Section 7.8 to be simplifying. Unfortunately, searching simplifying resolvents with the enhanced resolution rule shows to be computationally expensive, since there is no way to restrict significantly the search for fathers of the simplifying resolvent. We overcome the problem by filtering out cases that are not promising.

8.3.1 Simplifying Resolvents for Classical Clauses

We say that a set of classical clauses S has a *simplifying resolvent* if there exists a classical clause $L \geq 1 \in S$ and a resolvent $L' \geq 1$ of two classical clauses in S such that $L' \subset L$. Note that $\mathsf{Ext}(S) = \mathsf{Ext}((S \setminus \{L \geq 1\}) \cup \{L' \geq 1\})$ and, since $L' \geq 1 \prec L \geq 1$, we say we have simplified S when we replace S by $(S \setminus \{L \geq 1\}) \cup \{L' \geq 1\}$.

For determining a simplifying resolvent we could compute all possible resolvents and then check whether there is one strictly dominating a classical clause in S, which is too inefficient. As done for the diagonal sum rule, we try to construct for each classical clause in S a resolvent of two classical clauses in S strictly dominating it.

Let $L \geq 1 \in S$ be a classical clause for which we search a simplifying resolvent $L' \geq 1$ with $L' \subset L$. First, we restate the resolution rule. Two classical clauses have a resolvent if and only if there is exactly one Boolean variable X_i that occurs positively in one classical clause and negatively in the other. Therefore, two classical clauses admitting a resolvent are of the form

$$M \cup \{X_i\} \geq 1 \tag{8.18}$$
$$N \cup \{\overline{X_i}\} \geq 1 \tag{8.19}$$

with $M \cap \overline{N} = \emptyset$. The resolvent of (8.18) and (8.19) is then the classical clause $M \cup N \geq 1$. Since we search for a resolvent strictly dominating $L \geq 1$, we know that $M \cup N \subset L$ needs to hold.

First, suppose that either (8.18) or (8.19) is $L \geq 1$. We then have a simplifying classical resolvent strictly dominating $L \geq 1$ if and only if there exists a classical clause $M \cup \{\overline{L_i}\} \geq 1$ in S with $L_i \in L$ and $M \subset L$.

Next, suppose that neither (8.18) nor (8.19) is $L \geq 1$. Then there must be two classical clauses (8.18) and (8.19) in S such that neither X_i nor $\overline{X_i}$ occurs in L, since S is in normal form (Assumption 8.0.1), and $M \cup N \subset L$. Thus, it is sufficient to consider only classical clauses in S that contain exactly one literal that does not occur in L. Note that each classical clause in S that is different from $L \geq 1$ contains at least one literal that does not occur in L, since S is in normal form (Assumption 8.0.1). In the worst case searching a simplifying resolvent for a specific clause $L \geq 1$ is not better than just generating all resolvents and checking domination afterwards. But, in practice, the restriction that each clause that need to be considered must have exactly one literal that does not occur in L means that we can easily, i.e., in linear time w.r.t. the number of clauses, eliminate a large fraction of the candidates. Only for the remaining candidates we have to do a pairwise, i.e., quadratic, check.

We obtain the following algorithm that returns a simplifying resolvent for a classical clause $L \geq 1 \in S$ if one exists, and returns $\perp$ otherwise.

Algorithm 8.3.1 *Simplifying Resolvent for Classical Clauses*

```
class_simpres(L ≥ 1, S)
      S' := {M ∪ {L_i} ≥ 1 | M ∪ {L_i} ≥ 1 ∈ S, M ⊂ L and L_i ∉ L}
      if ∃M ∪ {L_i} ≥ 1 ∈ S' : L̄_i ∈ L then
             return L \ {L̄_i} ≥ 1
      endif
      forall M ∪ {X_j} ≥ 1 ∈ S' : X_j ∉ L do
             if ∃N ∪ {X̄_j} ≥ 1 ∈ S' : M ∪ N ⊂ L then
                    return M ∪ N ≥ 1
             endif
      endforall
      return ⊥
end class_simpres
```

We illustrate the simplification of a set of classical clauses with help of the resolution rule by an example.

Example 8.3.2 Let S be

$$\{X_1+X_2+X_3 \geq 1, \overline{X_3}+X_4 \geq 1, X_1+X_2+X_4+X_5 \geq 1, \overline{X_1}+X_2+X_4+X_6 \geq 1\}$$
$$(8.20)$$

and let us search a simplifying classical resolvent strictly dominating $X_1 + X_2 + X_4 + X_5 \geq 1 \in S$ following Algorithm 8.3.1. We start calculating S' and obtain

$$\{X_1 + X_2 + X_3 \geq 1, \overline{X_3} + X_4 \geq 1\} \ .$$

Since there is no simplifying resolvent where $X_1 + X_2 + X_4 + X_5 \geq 1$ is one of the fathers, we search for two classical clauses in S' whose resolvent strictly dominates $X_1 + X_2 + X_4 + X_5 \geq 1$. We select $X_1 + X_2 + X_3 \geq 1$ containing the positive literal X_3 that does not occur in $\{X_1, X_2, X_4, X_5\}$ and resolve with a classical clause in S' containing $\overline{X_3}$, i.e., with $\overline{X_3} + X_4 \geq 1$. We obtain the resolvent

$$X_1 + X_2 + X_4 \geq 1 \ ,$$

which indeed strictly dominates $X_1+X_2+X_4+X_5 \geq 1$, and thus we can replace the weaker classical clause $X_1 + X_2 + X_4 + X_5 \geq 1$ by $X_1 + X_2 + X_4 \geq 1$. Next, we try to find a classical clause strictly dominating $\overline{X_1} + X_2 + X_4 + X_6 \geq 1$. The only classical clause in the newly calculated S' is the previously generated $X_1+X_2+X_4 \geq 1$, which contains a negated literal of $\{\overline{X_1}, X_2, X_4, X_6\}$, namely X_1. We obtain the simplifying resolvent $X_2 + X_4 + X_6 \geq 1$, strictly dominating $\overline{X_1}+X_2+X_4+X_6 \geq 1$ by resolving $X_1+X_2+X_4 \geq 1$ and $\overline{X_1}+X_2+X_4+X_6 \geq 1$. No further simplifying resolvents can be found. The simplified set of classical clauses equivalent to (8.20) is

$$\{X_1+X_2+X_3 \geq 1, \overline{X_3}+X_4 \geq 1, X_1+X_2+X_4 \geq 1, X_2+X_4+X_6 \geq 1\} \ . \ (8.21)$$

8.3.2   Simplifying Resolvents for Extended Clauses

A set of extended clauses S has a *simplifying resolvent* if there is an extended clause $L \geq d \in S$ such that there is an extended clause in $\mathsf{SCP}(\mathsf{SRed}(M + N \geq d_1 + d_2))$, strictly dominating $L \geq d$, where $M \geq d_1$ and $N \geq d_2$ are two extended clauses in S (see Proposition 7.8.2). Checking whether a set of extended clauses has a simplifying resolvent is unfortunately a computationally expensive task. For a complete check we have to build all possible sums of all possible pairs of two extended clauses in S (which is of $O(|S|^2)$) and transform them into a set of equivalent extended clauses with the method of Chapter 7.

Note that the transformation itself may produce several extended clauses per pair. For each extended clause in S and each generated extended clause, we have to check domination, which is at least of $O(|S|^3)$. This approach is far too expensive.

As for classical clauses the idea is to select a specific extended clause $L \geq d \in S$ and to try to construct a simplifying extended clause strictly dominating $L \geq d$. Unlike for classical clauses we have found no way to restrict significantly the set of possible candidates in advance.

Example 8.3.3   [a] Let $X_1 + X_2 + X_3 + X_4 \geq 2 \in S$ be the extended clause for which we search a simplifying resolvent. Suppose that the extended clauses $X_5 + X_6 + X_7 \geq 2$ and $X_1 + X_2 + X_3 + \overline{X_5} + \overline{X_6} + \overline{X_7} \geq 3$ are in S. Their sum is the simplifying resolvent $X_1 + X_2 + X_3 \geq 2$, although the extended clause $X_5 + X_6 + X_7 \geq 2$ contains no literal also occurring in the extended clause to be dominated. Even worse, if S contains the extended clauses $X_5 + X_6 + X_7 \geq 2$ and $\overline{X_5} + \overline{X_6} + \overline{X_7} \geq 2$ whose sum is $\bot$. Then all extended clauses are dominated, although in both extended clauses none of the literals in the extended clause to be dominated needs to occur.

[b] Let $X_1 + X_2 + X_3 + X_4 + X_5 + X_6 + X_7 + X_8 + X_9 \geq 5 \in S$ be the extended clause for which we search a simplifying resolvent. Suppose that the two extended clauses $X_1 + X_2 + X_3 + X_4 \geq 3$ and $X_5 + X_6 + X_7 + X_8 \geq 3$ are in S. Their sum is the simplifying resolvent $X_1 + X_2 + X_3 + X_4 + X_5 + X_6 + X_7 + X_8 \geq 6$, although both extended clauses have a smaller right-hand side than the one to be dominated.

[c] Let $X_1 + X_2 + X_3 + X_4 \geq 1 \in S$ be the extended clause for which we search a simplifying resolvent. Suppose that the two extended clauses $X_1 + X_2 + X_3 + \overline{X_4} + \overline{X_5} + \overline{X_6} \geq 2$ and $X_1 + X_2 + X_3 + X_4 + X_5 + X_6 \geq 2$ are in S. Their sum is $2 \cdot X_1 + 2 \cdot X_2 + 2 \cdot X_3 \geq 1$, which dominates the simplifying resolvent $X_1 + X_2 + X_3 \geq 1$, although both extended clauses have a greater weakness than the one to be dominated.

Example 8.3.3 indicates that there is no easy check of whether or not an extended clause summed up with another extended clause strictly dominates a given extended clause. Hence, we cannot filter out a large amount of extended clauses in advance in order to reduce the computational effort. Therefore, we restrict ourselves to special cases, where reducing the number of candidates is possible. More precisely, we do not search for simplifying resolvents $L' \geq d'$ strictly dominating $L \geq d$ with $L' \supseteq L$ and $d' > d$. Note that some of these simplifying extended clauses are already generated by the diagonal sum rule as

in Section 8.2. We search for simplifying resolvents $L' \geq d'$ with $L' \subset L$ and $d' \geq d$.

Input Refutation

Given an extended clause $L \geq d$ in a set of extended clauses S, the goal is to find an extended clause

$$L \setminus \{L_i\} \geq d , \qquad (8.22)$$

dominated by S with $L_i \in L$. We know that (8.22) is dominated by S if and only if the negation of (8.22),

$$\overline{L} \setminus \{\overline{L_i}\} \geq |L| - d , \qquad (8.23)$$

together with S is unsatisfiable. In the following we present a method that will detect unsatisfiability of $S \cup \{\overline{L} \setminus \{\overline{L_i}\} \geq |L| - d\}$ by an input resolution like method, where we allow at most two steps in order to detect unsatisfiability. One step in the input resolution method means adding one extended clause starting with (8.23), plus some additional checks whether $\bot$ is derivable. First, we allow only one step and show that we get an input refutation if $L \geq d$ together with one extended clause dominates (8.22). The method is then expanded to two step input resolution, and we show that there is an input refutation if there are two extended clauses in S whose sum dominates (8.22). Furthermore, we present a sequential algorithm for two step input resolution that allows one to filter out extended clauses that are unlike to lead to $\bot$. We reduce the computational effort with most simplifying resolvents still being found.

One Step Input Refutation

The goal is to obtain $\bot$ starting with (8.23) by considering one extended clause in S. Note that the resolvent of $L \geq d$ and (8.23) is $L_i \geq 1$. Therefore, we already have shown unsatisfiability of $S \cup \{\overline{L} \setminus \{\overline{L_i}\} \geq |L| - d\}$ if we can derive $\overline{L_i} \geq 1$. We try to obtain $\overline{L_i} \geq 1$ by input resolution starting with the extended clause (8.23).

Example 8.3.4 Let $X_1 + X_2 + X_3 + X_4 + X_5 + X_6 + X_7 \geq 3$ be the extended clause in S for which we search a simplifying resolvent and suppose that S contains the extended clause $X_1 + X_2 + X_3 + \overline{X_5} + \overline{X_6} \geq 4$. The sum of both extended clauses is $2 \cdot X_1 + 2 \cdot X_2 + 2 \cdot X_3 + X_4 + X_7 \geq 5$, which dominates $X_1 + X_2 + X_3 + X_4 + X_7 \geq 3$, and thus, for example, $X_1 + X_2 + X_3 + X_4 + X_6 + X_7 \geq 3$, a simplifying extended clause which strictly dominates $X_1 + X_2 +$

$X_3 + X_4 + X_5 + X_6 + X_7 \geq 3$. Next, we show with help of an input refutation that $X_1 + X_2 + X_3 + X_4 + X_6 + X_7 \geq 3$ is dominated by S. The literal that is missing from $\{X_1, X_2, X_3, X_4, X_5, X_6, X_7\}$ is X_5. We start resolving on the negation of $X_1 + X_2 + X_3 + X_4 + X_6 + X_7 \geq 3$, i.e.,

$$\overline{X_1} + \overline{X_2} + \overline{X_3} + \overline{X_4} + \overline{X_6} + \overline{X_7} \geq 4 , \tag{8.24}$$

and know that unsatisfiability is detected if $\overline{X_5} \geq 1$ follows. We sum up (8.24) and $X_1 + X_2 + X_3 + \overline{X_5} + \overline{X_6} \geq 4$, and obtain the linear pseudo-Boolean inequality

$$\overline{X_4} + \overline{X_5} + 2 \cdot \overline{X_6} + \overline{X_7} \geq 5 , \tag{8.25}$$

which fixes all literals in it and thus dominates $\overline{X_5} \geq 1$. Together with $X_5 \geq 1$ we obtain $\perp$ and thus have derived unsatisfiability.

Typically, we do not know in advance which literal $L_i \in L$ can be eliminated. Therefore, the problem is whether one of the extended clauses represented by the compact extended clause set

$$L^{|L|-1} \geq d , \tag{8.26}$$

(see Definition 7.4.3) is valid w.r.t. S. This is the case if and only if one of the extended clauses of the compact extended clause set

$$\overline{L}^{|L|-1} \geq |L| - d , \tag{8.27}$$

i.e., the negation of (8.26), together with S is unsatisfiable. Resolving $L \geq d$ with (8.27) yields the compact extended clause set

$$L^1 \geq 1 ,$$

which is $L_i \geq 1$ if we have decided which literal L_i we eliminate, i.e., which of the extended clauses represented by (8.26) we select.

Let us add an extended clause containing a literal L_i to a compact extended clause set, where $\overline{L_i} \in S_j^{k_j}$ for some set of literals $S_j^{k_j}$ in the compact representation. We consider only expansions, where we select $\overline{L_i}$ from $S_j^{k_j}$. We obtain a valid compact extended clause if we replace $S_j^{k_j}$ by $\overline{L_i} + (S_j \setminus \{\overline{L_j}\})^{k_j-1}$. The sum of the extended clause and the valid compact extended clause set then contains the subterm $L_i + \overline{L_i} + (S_j \setminus \{\overline{L_j}\})^{k_j-1}$, which simplifies to $1 + (S_j \setminus \{\overline{L_j}\})^{k_j-1}$, where 1 can be brought to the right-hand side. Performing this simplification for all literals if possible yields the *resolvent* of a compact extended clause set and an extended clause.

We start the refutation sequence with (8.27). Note that we can delete ay any time some literal $\overline{L_i} \in \overline{L}$, and have shown unsatisfiability if $\overline{L_i} \geq 1$ is dominated.

Example 8.3.5 Let us again consider Example 8.3.4. We start resolving on the negation of $\{X_1, X_2, X_3, X_4, X_5, X_6, X_7\}^6 \geq 3$, namely

$$\{\overline{X_1} + \overline{X_2} + \overline{X_3} + \overline{X_4} + \overline{X_5} + \overline{X_6} + \overline{X_7}\}^6 \geq 4 \ , \qquad (8.28)$$

and add the extended clause $X_1 + X_2 + X_3 + \overline{X_5} + \overline{X_6} \geq 4$ yielding

$$\{\overline{X_4} + \overline{X_5} + \overline{X_6} + \overline{X_7}\}^3 + \overline{X_5} + \overline{X_6} \geq 5 \ . \qquad (8.29)$$

Since we have 5 literals in the left-hand side and the right-hand side is 5, we know that all literals need to be fixed. Because we have to derive $\overline{L_i} \geq 1$ for the literal that we delete, the literals in question are X_5 and X_6. We select X_5 and obtain $\overline{X_4} + \overline{X_7} + \overline{X_5} + 2 \cdot \overline{X_6} \geq 5$, which dominates $\overline{X_5} \geq 1$. Since $\overline{X_5} \geq 1$ is obtained by summing up $\overline{X_1} + \overline{X_2} + \overline{X_3} + \overline{X_4} + \overline{X_6} + \overline{X_7} \geq 4$ and $X_1 + X_2 + X_3 + X_4 + X_5 + X_6 + X_7 \geq 3$, we obtain $\perp$ and thus know that

$$X_1 + X_2 + X_3 + X_4 + X_6 + X_7 \geq 3$$

is dominated by S. Hence, we have a simplifying resolvent strictly dominating $X_1 + X_2 + X_3 + X_4 + X_5 + X_6 + X_7 \geq 3$.

Next, we give an Algorithm for detecting a simplifying resolvent of an extended clause $L \geq d \in S$ by an input refutation, where we resolve only with one additional extended clause in S.

Algorithm 8.3.6 *One Step Input Resolution*

```
onestep_simpres(L ≥ d, S)
    forall L' ≥ d' ∈ S do
        rhs := |L| − d + d' − |L ∩ L'|
        X := L̄ \ (L̄ ∩ L')
        Y := L' \ (L ∩ L')
        (* X^{|X|−1} + Y ≥ rhs *)
        (* L̄_i ≥ 1 is dominated (fixing) *)
        if |X ∩ Y| ≥ 1 ∧ |X| + |Y| − 1 ≤ rhs then
            L_i ∈ X ∩ Y
                return L \ {L_i} ≥ d
        endif
    endforall
    return ⊥
end onestep_simpres
```

The correctness of Algorithm 8.3.6 will be proved in Proposition 8.3.8. Algorithm 8.3.6 returns a simplifying resolvent for $L \geq d \in S$ if it finds one by resolving with one extended clause $L' \geq d' \in S$. We show that Algorithm 8.3.6 finds a simplifying resolvent for $L \geq d$ if and only if there is an extended clause $L' \geq d' \in S$ such that the linear pseudo-Boolean inequality $L + L' \geq d + d'$ dominates $L \setminus \{L_i\} \geq d$ for an $L_i \in L$. For this purpose we first investigate when a linear pseudo-Boolean inequality, obtained by summing up two extended clauses, dominates an extended clause.

The sum of two extended clauses is always of the form

$$2 \cdot L + L' \geq d , \tag{8.30}$$

where L is the set of literals occurring in both extended clauses, and L' is the set of literals whose variables occur once in both extended clauses. Literals that occur positively in one and negatively in the other extended clause are simplified to 1 and brought to the right-hand side. Next, we investigate conditions when (8.30) dominates the extended clause $L \cup L' \geq d'$.

Lemma 8.3.7 *The linear pseudo-Boolean inequality $2 \cdot L + L' \geq d$ dominates the extended clause $L \cup L' \geq d'$ if and only if*

$$\begin{array}{ll} d' \leq \lceil d/2 \rceil & \text{if } 2|L| \geq d \\ d' \leq d - |L| & \text{if } 2|L| < d . \end{array} \tag{8.31}$$

Proof. By Proposition 7.1.2 we know that $2 \cdot L + L' \geq d$ dominates the extended clause $L \cup L' \geq d'$ if and only if the right-hand side of the strongest extended clause $\mathsf{SCP}(2 \cdot L + L' \geq d)$ is greater than or equal to d'. It remains to show that

$$\beta := \begin{cases} \lceil d/2 \rceil & \text{if } 2|L| \geq d \\ d - |L| & \text{if } 2|L| < d \end{cases}$$

is the right-hand side of $\mathsf{SCP}(2 \cdot L + L' \geq d)$.

First, suppose that $2|L| \geq d$. Condition (7.4) for calculating β states that β is the smallest number of the largest coefficients such that their sum is greater or equal than d. Since the sum of the literals with coefficient 2 is already greater than d, we know that we have to sum up $\lceil d/2 \rceil$ times the coefficient 2.

Next, suppose that $2|L| < d$. Then we have to sum up all coefficients that are 2, i.e., $|L|$, plus as many times 1 as needed in order to reach d, i.e., $d - 2|L|$. Thus, we need to sum up at least $|L| + d - 2|L| = d - |L|$ coefficients. □

Note that a linear pseudo-Boolean inequality $2 \cdot L + 2 \cdot M + L' + M' \geq d$ dominates an extended clause $L + L' \geq d'$ if and only if its reduction $2 \cdot L + L' \geq d - 2|M| - |M'|$ dominates $L + L' \geq d'$.

Proposition 8.3.8 *If there exists $L \geq d \in S$ and $L' \geq d' \in S$ such that $L + L' \geq d + d'$ dominates a simplifying resolvent $L \setminus \{L_i\} \geq d$ with $L_i \in L$, then there is an input refutation, following Algorithm 8.3.6, for a simplifying resolvent of $L \geq d$.*

Proof. Let $L + L' \geq d + d'$ dominate a simplifying resolvent $L \setminus \{L_i\} \geq d$ with $L_i \in L$. Let $M := L \cap L'$, $N := L \cap \overline{L'}$, $Q := L \setminus (M \cup N)$, and $R := L' \setminus (M \cup \overline{N})$. Then $M \cup N \cup Q = L$, $M \cup \overline{N} \cup R = L'$, and $L + L' \geq d + d'$ is

$$2 \cdot M + Q + R \geq d + d' - |N| \ .$$

Since R and L are disjoint, we know that

$$2 \cdot M + Q \geq d + d' - |N| - |R| \tag{8.32}$$

dominates $L \setminus \{L_i\} \geq d$.

First, we show that $N \neq \emptyset$. Suppose otherwise, then $L = M \cup Q$, $L' = M \cup R$, and we know that (8.32), which is

$$2 \cdot M + Q \geq d + d' - |R| \ , \tag{8.33}$$

dominates $L \setminus \{L_i\} \geq d$. Since $L = M \cup Q$ we know that (8.33) dominates $L \geq d + 1$. From Lemma 8.3.7 we know that then

$$\begin{aligned} d + 1 &\leq \lceil (d + d' - |R|)/2 \rceil &&\text{if } 2|M| \geq d + d' - |R| \\ d + 1 &\leq d + d' - |R| - |M| &&\text{if } 2|M| < d + d' - |R| \ . \end{aligned}$$

Note that if $2|M| < d + d' - |R|$, then $d + 1 \leq d + d' - |R| - |M|$, which is equivalent to $|R| + |M| + 1 \leq d'$. But then $d' > |L'|$ and thus $L' \geq d'$ is $\perp$, which is not allowed. Therefore, we have $2|M| \geq d + d' - |R|$ and thus

$$d + 1 \leq \lceil (d + d' - |R|)/2 \rceil \ . \tag{8.34}$$

From (8.34) we have

$$\begin{aligned} 2d + 2 &\leq d + d' - |R| + 1 \\ d + 1 &\leq d' - |R| \\ d + 1 + |R| &\leq d' \ . \end{aligned}$$

Thus, $L' \geq d'$ dominates $M \cup R \geq d + 1 + |R|$, which in turn dominates its reduction $M \geq d + 1$. Therefore, $L' \geq d'$ dominates $L \geq d$, which contradicts the normal form condition. We conclude that $N \neq \emptyset$ and w.l.o.g. we have $L_i \in N$.

Therefore, $L \setminus \{L_i\} \geq d$ is dominated by (8.32) if and only if (8.32) dominates $M + Q \geq d$. From Lemma 8.3.7 we know that

$$
\begin{array}{ll}
d \leq \lceil (d + d' - |N| - |R|)/2 \rceil & \text{if } 2|M| \geq d + d' - |N| - |R| \\
d \leq d + d' - |N| - |R| - |M| & \text{if } 2|M| < d + d' - |N| - |R|
\end{array}
$$

holds. Note that if $2|M| < d + d' - |N| - |R|$, then $d \leq d + d' - |N| - |R| - |M|$, which is equivalent to $|N| + |R| + |M| \leq d'$. But then $d' \geq |L'|$, which is not allowed, since the weakness of $L' \geq d$ is less than or equal to 0. Thus, either unsatisfiability is detected or the literals in L' are fixed to 1. Therefore, we have $2|M| \geq d + d' - |N| - |R|$ and thus

$$d \leq \lceil (d + d' - |N| - |R|)/2 \rceil . \tag{8.35}$$

Next, we establish that $d = \lceil (d + d' - |N| - |R|)/2 \rceil$. Suppose otherwise, then we have

$$
\begin{array}{rcl}
d + 1 & \leq & \lceil (d + d' - |N| - |R|)/2 \rceil \\
2d + 2 & \leq & d + d' - |N| - |R| + 1 \\
d + 1 & \leq & d' - |N| - |R| \\
d' & \geq & d + 1 + |N| + |R| .
\end{array}
$$

Therefore, $L' \geq d'$ dominates $M \cup \overline{N} \cup R \geq d + 1 + |N| + |R|$, since $L' = M \cup \overline{N} \cup R$, which dominates its reduction $M \geq d + 1$. But then $L' \geq d'$ dominates $L \geq d$, since $M \subseteq L$, which contradicts the normal form condition. We conclude that $d = \lceil (d + d' - |N| - |R|)/2 \rceil$.

Let us now investigate an input refutation starting with $\overline{M} \cup \overline{N}^{|N|-1} \cup \overline{Q} \geq |M| + |N| + |Q| - d$. We add $M \cup \overline{N} \cup R \geq d'$, which yields

$$\overline{N} + \overline{N}^{|N|-1} + \overline{Q} + R \geq |N| + |Q| - d + d' . \tag{8.36}$$

Since (8.36) needs to dominate $\overline{L_i} \geq 1$, where L_i is the literal that is missing from $\overline{N}$ in $\overline{N}^{|N|-1}$, it remains to show

$$2|N| - 1 + |Q| + |R| \leq |N| + |Q| - d + d' , \tag{8.37}$$

which simplifies to $|N| + |R| + d \leq d' + 1$. We assume the converse,

$$|N| + |R| + d > d' + 1 ,\qquad(8.38)$$

which will lead to a contradiction. From (8.38) we have $|N| + |R| + d \geq d' + 2$.
Since $d = \lceil (d + d' - |N| - |R|)/2 \rceil$, we derive

$$|N| + |R| + \lceil (d + d' - |N| - |R|)/2 \rceil \geq d' + 2 ,$$

which implies

$$
\begin{aligned}
2|N| + 2|R| + d + d' - |N| - |R| + 1 &\geq& 2d' + 4 \\
|N| + |R| + d &\geq& d' + 3 \\
d &\geq& d' + 3 - |N| - |R| .
\end{aligned}
$$

Since $d \geq d' + 3 - |N| - |R|$, we know that $L \geq d$ dominates

$$M \cup N \cup R \geq d' + 3 - |N| - |R|$$

and thus dominates

$$M \geq d' + 3 .$$

But then $L \geq d$ dominates $L' \geq d'$, which again violates the normal form
condition.

Note that in Algorithm 8.3.6 X is $\overline{N} \cup \overline{Q}$, Y is $\overline{N} \cup R$, and rhs is $|N|+|Q|-d+d'$.
Thus $|X| + |Y| - 1 \leq rhs$ is equivalent to

$$2|N| + |R| + |Q| - 1 \leq |N| + |Q| - d + d'$$

which is (8.37). Furthermore, $X \cap Y = \overline{N}$ and thus we also ensure that N is
not empty.   □

Therefore, Algorithm 8.3.6 is a complete method checking whether there is an
extended clause $L' \geq d' \in S$, which dominates together with $L \geq d$ a simplifying
resolvent $L \setminus \{L_i\} \geq d$. A more general method is to check whether there are
two extended clauses in S whose sum dominates a simplifying resolvent for
$L \geq d$. We present a similar input refutation method for that problem.

Two Step Input Refutation

Let $L \geq d \in S$ be an extended clause for which we want to check whether there
are two extended clauses in S such that their sum dominates a simplifying
resolvent $L \setminus \{L_i\} \geq d$. We present an input refutation method starting with
$\overline{L}^{|L|-1} \geq |L| - d$, but allows two steps in order to derive unsatisfiability.

Example 8.3.9 Let the two extended clauses $X_1 + X_2 + X_5 + X_6 + X_7 \geq 2$ and $X_3 + X_4 + \overline{X_5} + \overline{X_6} + \overline{X_7} \geq 3$ be in S. Their sum $X_1 + X_2 + X_3 + X_4 \geq 2$ is a simplifying resolvent for $X_1 + X_2 + X_3 + X_4 + X_8 \geq 2 \in S$. We start an input refutation with $\{\overline{X_1}, \overline{X_2}, \overline{X_3}, \overline{X_4}, \overline{X_8}\}^4 \geq 3$, and add the two extended clauses $X_1 + X_2 + X_5 + X_6 + X_7 \geq 2$ and $X_3 + X_4 + \overline{X_5} + \overline{X_6} + \overline{X_7} \geq 3$ yielding $\{\overline{X_8}\}^0 \geq 1$, which is $\perp$.

We see that in a two step input refutation we may immediately obtain $\perp$. It is also possible to derive that some literals need to be fixed, and fixing these literals in $\overline{L}^{|L|-1} \geq |L| - d$ yields the desired $\perp$.

Example 8.3.10 Let $X_1 + X_2 + X_3 + X_4 + X_5 + X_8 + X_9 + X_{10} \geq 4$ and $X_1 + X_2 + X_3 + X_6 + X_7 + \overline{X_8} + \overline{X_9} + \overline{X_{10}} \geq 5$ be two extended clauses in S. Their sum $2 \cdot X_1 + 2 \cdot X_2 + 2 \cdot X_3 + X_4 + X_5 + X_6 + X_7 \geq 6$ dominates, for example, the extended clause $X_1 + X_2 + X_3 + X_4 + X_5 + X_6 \geq 3$, which is a simplifying resolvent for the extended clause $X_1 + X_2 + X_3 + X_4 + X_5 + X_6 + X_{11} \geq 3 \in S$. We start an input refutation with

$$\{\overline{X_1}, \overline{X_2}, \overline{X_3}, \overline{X_4}, \overline{X_5}, \overline{X_6}, \overline{X_{11}}\}^6 \geq 4 \ . \tag{8.39}$$

Adding both extended clauses yields $X_1 + X_2 + X_3 + X_7 + \{X_{11}\}^0 \geq 4$. Thus, the literals X_1, X_2, X_3 and X_7 need to be fixed to 1. The literal that needs to be eliminated is X_{11}. Fixing X_1, X_2 and X_3 to 1 in (8.39) yields $\{\overline{X_4}, \overline{X_5}, \overline{X_6}, \overline{X_{11}}\}^3 \geq 4$, which is $\perp$, and thus unsatisfiability is shown.

Unfortunately, these two cases are not sufficient. It is also possible that $\perp$ may only be obtained by adding again the initial compact extended clause set.

Example 8.3.11 Let $X_1 + X_2 + X_3 + X_4 + X_5 + X_6 + X_7 \geq 3$ and $X_1 + X_2 + X_3 + X_4 + X_5 + \overline{X_6} + X_8 \geq 3$ be two extended clauses in S. Their sum $2 \cdot X_1 + 2 \cdot X_2 + 2 \cdot X_3 + 2 \cdot X_4 + 2 \cdot X_5 + X_7 + X_8 \geq 5$ dominates the extended clause $X_1 + X_2 + X_3 + X_4 + X_5 + X_7 + X_8 \geq 3$, which is a simplifying resolvent for $X_1 + X_2 + X_3 + X_4 + X_5 + X_7 + X_8 + X_9 \geq 3 \in S$. We start an input refutation with

$$\{\overline{X_1}, \overline{X_2}, \overline{X_3}, \overline{X_4}, \overline{X_5}, \overline{X_7}, \overline{X_8}, \overline{X_9}\}^7 \geq 5 \ , \tag{8.40}$$

and add the two extended clauses yielding $X_1 + X_2 + X_3 + X_4 + X_5 + \{X_9\}^0 \geq 3$, which is neither $\perp$ nor fixes any literal. Note that the set of literals that occur in both extended clauses and in the extended clause to be dominated is relatively large, i.e., its cardinality is greater than or equal to the right-hand side. One way to eliminate these literals is to add again (8.40) yielding $\{\overline{X_7}, \overline{X_8}, \overline{X_9}\}^2 + \{X_9\}^0 \geq 3$, which is $\perp$, and thus we have shown unsatisfiability.

L	L_i	L_i	L_i	L_i	L_i	L_i	L_i	L_i	L_i				
L'	L_i	L_i	L_i	$\overline{L_i}$	$\overline{L_i}$	$\overline{L_i}$				L_i	L_i	L_i	
L''	L_i	$\overline{L_i}$		L_i	$\overline{L_i}$		L_i		$\overline{L_i}$	L_i	$\overline{L_i}$		L_i
Set	M	N	Q	P	M',T	Q',T	R	T	R',T	M'	N'	Q'	R'

Figure 8.1   Splitting literals

Based on these examples, we construct the following algorithm for detecting a simplifying resolvent of $L \geq d \in S$, where we resolve with two other extended clause in S. When we select $L' \geq d_1, L'' \geq d_2$, a pair of extended clauses in S, we build 9 disjoint subsets $(M, M', N, N', Q, Q', R, R', T)$ of the literals occurring in the extended clauses $L \geq d$, $L' \geq d_1$ and $L'' \geq d_2$ according to Figure 8.1. The first three lines indicate the occurrence of a literal, resp. its negation, in the sets of literals L, L' and L''. The fourth line indicates in which set to put L_i. For example, the seventh column reads "If L_i occurs in L, $\overline{L_i}$ occurs in L', and neither L_i nor $\overline{L_i}$ occurs in L'', then put $\overline{L_i}$ in the set Q' and put L_i in the set T". Figure 8.1 covers all possible cases exactly once. Note that $L = M \cup N \cup P \cup Q \cup R \cup T$, $L' = M \cup M' \cup N \cup \overline{P} \cup N' \cup Q \cup Q'$, and $L'' = M \cup M' \cup \overline{N} \cup P \cup \overline{N'} \cup R \cup R'$. This splitting enables us to express directly the combinations of the extended clauses and to reason about their properties like in Proposition 8.3.13.

Algorithm 8.3.12 *Two Step Input Resolution*

twostep_simpres$(L \geq d, S)$

forall $\begin{aligned} & M + M' + N + \overline{P} + N' + Q + Q' \geq d_1, \\ & M + M' + \overline{N} + P + \overline{N'} + R + R' \geq d_2 \end{aligned} \in S$ **do**

    $T := L \setminus (M \cup N \cup P \cup Q \cup R)$

    if $N = P = T = \emptyset$ **return** $\bot$ **endif**

    if $|M| + |N| + |P| \leq d_1 + d_2 - d - |N'| - 2|M'| - |Q'| - |R'|$ $\vee$

        $(d < |M| + 1$ $\wedge$

        $|M| + |N| + |P| - 1 = d_1 + d_2 - d - |N'| - 2|M'| - |Q'| - |R'|)$ $\vee$

        $(d \leq |M| - 1$ $\wedge$

        $2d < d_1 + d_2 + |N| - |N'| - 2|M'| - |Q'| - |R'| + 2)$

    then

        $L_i \in N \cup P \cup T$

        return $L \setminus \{L_i\} \geq d$

    endif

endforall
return ⊥
end twostep_simpres

The first **if**-condition checks whether a simplifying resolvent is possible, i.e., whether a literal of L is missing in the sum of the two extended clauses. The next **if**-condition checks (a) whether the sum of the two extended clauses and $\overline{L}^{|L|-1} \geq |L| - d$ is ⊥, (b) whether the sum of the two extended clauses and $\overline{L}^{|L|-1} \geq |L| - d$ forces fixing literals, and if yes whether fixing these literals in $\overline{L}^{|L|-1} \geq |L| - d$ yields ⊥, and (c) whether $|M|$ is large enough such that the special case of Example 8.3.11 may occur. If yes, it is tested if the sum of the two extended clauses plus two times $\overline{L}^{|L|-1} \geq |L| - d$ yields ⊥. It turns out that these three cases cover all possibilities.

Proposition 8.3.13 *If the sum $L' + L'' \geq d_1 + d_2$ of two extended clauses $L' \geq d_1$ and $L'' \geq d_2$ dominates an extended clause $L \setminus \{L_i\} \geq d$ with $L_i \in L$, but not $L \geq d + 1$, then there is an input refutation of $\overline{L}^{|L|-1} \geq |L| - d$ using these two extended clauses following Algorithm 8.3.12 and L_i is determined such that $L \setminus \{L_i\} \geq d$ is valid and strictly dominating $L \geq d$.*

Proof. The two extended clauses $L' \geq d_1$ and $L'' \geq d_2$ are of the form

$$M + M' + N + \overline{P} + N' + Q + Q' \geq d_1 \tag{8.41}$$
$$M + M' + \overline{N} + P + \overline{N'} + R + R' \geq d_2 \tag{8.42}$$

according to Figure 8.1. The sum of (8.41) and (8.42) is

$$2 \cdot M + 2 \cdot M' + Q + Q' + R + R' \geq d_1 + d_2 - |N| - |P| - |N'| . \tag{8.43}$$

Since (8.43) dominates $L \setminus \{L_i\} \geq d$, we know that the reduction

$$2 \cdot M + Q + R \geq d_1 + d_2 - |N| - |P| - |N'| - 2|M'| - |Q'| - |R'| \tag{8.44}$$

of (8.43) dominates $L \setminus \{L_i\} \geq d$. Note that $N \cup P \cup T \neq \emptyset$. Suppose otherwise, then $L = M \cup Q \cup R$ and thus we know that (8.44), which is

$$2 \cdot M + Q + R \geq d_1 + d_2 - |N'| - 2|M'| - |Q'| - |R'| , \tag{8.45}$$

dominates $M + Q + R \geq d + 1$, since it also dominates $L \setminus \{L_i\} \geq d$, which is $(M \cup Q \cup R) \setminus \{L_i\} \geq d$. But that case is excluded, thus, $N \cup P \cup T \neq \emptyset$. Therefore, we can safely suppose in the following that $L_i \in N \cup P \cup T$.

We start an input refutation with $\overline{L}^{|L|-1} \geq |L| - d$, which is

$$\overline{M} + \overline{Q} + \overline{R} + \{\overline{N} + \overline{P} + \overline{T}\}^{|N|+|P|+|T|-1} \geq |M| + |N| + |P| + |Q| + |R| + |T| - d \ . \tag{8.46}$$

We add the two extended clauses (8.41) and (8.42) to (8.46), and obtain

$$M + 2|M'| + Q' + R' + \{\overline{N} + \overline{P} + \overline{T}\}^{|N|+|P|+|T|-1} \geq d_1 + d_2 + |T| - d - |N'| \ , \tag{8.47}$$

which dominates its reduction

$$M + \{\overline{N} + \overline{P} + \overline{T}\}^{|N|+|P|+|T|-1} \geq d_1 + d_2 - d + |T| - |N'| - 2|M'| - |Q'| - |R'| \ . \tag{8.48}$$

We have shown unsatisfiability if

- inequality (8.48) is $\bot$, i.e., if

$$|M| + |N| + |P| \leq d_1 + d_2 - d - |N'| - 2|M'| - |Q'| - |R'| \ , \tag{8.49}$$

- or if the literals in $M + \{\overline{N} + \overline{P} + \overline{T}\}^{|N|+|P|+|T|-1}$ need to be fixed, and fixing these literals in (8.46) yields $\bot$, i.e., if

$$|M| + |N| + |P| - 1 = d_1 + d_2 - d - |N'| - 2|M'| - |Q'| - |R'| \tag{8.50}$$

and

$$|\overline{Q}| + |\overline{R}| + |\overline{N}| + |\overline{P}| + |\overline{T}| - 1 < |M| + |N| + |P| + |Q| + |R| + |T| - d \ , \tag{8.51}$$

where (8.51) simplifies to

$$d < |M| + 1 \ , \tag{8.52}$$

- or if $d \leq |M| - 1$ and the sum of $2 \cdot (8.46)$, (8.41) and (8.42) is $\bot$.

In the remaining part of the proof we investigate the sum of (8.41) and (8.42), which dominates $L \setminus \{L_i\} \geq d$. We show that always one of the previous three cases apply, which shows the proposition.

We know that (8.44) dominates $L \setminus \{L_i\} \geq d$ if and only if it dominates $M + Q + R \geq d$, since $L_i \in N \cup P \cup T$. From Lemma 8.3.7 we know that

$$
\begin{aligned}
d \leq \ & \lceil d_1 + d_2 - |N| - |P| - |N'| - 2|M'| - |Q'| - |R'|/2 \rceil \\
& \text{if } 2|M| \geq d_1 + d_2 - |N| - |P| - |N'| - 2|M'| - |Q'| - |R'| \\
d \leq \ & d_1 + d_2 - |N| - |P| - |N'| - 2|M'| - |Q'| - |R'| - |L| \\
& \text{if } 2|M| < d_1 + d_2 - |N| - |P| - |N'| - 2|M'| - |Q'| - |R'| \ .
\end{aligned}
$$

- First, suppose that $2|M| < d_1 + d_2 - |N| - |P| - |N'| - 2|M'| - |Q'| - |R'|$, and thus $d \le d_1 + d_2 - |N| - |P| - |N'| - 2|M'| - |Q'| - |R'| - |L|$. Since $L = M \cup N \cup P \cup Q \cup R \cup T$, we have

$$d \le d_1 + d_2 - 2|N| - 2|P| - |N'| - 2|M'| - |Q'| - |R'| - |M| - |Q| - |R| - |T| \; ,$$

and after a rearrangement we know that

$$\begin{aligned} |M| + |N| + |P| + |T| \; &\le \\ d_1 + d_2 - d - |N| - |P| - |N'| - 2|M'| &- |Q'| - |R'| - |Q| - |R| \; . \end{aligned}$$
$$(8.53)$$

We add the valid inequality $-|T| \le |N| + |P| + |Q| + |R|$ to (8.53) and obtain

$$|M| + |N| + |P| \le d_1 + d_2 - d - |N'| - 2|M'| - |Q'| - |R'| \; ,$$

which is (8.49) and thus we have shown unsatisfiability.

- Next, suppose that $2|M| \ge d_1 + d_2 - |N| - |P| - |N'| - 2|M'| - |Q'| - |R'|$, thus $d \le \lceil d_1 + d_2 - |N| - |P| - |N'| - 2|M'| - |Q'| - |R'|/2 \rceil$, and therefore

$$2 \cdot d \le d_1 + d_2 - |N| - |P| - |N'| - 2|M'| - |Q'| - |R'| + 1 \; . \qquad (8.54)$$

We assume that input refutation fails to exhibit unsatisfiability. First, suppose that

$$|M| + |N| + |P| - 1 > d_1 + d_2 - d - |N'| - 2|M'| - |Q'| - |R'| \; , \qquad (8.55)$$

i.e., (8.48) has weakness greater than 0, which is equivalent to

$$d_1 + d_2 - d - |N'| - 2|M'| - |Q'| - |R'| + 1 \le |M| + |N| + |P| - 1 \; . \qquad (8.56)$$

We sum up (8.56) and (8.54), and obtain $d \le |M| - 1$. In that case we add again (8.46) to the sum (8.47), resp. (8.48), obtained by the input refutation following Algorithm 8.3.12, which yields

$$\begin{aligned} \overline{Q} + \overline{R} + 2 \cdot \{\overline{N} + \overline{P} + \overline{T}\}^{|N| + |P| + |T| - 1} \; &\ge \\ |N| + |P| + |Q| + |R| + 2|T| - 2d + d_1 + d_2 - |N'| - 2|M'| &- |Q'| - |R'| \; . \end{aligned}$$
$$(8.57)$$

We have shown unsatisfiability if (8.57) is $\bot$, i.e., if

$$\begin{aligned} |Q| + |R| + 2|N| + 2|P| + 2|T| - 2 \; &< \\ |N| + |P| + |Q| + |R| + 2|T| - 2d + d_1 + d_2 - |N'| - 2|M'| &- |Q'| - |R'| \end{aligned}$$
$$(8.58)$$

holds. We assume the negation of (8.58), which simplifies to

$$2 \cdot d \geq d_1 + d_2 - |N| - |P| - |N'| - 2|M'| - |Q'| - |R'| + 2 \ . \qquad (8.59)$$

Since (8.59) contradicts (8.54), we know that (8.57) is $\bot$.
Second, suppose that

$$|M| + |N| + |P| - 1 = d_1 + d_2 - d - |N'| - 2|M'| - |Q'| - |R'| \ , \qquad (8.60)$$

thus we have

$$d_1 + d_2 - d - |N'| - 2|M'| - |Q'| - |R'| \leq |M| + |N| + |P| - 1 \ . \qquad (8.61)$$

We sum up (8.61) and (8.54), and obtain $d \leq |M|$, which is equivalent to $d < |M| + 1$, which is (8.52). But then input refutation, following Algorithm 8.3.12, exhibits unsatisfiability. $\qquad\qquad \square$

Example 8.3.14 We apply Algorithm 8.3.12 to the previous examples in this section.

[a] We again consider Example 8.3.9. We have $N' = \{X_5, X_6, X_7\}$, $R = \{X_1, X_2\}$, $Q = \{X_3, X_4\}$, $T = \{X_8\}$, and the other sets are empty. The first condition of Algorithm 8.3.12, i.e., (8.49), holds.

$$
\begin{aligned}
|M| + |N| + |P| &\leq d_1 + d_2 - d - |N'| - 2|M'| - |Q'| - |R'| \\
0 + 0 + 0 &\leq 2 + 3 - 2 - 3 - 0 - 0 - 0 \\
0 &\leq 0
\end{aligned}
$$

[b] Consider again Example 8.3.10. We have $M = \{X_1, X_2, X_3\}$, $N' = \{X_8, X_9, X_{10}\}$, $Q = \{X_4, X_5\}$, $R = \{X_6\}$, $R' = \{X_7\}$, $T = \{X_{11}\}$, and the other sets are empty. The second condition of Algorithm 8.3.12, i.e., (8.50), which is $d < |M| + 1 (\equiv 3 < 3 + 1 = 4)$, and (8.52), hold.

$$
\begin{aligned}
|M| + |N| + |P| - 1 &= d_1 + d_2 - d - |N'| - 2|M'| - |Q'| - |R'| \\
3 + 0 + 0 - 1 &= 4 + 5 - 3 - 3 - 0 - 0 - 1 \\
2 &= 2
\end{aligned}
$$

[c] Consider again Example 8.3.11. We have $M = \{X_1, X_2, X_3, X_4, X_5\}$, $N' = \{X_6\}$, $Q = \{X_7\}$, $R = \{X_8\}$, $T = \{X_9\}$, and the other sets are empty. The third condition of Algorithm 8.3.12, i.e.,

$$d \leq |M| - 1 (\equiv 3 \leq 5 - 1 = 4) \ ,$$

and (8.58) hold.

$$
\begin{aligned}
2d &< d_1 + d_2 + |N| + |P| - |N'| - 2|M'| - |Q'| - |R'| + 2 \\
6 &< 3 + 3 + 0 + 0 - 1 - 0 - 0 - 0 + 2 \\
6 &< 7
\end{aligned}
$$

Thus, Algorithm 8.3.12 finds a simplifying resolvent if there is one dominated by the sum of two extended clauses in S. The algorithm is of $O(|S|^2)$, since each pair of extended clauses in S needs to be considered. After splitting the set of literals in the extended clauses the test of whether there is a simplifying extended clause is reduced to simple arithmetic expressions only involving the cardinality of the split sets.

Restricted Two Step Input Refutation

Algorithm 8.3.12 still considers all possible pairs of extended clauses in S. The advantage of the presented two step input refutation is that we can start adding one extended clause and then skip cases that are not *promising*. Since the goal is to generate $\perp$ or force fixing literals, we may restrict ourselves to cases, where the number of literals of the left-hand side is already close to the right-hand side. We reformulate Algorithm 8.3.12 such that first one extended clause is added. The second extended clause is only added if a function `promising` decides to do so. Furthermore, we include the check for one step input resolution.

Algorithm 8.3.15 *Sequential One and Two Step Input Resolution*

```
seq_twostep_simpres(L ≥ d, S)
    forall L' ≥ d₁ ∈ S do
        rhs₁ := |L| - d + d₁ - |L ∩ L'|
        X, Y := L̄ \ (L̄ ∩ L'), L' \ (L ∩ L')
        if |X ∩ Y| ≥ 1 ∧ |X| + |Y| - 1 ≤ rhs₁ then
            (* one step input resolution *)
            Lᵢ ∈ X̄ ∩ Y
            return L \ {Lᵢ} ≥ d
        endif
        (* the current state is X^{|X|-1} + Y ≥ rhs₁ *)
        if promising(L ≥ d, L' ≥ d₁, X, Y, rhs₁) then
            forall L'' ≥ d₂ ∈ S do
```

(* add the second extended clause *)
$Y' := Y \setminus (\overline{\overline{Y} \cap L''})$ (* resolve, no choice *)
$\hat{L}'' := L'' \setminus (\overline{Y} \cap L'')$ (* remaining from L'' *)
$X' := X \setminus (\overline{\overline{X} \cap \hat{L}''})$ (* resolve, choice *)
$L''' := \hat{L}'' \setminus (\overline{X} \cap \hat{L}'')$ (* remaining from L'' *)
if $X' = \emptyset$ **then**
        (* no simp. res. possible, since $N = P = T = \emptyset$ *)
else
$rhs_2 := rhs_1 + d_2 - |\overline{X} \cap \hat{L}''| - |(\overline{Y} \cap L''|$
$M := L \cap L' \cap L''$
(* check if $\bot$; current state $X'^{|X'|-1} + Y' + L''' \geq rhs$ *)
if $(|X'| + |Y'| + |L'''| \leq rhs_2) \vee$ (* (a) *)
        $(|X'| + |Y'| + |L'''| - 1 = rhs_2 \wedge d < |M| + 1)$ (* (b) *)
then
        $L_i \in L \cap ((L' \cap \overline{L''}) \cup (\overline{L'} \cap L'')) \vee L_i \in L \setminus (L' \cup L'')$
        return $L \setminus \{L_i\} \geq d$
endif
if $d \leq |M| - 1$ **then** (* (c) *)
        (* add $\overline{L}^{|L|-1} \geq |L| - d$ again, X', Y' not affected *)
        $L'''' := L''' \setminus (L''' \cap L)$ (* resolve *)
        $rhs_3 := rhs_2 + |L| - d - |L''' \cap L|$
        if $|X'| + |Y'| + |L''''| + |\overline{L} \setminus \overline{L''' \cap L}| - 2 < rhs$ **then**
        $L_i \in L \cap ((L' \cap \overline{L''}) \cup (\overline{L'} \cap L'')) \vee L_i \in L \setminus (L' \cup L'')$
                return $L \setminus \{L_i\} \geq d$
        endif
endif
endif
endforall
        endif
    endforall
    return $\bot$
end `seq_twostep_simpres`

If the function `promising` always succeeds, i.e., all pairs of extended clauses are considered, then Algorithm 8.3.15 is equivalent to Algorithm 8.3.12. Note that:

$$
\begin{aligned}
L \cap L' &= M \cup N \cup Q \\
rhs_1 &= |P| + |R| + |T| - d + d_1 \\
X &= \overline{P} \cup \overline{R} \cup \overline{T}
\end{aligned}
$$

$$
\begin{aligned}
Y &= M' \cup \overline{P} \cup N' \cup Q' \\
\overline{Y} \cap L'' &= P \cup \overline{N}' \\
Y' &= M' \cup Q' \\
\hat{L}'' &= M \cup M' \cup \overline{N} \cup R \cup R' \\
\overline{X} \cap \hat{L}'' &= R \\
X' &= \overline{P} \cup \overline{T} \\
L''' &= M \cup M' \cup \overline{N} \cup R' \\
rhs_2 &= |T| - d + d_1 + d_2 - |N'| \\
|X'| + |Y'| + |L'''| &= |P| + |T| + 2|M'| + |Q'| + |M| + |N| + |R'|
\end{aligned}
$$

Therefore, we know that $|X'| + |Y'| + |L'''| \le rhs_2$ is equivalent to (8.49) and that $|X'| + |Y'| + |L'''| - 1 = rhs_2$ is equivalent to (8.50). Furthermore,

$$
\begin{aligned}
L''' \cap L &= M \, , \\
L'''' &= M' \cup \overline{N} \cup R' \, , \\
rhs_3 &= 2|T| - 2d + d_1 + d_2 - |N'| + |N| + |P| + |Q| + |R| \, , \\
\overline{L} \setminus \overline{L''' \cap L} &= N \cup P \cup Q \cup R \cup T \, ,
\end{aligned}
$$

and

$$
\begin{aligned}
|X'| + |Y'| + |L''''| + |\overline{L} \setminus \overline{L''' \cap L}| &= \\
2|P| + 2|T| + 2|M'| + |Q'| + 2|N| + |R'| + |Q| + |R| &\, .
\end{aligned}
$$

Thus, $|X'| + |Y'| + |L''''| + |\overline{L} \setminus \overline{L''' \cap L}| - 2 < rhs_3$ simplifies to

$$
|P| + 2|M'| + |Q'| + |N| + |R'| - 2 < -2d + d_1 + d_2 - |N'| \, ,
$$

which is equivalent to (8.58).

The main advantage of Algorithm 8.3.15 w.r.t. Algorithm 8.3.12 is that we can filter out combinations $\overline{L}^{|L|-1} + L' \ge |L| - d + d_1$ that are not likely to lead to the desired contradiction yielding a simplifying resolvent. The function promising decides whether a combination should be considered.

■ Note that at least one of the extended clauses $L' \ge d_1$ and $L'' \ge d_2$ needs to contain a literal in L, since otherwise the sum $L' + L'' \ge d_1 + d_2$ cannot dominate $L \setminus \{L_i\} \ge d$, except if it is $\bot$. Since we consider each extended clause in S as a candidate for $L' \ge d_1$ as well as for $L'' \ge d_2$, we can reject all combinations $\overline{L}^{|L|-1} + L' \ge |L| - d + d_1$ with $L' \cap L = \emptyset$. Thus, promising should always include the test

if $L' \cap L = \emptyset$ then   return false   endif

and Algorithm 8.3.15 remains still equivalent to Algorithm 8.3.12.

- We want to simplify each extended clause in S. Since checking for a simplifying resolvent is $O(|S|^2)$ for each extended clause, we have $O(|S|^3)$ in the worst case when checking for each extended clause in S whether there is a simplifying resolvent for it. We propose to reduce the computational effort by rejecting some combinations that will probably not lead to a simplifying resolvent.

  A possible measure is $|X| + |Y| - 1 - rhs$, the difference between the right-hand side and the number of literals on the left-hand side. Since we obtain $\bot$, resp. fixing literals, if the number of literals is greater than, resp. equal to, the right-hand side, we can include

  if $|X| + |Y| - 1 - rhs > b$ then   return false   endif

  in promising for filtering out combinations where for more than b literals their negation has to be added after adding the first extended clause. The smaller b, the better the probability that we will find a contradiction and the more cases are filtered out. For example, with $b = 2$ all presented examples still work. Note that we may lose simplifying resolvents with that restriction. An improvement is to apply the filtering only if $d \geq |L \cap L'|$, since otherwise we may lose simplifying resolvents constructed by adding twice $\overline{L}^{|L|-1} \geq |L| - d$.

8.4   EQUATIONS BETWEEN LITERALS

An equation $L_i = L_j$ between two literals L_i, L_j is equivalent to the set of extended clauses

$$\{L_i + \overline{L_j} \geq 1, \overline{L_i} + L_j \geq 1\} \ . \tag{8.62}$$

Since the constraints we work with are only linear pseudo-Boolean inequalities and extended clauses, the best we can get whenever $L_i = L_j$ is dominated by the current constraint store, is that we have two different extended clauses in the constraint store, each of them dominating one of the extended clauses in (8.62). Note that for (8.62) no further simplifications apply.

But, the information $L_i = L_j$ can be used in order to simplify the constraint store. We can replace each occurrence of L_i by L_j and each occurrence of $\overline{L_i}$ by $\overline{L_j}$ without changing the solution space. After bringing the formulas in the

constraint store into pseudo-Boolean normal form subsequent simplifications may be possible.

Example 8.4.1 Consider the linear pseudo-Boolean inequality

$$5 \cdot X_1 + 4 \cdot X_2 + 3 \cdot X_3 + 2 \cdot X_4 \geq 6$$

and suppose that $X_1 = X_2$ holds. After applying the equation to the linear pseudo-Boolean inequality and normalization we obtain

$$6 \cdot X_2 + 3 \cdot X_3 + 2 \cdot X_4 \geq 6 \ ,$$

which dominates $X_2 \geq 1$, i.e., we can fix X_2, and thus X_1, to 1. Given only the extended clauses $X_1 + \overline{X_2} \geq 1$ and $\overline{X_1} + X_2 \geq 1$ the same deduction is possible, but more steps are needed.

Transformation of $5 \cdot X_1 + 4 \cdot X_2 + 3 \cdot X_3 + 2 \cdot X_4 \geq 6$ gives

$$\{X_1 + X_2 \geq 1, X_1 + X_2 + X_3 + X_4 \geq 2\} \ .$$

Resolving $X_1 + \overline{X_2} \geq 1$ and $X_1 + X_2 \geq 1$ then generates $X_1 \geq 1$ and fixing X_1 to 1 in $\overline{X_1} + X_2 \geq 1$ then fixes X_2 to 1.

The crucial point in Example 8.4.1 is that we have to transform completely a linear pseudo-Boolean inequality and that we have to search for simplifying resolvents. Since transforming a linear pseudo-Boolean inequality is a computationally hard task, and since it is not sure that any simplifications or fixings of literals will happen, the task may be delayed. On the other hand, the application of an equality between Boolean variables is always useful, since the problem dimension is reduced, and thus should be performed immediately.

8.4.1 Equation Detection

Since an equation between literals simplifies the current constraint store, we show how to detect some equations of the form

$$L_i = L_j \tag{8.63}$$

dominated by a set of extended clauses. Since detecting equations is NP-complete[3], we restrict ourselves to the case that each of the two extended

---

[3] A problem is unsatisfiable if $X = \overline{X}$ can be derived.

clauses

$$L_i + \overline{L_j} \geq 1 \qquad\qquad (8.64)$$
$$\overline{L_i} + L_j \geq 1 \qquad\qquad (8.65)$$

are dominated by an extended clause in a set of extended clauses S. We thus overcome the loss of naturally expressing equations in our solved form.

Since both (8.64) and (8.65) have weakness 1, we know by Lemma 8.1.2 that if there are extended clauses in S dominating (8.64) and (8.65), then they must also have weakness 1^4. Thus, it is sufficient to consider only the set of extended clauses, i.e., cliques (see Definition 7.7.5),

$$S' := \{L \geq |L| - 1 \mid L \geq |L| - 1 \in S\} \; .$$

Given a set of extended clauses S' containing only extended clauses with weakness 1, we show how to decide whether there are extended clauses (8.64) and (8.65), each of them dominated by one extended clause in S'.

An extended clause $L \geq |L| - 1$ dominates the classical clauses $L_i + L_j \geq 1$ for all $L_i, L_j \in L$ with $L_i \neq L_j$. Let us collect for all literals L_i the set of literals L_j such that $L_i + L_j \geq 1$. Suppose that these sets are stored in an array lits, indexed by the set of all literals whose variables occur in S'. Then we know that $L_i + \overline{L_j} \geq 1$ is dominated by an extended clause in S' if and only if $\overline{L_j} \in \text{lits}[L_i]$ and that $\overline{L_i} + L_j \geq 1$ is dominated by an extended clause in S' if and only if $L_j \in \text{lits}[\overline{L_i}]$. Thus, we can deduce $L_i = L_j$ if

$$L_j \in \text{lits}[\overline{L_i}] \cap \overline{\text{lits}[L_i]} \; . \qquad\qquad (8.66)$$

Note that if $L_i = L_j$, then also $L_j = L_i$ and thus we can deduce $L_i = L_j$ if

$$L_i \in \text{lits}[\overline{L_j}] \cap \overline{\text{lits}[L_j]} \; .$$

We can save space and computation time by just trying to detect equations $L_i = L_j$, where $L_i \lhd L_j$ and condition (8.66) holds. The ordering $\lhd$ for literals was defined on page 164. Note that if $X_i \lhd X_j$, then $L_k \lhd L_l$ for all $L_k \in \{X_i, \overline{X_i}\}$ and for all $L_l \in \{X_j, \overline{X_j}\}$. Therefore, it is sufficient to store only literals L_j in lits$[L_i]$ with $L_i \lhd L_j$. Since it is convenient to look for equations $L_i = \overline{L_j}$, which is obviously no restriction, condition (8.66) becomes

$$L_j \in \overline{\text{lits}[\overline{L_i}]} \cap \text{lits}[L_i] \; . \qquad\qquad (8.67)$$

---

^{4}Note that extended clauses with weakness 0 fix all their literals. Thus, they are already removed and the fixed literals are collected elsewhere.

Next, we present an incremental algorithm that updates the array lit given a new clique inequality $L \geq |L| - 1$ and returns all equations between literals that are deducible.

Algorithm 8.4.2 *Equation Detection*

$$eq\_detect(L \geq |L| - 1)$$
$$Eq := \emptyset$$
$$\textbf{forall } L_i, L_j \in L \wedge L_i \lhd L_j \textbf{ do}$$
$$\textbf{if } L_j \notin \text{lit}[L_i] \textbf{then}^*$$
$$\text{lit}[L_i] := \text{lit}[L_i] \cup \{L_j\}$$
$$\textbf{if } \overline{L_j} \in \text{lits}[\overline{L_i}] \textbf{ then}$$
$$Eq := Eq \cup \{L_i = \overline{L_j}\}$$
$$\textbf{endif}$$
$$\textbf{endif}$$
$$\textbf{endforall}$$
$$\textbf{return } Eq$$
$$\textbf{end } eq\_detect$$

Algorithm 8.4.2 should be called with $eq\_detect(L \geq |L| - 1)$ whenever a new clique $L \geq |L| - 1$ enters the constraint store. The returned equations are immediately applied, i.e., for each $L_i = \overline{L_j} \in eq\_detect(L \geq |L| - 1)$ we replace in all linear pseudo-Boolean inequalities and extended clauses in the constraint store the literals L_i by $\overline{L_j}$ and the literals $\overline{L_i}$ by L_j. After bringing the updated constraints into normal form other simplifications may arise.

Note that after detecting an equation $L_i = \overline{L_j}$ we can immediately update $\text{lits}[L_i]$ by adding $\text{lits}[\overline{L_j}]$ and update $\text{lits}[\overline{L_i}]$ by adding $\text{lits}[L_j]$ and thus even more equations may immediately be detected. Since the returned equations are applied to the original constraint store, we get new cliques and the remaining equations are detected in the next round. In order to speed up searching and save space all literals L_i and $\overline{L_i}$ in all $\text{lits}[L_j]$ with $L_j \lhd L_i$ should be deleted.

8.4.2 Fixing Literals

Since we already maintain the data structure lits, we can use it also for the detection of fixed literals. Suppose there are literals L_i and L_j such that L_j and $\overline{L_j}$ are in $\text{lits}[L_i]$. Therefore, the extended clauses $L_i + \overline{L_j} \geq 1$ and

$L_i + L_j \geq 1$ are dominated by the current constraint store. Since resolving on the two extended clauses gives $L_i \geq 1$, and thus fixes L_i to 1, we have a simple method for checking whether there are literals that can be fixed. Similarly, we can deduce from $L_j \in \text{lits}[L_i]$ and $L_j \in \text{lits}[\overline{L_i}]$ that L_j needs to be fixed to 1.

We can insert in Algorithm 8.4.2 the lines

> **if** $\overline{L_j} \in \text{lits}[L_i]$ **then** $Eq := Eq \cup \{L_i = 1\}$ **endif**
> **if** $L_j \in \text{lits}[\overline{L_i}]$ **then** $Eq := Eq \cup \{L_j = 1\}$ **endif**

after the **then*** and thus additionally collect equations of the form $L_i = 1$ whenever deducible. Equations of that form are handled by pseudo-Boolean unit resolution, introduced in Chapter 5.

LINEARIZATION

In order to handle non-linear pseudo-Boolean constraints with a constraint solver for linear pseudo-Boolean inequalities, we have to linearize the non-linear pseudo-Boolean constraints in advance. It is sufficient to consider only non-linear pseudo-Boolean inequalities in normal form like in Definition 3.1.8, since others can be brought into that form with (3.3). Thus, the problem is to compute a set of linear pseudo-Boolean inequalities equivalent to a non-linear pseudo-Boolean inequality in normal form. After a review of well-known linearization techniques, we present a linearization method that fits well into the context of constraint logic programming.

9.1 PREVIOUS WORK

The first linearization method for non-linear pseudo-Boolean constraints was introduced by Fortet [For59, For60] and Dantzig [Dan60]. Consider a non-linear pseudo-Boolean inequality in normal form

$$\sum_{I \in \Omega} c_I \prod_{i \in I} X_i \geq d \qquad (9.1)$$

like in Definition 3.1.8. The idea of Fortet and Dantzig is to replace each product term $\prod_{i \in I} X_i$ by a new Boolean variable X_I yielding

$$\sum_{I \in \Omega} c_I X_I \geq d \qquad (9.2)$$

and add the linear pseudo-Boolean inequalities

$$X_I + \sum_{i \in I} \overline{X_i} \geq 1 \tag{9.3}$$

$$|I| \cdot \overline{X_I} + \sum_{i \in I} X_i \geq |I| \tag{9.4}$$

for all $I \in \Omega$. Since (9.3) forces $X_I = 1$ if $X_i = 1$ for all $i \in I$, and (9.4) forces $X_I = 0$ if $X_i = 0$ for some $i \in I$, we know that the non-linear pseudo-Boolean inequality (9.1) is equivalent to the set of linear pseudo-Boolean inequalities

$$\{\sum_{I \in \Omega} c_I X_I \geq d\} \cup \{|I| \cdot \overline{X_I} + \sum_{i \in I} X_i \geq |I|, X_I + \sum_{i \in I} \overline{X_i} \geq 1 \mid \text{ for all } I \in \Omega\} \ . \tag{9.5}$$

Therefore, we have a simple method for replacing a non-linear pseudo-Boolean inequality by an equivalent set of linear pseudo-Boolean inequalities. Glover and Wolsey [GW73] modify the method in order to decrease the number of linear pseudo-Boolean inequalities in (9.5) while preserving equivalence.

The introduction of new Boolean variables is the main problem of the Fortet-Dantzig linearization, since the dimension of the problem is increased. As reported by Hansen et al. [HJM93] the Fortet-Dantzig linearization is adequate if there are only a few non-linear pseudo-Boolean terms. In the context of constraint logic programming the Fortet-Dantzig linearization is not suitable, since the new Boolean variables have to be eliminated at the end of computation.

Balas and Mazzola [BM84a] present linearization techniques based on the work of Granot and Hammer [GH75] that do not introduce new Boolean variables. Their basic idea is to generate sufficiently many cutting plane inequalities until equivalence is established [HJM93, BM84a, BM84b]. We develop a linearization method that takes into account the current constraint store in order to obtain immediately stronger linear pseudo-Boolean inequalities whenever possible.

9.2 A LINEARIZATION METHOD

We present a linearization method that fits well into the context of constraint logic programming, since the current constraint store can be used to influence the linearization process. Furthermore, the linearization method does not introduce new Boolean variables. The principal idea is to successively split a non-linear pseudo-Boolean inequality into two others that are in some sense

more linear. The process is repeated until only linear pseudo-Boolean inequalities remain. While splitting the non-linear pseudo-Boolean inequalities, we need to derive lower bounds for non-linear pseudo-Boolean terms. By taking into account the constraint store when deriving these bounds, we can derive stronger linear pseudo-Boolean inequalities. Furthermore, the method coincides nicely with the compact representation of linear pseudo-Boolean constraints presented in Section 7.4.

We do not require that the non-linear pseudo-Boolean inequality is in normal form, but we allow non-linear pseudo-Boolean inequalities of the form

$$\sum_{I \in \Omega} c_I \prod_{i \in I} L_i \geq d \ , \tag{9.6}$$

where for all $i, j \in I$ we have $\mathsf{Var}(L_i) \neq \mathsf{Var}(L_j)$ for all $I \in \Omega$. The main difference w.r.t. the normal form of Definition 3.1.8 is that we allow literals and not only variables in the product terms. First, we show how to split the left-hand side of (9.6) w.r.t. a variable X_j occurring in (9.6).

Lemma 9.2.1 *A non-linear pseudo-Boolean inequality* $\sum_{I \in \Omega} c_I \prod_{i \in I} L_i \geq d$ *containing a variable X_j is equivalent to the inequality*

$$X_j \cdot \left(\sum_{I \in \Omega : \forall i \in I : L_i \neq \overline{X_j}} c_I \prod_{i \in I : L_i \neq X_j} L_i \right) + \overline{X_j} \cdot \left(\sum_{I \in \Omega : \forall i \in I : L_i \neq X_j} c_I \prod_{i \in I : L_i \neq \overline{X_j}} L_i \right) \geq d \ . \tag{9.7}$$

Proof. The pseudo-Boolean term that is multiplied by X_j is the sum over all product terms of (9.6), where either X_j occurs or neither X_j nor $\overline{X_j}$ occurs. Similarly, the pseudo-Boolean term that is multiplied by $\overline{X_j}$ is the sum over all product terms of (9.6), where either $\overline{X_j}$ occurs or neither X_j nor $\overline{X_j}$ occurs. In both terms X_j and $\overline{X_j}$ is deleted. By multiplying X_j, resp. $\overline{X_j}$, into the corresponding pseudo-Boolean term we obtain all product terms of the left-hand side of (9.6), where X_j or $\overline{X_j}$ occurs, plus the pseudo-Boolean terms

$$X_j \cdot c_I \prod_{i \in I} L_i + \overline{X_j} \cdot c_I \prod_{i \in I} L_i \tag{9.8}$$

for all product terms of the left-hand side of (9.6) not containing X_j or $\overline{X_j}$. Since (9.8) is equivalent to $c_I \prod_{i \in I} L_i$, we have shown equivalence of (9.6) and (9.7). $\square$

Theorem 9.2.2 *A non-linear pseudo-Boolean inequality* $\sum_{I \in \Omega} c_I \prod_{i \in I} L_i \geq d$ *is equivalent to the two pseudo-Boolean inequalities*

$$(d - l_1) \cdot \overline{X_j} + \sum_{I \in \Omega : \forall i \in I : L_i \neq \overline{X_j}} c_I \prod_{i \in I : L_i \neq X_j} L_i \geq d \tag{9.9}$$

$$(d - l_2) \cdot X_j + \sum_{I \in \Omega : \forall i \in I : L_i \neq X_j} c_I \prod_{i \in I : L_i \neq \overline{X_j}} L_i \geq d , \tag{9.10}$$

where l_1 is a lower bound for

$$\sum_{I \in \Omega : \forall i \in I : L_i \neq \overline{X_j}} c_I \prod_{i \in I : L_i \neq X_j} L_i \quad \text{subject to} \quad \{(9.6), X_j = 0\}$$

and l_2 is a lower bound for

$$\sum_{I \in \Omega : \forall i \in I : L_i \neq X_j} c_I \prod_{i \in I : L_i \neq \overline{X_j}} L_i \quad \text{subject to} \quad \{(9.6), X_j = 1\} .$$

Proof. We abbreviate (9.7) by

$$X_j \cdot t_1 + \overline{X_j} \cdot t_2 \geq d .$$

Thus, inequality (9.9) is equivalent to $(d - l_1) \cdot \overline{X_j} + t_1 \geq d$ and (9.10) is equivalent to $(d - l_2) \cdot X_j + t_2 \geq d$, where l_1 is a lower bound for t_1 subject to $\{(9.6), X_j = 0\}$ and l_2 is a lower bound for t_2 subject to $\{(9.6), X_j = 1\}$. Note that if the constraint $\{(9.6), X_j = c\}$ is unsatisfiable for $c = 0$, resp. $c = 1$, then l_1, resp. l_2, is arbitrary. We show

$$\mathsf{Ext}(X_j \cdot t_1 + \overline{X_j} \cdot t_2 \geq d) = \mathsf{Ext}(\{(d - l_1) \cdot \overline{X_j} + t_1 \geq d, (d - l_2) \cdot X_j + t_2 \geq d\})$$

in order to prove the theorem.

$\subseteq$: Let α be in $\mathsf{Ext}(X_j \cdot t_1 + \overline{X_j} \cdot t_2 \geq d)$. First, suppose that $\alpha(X_j) = 1$. Then $\alpha(X_j \cdot t_1 + \overline{X_j} \cdot t_2 \geq d)$ simplifies to $\alpha(t_1) \geq d$. Since $\alpha((d - l_1) \cdot \overline{X_j} + t_1) = \alpha(t_1)$ and $\alpha(t_1) \geq d$, we have $\alpha \in \mathsf{Ext}((d - l_1) \cdot \overline{X_j} + t_1 \geq d)$. Furthermore, $\alpha((d - l_2) \cdot X_j + t_2) \geq d$ simplifies to $d - l_2 + \alpha(t_2) \geq d$ and after bringing the constants to the right hand side we have $\alpha(t_2) \geq l_2$. Since l_2 is a lower bound for t_2 for all $\alpha' \in \mathsf{Ext}(X_j \cdot t_1 + \overline{X_j} \cdot t_2 \geq d)$ with $\alpha'(X_j) = 1$, we know that $\alpha(t_2) \geq l_2$. Thus, $\alpha \in \mathsf{Ext}((d - l_2) \cdot X_j + t_2 \geq d)$. Similarly, for $\alpha(X_j) = 0$.

$\supseteq$: Let α be in $\mathsf{Ext}(\{(d - l_1) \cdot \overline{X_j} + t_1 \geq d, (d - l_2) \cdot X_j + t_2 \geq d\})$. First, suppose that $\alpha(X_j) = 1$. From $\alpha((d - l_1) \cdot \overline{X_j} + t_1) \geq d$ we derive $\alpha(t_1) \geq d$ and thus $\alpha(X_j \cdot t_1 + \overline{X_j} \cdot t_2) \geq d$, because $\alpha(\overline{X_j} \cdot t_2) = 0$. Therefore, $\alpha \in \mathsf{Ext}(X_j \cdot t_1 + \overline{X_j} \cdot t_2 \geq d)$. Similarly, for $\alpha(X_j) = 0$. $\qquad\square$

Theorem 9.2.2 enables us to split a non-linear pseudo-Boolean inequality into two others. In order to give a complete linearization algorithm, we define a measure of non-linearity of non-linear pseudo-Boolean inequalities.

Definition 9.2.3 A Boolean variable X_j has a *non-linear* occurrence in a non-linear pseudo-Boolean inequality $\sum_{I \in \Omega} c_I \prod_{i \in I} L_i \geq d$ if there is an $I \in \Omega$ such that $|I| \geq 2$ and there exists an $i \in I$ such that $\mathsf{Var}(L_i) = X_j$. A Boolean variable has a *linear* occurrence in a non-linear pseudo-Boolean inequality if it occurs in the inequality, but has no non-linear occurrence. We call $\sum_{I \in \Omega} \max(0, |I| - 1)$ the *non-linearity* of a non-linear pseudo-Boolean inequality $\sum_{I \in \Omega} c_I \prod_{i \in I} L_i \geq d$.

Since t_1 and t_2 of Theorem 9.2.2 do not contain the variable X_j, the occurrence of the variable X_j in the pseudo-Boolean inequalities (9.9) and (9.10) is linear. If we have split on a variable X_j having a non-linear occurrence in (9.6), then the resulting two pseudo-Boolean inequalities (9.9) and (9.10) are *more linear* than (9.6), since the non-linearity of (9.9) and (9.10) is smaller than the non-linearity of (9.6). Note that linear product terms, i.e., product terms containing at most one literal, do not count for the non-linearity. Furthermore, for each non-linear occurrence of X_j in a product term, the number of literals in this product term is decreased. If there are no non-linear occurrences of Boolean variables, then the pseudo-Boolean inequality is linear. We obtain the following linearization algorithm transforming a non-linear pseudo-Boolean inequality into an equivalent set of linear pseudo-Boolean inequalities.

Algorithm 9.2.4 *Linearization of non-linear pseudo-Boolean inequalities*

```
linearize(t ≥ d)
    if ∃Xⱼ having a non-linear occurrence in t ≥ d then
            reformulate t ≥ d to Xⱼ · t₁ + X̄ⱼ · t₂ ≥ d (* Lemma 9.2.1 *)
            l₁ := nlpbt_lower_bound(t₁, t ≥ d, {X̄ⱼ})
            l₂ := nlpbt_lower_bound(t₂, t ≥ d, {Xⱼ})
            return (linearize((d − l₁) · X̄ⱼ + t₁ ≥ d)∪
                    linearize((d − l₂) · Xⱼ + t₂ ≥ d))
    else
            return {t ≥ d}
    endif
end linearize
```

We assume the existence of a function $\mathsf{nlpbt\_lower\_bound}(t', t \geq d, F)$ that computes a lower bound for a non-linear pseudo-Boolean term t' subject to the

set of pseudo-Boolean constraints $\{t \geq d, F \geq |F|\}$, where F is a set of literals to be fixed. A naive implementation of nlpbt_lower_bound just computes the sum of all negative coefficients of t'. Better lower bounds, and thus stronger linear pseudo-Boolean inequalities, are obtained by taking into account the constraints $t \geq d$ and $F \geq |F|$.

Example 9.2.5 Let

$$A \cdot B + A \cdot C + B \cdot C \geq 1 \qquad\qquad (9.11)$$

be the non-linear pseudo-Boolean inequality that is to be linearized. First, we split on A and obtain

$$A \cdot (B + C + B \cdot C) + \overline{A} \cdot (B \cdot C) \geq 1 \ .$$

A naive lower bound for both terms is 0. Thus, by Theorem 9.2.2, we obtain the set of pseudo-Boolean inequalities

$$\{\overline{A} + B + C + B \cdot C \geq 1, A + B \cdot C \geq 1\} \ ,$$

which is equivalent to $A \cdot B + A \cdot C + B \cdot C \geq 1$. Next, we split the first non-linear pseudo-Boolean inequality on B and obtain

$$B \cdot (\overline{A} + 1 + 2 \cdot C) + \overline{B} \cdot (\overline{A} + C) \geq 1$$

With the lower bound 1 for the first and 0 for the second term we get

$$\{(1 - 1) \cdot \overline{B} + \overline{A} + 1 + 2 \cdot C \geq 1, B + \overline{A} + C \geq 1\} \ ,$$

which is equivalent to $\overline{A} + B + C + B \cdot C \geq 1$. Note that the first inequality is $\top$ and can be eliminated. It remains to linearize $A + B \cdot C \geq 1$. We split on B and obtain

$$B \cdot (A + C) + \overline{B} \cdot A \geq 1 \ .$$

According to Theorem 9.2.2 we derive with the lower bound 0 the set of pseudo-Boolean inequalities

$$\{\overline{B} + A + C \geq 1, B + A \geq 1\} \ ,$$

which is equivalent to $A + B \cdot C \geq 1$. There are no more pseudo-Boolean inequalities that need to be linearized. Therefore,

$$\{\overline{A} + B + C \geq 1, A + \overline{B} + C \geq 1, A + B \geq 1\}$$

is equivalent to $A \cdot B + A \cdot C + B \cdot C \geq 1$.

Let us again linearize (9.11), but take into account the constraints while calculating the lower bounds. We again split $A \cdot B + A \cdot C + B \cdot C \geq 1$ on A and obtain

$$A \cdot (B + C + B \cdot C) + \overline{A} \cdot (B \cdot C) \geq 1 \ .$$

While calculating a lower bound for $B + C + B \cdot C$ we have the additional constraint

$$\{A \cdot B + A \cdot C + B \cdot C \geq 1, A = 0\} \ ,$$

which simplifies to $B \cdot C \geq 1$ and thus $B = C = 1$. Therefore, a lower bound for $B + C + B \cdot C$ is 3. Likewise, we calculate the lower bound 0 for $B \cdot C$ subject to $\{A \cdot B + A \cdot C + B \cdot C \geq 1, A = 1\}$, which simplifies to $B + C + B \cdot C \geq 1$. We obtain the set of pseudo-Boolean inequalities

$$\{2 \cdot A + B + C + B \cdot C \geq 3, A + B \cdot C \geq 1\} \ ,$$

which is equivalent to $A \cdot B + A \cdot C + B \cdot C \geq 1$. Next, we linearize $2 \cdot A + B + C + B \cdot C \geq 3$. We split on B and obtain

$$B \cdot (2 \cdot A + 1 + 2 \cdot C) + \overline{B} \cdot (2 \cdot A + C) \geq 3 \ .$$

We get the lower bound 5 for $2 \cdot A + 1 + 2 \cdot C$ subject to $2 \cdot A + C \geq 3$ and the lower bound 0 for $2 \cdot A + C$ subject to $2 \cdot B \geq 0$. According to Theorem 9.2.2 we know that

$$\{2 \cdot B + 2 \cdot A + 2 \cdot C \geq 4, 3 \cdot B + 2 \cdot A + C \geq 3\}$$

is equivalent to $2 \cdot A + B + C + B \cdot C \geq 3$. If we transform $2 \cdot B + 2 \cdot A + 2 \cdot C \geq 4$ with the method described in Chapter 7, we obtain the single extended clause $A + B + C \geq 2$. Transforming all other linear pseudo-Boolean inequalities obtained by the linearization process yields only extended clauses that are dominated by $A + B + C \geq 2$. Thus, the non-linear pseudo-Boolean inequality

$$A \cdot B + A \cdot C + B \cdot C \geq 1$$

is equivalent to the single extended clause

$$A + B + C \geq 2 \ .$$

9.3 DERIVING LOWER BOUNDS

Example 9.2.5 indicates that calculating good lower bounds is worthwhile. In principle we can calculate the best lower bound for t' subject to $t \geq d$ by solving the non-linear pseudo-Boolean optimization problem

$$\min t' \quad \text{subject to} \quad t \geq d \ . \tag{9.12}$$

Since this is computationally too expensive, we approximate the best possible lower bound as follows. First, we fix all literals that can be fixed. Afterwards, we check whether a product term has to evaluate to 1, i.e., if further fixings are implied. This process is repeated until no more obvious fixings apply. A lower bound is then obtained by summing up all remaining negative coefficients. Fixing literals in a non-linear pseudo-Boolean term is done by nl_fixing defined as:

$$\texttt{nl\_fixing}(\sum_{I \in \Omega} c_I \prod_{i \in I} L_i \geq d, F) := \sum_{I' \in \Omega'} c_{I'} \prod_{i \in I'} L_i \geq d \quad \text{where}$$
$$\Omega' = \{I' \mid I \in \Omega \wedge \forall i \in I : \overline{L_i} \notin F \wedge I' = I \setminus F\}$$

(9.13)

If any simplifications are possible, like bringing constants on the right-hand side and grouping identical product terms, these are performed by bringing the non-linear pseudo-Boolean inequality into normal form. We relax the detection of fixed literals by viewing each product term as a single Boolean variable. Thus, the task becomes computationally manageable and is similar to fixed in (5.7).

$$\texttt{nl\_fixed}(\sum_{I \in \Omega} c_I \prod_{i \in I} L_i \geq d) := \begin{cases} \{L_j \mid \forall j \in J\} & \text{if } \sum_{I \in \Omega' \setminus \{J\}} c_I - c_J < d \\ & \text{where} \\ & \Omega' = \{I \mid I \in \Omega \wedge c_I \geq 0\}, \\ & J \in \Omega, \text{and} \\ & c_J \geq c_I \text{ for all } I \in \Omega \\ \bot & \text{otherwise} \end{cases}$$

(9.14)

Note that we can only consider positive coefficients. Hence, some obvious fixings may not be detected. We can overcome that problem by reformulating the non-linear pseudo-Boolean inequality such that only positive coefficients occur with help of the following equation.

$$c_I \cdot \prod_{i \in I} L_i = c_I \cdot \prod_{i \in I \setminus \{j\}} L_i + (-c_I) \cdot \overline{L_j} \cdot \prod_{i \in I \setminus \{j\}} L_i \quad \text{where } j \in I \qquad (9.15)$$

Let c_I be negative and let us apply (9.15) recursively to the product term $c_I \cdot \prod_{i \in I \setminus \{j\}} L_i$. Since this product term contains only $|I| - 1$ literals, we end up with the negative constant c_I, which can be brought to the right-hand side, and a sum of product terms having the positive coefficient $-c_I$. Note that a product $c_I \cdot \prod_{i \in I} L_i$ with $c_I < 0$ expands to at most $|I|$ products with positive coefficients. Therefore, we have a method for reformulating a non-linear pseudo-Boolean inequality such that only positive coefficients occur and more fixings of literals will be detected in nl_fixed. Next, we give a possible implementation of nlpbt_lower_bound, which computes a lower bound for a non-linear pseudo-Boolean term t by first doing all possible fixings and then computing a naive lower bound.

Algorithm 9.3.1 *Lower bound for a non-linear pseudo-Boolean term*

```
nlpbt_lower_bound(t', t ≥ d, F)
        while F ≠⊥
            t ≥ d := nl_fixing(t ≥ d, F)
            t' := nlpbt_fixing(t', F)
            F := nl_fixed(t ≥ d)
        endwhile
        return naive_lower_bound(t', t ≥ d)
end nlpbt_lower_bound
```

We assume the existence of a function `nlpbt_fixing`, which is similar to `nl_fixing`, but fixes the literals in a pseudo-Boolean term only and collects the constants separately.

$$\texttt{nlpbt\_fixing}(\sum_{I\in\Omega} c_I \prod_{i\in I} L_i, F) := \sum_{I'\in\Omega'} c_{I'} \prod_{i\in I'} L_i \quad \text{where} \tag{9.16}$$
$$\Omega' = \{I' \mid I \in \Omega \wedge \forall i \in I : \overline{L_i} \notin F \wedge I' = I \setminus F\}$$

We also assume the existence of a function `naive_lower_bound` that returns a lower bound for a non-linear pseudo-Boolean term t'. A simple implementation of `naive_lower_bound` calculates the sum of all negative coefficients of t' plus the constant terms of t'.

Example 9.3.2 Consider again Example 9.2.5 and let us calculate a lower bound for $B + C + B \cdot C$ subject to $\{A \cdot B + A \cdot C + B \cdot C \geq 1, A = 0\}$ with `nlpbt_lower_bound`. We call

$$\texttt{nlpbt\_lower\_bound}(B + C + B \cdot C, A \cdot B + A \cdot C + B \cdot C \geq 1, \{\overline{A}\})$$

and get in the first iteration of the **while**-loop

$$\begin{aligned} t \geq d &= B \cdot C \geq 1, \\ t' &= B + C + B \cdot C, \\ F &= \{B, C\} \ . \end{aligned}$$

Since $F \neq \perp$, we continue and get in the second iteration of the **while**-loop

$$\begin{aligned} t \geq d &= \top, \\ t' &= 3, \\ F &= \perp \ . \end{aligned}$$

Thus, we return the naive lower bound 3. The presented `nlpbt_lower_bound` calculates the same lower bounds as in Example 9.2.5.

Next, we improve `naive_lower_bound` based on the observation that the non-linear pseudo-Boolean optimization problem (9.12) has a special form. Typically, many product terms that occur in t' also occur in t.

Example 9.3.3 Let

$$5 \cdot L_1 + 4 \cdot L_2 + 3 \cdot L_3 \cdot \overline{L_5} + 2 \cdot L_4 + L_5 \cdot L_6 \geq 6$$

be the non-linear pseudo-Boolean inequality to be linearized. We split on L_5 and obtain an optimal lower bound for $t' = 5 \cdot L_1 + 4 \cdot L_2 + 2 \cdot L_4 + L_6$ by solving the non-linear pseudo-Boolean optimization problem

$$\min 5 \cdot L_1 + 4 \cdot L_2 + 2 \cdot L_4 + L_6 \quad \text{subject to} \quad 5 \cdot L_1 + 4 \cdot L_2 + 3 \cdot L_3 + 2 \cdot L_4 \geq 6 \ .$$

We eliminate the product terms in the constraint that do not occur in the objective function, which yields the valid non-linear pseudo-Boolean inequality

$$5 \cdot L_1 + 4 \cdot L_2 + 2 \cdot L_4 \geq 3 \ ,$$

whose left-hand side is a subterm of the objective function. Thus, we can derive the lower bound 3 and get the linear pseudo-Boolean inequality

$$3 \cdot \overline{L_5} + 5 \cdot L_1 + 4 \cdot L_2 + 2 \cdot L_4 + L_6 \geq 6 \ .$$

Just summing up the constant and all negative coefficients gives the lower bound 0. Hence, with `naive_lower_bound` only the weaker linear pseudo-Boolean inequality

$$6 \cdot \overline{L_5} + 5 \cdot L_1 + 4 \cdot L_2 + 2 \cdot L_4 + L_6 \geq 6$$

can be constructed.

Many product terms are shared between the objective function and the left-hand side of the constraint, since the objective function is obtained by selecting all product terms not containing the negation of a specific literal L, whereas the left-hand side of the constraint is obtained by fixing L to 0. By taking into account these shared products terms, we obtain a valid lower bound for a pseudo-Boolean term

$$\sum_{I \in \Omega_1} c_I \prod_{i \in I} L_i + \sum_{I \in \Omega_2} c_I \prod_{i \in I} L_i + \sum_{I \in \Omega_3} c_I \prod_{i \in I} L_i$$

w.r.t.

$$\sum_{I \in \Omega_1} c_I \prod_{i \in I} L_i + \sum_{I \in \Omega_4} c_I \prod_{i \in I} L_i + \sum_{I \in \Omega_5} c_I \prod_{i \in I} L_i \geq d \ ,$$

where $c_I > 0$ for all $I \in \Omega_2 \cup \Omega_4$ and $c_I < 0$ for all $I \in \Omega_3 \cup \Omega_5$, is

$$d - \sum_{I \in \Omega_4} c_I + \sum_{I \in \Omega_3} c_I . \tag{9.17}$$

Note that Ω_1 represent all product terms that occur in both the objective function and the constraint. The set Ω_2, resp. Ω_3, represents the product term with positive coefficients, resp. negative coefficients in the objective function that do not occur in the constraint. Vice versa for the Ω_4 and Ω_5. Since the objective function and the left-hand side of the constraint typically share many product terms, we know that Ω_4 and Ω_3 are small and we may obtain a good lower bound. Thus, we propose to replace `naive_lower_bound` by `improved_lower_bound`, where we view a sum of product terms as a set of product terms.

Algorithm 9.3.4 *Improved Lower Bound*

```
improved_lower_bound(t', t ≥ d)
```
$$O_4 := \{c_I \mid c_I > 0 \wedge c_I \prod_{i \in I} L_i \in (t \setminus t')\}$$
$$O_3 := \{c_I \mid c_I < 0 \wedge c_I \prod_{i \in I} L_i \in (t' \setminus t)\}$$
(* equation (9.17) *)
$$NLB_1 := d - \sum_{c_I \in O_4} c_I + \sum_{I \in O_3} c_I$$
(* sum of constants and negative coefficients *)
$$NLB_2 := \sum_{I : c_I \prod_{i \in I} L_i \in t' \wedge (c_I < 0 \vee I = \emptyset)} c_I$$
```
    return max(NLB₁, NLB₂)
end improved_lower_bound
```

Example 9.3.5 Let

$$5 \cdot A + 4 \cdot B + 3 \cdot C + 2 \cdot D + E \cdot F \geq 10$$

be the non-linear pseudo-Boolean inequality to be linearized. Using the improved lower bounds of Algorithm 9.3.4 we get the set of linear pseudo-Boolean inequalities

$$\{5 \cdot A + 4 \cdot B + 3 \cdot C + 2 \cdot D + E \geq 10,$$
$$5 \cdot A + 4 \cdot B + 3 \cdot C + 2 \cdot D + F \geq 10\} .$$

Just summing up the constants and the negative coefficients yields the weaker linear pseudo-Boolean inequalities

$$\{10 \cdot \overline{E} + 5 \cdot A + 4 \cdot B + 3 \cdot C + 2 \cdot D + F \geq 10,$$
$$10 \cdot E + 5 \cdot A + 4 \cdot B + 3 \cdot C + 2 \cdot D \geq 10\} .$$

So, the better the lower bound, the stronger the linear pseudo-Boolean inequalities that result. By taking into account the constraint store when calculating the lower bounds, we perform *constrained linearization*, which is suitable in the context of constraint logic programming. For example, the set of fixed literals calculated in Algorithm 9.3.1 can be temporarily fixed in the current constraint store. Fixings that result from this operation then can be propagated into nlpbt_lower_bound, i.e., further literals can be fixed. Thus, stronger lower bounds w.r.t. the current constraint store result and stronger linear pseudo-Boolean inequalities are generated while equivalence w.r.t. the current constraint is still preserved.

The presented linearization algorithm compares well with the linearization method of Balas and Mazzola [BM84a, BM84b] on the examples found in their paper. They reformulate the non-linear pseudo-Boolean inequality (Example 6 [BM84a])

$$10 \cdot X_1 \cdot X_9 + 9 \cdot X_2 \cdot X_8 + 8 \cdot X_3 \cdot X_7 + 8 \cdot X_1 \cdot X_6 + 8 \cdot X_3 \cdot X_4 + 5 \cdot X_2 \cdot X_5 \leq 20$$

into an equivalent set of 20 cover inequalities. With our approach, not including improvements, we generate 4 linear pseudo-Boolean inequalities, that, when transformed, are equivalent to 25 extended clauses. They reformulate the non-linear pseudo-Boolean inequality (Example 3 [BM84b])

$$6 \cdot X_1 \cdot X_2 \cdot X_3 \cdot X_4 + 4 \cdot X_1 \cdot X_5 - 3 \cdot X_3 \cdot X_4 \cdot X_6 + 2 \cdot X_1 \cdot X_2 \cdot X_4 \cdot X_7 + 2 \cdot X_3 \cdot X_4 \cdot X_8 \leq 7$$

with an improved method into the single equivalent linear pseudo-Boolean inequality

$$7 \cdot \overline{X_1} + 7 \cdot \overline{X_2} + 7 \cdot \overline{X_3} + 7 \cdot \overline{X_4} + 4 \cdot \overline{X_5} + 3 \cdot \overline{X_6} + 2 \cdot \overline{X_7} + 2 \cdot \overline{X_8} \geq 7 \ .$$

Our method computes the same inequality.

9.4   FURTHER IMPROVEMENTS

The variable X_j on which to split in Theorem 9.2.2 is important for the efficiency of the presented algorithm. We propose to split on the variable having the largest number of non-linear occurrences, since then the sum of the non-linearity of the resulting two pseudo-Boolean inequalities is minimal.

The worst case occurs if each Boolean variable has exactly one occurrence in the non-linear pseudo-Boolean inequality to linearize. Then each Boolean

variable, except one in each product term, has to be eliminated. Exactly for this case, we know of a better representation; the compact representation of linear pseudo-Boolean inequalities introduced in Section 7.4. Since we may have negative coefficients in a non-linear pseudo-Boolean inequality, we need to drop the condition of Definition 7.4.1 that the coefficients are all positive and ordered. Alternatively, we can reformulate a product term with a negative coefficient into one having only positive coefficients with help of (9.15).

Proposition 9.4.1 *Let the non-linear pseudo-Boolean inequality*

$$\sum_{I \in \Omega} c_I \prod_{i \in I} L_i \geq d \qquad (9.18)$$

contain each Boolean variable only once, i.e., for all $i, j \in I$ we have $\mathrm{Var}(L_i) \neq \mathrm{Var}(L_j)$ for all $I \in \Omega$. W.l.o.g. assume that $c_I \geq 1$ for all $I \in \Omega$. Then (9.18) is equivalent to the compact pseudo-Boolean inequality set

$$\sum_{I \in \Omega} c_I \{ L_i \mid i \in I \}^1 \geq d \ . \qquad (9.19)$$

Proof. We show that the extension of (9.18) is the same as the extension of (9.19).

"$\subseteq$:" Let α be in the extension of (9.18). Let Ω_1 be those $I \in \Omega$ for which $\alpha(\prod_{i \in I} L_i) = 1$ and let Ω_2 be $\Omega \backslash \Omega_1$. Then $\sum_{I \in \Omega_1} c_I \geq d$ and for all $I \in \Omega_1$ we have $\alpha(L_i) = 1$ for all $i \in I$. Each linear pseudo-Boolean inequality in the expansion of (9.19) is of the form $\sum_{I \in \Omega_1} c_I L_{I_i} + \sum_{I \in \Omega_2} c_I L_{I_i} \geq d$ with $I_i \in I$ for all $I \in \Omega$. Since for all $I \in \Omega_1$ we have $\alpha(L_{I_i}) = 1$ for all $I_i \in I$, we know that $\alpha(\sum_{I \in \Omega_1} c_I L_{I_i}) = \sum_{I \in \Omega_1} c_I \geq d$, and thus $\alpha(\sum_{I \in \Omega_1} c_I L_{I_i} + \sum_{I \in \Omega_2} c_I L_{I_i}) \geq d$. Therefore, α is in the extension of each linear pseudo-Boolean inequality in the expansion of (9.19) and thus in the extension of (9.19).

"$\supseteq$:" We show that if α is not in the extension of (9.18), then α is not in the extension of (9.19). Let α be not in the extension of (9.18). Let Ω_1 be those $I \in \Omega$ for which $\alpha(\prod_{i \in I} L_i) = 0$ and let Ω_2 be $\Omega \setminus \Omega_1$. Then $\sum_{I \in \Omega_2} c_I < d$ and for each $I \in \Omega_1$ there is a literal $L_{I_i}, I_i \in I$, such that $\alpha(L_{I_i}) = 0$. Let us consider the linear pseudo-Boolean inequality in the expansion of (9.19), where we have selected exactly that literal L_{I_i} for each $I \in \Omega_1$ and an arbitrary literal for each $I \in \Omega_2$. Since then $\alpha(\sum_{I \in \Omega_1} c_I L_{I_i} + \sum_{I \in \Omega_2} c_I L_{I_i}) = \alpha(\sum_{I \in \Omega_2} c_I L_{I_i}) < d$, because $\alpha(\sum_{I \in \Omega_1} c_I L_{I_i}) = 0$, we know that α is not in the extension of that

linear pseudo-Boolean inequality in the expansion of (9.19), and thus not in the extension of (9.19).   □

We can use Proposition 9.4.1 in order to enhance our linearization method. We propose to split only on a Boolean variable if it has at least two occurrences and at least one of them is non-linear. If there is no such Boolean variable, we can linearize the non-linear pseudo-Boolean inequality directly by expanding the compact pseudo-Boolean inequality set that is equivalent to the non-linear pseudo-Boolean inequality as shown in Proposition 9.4.1.

Given a pseudo-Boolean constraint solver working directly with the compact set representation of pseudo-Boolean constraints, we can stop the linearization process if there is no Boolean variable having at least two occurrences, where at least one of them is non-linear. Instead of linearizing, we add the corresponding compact pseudo-Boolean inequality set of Proposition 9.4.1 directly to the constraint store.

10

PROJECTION

At the end of computation of a CLP($\mathcal{PB}$)-program we have to reformulate the set of collected constraints such that only Boolean variables that appear in the top-level goal remain. The so computed constraint set is the answer constraint of the top-level goal.

Let S be the set of pseudo-Boolean constraints collected at the end of a computation and let V' be the set of Boolean variables occurring in the corresponding top-level goal. We search a set of pseudo-Boolean constraints S' containing only variables in V' such that $\text{Ext}(S')$ equals $\text{Ext}(S)$ restricted to the variables in V' according to the following definition.

Definition 10.0.1 Let S be a set of pseudo-Boolean constraints and let V' be a set of Boolean variables. A *projection* $S|_{V'}$ of S on V' is a set of pseudo-Boolean constraints containing only variables in V' such that

[a] for all $\alpha \in \text{Ext}(S)$ there exists an $\alpha' \in \text{Ext}(S|_{V'})$ with $\alpha(X_i) = \alpha'(X_i)$ for all $X_i \in V'$ and

[b] for all $\alpha' \in \text{Ext}(S|_{V'})$ there exists an $\alpha \in \text{Ext}(S)$ with $\alpha(X_i) = \alpha'(X_i)$ for all $X_i \in V'$.

The first condition of Definition 10.0.1 assures that we do not miss any satisfying solution, whereas the latter assures that all solutions of the reformulated set of pseudo-Boolean constraints are correct. Let V be the set of Boolean variables occurring in S. Then projecting S on V' can also be seen as a *variable elimination* problem. We say we have eliminated the Boolean variables $V \setminus V'$ in the projection $S|_{V'}$ of S.

10.1 PROJECTION FOR PRIME EXTENDED CLAUSES

Projecting a set of prime extended clauses on a set of variables is easy. It suffices to eliminate all variables that need to be projected away for each prime extended clause separately, but that just means to compute strict reductions.

Proposition 10.1.1 *Let S be the set of all prime extended clauses of a set of pseudo-Boolean constraints and V' be a set of Boolean variables. Let*

$$S' := \{L \setminus L' \geq d - |L'| \mid L \geq d \in S \wedge L' = L \cap (V' \cup \overline{V'})\} \tag{10.1}$$

be the set of all strict reductions of the extended clauses in S, where all literals whose variables are not in V' are eliminated. Then S' is a projection of S on V'.

Proof. We need to show Definition 10.0.1 [a] and [b].

[a] Since an extended clause dominates all its reductions, we know that each extended clause in S' is dominated by an extended clause in S and thus S dominates S'. Therefore, $\mathsf{Ext}(S) \subseteq \mathsf{Ext}(S')$ and Definition 10.0.1 [a] is fulfilled.

[b] Suppose that Definition 10.0.1 [b] does not hold. Then there exists an $\alpha' \in \mathsf{Ext}(S')$ such that for all $\alpha \in \mathsf{Ext}(S)$ there is an $X_i \in V'$ with $\alpha(X_i) \neq \alpha'(X_i)$. Therefore, α' is not in the extension of S. Let $L = \{L_i \mid \alpha'(L_i) = 1 \wedge \mathsf{Var}(L_i) \in V'\}$ be the set of literals containing the variables in V' that are mapped to 1 by α'. Since α' is not in the extension of S, we know that fixing the literals in L to 1 in the problem S yields an unsatisfiable set of extended clauses, i.e., $S \cup \{L \geq |L|\}$ is unsatisfiable. Thus, S dominates $L < |L|$ and therefore S dominates $\overline{L} \geq 1$. Since S is a complete set of prime extended clauses, we know that there is an extended clause $L' \geq d' \in S$ that dominates $\overline{L} \geq 1$. Let $L'' \geq d'' \in S'$ be the strict reduction of $L' \geq d'$ obtained by eliminating all literals in $V \cup \overline{V}$. Since none of the literals that are eliminated occur in $\overline{L} \geq 1$, we know that $L'' \geq d''$ dominates $\overline{L} \geq 1$. Since $\alpha'(\overline{L}) = 0$, we have $\alpha' \notin \mathsf{Ext}(\overline{L} \geq 1)$. Thus, $\alpha' \notin \mathsf{Ext}(L'' \geq d'')$ and therefore $\alpha' \notin \mathsf{Ext}(S')$, which is a contradiction.   □

With Proposition 10.1.1 the projection on a set of variables for a complete set of prime extended clauses of a set of pseudo-Boolean constraints is computationally no problem. Furthermore, the projection by Proposition 10.1.1 of a

set of all prime extended clauses of a set of pseudo-Boolean constraints is the set of all prime extended clauses of the projection of the set of pseudo-Boolean constraints. Hence, we immediately obtain the solved form.

Proposition 10.1.2 *Let S be the set of all prime extended clauses of a set of pseudo-Boolean constraints T and V' be a set of Boolean variables. Let S' be defined by (10.1), then S' is the set of all prime extended clauses of $T|_{V'}$.*

Proof. By Proposition 10.1.1 we know that S' is equivalent to $S|_{V'}$ and thus to $T|_{V'}$. It remains to show that S' consists of all prime extended clauses of $S|_{V'}$. Let $L' \geq d'$ be an extended clause that is dominated by S'. Since S dominates S' and S is the set of all prime extended clauses, we know that there is an extended clause $L \geq d$ in S that dominates $L' \geq d'$. The reduction of $L \geq d$, where we have eliminated all literals in $V' \cup \overline{V'}$, also dominates $L \geq d$, since only literals not occurring in $L' \geq d'$ are eliminated. Since that reduction is in S' by construction, we know that there is a single extended clause in S' that dominates $L' \geq d'$. Since $L' \geq d'$ is arbitrary, we know that any extended clause dominated by S' is dominated by a single extended clause in S'. Thus, S' consists of all prime extended clauses of $S|_{V'}$. □

Given the complete solved form, we see that projection can easily be done. Typically, we do not have the complete solved form, i.e., the set of all prime extended clauses of the set of pseudo-Boolean constraints collected so far. Hence, we need to project arbitrary sets of pseudo-Boolean constraints on a set of Boolean variables. We assume that we have reformulated the set of pseudo-Boolean constraints into an equivalent set of extended clauses. Thus, it suffices to consider the projection of a set of extended clauses onto a set of Boolean variables.

10.2 PROJECTION FOR EXTENDED CLAUSES

Projecting an arbitrary set of extended clauses on a set of Boolean variables is NP-complete[1] and practically a hard problem. We have to build all possible resolvents on the Boolean variables that are to be eliminated. We develop a projection algorithm that is similar to the Fourier-Motzkin variable elimination algorithm for linear constraints over the real numbers.

---

[1] By eliminating all variables we can decide satisfiability of a set of extended clauses.

Let S be a set of extended clauses and let X be a Boolean variable that needs
to be eliminated. The problem is to find a projection $S|_{V \setminus \{X\}}$ of S, where V
is the set of all Boolean variables that occur in S. Let

$$
\mathbf{res}(S, X) := \left\{ L \geq d \; \middle| \; \begin{array}{l} L \geq d \in \mathsf{SCP}(\mathsf{SRed}(L' + L'' \geq d' + d'')), \\ L' \geq d' \in S, L'' \geq d'' \in S, \\ X \in L' \text{ and } \overline{X} \in L'' \end{array} \right\} \; , \quad (10.2)
$$

then for each possible resolvent on X for any two extended clauses in S,
$\mathbf{res}(S, X)$ contains an extended clause that dominates the resolvent by Proposition 7.8.2. Furthermore, all extended clauses in $\mathbf{res}(S, X)$ do neither contain
X nor $\overline{X}$.

We show that the set of reductions as defined in Proposition 10.1.1 together
with $\mathbf{res}(S, X)$ are a projection of S on $V \setminus \{X\}$. For this purpose we need two
lemmas for reasoning on classical clauses.

Lemma 10.2.1 *Let S be a set of extended clauses. We define the set of
classical clauses*

$$
SC := \{L' \geq 1 \mid L \geq d \in S \wedge L' \subseteq L \wedge |L'| = |L| - d + 1\} \; .
$$

*Then $\mathsf{Ext}(S) = \mathsf{Ext}(SC)$ and for each classical clause $L' \geq 1$ that is dominated
by S, classical resolution on SC can generate a classical clause that dominates
$L' \geq 1$.*

Proof. Since SC consists only of reductions of extended clauses in S, we know
that S dominates SC. On the other hand, each extended clause of S can
be generated by the diagonal sum rule from the classical clauses in SC by
construction. Thus, SC dominates S and therefore $\mathsf{Ext}(S) = \mathsf{Ext}(SC)$.

Let $L \geq 1$ be a classical clause that is dominated by S, then SC dominates
$L \geq 1$. Since resolution is complete on classical clauses, i.e., can generate
all prime implicates of a set of classical clauses [Qui52, Qui55], we know that
resolution can generate a classical clause dominating $L \geq 1$.   □

Lemma 10.2.2 *Let SC be a set of classical clauses. Let $L \geq 1$ be a classical
clause dominated by SC and let X be a Boolean variable such that neither X
nor $\overline{X}$ occurs in L. Then $SC' \cup \mathbf{res}(SC, X)$ dominates $L \geq 1$ with $SC' :=
\{L' \geq 1 \mid L' \geq 1 \in SC$ and $X, \overline{X} \notin L'\}$.*

Proof. We rely on Tison's method [Tis67] for generating prime implicates of a set of classical clauses[2]. Let V be the set of all variables occurring in the set of classical clauses SC. All prime implicates of SC are generated by the following algorithm due to Tison [Tis67].

$$PI := SC$$
$$\textbf{forall} \quad X \in V \quad \textbf{do} \quad PI := PI \cup \textbf{res}(PI, X) \quad \textbf{endforall}$$

At the end of computation PI is the set of all prime implicates of SC. In the above algorithm PI is always kept in normal form, i.e., PI does not contain classical clauses that are dominated by another classical clause in PI. The correctness proof of Tison's method can be found in [LB82].

Next, we show that $SC' \cup \textbf{res}(SC, X)$ dominates $L \geq 1$. Since SC dominates $L \geq 1$, we know that there is a prime implicate $L' \geq 1$ of SC that dominates $L \geq 1$. Since neither X nor $\overline{X}$ occur in L, we know that this prime implicate $L' \geq 1$ of SC does not contain X or $\overline{X}$. Furthermore, we know that Tison's method will generate $L' \geq 1$. Suppose that we start the loop in Tison's method by resolving on all classical clauses containing X. Note that the order of the variables on which to resolve is arbitrary. After that step we do no longer resolve on X. Therefore all classical clauses that contain X or $\overline{X}$ generate only classical clauses that also contain X or $\overline{X}$. Thus, $L' \geq 1$ must either be already in $SC' \cup \textbf{res}(SC, X)$ or is generated by Tison's method, where all classical clause still containing X or $\overline{X}$ are eliminated. Therefore, we know that $L' \geq 1$ is dominated by $SC' \cup \textbf{res}(SC, X)$. □

Proposition 10.2.3 *Let S be a set of extended clauses. Let X be a Boolean variable and let*

$$S' := \{L \setminus L' \geq d - |L'| \mid L \geq d \in S \text{ and } L' := L \cap \{X, \overline{X}\}\}$$

similar to (10.1). Then $S' \cup \textbf{res}(S, X)$ is a projection of S on $V \setminus \{X\}$.

Proof. We need to show Definition 10.0.1 [a] and [b].

[a] S dominates both S' and $\textbf{res}(S, X)$.

[b] Suppose that Definition 10.0.1 [b] does not hold. Then there exists an $\alpha' \in \textsf{Ext}(S' \cup \textbf{res}(S, X))$ such that for all assignments $\alpha \in \textsf{Ext}(S)$ there is an $X_i \in V \setminus X$ with $\alpha(X_i) \neq \alpha'(X_i)$. Therefore, α' is not in the extension of S. Let $L := \{L_i \mid \alpha'(L_i) = 1 \wedge \textsf{Var}(L_i) \in V \setminus \{X\}\}$ be the set of literals

---

[2]Tison's method was originally developed for the disjunctive normal form and the consensus operation. By duality all results hold for conjunctive normal form, i.e., classical clauses and resolution.

containing the variables in $V \setminus \{X\}$ that are mapped to 1 by α'. Similar to the proof of Proposition 10.1.1, we derive that S dominates $\overline{L} \geq 1$. By Lemma 10.2.1 we know that there is a classical clause dominating $\overline{L} \geq 1$ that is derivable by classical resolution from the set SC of classical clauses equivalent to S. By Proposition 7.8.2 we know that for each possible resolvent on X for any two extended clauses in S, $\mathbf{res}(S, X)$ contains an extended clause that dominates that resolvent. Let $T = S' \cup \mathbf{res}(S, X)$ and TC be the set of classical clauses that is equivalent to T obtained by applying Lemma 10.2.1 on T. Then by Lemma 10.2.2 we know that the classical clause dominating $\overline{L} \geq 1$ can be derived by classical resolution from TC. Therefore, $S' \cup \mathbf{res}(S, X)$ dominates $\overline{L} \geq 1$. Since $\alpha'(\overline{L}) = 0$, we know that $\alpha' \notin \mathsf{Ext}(S' \cup \mathbf{res}(S, X))$, which is a contradiction.   □

With help of Lemma 10.2.1 we transform our problem to a problem for classical clauses, which is then solved using Lemma 10.2.2. Note that the diagonal sum rule need not be applied for calculating a projection.

We obtain a projection of a set of extended clauses S on a set of Boolean variables V' by eliminating one after the other all variables in $V \setminus V'$, where V is the set of Boolean variables occurring in S.

Example 10.2.4 Let us eliminate the Boolean variable C in the set of extended clauses

$$S = \{A+B+C+D \geq 2, A+\overline{C}+\overline{D}+E+F \geq 3, \overline{A}+C+E \geq 1, D+\overline{C}+F \geq 1\} \ .$$

We build all linear combinations of two extended clauses, where one contains C and the other one contains $\overline{C}$, yielding the set of linear pseudo-Boolean inequalities

$$\{2 \cdot A+B+E+F \geq 3, 2 \cdot D+A+B+F \geq 2, 2 \cdot E+\overline{D}+F \geq 2, \overline{A}+D+E+F \geq 1\} \ .$$

We transform these linear pseudo-Boolean inequalities into an equivalent set of extended clauses and obtain

$$\mathbf{res}(S, C) = \begin{array}{l} \{A + E \geq 1, A + B \geq 1, A + F \geq 1, A + B + E + F \geq 2, \\ B + D + F \geq 1, E + F \geq 1, \overline{D} + E \geq 1\} \ , \end{array}$$

where dominated extended clauses have been deleted. The set of strict reductions of S, where C and $\overline{C}$ are eliminated, is

$$S' = \{A + B + D \geq 1, A + \overline{D} + E + F \geq 2\} \ .$$

Since $A + B + D \geq 1$ is already dominated by an extended clause in $\mathbf{res}(S, C)$, we know that

$$S|_{\{A,B,D,E,F\}} = \begin{array}{l} \{A + E \geq 1, A + B \geq 1, A + F \geq 1, \\ A + B + E + F \geq 2, B + D + F \geq 1, \\ E + F \geq 1, \overline{D} + E \geq 1, A + \overline{D} + E + F \geq 2\} \end{array}.$$

Next, we eliminate A. Since A occurs only positively in $S|_{\{A,B,D,E,F\}}$, we know that $\mathbf{res}(S|_{\{A,B,D,E,F\}}, A) = \emptyset$. Thus, the projection $S|_{\{B,D,E,F\}}$ consists only of the strict reductions

$$\{E + F \geq 1, B + D + F \geq 1, \overline{D} + E \geq 1\}$$

of $S|_{\{A,B,D,E,F\}}$, where we have eliminated A.

The presented variable elimination method for eliminating a Boolean variable is closely related to the Fourier-Motzkin variable elimination method for linear inequalities over the real numbers [Fou27, Mot36, Sch86]. We briefly recall the Fourier-Motzkin variable elimination method. Let A be a set of linear inequalities over the real numbers. Let V be the set of real variables occurring in A, and let X be a real variable that has to be eliminated. Each inequality can be brought into one of the following three forms

$$-X + \sum_{Y \in V \setminus \{X\}} c_i Y \geq d \tag{10.3}$$

$$+X + \sum_{Y \in V \setminus \{X\}} c_i Y \geq d \tag{10.4}$$

$$\sum_{Y \in V \setminus \{X\}} c_i Y \geq d . \tag{10.5}$$

Let $\mathbf{fm}(A, X)$ be the set of all linear inequalities obtained from adding an inequality of the form (10.3) to one of the form (10.4), then $\mathbf{fm}(A, X)$ does no longer contain X. We know that the set of linear inequalities $\mathbf{fm}(A, X)$ plus all inequalities of the form (10.5) describe a projection of A on $V \setminus \{X\}$ [Sch86]. Note that $\mathbf{fm}(A, X)$ corresponds to the resolvents $\mathbf{res}(S, X)$ in our variable elimination method. What is missing is the set of strict reductions in S'. Note that we also have the trivial inequalities $-X_i \geq -1$ and $X_i \geq 0$ for all Boolean variables X_i. Since they are of the form (10.3), resp. (10.4), they need also be considered in the Fourier-Motzkin elimination method. But then we obtain all strict reductions in S'. Thus, our variable elimination method for extended clauses is essentially the Fourier-Motzkin variable elimination method

for real constraints, plus the transformation of linear pseudo-Boolean inequalities into an equivalent set of extended clauses. Williams [Wil76] strengthened the Fourier-Motzkin elimination method by certain reduction and rounding operations to work for integer programming problems. Equation (10.2) can be seen as a specialized version of these operations that work for extended clauses. Hooker [Hoo92b] presents a specialized method for classical clauses.

10.3   IMPROVEMENTS

The presented variable elimination method is a computationally expensive task. In the worst case we may generate a quadratic number of linear pseudo-Boolean inequalities that need to be transformed and added to the constraint store for each variable to be eliminated. A possible improvement of the method is to first check whether an extended clause containing a variable that is to be eliminated is dominated by an extended clause not containing that variable.

Let $L + X \geq d \in S$ and suppose that we want to eliminate the Boolean variable X. If S dominates $L \geq d$, we can replace $L + X \geq d$ by $L \geq d$. In the variable elimination process we then need not compute any linear combination with $L + X \geq d$. We can check whether $L + X \geq d$ is redundant with the techniques presented in Section 6.3. We know that S dominates $L \geq d$ if and only if $\texttt{entail\_extendedclause}(S, L \geq d) = (S', \top)$ Similarly, for extended clauses of the form $L + \overline{X} \geq d$. Since a complete test of entailment by $\texttt{entail\_extendedclause}$ may be computationally too expensive for all extended clauses that contain the variable to be eliminated, we may restrict the test by selecting only some promising extended clauses or limit the computational effort spent for the entailment test. Note that the simplifying resolvents of Section 8.3 have already the property to construct some of these dominated extended clauses. Whether or not a complete entailment test is worthwhile in practice remains to be evaluated.

Typically, we do not only eliminate a single Boolean variable but many Boolean variables. Although we have to eliminate each Boolean variable one after the other, the order is arbitrary and can influence the performance of the variable elimination algorithm. Obviously, it is a good idea to eliminate first all Boolean variables X that occur only positively or only negatively in S, since then $\texttt{res}(S, X) = \emptyset$. As a heuristic rule we propose to choose the Boolean variable that minimizes the number of linear pseudo-Boolean inequalities that are generated by $\texttt{res}(S, X)$. Let $\texttt{occ}(S, L_i) := \{L \geq d \mid L \geq d \in S \text{ and } L_i \in L\}$ be

set of all extended clauses in S where the literal L_i occurs. First, we eliminate the Boolean variable X that minimizes

$$|\text{occ}(S, X)| \cdot |\text{occ}(S, \overline{X})| \ .$$

Thus, we minimize the number of generated linear pseudo-Boolean inequalities. We obtain the following Boolean variable elimination algorithm for extended clauses.

Algorithm 10.3.1 *Boolean variable elimination for extended clauses*

```
var_elim(S, V′)
   while V′ ≠ ∅
      S := ve_simplify(S, V′)
      M := min_{Y∈V′}(|occ(S, Y)| · |occ(S, Ȳ)|)
      select X such that |occ(S, X)| · |occ(S, X̄)| = M
      S := {L \ L′ ≥ d − |L′| | L ≥ d ∈ S, L′ = L ∩ {X, X̄}} ∪ res(S, X)
      V′ := V′ \ {X}
   endwhile
end var_elim
```

We assume the existence of a function **ve_simplify** that performs some of the simplifications possible by a complete entailment check. Algorithm 10.3.1 calculates a projection S' of S on a set of Boolean variables V' when called as

$$S' := \text{var\_elim}(S, V \setminus V') \ ,$$

where V is the set of Boolean variables occurring in S.

11

CONCLUSION

We have presented a complete collection of techniques for solving pseudo-Boolean constraints in the constraint logic programming language $\mathrm{CLP}(\mathcal{PB})$. We can use the methods to ensure global consistency (if desired) and to provide an appropriate solved form.

On one hand, pseudo-Boolean constraints are a powerful extension of Boolean constraints. On the other hand, pseudo-Boolean constraints are a restriction of finite domain constraints that allow the fulfillment of the requirements imposed in the context of constraint logic programming, i.e., providing a solved form and ensuring global consistency. The class of treatable problems still covers an important class of typical problems arising in operations research and artificial intelligence.

The set of all prime extended clauses as ideal solved form fits exactly into the context of constraint logic programming. Furthermore, it provides an intuitive and user-friendly understanding because of the natural d out of n interpretation. Since the ideal solved form is typically exponential in size w.r.t. the constraint set, the crucial idea is to approximate the solved form as long as questions imposed by the CLP-environment are not yet answered. The incremental logic cut algorithm of Chapter 6 allows the approximation of the solved form as closely as necessary and furthermore handles entailment questions. Thus, it constitutes the core of our complete pseudo-Boolean constraint solver. The presented simplification techniques enhance the efficiency of the constraint solver and are an attempt to make the theoretical power of cutting plane proofs available for practical use.

A complete pseudo-Boolean constraint solver embedded in $\text{CLP}(\mathcal{PB})$ encourages a more declarative programming style, since inconsistency can be detected immediately. For many typical problems, i.e., optimization problems, there is no performance penalty when ensuring global consistency. For some CLP-programs efficiency is enhanced or, even better, termination ensured. From a software-engineering point of view it is important that if global consistency is ensured, the program behavior does not change if the underlying constraint solving techniques are modified. In the context of concurrent constraint logic programming the presented constraint solver provides a basic functionality, namely deciding entailment.

11.1 SUMMARY OF RESULTS

All relevant parts of a complete symbolic pseudo-Boolean constraint solver for $\text{CLP}(\mathcal{PB})$ are covered in this book. The investigation of extended clauses, which are a useful generalization of classical clauses that remains computationally tractable, is a main part of this work. They constitute the solved form of our constraint solver.

The transformation of linear pseudo-Boolean inequalities into an equivalent set of extended clauses is the basic method for handling arbitrary pseudo-Boolean constraints by specialized methods for extended clauses. Encouraging computational results show that the number of extended clauses is typically much smaller than the number of classical clauses needed to represent a linear pseudo-Boolean inequality. Furthermore, the transformation technique is also applicable in the context of classical, polyhedral-based, 0-1 integer programming, i.e., it may serve as a cut generator in a branch-and-cut algorithm.

The deductive system *Generalized Resolution* introduced by Hooker is a complete inference system for linear pseudo-Boolean constraints. We have studied the inference rules of *Generalized Resolution* and specialized them for extended clauses. Applying these inference rules only if they *simplify* the current set of constraints has been shown to carry over the theoretical power of cutting plane proofs into a practical method. We have presented conditions and methods that enable an efficient search for these simplifications. Like the transformation method, the simplification methods can be used as cut generators in the context of classical linear programming based 0-1 integer programming.

The linearization method allows us to handle non-linear pseudo-Boolean constraints in CLP($\mathcal{PB}$). In the context of constraint logic programming a variable elimination algorithm for extended clauses is needed in order to project on the Boolean variables appearing in the top-level goal. We have developed a Fourier-Motzkin like variable elimination algorithm for projecting extended clauses on a set of Boolean variables for this purpose.

The presented pseudo-Boolean constraint solver is a logic-based method for solving pseudo-Boolean problems. As discovered by Hooker [Hoo94b, Hoo94a], logic-based methods and polyhedral methods have many parallels when replacing the polyhedral concepts by their logical counterparts. We have introduced a discrete relaxation, namely pseudo-Boolean unit relaxation, which replaces the linear programming relaxation. Computational results indicate that a pure branch-and-bound algorithm based on pseudo-Boolean unit relaxation is comparably efficient w.r.t. state-of-the-art linear programming based branch-and-bound methods. Furthermore, a pure logic cut algorithm has been given that corresponds to a pure polyhedral cut method for solving linear pseudo-Boolean problems.

One reason for the great success of polyhedral methods in 0-1 integer programming is the number of sophisticated problem-specific polyhedral cut generation methods. Hooker [Hoo94b, Hoo94a] starts the investigation of problem-specific logic cut generation methods. The presented simplification techniques can be seen as general problem independent logic cut generation methods, as needed for a general purpose pseudo-Boolean constraint solver.

11.2 RELATED AND FUTURE RESEARCH

Using logic cut methods in a constraint solver for CLP($\mathcal{PB}$) is the dual approach of the polyhedral cut method for constraint logic programming proposed by Bockmayr [Boc94]. The advantages of polyhedral cutting plane methods in the context of constraint logic programming carry over to logic cut methods. The investigation of strong polyhedral cut generation methods for general linear 0-1 problems and their incorporation into constraint logic programming is currently an active research area.

The investigation of the logic cut approach by Hooker [Hoo94b, Hoo94a] based on the deductive system *Generalized Resolution* [Hoo92a] is a promising alternative to classical linear programming based 0-1 integer programming. But, logic

cut and polyhedral cut generation methods do not exclude each other. Transferring methods from one field to the other and comparing both approaches w.r.t. their problem-specific applicability is an interesting topic for future research.

REFERENCES

[AB93]   A. Aggoun and N. Beldiceanu. Extending CHIP in order to solve
            complex scheduling and placement problems. *Mathl. Comput.
            Modelling*, 17(7):57–73, 1993.

[AK93]   H. Aït-Kaci. An introduction to LIFE – programming with logic,
            inheritance, functions and equations. In D. Miller, editor, *Pro-
            ceedings of the International Symposium on Logic Programming*,
            pages 52–68, Vancouver, Canada, 1993. MIT Press.

[ASS⁺88]   A. Aiba, K. Sakai, Y. Sato, D. J. Hawley, and R. Hasegawa. Con-
            straint logic programming language CAL. In *Proceedings Interna-
            tional Conference on Fifth Generation Computer Systems*, pages
            263–276, Tokyo, Japan, 1988. Springer-Verlag.

[Bar92a]   P. Barth. CLP($\mathcal{PB}$) A Meta-interpreter in CLP($\mathcal{R}$). Technical
            Report MPI-I-92-233, Max-Planck-Institut für Informatik, Saar-
            brücken, 1992.

[Bar92b]   P. Barth. A complete symbolic 0-1 constraint solver. In *AC-
            CLAIM Kick-Off Workshop*, Stockholm, Sweden, November 1992.

[Bar93a]   P. Barth. A complete symbolic 0-1 constraint solver. In A. Bock-
            mayr and F. J. Radermacher, editors, *Künstliche Intelligenz und
            Operations Research, Workshop, Extended Abstracts*, MPI-I-93-
            234, pages 11–13, Berlin, Germany, September 1993.

[Bar93b]   P. Barth. A complete symbolic 0-1 constraint solver. In F. Ben-
            hamou, A. Colmerauer, and G. Smolka, editors, *Third Work-
            shop on Constraint Logic Programming WCLP*, Marseille, France,
            March 1993.

[Bar93c]   P. Barth. Linear 0-1 inequalities and extended clauses. In *Pro-
            ceedings International Conference on Logic Programming and Au-
            tomated Reasoning LPAR*, pages 40–51, St. Petersburg, Russia,
            July 1993. Springer, LNAI 698.

[Bar94]   P. Barth. Linear 0-1 inequalities and extended clauses. Technical Report MPI-I-94-216, Max-Planck-Institut für Informatik, Saarbrücken, April 1994.

[Bar95]   P. Barth. A Davis-Putnam based enumeration algorithm for linear pseudo-Boolean optimization. Technical Report MPI-I-95-2-003, Max-Planck-Institut für Informatik, Saarbrücken, January 1995. System available:
            `ftp.mpi-sb.mpg.de:pub/guide/staff/barth/opbdp/opbdp.tar.Z`,
            `http://www.mpi-sb.mpg.de/~barth/opbdp/opbdp.html` .

[BB93]   P. Barth and A. Bockmayr. Solving 0-1 problems in CLP($\mathcal{PB}$). In *Proceedings 9th Conference on Artificial Intelligence for Applications CAIA*, pages 263–269, Orlando, Florida, 1993. IEEE.

[BB95]   P. Barth and A. Bockmayr. Finite domain and cutting plane techniques in CLP($\mathcal{PB}$). In L. Sterling, editor, *Proceedings 12th International Conference on Logic Programming ICLP*, pages 133–147, Kanagawa, Japan, 1995. MIT Press.

[BBI92]   R. E. Bixby, E. A. Boyd, and R. Indovina. MIPLIB: A Test Set of Mixed-Integer Programming Problems. *SIAM News 25*, page 16, 1992. ftp: softlib.cs.rice.edu.

[BC94]   N. Beldiceanu and E. Contejean. Introducing global constraints in CHIP. *Mathl. Comput. Modelling*, 20(12):97–123, 1994.

[BCC93a]   E. Balas, S. Ceria, and G. Cornuéjols. A lift-and-project cutting plane algorithm for mixed 0-1 programs. *Mathematical Programming*, 58:295–324, 1993.

[BCC93b]   E. Balas, S. Ceria, and G. Cornuéjols. Solving mixed 0-1 programs by a lift-and-project method. In *Symposium on Discrete Algorithms SODA*, Austin, Texas, 1993. ACM – SIAM.

[BCC94]   E. Balas, S. Ceria, and G. Cornuéjols. Mixed 0–1 programming by lift-and-project in a branch-and-cut framework. Technical report, GSIA, Carnegie Mellon University, February 1994.

[BDP93]   P. Boizumault, Y. Delon, and L. Péridy. Solving a real-life planning exams problem using constraint logic programming. In M. Meyer, editor, *Constraint Processing: Proceedings of the International Workshop at CSAM'93*, Research Report RR-93-39, pages 107–112, St. Petersburg, Russia, July 1993. DFKI Kaiserslautern.

[Bea85]   J. Beasly. Bounds for two-dimensional cutting. *Operational Research Society*, 36(1):71–74, 1985.

[Ben93]   F. Benhamou. Boolean algorithms in Prolog III. In F. Benhamou and A. Colmerauer, editors, *Constraint Logic Programming – Selected Research*, chapter 17, pages 307–326. MIT Press, 1993.

[Ber88]   F. Berthier. Managing underlying assumptions of a financial planning model in CHIP. Technical Report TR-LP-39, ECRC, Munich, Germany, 1988.

[Ber90]   F. Berthier. Solving financial decision problems with CHIP. In J.-L. Le Moigne and P. Bourgine, editors, *CECOIA 2: Proceedings 2nd Conference on Economics and Artificial Intelligence*, pages 233–238, Paris, France, 1990.

[BJL86]   C. E. Blair, R. G. Jeroslow, and J. K. Lowe. Some results and experiments in programming techniques for propositional logic. *Computers and Operations Research*, 13(5):633–645, 1986.

[BL95]   S. Breitinger and H. C. R. Lock. Using constraint logic programming for industrial scheduling problems. In C. Beierle and L. Plümer, editors, *Logic Programming: Formal Methods and Practical Applications*, Studies in Computer Science and Artificial Intelligence, chapter 9, pages 273–299. Elsevier, 1995.

[BLPN95]   P. Baptiste, C. Le Pape, and W. Nuijten. Incorporating efficient operations research algorithms in constraint-based scheduling. In J. N. Hooker and M. Ginsberg, editors, *Proceedings First International Workshop on Artificial Intelligence and Operations Research*, Oregon, 1995.

[BM84a]   E. Balas and J. B. Mazzola. Nonlinear 0-1 programming: I. Linearization techniques. *Mathematical Programming*, 30:1–21, 1984.

[BM84b]   E. Balas and J. B. Mazzola. Nonlinear 0-1 programming: II. Dominance relations and algorithms. *Mathematical Programming*, 30:22–45, 1984.

[BMvH94]   F. Benhamou, D. McAllester, and P. van Hentenryck. CLP(Intervals) revisited. In M. Bruynooghe, editor, *Proceedings International Symposium on Logic Programming ILPS*, pages 124–138, Santa Margherita Ligure, Italy, 1994. MIT Press.

[BO93]   F. Benhamou and W. Older. Applying interval arithmetic to real, integer and Boolean constraints. *Logic Programming: The ALP Newsletter*, 6(2):13–14, 1993. (Extended Abstract).

[Boc91]   A. Bockmayr. Logic programming with pseudo-Boolean constraints. Technical Report MPI-I-91-227, Max-Planck-Institut für Informatik, Saarbrücken, 1991.

[Boc92a] A. Bockmayr. 0-1 constraints and 0-1 optimization. In *ACCLAIM Kick-Off Workshop*, Stockholm, Sweden, November 1992.

[Boc92b] A. Bockmayr. Embedding OR techniques in constraint logic programming. In *Operations Research '92. 17th Symposium on Operations Research*, Hamburg, Germany, 1992.

[Boc93a] A. Bockmayr. 0-1 constraints and 0-1 optimization. In F. Benhamou, A. Colmerauer, and G. Smolka, editors, *Third Workshop on Constraint Logic Programming WCLP*, Marseille, France, March 1993.

[Boc93b] A. Bockmayr. Logic programming with pseudo-Boolean constraints. In F. Benhamou and A. Colmerauer, editors, *Constraint Logic Programming – Selected Research*, chapter 18, pages 327–350. MIT Press, 1993.

[Boc93c] A. Bockmayr. Using strong cutting planes in constraint logic programming. In *Operations Research '93. 18th Symposium on Operations Research*, Köln, Germany, 1993.

[Boc94]   A. Bockmayr. Cutting planes in constraint logic programming. Technical Report MPI-I-94-207, Max-Planck-Institut für Informatik, Saarbrücken, Saarbrücken, February 1994.

[Boc95]   A. Bockmayr. Solving pseudo-Boolean constraints. In A. Podelski, editor, *Constraint Programming: Basics and Trends*, pages 22–38. Springer, LNCS 910, 1995.

[BR89]   A. Bockmayr and H. H. Rath. Algorithms for Boolean unification. In *Proceedings FAW Workshop on Boolean Functions, Propositional Logic, and AI Systems*. FAW Ulm, Germany, 1989.

[Bry86]   R. E. Bryant. Graph-based algorithms for Boolean function manipulation. *IEEE Transactions on Computers*, C-35:677–691, 1986.

[Bry92]   R. E. Bryant. Symbolic Boolean manipulation with ordered binary-decision diagrams. *ACM Computing Surveys*, 24(3):293–318, 1992.

[Brz91]   C. Brzoska. Temporal logic programming and its relation to constraint logic programming. In V. Saraswat and K. Ueda, editors, *Proceedings International Logic Programming Symposium ILPS*, pages 661–677, San Diego, 1991. MIT Press.

[BS87]   W. Büttner and H. Simonis. Embedding Boolean expressions in logic programming. *Journal of Symbolic Computation*, 4(2):191–205, 1987.

[BS92]   B. Benhamou and L. Sais. Theoretical study of symmetries in propositional calculus and applications. In D. Kapur, editor, *Proceedings 11th International Conference on Automated Deduction CADE*, pages 281–294, Saratoga Springs, NY, 1992. Springer, LNCS 607.

[CCT87]   W. Cook, C. R. Coullard, and G. Turán. On the complexity of cutting plane proofs. *Discrete Applied Mathematics*, 18:25–38, 1987.

[CD93]   P. Codognet and D. Diaz. Boolean constraint solving using clp(FD). In D. Miller, editor, *Proceedings International Symposium on Logic Programming*, pages 525–529, 1993.

[CD94]   P. Codognet and D. Diaz. clp(B): Combining simplicity and efficiency in Boolean constraint solving. In M. Hermenegildo and J. Penjam, editors, *Programming Language Implementation and Logic Programming PLILP*, pages 244–260, Madrid, Spain, 1994. Springer, LNCS 844.

[CFGG95]   A. Chamard, A. Fischler, B. Guinaudeau, and A. Guillaud. CHIC lessons on CLP methodology. Technical Report ESPRIT EP5291 / D2.1.2.3, CHIC Project, Dassault Aviation, Bull, 1995.

[CG93]   M. Carlsson and M. Grindal. Automatic frequency assignment for cellular telephones using constraint satisfaction techniques. In D. S. Warren, editor, *Proceedings 10th International Conference on Logic Programming ICLP*, pages 647–665, Budapest, Hungary, 1993. MIT Press.

[Chv73]   V. Chvátal. Edmund polytopes and a hierarchy of combinatorial problems. *Discrete Mathematics*, 4:305–337, 1973.

[CJP83]   H. Crowder, E. L. Johnson, and M. Padberg. Solving large-scale zero-one linear programming problems. *Operations Research*, 31(5):803–834, September 1983.

[CKPR73]   A. Colmerauer, H. Kanouia, R. Pasero, and P. Roussel. Un système de communication homme-machine en français. Technical report, Université d'Aix-Marseille II, Groupe Intelligence Artificielle, 1973.

[CL94]   C. K. Chiu and J. H. M. Lee. Towards practical interval constraint solving in logic programming. In M. Bruynooghe, editor, *Proceedings International Symposium on Logic Programming ILPS*, pages 109–123, Santa Margherita Ligure, Italy, 1994. MIT Press.

[CM87]   W. F. Clocksin and C. S. Mellish. *Programming in Prolog*. Springer, 1987. Third revised and extended edition.

[Col75]   G. E. Collins. Quantifier elimination for the elementary theory of real closed fields by cylindrical algebraic decomposition. In H. Brakhage, editor, *Automata Theory and Formal Languages, 2nd GI Conference*, volume 33, pages 134–183, Kaiserslautern, West Germany, 1975. Springer, LNCS 33.

[Col86]   A. Colmerauer. Note sur Prolog III. In *Actes du Seminaire 1986 - Programmation en Logique*, pages 159–173, Tregastel, France, Mai 1986. CNET.

[Col87]   A. Colmerauer. Introduction to PROLOG III. In *Fourth Annual ESPRIT Conference*, Bruxelles, 1987. North Holland.

[Col90]   A. Colmerauer. An introduction to Prolog III. *Communications of the ACM*, 33(7):69–90, 1990.

[Coo71]   S. A. Cook. The complexity of theorem proving procedures. In *Proceedings Third ACM Symposium on the Theory of Computing*, pages 151–158. ACM, 1971.

[Cra93]   J.-I. Cras. A review of industrial constraint satisfaction tools. AI perspectives report, AI Intelligence, Oxford, 1993.

[CW77]   N. Christofides and C. Whitlock. An algorithm for two-dimensional cutting problems. *Operations Research*, 25(1):30–44, 1977.

[CW90]   M. Carlsson and J. Widen. *SICStus Prolog Users Manual*. Swedish Institute of Computer Science, 1990. SICS/R-88/88007C.

[Dan57]   G. B. Dantzig. Discrete variable extremum problems. *Operations Research*, 5:266–277, 1957.

[Dan60]   G. B. Dantzig. On the significance of solving linear programming problems with some integer variables. The Rand Corporation document P1486 (1958), 1960. also published in *Econometrica* 28 (1961), 30–44.

[DC93]   D. Diaz and P. Codognet. A minimal extension of the wam for clp(fd). In D. S. Warren, editor, *Proceedings 10th International Conference on Logic Programming ICLP*, pages 774–792, Budapest, Hungary, 1993. MIT Press.

[DEC93]   B. L. Dietrich, L. F. Escudero, and F. Chance. Efficient reformulation for 0-1 programs – Methods and computational results. *Discrete Applied Mathematics*, 42:147–175, 1993.

[DP60]   M. Davis and H. Putnam. A computing procedure for quantification theory. *Journal of the ACM*, 7:201–205, 1960.

[DSvH88a]   M. Dincbas, H. Simonis, and P. van Hentenryck. Solving a cutting-stock problem in constraint logic programming. In R. Kowalski and K. Bowen, editors, *Proceedings Fifth International Conference and Symposium on Logic Programming*, pages 42–58, Seattle, Washington, 1988. MIT Press.

[DSvH88b]   M. Dincbas, H. Simonis, and P. van Hentenryck. Solving large scheduling problems in logic programming. In *Proceedings EURO-TIMS Joint International Conference on Operations Research and Management Science*, Paris, France, 1988.

[DSvH88c]   M. Dincbas, H. Simonis, and P. van Hentenryck. Solving the car sequencing problem in constraint logic programming. In *Proceedings European Conference on Artificial Intelligence ECAI*, pages 290–295, Munich, Germany, 1988.

[DSvH90]   M. Dincbas, H. Simonis, and P. van Hentenryck. Solving large combinatorial problems in logic programming. *Journal of Logic Programming*, 8(1–2):75–93, 1990.

[DvHS+88a] M. Dincbas, P. van Hentenryck, H. Simonis, A. Aggoun, and T. Graf. The constraint logic programming language CHIP. In *Proceedings International Conference on Fifth Generation Computer Systems*, pages 693–702, Tokyo, Japan, 1988. Springer-Verlag.

[DvHS⁺88b] M. Dincbas, P. van Hentenryck, H. Simonis, A. Aggoun, and T. Graf. Applications of CHIP to industrial and engineering problems. In *Proceedings First International Conference on Industrial and Engineering Applications of Artificial Intelligence and Expert Systems*, Tullahoma, Tennessee, 1988.

[Fag93]   F. Fages. On the semantics of optimization predicates in CLP languages. In P. Kanellakis, J.-L. Lassez, and V. Saraswat, editors, *First International Workshop on Principles and Practice of Constraint Programming PPCP*, Newport, Rhode Island, 1993.

[FGGB66]   R. J. Freeman, D. C. Gogerty, G. W. Graves, and R. B. S. Brooks. A mathematical model of supply support for space operations. *Operations Research*, 14:1–15, 1966.

[FGK90]   R. Fourer, D. M. Gay, and B. W. Kernighan. A modelling language for mathematical programming. *Management Science*, 36:519–554, 1990.

[FHJ91]   T. Franzén, S. Haridi, and S. Janson. An overview of the andorra kernel language. In L.-H. Eriksson, L. Hallnäs, and P. Schroeder-Heister, editors, *Proceedings Second International Workshop on Extensions of Logic Programming ELP*, pages 163–180, Stockholm, Sweden, 1991. Springer, LNAI 596.

[For59]   R. Fortet. L'algèbre de Boole et ses applications en recherche opérationelle. *Cahiers du Centre d'Études de Recherche Opérationelle*, 1(4):5–36, 1959.

[For60]   R. Fortet. Applications de l'algèbre de Boole en recherche opérationelle. *Revue Française d'Informatique et de Recherche Opérationelle*, 4(14):17–25, 1960.

[Fou27]   J. B. Fourier. [reported in:] Analyse de travaux de l'Académie Royale des Sciences, pendant l'année 1824, Partie mathématique; Histoire de l'Académie Royale des Sciences de l'Institut de France, 1827. Partial English Translation in *Translation of a Report by Fourier on his work on linear inequalities*, Operations Research 10 (1973) 38–42.

[Ger94]   C. Gervet. Conjuncto: Constraint logic programming with finite set domains. Technical Report ECRC-94-15, ECRC, 1994.

[GG80]   D. Granot and F. Granot. Generalized covering relaxation for 0-1 programs. *Operations Research*, 28:1442–1450, 1980.

[GH71]   F. Granot and P. L. Hammer. On the use of Boolean functions in
           0-1 programming. *Methods of Operations Research*, 12:154–184,
           1971.

[GH75]   F. Granot and P. L. Hammer. On the role of generalized cover-
           ing problems. *Cahiers du Centre d'Études de Recherche Opéra-
           tionelle*, 17:277–289, 1975.

[GJ79]   M. R. Garey and D. S. Johnson. *Computers and Intractability:
           A Guide to the Theory of NP-Completeness.* Freeman, San Fran-
           cisco, CA, 1979.

[Gom58]   R. E. Gomory. Outline of an algorithm for integer solutions to
           linear programs. *Bull. AMS*, 64:275–278, 1958.

[GU89]   G. Gallo and G. Urbani. Algorithms for testing the satisfiability of
           propositional formulae. *Journal of Logic Programming*, 7:45–61,
           1989.

[GW73]   F. Glover and E. Wolsey. Further reduction of zero-one polyno-
           mial programs to zero-one linear programming problems. *Opera-
           tions Research*, 21(1):156–161, 1973.

[Hak85]   A. Haken. The intractability of resolution. *Theoretical Computer
           Science*, 39(2 & 3):297–308, 1985.

[Hal35]   P. Hall. On representatives of subsets. *Journal of the London
           Mathematical Society*, 10:26–30, 1935.

[Ham64]   P. L. Hammer. Systems of pseudo-Boolean equations and in-
           equalities. *Bulletin de l'Academie Polonaise des Sciences-Serie
           des Sciences Math. , Astr. et Phys.*, XII(11):673–680, 1964.

[Ham68]   P. L. Hammer. Plant location – a pseudo-Boolean approach. *Israel
           Journal of Technology*, pages 350–362, 1968.

[HF90]   J. N. Hooker and C. Fedjki. Branch-and-cut solution of infer-
           ence problems in propositional logic. *Annals of Mathematics and
           Artificial Intelligence*, 1:123–139, 1990.

[HHT94]   F. Harche, J. N. Hooker, and G. L. Thompson. A computational
           study of satisfiability algorithms for propositional logic. *ORSA
           Journal on Computing*, 6(4):423–435, 1994.

[HJ90]   S. Haridi and S. Janson. Kernel Andorra Prolog and its computation model. In D. H. Warren and P. Szeredi, editors, *Proceedings 7th International Conference on Logic Programming ICLP*, pages 31–48, Jerusalem, Israel, 1990. MIT Press.

[HJM+92]   N. C. Heintze, J. Jaffar, S. Michaylov, P. J. Stuckey, and R. Yap. The CLP($\mathcal{R}$) programmer's manual – version 1.2. Technical report, IBM Thomas J. Watson Research Center, September 1992.

[HJM93]   P. Hansen, B. Jaumard, and V. Mathon. Constrained nonlinear 0-1 programming. *ORSA Journal on Computing*, 5(2):97–119, 1993.

[HJO+92]   W. Havens, J. Jones, R. Ovans, S. Sidebottom, and G. Sidebottom. Echidna: A constraint logic programming shell. In *Proceedings Pacific Rim Conference on AI*, pages 165–171, 1992.

[HL88]   T. Huynh and C. Lassez. A CLP($\mathcal{R}$) options trading analysis system. In R. Kowalski and K. Bowen, editors, *Proceedings Fifth International Conference and Symposium on Logic Programming*, pages 59–69, Seattle, Washington, 1988. MIT Press.

[HMS87]   N. Heintze, S. Michaylov, and P. Stuckey. CLP($\mathcal{R}$) and some electrical engineering problems. In J.-L. Lassez, editor, *Proceedings 4th International Conference on Logic Programming ICLP*, pages 675–703, Melbourne, Australia, May 1987. MIT Press.

[HMSY89]   N. C. Heintze, S. Michaylov, P. J. Stuckey, and R. Yap. On meta-programming in CLP($\mathcal{R}$). In E. Lusk and R. Overbeek, editors, *Proceedings of the North American Conference on Logic Programming*, pages 52–68. MIT Press, October 1989.

[Hol95]   C. Holzbaur. OFAI clp(q,r) manual, edition 1.3.3. Technical Report TR-95-09, Austrian Research Institute for Artificial Intelligence, Vienna, 1995.

[Hon90]   H. Hong. *Improvements in CAD-Based Quantifier Elimination*. PhD thesis, Ohio State University, 1990.

[Hon92]   H. Hong. Non-linear constraints solving over real numbers in constraint logic programming (introducing RISC-CLP). RISC-Linz Report Series 92-08, Research Institute for Symbolic Computation,Johannes Kepler Institute, A-4040 Linz, Austria, Europe, January 1992.

[Hoo88a]   J. N. Hooker. A quantitative approach to logical inference. *Decision Support Systems*, 4:45–69, 1988.

[Hoo88b]   J. N. Hooker. Resolution vs. cutting plane solution of inference problems: some computational experience. *Operations Research Letters*, 7(1):1–7, 1988.

[Hoo89]   J. N. Hooker. Input proofs and rank one cutting planes. *ORSA Journal on Computing*, 1:137–145, 1989.

[Hoo92a]   J. N. Hooker. Generalized resolution for 0-1 linear inequalities. *Annals of Mathematics and Artificial Intelligence*, 6:271–286, 1992.

[Hoo92b]   J. N. Hooker. Logical inference and polyhedral projection. *ORSA Journal on Computing*, 1(3):137–145, 1992.

[Hoo93]   J. N. Hooker. Solving the incremental satisfiability problem. *Journal of Logic Programming*, 15:177–186, 1993.

[Hoo94a]   J. N. Hooker. Logic-based methods for optimization. *ORSA CSTS Newsletter*, 15(2):4–11, 1994.

[Hoo94b]   J. N. Hooker. Logic-based methods for optimization: A tutorial. Working Paper 1994-05, GSIA, Carnegie-Mellon-University, 1994.

[HR68]   P. L. Hammer and S. Rudeanu. *Boolean Methods in Operations Research and Related Areas*. Springer-Verlag, 1968.

[HRR63]   P. L. Hammer, I. Rosenberg, and S. Rudeanu. Application of discrete linear programming to the minimization of Boolean functions. *Rev. Math. Pures Appl.*, 8:459–475, 1963. (in Russian).

[HV94]   J. N. Hooker and V. Vinay. Branching rules for satisfiability. In *Third International Symposium on Artificial Intelligence and Mathematics*, Fort Lauderdale, Florida, January 1994. to appear in Journal of Automated Reasoning.

[IFP95]   IF-prolog 5.0, 1995. IF Computer GmbH, Siemens/Nixdorf.

[Jac92]   P. Jackson. Computing prime implicates incrementally. In D. Kapur, editor, *Proceedings 11th International Conference on Automated Deduction CADE*, pages 253–267, Saratoga Springs, NY, 1992. Springer, LNCS 607.

[JKS85]   E. L. Johnson, M. M. Kostreva, and U. H. Suhl. Solving 0-1 integer programming problems arising from large scale planning models. *Operations Research*, 33(4):803–819, July 1985.

[JL87]   J. Jaffar and J.-L. Lassez. Constraint logic programming. In *Proceedings 14th ACM Symposium on Principles of Programming Languages*, pages 111–119, München, Germany, January 1987. ACM.

[JM94]   J. Jaffar and M. J. Maher. Constraint logic programming: A survey. *Journal of Logic Programming*, 19/20:503–581, 1994.

[JMSY90]   J. Jaffar, S. Michaylov, P. Stuckey, and R. Yap. The CLP($\mathcal{R}$) language and system. Technical Report RC 16292 (#72336) 11/15/90, IBM Research Division, November 1990.

[JP90]   P. Jackson and J. Pais. Computing prime implicants. In M. Stickel, editor, *Proceedings 10th International Conference on Automated Deduction CADE, Kaiserslautern*, pages 543–557. Springer, LNCS 449, 1990.

[JW90]   R. G. Jeroslow and J. Wang. Solving propositional satisfiability problems. *Annals of Mathematics and AI*, 1:167–187, 1990.

[Kar72]   R. M. Karp. Reducibility among combinatorial problems. In R. E. Miller and J. W. Thatcher, editors, *Complexity of Computer Computations*, pages 85–103. Plenum Press, New York, 1972.

[Kar88]   K. Karplus. Representing Boolean functions with if-then-else DAGs. Technical Report UCSC-CRL-88-28, Computer Research Laboratory, Univ. of California, Santa Cruz, Nov. 1988.

[KGV83]   S. Kirkpatrick, C. D. Gelatt, and M. P. Vecchi. Optimization by simulated annealing. *Science*, 220:671–680, 1983.

[Kow74]   R. A. Kowalski. Predicate logic as programming language. In *Proceedings of the IFIP Congress*, pages 569–574, Amsterdam, Netherlands, 1974. North Holland.

[KT90]   A. Kean and G. Tsiknis. An incremental method for generating prime implicants/implicates. *Journal of Symbolic Computation*, 9:185–206, 1990.

[Kum92]   V. Kumar. Algorithms for constraint-satisfaction problems: A survey. *A.I. Magazine*, 13(1):32–44, 1992.

[LB82]   M. C. Loui and G. Bilardi. The correctness of Tison's method for generating prime implicants/implicates. Technical Report R-952, UILU-ENG 82-2218, Coordinated Science Laboratory, University of Illinois at Urbana-Champaign, 1982.

[LMY87]   C. Lassez, K. McAloon, and R. Yap. Constraint logic programming and options trading. *IEEE Expert, Special Issue on Financial Software*, 2(3):42–50, 1987.

[Lov78]   D. W. Loveland. *Automated theorem proving : A logical basis*, volume 6 of *Fundamental studies in computer science*. North-Holland, Amsterdam, 1978.

[LP94]   C. Le Pape. Implementation of resource constraints in Ilog schedule: A library for the development of constraint-based scheduling systems. *Intelligent Systems Engineering*, 3:55–66, 1994.

[Mac77]   A. K. Mackworth. Consistency in networks of relations. *Artificial Intelligence*, 8:99–118, 1977.

[MAC+89]   M. Meier, A. Aggoun, D. Chan, P. Dufresne, R. Enders, D. H. de Villeneuve, A. Herold, P. Kay, B. Perez, E. van Rossum, and J. Schimpf. SEPIA – an extendible Prolog system. In *Proceedings 11th Word Computer Congress IFIP'89*, pages 1127–1132, San Francisco, 1989.

[MB93]   A. Meeraus and A. Brooke. *GAMS: A User's Guide*. Boyd and Fraser publishing, 1993.

[MN86]   U. Martin and T. Nipkow. Unification in Boolean rings. In J. H. Siekmann, editor, *Proceedings 8th International Conference on Automated Deduction CADE*, pages 506–513, Oxford, UK, 1986. Springer, LNCS 230.

[MN88]   U. Martin and T. Nipkow. Unification in Boolean rings. *Journal of Automated Reasoning*, 4:381–396, 1988.

[MN89]   U. Martin and T. Nipkow. Boolean unification – the story so far. *Journal of Symbolic Computation*, 7:275–293, 1989.

[Mot36]   T. S. Motzkin. *Beiträge zur Theorie der linearen Ungleichungen*. PhD thesis, (Inaugural Dissertation Basel), Azriel, Jerusalem, 1936.

[MR91]   I. Mitterreiter and F. J. Radermacher. Experiments on the run-
           ning time behavior of some algorithms solving propositional logic
           problems. Technical report, FAW Ulm, 1991.

[MS85]   B. Monien and E. Speckenmeyer. Solving satisfiability in less than
           2^n steps. *Discrete Applied Mathematics*, 10:287–295, 1985.

[MS94]   K. Marriott and P. J. Stuckey. Semantics of constraint lo-
           gic programs with optimization. In *Integration of Declara-
           tive Paradigms. Proceedings ICLP'94 Postconference Workshop*,
           Santa Margherita Ligure, Italy, June 1994.

[MW89]   K. I. M. McKinnon and H. P. Williams. Constructing integer pro-
           gramming models by the predicate calculus. *Annals of Operations
           Research*, 21:227–246, 1989.

[NSS94]   G. L. Nemhauser, M. W. P. Savelsbergh, and G. Sigismondi.
           MINTO, a Mixed INTeger Optimizer. *Operations Research Let-
           ters*, 15:47–58, 1994.

[NW88]   G. L. Nemhauser and L. A. Wolsey. *Integer and Combinatorial
           Optimization*. Series in Discrete Mathematics and Optimization.
           Wiley–Interscience, 1988.

[OB93]   W. Older and F. Benhamou. Programming in CLP(BNR). In
           P. Kanellakis, J.-L. Lassez, and V. Saraswat, editors, *First In-
           ternational Workshop on Principles and Practice of Constraint
           Programming PPCP*, Newport, Rhode Island, 1993.

[OMT89]   A. Oplobedu, J. Marcovitch, and Y. Tourbier. Charme: Un lan-
           gage industriel de programmation par contraintes, illustré par
           une application chez Renault. In *9th International Workshop on
           Expert Systems and their Applications: General Conference*, vol-
           ume 1, pages 55–70, Avignon, France, May 29th – June 2nd 1989.

[OV90]   W. Older and A. Vellino. Extending Prolog with constraint arith-
           metic on real intervals. In *Proceedings Canadian Conference on
           Electrical and Computer Engineering*, pages 14.1.1–14.1.4, 1990.

[PR91]   M. Padberg and G. Rinaldi. A branch-and-cut algorithm for the
           resolution of large-scale symmetric traveling salesman problems.
           SIAM Review, 33(1):60–100, 1991.

[PS95]   A. Podelski and G. Smolka. Operational semantics of constraint
           logic programming with coroutining. In L. Sterling, editor, *Pro-
           ceedings 12th International Conference on Logic Programming
           ICLP*, pages 449–463, Kanagawa, Japan, 1995. MIT Press.

[Pug94]   J.-F. Puget. A C++ implementation of CLP. In *Proceedings Second Singapore International Conference on Intelligent Systems*, Singapore, 1994.

[PWW69]   A. B. Pritsker, L. J. Watters, and P. M. Wolfe. Multiproject scheduling with limited resources: a zero-one integer programming approach. *Management Science*, 16(1):93–108, 1969.

[Qui52]   W. V. Quine. The problem of simplifying truth functions. *American Mathematical Monthly*, 59:521–531, 1952.

[Qui55]   W. V. Quine. A way to simplify truth functions. *American Mathematical Monthly*, 62:627–631, 1955.

[Rhy70]   J. Rhys. A selection problem of shared fixed costs and networks. *Management Science*, 17:200–207, 1970.

[Rob65]   J. A. Robinson. A machine-oriented logic based on the resolution principle. *Journal of the ACM*, 12(1):23–41, 1965.

[Sar88]   V. A. Saraswat. A somewhat logical formulation of CLP synchronization primitives. In R. Kowalski and K. Bowen, editors, *Proceedings Fifth International Conference and Symposium on Logic Programming*, pages 1298–1314, Seattle, Washington, 1988. MIT Press.

[Sar89]   V. A. Saraswat. *Concurrent Constraint Programming Languages*. PhD thesis, Carnegie-Mellon University, 1989. Revised version appears as [Sar93].

[Sar93]   V. A. Saraswat. *Concurrent Constraint Programming*. MIT Press, 1993.

[Sch86]   A. Schrijver. *Theory of Linear and Integer Programming*. John Wiley, 1986.

[SD90]   H. Simonis and M. Dincbas. Propositional calculus problems in CHIP. Technical report TR-LP-48, ECRC, May 1990. full version of [SD93].

[SD93]   H. Simonis and M. Dincbas. Propositional calculus problems in CHIP. In F. Benhamou and A. Colmerauer, editors, *Constraint Logic Programming – Selected Research*, chapter 15, pages 269–285. MIT Press, 1993.

[SHW93a]   G. Smolka, M. Henz, and J. Würtz. Object-oriented concurrent constraint programming in Oz. Research Report RR-93-16, Deutsches Forschungszentrum für Künstliche Intelligenz, April 1993. Previous version appeared as [SHW93b].

[SHW93b]   G. Smolka, M. Henz, and J. Würtz. Oz – a programming language for multi-agent systems. In *Proceedings International Joint Conference on Artificial Intelligence*, pages 404–409, Chambéry, France, 1993. Morgan Kaufmann Publishers.

[Smo94]   G. Smolka. A calculus for higher-order concurrent constraint programming with deep guards. Research Report RR-94-03, Deutsches Forschungszentrum für Künstliche Intelligenz, February 1994.

[SND88]   H. Simonis, H. Nguyen, and M. Dincbas. Verification of digital circuits using CHIP. In G. J. Milne, editor, *Proceedings of the IFIP WG 10.2 International Working conference on the Fusion of Hardware Design and Verification*, Glasgow, Scotland, July 1988. IFIP, North-Holland.

[SSW94]   C. Schulte, G. Smolka, and J. Würtz. Encapsulated search and constraint programming in Oz. In A. Borning, editor, *Second International Workshop on Principles and Practice of Constraint Programming PPCP*, pages 134–150, Orcas Island, Seattle, 1994. Springer, LNCS 874.

[Tah71]   H. A. Taha. Sequencing by implicit ranking and zero-one polynomial programming. *AIIE Transactions*, 3:299–308, 1971.

[Tar51]   A. Tarski. *A Decision Method for Elementary Algebra and Geometry*. University of California Press, Berkeley and Los Angeles, 1951.

[Tis67]   P. Tison. Generalized consensus theory and application to the minimization of Boolean functions. *IEEE Transaction on Electronic Computers*, EC-16(4):446–456, 1967.

[Tri93]   M. Trick. The second dimacs international algorithm implementation challenge: Clique, graph coloring, and satisfiability. ftp: dimacs.rutgers.edu, 1993.

[Tsa93]   E. Tsang. *Foundations of Constraint Satisfaction*. Academic Press, 1993.

[vG84]   A. van Gelder. A satisfiability tester for non-clausal proposi-
            tional calculus. In R. E. Shostak, editor, *Proceedings 7th In-
            ternational Conference on Automated Deduction CADE*, pages
            101–112, Napa, CA, May 1984. Springer, LNCS 170.

[vH89a]   P. van Hentenryck. *Constraint satisfaction in logic programming.*
            MIT Press, 1989.

[vH89b]   P. van Hentenryck. A logic language for combinatorial optimiza-
            tion. *Annals of Operations Research*, 21:247–274, 1989.

[vH92]   P. van Hentenryck. Scheduling and packing in the constraint lan-
            guage cc(FD). Technical Report CS-92-43, Department of Com-
            puter Science, Brown University, September 1992.

[vHSD92]   P. van Hentenryck, H. Simonis, and M. Dincbas. Constraint satis-
            faction using constraint logic programming. *Artificial Intelligence*,
            58:113–159, 1992.

[Wal94]   M. Wallace. Applying constraints for scheduling. In B. Mayoh,
            E. Tyugu, and J. Penjam, editors, *Constraint Programming: Pro-
            ceedings 1993 NATO ASI*, NATO Advanced Science Institute Se-
            ries, pages 161–180, Parnu, Estonia, 1994. Springer.

[Wil76]   H. P. Williams. Fourier-Motzkin elimination extension to inte-
            ger programming. *Journal of Combinatorial Theory*, 21:118–123,
            1976.

[Wil90]   H. P. Williams. *Model Building in Mathematical Programming.*
            Wiley–Interscience, third edition, 1990.

[WYO81]   T. Watanabe, C. Yasunobu, and M. O'Kuma. Fault diagnosis
            by mathematical programming. *Transactions of Reliability*, R-
            30(4):345–352, 1981.

[Zha93]   H. Zhang. SATO: a decision procedure for propositional logic.
            Association of Automated Reasoning Newsletters, 22:1–3, March
            1993.

Index

Symbols

A

B

C

D

E